Special Edition
Using
Director 8.5

Gary Rosenzweig

201 W. 103rd Street
Indianapolis, Indiana 46290

Contents at ~~a~~ ~~Glance~~

G000144894

SPECIAL EDITION USING DIRECTOR 8.5

Copyright © 2002 by Que

International Standard Book Number: 0-7897-2667-X

Library of Congress Catalog Card Number: 2001094249

Printed in the United States of America

First Printing: November 2001

02 01 00   4 3 2 1

Trademarks

Warning and Disclaimer

Executive Editor
Jeff Schultz

Development Editor
Damon Jordan

Managing Editor
Thomas F. Hayes

Project Editor
Karen S. Shields

Copy Editor
Julie McNamee

Indexer
Erika Millen

Proofreader
Kaylene Riemen

Technical Editors
Paul Cantanese
Jonathan Powers

Team Coordinator
Sharry Lee Gregory

Media Developer
Michael Hunter

Interior Designer
Anne Jones

Cover Designers
Alan Clements

Illustrations
William Follett

Page Layout
Stacey Richwine-DeRome

CONTENTS

V **Using Behaviors**

14 **Creating Behaviors 255**

ABOUT THE AUTHOR

Gary Rosenzweig is the chief engineer, founder, and owner of CleverMedia, a game and multi-media development company in Denver, Colorado. This is his sixth book on Director.

Before the multimedia industry started, he was a computer science student at Drexel University in Philadelphia. There, he took a greater interest in journalism than computers. After working for years in various positions at the student newspaper, he eventually rose to the position of editor-in-chief.

Gary followed his journalistic interests to the University of North Carolina at Chapel Hill, where he earned a master's degree. As an undergraduate, he found that he was someone who knew a lot about publishing at a school where everyone was a computer expert. In graduate school, he found that he was someone who knew a lot about computers at a school where everyone was involved in publishing.

While in school, he got his first taste of a scripting language with Hypercard 1.0. Although class projects were done in Pascal, C, and other "serious" programming languages, Gary found that he was able to build programs for freelance jobs with Hypercard in a fraction of the time.

After school, rather than enter one field or another, Gary combined both and began freelancing for publications to build multimedia products. Shortly thereafter, he moved to Denver to take a job at Ingenius, an educational news service partially owned by Reuters. It was there that he began using Director all day, every day.

As a serious developer, Gary went to bookstores to find books on Director. Seeing none, he decided to write one. He then published the book, free, on the Internet. Soon after that, he was paid to rewrite and update the book as *The Comprehensive Guide to Lingo*.

After the book was published, Gary left Ingenius and started his own company, CleverMedia. This was made possible because of Shockwave, which gives users the capability to play Director movies on the Web. Demand for Shockwave applets rose and CleverMedia was hired by many companies, both large and small, to build Shockwave applets. Today, CleverMedia owns four of the largest Shockwave and Flash game sites on the Web and creates games for many of the others.

Gary lives in Denver, Colorado, with wife Debby, a cat named Lucy, and a dog named Natasha. Other than computers and the Internet, he also enjoys film, camping, classic science fiction books, and writing.

Personal Home Page: http://www.garyrosenzweig.com

E-mail: http://www.garyrosenzweig.com/email.html

DEDICATION

To my brother, Larry Rosenzweig, who I used to be able to beat at video games.

ACKNOWLEDGMENTS

Very special thanks go to William Follett, Justin Gitlin, Kenny Kaplan, Brian Robbins, Leif Saul, and Jay Shaffer, my co-workers at CleverMedia. They make developing games even more fun than playing them.

Thanks also to the team at Que for making this edition the best to date.

Thanks to the many people who participate in the Hopper-Ex and DXR mailing lists, DOUG and the Director 8 and 8.5 Beta Lists: Darrel Plant, Colin, Holgate, Ron Manke, Ely Greenfield, Hudson Ansley, Alex Zavatone, Bruce Epstein, Phillip Kerman, Emmanuel Beuque, Mark Reijnders, Terry Schussler, Rebecca Lovelace, Scott Flowers, Dave Cole, James Newton, Andrew White, Roy Pardi, Alan Levine, Ron Bearry, Eric Coker, Dorian Dowse, Julian Baker, Marvyn Hortman, Oogie McGuire, Raul Silva, Paul Hertz, Rob Dillon, Gretchen MacDowel, Matt Craig, Miles Lightwood, Mark Hagers, Glenn Picher, Peter Lundholm, Simon Biggs, Ian Chia, Zac Belado, Patrick McClellan, and all the rest.

Thanks to all of the Macromedia Director team, including John Thompson, Buzz Kettles, Karen Silvey, James Khazar, Chris Nuuja, David Mendels, Jake Sapirstein, Glenn Ruehle, Mike Edmunds, Werner Sharp, Gordon Smith, Dan Sadowski, Tracy Stampfli, Tom Higgins, Sarah Allen, Peter Grandmaison, Perihan Cumali, Lalit Balchandani, Ken Day, Karl Miller, Joe Schmitz, Jim Corbett, Jenny Suter, John Dowdell, Jay Armstrong, David Calaprice, Christophe Leske, Chris Nuuja, Alex Lelievre, Kraig Mentor, Greg Yachuk, Eliot Greenfield, Doug Wyrick, and the rest.

Thanks to my family for their continuing lifetime of support: Jacqueline, Jerry, and Larry Rosenzweig; Rebecca Jacob; Barbara and Richard Shifrin.

The most thanks go to my wife, Debby, for her love and support.

TELL US WHAT YOU THINK!

As the reader of this book, *you* are our most important critic and commentator. We value your opinion and want to know what we're doing right, what we could do better, what areas you'd like to see us publish in, and any other words of wisdom you're willing to pass our way.

As an Executive Editor for Que, I welcome your comments. You can, e-mail, or write me directly to let me know what you did or didn't like about this book—as well as what we can do to make our books stronger.

Please note that I cannot help you with technical problems related to the topic of this book, and that due to the high volume of mail I receive, I might not be able to reply to every message.

When you write, please be sure to include this book's title and author as well as your name and phone or fax number. I will carefully review your comments and share them with the author and editors who worked on the book.

E-mail: ctfeedback@quepublishing.com

Mail: Jeff Schultz
          Executive Editor
          Que
          201 West 103rd Street
          Indianapolis, IN 46290 USA

INTRODUCTION

I love working with Director. By education, I am a computer scientist and a journalist. By nature, I am a problem solver. I love using both logic and imagination. Director requires me to use all these things.

If you have a job in which you work all day with Director, consider yourself lucky. You probably already do. In fact, you have probably said to yourself before: "I can't believe I get paid for this!"

Director is a great tool for creating software. On one hand, you can quickly bring to life your ideas. On the other hand, Director is an environment that inspires new ideas as you explore it.

The possibilities for animators are incredible, even if they never choose to do any programming. Director also has built-in programs called behaviors that expand the possibilities a thousand times for those looking to make interactive presentations.

If you are willing to go on to learn Lingo, the programming language of Director, the possibilities for your creations become virtually limitless. There are more than 800 Lingo keywords in Lingo including all standard programming language structures. This makes Lingo every bit as powerful as languages such as C++, Pascal, and Java. In some cases, it's even more powerful.

The results of your work can be easily distributed to the world. You can create standalone applications to send over the Internet or burn into CD-ROMs. You can embed your creations into HTML pages for the Web. You can even create a Java applet.

Many people in the computer industry still think of Director as it was in version 3: an animation tool with a simple scripting language. However, each version since then has added a huge array of powerful features. Director is now the most advanced animation tool ever, with one of the most advanced programming languages.

Anyone who says, "You can't do that in Director," doesn't really understand the power or depth of Director 8.5.

DO YOU NEED TO UPDATE YOUR BOOK?

If you already have the previous edition, "*Special Edition Using Director 8*," then you are probably wondering what is new in this version. The changes in this book reflect the changes in Director itself. So, for instance, when it comes to sound, there are no changes from Director 8.0 to 8.5, so I didn't see the need to make any changes in the book either.

The main reason to upgrade to this book is the addition of two large chapters on the new Director 8.5 3D engine (Chapters 38, "Using 3D Media," and 39, "3D Lingo"). There is so much new material there that these two chapters are almost like a book inside a book.

In addition, I added a lot to the Multiuser Server chapter to cover the new Multiuser Server features. The Lingo Reference guide at the back of the book now includes almost 400 new 3D commands and functions. Chapter 4, "Text and Field Members," has been updated to talk about 3D text. Chapter 20, "Controlling Vector Graphics," has been updated with the new Lingo Flash commands. I even added some 3D terms to the glossary.

The one chapter that I removed from the book was the old Chapter 37, "Creating Java Applets." Why did I remove it? Well, the "Save As Java" feature of Director is now gone. Macromedia removed this feature from Director 8.5 due to lack of use.

So if you already have *Special Edition Using Director 8* and you are trying to decide whether to upgrade to this book, you have to ask yourself if you plan to use these new features.

People will also vary on how important it is to them to have an up-to-date reference. Some will decide to get by on the older edition, while others must have the latest and greatest.

WHO SHOULD READ THIS BOOK?

Chapter 1, "Animation with Director," assumes that you are a total beginner and have never used Director before. However, it does not assume that you lack intelligence.

The first two chapters move quickly through the basics. Those chapters, like the rest of this book, state concepts and techniques clearly, and never assume you know something about Director before it is taught in the book.

The idea is to not waste time by walking you step-by-step through basic and simple tasks. Instead, this book assumes that you are a motivated learner, wanting to read, absorb, understand, and then move on to the next piece of information.

If you are an animator or are simply using Director to create presentations, Chapters 1 through 11 are for you. They go into detail about making animations and presentations without using any Lingo programming.

If you want to learn Lingo, Chapter 12, "Learning Lingo," and the following chapters teach you from the ground up. Like Chapters 1 and 2, these chapters do not assume you know anything about Lingo or programming in advance. However, they move quickly, and a motivated learner can be programming in Lingo in a matter of hours.

If you are interested in advanced Lingo techniques, the later chapters are filled with high-level Lingo programs. I have continued the practice of my earlier books in providing more advanced Lingo concepts than any of the other books on the market.

If you are already familiar with Director and Lingo, but want to get up to speed on the new 3D engine, then you could jump right to Chapters 38 and 39.

Finally, if you are seeking a good reference book on Director, this book will beat or rival any other. I have tried to cover all topics, even ones that other books do not explore. In addition, I have made the reference section comprehensive. It features a full Lingo dictionary and many other useful appendixes.

WHAT THIS BOOK DOESN'T HAVE

This book has a lot of useful information crammed in between the covers. But it doesn't have everything.

Director is such a huge program that there is no way to go into detail about everything. There is no way to cover every aspect of Director for beginner, intermediate, and advanced users.

There's not even a consensus about what "beginner," "intermediate," and "advanced" mean. I've seen some users who call themselves advanced, but they can hardly program enough Lingo to make a single button, while other "advanced" users are extending Lingo by writing their own Xtras.

Bill Cosby once said, "I don't know the key to success, but the key to failure is trying to please everyone."

This book will not please everyone. No Director book will. I don't even go into features that are rarely used, like the XML Xtra and RealMedia. If I tried to include everything, then the book would be several thousand pages long, cost a lot more to buy, and wouldn't have been finished until well after Director 9 was released.

I have tried very hard to provide an intermediate to advanced guide to Director 8.5. I have also tried to make this the best general-purpose Director book on the market. Other books may cover a topic or two better than this one, but I believe that this is the book that covers Director as a whole better than any other book you will find.

THIS BOOK IS ABOUT DIRECTOR 8 AND 8.5

One thing to note is that this book is really for Director 8 and 8.5, not earlier versions of Director. In the past, many people have bought my Director 7 book and tried to use it to learn Director 5 or 6. They, of course, ran into problems.

The differences between Director 7 and Director 8 mean that many of the things in this book will not work in Director 7. In addition, all the examples on the CD-ROM are in either Director 8 or Director 8.5 format and cannot be opened with Director 7. I have tried to make as many example files in Director 8 format so that you can use this book with both Director 8 and 8.5.

Macromedia is definitely not one of those companies that fixes a few bugs and calls it an upgrade. It has added a large number of new features. Other companies should take a lesson from Macromedia about creating upgrades that are really worth the upgrade price.

If you consider yourself a serious developer, you should be using Director 8.5 by the time you read this. Director 7 is a great tool, but Director 8.5 is better. It will empower you to create better products.

HOW TO USE THIS BOOK

You can read this book through, or use it for random access reference. If you are just learning Director, or are looking to expand your skills, you can pick a point in the book that seems to match your current skill level and start reading there.

Each chapter makes the general assumption that you know the basics of the material in the previous chapters. However, enough context is given in each chapter for you to fill in the gaps in your knowledge as you go along. There are "See Also" markers throughout the book that refer you both forward and backward in the book to places where a similar topic is covered.

Chapters 1 and 2 are meant to teach the basics, from using Director as an animation tool to using Director as a presentation tool. Chapters 3 through 11 then add to those basics with information about each media type and some more advanced techniques. No Lingo knowledge is required or taught during these chapters.

Chapters 12 through 14 teach Lingo basics. Then, Chapters 15 through 20 build on that knowledge by showing how Lingo can control various types of media. Chapters 21 through 26 are about even more advanced Lingo techniques.

Chapters 27 to 32 are very different from the rest of the book, and from material found in other books. They provide examples of Director movies. An explanation of what each movie does and how it does it, plus the source code for each movie, is given. These are examples that you can use to see how Lingo code is put to use in real-life situations. These chapters also include suggestions for how you can alter and adapt them to make your own movies.

Chapter 37 deals with the Multiuser Server, including the new server-side scripting ability.

Chapters 38 and 39 are new to this edition of the book, and deal with the 3D engine. These are large chapters that can almost be treated as a book inside a book.

The rest of the chapters have information useful for completing a project, such as debugging, performance issues, and building projectors and Shockwave pages.

To round out the book as a reference guide, I have added a complete Lingo quick reference section and many tables and charts as appendixes.

The following list contains a few goals that developers might have for this book and how to go about using the book to accomplish them:

- Learn Director as a beginner: Start at Chapter 1 and read through Chapter 11, trying all of the examples along the way. Continue to learn Lingo in Chapter 12 when you feel you have mastered Chapters 1–11.

- Learn to create animation with Director: Read Chapters 1–10.

- Learn to add interactivity to your animation: Read Chapter 2, and then Chapters 9–11.

- Learn to create presentations: Read Chapters 1–11.

- Learn how to create behaviors without using Lingo: Read Chapter 11.

- Learn how to program basic Lingo: Read Chapters 12–15.

- Learn how to create behaviors with Lingo: Read Chapter 14.

- Increase your Lingo skills beyond the basics: First review Chapters 12–15, and then continue to read Chapters 16–26.

- Learn advanced Lingo techniques: Read Chapters 21–26.

- Find useful source code that you can reuse: Scan through Chapters 14–26, and then refer to Chapters 27–32 for larger examples.

- Learn how to optimize and complete a project: Read Chapters 33–36.

- Learn how to translate your CD-ROM-building Director knowledge to make Shockwave movies: See Chapters 9, 22, 31, 35, and 36.

- Fill in your existing Director knowledge with a greater understanding of members and techniques: Read Chapters 3–8 to learn about members, 16–20 to learn about Lingo related to these members, and then 21–26 for advanced techniques.

- Learn how to create 3D Director movies: If you are already familiar with the rest of Director, then you can go to Chapters 38 and 39 to learn all about 3D.

- Use this book as your Director 8 reference guide: Familiarize yourself with the table of contents and index to learn where things are in the book. Also scan the appendixes to get an idea of the content there.

CONVENTIONS USED IN THIS BOOK

The following conventions are used to differentiate Lingo keywords from user-defined keywords and any other text with special emphasis:

- Italic—Used for official Lingo keywords. This includes handlers, commands, properties, and anything found in the official Macromedia documentation. Examples: *on mouseUp*, *on exitFrame*, *puppetSprite*, and the *ticks*.

- Quotation marks—Anything made up by the programmer or the author. These keywords can't be found in the official documentation, because they don't exist until the programmer creates them. Examples: "on myHandler" and "myVariable".

Messages. A message is an invisible thing that is sent through the Director environment. They have names only as a way to relate to the reader what is going on. Examples: "mouseUp" and "exitFrame". They look like official keywords, but are not.

Values. When I want to say something such as: the value of this variable is "hello world", the value returned is shown in quotes.

- Monospace—Lines of code and commands that the programmer is asked to type into Director appear in monospace and bold, regardless of keyword type. For example: `put 41+1`.

This formatting reflects the importance of showing the difference between official Lingo keywords and made-up words.

At the end of most chapters you will find two sections: "Troubleshooting" and "Did You Know?" The first presents some common problems that developers face and how to avoid them. This is in addition to troubleshooting advice found throughout many chapters.

The "Did You Know?" section is something a little different. It contains extra information about the topic. Sometimes the information is a little more advanced than the level of the chapter. Other times it highlights little-known facts or undocumented Lingo. On occasion it simply contains an idea for an interesting application of the information taught in the chapter. In addition, "Tips" and "Notes" placed throughout the chapters provide interesting ideas and methods you might not have considered.

BEFORE YOU BEGIN

There are several ways that I recommend beginning to use this book. The first suggestion is for first-time Director users. Play with Director first. Just open the program and play with it. Try all the menu commands and look at some of the tutorials that come with Director.

Another thing that beginners should do is check out as many Shockwave movies on the Web as you can. These give you an idea of what is possible. If you need a place to start, try `http://clevermedia.com`, a site created by my company, CleverMedia, and me.

Getting grounded by playing with Director and surfing the Web will give you some context as you start reading this book.

If you are a Director user who has just upgraded to Director 8 or 8.5, you should check the next section of this book, "What's New in Director 8 and 8.5." It has, of course, a list of most of the features new to Director 8 and 8.5.

There are so many new features, I honestly recommend that even an experienced Director 7 user start this book at Chapter 1. However, such a user would be able to move through most of the early chapters quickly.

Another way to use this book is to simply place it next to your computer as a reference. Need to know about using the Behavior Inspector? Chapter 11, "Advanced Techniques." Need to remember the basics for creating a behavior? Chapter 14, "Creating Behaviors." Need to create or alter a vector shape? Chapter 20, "Controlling Vector Graphics." Want to make a game? Chapter 32, "Games." You get the idea. All in all, there is a lot in this book for every level of Director user. I hope you enjoy reading this book as much as I enjoyed writing it!

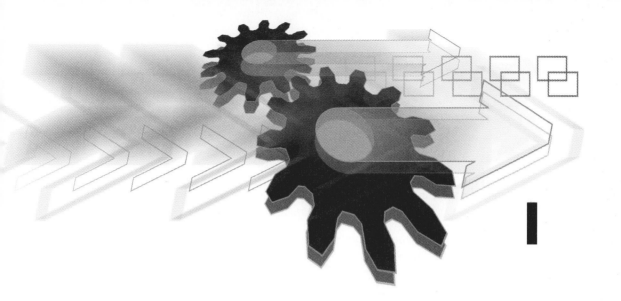

DIRECTOR BASICS

IN THIS PART

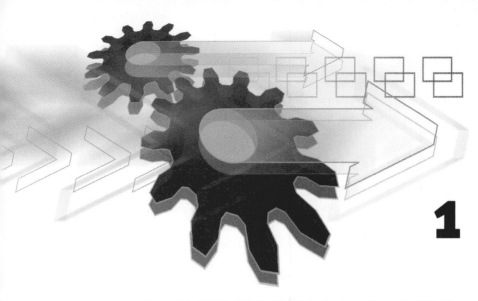

1

ANIMATION WITH DIRECTOR

To many people, Director is only an animation tool. Indeed, it evolved from one. Although it's capable of much more than just animation, much of how Director looks and works is based on its use as an animation tool. Learning the animation side of Director is a good place for you to begin.

AN INTRODUCTION TO DIRECTOR

Macromedia Director 8 is a complete environment for the creation of multimedia. Think of it as an artist's canvas. Or, to use the metaphor that Director follows, a stage.

You can fill this stage with your own production. Any element in the production is called a cast member or simply a member. The computer screen where the action takes place is a window called the *Stage*.

The rest of the elements in Director also follow a theater/film metaphor, although some element names follow it better than others.

The Theater Metaphor

Assume that you have an image drawn in another program that you want to place in Director. Let's look at how this is done, leaving the details for later.

When you import this image into Director, it becomes a cast member. The Cast window displays a list of all the cast members. This list is called the *cast library* or sometimes simply the *Cast*. Members can be of different types: bitmap images, text, sounds, shapes, and so on. In this case, let's assume that you have a bitmap image, commonly called a *bitmap*.

You can take this bitmap and place it onto the Stage by simply dragging and dropping it there. It actually appears both on the Stage and in the Score. The *Score* is a chart that shows which members appear on the Stage at certain times. A moment in time is called a *frame*. The Score shows which members appear in which frames. The Stage shows the positions of each member on the Stage during a particular frame.

The users see the Stage only when they are finished with their project. The Cast window and Score window are tools used only by you, the author of the Director project.

A member that is in the Score is called a sprite. This term does not describe the member, but rather the combination of the member and its placement in the Score and on the Stage. A *member* is simply a bitmap or other media element, whereas a *sprite* is the description of which member is being used, which frame of the Score it is in, and where it is located on the Stage, as well as many other properties. For instance, a member might be a picture, and a sprite is that member placed on the Stage.

Figure 1.1 illustrates Director's primary metaphor. The actors, both on and off the Stage, are members. The two actors on the Stage are also sprites because they are taking an active part in the production.

Director is great at giving you a lot of options. Bitmap images can be just about any image format, including PICT, BMP, JPEG, GIF, or even a file in native PhotoShop format.

The Cast

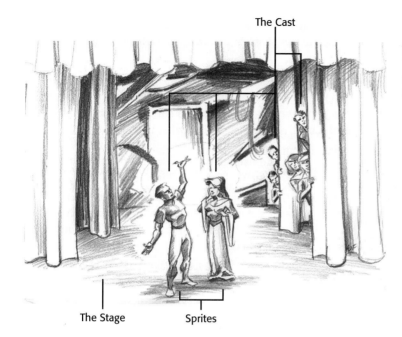

The Stage   Sprites

Figure 1.1
This illustration demonstrates the difference between cast members and sprites.

A Director production is called a *movie*. This term is more accurately used to describe the file that contains all your work. A Director project can actually contain many movies, or just one. A movie can have many cast members, but only one Score.

Understanding Director's terminology is the first step toward learning to use the program:

- **Movie**—The primary Director file. It contains one or more cast libraries and a Score. It's the only Director file you need for most productions.

- **Cast**—The list of cast members used in a movie.

- **Member**—A single element, such as a bitmap, some text, a sound, a shape, a vector drawing, or a piece of digital video.

- **Score**—A chart showing which members appear on the Stage at certain times.

- **Frame**—An instant of time in Director. While you are working on a movie, the Stage shows a single frame. While the movie is animating, the Stage moves through frames to create the visual effect of animation.

- **Channel**—A numbered position in the Score. Every sprite occupies a channel over a series of frames. The Score can have as many as 1,000 channels, as well as a few special channels at the top. The specific channel a sprite is in determines whether it gets drawn over or under another sprite.

- **Sprite**—The description of which member is shown, where it is in the Score, where it appears on the Stage, and many other properties.

Using only the preceding elements, you can create animations with Director. They are the primary parts of the program and are used in the simplest of movies as well as in the most complex.

However, several other important elements are required to create anything but the simplest projects in Director. The most critical element is the *script*.

If you want to stick with the theater/film metaphor, a script is like stage direction. Using a programming language in Director called Lingo, you can tell sprites what to do. Although it is possible to animate a sprite using only the Stage and Score, more complex movements and interaction with the users require you to learn and use Lingo. You'll learn more about using Lingo in Chapter 12, "Learning Lingo," and Chapter 13, "Essential Lingo Syntax."

A Lingo script that is attached to a sprite in the Score is called a *behavior*. This type of script shows a sprite how to behave under different circumstances. A script attached to a whole frame is called a *frame script*, and a script that controls the entire movie is called a *movie script*. You'll find more information about scripts and scripting later in the book.

These terms will become important to you after you have mastered the basic skills of Director and begin to make professional projects. Here is a review of some more advanced Director terms:

* **Script**—A set of Lingo commands that controls sprites and other elements of the movie.

* **Lingo**—The programming language of Director.

* **Behavior**—A script that controls a sprite.

* **Frame Script**—A script that controls a frame.

* **Movie Script**—A script that controls the entire movie.

* **Projector**—A standalone application program created from a Director movie.

* **Shockwave**—Technology that enables users to play Director movies in Web browsers.

Playback Options

After you have created a movie and want to make a standalone computer application, you create a *projector*. This is simply a program that can be distributed to your users. It runs your Director movie without requiring Director.

Another way to distribute your finished Director movie is to embed it in Internet Web pages. People without Director can use Shockwave to play your movies. They can view your original Director movie file, or a special protected and compressed version of it. Shockwave most commonly comes in the form of a Web browser plug-in for Netscape Navigator and Microsoft Internet Explorer.

When a Director movie plays, it begins by displaying frame 1 on the Stage. Which members are shown on the Stage is determined by what is in the Score. The positions of the members on the Stage are determined by how you placed them there. After frame 1 is displayed, Director waits an appropriate amount of time, usually a fraction of a second, and then displays frame 2.

If frame 1 and frame 2 look the same, you will see no difference. However, if the locations of the sprites differ from frame to frame, they appear to move. As the movie goes from one frame to the next, changes in the locations of sprites create the illusion of movement.

As the movie progresses, each sprite starts and ends. Some sprites exist throughout the entire movie, whereas others begin at a certain frame and end at another. Some sprites may appear in only one frame.

When the last frame is reached, the movie stops. You might want to simply have the movie loop back to the beginning and start again. However, you also can use Lingo to have the movie jump to any other frame.

Movie Example

A simple example will help you understand how Director movies are made. It includes three bitmap cast members and 28 frames of animation. Figures 1.2 and 1.3 show the Cast window with all three members. You can open the Cast window by choosing Window, Cast in the menu bar. The shortcut for this action is ⌘+3 on the Macintosh and Ctrl+3 in Windows.

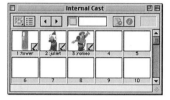

Figure 1.2
The Internal Cast window with three bitmap members. The name of the window refers to the name of the Cast: Internal (the default name for the main Cast).

This example, like all the examples in this book, is located on the CD-ROM that comes with the book. A folder exists for each chapter, and inside that folder is a variety of Director movies named in such a way that you can easily find the file that corresponds to the example in the book. The file for this example is called 01romeo.dir.

Figure 1.3 shows an alternative view of the Cast window. In Director 8, you can view the Cast as a set of image thumbnails (refer to Figure 1.2), or as a list, as shown in Figure 1.3. The second button from the left at the top of the Cast window allows you to switch between these two views.

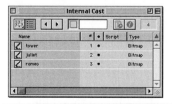

Figure 1.3
The Internal Cast window with the same three bitmap members as shown in Figure 1.2, but this time in list format.

Note in Figures 1.2 and 1.3 that I have also named these three members. You can name members by selecting a member and editing its name in the text area at the top of the Cast window. In Figure 1.2, shown earlier, the Cast window shows miniature images of each bitmap, called *thumbnails*. When the Cast window is set to list format, small icons are shown on the left to signify which type of member each item is.

To continue building the movie, take the first member, the tower, and place it on the Stage by clicking and dragging the member from the Cast window to the Stage window. Because the image was drawn to be placed on the right side of the Stage, you put it there.

Placing the member on the Stage also places it in the Score in the first available channel, which in this case is channel 1. Figure 1.4 shows the Stage with the member placed, as well as the Score window on top of it. More details about all these windows can be found later in the chapter. Right now, just notice that the sprite appears in channel 1 and stretches from frame 1 to frame 28.

Figure 1.4
Both the Stage and the Score window are shown. The bitmap of the tower corresponds to the sprite shown in channel 1, from frames 1 to 28.

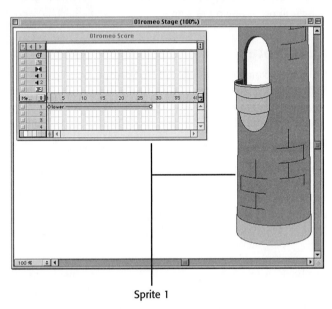

Sprite 1

The Stage window contains the bitmap from member 1. The Score shows a sprite that will display member 1 from frames 1 to 28.

If you play the movie now, not much happens. You will see an indicator in the Score window move from frame 1 to 28. The bitmap stays in the same place on the Stage because you have not told it to do otherwise.

Now add a second element to the movie. Drag the picture of the woman onto the Stage. It then appears in channel 2 in the Score. If you move the woman over to the tower, you see an interesting result. Figure 1.5 shows the woman (Juliet) and the tower on the Stage as well as in the Score. The woman appears to be outside the tower. Her sprite is drawn after the tower's sprite because it appears in a higher Score channel.

The reason that I show a 28-frame sprite in the example here is because Director's default setting is to make all new sprites 28 frames long. After you get in the Score, you can adjust the sprite's length. You can also change the default sprite span to something other than 28. If you do not get a 28-frame sprite when you create a new sprite, the preferences for your copy of Director have been modified. Choose File, Preferences, Sprite to change this setting.

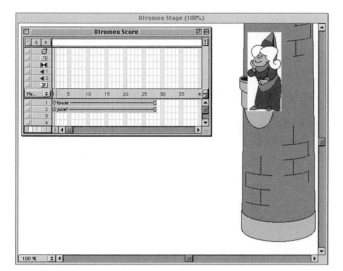

Figure 1.5
The Stage shows two members: a woman and a tower. The woman is drawn on top of the tower because her sprite is in a higher Score channel.

You can fix this problem by swapping the two sprites. If you move the woman's sprite to channel 1 and the tower's sprite to channel 2, the tower then covers the woman rather than the other way around. You can swap the sprites by simply dragging them around the Score window. Move the tower to channel 3, the woman to channel 1, and then the tower back to channel 2.

The desired effect, however, is not to completely cover the woman with the tower, but instead to have her show through the tower window. You can do this by applying an ink to the sprite.

Sprites are more than just a member, a Stage location, and a frame range. They also have properties, such as inks. An ink determines how a sprite is drawn on the Stage. The default ink is copy, which means that a bitmap member blocks out everything under its rectangular boundaries. This is what you have been using, which is why the woman is completely obscured by the tower.

However, if you set the ink of the tower sprite to Background Transparent, the tower sprite draws differently. This ink setting causes all pure white pixels in the drawing to appear as transparent, so the sprites behind them show through. Setting the tower sprite to Background Transparent gives you the result seen in Figure 1.6.

Now you have a movie with two sprites, but it still does not include animation. Drag the bitmap of the man (Romeo) on the Stage and place him somewhere toward the bottom. You want to have him slide in from the left. For now, he appears as sprite 3, which spans the same frames as the other two sprites.

Take a close look at the sprites as represented in the Score. Notice that a small circle appears in the first frame of each sprite and a small rectangle appears in the last frame. The circle signifies a *keyframe*, which describes a frame where the graphic is locked into a position on the Stage. You can see these in Figure 1.7.

Figure 1.6
Now the woman shows through the window of the tower on the Stage. This effect is achieved by having the tower sprite set to Background Transparent ink.

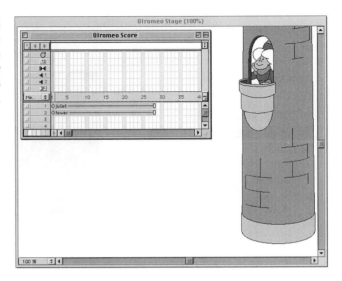

In any frame of a sprite that does not include a keyframe, Director positions the sprite on the Stage relative to the last and next keyframe. This process is known as *tweening*. With it, you can define simple animations by just showing Director the starting and ending points of a sprite.

The small rectangles at the right side of each sprite span changes into a small circle if you grab the sprite on that frame and move it onto the Stage. This turns the last frame into a keyframe. Now, each of the two keyframes of each sprite represent different Stage positions for that sprite. The nonkeyframe spaces in between determine how to position the sprite by using a position somewhere between the two keyframes. So, halfway between the two keyframes, the sprite appears on the Stage halfway between the two positions.

For instance, suppose you have a sprite that is three frames long. The first frame is always a keyframe; otherwise, Director would not know where to start the animation. In most cases, the last frame is also a keyframe, so Director knows where to end the animation. If you position the sprite on the left side of the screen in frame 1, and the right side of the screen in frame 3, you have set the locations of both keyframes.

Director then determines that for frame 2 the sprite needs to be in the middle of the Stage, directly between the first and last locations. You never have to show Director where to place the sprite in frame 2; it just figures it out by looking at the keyframes before and after it.

You can position the man's sprite over to the left of the Stage in frame 1, and then place him closer to the tower in frame 28. Do this by using the Score window to select which frame to edit. Just click anywhere in that frame's column to move to that frame. Move to frame 1 and position the man, and then move to frame 28 and position him again.

The result is that he will animate from frame 1 to 28, moving across the Stage from left to right. Figure 1.7 shows this animation somewhere in the middle.

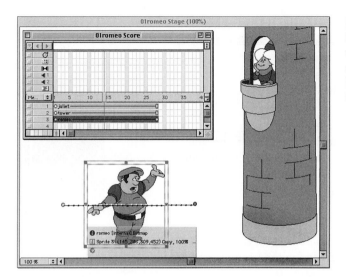

Figure 1.7
Sprite 3 moves from left to right, which results from having different settings for the initial and final keyframes of the sprite in the Score.

Later in this book, you will find out how to add more than one keyframe to a sprite, how to use many different inks, and even how to make sprites move in directions other than straight lines and constant speeds.

*For more information about inks, **see** "Setting Sprite Inks," **p. 176** (Chapter 10, "Properties of Sprites and Frames")*

THE CAST

Recall that when you import an image into Director, it becomes a cast member. The Cast window displays a list of all the cast members. This list is called the *Cast*. Members can be of different types: bitmap images, text, sounds, shapes, and so on. This section discusses the various types of cast members in more detail.

Types of Cast Members

The most basic elements of any Director movie are the cast members. You can't do any work in the Score or on the Stage without first having some members to work with.

In the last section, you saw examples of bitmap members. You can also use many more types of members. Basically, any form of media can be represented in Director as a cast member.

Each type of cast member has its own editing window, its own Properties dialog box, or both. For instance, the Paint window enables you to edit a bitmap member. It resembles a standalone image-editing application, but with an emphasis on editing the bitmap for use in Director.

In some cases, you can assign external editors to cast member types. You can use Adobe PhotoShop to edit bitmap members if you want.

Every cast member also has a name and a number. The number corresponds to its position in the Cast window while using the thumbnail view of the Cast. The number is also shown in the list view of the Cast window, in a column titled with a #. The name, however, is anything you want it to be.

You should always assign every cast member a unique name. Named cast members will come in handy when you begin scripting with Lingo.

Earlier in this chapter, Figures 1.2 and 1.3 showed typical Cast windows. A Cast window is really just one continuous list of members. You can stretch or shrink the window to display more or fewer members at a time.

You already know that you can add a member to the Score or Stage by dragging from the Cast window. You can edit a member by double-clicking its thumbnail or icon. A single click on a member selects it, and then you can click the information button in the Cast window to view its properties.

The information button—a blue box with a lowercase *"i"*—appears in the upper-right corner of many windows in Director. Clicking it shows you the properties of the selected cast member. Sometimes you can edit important properties of the member this way.

Cast member types vary greatly. Some can be created and edited in Director. Others need to be created in programs such as video or sound-editing tools and then imported. The following list summarizes most of the possible member types. Chapter 3, "Bitmap Members," provides more details.

- **Bitmaps**—A bitmap is essentially a graphic or image. It can be a drawing, photograph, or even an image generated by a 3D program. You can use the Paint window to edit most bitmaps in Director.

- **Text**—A text member contains formatted characters. You can create them in Director with the text-editing window, or you can import files created in word processing programs. Director has the capability to display graphically pleasing anti-aliased text. This means that the edges of characters are smooth rather than jagged. Director 8 also enables you to create text members that use fonts that don't need to be on the user's machine to display properly.

- **Fields**—These are like text members, but date back to earlier versions of Director, in which fields were the only text display option. Although they can't be anti-aliased and you cannot import word processing files as fields, they have other advantages. Mostly, they take up less file space and are more suited to general text use in which file size is important.

- **Sounds**—Director can import many different types of sound formats, but does not have the capability to create or edit sounds. Sounds can be quick, simple buzzes and beeps or long music pieces.

- **Shapes**—Director has a few special cast member types called *shapes*. You can draw lines, ovals, rectangles, and rounded rectangles. All but lines can be either filled or outlines. You can use these shapes to add quick graphic elements to your movies without having to create bitmaps for them.

- **Vectors**—You can also create unique, complex shapes called *vectors*. These are similar to the media created with programs such as Macromedia FreeHand and Adobe Illustrator. A vector member is one or more long lines that can be bent and curved. A closed loop in a vector member can be filled. Vector members can be scaled to any size and still maintain their shape and clarity.

- **Flash**—Another authoring program made by Macromedia is Flash. In Flash, you also create "movies." Flash differs from Director in many ways, including the fact that it uses vector-based graphics for a majority of its elements, and it does not have a robust programming language, such as Lingo. However, you can make Flash movies and then import them into Director as members. These can either be static graphics, animated sequences, or interactive elements.

- **Buttons**—You can make quick, simple buttons in Director. These buttons have a generic look and feel. They are mostly useful for prototyping and pre-release versions of your project. You will eventually want to replace them with bitmaps that act as buttons.

- **Digital Video**—Video members can come in a variety of sources but are usually in Apple QuickTime format or Windows AVI format. Most of the time, these members are merely links to external files that contain the real media. This category can be extended to hold a variety of QuickTime formats, such as QuickTime VR and MIDI files.

- **Scripts**—Cast members that hold scripts appear to be similar to field members. They hold the Lingo instructions that control the elements of the movie.

- **Xtra Members**—Macromedia and third parties develop extensions to Director that add or enhance functionality. These are called Xtras. Some of these Xtras enable you to have new types of cast members, such as cursor cast members or 3D graphics.

As you explore Director's different cast members, you will find that they relate to one another in many ways. For instance, most cast members can have a script attached to them. The script is not a separate cast member, but a property of that single cast member. You can, therefore, create a bitmap image that has a script in it. That script enables it to react to the users clicking it. But you can also use that bitmap without any script attached to it. Instead, you attach a separate script member, known as a behavior, to the same sprite in the Score.

Cast Window Properties and Settings

The Cast window is one of your primary tools for using Director. The customizable features may help you better organize your work. First, take a look at the toolbar area of a Cast window. Figure 1.8 shows an Internal Cast window with some members. You can see several icon buttons in the toolbar.

Figure 1.8
An Internal Cast window in thumbnail view, with several sample
members. There are three
bitmaps, a behavior script, a
shape, a button, and a sound.

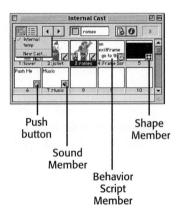

Push
button

Sound
Member

Behavior
Script
Member

Shape
Member

The first button on the left, the Choose Cast pop-up, enables you to browse the various cast libraries contained in, or attached to, the movie. You can have many internal and external Casts. More information about this feature appears later in the chapter.

The second button allows you to switch between the thumbnail view and list view of the Cast window. Earlier in this chapter, Figures 1.2 and 1.8 showed the thumbnail view, whereas Figure 1.3 showed the list view.

While in the list view, you can click any column title to force the Cast window to sort your members by that column. On the Macintosh, you will see a little pyramid-like button just to the right of all the column titles. By clicking this button, you can change the sort order of the Cast window from ascending to descending and back again. In Windows, this button is not present, and you simply click the column title a second time to change the sort order.

The rest of the buttons are pretty simple. The arrows enable you to select the next or previous member in the Cast. The square is a button that you can click and drag to the Stage or Score. Doing so places the selected cast member or members there. The Member Script button enables you to add or edit a script to most members. For script members, it simply opens the script-editing window. The Member Properties button, as you have seen before, shows you the Properties dialog box for the selected member or members.

In addition to these buttons, the toolbar shows you the name and number of the cast member. You can edit the name of the member within the toolbar.

Now look at the members in this Cast shown earlier in Figure 1.2. Every member shown has a thumbnail repre-sentation of the contents of the member. In the case of a bitmap, it is simply a resized version of the image. In other cases, such as with scripts and buttons, the text is displayed. In addition to this image, an icon appears in the lower-right corner of each box that tells you what type the member is. A little paintbrush shows you that it is a bitmap.

You can select one or many cast members in the Cast window. Using the Shift key, you can select a set of continuous members. Using the ⌘ key on the Macintosh and the Ctrl key in Windows, you can add single members to your current selection. You can drag members around the Cast window in thumbnail view. You can also drag members to the Score or Stage.

Another icon sometimes appears in the lower-left corner of each box. This icon tells you that a script is attached to this member. It is not important for a beginner to understand these icons right away. They are simply there to help you quickly identify items in the cast.

You can customize Cast windows to an extent. Choose File, Preferences, Cast to bring up the Cast Window Preferences dialog box. Figure 1.9 shows this dialog box for the Internal Cast window.

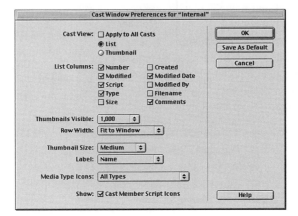

Figure 1.9
The Cast Window Preferences dialog box enables you to customize the appearance of the Cast window.

The first half of the Cast Window Preferences dialog box enables you to set the default way in which a Cast window first appears. You can select either the list or thumbnail view. You can also choose which columns you want to be present in the list view.

The various settings in the rest of the dialog box are fairly self-explanatory. You can use the Row Width setting to fix the number of members shown in the thumbnail view on each row regardless of the present size of the window. You can also set the Thumbnail Size, Label display, and Media Type Icons display options.

Multiple Cast Libraries

In the days of Director 4, all cast members had to be contained in one Cast. This sometimes meant a huge Cast with hundreds of cast members. The only option for sharing members between movies was to have one specially labeled movie that acted as a shared Cast. Director 5 introduced the idea of multiple cast libraries. The main advantage is that you can better organize the members.

Each cast library has a name. Each movie must have at least one cast library. This first cast library is named "Internal" by default, but you can change that.

Use the Cast icon that appears as the leftmost button in the Cast window toolbar to create a new Cast. You are then prompted for its name.

Setting the row width option to "10 thumbnails" can sometimes help you organize your cast members. However, if you set the window width on the screen to be less than 10 members across, you won't be able to see a continuous set of members. For instance, you might see members 1 to 8, 11 to 18, 21 to 28, and 31 to 38. You might end up wasting time searching for lost members that are simply outside the viewable window area.

Organizing your members into multiple Casts is a requirement for some developers, whereas others still prefer to use just one Cast. In practice, it depends on the type of project you are working on.

If you are creating a simple, linear animation that has only a few members, it is probably best to keep your movie to one Cast. However, multiple casts help when you have more than a few dozen members.

Some developers organize their casts by member type, placing bitmaps in one Cast, scripts in another, sounds in another, and so on. Others mix member types in a Cast, but place items according to when they are used, such as placing members that are part of an introduction screen together and members that are in the main animation together.

External Cast Libraries

Not all your Casts have to be contained inside a single movie. You can have Casts that exist as their own files—these are called *external cast libraries*.

By their very nature, these external Casts have some interesting properties. For one, they can be shared by multiple movies. For instance, you can have a series of photographs in an external Cast. One movie can use some of these members in a slideshow presentation. A separate movie can use these same images in a puzzle game. The cast library needs to be included only once, even though it is being used twice.

The inverse of this property of external Casts is that you can easily switch Casts in one movie without editing the movie. For instance, a Cast called *images.cst* might contain pictures of famous buildings in New York. A movie called *slideshow.dir* can use these images in a slideshow presentation. If you take another cast file also called *images.cst* and replace the first one with it, you could have a slideshow of famous buildings in San Francisco instead.

External Cast libraries also make it easier for multiple people to work on a project together. You could have an artist working on one cast file, a sound engineer on another, and a multimedia author on the main movie. When the artist and engineer are done, you can plug the new cast libraries right in.

If you are using multiple cast libraries, you might find it necessary to look at more than one Cast at a time. You can do this by holding down the Option key on the Macintosh or the Alt key in Windows and selecting the second Cast from the list presented when clicking the Cast icon on the left side of the Cast window toolbar. A second Cast window opens. You can drag members between windows.

In Windows, dot-three extensions are still necessary to enable the operating system to recognize the contents of a file. Dot-three names are also used by most Internet servers. Director movies use a .dir extension. External Cast libraries use a .cst extension. You can make protected versions of either type of file so that other developers cannot see your code or access your media. These files have .dxr and .cxt extensions. If you compress the files for Internet delivery, the extensions are .dcr and .cct. Projectors, of course, are executable applications and use the .exe extension. Even if you are developing on a Macintosh, it's useful to name your files this way to avoid problems when making a cross-platform version of your project.

THE STAGE

TheStage is the only window that the end users will actually see. It is where all the visual action of a movie takes place, at least until you start using some advanced techniques.

During authoring, the main purpose of the Stage is to show you a preview of what the users will see. While the movie is stopped, you see a frozen moment in time: one single frame of the movie.

The Stage also acts as your primary placement tool. You can drag cast members to either the Stage or the Score to use them on the Stage. However, only on the Stage can you position them. With the Score and other tools, you are limited to positioning the sprites by tweaking numbers. On the Stage, you can position sprites by dragging them with the mouse.

It is important to differentiate the Stage window in Director with the actual Stage. The Stage is the area where your Director movie is seen. The end user will see only this area. However, the Stage window in Director 8 can show this area, plus the area that surrounds the Stage.

Because it is impossible to change an internal cast to an external cast, and vice versa, decide at the beginning of your project how you are going to organize your casts. Otherwise, you might find yourself needing to move large amounts of media from cast to cast by dragging and dropping it.

The Stage in Director 8 is a separate window. You can make the window temporarily disappear by pressing ⌘+1 on the Macintosh or Ctrl+1 in Windows. You can make it reappear the same way.

Figure 1.10 shows the Stage window. In this case, the Stage window view is set to 100%, so the Stage fills the entire Stage window.

Figure 1.10
The Stage is shown inside the Stage window at 100% zoom, with the Stage window matching the Stage in size exactly.

You can stretch the Stage window just like most other windows on the Mac or Windows operating system. If you stretch the window to be larger than the Stage size, you can see space surrounding the Stage as grayish areas (see Figure 1.11).

Figure 1.11
The Stage is shown inside the Stage window at 100% zoom, with the Stage window stretched so that the Stage and some surrounding area can be seen.

The Stage window can also be shrunk or magnified in a number of ways. One is to use the pop-up menu shown previously at the bottom left of both Figures 1.10 and 1.11. You can also use the keyboard shortcuts ⌘+= and ⌘+- on the Mac, and Ctrl+= and Ctrl+- in Windows. This zooming feature helps you arrange objects on the Stage, but does not affect playback for the end user.

The size of the actual Stage, as opposed to the size of the Stage window, can be changed by choosing Modify, Movie, Properties. You can change the size of the Stage as well as its default position on the screen.

A common Stage size is 640 pixels wide and 480 pixels high, because that screen size was the standard for personal computers for a long time. Today, 800×600 seems to be the most common size, but enough people still use 640×480 screens that it is the default size of multimedia presentations.

Stage size depends on what you expect your users to have. It also depends on other factors. For instance, if your movie will end up on the Web and be played with Shockwave, take into account the window borders of the Netscape and Internet Explorer windows. You will examine this more closely when you read about projectors and Shockwave in Part VIII, "Using Director to Create Professional Applications."

When you choose Modify, Movie, Properties, a palette window appears called the *Property Inspector*. This same window is used to change the properties of a number of elements in your movie, including the Stage, sprites, and members. We will be looking closer at this new feature of Director 8 later in this chapter, and then in detail in Chapter 9, "The Director Environment."

Another property of the Stage is its background color. You can set the background color of the Stage in the same place that you set the Stage size. The default is white and the second most common setting is black, but you can use any color.

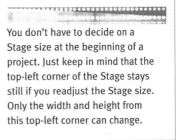

You don't have to decide on a Stage size at the beginning of a project. Just keep in mind that the top-left corner of the Stage stays still if you readjust the Stage size. Only the width and height from this top-left corner can change.

➪ *For more information about the Movie Preferences dialog box, **see** "Movie Properties," **p. 160** (Chapter 9, "The Director Environment")*

THE SCORE

The real heart and soul of a movie is the Score. As you can see in Figure 1.12, it really is just a chart of the contents of the movie. Time, represented by frames, goes across the Score, whereas sprite channels and other elements are listed as rows in the chart.

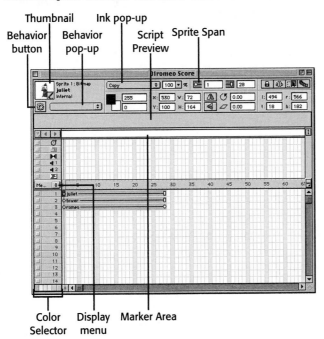

Thumbnail   Ink pop-up

Behavior button   Behavior pop-up   Script Preview   Sprite Span

Color Selector   Display menu   Marker Area

Figure 1.12
The Score window shows frames horizontally and channels vertically. Other elements appear near the top, and many buttons and icons provide other functions.

Elements of the Score Window

The Score window is much more complex than the Cast window. Notice that the toolbar at the top contains dozens of items. Each item corresponds to a property of the selected sprites.

Moving from left to right across the top, you can see the thumbnail of the sprite's cast member, a pop-up menu for the ink setting, a percentage for a property called the blend, the starting and ending frames of the sprite, and four sprite properties known as lock, editable, movable, and trails.

Starting on the left across the bottom of the toolbar you can see a button and a pop-up menu that relate to any behavior scripts attached to the sprite. Next are the foreground and background colors for the selected sprite. Most of the rest of the settings correspond to the position and size of the sprite on the Stage. You can also see buttons and fields for flipping, skewing, and rotating the sprites. For simple animation, most of this information can be ignored, so don't let it overwhelm you right now.

Below the toolbar is an area that would show a script preview if you had selected a sprite with a script. In Figure 1.12, shown previously, this is simply a blank space. Clicking this space provides a shortcut for adding or editing a script.

Under the script preview area is the marker area. You can mark special frames in your movie with text called *labels*. A typical marker label may be "introduction" or "main animated loop." You add a marker by simply clicking in the marker area. The small down-arrow button on the left enables you to see a list of markers or even to open a dialog box that lists all the markers. The two other arrows enable you to jump between frames that have markers.

The toolbar at the top of the Score window is optional. While the Score is the selected window, choose View, Sprite Toolbar to show or hide the toolbar portion of the Score.

Sprites can have more than one behavior script attached to them. In this case, the behavior-related elements in the Score window are not very useful. Another window, called the Behavior Inspector, enables you to manipulate multiple behaviors. You will learn more about it in Chapter 11, "Advanced Techniques."

Markers can be used to organize your project. When you begin programming with Lingo, markers are even more important because you can refer to them in your code.

Under the marker area are some rows that contain special channels. Likethe Sprite channels below them, some of these channels refer to cast members. For instance, the two Sound channels, marked with sound speaker icon, can refer to sound cast members that are supposed to play during those frames. These special channels are defined as follows:

- **Tempo channel**—This is the first channel, the one with the clock icon. You can use this channel to specify the speed at which the movie moves through this frame. Double-clicking this row brings up a dialog box. You can specify the rate at which this movie should be progressing in frames per second (fps). This setting persists until another frame contains a new setting to override it.

    You can also set the Tempo channel to pause for a certain number of seconds. This is useful for slow animations, such as automatic slideshows. Other settings include having the movie stop altogether until the mouse is clicked, and having the movie wait for a sound or video cue point.

For more information about using the Tempo channel to wait for sounds, **see** "Waiting for Sounds and Cue Points," **p. 115** (Chapter 5, "Sound Members")

- **Palette channel**—This channel controls the palettes. Color palettes, discussed in Chapter 3, are sets of 256 colors that the computer uses to display graphics. If a computer is capable of displaying only 256 colors, a palette defines which 256 colors can be used at one time. You can use the Palette channel of the Score to set which palette is used in which frame. There are also a few palette special effects that can be performed.

  Because most home computers can now support more than 256 colors, it's becoming more common to ignore palettes and simply work in a thousands- or millions-of-colors mode. Director 7 was the first version of Director to support the use of millions of colors as the basis for the movie's color scheme, as opposed to requiring you to select a palette.

- **Transition channel**—The next channel is the Transition channel. Director has a number of predefined visual transitions that can be applied to a frame. The transition defines how that frame appears as the movie goes from the preceding frame to the current one. For instance, you can have the screen wipe from left to right, or you can have one frame dissolve into the next.

- **Sound channels**—The two Sound channels enable you to overlap sounds. You can have background music playing in Sound channel 1, and voice narration in Sound channel 2. With Lingo, you can use even more Sound channels.

- **Frame Script channel**—In the Frame Script channel, you can place Lingo script members that are meant to control that specific frame, the sprites on it, and the entire Director environment, as long as the movie is passing through that frame.

The rest of the Score shows the numbered Sprite channels. You can have from 1 to 1,000 channels in a movie. The total number of channels depends on a movie properties setting that you can access by choosing Modify, Movie, Properties.

Customizing the Score Window

You can customize the Score window in several ways. Some methods involve buttons and menus incorporated into the window itself, and others involve setting Director preferences.

The Display menu is a little pop-up menu that appears just under the Script channel and all the way to the left. It offers a variety of ways to label the sprites in the Score. In the earlier figures that contained the Score window, you saw this setting set to "Member." This means that it will display the member number and name in the Sprite channel. Here is a rundown of all the possible settings:

It is best to stick to the lowest number of channels that you can. Some overhead is involved with processing all the channels in every frame, and Director may perform better if you set your channel limit as low as possible. The default setting of 120 channels is a good start.

- **Member**—Shows the cast member of the sprite. The default setting shows the number of the cast member followed by the name if there is room in the span. To change this setting so that the name of the cast member is displayed, select Cast from the Preferences submenu of the File menu and change the Label pop-up to Name.

- **Behavior**—Displays the behavior number associated with the sprite, if a script is attached.

- **Location**—When the cursor is over a particular sprite span, displays the horizontal and vertical coordinates of the sprite in the frame in which you currently have the cursor.

- **Ink**—Displays the ink applied to the sprite span from the Ink pop-up menu to the right of the sprite thumbnail at the top of the Score.

- **Blend**—Displays the blend percentage as set in the Blend pop-up menu to the right of the Ink menu in the Score or under Sprite Properties in the Modify menu.

- **Extended**—Displays the cast member number, the behavior, the location, the ink, and the blend, as well as changes in the X and Y location. To customize the extended display options, choose File, Preferences, Score.

Directly across from the Display Options menu, on the right side of the window, is the Zoom pop-up. You can use this pop-up to adjust the width of frame columns in the display. Larger sizes might make it easier for you to examine the contents of individual frames. With smaller sizes, you can see more frames at one time in the window.

Also on the right side, directly next to the marker area, is a button that enables you to show or hide most of the special Sprite channels. Clicking it toggles between showing and not showing the Tempo, Palette, Transition, and Sound channels. When you get into creating interactive applications, you will find that it's more important to see more Sprite channels below than these special channels at the top. The frame script window is always displayed, regardless of this setting.

Another useful feature of the Score window is the Color Selector. You can use these little chips of color, located at the bottom-left corner of the window, to add color to the Score. This has absolutely no effect on movie playback. It is simply there to help you better organize your Score. To use it, first select a sprite, and then click a color chip to change its color.

If you are dealing with animations that span more than 20 frames at a time, a zoom of 100% or less is easier to work with.

Score Window Preferences

Figure 1.13 shows the Score Window Preferences dialog box. You can bring this up by choosing File, Preferences, Score. This dialog box has only a few settings.

You can quickly select the Score Preferences dialog box by pressing the Ctrl key and clicking (on the Mac) or right-clicking (in Windows) any empty space in the Score Window toolbar and selecting Score Preferences.

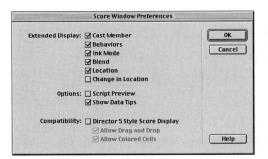

Figure 1.13
The Score Window Preferences dialog box enables you to customize the sprite display.

The first part of this dialog box enables you to specify which properties of a sprite are displayed when you select Extended in the Display Options of the Score. For instance, you can decide that you want to see both the member name and the ink. The default for this option is to show almost all the available information.

Next, you can choose to show or hide the script preview area. The script preview is handy not only because you can see the first few lines of code of a behavior script, but because you can also click it to create or edit the script. If this is not important to you and you would rather have the extra space in the window, turn this off.

Data tips are those little yellow labels that appear over sprites when you hover the cursor over them. They are mostly useful when you have small, single-frame sprites. In this case, there's not enough room in the Score window to display the member number and name. Instead, you can just roll the cursor over the sprites and see the information you want as data tips. The Preferences dialog box enables you to turn this function off if you want.

The last set of options gives you the chance to make the Score appear like a Director 5 Score. This was useful for developers who became attached to the way Director 4 and 5 displayed the Score information. However, using the Director 5 Score option is not recommended. The Director 6/7/8 Score window displays more information in a way more similar to how things are actually represented in Director. For those more familiar with the Director 5 Score, it can be a hard transition to the next Score window. However, when that transition is complete you will find that you have more control and are able to accomplish tasks faster.

For more information about Score window preferences, ***see*** *"Setting Preferences,"* **p. 157** *(Chapter 9, "The Director Environment")*

Sprite Preferences Dialog Box

Choosing File, Preferences, Sprite brings up the Sprite Preferences dialog box, as shown in Figure 1.14. Because sprites and the Score window go hand in hand, it should be discussed here.

You can quickly switch between the Director 8 and Director 5 Scores by Ctrl+clicking (on Macintosh computers) or right-clicking (in Windows) any empty gray area in the Score window toolbar and selecting Director 5 Style Display.

Figure 1.14
The Sprite Preferences dialog box enables you to alter the default settings for sprites.

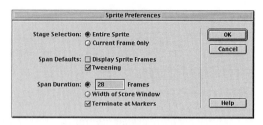

The first option, Stage Selection, enables you to specify what happens when you click a sprite on the Stage. The first choice is to have this action select the entire sprite in the Score, including the frames before and after the current one, if any. If you choose the second option, however, clicking the sprite on the Stage selects only that one frame of the sprite in the Score.

The Display Sprite Frames option enables you to set the default setting for adding keyframes to a sprite. A sprite can be set to add keyframes automatically whenever you change something about the sprite in a single frame. Or, the sprite can be set to require you to use the Insert, Keyframe menu options to create a new keyframe.

You can switch between these options for any sprite by using the Edit Sprite Frames and Edit Entire Sprite options in the Edit menu. Checking the Display Sprite Frames option in the Sprite Preferences dialog box makes every new sprite you create start out as if the Edit Sprite Frames option was turned on.

The Tweening option works in a similar way. Sprites have various tweening options set by the Tweening dialog box that you will examine later in this chapter. Checking the Tweening option in the Sprite Preferences dialog box makes all new sprites use tweening for size and position by default.

The last set of options enables you to specify the length of a new sprite. The default in Director is to set sprites to be 28 frames long. However, you can change this to a specific number or have the new sprites fill the Score window. As a further modification, you can limit the size of new sprites to end just before the next marker in the Score.

Other Score and Sprite Settings

Director is a very customizable development environment. If you don't like the way something works in the environment, chances are there is an option to change it. Here are some more useful options:

- The View menu holds a few more items that change the way the Score looks and works.

- The Sprite Toolbar option enables you to choose whether Director will show or hide the entire toolbar area of the Score. The only advantage to hiding it is if you need the screen space to display more sprites at one time. Access the Sprite toolbar by choosing Windows, Toolbar.

You can quickly select the Sprite Preferences dialog box by Ctrl+clicking (on the Mac) or right-clicking (in Windows) any empty space in the Score Window toolbar and selecting Sprite Preferences.

I always use a default span duration of 1. I find it more convenient to start with a small sprite and stretch it to the length I need.

- The Keyframes menu item offers an option to show or hide the little dots in the sprite spans that signify keyframes. When you turn this off, the sprite number is usually repeated at the end of the sprite span rather than with the final keyframe dot. Access the keyframes item by choosing View, Keyframes.

- The Sprite Labels submenu enables you to specify how often you want the label of the sprite to be displayed in the Score. You display it only in the first frame, every keyframe, only where changes occur, every single frame, or not at all. The label information depends on your settings in the Score Preferences dialog box. Access the Sprite Labels submenu by choosing View, Sprite Labels.

OTHER CONTROLS

Several other control windows round out the Director interface. The Control Panel enables you to move the playback head and control some other functions. The Tool Palette enables you to quickly create cast members and sprites. The Property Inspector enables you to examine and change some properties of a sprite without using the Score window. Each of these controls is discussed in the following sections.

The Control Panel

The Control Panel is small and simple. It has all the functions available to manipulate the play-back head. Choose Control Panel from the Window menu or press ⌘+2 on the Mac, or Ctrl+2 in Windows. Figure 1.15 shows all the Control Panel functions.

Starting at the top-left side of the panel, the functions are as follows:

- **Step Backward and Step Forward buttons**— These two buttons move the playback head forward or backward one frame. Holding down either button scans the movie quickly in the corresponding direction.

- **Frame Counter**—Displays the current position of the playback head. Entering a number in the frame counter and pressing Return/Enter advances you to that frame. Dragging the mouse in the frame counter, Option+dragging on the Mac, or Alt+dragging in Windows moves the playback head quickly forward or backward.

- **Tempo Mode**—This pop-up menu determines how the tempo is displayed. The choices are frames per second (fps) or seconds per frame (spf).

- **Tempo**—This is the area to the right of the Tempo Mode and left of the Loop Playback button. This is the assigned speed of the selected frame in either fps or spf. Entering a new tempo into the field and pressing Return or clicking the arrow buttons changes the tempo.

- **Loop Playback button**—Sets the movie to play again after the last frame or to play only once.

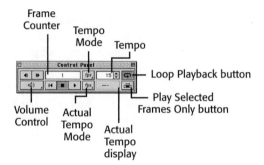

Figure 1.15
The Control Panel is used to move the playback head, to start and stop your movie, and to get information about the frame rate.

- **Volume Control**—This pop-up menu sets the volume for the entire movie. It can be overridden by Lingo commands.

- **Rewind button**—Rewinds the movie to frame 1. You can also select Rewind from the Control menu or press ⌘+Option+R on the Mac or Ctrl+Alt+R in Windows.

- **Stop button**—Stops the movie on the current frame. Select Stop from the Control menu or press ⌘+. (period) on the Mac or Ctrl+. (period) in Windows.

- **Play button**—Plays the movie from the current frame. Select Play from the Control menu or press ⌘+Option+P on the Mac or Ctrl+Alt+P in Windows.

- **Actual Tempo Mode**—This pop-up list sets the display mode of the actual tempo to the right of this setting. The choices are frames per second (fps), seconds per frame (spf), Running Total, and Estimated Total. Running Total is the elapsed time since the start of the movie. Estimated Total is a more accurate, although slower, calculation of elapsed time.

- **Actual Tempo display**—This number shows the actual tempo that Director is achieving in the current frame. Depending on how much activity is taking place on the Stage, the actual tempo could be less than the assigned tempo on slower machines. It never exceeds the assigned tempo.

- **Play Selected Frames Only button**—Toggle this button on or off to set the movie to play only the selected frames in the Score window. A green line at the top of the Sprite channels indicates the selected frames. If the movie is looped, only the selected frames play over and over.

The Tool Palette

The Tool Palette, shown in Figure 1.16, contains a variety of buttons. Most of them enable you to quickly create both a cast member and a sprite at the same time by placing a new element on the Stage. To open or close the Tool Palette, press ⌘+7 on the Mac or Ctrl+7 in Windows.

The topmost two tools in the Tool Palette are the Selection tool and the Rotate/Skew tool. Picking the Selection tool enables you to select sprites on the Stage with the arrow cursor.

Usually, clicking a sprite once selects it and enables you to move it around the Stage. If a sprite is editable, as a bitmap sprite is, double-clicking brings up the editing window. Some sprites, such as text members, can be edited directly on the Stage.

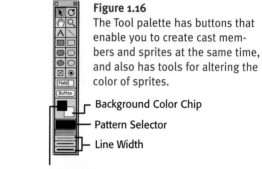

Figure 1.16
The Tool palette has buttons that enable you to create cast members and sprites at the same time, and also has tools for altering the color of sprites.

— Background Color Chip

— Pattern Selector

— Line Width

Foreground Color Chip

The Hand and Magnifying Glass tools are new to Director 8. When you select the Hand tool, you can drag the actual Stage around inside the Stage window. Use this to reposition the Stage so you can work with a specific area while you have the Stage zoomed past 100%.

The Magnifying Glass tool allows you to zoom in on a spot of the Stage. Hold the Option key down on the Mac, or the Alt key in Windows, to zoom back out.

The Rotate and Skew tool enables you to grab certain types of sprites and rotate them at any angle. You can also grab the corners of sprites and pull them to distort the image. This does not change the cast member at all, just its appearance on the Stage as that particular sprite.

The main set of tools in the Tool palette changes the cursor to notify you that clicking the Stage creates a new member and sprite. When you select one of these tools and click the Stage, a new member is added in the Cast in the new available spot. This member is automatically placed on the Stage and in the Score in the form of a sprite.

Two tools enable you to create text. The first is represented by the letter A. This Text tool enables you to create text cast members. Text members can be anti-aliased and can use a variety of formatting.

The Field tool enables you to create field members. Field members are more basic than text members, but have a few special features of their own. You can read more about the difference between text and field members in Chapter 3.

Many of the buttons in the Tool palette are there to let you create simple shapes, such as the Line tool, Oval tool, Rounded Rectangle tool, and Rectangle tool. The last three have both filled and outline options as well: Filled Rectangle, Outline Rectangle, Filled Rounded Rectangle, Outline Rounded Rectangle, Filled Oval, and Outline Oval.

The Radio Button, Check Box, and Pushbutton tools enable you to create control items. The first two require some Lingo programming to work properly. The Pushbutton tool (marked with the word "button") creates a standard Director-style button to which Lingo scripts can be attached.

Below all these tools are the color chips. These buttons represent the foreground and background colors of the selected sprites. You can change these colors by clicking and holding over one of the chips. Doing so brings up a small color palette from which you can pick a new color.

Changing colors works for only those sprites that have active foreground and background color properties. You can change the color of all shapes, for instance, or for 1-bit (black-and-white) artwork. You can change only the background color of fields, but you must select the field and edit it first.

> Use the foreground color chip to change the color of a shape or 1-bit bitmap. You can drag the same shape member to the Score multiple times and apply a different color to each one. The result is that you can have many different-colored shapes on the Stage, but use only one cast member.

Below the color chips is the Pattern Selector area, which is usually plain black. Clicking the Pattern Selector enables you to select a pattern for the sprite. Patterns are tiled bitmap images that repeat over the duration of the sprite area. You can use them only on filled shape sprites.

The last item on the toolbar is the Line Width Selector. You can set the line width of any line or outlined shape. The options here are limited, but Lingo enables you to use other sizes as well.

The Property Inspector

The Property Inspector is a new tool in Director 8. It replaces the Sprite Inspector, as well as a variety of other windows.

The Property Inspector is a chameleon. It changes depending on the element of Director you have selected. For instance, if you have selected a sprite in the Score or on the Stage, you get a Property Inspector that looks like Figure 1.17. This version of the window is similar to the top toolbar of the Score. However, with the rest of the Score window left behind, you have a more compact sprite-editing tool.

Figure 1.17
The Property Inspector is similar to the top portion of the Score window.

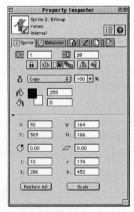

The Sprite Inspector shows you many of the properties of the selected sprites. You can edit these properties, or watch them change as you drag, rotate, or skew a sprite.

The Property Inspector actually has two sizes. There is a little triangle/arrow button halfway down the left side of the window. You can see this in Figure 1.17 shown previously. Clicking this arrow hides the information below the line. Clicking it again shows this information. This way, you can fit the window around the others you are currently working on.

Sprite Overlays

The Sprite Overlay tool is one you either love or hate. The sprite overlay is a gray box below each sprite that enables you to access sprite information. It contains some information about the sprite, such as which member it uses, as well as a few buttons to quickly bring up more windows. Figure 1.18 shows a Stage with sprite overlays turned on for all sprites.

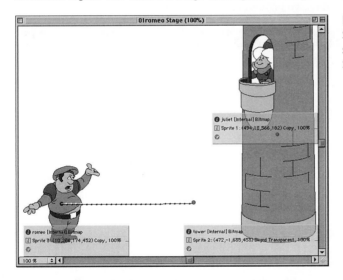

Figure 1.18
Sprite overlays show you some sprite information right on the Stage.

You can turn on sprite overlays, as well as change settings, by choosing View, Sprite Overlay. The settings are self-explanatory. You can choose where the overlays appear: either on every sprite, on only selected sprites, or only on sprites that are under the cursor. You can also choose the color of the text if black is not readable because of the colors on your Stage.

In addition to member and sprite information, sprite overlays give you three small buttons. You can use them to quickly bring up the Member Information dialog box, the Sprite Information dialog box, and the Behavior Inspector. You will be introduced to behaviors in the next chapter.

Another aspect of sprite overlays is their capability to show animation paths. An *animation path* is a curve on the screen that shows the complete animated path of a sprite. You find out more about this later in this chapter.

> There is a tiny little line at the right side of sprite overlays that you can click and drag up and down. This will change the opacity of the overlay.

The Toolbar

Although many windows in Director have toolbars at the top, "the toolbar" refers to a long strip of buttons that appears just under the menu bar at the top of the screen. It contains various buttons that correspond to menu items and controls. No functions are found in the toolbar only. All the buttons on the toolbar act merely as shortcuts. You can quickly show and hide the toolbar using ⌘+Shift+Option+B on the Mac or Ctrl+Shift+Alt+B in Windows.

Sprite overlays are sometimes useful to quickly track down information on a single frame. If you want to quickly turn on and off sprite overlays, use ⌘+Shift+Option+O on the Mac or Ctrl+Shift+Alt+O in Windows.

Some developers never use the toolbar. Others can't live without it. It all depends on what you are comfortable with. Because many Director functions have window or palette buttons, menu items, and keyboard shortcuts, you can operate in different ways.

ANIMATING WITH THE CAST, STAGE, AND SCORE

You can use members in the Cast, frames in the Score, and positions on the Stage to animate graphics over time. There are several methods to create these animations.

Step Recording

The easiest type of animation is called *step recording*. It enables you to specify the position of a sprite in every frame.

To perform step recording, you first have to open the correct windows and prepare a sprite to animate. Create or import a bitmap member and place it on the Stage. Be sure that the sprite covers many frames in the Score. If not, stretch it so that it does.

Now close the Cast window and move the Score window away from the area on the Stage where the sprite is to animate. Be sure you can see the Control Panel. Although it isn't necessary, turn on the Sprite Overlay, Show Paths function by choosing View, Sprite Overlay, Show Paths. This enables you to see the animation path as you create each step.

To begin animating, select the first frame of the sprite in the Score. Then, choose Control, Step Recording. Now you are ready to begin.

The position of the sprite is probably where you want it to be for frame 1, so proceed to frame 2. Click the Step Forward button in the control panel. The Score should reflect that you are now working in frame 2.

Click and drag the sprite on the Stage. A line should form from the center of the original placement of the sprite to the current placement as you drag. This is the sprite overlay showing you the animation path.

Drop the sprite where you want it to be in frame 2. Click the Step Forward button again to go to frame 3. Set the third position for the sprite. You will see that the sprite overlay feature shows you all the locations of the sprite in each frame. Your screen should look similar to Figure 1.19.

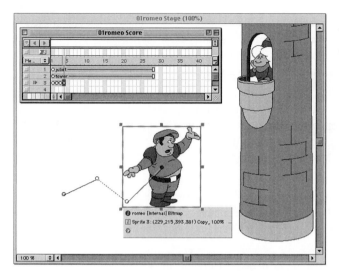

Figure 1.19
The Sprite Overlay feature reflects a step animation in progress.

You can continue this way, advancing one frame at a time, until your animation is complete. You can delete any leftover sprite cells by selecting those frames and deleting them. You can also go back and edit the animation positions on each frame by using the Step Forward and Step Backward buttons or by clicking in the Score. Doing so halts the step recording process and you will have to reselect the menu item later to continue.

After you are finished with step recording, or any animation technique, you can go back and animate other sprites relative to the ones you have completed. As you step through the frames, you will see the sprites you have already worked with move through their paths.

Real-Time Recording

Step recording is good for small animation sequences. However, if you want to animate 200 frames, it can take a long time. For cases such as this, you should use real-time recording.

You set up a real-time recording session in the same way as a step-recording session. After the first frame of the sprite is selected, you can start. Choose Control, Real-Time Recording from the menu. Nothing happens until you click the sprite on the Stage again.

What you want to do is click and hold down the mouse on the sprite. The movie starts going and the frame indicator on the Score moves with it. Drag the sprite around the Stage to change its position. This all happens quickly.

When you are editing an animation path, simply clicking and dragging the sprite results in your dragging the entire animation sequence. Clicking and dragging the sprite overlay circle for each frame enables you to move just that one frame of animation.

In both step recording and real-time recording, the sprite automatically grows in the Score if you add more frames of animation than the sprite was originally sized to hold.

When you are finished, the result is similar to step recording. You can go back and edit individual frames of animation. After some practice, you can even combine step and real-time animation techniques to make precisely the animations you want.

Real-time recording happens at the speed of the tempo of the movie. Adjust this in the Control Panel. It is a good idea to lower the tempo for real-time recording, perform your animation in slow motion, and then reset the tempo to play it back. This gives you better control over the placement of each step.

Space to Time Recording

An animation technique that is not used much anymore is called *space to time*. You can place several sprites in the same frame, but in different channels, to represent different steps in the animation. The sprites can use the same cast member, and very often do. You should arrange them so that each step is placed in descending order with the first step in the lowest Sprite channel.

When you have all the sprites in place, select them in the Score. This can be done by clicking the first sprite, holding down the Shift key, and clicking the last sprite. Then choose Modify, Space to Time. This menu item is active only if you have properly selected consecutive, single-framed sprites in the Score.

You are then prompted by a dialog box asking you how far apart you want the sprites placed. This simply adds extra frames in the Score between each animation keyframe.

The result of a space to time operation is that all the selected sprites are removed from the Score. They are replaced with a horizontal animated sequence consisting of the member and position of each sprite. This sequence exists in one Sprite channel.

Uses for this technique are limited. Because you must place each sprite individually first, it isn't ideal for long animations. However, because you can quickly place sprites that use different members, it's good for multiple-member animation.

For example, you might want to animate a bird flying using three different drawings. You can see each step of the animation on one frame, and easily swap members for some steps before using the space to time command. You can create the same animation using any other animation technique as well, but some people might find it easier to use space to time.

Cast to Time Recording

A similar technique to space to time is *cast to time*. Here, you can use the Cast window rather than the Score to set up the animation.

To start, place an animated sequence of members in the Cast in consecutive members. For instance, if you have a seven-member sequence that shows a man walking, place each member in member slots 1 through 7. Looking at the Cast window thumbnails should give you a preview of what the animation will look like, as if it were laid out on individual sheets of paper.

Select all those cast members and then open the Score window. Select the Sprite channel and frame where you want the animation to start. Choose Control, Cast to Time to place the animation.

This technique is mostly useful for animations where each step uses a different cast member.

Tweening

Each of the preceding techniques relies on each step of the animation being represented by a specific location on the Stage. If you have a 30-frame animation, you will have 30 keyframes, each with a specific location as a property.

However, there is a better way to make animations. With tweening, you set two positions in the animation and have Director automatically fill in the rest. The result is that each frame in between the two positions shows one step in the progression of movement from the first point to the last.

Figure 1.20 shows the Stage and the Score with the simplest of tweening animations. In fact, this is the same example you saw earlier in this chapter. The only difference is that sprite overlay paths have been turned on.

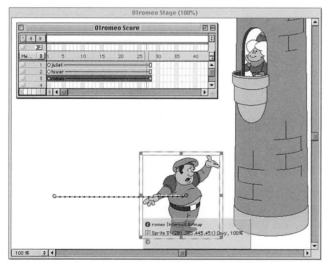

Figure 1.20
A simple animation that uses two keyframes and tweening.

The sprite overlay animation line shows you exactly what is going on here. The two large dots show the two keyframes: the first frame and the last frame. The line between them is the animation path. The small dots on the line show the positions that the sprite will occupy during each frame of the animation. You didn't have to set any of these positions because the tweening function does it for you.

What makes tweening so powerful is that you can reposition any keyframe point and the rest of the animation adjusts automatically. If you move the position of the sprite in the last frame up to the top of the screen, the animation line goes from the initial point up to the top of the screen. All the intermediate points reposition themselves as expected.

You can even lengthen or shorten the sprite span. The example shown previously in Figure 1.20 shows an animation 28 frames long. The first and last frame are keyframes and there are 26 intermediate frames. If you were to drag the end of the sprite out to frame 40, there would be 38 intermediate frames. The animation would take longer, but it would run smoother because smaller steps would be involved.

But the power of tweening doesn't end there. You can do more than just straight lines. You can actually use tweening to define a curve with three or more points.

Figure 1.21 shows an animation with three keyframe points. The first keyframe starts the animation on the left side of the screen and in frame 1. The last keyframe puts the sprite on the right side of the screen and a little lower. A third keyframe is at frame 10. The position of the sprite at this keyframe is higher and to the right of both the start and finish points.

Figure 1.21
A three-keyframe sprite animation. Tweening is used to interpolate the points in between.

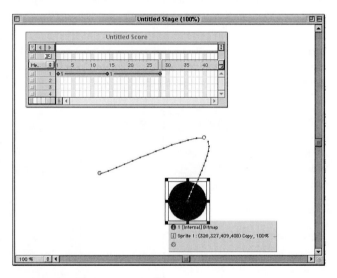

As Figure 1.21 shows, the result is not a straight line between the keyframes. Instead, Director interprets a natural curve for you. But this doesn't mean that you can't make the path a straight line. Nor does it mean that you are stuck with the curve shape shown.

Tweened animations have a variety of settings that can be adjusted for each sprite. You can change these settings by choosing Modify, Sprite, Tweening, or by pressing ⌘+Shift+B on the Mac or Ctrl+Shift+B in Windows. Figure 1.22 shows the dialog box that appears.

At the top of the Sprite Tweening dialog box is a set of check boxes. You can use these options to decide which sprite properties are tweened. The examples so far have used only position tweening. However, because you have

To create a keyframe, click a specific frame in a sprite span in the Score. The red line drawn vertically in the Score shows you precisely which frame of the sprite is selected. To create a keyframe, choose Insert, Keyframe from the menu bar or press ⌘+Option+K on the Mac or Ctrl+Alt+K in Windows.

not changed the size or other properties of the sprite in any keyframe, the other options could be turned on and would have no effect.

Figure 1.22
The Sprite Tweening dialog box enables you to control which properties of a sprite are tweened and how.

Tweening the other properties has the obvious result. For instance, if you stretch the sprite in the last keyframe, the sprite stretch is applied gradually from the second-to-last keyframe. Rather than becoming a new size suddenly, the sprite changes size over time. You can get the same result by tweening the rotation or skew of a sprite. Changing the forecolor or backcolor of a sprite affects only sprites in which color changes can change the appearance of the sprite, as in a 1-bit bitmap sprite. Changing the blend gradually alters the blend property of the sprite, something you can read more about in Chapter 4, "Text and Field Members."

Below the check boxes is a slider bar that enables you to alter the curvature of the tween. The farther to the left you position the slider, the closer the path comes to being a straight line. Placing the slider on the Normal setting gives you Director's best curved path. If you want a more unusual curve, adjust the slider toward Extreme. The effect varies according to the positions and number of keyframes. In general, you should have at least three keyframes to create curved paths.

The Continuous at Endpoints option is primarily for circular paths. If your animation moves through a circle and ends at the same point that it began (the first and last keyframes have the same position), turn this option on to create a smoother transition between one cycle and the next.

The Ease-In and Ease-Out sliders enable you to alter the apparent speed of the sprite as it moves through the animation. All it really does is space the path points at a slight difference to create the illusion of acceleration or deceleration. The two sliders are related to each other, so they cannot add up to more than 100%. If you try to adjust a slider too far, the other adjusts itself automatically to compensate.

The two options for the speed of the tween affect how abrupt the changes are when the sprite is traveling between keyframes. In most animations, it is hard to tell the difference. The most dramatic effect is when you are using Ease-In or Ease-Out. Try both speed settings to determine which one you like better.

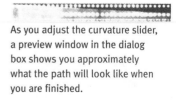

As you adjust the curvature slider, a preview window in the dialog box shows you approximately what the path will look like when you are finished.

Working with Sprites

The five animation techniques that Director 8 offers are not the only ways to create moving objects on the Stage. You can also force animation by placing new sprites on each frame and manually building each frame.

It wouldn't make sense to build an entire animation this way, but it sometimes does make sense to mix this strategy in with the other techniques. You might have 100 frames of tweened animation, another 100 frames of animation built with real-time recording, and a few manually constructed frames in between.

To construct frames of animation manually, you should become familiar with a few Director commands. TheInsert menu, for instance, not only enables you to insert and remove keyframes in a sprite, but it enables you to insert and remove frames for all Sprite channels. Inserting a frame stretches a sprite span that crosses that frame. Any tweening adjusts automatically to reflect this extra frame.

The Modify menu enables you to split and join sprite spans. Splitting a sprite enables you to break free from a previous tweened path and start with a fresh keyframe point. Joining sprite spans automatically tweens their properties provided that those tweening options are turned on for the new sprite.

You can also extend a sprite by selecting the sprite, and then selecting a frame in the Score that is beyond the current sprite span. Choosing Modify, Extend Sprite brings the last frame of the sprite out to the new location.

A variety of other tools exist to help you position sprites on the Stage. The Modify menu contains access to the Align and Tweak tools. The Align tool enables you to line up sprites horizontally or vertically, according to their sides, registration points, or centers. The Tweak tool is a small window that enables you to specify an exact amount of movement for the sprite. You can set horizontal and vertical numbers, in pixels, and then execute this movement for any sprite or group of sprites.

To space out the sprite vertically, access the Tweak tool by choosing Modify, Tweak, while a sprite is selected. Type **-60** into the vertical change field. Select the first sprite in the Score. Click the Tweak button twice. This moves the first sprite up 120 pixels. Select the second sprite in the Score and click the Tweak button once to move it up 60 pixels. Now change the vertical setting in the Tween tool to be 60 pixels (remove the negative sign). Use tweak to move the fourth sprite down 60 pixels and the fifth sprite down 120. Now the sprites are vertically spaced 60 pixels apart.

Any tools that enable you to position sprites work while you are using step recording. They can give you more precise control over your animations.

A common shortcut for moving sprites is to use arrow keys along with the Shift key. Doing so moves the sprite 10 pixels at a time. Therefore, you could get the same result by selecting a sprite and pressing the up arrow key six times while holding the Shift key, that you did when using the Tweak tool set to **-60** vertical change.

A minor detail is that the sprites are still horizontally aligned to the center of the Stage. You can align the left sides of the sprites with each other, instead, by using the Align tool. Bring it up by selecting Modify, Align, and set the second pop-up menu to Align Lefts. Click the Align button to make the change. You will see some of the sprites shift.

Dragging all the sprites at once to the left of the Stage is one way to complete the example. However, there are some other ways of doing this.

Grids and Guides

 Using grids and guides is another way to quickly position sprites. You can find the menu items that pertain to grids and guides by choosing View, Grids and Guides.

The grid is a set of evenly spaced lines on the Stage that you can simply have as a visual guide, or as something that your sprites lock to as you rearrange them on the Stage. You can set horizontal and vertical amounts for the grid, and then specify whether you want to have sprites snap to the grid. This is useful when you want to quickly lay out items in precise positions relative to each other.

Figure 1.23 shows the Stage with grids turned on and visible. Each grid point is spaced exactly 64 pixels horizontally and 64 pixels vertically from each other.

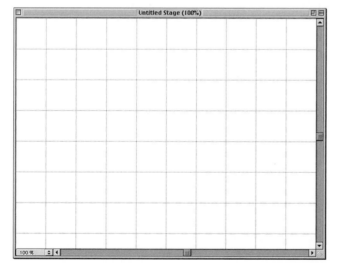

Figure 1.23
A Stage with the grid visible. Each grid line is set to be 64 pixels apart.

Guides are like the grid, but you can individually place each guide line. You can place horizontal and vertical guides, and you have the option to display them visibly, or not, and have sprites snap to them, or not. Figure 1.24 shows the Stage with guides visible, and several guides placed.

Figure 1.24
This Stage has two horizontal guides and one vertical guide visible.

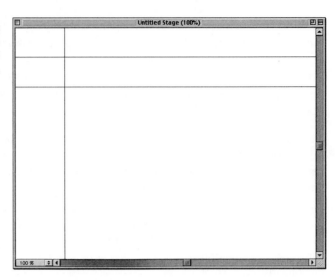

You can turn grids and guides on and off and set their preferences by selecting View, Grids and Guides, Settings. This brings up the Property Inspector with the Guides and Grid settings properties (see Figure 1.25). You can change the color of the grid and guides here. You can also click the horizontal and vertical guide buttons, next to the New label and above the Remove All button, to add guides.

Figure 1.25
The Property Inspector with the Guides and Grid properties shown.

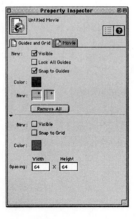

To align the sprites in a movie, you can simply turn on grids or guides. You can set the vertical grid to 60 pixels and space each sprite by just dragging it until it locks onto a grid line. You can position the sprites to a vertical grid line as well, which accomplishes the left-side alignment. Or, use guides and create a guide line that you want the sprites to snap to.

You can also use the Property Inspector or the toolbar at the top of the Score to manually set the locations of all the sprites. Although this sounds complex, it actually takes about the same amount of time.

All in all, there are many ways to move sprites around in Director. The idea of having more than one way to do something is present throughout Director, from simple animation to complex Lingo scripts. Director almost always gives you two or more ways to accomplish a task, which makes Director an easy-to-learn and flexible environment.

EXPORTING ANIMATIONS

After you finish creating an animation, you can do three things with it: You can make a projector, you can make a Shockwave movie, or you can export it to a variety of file types. The last section of the next chapter introduces projectors and Shockwave files. Exporting, however, is usually used with animation only.

To export an animation, first check to see which elements in your movie cannot be exported. You cannot export scripts, for instance, because file formats, such as PICS files and Video for Windows, can't do anything with them. Basically, you can export only pictures of the Stage, frame for frame.

To export, choose File, Export. This brings up the Export dialog box shown in Figure 1.26.

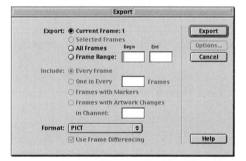

Figure 1.26
The Export dialog box on the Macintosh (shown here) has slightly different format options than in Windows.

The primary option is the format of the exported files. This option is at the bottom of the dialog box. The following is a rundown of the types of files you can export:

- **PICT**—The standard image file for Macintosh computers; choosing this option gives you a numbered series of PICT files. Available on the Macintosh only.

- **Scrapbook**—If you choose this option, Director outputs a Macintosh scrapbook file, similar to the one found in the system folder. Some video programs can import this type of file. Available on the Macintosh only.

- **PICS**—A single file that contains multiple images. This type of file can be imported into a variety of programs. It can also be imported into Director as a film loop and series of members. Available on the Macintosh only.

- **QuickTime**—The standard video format for Macintosh computers and also used by about 50% of all Windows machines. This is the only option that preserves some of the tempo changes in your animation. Available as an export option on Macintosh computers only.

- **DIB File Sequence**—A single file that contains a series of images. Available in Windows only.

- **Video For Windows**—The video format built in to Windows. Sometimes called AVI files. Available in Windows only.

Most of the formats you can export to are useful only if you plan on bringing the file into another editing program. QuickTime and Video For Windows, however, can be played by small video players on most computers and can be used by other presentation software.

The export for each of these formats is basically the same. Director moves though the frames you specify and takes a snapshot of the Stage each time. Each image is incorporated into the export as the next file or the next portion of the file. In most cases, scripting, tempo changes, and transitions are not considered.

The export to QuickTime capability, however, is a little more powerful. You can specify a variety of settings by using the additional QuickTime Options dialog box. Figure 1.27 shows this dialog box.

Most of the options in the QuickTime Options dialog box are self-explanatory. Note that the compression options depend on the version of QuickTime you are using and any additional compression algorithms you might have added to QuickTime on your machine.

The Frame Rate option determines how the frames are written out to the QuickTime movie. If you set this option to Real Time, the export becomes much more complex. It is essentially recording the progress on the screen as the movie plays. This means it is taking changes in tempo into account. Otherwise, you just get a frame-by-frame dump of the movie as a QuickTime file.

Figure 1.27
The QuickTime Options dialog box is available only on Macintosh versions of Director.

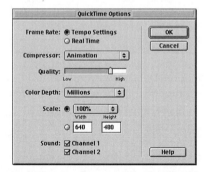

In Windows, the export to Video For Windows (.avi) option is not as flexible. You cannot capture in real-time mode. However, you can set the frame rate independent of the movie's tempo, and you can set the quality and compression technique.

Even these built-in export options might not give you what you want. If, for instance, you have scripts that move the movie about in a nonlinear fashion, or you want user-initiated events recorded, you can always record the video directly from your computer's output. Many computers come with a video outfeed that can be plugged into standard and S-video videotape recorders. Or, you can always have one computer capture a screen directly from another computer playing a Director movie. This is, of course, providing they both have appropriate video capabilities.

Another approach is to use a screen-capture utility that takes a snapshot of the screen automatically every fraction of a second. In practice, to play an animation and record it at the same time is a heavy task for even a production machine.

TROUBLESHOOTING ANIMATION

- If you cannot find some feature mentioned in this chapter, it might be because your copy of Director has its preference settings set in a different way. Many preferences show or hide different features of the authoring environment.

- It is not uncommon for a developer to create an animation with real-time recording or tweening and not get it quite right the first time. That's what the Delete key is for. Just select the sprites, delete them, and start again.

- If tweening doesn't seem to be working, check the sprite properties by choosing Modify, Sprite, Tweening. Tweening may simply be turned off for that sprite.

- If you are exporting animation and are also using more advanced techniques, such as behaviors and other scripting, the changes made by Lingo might not be reflected in the exported animation. Exporting is really just for Score animation, not Lingo animation.

- Getting little white edges around images set to Background Transparent or Matte ink? These appear when the image is anti-aliased around the edges to white, which happens very often. You can either manually edit these pixels out of the image, or use PhotoShop to create images with an alpha-channel that will properly anti-alias the edges.

- Does your animation play too fast on some machines or too slow on others? Choose a frame rate that your target machine can handle. Many older PCs cannot handle more than a few frames per second when many bitmaps with different inks are used.

DID YOU KNOW?

- If you are having trouble making your first movie, try to open a simple sample movie first, such as one on the Director 8 CD-ROM or one on this book's CD-ROM. Play around with it first before trying to create your own movie.

- Most preference windows can be reached by ⌘+clicking on the Macintosh, or right-clicking in Windows on the element or window that you want to affect. Many times the contextual menu brought up by this click will have some commonly used options available in the menu, in addition to a menu item that will bring up the complete preferences window.

- You can export a single frame of a movie to an image by selecting only that one frame as the export range and an image format as opposed to a video format.

- Grids always start in the upper-left corner. If you want to have a grid that starts a little farther in, such as a 20×20 grid that starts at 10×10, you can just use the 20×20 grid as is, and then move all the sprites over and down by 10 pixels when you are done. This way, your grid starts at 10 horizontally and vertically, and it continues to 30, 50, 70, and so on.

PRESENTATIONS WITH DIRECTOR

IN THIS CHAPTER

Source movies for this chapter can be found on the CD-ROM in the "Book Movies" folder under folder 2.

Presentations, unlike animations, are interactive Director movies. Instead of the end users being passive watchers, they need to participate with the playback of a presentation, even if that simply means clicking the mouse to tell the movie that it is okay to continue from a stopping point.

A typical presentation appears much like a slideshow, wherein a variety of screens are displayed on the monitor, all containing sequential information of some sort. A simple presentation shows a series of ordered slides, whereas a complex one includes navigation buttons that enable the contents to be browsed by the users. This chapter covers all types of presentations, including linear and nonlinear. The first step to every presentation is designing the screens.

> It might help you to know that an inch usually comprises 72 pixels. This is an arbitrary standard; the size of a pixel depends on the size of a user's monitor and other settings. To confuse things further, some computer documentation refers to an inch as 96 pixels.

DESIGNING SCREENS

A presentation can be broken into a number of screens. Each screen presents some information, usually through text and graphics. Before designing an entire presentation, you should put some thought into how you plan to design your screens.

In Director, a screen appears as a frame in the Score. A simple way to organize this is to have frame 1 be your first screen, frame 2 your second, and so on. You might also decide to space frames farther apart—say every five frames—if this is easier for you to manage.

On the Stage, sprite positions are measured in pixels. A pixel is equal to exactly one "dot" on the screen; it is the smallest graphic element on computer screens. When one reads that the Stage is 640×480, for example, this means that the Stage is 640 pixels across and 480 pixels down. The pixel at the top-left corner of the Stage is pixel 0,0.

Planning a Consistent Design

Before starting to build the presentation, think about what you want on each screen. Will background elements appear on every screen? Will a title appear across the top on every screen? Will all the screens have a similar design or will they vary greatly?

Figure 2.1 shows a typical presentation design. It has a title across the top, a matching graphic element across the bottom, a picture on the right, and text on the left.

This layout has six elements. They correspond to six sprites in the Score. Figure 2.2 shows the Score for this layout. Sprite 1 contains a solid-colored box that is used as the backing for the title area. Sprite 2 is a text member that contains the title. Sprite 3 contains the same cast member as sprite 1. It's the same box, but this time it is positioned at the bottom of the Stage and is a little smaller. Sprite 4 is a bitmap image of an arrow. You can use this as the button to enable the users to go to the next screen.

> To create screens that are equivalent to one frame in the Score, set your sprite preferences to use a default width of 1. Choose File, Preferences, Sprite to adjust this setting.

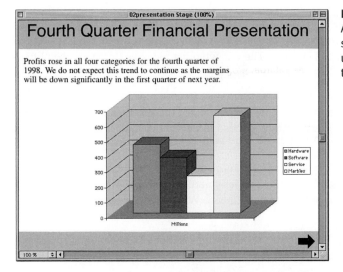

Figure 2.1
A typical presentation screen. You should decide on one layout and use it, or versions of it, throughout the presentation.

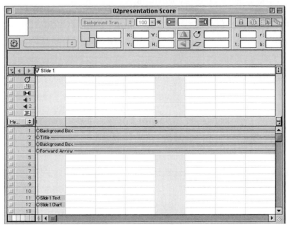

Figure 2.2
The Score shows six sprites being used to make the screen shown in Figure 2.1.

After sprite 4 are six empty sprite channels. Leaving sprite channels empty in this example is just a way to better organize the Score. Everything above these channels appears in every frame. Everything below these channels appears in only one screen.

Sprite 11 contains the text for this one screen and sprite 12 contains the image. These elements will change on every screen. On some screens, you might add additional sprites after sprite 8. For instance, if a screen has more than one image or if an arrow graphic is needed to point something out in an image, you need to add sprites to that specific screen for those elements.

You can use empty channels to help visually divide your Score. Otherwise, you end up with all your sprites in consecutive channels, which can make it hard to find a specific sprite quickly.

Tools for Screen Design

When designing your screens, take advantage of some of the tools that you learned about in Chapter 1, "Animation with Director." The following list includes the most useful tools for screen design:

- **Guides and Grid**—You can position your sprites more precisely and quickly if you use grids and guides. Use them in visible mode to see guidelines on the Stage. Use the Snap To feature to line up items quickly. Choose View, Guides and Grid to access the grids and guides options.

- **Property Inspector**—If you like sprites to be at precise locations, the Property Inspector enables you to manually edit the horizontal and vertical locations, as well as the width, height, rotation, and other properties. Choose Windows, Inspectors, Property to open the Property Inspector.

- **Sprite Overlay**—This tool shows you sprite information and enables you to gain access to the Properties windows without having the Score and Cast windows open. Choose View, Sprite Overlay to access the Sprite Overlay options.

- **Align tool**—You can select groups of sprites and align them horizontally or vertically based on their left, right, top, bottom, center, or registration points. Choose Modify, Align to bring up the Align tool.

- **Tweak tool**—This tool enables you to move a sprite or group of sprites a precise number of pixels in any direction. Choose Modify, Tweak to bring up the Tweak tool.

- **Arrow keys**—You can move any sprite or group of sprites one pixel at a time with the arrow keys. Select a sprite or group of sprites, and then hold the Shift key down and you can move sprites 10 pixels at a time.

- **The Score window**—The Score window combines all the elements of the Sprite Inspector and sprite overlays, plus much more. It's the only tool that enables you to move sprites up and down in the Sprite channels, and thereby over and under other sprites. Choose Window, Score to bring up the Score window.

➪ *For more information about the Score window,* **see** *"Customizing the Score Window," **p. 28** and "Score Window Preferences," **p. 28** (Chapter 1, "Animation with Director")*

➪ *For more information about sprite overlays,* **see** *"Sprite Overlays," **p. 35** (Chapter 1)*

➪ *For more information about sprites,* **see** *"The Property Inspector," **p. 34** (Chapter 1)*

LINEAR PRESENTATIONS

The simplest type of presentation is a linear presentation. Linear presentations are sometimes referred to as *slideshows* because they resemble the process of showing visuals with a slide projector.

The objective of a linear presentation is to present screens of information in a defined sequence. The movie should move from one screen to the next either automatically, after a period of time, or after some input, such as a keyboard press or a mouse click. You might even want to give the users the capability to back up one screen, just as a slide projector would.

Creating Your Presentation

To start, create your presentation, screen for screen. Each screen should be in a different frame. If you aren't using every frame, you should name each screen frame with a label in the marker area of the Score. This will help you later. Label frames by clicking in the marker area directly above the Tempo channel in the Score.

There are several ways to stretch a sprite span. You can grab the keyframe, shown as a large dot in the last frame, and pull it. You can also select the sprite, click in the frame number area at the top of the Score of the frame to which you want to stretch it, and press ⌘+B on the Mac or Ctrl+B in Windows. Or, you can use the Start Frame and End Frame fields in the Score window.

If some elements are used in more than one frame, you don't need to place them in every frame individually. Instead, stretch them so that their sprite spans cover all the screen frames. For example, sprites 1 through 4 of the example shown previously in Figure 2.2 can be stretched to cover all the frames of the movie, which places the title bar, bottom bar, and Forward button on every screen.

Arrangement in the Cast is another matter. In the sample presentation, you end up with a few cast members that represent graphics used in every screen: the title bar text, the boxes, and the Forward button. The rest of the cast members are graphics that appear in only one frame.

You could have one cast library for the reused graphics, and one cast library for the text and images. Or, you could have everything in one Cast. If the screens were more complex and had dozens of members, you might even want to consider a new cast library for every frame. However, schemes such as this can cause problems when you want to use a member in more than one frame, such as a photo of the company headquarters that is used on both the introduction screen and the corporate summary screen of a financial presentation.

Whichever way you decide to arrange your Cast, keep in mind that you may be adding graphics and text for each screen. If you have 100 screens in your presentation, you will have a lot of members.

Adjusting the Tempo

Running the movie now results in anything but a nice presentation. If you have all your screens in consecutive frames, the entire presentation flies by as quickly as Director can display it. If you skipped frames, the presentation flashes by, alternating screens and blank Stages.

You need the movie to pause on each frame. The simplest way to do this is to use the Tempo channel. First, be sure

Cast arrangement is something you can worry about later. You can drag and drop cast members within the Cast window, or open a second Cast window and drag and drop between them. This second window can be another cast library or even another view of the same cast library.

that the special Score channels are visible in the Score window. Click the Hide/Show Effects Channels button (two arrows pointing up and down at each other) on the right side of the Score to make them visible.

The first channel, Tempo, is marked with a small clock icon. Double-click the Tempo channel in the current frame to bring up the Frame Properties: Tempo dialog box, shown in Figure 2.3. You can see that one of the options is Wait for Mouse Click or Key Press. Select that option and click OK to close the dialog box.

Figure 2.3
The Frame Properties: Tempo dialog box enables you to stop the movie until a key is pressed.

The Tempo channel now reads "Click" to remind you of your choice. When you play the movie now, Director pauses on that frame until you click the mouse. The cursor changes to an animated cursor, which indicates to the user that a mouse click is needed.

This way of pausing the movie and enabling the users to control the forward movement of the presentation works well. However, this method is generic in that it contains no alternatives for the way in which it works or for the cursor that is used. Additionally, the little "click now" cursor animation can be distracting to the viewers.

Another way to control tempo is to pause the movie on that frame and then use the Forward button to go to the next screen. To do this, you must use some scripting. Fortunately, you do not have to do the scripting yourself. Director comes with many behaviors ready to be dragged and dropped into the Score.

To access the behaviors in the libraries, choose Window, Library Palette. Figure 2.4 shows the Library palette.

To use a behavior from the Library palette, first select the library from the pop-up menu at the upper-left corner of the window. Then, drag and drop the appropriate behavior onto the Score. If you want the behavior applied to the frame, drop it into the Frame Script channel. Otherwise, drop it on top of a sprite.

To use a behavior from the Library palette, follow these steps:

1. Choose Window, Library Palette.

2. Using the pop-up menu in the upper-left corner, shown in Figure 2.4, choose the library name.

3. Click the behavior you need and drag it onto a sprite on the Stage or in the Score.

4. If the behavior needs more information, it prompts you with a dialog box.

You can copy, cut, and paste in the Score just as you can in a word processor or spreadsheet program. For example, after selecting a Tempo channel setting for one frame, you can copy and paste this setting into any other channel. You can also hold down the Option key on the Mac or the Alt key in Windows and click and drag the Tempo channel to stretch that setting over several frames.

Figure 2.4
The Library palette contains some behaviors that are built in to Director 8.

To get the movie to pause on a frame, select the Navigation category in the Library palette and drag and drop the behavior named "Hold on Current Frame" onto one of the screen frames in the Score. You can drag and drop it onto each one of the frames you use, use Copy and Paste to spread it around to all the frames, or simply stretch its sprite span to encompass all the frames.

The Library palette can also contain other behaviors that you can get from third-party companies. You can also add behaviors that you write yourself.

Now you have a presentation that pauses correctly over each frame. The next step is to activate the Forward button so that the users can go to the next frame. You can use another behavior from the library to do this. Just drag and drop the Go Next Button behavior onto the forward arrow sprite.

The Go Next Button behavior causes the action to be initiated when the users complete a click on the sprite. Be sure that you have just one sprite for the Forward button that covers all the frames in your movie. When you apply the behavior to it, the behavior works throughout the entire sprite span.

When you select a behavior from the library, it copies that behavior from the library to your Cast. The behavior that you are using then actually comes from your own movie's Cast. This way, you don't have to provide the library to the users with the rest of your project.

The Go Next Button behavior makes the movie jump forward to the next frame that has a marker label. For it to work, you need to label each frame that is used as a screen. The behavior skips any frame that has no label, even if sprites are on it.

The presentation now behaves as desired. It begins at frame 1 and waits. When the users click the Forward button, the movie advances to the next labeled frame and waits again.

This simple presentation design can be used for anything from showing your vacation photos to presenting your company's financial data. But it is only the tip of the iceberg as far as Director's capabilities are concerned. The next section discusses how nonlinear presentations are accomplished in Director.

NONLINEAR PRESENTATIONS

The next step in creating advanced presentations is to give users the capability to navigate throughout the presentation in any direction. The previous presentation only moves forward. What if users want to go back one screen? Or, what if they want to return to the beginning?

Adding Back and Home Buttons

Creating a button that enables the users to move back in the presentation is easy. You saw how to create a button that moved the users forward, which was done with the Go Next Button behavior. There is also a behavior called Go Previous Button. All you need to do is create a new bitmap, add it to the Score, and place the Go Previous Button behavior on it from the Library palette. Figure 2.5 shows the addition of the Go Previous button (shown as a back arrow bitmap).

Figure 2.5 also shows a button labeled "Home" that takes the users back to the first frame. The behavior you need to use to accomplish this is the Go to Frame X Button behavior also found in the Library palette.

Figure 2.5
The presentation screen now includes a back (Go Previous) arrow and a Home button.

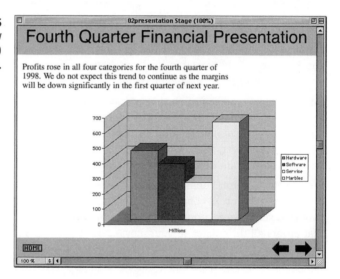

When you drag the Go to Frame X Button behavior to the sprite with the bitmap you've created for the new button, a dialog box appears that enables you to specify a frame number. Figure 2.6 shows this dialog box. You should type the number of the frame labeled "Home" here.

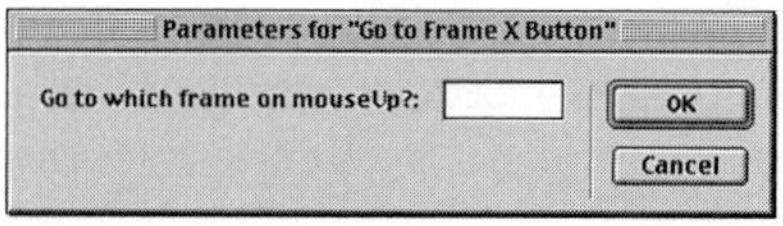

Figure 2.6
Some behaviors display a dialog box when you place them on a sprite or a frame. These dialog boxes ask you to specify information about how you want the behavior to act.

Now that you know how to add a button that moves the presentation to any frame, you can add buttons as necessary. If your presentation is easily broken into three main sections, you can have buttons that take the users to the first frame of each section.

Also, remember that you don't necessarily have to have the same buttons on each frame. If you have multiple sections in your presentation, you can have buttons that take the users forward or back to the next or previous sections.

To do this, use the same cast member buttons, but create separate sprites that cover each section. If the first section covers frames 1 to 17 and the second section covers frames 20 to 34, place one sprite from frame 1 to 17 and a second sprite from frame 20 to 34. You can use the same Sprite channel, but be sure that the sprites are not joined to each other.

> You can leave the Next Section button out in the last section. Or, you can place a new cast member, such as a dimmed or grayed version of the button, in its place. Don't place any behavior on this sprite, so nothing happens if the users try to click it. The same can be done for the Previous Section button in the first section.

When you apply the Go to Frame X Button behavior to each sprite, just input a different frame number for each. You can specify that the Next Section button for section 1 is to take the users to the first frame of section 2. The Next Section button in section 2 takes the users to the first frame of section 3. You need to have only one cast member and use only one behavior for this. The only difference between the sprites is the destination frame property of the behavior.

Adding a Menu Screen

You could call the area at the bottom of the sample presentation a toolbar. It contains elements such as the Forward and Back buttons. After you start adding buttons that take the users to specific sections, it becomes more like a menu.

If you want to add a table of contents to the presentation, the toolbar or menu area might start to get a little crowded. If you have 100 frames of screens and eight sections, you can have a lot of buttons. Rather than crowd this area with buttons, you might want to consider adding a menu screen, otherwise known as a table of contents screen.

With a menu screen, you can have just a few buttons in the toolbar: Forward, Back, and Main Menu. The Main Menu button takes users to the menu screen. From there, they can navigate to any section of the presentation. Because you have an entire screen to dedicate to this, you can be more descriptive about each section, rather than trying to simplify the sections into a single button.

Figure 2.7 shows an example of a menu screen. The title bar remains, but the toolbar is not necessary. You might decide otherwise when designing your presentation. Notice that no buttons are on the screen. Instead, what appears to be a text member shows a list of the sections. This is actually not one text member, but five. Each line is its own member. This enables you to place a separate behavior on each line.

You can create these text members by simply selecting the Text tool (not the Field tool), which looks like the letter A, in the Tools palette, and clicking the Stage. Be sure to check the Score afterward to ensure that the sprites have been placed in channels that make sense. Move them around and group them together if you want.

Figure 2.7
A presentation menu. Each line of text is a separate member and sprite.

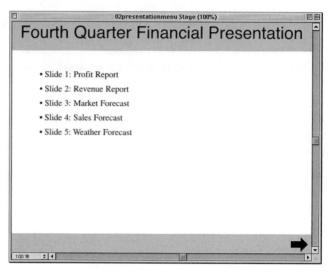

Drag the Go to Frame X Button behavior from the Library palette onto each of these sprites separately. This enables you to enter the destination frame for each sprite. This is all it takes to set up your menu screen. You will want to arrange the sprites and probably use the Grid or Align tool to set them up on the Stage.

⇨ *For more information on using text in your presentations,* **see** *"Using Text Members,"* **p. 94** *(Chapter 4, "Text and Field Members")*

A presentation with a set of toolbar buttons and a menu screen can be used for almost any purpose. This sort of presentation can even be used to prototype software, whereby you show each screen of the software and enable users to browse its functions in a nonlinear fashion.

⇨ *For more information about behaviors,* **see** *"Building Your Own Behaviors,"* **p. 190** *(Chapter 11, "Advanced Techniques")*

If you enter the wrong destination frame, or want to edit it later, you can access the sprite's behavior properties by bringing up the Behavior Inspector. A button for this appears on the left side of the Score toolbar. It looks like a pair of gears.

You can also press ⌘+Option+; (semicolon) on the Mac or Ctrl+Alt+; (semicolon) in Windows. When the Behavior Inspector appears, you see the list of behaviors applied to the sprite. Use the Parameters button, which looks like a pair of gears, to change the properties. Chapter 11, "Advanced Techniques," describes the Behavior Inspector in more detail.

ADVANCED PRESENTATIONS

You can add functionality to your presentations in many ways without learning Lingo. You can make your buttons a little nicer, use the cursor to guide the users, and even add sounds and transitions.

Play and Return

Suppose you want to have a side topic referenced in your presentation. For example, if you present a list of products that your company sells, you can have a button that links to a screen with more information about those products.

In this example, you might not want to have the presentation leap to a new frame. You might want it to remember where it came from, and return to that frame when the users are finished. This way, you can have the presentation jump to a frame from several places, and then a button on the destination frame returns the users to the original frame.

You can do this with the Play Frame X behavior from the Library palette. This behavior causes the presentation to jump to a frame, just as the Go to Frame X behavior does. However, it remembers the frame it came from. When a button with a Play Done behavior is clicked, the presentation returns to the original frame.

Button Highlights

Chapter 14, "Creating Behaviors," describes how to make complex button behaviors, such as buttons that have rollover and down states. For now, you can learn a simple way to provide the users with some feedback when they click a button.

Select any bitmap from the Cast. For example, select the forward arrow button bitmap. Click the Information button at the top of the Cast window, which looks like a white "I" with a blue circle around it. This Information button brings up the Property Inspector with the member's properties shown. One property is Highlight When Clicked. When this property is turned on, the bitmap appears highlighted when it is clicked by the user. It's a generic effect, but much better than having none at all.

Turn this option on for all your bitmap presentation buttons. Ideally, you want to define the down state of a button with another bitmap entirely. This enables you to customize the look of the button as it is clicked. For now, however, this behavior suffices. Unfortunately, you can use this option only on bitmaps. Your text members used in the menu screen do not change appearance as they are clicked.

Cursor Changes

Cursor changes work on any cast member type. The idea is to have the cursor change when the users position it over a button. The behavior for this is called the Rollover Cursor Change. You can find it in the Animation category in the Library palette, under the Interactive subcategory.

Upon dragging and dropping this behavior from the Library palette onto a sprite, you are prompted by the behavior's parameter box. You need to worry about only one property of the behavior. The first property enables you to choose from some standard cursors that are built in to Director 8. The best choice for this purpose is probably the "finger" cursor. It is similar to the cursor used by Web browsers when users roll over a hypertext link. The rest of the properties are used when you want to make your own cursor.

⇨ *For more information on button behaviors, **see** "Creating A Simple Button Behavior," **p. 265** and "Building A Complete Button Behavior," **p. 60** (Chapter 14, "Creating Behaviors")*

⇨ *For more information about using cursors, **see** "Using Cursors," **p. 430** (Chapter 21, "Controlling the Director Environment")*

Transitions

The next step to jazzing up your presentations is adding some transitions. Up until now, the frames advanced in an abrupt manner, whereby the new frame suddenly replaced the old. You can soften these changes by using *transitions*, which are designs such as dissolves and wipes that change one screen into another.

Transitions are applied by using the Transitions channel at the top of the Score, directly under the Tempo and Palette channels. Double-clicking the Transitions channel on a frame presents you with a list of transitions and a few options. You become more familiar with the different types of transitions in Chapter 10, "Properties of Sprites and Frames." For now, use any dissolve transition with its default settings.

A transition on a frame occurs as the movie enters the frame. This means that the dissolve occurs between the preceding frame that the movie displayed and the new one. It does not matter whether the preceding frame was the frame directly before the new one in the Score. Transitions work just fine even when you jump from frame 45 to frame 23, as long as the transition is on frame 23.

You cannot, however, simply add transitions such as this to a frame when you have placed a Hold on Current Frame behavior in the Frame Script channel of that frame. This is because that behavior actually sends the movie back to the current frame when the frame is done. It is, in effect, looping on one single frame. Therefore, if you had a transition on that frame, the transition would be repeated over and over.

Assume, for example, that a button took the users from frame 12 to frame 14, and there was a dissolve transition and a "Hold on Current Frame" behavior on frame 14. The Stage would first show a dissolve from frame 12 to frame 14 and then repeat a dissolve from frame 14 to frame 14. The result would be that certain reactions, such as mouse clicks, would slow way down as the complex dissolve transition was performed over and over.

If you need to remove behaviors from a sprite, bring up the Behavior Inspector by choosing Window, Inspectors, Behavior or by clicking the Behavior Inspector icons that appear in the Score, the Property Inspector, and other windows. This shows you all the current behaviors and enables you to select and delete any of them. You can also use the behavior pop-up menu in the Score to clear all the behaviors and start over.

When you add a transition to the Score for the first time, it creates a transition cast member automatically. You can then use this cast member again by dragging it to a new position in the Transition channel of the Score window. If you double-click the Transition channel again, it creates another new cast member, even if the transition is exactly the same as the one you previously created. The advantage to having one transition cast member and applying it throughout the Score is that you have to change that one member's settings only once to change all the transitions.

Avoiding this pitfall is easy. You need to create two frames for each presentation screen. All the sprites in each frame should be the same. However, the first frame features the transition in the Transition channel. It has no frame script, and so the movie flows naturally from that frame to the next. The second frame does not contain any transition, but does have the Hold on Current Frame behavior. The marker label should appear on the first frame of the pair. Figure 2.8 shows an example.

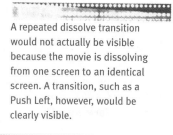

A repeated dissolve transition would not actually be visible because the movie is dissolving from one screen to an identical screen. A transition, such as a Push Left, however, would be clearly visible.

Transition Frames

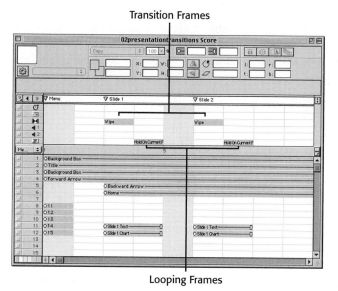

Looping Frames

Figure 2.8
The Score shows a dual-frame setup for each presentation screen. The first frame of each pair has the marker and transition. The second frame uses the Hold on Current Frame behavior.

Note that you don't need to actually create an entire separate set of sprites to make this second frame. Instead, you can stretch all the sprites of one frame. Do this by selecting the first frame, moving the playback head of the movie forward one frame, and then choosing Modify, Extend Sprite.

You can create sounds with Macromedia's SoundEdit 16 or Peak LE on the Mac, or SoundForge in Windows or with many other sound-editing programs. Many are available as shareware on the Internet.

Adding Sounds

You can add sounds to your presentations in a few simple ways. First, you need to import some sounds into the Cast. Choose File, Import to bring in a sound.

Try adding sounds to the buttons. It is sometimes nice to have the button actually make a noise when the users click it. The Play Sound Member behavior enables you to do this. You can find it in the Media category of the Library palette, under the subcategory Sound.

This behavior prompts you for a sound, channel, initializing event, and loop setting. You can see the Parameters dialog box created by the behavior in Figure 2.9.

Figure 2.9
The Parameters dialog box for the Play Sound Member library behavior asks for a Sound to play, a Sound channel, When to play sound, and Number of loops.

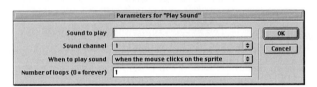

Choose the sound from the pop-up menu. It should list all the sound cast members available. Keep the channel at 1, and choose mouseDown as the initializing event. You need to do this because the event mouseUp is already being used by one of the other behaviors that you have assigned to the button sprites.

For more information about messages and behaviors, **see** "Building Your Own Behaviors," **p. 190** (Chapter 11, "Advanced Techniques")

The buttons now play a sound when the users click them. You can define different sounds for each type of button if you like.

Another way to use sounds is to make a sound play when the presentation enters a new frame. Adding sounds such as this is even easier. All you need to do is place a sound in the Sound channel of any frame. You can double-click the Sound channels and add sounds the same way you add transitions. Or, you can drag a sound from the Cast to the Score. You can even drag and drop a sound member onto the Stage to add it to the Score.

An extension of this is to add a background sound to a frame. Background sounds look the same as any other sound to Director, but they are typically longer pieces with music or some sort of ambient noise, such as wind. Often these background sounds are built so that they loop. When the sound ends, it can start playing again in a manner that makes the loop seem seamless.

When you have a looping sound, you need to tell Director what it is. Do this by editing the properties of a sound cast member. The only available option is to let Director know that it is a looping sound. Director then plays the sound continuously as long as it appears in the Sound channel of the frame currently playing.

Add a background sound to the Score in the same way that you added the previous sound to the Score. Be sure that you are not using this Sound channel for anything else. For instance, if you have a button sound that plays in Sound channel 1, place the background sound in channel 2. Otherwise, the button sound interrupts the background sound.

Notice that there is also a Sound Beep behavior in the Media: Sound library. This behavior plays the system beep instead of a cast member sound. Using this option is not recommended, however, because many users have customized their system sounds. You never really know what sounds will play on various machines. However, it's a quick and easy way to create sound feedback when you don't have a custom sound available.

For more information on using sound, **see** "Using Sound in Director," **p. 115** (Chapter 5, "Sound Members")

Adding Animation in Presentations

Don't forget that Director is a fantastic animation tool. Just because you are creating a slideshow-like presentation doesn't mean that you can't have moving objects. The two frames per screen design shown in the previous examples can easily be expanded to include animation.

To make an animated presentation screen, just create your animated sequence in a set of frames. Label the first frame, but not any others. Do not place any frame scripts in any of the animation frames except the last. In the last frame, use the Hold on Current Frame behavior as the frame script. This causes the movie to pause when the last frame is reached. The movie continues to loop until the users break the pattern by using a button to jump to another set of frames. Figure 2.10 shows this sort of setup.

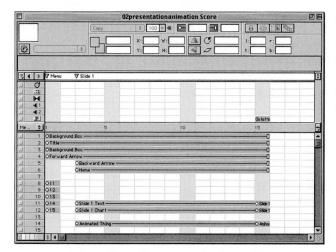

Figure 2.10
The Score shows an animated presentation screen. The playback head moves from the frame label "Slide 1" to the end of that animation sequence and then loops on the last frame.

You could also have the screen animate until it reaches a certain point and then stop. To do this, simply use a Hold on Current Frame behavior in the last frame. This means that the animation will not loop, but instead plays itself out and then pauses on the last frame.

Adding animation to a presentation can really spice it up. You can have elements slide into the screen, or even have animated characters that introduce the next screen.

For more information about animation, **see** "Animating with the Cast, Stage, and Score," **p. 36** (Chapter 1)

SHOWING YOUR PRESENTATION

After you have completed a presentation, you have basically three options for presenting the final product. You can use Director to present it, create a standalone projector, or compress the movie for use on the Internet or an intranet. Each of these options is discussed in the following sections.

> **Caution**
>
> If you are sending the Director movie to someone else, remember that he can see all your source code, the Score, cast members, and so on.

Using Director to Show Your Presentation

This option makes sense only for presentations meant to be shown at a certain time and place, such as a business meeting or a sales pitch. To show a raw movie, you must have Director present on the machine. If you plan to show the presentation yourself, this poses no problem. Otherwise, make sure the person showing the presentation has the same version of Director that you do. Be sure also to test your presentation on the playback machine. Slight differences in computers can cause the presentation to look different. The playback machine could be missing fonts or have different monitor bit-depth settings.

> By choosing View, Full Screen, you can present your movie in Director, but without the rest of the Director interface, or even the menu bar, present. The keyboard shortcut for this is ⌘+Option+1 on the Mac and Ctrl+Alt+1 in Windows. Use the keyboard shortcut to return to the normal display, or press the Esc key.

The advantage to showing a movie in Director is that you don't have to spend time building and testing projectors. You can also edit the presentation seconds before showing it, or even while it is playing.

Creating a Standalone Projector

This is the most common way of showing a presentation project. A projector is a standalone application that other people can play on their computers without having Director. Issues such as fonts and monitor settings are still valid, but if the movie is authored correctly it should run fine on all similar computer systems.

To create a projector, follow these steps:

> Director cannot create a cross-platform projector. There is no such thing. A Mac version of Director can create a Mac projector and a Windows version of Director can create a Windows projector. You'll have to buy two copies of Director to create projectors on both platforms.

1. Choose File, Create Projector. This brings up the Create Projector dialog box shown in Figure 2.11.

2. Specify which file or files you want to incorporate in the projector. The Create Projector dialog box prompts you to add movie and cast files. Do this by selecting the files and clicking the Add button. In most cases, you will be adding only one movie file. However, you can have a projector play several movie files sequentially by adding more than one.

3. Decide on the projector options by clicking the Options button to go to the Projector Options dialog box, shown in Figure 2.12.

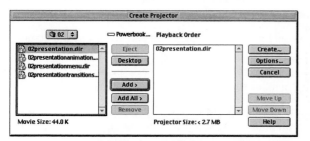

Figure 2.11
The Create Projector dialog box is the first step in making stand-alone applications from Director movies. This is the Macintosh version of the dialog box. The Windows version is slightly different, but offers the same settings.

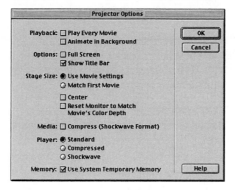

Figure 2.12
The Mac version of the Projector Options dialog box. (The Windows version is similar.)

The Projector Options dialog box has the following options to choose from:

- **Play Every Movie**—This option causes the projector to play each movie in the list sequentially. If this option is not selected, only the first movie is played. The other movies included in your list can still be called from Lingo.

- **Animate in Background**—This option determines whether the movie continues to play if it is not the frontmost application on the computer. If this option is not turned on and the users click another application, or use the Windows Alt+Tab function, the movie pauses. Unless your movie is a straightforward animation, you should turn this option on.

- **Full Screen**—You can choose to have your movie take over the full screen when the projector runs. This means that the rest of the screen will be blanked out, using the background color of the Stage. If you are creating a presentation or an animation, this is a desired option. However, if you are creating something that you want to look like a normal Mac or Windows application, don't use this option.

- **Show Title Bar**—This option will put a standard title bar above the Projector's window. The user can see the windows's title, and use the bar to move the window.

- **Stage Size (Use Movie Settings and Match First Movie options)**—The two options for Stage size enable you to decide how the projector handles multiple movies that are different sizes. If you have two movies in your projector, for instance, and the first is 640×480 and the second is 320×240, choosing the Match First Movie option forces the second movie to be contained in a larger, 640×480 Stage. The use Movie Settings option resizes the Stage when the other movie starts.

- **Center**—This option should always be selected unless you want the Stage to appear at a specific location on the user's monitor. If Center is not selected, the Stage appears at the same location as it does when you are authoring in Director. This can be dangerous if you are not sure what size monitor the playback machine will have.

- **Reset Monitor to Match Movie's Color Depth**—This option is available only for Mac projectors. On the Mac, a program such as a projector can automatically adjust the monitor itself. This means that you can switch the monitor to thousands or millions of colors, if that is what your movie requires.

- **Media: Compress (Shockwave Format)**—You have several options that affect the size of the final projector. You can choose to have Director compress media for you before placing the movie in the projector. This uses the same compression technique that you use when you create a Shockwave movie.

- **Player: (Standard, Compressed, and Shockwave options)**—You can also choose to make a Shockwave projector that relies on the user's computer system having Shockwave installed. The users would get Shockwave from Macromedia's Web site, if they do not already have it from playing Shockwave content off the Web. The Shockwave engine contains most of the code that a Projector needs to run. It is a standalone application that does not require a browser to run. A Shockwave Projector will be a lot smaller in size, because it uses the Shockwave engine. If users do not have Shockwave, the projector prompts them to download it.

- **Use System Temporary Memory**—This option is available only on the Mac. It enables the projector to steal memory not being used by other programs. It is not used if virtual memory is turned on, so it isn't likely to be a factor in most cases. However, it might give a large presentation a speed boost on some machines.

When you finish with the options, the only thing left to do is choose a filename. The result is an application program on the Mac and an .exe file in Windows. Chapter 36, "Delivering the Goods," goes into more detail about creating projectors.

➪ *For more information about building projectors,* **see** *"Making Projectors,"* **p. 710** *(Chapter 36, "Delivering the Goods")*

Creating a Shockwave Movie

A big misconception about Shockwave movies is that you have to "shock" (compress) them. This is not true. You can take a normal Director movie file and play it back in a Web browser with Shockwave.

What is normally referred to as "shocking a movie" is actually just compressing it. The new file is a copy of the movie with images, text, sounds, and Score information compressed. The difference is usually very large; often the file is less than half the size of the original. This makes it much easier for Internet users to download Director movies, especially when they are using modems. The code in a Shockwave file is also protected so that users cannot see the source code.

> **Caution**
>
> Compressing a Director movie also protects it from being opened by other people who have Director. Otherwise, they could steal your code and media.

To make a Shockwave movie, simply choose File, Publish. This outputs the movie as a compressed Shockwave movie, along with a sample HTML page.

Shockwave movies, as these compressed files are called, always have .dcr as a file extension. Web servers use this extension to identify them as Shockwave movies and tell the browser to use the Shockwave plug-in to play them.

The process for placing Shockwave movies on your Web server depends on your file transfer protocol (FTP) software. In most cases, you have the option to upload the file in text or binary format. You must select binary for the file to be properly transferred.

To place the Shockwave movie inside a Web page, you need to use an <OBJECT> tag for Internet Explorer on Windows, and an <EMBED> tag for Netscape on Windows and Mac, and Internet Explorer on Mac. However, you can just view the HTML code in the same page that the Publish command outputs.

➪ *For more information about building Shockwave movies,* **see** *"Making Shockwave Movies,"* **p. 712** *(Chapter 36)*

TROUBLESHOOTING DIRECTOR

- Be sure to set your Span Duration to 1 if you plan on placing a lot of single-frame sprites. Do this by choosing File, Preferences, Sprite.

- If a sprite or frame is behaving strangely, use the Behavior Inspector to ensure that only the behavior(s) you want are present. You can also use it to check the behavior's parameters.

- Remember to reuse transitions that have been added to the Cast when you can, rather than creating a new transition member each time.

- Always check your Projector options before making a projector.

- Don't assume that a playback computer will have compatible fonts, monitor size, and other options. Always test projectors on the playback machine, or on as many machines as possible.

DID YOU KNOW?

- When you add a behavior from the library, a copy is placed in your Cast. You can open this script and examine the code and comments if you are interested.

- You can import PowerPoint presentations into movies that will then look much like the examples described here. Just choose Xtras, Import PowerPoint File.

- In addition to the transitions built in to Director, you can purchase third-party Xtras that add more transitions.

- If you always use the Play behavior rather than the Go behavior to go to a frame, a Play Done button acts just like a Back button in a Web browser. It takes the users back through their navigation paths.

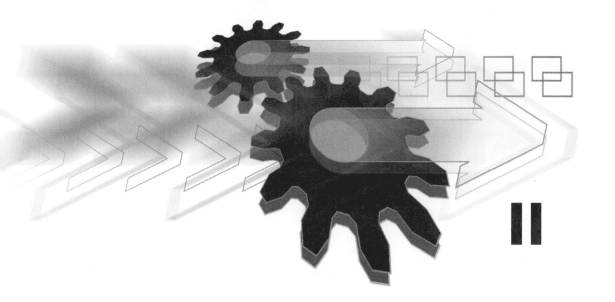

MEMBERS IN DETAIL

IN THIS PART

3

BITMAP MEMBERS

Images, graphics, illustrations, photographs, and renderings: These are all different names for the same thing as far as Director is concerned. They are all bitmaps: arrangements of colored pixels in computer format. For such content, Director has the bitmap member type.

You can create bitmaps in a variety of programs, and then you can bring these images into Director by importing from a variety of standard formats. You can also create and edit bitmaps by using Director's Paint window. This chapter is dedicated to explaining the bitmap member type and the tasks that Director can do with it.

TYPES OF BITMAPS

The biggest difference between types of bitmaps is that they can be of different bit depths. There are five different bit depth settings. Bits refer to the amount of information stored for each pixel of a graphic. A 1-bit image has only one piece of information: on or off. An 8-bit image has eight pieces of information, which corresponds to 256 possible combinations. This means that every pixel can have 256 possible colors. Here is a rundown of some of the possible bit depths:

- A 1-bit bitmap contains only black-and-white pixels. It's small, because only "on" or "off" data has to be stored for each pixel, not a color value. 1-bit bitmaps can be useful because you can define the colors of the two types of pixels in them to different colors depending on the sprite. So, a single 1-bit member can be used multiple times to display graphics with different colors.

- A 4-bit bitmap contains 16 colors. On the Macintosh, you can customize these 16 colors. In Windows, you can use only one 16-color palette: the Microsoft VGA palette. If you are making your Director movie for a 4-bit machine and intend to distribute it cross-platform, use the Windows VGA palette.

- An 8-bit bitmap contains 256 colors. These 256 colors correspond to a color palette. This palette contains black, white, a small range of grays, and a general selection of basic colors. You can customize an 8-bit palette both on the Macintosh and in Windows. Director ships with a number of built-in 8-bit palettes. You also can import custom 8-bit palettes into your Director movie either with images that use them, or on their own in the standard palette format (PAL). They are then stored as cast members.

- The 16-bit, or thousands of colors, color depth contains 65,536 colors. This color depth was created to closely match the color values of a normal television set. This color depth does not have a palette associated with it.

- The 24/32-bit, or millions of colors, color depth contains 16,777,216 colors. This is the maximum numbers of colors that can be viewed on a computer monitor. This number is actually overkill because a person with normal vision can perceive only about nine million colors. This color depth does not have a palette associated with it.

  The notation 24/32 might seem a bit odd. The 32 refers to total bits of information: 24 bits for everyday colors and 8 bits that deal with Alpha channel information or other special effects. You can't, however, work in 24 bits; when 24-bit terminology is used, it actually means a 32-bit resolution.

Using 8-bit images wherever possible is a good idea. An 8-bit image draws faster than a 16- or 32-bit image because the computer can process the smaller 8-bit image faster than a larger one. However, if your movie requires better color, use a higher setting.

An 8-bit bitmap can use only 256 colors at one time. However, a technique known as dithering can make the color range look wider. *Dithering* is the process of approximating a color by placing pixels of different, but similar, colors next to one another.

Two things are conspiring to make 8-bit images obsolete. First, just about every consumer-level computer sold in the last three years is capable of displaying 32-bit color. Second, Director's bitmap compression and JPEG compression for Shockwave movies can often make 32-bit images almost as small as their 8-bit counterparts, and these 32-bit images look much better.

Using Palettes

You can use Director and bitmaps without knowing much at all about palettes, but it helps to understand them. Several palettes are built in to Director. These include the Mac system palette and the Windows system palette. Each acts as a default palette for Director running on the system.

Strangely enough, these palettes are not the same. This is where a lot of trouble begins. If you decide to make your movie work with 8-bit graphics, you must choose a palette in the Movie Properties dialog box. But which standard palette do you use? The Mac palette displays fine on Macintosh computers, but not on some Windows machines, and vice versa.

In fact, if the user's monitor is set to use 16- or 32-bit color, the palette issue will never arise. This monitor has enough colors available to display any palette. However, if a computer is set to use an 8-bit monitor setting, it means that it can display only 256 colors at one time.

Showing a movie that uses a palette that differs from the one the system uses causes the computer to adjust and shift to your movie's palette. This is fine as long as the movie takes over the entire computer screen. However, if a window of another application or the desktop shows through, it will display in the wrong colors.

In addition, showing two 8-bit images that use different palettes also causes problems. Two totally different palettes would mean that you are asking the computer to display 512 colors at one time. Because it can't do this, some of the colors shift.

Using graphics that are 16- or 32-bit also causes problems for users with 8-bit displays. The graphics probably use far more than 256 colors, so Director attempts to compromise when displaying them. The result might be that your graphics do not look very good.

If you want to use 8-bit images and you don't need to stick to a standard palette, it might be a good idea to create a new palette that is optimized to display your collection of graphics as best as possible. This palette can be imported as a cast member and referred to just like the built-in palettes. Programs like DeBabelizer on the Mac and Brenda in Windows can create custom palettes for you. Also, the PhotoCaster Xtra can import a series of PhotoShop images and create a new palette at the same time.

Choosing the Bit Depth

You should think about palettes and bit depth before starting your project. What will your users be using? If they have 32-bit monitors, you know that you have the option to use 32-bit graphics. If many have only 8-bit capability, 8-bit might be your only option.

The Web palette uses only 216 colors that are shared by both palettes. The rest of the colors are not used, but are reserved to enable the system to display the desktop and other elements.

If your project is focused on deep, complex images, such as photographs, you might want to consider 16- or 32-bit graphics if possible. However, remember that they are two or four times larger than 8-bit bitmaps. Your Director movies will be much larger as a result. However, much of this excess file size disappears when you make Shockwave movies for either the Web or a projector.

If you know that most of your users have either Macintosh computers or Windows, the choice of a palette is obvious. Otherwise, consider which one is appropriate for both platforms or per-haps construct a new one. If your movie will end up as a Shockwave movie on a Web site, using Director's built-in Web palette might be the answer. It displays well on both Mac and Windows.

The options can be confusing. If you are just learning Director, stick to using the default palette of your system for now.

➪ *For more information on cross-platform development, see "Developing for Both Mac and Windows" p. 700 (Chapter 35, "Cross-Platform Development")*

IMPORTING BITMAPS

Even though there is only one bitmap member type, a variety of formats can be imported into this bitmap member type. You can import any one of these types of formatted files:

- **BMP**—A common Windows graphic format.

- **GIF**—A format originally used by CompuServe known as the Graphic Interchange Format. It's now one of the two standard image formats of the Internet.

- **JPEG**—Defined by the Joint Photographic Experts Group as a high-quality compressed image format. It is also a standard image format of the Internet.

- **LRG**—The native format of Macromedia's xRes image editor.

- **PhotoShop**—The native format of Adobe PhotoShop.

- **MacPaint**—An older Macintosh image format.

- **PNG**—Portable Network Graphics format. There is some momentum behind this format to be the new standard for the Internet.

- **PICT**—Originally defined for the Apple Lisa computer, now a standard Macintosh image format.

- **Targa**—Also known as the .tga format. Targa was the name of the Truevision graphics card that first used the .tga format.

- **TIFF**—Tag Image File Format.

After you import any of these file formats into Director as a bitmap, it no longer matters what the original format of the document was; it is now a bitmap cast member.

By default, however, JPEG, GIF, and PNG files retain their original file data inside Director until you edit them. These originals are then used as the compressed image data when a Shockwave movie is made. The result is that the Shockwave movie is far smaller than the original Director movie, which contained both the original file data and the Director-formatted bitmap.

To import a bitmap image, choose File, Import. This brings up Director's Import dialog box. Figure 3.1 shows this complex window. You can import most media from here, including sound and video.

Figure 3.1
This is the Macintosh Import dialog box. It looks slightly different on the Windows platform, but the functions are basically the same.

You can choose one or more images and add them to your import list. When you are done, click Import to bring them in. If the graphics are set to the same bit depth as the monitor, and use the same palette as the movie does, they are immediately brought in. Otherwise, you are prompted with the Image Options dialog box shown in Figure 3.2.

In the Image Options dialog box, you are given the choice of bringing in the bitmap using its bit depth or palette, or converting it to the bit depth of the movie. The Trim White Space option allows you to remove any excess white pixels from around the image. Selecting the Dither option smoothes over any color changes that need to be made. The final option, Same Settings for Remaining Images, enables you to bypass this dialog box for the rest of the images that you have selected in that single import.

Figure 3.2
The Image Options dialog box enables you to specify how to translate images that use a different bit depth or palette than the movie.

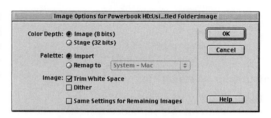

After you have imported a bitmap, you can still change its bit depth or palette. Just select a bitmap or bitmaps in the Cast and choose Modify, Transform Bitmap. This command also enables you to resize the image.

USING THE PAINT WINDOW

Some people love the Paint window and others hate it. Those who dislike it point to its weakness when compared with programs such as PhotoShop, plus its odd quirks and idiosyncrasies. Those who love it, including me, point to its speed, ease of use, and its unique tool set.

You can open the Paint window by double-clicking a bitmap cast member or choosing ⌘+5 on the Mac or Ctrl+5 in Windows. Figure 3.3 shows an empty Paint window. Notice that it has a toolbar both on the top and on the left side of the window. It also has a typical set of buttons and the name field at the top of the window.

The tools on the left side of the window are used to edit or add to the bitmap. Notice that some of them have a small arrow at the right-bottom corner of the button. This means that you can click and hold over that button to see a small pop-up list of tool options.

The Trim White Space feature of the Image Options dialog box defaults to on. You might want to turn it off when you are importing graphics that use whitespace around them to cause each graphic to line up on the screen with the others. This often happens when importing a group of related images, such as images exported from PowerPoint, or a set of images exported from a 3D graphics tool.

It's always best to convert your graphics to the desired bit depth and palette in the program that you originally used to create them. PhotoShop, for instance, generally does a better job of converting and dithering an image down to 8-bit than Director does.

Lasso and Marquee Tools

The first two tools, the Lasso and Marquee tools, are the selection tools. They enable you to select an area of the image to manipulate, move, or delete. The Lasso tool has three options and the Marquee tool has four, as follows:

- **Marquee, Shrink**—On selection of an element, the selection marquee shrinks to the outside edges of the artwork to create a rectangular selection. All white pixels contained within this selection are seen as opaque white.

- **Marquee, No Shrink**—On selection of an element, the selection marquee remains in the dragged position as a rectangular selection. All white pixels contained within this selection are seen as opaque white.

- **Marquee, Lasso**—On selection of an element, the color of the pixel where the drag was started and all same-colored touching pixels are ignored. All other colors within the selection are selected within a flat-sided selection. All white pixels contained within this selection are seen as opaque white.

- **Marquee, See Thru Lasso**—This option behaves the same as Marquee, Lasso except all white pixels contained within this selection are seen as transparent (no value).

- **Lasso, No Shrink**—The area drawn with the Lasso tool retains its shape and selects all its content. All white pixels contained within this selection are seen as opaque white.

- **Lasso, Lasso**—On selection of an element, the color of the pixel where the drag was started and all same-colored touching pixels are ignored. All other colors within the selection are selected within the drawn area. All white pixels contained within this selection are seen as opaque white.

- **Lasso, See Thru Lasso**—This option behaves the same as Lasso, Lasso, except that all white pixels contained within this selected area are seen as transparent (no value).

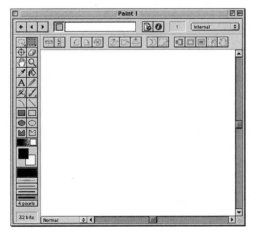

Figure 3.3
The Paint window has more than 50 buttons and other items that enable you to alter bitmap images.

Registration Point Tool

The next tool, shown as a target sight, can be used to view or reset the registration point of a member. A registration point is a location in the bitmap that the Stage uses to decide the placement of the sprite. By default, the registration point is at the center of the image. A bitmap displayed at location 50, 120 on the Stage, would then be centered at 50, 120. However, you can use the Registration Point tool to shift that point from the center of the image, and thus have it displayed according to the new registration point.

Why would you want to do this? If you are animating something that requires a series of members—a man jumping, for example—you would expect the center of the graphic to change as the animation progresses. In the middle of the jump, for instance, the center of the man would be higher than at the start. You can move that portion of the sprite higher on the Stage when creating the animation.

However, by using different registration points, you can have each bitmap in the animation stay at the same Stage location, and let the offset of registration points do the movement for you. You can then easily reuse this set of cast members as an animation without having to reposition every sprite.

Bitmap members use the center of the bitmap as the default registration point. However, text and field members use the upper-left corner of the sprite as their registration points. You can't change the registration points of text or field members.

If you open a bitmap member where the registration point is not in the center, you can double-click the Registration Point tool button to recenter it.

Eraser Tool

Next to the Registration Point tool is the Eraser tool. You can choose this tool to paint white pixels on the bitmap. This has the same effect as using the Paintbrush tool with the color set to white, except that the eraser paints in a different shape. Double-clicking this button erases the entire image in the window.

Hand Tool

The Hand tool is one way to move artwork around in the Paint window. It does the same job as the window's scrollbars. You can quickly access the Hand tool by pressing the spacebar.

The Paint window has no real boundaries, so it's easy to move the paint object so far away from the center of the visible window that you can't find it again. In this situation, simply close and reopen the Paint window and the artwork again appears in the middle.

Zoom Tool

The capacity of the Paint window to enable you to zoom in on artwork with the Zoom tool is one of its best features. You can edit your graphic's pixels much more easily this way. You can zoom up to 800%.

The Paint window changes somewhat when you zoom in. The upper-right corner of the window contains an actual-size version of what you see in the main, zoomed area of the window. When you make changes to the bitmap, both images update. Because the number of pixels that fit in the Paint window changes as you zoom, this actual-size area also shrinks as you zoom in.

The result is that at 200% zoom, one quarter of the window shows the actual-size view. At 400%, only 1/16 of the window is occupied by it. This makes editing at 400% and 800% much more effective than at 200%. You can click the actual-size area to immediately zoom all the way back out again. Figure 3.4 shows the Paint window with a zoom of 400%.

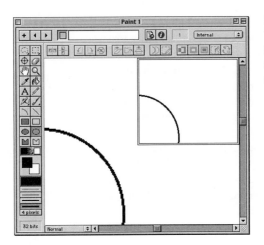

Figure 3.4
The Paint window here is zoomed at 400%. The upper-right corner shows the same image, but actual size.

A few shortcuts enable you to zoom in and out in the Paint window. You can press the ⌘++ (plus) and ⌘+- (minus) on the Mac, or Ctrl++ (plus) and Ctrl+- (minus) in Windows to quickly zoom in and out. While using most Paint window tools, you can also hold down the ⌘ key on the Mac and the Control key in Windows and click in the Paint window to zoom in. The ⌘+Shift keys on the Mac and the Ctrl+Shift keys in Windows enable you to zoom back out.

Eyedropper Tool

The Eyedropper tool enables you to select a color in the Paint window to use as the foreground color. If you hold down the Shift key, that color becomes the background color. If you hold down the Option key on the Mac or the Alt key in Windows, that color becomes the gradient destination color.

As in other drawing programs, you can hold down the Option key on the Mac or the Alt key in Windows to temporarily use the Eyedropper tool without selecting it from the tool area. You can also hold down the Shift key at the same time to grab a background color.

Paint Bucket Tool

This tool enables you to fill an area with the foreground color. The fill begins at the hot spot of the fill cursor, which is the tip of the pouring paint. The fill changes the color of the selected pixel and all pixels of that color that surround it. Double-clicking the Paint Bucket button brings up the Gradient Settings dialog box.

Text Tool

You can paint text into a bitmap member with the Text tool. Selecting this tool changes the cursor to a text insert cursor. You can then click in the Paint window to set the start position of the text. A blinking cursor appears and you can start to type. While typing, you can double-click the Text tool button to bring up the Font dialog box, with which you can change the font, size, and style of the text you are inserting.

After you have clicked another tool, or clicked in the Paint window to start typing another piece of text, the text you type becomes a permanent part of the image. You can, however, use Undo to restore the bitmap to its preceding state.

> Text entered into the Paint window is not anti-aliased, nor is it editable. To create members that are purely text, use the text member type instead.

Pencil Tool

This tool is the simplest, and yet the most useful, tool in the Paint window. You can draw one pixel at a time with this tool, something that is not easy to do in PhotoShop or other image-editing programs. Pixel editing is a must for creating precise graphics to be displayed on the computer screen.

> Holding down the Shift key before clicking the screen constrains the Pencil tool to drawing a straight line, either horizontally or vertically.

Air Brush Tool

The effect the Air Brush tool creates, at first, might not look like paint being sprayed out of an air brush. To get a very smooth spray, the pixels must be smoothed out or anti-aliased, something you generally don't want to do in a Director animation. The Air Brush tool can create some fun patterns despite its limitations. This tool has five fixed settings, ranging from small to large, and a custom setting dialog box to set up your own air brush pattern. Click the Air Brush tool to activate the pop-up menu. Choose Settings or double-click the Air Brush tool to open the Air Brush Settings dialog box.

The Air Brush Settings dialog box is shown in Figure 3.5. The options are as follows:

Figure 3.5
The Air Brush Settings dialog box allows you to customize the Air Brush tool to create a number of different effects.

- **Flow Rate**—How fast the paint comes out of the gun. The higher the setting, the quicker the paint dots come out of the gun.

- **Spray Area**—How much area the dots can cover for each click of the mouse. If the mouse is clicked and held in one place for a period of time, the paint dots eventually fill the entire spray area.

- **Dot Size**—Size of the paint dots that hit the canvas.

- **Uniform Spray**—Sprays an even amount of paint from the tool.

- **Random Sizes**—Sprays paint dots of random sizes.
- **Current Brush**—Sets the paint dot to the shape of the Brush tool. Double-click the Brush tool to set this option.

Brush Tool

The Brush tool is used for freehand drawing. It uses one of five brush settings. Click and hold the button to choose which setting you want to use, or open the Brush Settings dialog box.

You can preset up to five brushes in the Paint window at any one time. Figure 3.6 shows the Brush Settings dialog box, which includes some standard brush shapes and a brush-editing area. You can get to this dialog box by double-clicking the Brush tool in the Paint window. This dialog box enables you to edit the currently selected brush.

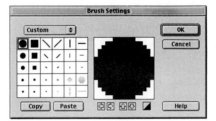

Figure 3.6
The Brush Settings dialog box enables you to set the shape of one of five brushes.

In the Brush Settings dialog box, you can choose one of the preset Standard brush tips. These brush tips appear in a box on the left in the dialog box. You can also access the brush tips by clicking the pop-up menu at the top of the dialog box to customize one of the Standard settings.

The palette of standard brush settings is fully customizable via the Brush Settings window. With the Brush Settings dialog box open, select an area outside the dialog box and a black-and-white image of what is under the cursor is placed in the custom brush creation canvas, shown in the box on the right side of the Brush Settings dialog box.

Within the Brush Settings dialog box, pixels can be added or removed from the enlarged brush creation canvas. You can use the move arrow buttons below the brush creation canvas to shuffle the pixels up, down, right, and left one pixel. The pixels in the blown-up area can also be swapped or inverted: white to black or black to white. In addition, brushes can be copied to or from the Clipboard.

Arc Tool

The Arc tool draws an arched line on the canvas the thickness of the line set in the line weight selection area of the Tool palette. Pressing the Shift key when an arc is created causes the arc to constrain to a circular radius.

Line Tool

The Line tool creates straight lines. The width of a line in the Paint window can be between 1 and 64 pixels. Click the default one-, two-, and three-pixel line width settings, or double-click the Other Line Width setting to select a larger width. Pressing the Shift key before starting to draw a line causes the line to constrain to a 45° angle.

Shape Tools

The Rectangle and Ellipse tools create basic shapes on the canvas. These bitmapped shapes can be filled or unfilled, depending on which tool you select. The line weight of the shape is set with the Line Weight selectors.

Pressing the Shift key as the bitmapped rectangle or ellipse is being created constrains the shape to square or circular, respectively.

The Polygon tools create both filled and outlined polygons. Each click you make on the Paint window with the Polygon tool becomes a corner of the desired shape. The shape can be finished by either double-clicking to close the shape or by clicking the last position over the top of the first position.

Color Chips

Four color chips are in the left-side tool area of the Paint window. They correspond to the foreground color, the gradient destination color, the foreground color, and the background color. You will notice that two color chips represent the foreground color. They behave as you might expect, with a change made to one of these two affecting both. So, despite the four color chips, there are really only three color settings.

The foreground color is used by just about all the tools as the primary painting color. The background color is used when you are drawing or filling an area with a pattern. It is also used as the background color when you are drawing text in the Paint window. The gradient destination color is used when you are filling or painting with a gradient, rather than a solid color.

To change any of these colors, click and hold the chip. A color palette appears, in which the current color is selected. You can drag the cursor to the new color and release. This little Palette selector also includes a group of favorite colors and a Color Picker tool option for selecting 32-bit colors. Figure 3.7 shows what this Palette selector looks like.

Figure 3.7
The Palette selector enables you to choose a color. It is used in the Paint window, as well as many other Director tools.

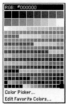

Gradients

Between the first foreground color chip and the gradient destination color chip is a small area in which you can specify a gradient for use with the Paint Bucket tool and some other tools. You can select options such as Top to Bottom, Bottom to Top, Left to Right, Right to Left, Directional, Shape Burst, and Sun Burst. You can also choose to bring up the Gradient Settings dialog box, shown in Figure 3.8.

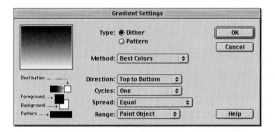

Figure 3.8
The Gradient Settings dialog box enables you to choose many options. Experimentation is the best way to understand them all.

After you have set the gradient options, you still need to select Gradient as your ink effect for a specific tool. To do this, select the tool you want, such as the Paint Bucket, and then select Gradient from the pop-up menu at the bottom of the Paint window. You can find out more about this pop-up menu a little later in this chapter.

Patterns

Most of the time, you will want to draw and fill with solid colors. However, Director includes a set of patterns that you can use instead. Clicking the area directly below the background color chip brings up the palette of patterns shown in Figure 3.9. The patterns should display using your current foreground and background colors.

Figure 3.9
The Pattern selector enables you to specify a pattern with which to paint and fill.

After you select a pattern, tools such as the Paintbrush and the Paint Bucket will use that pattern, with the current colors, to draw. The Pencil tool remains a single-pixel editing tool, however.

Line Weight Settings

Five choices for line weights are given at the bottom-left corner of the Paint window. The first is to have no line. The others are widths 1 through 3. The last line width choice is a custom setting. Double-clicking the last line width choice brings up the Paint Window Preferences dialog box, where you can set it.

Paint Window Inks

A small pop-up menu at the bottom of the Paint window usually reads "Normal." This pop-up enables you to set the ink of a drawing tool, such as the Paintbrush tool or the Rectangle tool. These are different from sprite inks in that they apply only to the result of editing in the Paint window. Not all inks are available to all painting tools. The ink options are as follows:

- **Normal**—The default ink draws with the foreground color or selected pattern.

- **Transparent**—When used with a pattern, this ink draws only the foreground color and leaves the background areas (white pixels) of the pattern with their existing colors.

- **Reverse**—This ink reverses the color of anything drawn over. If used with a pattern, only the black pixels of the pattern reverse the pixels under them.

- **Ghost**—This ink draws with the current background color. If you are using black and white, white pixels are drawn in such a way that they show up over a black background.

- **Gradient**—This ink uses the gradient settings and draws appropriately. Use with the Paint Bucket tool or a shape drawing tool.

- **Reveal**—This unusual ink uses the image of the previous bitmap member in the Cast. As you paint, you are actually painting with colors from that member, mapped onto the current bitmap.

- **Cycle**—This ink causes the Paintbrush tool to cycle through colors in the palette as you draw. It starts with the foreground color and cycles through all the colors until it reaches the background color. It can then repeat the sequence or move through the sequence in reverse, depending on your setting in the Paint Window Preferences dialog box.

- **Switch**—This ink causes any pixels that use the foreground color to switch to the destination color. You should have your monitor set to 8 bits for this to work properly.

- **Blend**—This ink enables you to blend the foreground color with the color of the pixels underneath it. It works best with 16- or 32-bit bitmaps.

- **Darkest**—This ink draws the foreground color only when it is darker than the pixels you are drawing over.

- **Lightest**—This ink draws the foreground color only when it is lighter than the pixels you are drawing over.

- **Darken**—This ink darkens the pixels as you paint over them.

- **Lighten**—This ink lightens the pixels as you paint over them.

- **Smooth**—This ink smoothes differences between adjoining pixels. The current color settings have no effect on the operation of this ink.

- **Smear**—This ink creates an effect similar to smearing paint across the image. The current color settings have no effect on the operation of this ink.

- **Smudge**—This ink is similar to smear, but the colors do not carry as far.

- **Spread**—This ink is similar to using the Eyedropper tool and then painting. Each time you click in the Paint window, the spread ink picks up the color under the brush and uses it to paint that stroke. It even works when several different colors are under the paintbrush. It just repeats that pattern as you draw.

- **Clipboard**—This ink draws with the clipboard image as the paintbrush shape and color pattern.

Paint Window Preferences

The Paint Window Preferences dialog box, shown in Figure 3.10, enables you to set a variety of options. In the middle, you can see the custom line width setting ("Other" Line Width), mentioned previously. Most of the rest of the options deal with the different inks.

The Remember Color and Remember Ink options enable you to specify whether you want Director to remember the last color set and ink used with each brush. The Interpolate by option determines whether the Cycle ink is to cycle between colors in the palette or real colors.

The Paint window also has a ruler that you can turn on or off. You can do this by choosing View, Rulers. After rulers are turned on, you can click a small area in the upper-left corner of the Paint window to change the type of units that the ruler displays.

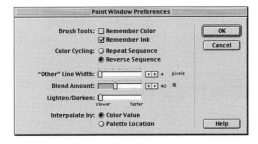

Figure 3.10
Open the Paint Window Preferences dialog box by choosing File, Preferences, Paint or by double-clicking the custom line width tool.

You can also hide or show the Paint window tools in the View menu. The tools still work, but you won't be able to change them unless you use keyboard shortcuts.

The Effects Toolbar

Above the paint area is another toolbar space with a few buttons that represent certain tools. To use these tools, first select an area in the bitmap. These tools are defined as follows:

- **Flip**—The Flip Horizontal and Flip Vertical tools flip a selected element across a horizontal or vertical axis.

- **Rotate**—Selected elements can be rotated 90° clockwise or counterclockwise. The Free Rotate tool enables the selected element to rotate freely around its center. The selection places handles on each of the element's corners. Drag these handles to a new position to produce the rotation.

- **Distort**—The next three buttons can create interesting effects. The Skew tool skews selected elements by slanting the sides of an element equally, leaving the top and bottom of the element perpendicular to one another. The Warp tool enables handles of the selected element to be pulled around to create a smashed or twisted effect. The Perspective tool shrinks or expands the edges of the selected element to give the illusion of depth.

- **Smooth**—This toolenables smoothing of pixels within a selected area of artwork. The smoothing effect functions only when the bit depth of the cast member is set to 8 bits.

- **Trace Edges**—This tool creates a new 1-pixel thick line around the edges of the original pixels of the artwork, leaving the original pixels white.

- **Invert**—When clicked, Invert causes the selection to change its black pixels to white, and white pixels to black. Colors in the active 8-bit palette flip to the opposite side of the palette. To see the exact place a color occupies in a palette, open the Color Palettes window from the Window menu. If an image has a color depth higher than 8-bit, the Invert button replaces the colors with their RGB complement colors.

- **Lighten and Darken**—Selected elements grow lighter or darker in their palette of colors. This command is unavailable in a 16-bit color space.

- **Fill**—This tool fills any selected area with the current foreground color or pattern.

- **Switch Colors**—This tool changes the color of identically colored pixels in a selected area. Pixels that match the foreground color are changed to the destination color. Switch Colors works only when the cast member is set to a palette of 256 or fewer colors.

BITMAP MEMBER PROPERTIES

Bitmaps have a few options that can be set in the Property Inspector, shown in Figure 3.11. You bring up Property Inspector with the bitmap settings showing by clicking the *i* button at the top of the bitmap Paint window.

At the top of the Property Inspector bitmap member settings area is a pop-up menu with a list of palettes. This will have an effect on the image only when the bitmap is set to 8-bit. It enables you to change the palette for the member without actually transforming it. The new palette is applied, regardless of the changes to the colors of the pixels.

The first option, Highlight When Clicked, was mentioned in Chapter 2, "Presentations with Director." It enables you to have the bitmap automatically invert itself when users click it. This can be used to make quick-and-dirty buttons that react to mouse clicks.

Figure 3.11
The Properties Inspector enables you to set a bitmap's options when a bitmap is selected in the Cast, or the Paint window is open.

The next option, Dither, comes into play if you scale or rotate the image. The image might display better with a dither, but dithering might hurt your animation speed.

A new feature of Director 8 is the Trim White Space option for bitmap images. Previously, this was something that could be done only when an image was initially imported. This option retains white pixels around the bitmap, even if it is edited in the Paint window.

The next option, Use Embedded Alpha, decides whether the Alpha channel of the bitmap is used when it is displayed on the Stage.

Alpha channels are a fourth channel of image data. The others are the Red, Green, and Blue channels. The Alpha channel defines how transparent each pixel is. If you create a 32-bit image with an Alpha channel, you can anti-alias the edges of the image, or make some of it transparent. You can use the Use Embedded Alpha option to make graphics that are semi-transparent or have edges that blend nicely with any background.

Director 8 also has a new Compression setting for bitmaps. This setting enables you to decide how the image is compressed when the movie is saved as a Shockwave movie. You can use the normal bitmap compression, which is similar to how Director 5 and 6 saved all bitmaps, or you can opt to use JPEG compression for the image. You can also choose the Movie Setting option from the Compression list, which means that the cast member will follow the preferences set by the Publish Settings dialog box.

JPEG compression is best used for photographic images and other things that do not require precision. Depending on the Quality setting, JPEG compression will blur your image more and more to squeeze it into a smaller file space.

In addition to being able to use JPEG compression, you can choose the Optimize in Fireworks button if you have the Macromedia Fireworks program installed. This option allows you to use the excellent compression techniques that Fireworks has available.

The Alpha Click Threshold defines how much of a role the Alpha channel plays in defining where the users can click the image. If the image is set to transparent, the Alpha channel is used to define the clickable area.

ONION SKINNING

Director operates on the principle that you have not just one image, but many images. Rarely does a movie have only one bitmap. Often, bitmaps relate to one another. If you are drawing a man jumping, for example, the second step of the jump animation is probably based on the first step. This is where *onion skinning* comes into play.

In cases such as this, it's useful to be able to see two bitmap members at once. You can do this by using the Option key on the Mac or the Alt key in Windows to open two Paint windows. However, all you see are the two members in different parts of your screen. Onion skinning enables you to see two or more members in the same Paint window. You can draw on only one of those members, but the others remain visible for reference.

To turn on onion skinning, first open the Onion Skin tool by choosing View, Onion Skin. A small tool window, shown in Figure 3.12, appears. It includes a few buttons and two number settings. You should also have the Paint window open, because it's the only window in which the Onion Skin tool works.

Figure 3.12
The Onion Skin tool enables you to see more than one member in the Paint window at one time.

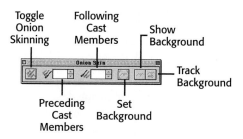

Toggle Onion Skinning · Following Cast Members · Show Background · Track Background · Preceding Cast Members · Set Background

You must have at least two bitmap members for the Onion Skin tool to work. You then need to turn onion skinning on by clicking the leftmost button in the tool (Toggle Onion Skinning).

The default settings for the Onion Skin tool are to show a single preceding bitmap member. You can actually show many more preceding bitmaps and even show many following bitmaps. The two number settings in the tool enable you to set this. Each bitmap shown appears dimmed slightly and always behind the paint image of the bitmap you are editing. If you are showing more than one bitmap in the background, each image is successively dimmed. Figure 3.13 shows this effect.

These images are shown so that you can draw on top of them and create artwork that is relative to another member. You can also adjust the registration point of the current member to match it to the background image.

Try using onion skinning while painting with the Reveal ink. It enables you to preview the image that is being revealed before you draw.

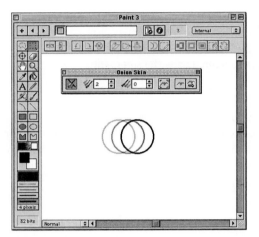

Figure 3.13
This Paint window is using onion skinning to show the two preceding members.

In addition to using the standard method for onion skinning, you can also use the tool to set a fixed background image. This image remains in the background no matter which other member you edit. Use this tool by first selecting the background bitmap. Click the Set Background button in the Onion Skin tool. To use that background image as your background, turn on onion skinning, set both numbers to 0, and then click the Show Background button. You will see that background image used as the background of any bitmap that you edit.

You can also combine background onion skinning with regular onion skinning and have several background images. Although normal onion skinning images change as you move from bitmap to bitmap, the background image remains the same.

In addition, you can turn on background tracking and have the background image used by the Paint window change relative to the bitmap you are editing. For instance, if you choose member 20 as your background, and then edit member 35, you will see member 20 act as the background to member 35, member 21 act as the background to member 36, and so on. Onion skinning is a powerful tool and one you will need to experiment with for a while before you become proficient with it.

PHOTOSHOP FILTERS

Although not all the features of programs such as PhotoShop are available in the Paint window, one powerful feature, *filters*, can be borrowed. If you are a PhotoShop user, you probably already know about filters and what they can do. From a simple blur to a complex rendering, filters can alter an entire graphic or part of one. They are really just special effects for still images.

In PhotoShop, you place filters in a plug-ins folder and access them through the Filter menu. You can apply the transformation, such as a blur effect, to the entire image, or to just an area.

Director can borrow these PhotoShop filters and use them on cast members or in the Paint window. First, you need to tell Director where the filters are. This can be as easy as making an alias or shortcut to your PhotoShop filters folder and placing it in the Director Xtras folder. You can also copy filters or folders of filters into the Xtras folder.

The simplest way to use filters is to apply them to an entire single cast member. Select that cast member in the Cast and choose Xtras, Filter Bitmap. This brings up the Filter Bitmap dialog box, which organizes the filters into categories (see Figure 3.14).

In addition to the filters that come with PhotoShop, several third-party companies make filters that work with both PhotoShop and Director.

Figure 3.14
The Filter Bitmap dialog box contains different items depending on which filters you have available.

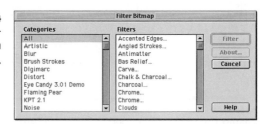

If no filters show up in your dialog box, it means that you have no filters in your Xtras folder, or the filters that you have are not compatible with Director. You also might be missing the PhotoShop Filters Xtra, which should have been installed when you initially installed Director.

To use a filter, select it and click the Filter button. If the filter has its own dialog box, as most do, you see that dialog box first and can then choose your options. The filter is then applied to the cast member.

If you are looking for some good special effects filters, check out Kai's Power Tools from MetaCreations, Inc. It is one of the most powerful and popular filter sets available.

A powerful feature of using filters with Director is that you can apply a filter to more than one cast member at a time. Simply select multiple cast members in the Cast window and filter. Each of the members gets the same filter, with the same settings, applied to it.

You can also use filters by selecting an area in the Paint window. In that case, the filter is applied to only that area in that one bitmap.

Director also has an auto filter function. Choose Xtras, Auto Filter to use it. Its purpose is to create a series of bitmaps based on a filter that changes slightly over time. However, very few filters are built to have a filter-over-time function. The dialog box that appears lists only the filters that do. Do not be disappointed if no filters are shown. Hopefully, more filters will be written in the future to take advantage of this feature.

If you don't get as nice an effect as you expected, check the bit-depth settings of the bitmap. Most filters only work well with 32-bit images. If you have an 8-bit image that you want to filter, convert it first to 32-bit, filter it, and then convert it back to 8-bit.

When working with filters, use a lot of caution. Filters are written by third-party companies that rarely test their filters on Director. Some filters do not work, others work in strange ways, and some will crash Director. Save your movie and Casts just before trying to apply a filter. If a filter does not work at first, add more memory to the Director application and try again.

TROUBLESHOOTING BITMAP IMAGES

- The Paint window has always had a few quirks. The Paint window was overhauled between Director 6 and 7, which removed many of the older quirks and created some new ones. At the time of this writing, it is hard to determine which quirks will stick around and which might get fixed in the final version of Director 8, or subsequent updates. Just don't worry so much if something doesn't seem to work quite as it should. There are many ways to perform the same task in the Paint window.

- If you are trying to use a PhotoShop filter and Director crashes, it's probably because the filter is not compatible with Director. Most filter developers test their products only on PhotoShop, and they may not be 100% compatible with Director. Make a note when a filter doesn't work so that you do not crash again.

- Director imports JPEGs and GIFs in their native format, which is not editable. When you try to edit one of these images, Director asks you first whether you want to convert it to a bitmap. This is normal. However, if you want to keep using the JPEG or GIF image, you must edit the image in an external application, such as PhotoShop or Fireworks, and re-import the changed file. You can set your editing application by choosing File, Preferences, Editors.

- Getting strange patches of white or black around the image when it is displayed on the Stage? This could be because the image has a bad Alpha channel, and you have Use Embedded Alpha turned on for the bitmap. If you don't care about the Alpha channel, just turn this option off.

- If you need to edit a 1-bit member in the Paint window, note that the Pencil tool does not always switch black to white and white to black as it should. However, converting the image to 8-bit and editing it there works fine; then, you can convert back to 1-bit when you are done.

DID YOU KNOW?

- You can cut, copy, and paste between the Paint window and other image programs.

- On the Mac, you can drag and drop a graphics file from the desktop to the Cast window.

- After you use one of the Distort tools in the Paint window, you can then choose Xtras, Auto Distort. This creates new cast members that are copies of the original image, but include the distortion you last used. So, if you rotate the image about 10°, and use Auto Distort to create six new members, the new members will be rotated 10, 20, 30, 40, 50, and 60°.

- You can convert a color image to black-and-white by using Transform Bitmap and then changing the color depth to 8-bit and the color palette to grayscale. You can then convert it to another palette if you need to.

- You can create a selected area in one bitmap member and then select that same area in another member. First, use the Lasso tool to select the area. Then, copy it. Go to the second bitmap image. Choose Edit, Paste, and then immediately choose Edit, Undo. The pasted image goes away, but the selection lasso remains.

- If you really don't like the Paint window, you can set Director so that it launches another application, such as PhotoShop or Fireworks, every time you edit a bitmap. Just choose File, Preferences, Editors. You can even opt to have an external application launch for certain types of bitmaps.

4

TEXT AND FIELD MEMBERS

Source movies for this chapter can be found on the CD-ROM in the "Book Movies" folder under folder 4.

Director 8 uses two types of text members. One is simply referred to as a text member and the other is called a field. Fields have been around in Director for a long time. Text members are relatively new, first appearing in Director 5, and undergoing significant improvements in Director 7.

Until Director 7, the difference between text and field members was clear: Text members are anti-aliased, use fonts without requiring that those fonts be present on the user's system, and are not editable; whereas fields use the user's system's fonts, are not anti-aliased, and are editable.

Since Director 7, text members have the capability to be edited. This blurs the line between text and field members. Differences, however, still exist, and there's definitely good reason to use field members whenever possible.

USING TEXT MEMBERS

Text members are complex, involving many options and features. However, you can create a simple text member without much trouble. Just select the Text tool, which looks like a letter A, in the Tool palette, and click the Stage. This creates a text cast member and at the same time places that member on the Stage and in the Score. You are then in edit mode, and can type text into this member on the Stage. Figure 4.1 shows this type of procedure in action.

Figure 4.1
You can simply click the Stage with the Text tool and start typing text. This text actually goes into the new text member.

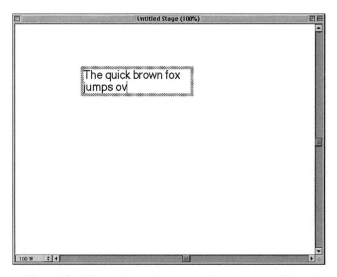

After you finish typing your text, you can click elsewhere on the Stage to deselect the text member. There are actually two ways to select a text member. The first, achieved by simply clicking it, enables you to drag the sprite around the Stage. You can also stretch and shrink the sprite's Stage area. If you double-click the sprite, you can once again edit the text inside it. In this mode, you cannot move or resize the sprite.

Text Editing

Although editing on the Stage is quick and easy, it doesn't give you as much control over the text as editing the member in a text window. You can open the member in a text window by double-clicking it in the Cast. You can also ⌘+click (on the Mac) or right-click (in Windows) the sprite to bring up a context menu. From here, you can select Edit Cast Member.

Figure 4.2 shows the text-editing window with the typical options. A simple toolbar at the top of the window gives you tools to change the font, size, style, alignment, line spacing, and kerning of any selection. A standard text ruler also enables you to add and adjust tabs.

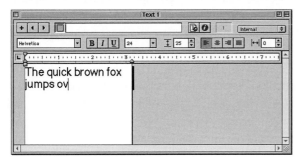

Figure 4.2
The text window has functions similar to that of a simple word processor.

The tools in this toolbar are self-explanatory. Line spacing enables you to set how many pixels apart each line begins. *Kerning* is an adjustment that you can make to the spacing of each character. Although each character has a different width—an *m* being wider than a *l* for instance—you can add or subtract from the width of each character space. This does not change the actual shape of the character, only the amount of space between that character and the next.

Using the tabs in the ruler is fairly simple, as well. Click the Tab button, which appears to the left of the ruler, to change the type of tab you want. You can have tabs that left-justify, right-justify, and center text. You can also have a decimal tab that lines up columns of numbers on their decimal points. To add a tab, click in the ruler. To remove a tab, click and drag that tab away from the ruler.

You can specify left, right, and first-line indents for paragraphs in the ruler as well. The thick markers along the top and bottom of the ruler can be dragged left and right. You can also grab the black bar to the right of the text area to stretch or shrink the page width. This bar brings the right margin along with it. Figure 4.3 shows a text member with some complex formatting.

Justified text, the last option of the four justification buttons, aligns both the left and right sides of lines of text. This is commonly used in newspapers. Although this technique looks nice at first, it can be distracting to the reader if the text columns are too narrow. Make sure you use it only for wide columns of text where many words appear on each line.

When setting any text property, whether it's font, size, tabs, or indents, remember that the property affects only the selected text, or the text in the paragraph in which the cursor is located. To have the change affect the whole member, select all the text first.

Figure 4.3
This text member uses tabs and
various fonts and sizes to create a
complex table.

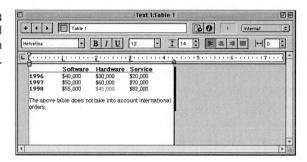

Text Importing

Although the text window is great for editing text, larger pieces of text are likely to come from an outside source, such as a word processor. You can easily import text of various formats into Director. Director can even remember most of the various styles and settings of that text.

Three primary file formats can be read by Director: text, rich text (RTF), and hypertext markup language (HTML). The first type of file does not have any formatting; it's just a simple stream of characters. You can still style these characters after they are in a text member, but they have no styling when they first arrive.

The other two formats can contain a variety of styles and formats. Rich text contains a similar set of styles and formatting options to the text-editing window. There are more advanced forms of RTF files, but the basic idea behind rich text is to accommodate different fonts, sizes, styles, and paragraph formatting. As long as your RTF files stick to these basics, you should be able to import them completely.

Some RTF files, such as those created from complex Microsoft Word documents, can include tables, images, and drawings. Director skips these elements when it imports the RTF file because the text member type does not support these options. All in all, rich text is your best bet for importing general text that uses only some formatting.

Since version 7, Director allows you to import HTML files, as well. You can create these files with some modern word processors, but they are commonly created with HTML editing programs. Netscape Communicator also enables you to create and edit HTML.

Director cannot import all the elements and formats used in modern HTML, but it does a fairly good job with those it can. Standard styles, font size changes, paragraphs, line breaks, and the most basic tags are all supported. Director even goes as far as importing tables. This is probably the most powerful aspect of the HTML import.

After the HTML text has been imported, you can edit it in the text editor window. However, because HTML is more complex than the features of the window, you might be better off editing the original HTML document in an HTML editor. Of course, if your text is only a few lines or plain paragraphs, it doesn't matter.

Text Member Options

You can set a variety of options to change the appearance of your text member. To change text member properties, use the Property Inspector. One way to get to these settings is to click the Information button in the text-editing window, or use the context menu on the Stage. The Property Inspector appears as shown in Figure 4.4.

Figure 4.4
You can use the Property Inspector to make decisions about how the member will look on the Stage.

The Display option gives you two choices. The first is "Normal" where the text member will display exactly as it did in Director 8.0. The second option, which is new to Director 8.5, allows you to select "3D Mode." We'll look at what 3D text is like towards the end of this chapter.

With the Framing option, you can decide to have the sprite's size adjust to automatically fit the amount of text in it. This adjustment is made with only the height of the box, because the width of the box is determined by the width of the member. Another choice is to have the size of the sprite fixed. Fixing the sprite size enables you to manually stretch or shrink the sprite, and the text in it is cropped if it can't fit. This option is useful if you plan on doing exact screen layouts and you want to make sure that the text will never overlap another element. Of course, the drawback is that this sprite might not display some text if there is too much to fit.

The third framing choice is to use a scrolling frame, which enables you to set the exact size of the text sprite. If the text doesn't fit, the scrolling bar on the sprite becomes active and the users can scroll through the text.

The Editable option enables you to make the text editable. You can make the member editable with this option, or you can make it editable as a sprite. Making it editable as a member means that every time the member appears on the Stage, it is editable. However, if you make it editable in the Score, it is editable only for that single sprite instance, and not every time the member appears as a sprite on the Stage.

The Word Wrap option is new to Director 8. Previously, all text members wrapped words automatically. However, this feature is useful when you have long lines of text that you want to keep to a single line, rather than wrapping them to a second or more. If a line of text is longer than the width of the text member, the rest of the line is simply not seen.

If you make a text member editable, you can also use the Tab to Next Editable Item option to instruct Director to accommodate a common text editing technique. This property enables the users to use the Tab key to move from editable text member to editable text member on the Stage. Mac and Windows applications, including Web browsers, work this way. Turn this option on if you plan on having more than one text member on the Stage at a time.

The Direct to Stage option speeds up the presentation of the text by ignoring other sprites drawn under it. If you are using background transparent ink, turning this option on blocks out underlying sprites. If you are using the Copy ink, however, you are already blocking the appearance of sprites underneath, so you should turn this option on.

The Use Hypertext Styles option works only when you have imported HTML to create your member. Any links in the hypertext then appear as blue and underlined, just as they typically do in a Web browser. When the users click them, they turn a purple color to signify that they have already been used. You can find out how to use hypertext in Chapter 16, "Controlling Text."

➡️ *For more information on hypertext, **see** "HTML and Hypertext," **p. 352** (Chapter 16, "Controlling Text")*

The next set of options enables you to determine when Director should anti-alias the text in the field. For those unfamiliar with anti-aliased text, look at Figure 4.5 to see the difference it can make.

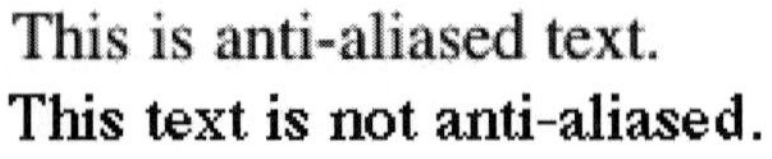

Figure 4.5

The anti-aliased text shown on the top appears smoother than the jagged characters below. The image is magnified 400% to show detail.

This is anti-aliased text.
This text is not anti-aliased.

You might be tempted to use anti-aliasing all the time. However, it has a few disadvantages. First, anti-aliased text renders more slowly than plain text. If you are making a speed-sensitive movie, you must consider this effect. Also, some fonts and sizes just don't look very good anti-aliased. However, titles that use large font sizes are good places to use anti-aliased text. At the same time, very small text, such as 9-point Arial, is more readable anti-aliased.

You can use the options in the Text Properties dialog box to specify whether you want all text anti-aliased, no text anti-aliased, or only text that is above a certain point size anti-aliased. This setting affects only the selected cast member.

A good rule is to use anti-aliased text for small text portions and use plain text for longer text that the users will have to read, as opposed to glance at. But this rule can be applied on a case-by-case basis. Experimentation usually reveals the best method.

You can assign the same set of conditions to text kerning. Kerning is spacing between individual characters. This could come in handy if you have set kerning universally throughout the text member, but really want only larger font sizes affected.

A common pitfall happens when a text member is set to use prerendering, but with an ink different than that used by the sprite on the Stage. Make sure you check the inks used by these text member sprites.

The Pre-Render options were added to Director in version 7.0.2. These options enable you to have Director create the image for the text member before it is displayed on the screen, thus speeding up the display. However, it also means that the text won't be editable or changeable by Lingo during playback.

In Figure 4.4, shown previously, you see the Pre-Render option set to None. You must choose Copy Ink or Other Ink to use pre-rendering. Copy Ink works only when you display the text member in a sprite using copy ink. Other Ink works with other inks, but doesn't work with copy ink.

In addition, if you select Save Bitmap, Director stores a copy of the bitmap it makes while you are in the authoring environment in the member. Then, when the member is displayed in Shockwave or a Projector, you see this stored bitmap, rather than a rerendered text member. The users do not need to have the font on their machines, nor do you have to rely on that machine to render the font. This is particularly useful for solving cross-platform font issues, in which fonts can be rendered slightly differently between Mac and Windows.

The Text Inspector

Although the text window's toolbar contains just about everything you need to style and format text, it's not always convenient to have this window open. Instead, you can edit text directly on the Stage, as shown previously, and use the Text Inspector to make some style and format changes. Figure 4.6 shows the Text Inspector. You can access it by choosing Windows, Inspectors, Text.

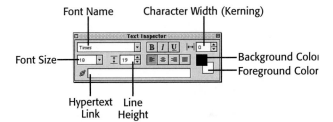

Font Name   Character Width (Kerning)

Font Size —

Background Color
Foreground Color

Hypertext Line
Link Height

Figure 4.6
The Text Inspector can be used to style and format text in text members, fields, scripts, and even in the Paint window.

In addition to the style and format tools, the Text Inspector has two color chips. You can use the foreground color chip to change the color of any selected text. The background color chip works on the entire text member that is being edited. A text member can have only one background color. This color is ignored if you are displaying the sprite in a background transparent ink.

You can also use the Text Inspector to add hyperlinks. For now, this just colors and underlines the text for you. When you read about the Lingo involved in hyperlinks, you will see how this can be used for navigation and control.

The Font Dialog Box

Although you can change fonts with either the toolbar in the text-editing window or the Text Inspector, you can also bring up a Font dialog box that contains detailed information about your selected text. Figure 4.7 shows this dialog box.

Figure 4.7
Choose Modify, Font to access the Font dialog box. You can also use ⌘+Shift+T on the Mac or Ctrl+Shift+T in Windows.

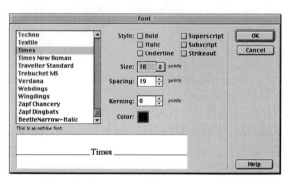

You have three more style choices in the Font dialog box: Superscript, Subscript, and Strikeout. Superscript and Subscript adjust the vertical position of the selected text. Strikeout places a line through the center of the text.

You also have a much nicer font selection method in the Font dialog box. The scrolling list is easier to look through than the pop-up menu. In addition, the Font dialog box can tell you which fonts are capable of displaying as anti-aliased text. Bitmapped fonts cannot be anti-aliased, whereas TrueType fonts can.

Only fonts that can be anti-aliased appear in the list when you choose Insert, Font. If you select some text in a text member and choose Modify, Font, you get the font dialog box seen in Figure 4.7. As you select fonts, you see either "This is an outline font" or "This font cannot be anti-aliased" under the font list.

The Paragraph Dialog Box

The Paragraph dialog box, shown in Figure 4.8, enables you to set the left, right, and first-line indents. Unlike the actual text-editing window, the Paragraph dialog box enables you to set these indents to precise numbers. You will find that this comes in handy when you are trying to match settings between two or more text members. Clicking and dragging the indent tabs does not give you precise enough control.

Inches? Yep, the margin settings in the Paragraph dialog box are in inches. If you would rather use pixels, then you can change this preference in File, Preferences, General and choosing the "Text Units" setting.

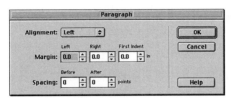

Figure 4.8
Choose Modify, Paragraph to access the Paragraph dialog box when you have text selected. You can also use ⌘+Shift+Option+T on the Mac or Ctrl+Shift+Alt+T in Windows.

You can also use the Paragraph dialog box to set extra space between paragraphs. Specified in points, you can set the spacing before and spacing after so that paragraphs are spaced farther apart than normal lines of text. This is a technique sometimes used to increase the readability of large text blocks.

➪ For more information on formatting text, **see** "Using Text Members and Fields," **p. 330** in Chapter 16

USING FIELD MEMBERS

Once the only text option in Director, field members are still useful for a variety of tasks. For one, they take up much less file space than text members. A text member with the phrase "This is a test" placed in it is about 1,600 bytes, whereas a field containing the same text is only about 700 bytes. The difference is even more dramatic when you use anti-aliased text in the text member.

A Field Member editing window, shown in Figure 4.9, looks different from a text member editing window. For one thing, the ruler is gone. Field members do not have the capability to recognize indents or tabs. However, you can still adjust the width of the field.

Figure 4.9
The Field Member editing window is similar to the Text Member editing window, except fewer options are available.

You also cannot fully justify text; only left, center, and right justification is possible. The Justify button is inactive.

Fields cannot be imported. Instead you have to copy and paste text into the field-editing window if you want to use text generated by an outside program. You can't anti-alias text within fields either.

Developers can use fontmap.txt to have more control over how fonts are mapped on other machines, across platforms. See the "Developing for Both Mac and Windows," section in Chapter 35, "Cross-Platform Issues," for more information.

Figure 4.10 shows the Property Inspector with the field member properties. You do not have as many options available as you do with text members.

Figure 4.10
The Field Cast Member Properties dialog box offers different options than the Text Cast Member Properties dialog box.

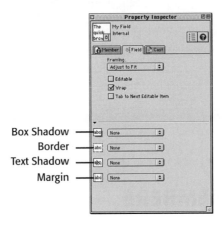

You can take advantage of four settings to add border-like elements to fields. You can find these in the lower portion of the Property Inspector, shown previously in Figure 4.10. The available border settings are Box Shadow, Border, Text Shadow, and Margin. Each one offers six options: None and the 1 through 5 pixels.

The Box Shadow option places a black shadow to the bottom and right of the field. This classic computer display effect can help make fields stand out, but can also be easily overused.

The Border setting enables you to add a plain black border around the field. You can add a border that is any size from 1 to 5 pixels wide.

> If you are using a border, you should always use a margin. One of the most common mistakes that Director developers make is to not include a margin on their fields. This makes the text bump right up against the border, which makes it look unprofessional. A two- or three-point margin should be used.

The Text Shadow option comes in handy when you are trying to display text over a background that makes the text hard to read. Figure 4.11 shows how this might work. The field is displayed with the background transparent ink so that the image shows through. The 1-point text shadow places a black shadow behind the text and helps it to stand out.

You can use the Margin option to add a margin inside the field. This places extra pixels between the border and the area that contains the text.

Figure 4.11
Using a text shadow can help fields stand out when they are placed on top of a background image.

Text without a text shadow
Text with a text shadow

➡ *For more information on field members, **see** "Using Text Members and Fields," **p. 330** in Chapter 16*

KNOWING WHEN TO USE TEXT AND FIELDS

When deciding whether to use text or field members, you must take a variety of factors into account. Table 4.1 can help you decide. In most cases, you will find reasons to use both types. To choose which to use, you must decide which factor is a priority.

Table 4.1 Factors in Deciding Between Text and Field Members

Factor	Use
Must look smooth	Text
Must display quickly	Field
Must not add too much to the file size	Field
Must be capable of displaying indents	Text
Consistent line spacing	Text
Must be capable of displaying tables	Text
Must be capable of receiving imported RTF and HTML files	Text
Must be able to add borders and margins easily	Field
Must be able to add a text shadow easily	Field
Must be able to add hypertext links easily	Text
Must never change appearance from platform to platform	Text

A good rule of thumb is to use text members unless you need to use one of the features of a field. You will find that text members are more versatile and easier to use.

USING FONT MEMBERS

A powerful feature of Director is the capability to import fonts as cast members. This feature enables you to use fonts in your movies that the users do not have on their machines. Otherwise, you have to use noneditable text members to display special fonts, or stick to fonts that you know the users have on their machines.

To import a font, choose Insert, Media Element, Font. This creates a new font cast member. The Font Cast Member Properties dialog box, shown in Figure 4.12, is immediately displayed. In this dialog box, you can choose the font that this cast member will display. The only fonts listed are those compatible with your machine.

You can choose any font to be represented by that cast member. After import, the font thereafter appears in font pop-up menus as a font with the same name, but followed by an asterisk. The asterisk signifies that this is a font internal to this movie. However, Director does not convert the field and text members that use the original font to now use the new internal font. You have to change them yourself. When you create new field and text members, you can select the new internal font.

Figure 4.12
The Font Cast Member Properties dialog box enables you to set the options for a font member.

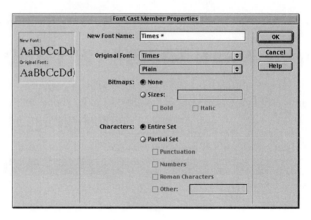

Director also enables you to decide how much of that font to import. If you want only the basic font, leave the bold and italic check boxes off. However, if you do want these versions of the font, check them. This increases the size of the font cast member. These members are compressed in Shockwave movies and compressed projectors, but it's a good idea to leave out whatever you don't use.

You can also specify the exact characters you want to import. This can further shrink the size of the font member. Another option enables you to include bitmap versions of fonts. Many fonts include bitmap versions to display perfect text at certain sizes. Include these by typing in font sizes separated by commas.

According to Macromedia, no legal issues are involved in distributing fonts inside a Director movie. There is no way for users to export and then redistribute them as fonts again. So, as long as you have the right to display the fonts on your authoring machine, you should be allowed to use them in your movies.

After you have a font member and are using it in text members and fields, do not try to delete or replace the font member. This will confuse your text and field members.

A good way to use imported fonts is to decide which fonts you want to use before authoring the movie. Import all your fonts first. You can also create external cast libraries that hold a variety of font members. You can then copy and paste these members into your current movie. This saves you from having to have these fonts on your system.

Another useful side-effect of using font members is that you can have custom-built fonts that display a variety of simple images. Using a program such as Macromedia Fontographer, you can create a vector graphic disguised as a font and import it into Director. You can then have text members that use these images. It's like having dozens of vector graphics embedded in a single member.

USING 3D TEXT

Thanks to the 3D engine inside Director and Shockwave, simple text members can now pop out of the 2D world and use a variety of 3D special effects. Making your text members 3D is easy—almost too easy. This is a lavish special effect that should be used rarely.

Figure 4.13 compares two text members that are exactly the same, except that the second member has been set to "3D Mode" using the text member's display property seen back in Figure 4.4.

Figure 4.13
The first text member is normal, but the second is the same member with its display type set to "3D Mode."

As you can see, this is an effect that is really meant for screen titles or special highlighting. If you made entire sentences or paragraphs of text that used the 3D mode, it would be very hard for users to read.

There are a variety of options that you can set for 3D text. They can all be found with the Property Inspector. Select the text member in the score, bring up the Property Inspector, and search the tabs at the top for the "3D Extruder" tab. When you select it, you will see a property inspector that looks like the one in Figure 4.14.

The first set of options defines the camera position and angle. When talking about any 3D object, like text in this case, the camera defines the point in space that the user is looking through to see the 3D object. In the case of 3D text, the camera is in front of the text looking straight at the text. This gives you the view seen in Figure 4.13.

There are six parameters that define the camera. The first three are the x, y and z positions of the camera. The x and y positions are simply the horizontal and vertical location. The z position is the third dimension, so to speak. It is the *depth*. So the position shown in Figure 4.14 is 90 units to the right of center, 55.5 units down from the center, and 177.04 units back from the center. This can also be represented as (90,55.5,177.04).

Displaying 3D text relies on the new Director 8.5 engine. This engine, in turn, relies of the user's computer's abilities to display 3D. If the user has a 3D video card, for instance, then the 3D text will appear faster and nicer than if the user's computer has to render the text in software mode. You can find out more about 3D display performance in Chapter 38, "Using 3D Media."

For a complete primer on how 3D computer graphics work, see the beginning of Chapter 38.

Why these numbers? Director created them when you decided to set the text to 3D mode. The text itself is placed in the 3D world at such a location so that the bottom left corner of the text is at the world center, (0,0,0). Moving the camera to the position (90,55.5,177.04) places the camera where it appears to be looking directly into the center of the text and the camera is far enough away so that the text appears to be the proper size on the screen.

Figure 4.14
The "3D Extruder" panel of the Property Inspector displays a variety of options that determine how your 3D text will look.

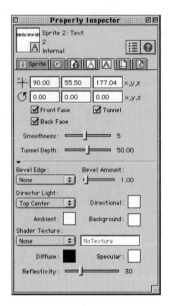

The six parameters at the top of Figure 4.14 give you complete control over the position of the camera. The most immediately useful are the two z values. The z position will allow you to easily move the camera toward or away from the text. The z rotation value will allow you to spin the text around the visual center of the text.

The next set of options are three check boxes called "Front Face," "Tunnel," and "Back Face." These are the three portions of the extruded text. You probably never want to turn off "Front Face" and leave the other two on, but combinations like "Front Face" and "Back Face" or just "Front Face" could create useful effects.

The "Smoothness" setting allows you to modify the 3D detail in the model. Larger numbers will mean that the text is constructed with more polygon faces. The downside is that the model is more complex and may be harder for slow, non-3D machines to render.

The "Tunnel Depth" setting is simply how long the distance is between the front and back face of the text. A smaller amount would mean that the letters simply appear as solid shapes, while a larger amount would suggest flying, zooming text like you sometimes see in movie titles.

A much easier way to control the appearance of the 3D text is to use Director 8.5's new Shockwave 3D window. You can open it by choosing Window, Shockwave 3D, or by the keyboard shortcut Command+Shift+W on Mac, Ctrl+Shift+W in Windows. You must also have the text member selected in the Cast window, as selecting the sprite might not be enough. Once the window is open, you can move and rotate the text. A button at the top called "Set Camera Transform" at the top of this window will make any changes to the camera permanent; otherwise, they will not affect the real cast member. This window and its functionality will be covered in more detail in Chapter 38.

The second half of the 3D Extruder properties as seen in Figure 4.14 contains some more advanced options. A Bevel Edge will make the edges of the letters, at the point where the front face and the tunnel meet, look rounded. The effect is very slight, so a figure here would do very little to demonstrate it. Play with the bevel settings, both "Round" and "Miter" (angled) and the amounts to see what sort of effect it has on text of your choice.

The "Director Light" on the other hand, has a very pronounced effect. You can change the main light that shines on the text to be in a variety of positions. You can also change the color of this light by selecting a color for the "Directional" light. Unless you want to tint the text a different color, you will want to stick with varieties of white, black, and grays.

> **Caution**
>
> This is one of many places where the documentation that comes with Director 8.5 is wrong. It states that "background light appears to come from behind the camera." This doesn't make any sense. The background setting for text clearly just defines the background color of the text. It is not a light, and it certainly does not come from behind the camera.

The "Ambient" light is a glow that comes from all directions and hits the text evenly throughout. You can easily set either the Directional or the Ambient light to black (turned off) and just use one of the two lights. Experimentation with these settings will usually pay off by giving you the perfect lighting effect.

The "Background" color doesn't affect the text at all, but simply changes the color of the pixels behind it. If you set the sprite to use Background Transparent ink, then this setting doesn't matter.

The last set of controls allows you to determine what texture is applied to the text. The default is to use "None," which produces an even, solid color. The "Diffuse" setting controls the overall reaction of the model to light, while the "Specular" color is used for highlights were the light is hitting the model almost directly. With "Shader Texture" set to "None," these two colors control the color of the model completely.

You can also set the "Shader Texture" to "Default," which will use a red and white checkerboard pattern, or the far more useful "Member" setting, which allows you to select a bitmap member as the texture. Figure 4.15 shows some 3D text that has been given a texture.

Figure 4.15
The text model has been given a texture applied from a bitmap cast member.

The last setting, "Reflectivity," determines how much light is reflected from the texture. The lower the number, the more washed-out the texture will appear as more of the directional light is reflected from the surface. It will look very shiny, to put it simply.

Later in the book, in Chapter 16, you will learn how to manipulate 3D text more precisely with Lingo. You will also learn how to manipulate and animate 3D cast members in Chapters 38 and 39, "3D Lingo." Most of these techniques can be applied to 3D text members as well.

TROUBLESHOOTING TEXT AND FIELD MEMBERS

- If you are trying to import an RTF file or an HTML file and you aren't getting the results you want, it's probably because the file uses an RTF or HTML feature that Director does not support. Try eliminating that part of the text or converting it to a simpler layout.

- Using fields means that the spacing between lines will differ on Mac and Windows. Sometimes, this happens with text members as well. You will learn how to set the line spacing of fields in Chapter 16, but it's a good idea to use text members rather than fields if line spacing is important.

- Bolded or italicized text will be displayed completely wrong if you do the following: use an embedded font, set the font member to use the "plain" version of that font, and then go ahead and make the font bold or italic in the displayed text. I've only seen this happen in Windows, so if you are developing on a Mac, make sure you avoid changing the font style if using embedded fonts; otherwise, your text will look very messed up when a Windows user sees it.

- There are a lot of cross-platform issues with fonts. The same font can differ on Mac and Windows, especially when it comes to special characters. See Chapter 35 for information about font mapping.

DID YOU KNOW?

- Some fonts, such as Courier and Courier New, are monospaced, which means that each character is the same width. You can use these fonts to create simple tables in which each column lines up exactly.

- In most fonts, all the number characters are monospaced.

- A common design mistake in Director is to use a field with a border, but not to set a margin. Any field that uses a border should have at least a 2-pixel margin.

- Because you can import fonts and specify which characters you need to keep, you can use the special Dingbats font and keep only one or two members. Then, use these members in text member sprites as graphics. They take up very little space, and are scalable by setting the font size.

5

SOUND MEMBERS

Source movies for this chapter can be found on the CD-ROM in the "Book Movies" folder under folder 5.

There are many reasons to include sounds in your movies. Sounds can be small button feedback noises, background music, audio narration, animation soundtracks, special effects, and more. Remember, this is called "multimedia" because it's more than just images.

SOUND FILE FORMATS

Like images, sound files come in a variety of formats. Director can import a large number of these formats. Inside each sound file, the sound is represented in a variety of sample rates and bit depths.

The Audio Interchange File Format (AIFF) is the most common format used on Macintosh computers. It is also used in the digital music recording industry. You will see these files on both Mac and Windows machines, usually represented as an .aif file.

The .wav or wave file is a Windows file format that is widely supported by most Windows and Mac programs. Both the AIFF and wave files can be imported into Director with no problems. You can also import System 7 sounds on the Mac and even MP3 (MPEG 3) formatted sounds.

If a sound file comes in another format, it is usually easy to find a program that will convert it to either an AIFF or wave file. You can even convert CD audio tracks to AIFF files by using a program such as Macromedia's SoundEdit 16 on the Mac.

After you have your sound files formatted properly, you can use them in three ways in Director. The first is to import them as cast members by choosing File, Import. You can place the members in the Score's Sound channels by dragging them to the Score, or you can use Lingo. Although sound members can be large, when you save the movie as a compressed Shockwave file or projector, Director can compress them for you.

Another way to use sound files in Director is as external files. You can import sound files using the Link to External File option, which is a check box in the Import dialog box. This action creates a cast member that contains no data, but represents the external file. You can place this member in the Score as well. Director accesses the external file as needed. You can also play external sound files with a Lingo command, even if the sound is not represented by a member.

You can also create Shockwave audio files. You create these files by exporting a file from your sound-editing program in Shockwave audio format. The resulting files are precompressed external files that can be called with Lingo. These files can also be *streamed*, meaning Director can play them over the Internet as the files are downloaded. Shockwave audio files can be created on the Mac inside SoundEdit 16. In Windows, you can use a Director Xtra, which converts wave files to Shockwave audio files.

FREQUENCY AND BIT DEPTH

Two measurements are used to set the quality of a sound file: sample frequency and bit depth. *Sample frequency* is the measurement of how often the samples of the sound are taken and stored as digital data. *Bit depth* is the range of information stored in each sample.

The rate at which audio is sampled is similar to the resolution of a scanned image, and defines how many samples are to be taken in a given time or space. The sample rate defines the detail of the sound wave. More samples can accommodate more detail, which means higher-pitched sounds can be recorded. Natural sounds contain a wide range of frequencies from low to high. The capability to record high-pitched sounds adds to the clarity of the overall sound. Examples of common sample rates include 44.1KHz, 22.05KHz, and 11.025KHz.

The depth at which the samples are measured is similar to the color depth of an image: 256 colors (8-bit), thousands of colors (16-bit), and millions of colors (32-bit). Digital audio can be commonly sampled at 16 bits per sample or 8 bits per sample. Lower bit depths are unacceptable and unpleasant to listen to due to the lack of clarity. Bit depth controls the signal-to-noise ratio, measured in decibels (dB), and refers to the number of times the quietest sound must be amplified to match the loudest sound.

The relationship between sample rate and sample depth can be varied to accommodate differing quality and playback requirements. An 11.025KHz audio file that uses eight bits, for example, sounds like a scratchy telephone line. The same rate used with 16 bits improves the dynamics of the sound but not the clarity. The 8-bit file, however, requires half the storage space that a 16-bit file does. The best results come from using the highest sample rate with the largest bit depth, which creates the largest file size. The tradeoff between quality and memory requirements is a familiar one, which applies to many aspects of multimedia and computer work in general.

Use the following guidelines when sampling or resampling audio for multimedia:

- **5.564KHz**—Poor quality, speech only. Intended for voice annotations rather than multimedia. Voice annotations are sound files attached to documents intended for comments, memos, and so on. The file sizes are very small (suitable for floppy disks and slow networks), but the quality is lower than a pocket dictation machine.

- **7.418KHz**—The lowest recommended quality for speech (Macintosh only). Very small file sizes, although Shockwave audio can provide similar sizes in powerful machines.

- **11.025KHz (CD)**—A good choice for playback on older Windows and Macintosh computers. Some distortion and background noise (equivalent to a telephone line). Use for low-quality music or medium-quality speech.

- **11.127KHz**—This was the original standard frequency for older Macintosh computers. New Macintosh computers have adopted the IBM 11.025KHz frequency. This frequency is not recommended when you are producing a cross-platform production. Some PC sound cards will not play this frequency.

- **22.050KHz**—The most popular choice for Macintosh and Windows. Good-quality music and narration, similar to a strong AM radio broadcast.

- **22.225KHz**—The old, high-quality Macintosh standard. Suffers compatibility problems on Windows machines.

- **44.100KHz**—Standard compact disc (CD) audio rate.

You should record sound at the highest level possible—44.1KHz and 16 bits—for example, and then *downsample* to the quality that you need in your Director movie. This results in a better-quality sound. In addition, it gives you the high-quality sound to fall back on if you want to re-import your sounds at a different quality later.

You have to do this downsampling in your sound-editing program, because Director has no way of doing it. By downsampling, you are just converting the sound to a lower quality, and thus a smaller file size.

⇨ *For more information on sounds, **see** "Sound Commands,"*
   p. 364-366 (Chapter 17, "Controlling Sound")

INTERNAL SOUND MEMBERS

You can import sounds into Director with the same import function used for bitmaps and text. Choose File, Import, and select the sound file or files you want to import.

A recommended quality setting for sounds imported into Director is 22.050KHz and 16 bits. This is half the size of a 44.1KHz sound, but the quality is nearly the same. Although this is much larger than an 11.025KHz, 8-bit sound, Shockwave audio compression can be used when you make your Shockwave movie or projector compress the sound further.

⇨ *For more information about importing, **see** "Importing Bitmaps," **p. 74** (Chapter 3, "Bitmap Members")*

After the sound is in the Cast, you can use the Property Inspector, shown in Figure 5.1, to see information about the sounds. You can bring up the Property Inspector by pressing the "*i*" button at the top of the Cast window while the sound member is selected.

Figure 5.1
Sound Cast Member Properties can be seen with the Property Inspector.

As you can see in Figure 5.1, sounds have only one available option. The Loop option enables you to tell Director whether the sound is a looping one.

If looping is turned on, Director plays this sound over and over as long as the sound is in one of the Sound channels in the Score. As soon as you jump to a frame that does not have this sound, it stops.

You can record sounds in Director only on the Mac. If you choose Insert, Sound, a Mac system sound recording dialog box appears that enables you to record a sound from the current sound source, usually the microphone. No editing options are available, so this technique can be used only to create temporary placeholder sounds.

EXTERNAL SOUNDS

Sounds tend to be large and add significantly to the file size of a Director movie. For this reason, you might want to consider keeping sounds as external files and creating a linked cast member that uses this external sound. You can create a linked sound member by choosing File, Import to get the Import dialog box, and then selecting Link to External File instead of Standard Import.

Another method for using an external sound involves no cast member at all, but simply playing a file directly with a Lingo command. You will learn about sound-related Lingo commands in Chapter 17, "Controlling Sound."

An even more compelling reason to use external sounds is that internal sounds need to be completely loaded into memory before being played. If a sound is 1MB, and the user's machine does not have the extra memory to store it, the sound simply does not play. However, an external sound does not have to be completely loaded to start playing. This might be your only option for playing larger sounds.

Starting speed is another issue. A large sound inside the Director movie might take some time to load and begin playing. However, an external file might also take some time to start because hard drives and CD-ROM drives have to search for the beginning of the sound file.

⇨ *For more information on controlling sounds, **see** "Sound Commands," p. 364-366 (Chapter 17)*

SHOCKWAVE AUDIO

For audio to stream over a network, the data rate has to be small and regular. This means that the size of the file devoted to the first second of sound and the second second of sound has to be exactly the same. This is known as the *bit rate* of the sound.

A typical streaming sound may be 16 kilobits per second (Kbps), or 16 times 1,024 bytes of information. A file with this bit rate can be streamed over a 28.8 modem that gets data at 28.8Kbps. However, a 32Kbps sound cannot stream smoothly.

Even a 24Kbps sound will probably not stream smoothly over a 28.8 modem because a 28.8 modem rarely gets a continuous stream of data at 28.8Kbps. The measurement is really telling you the maximum that the modem can receive.

Shockwave audio is typically produced by SoundEdit 16 or Bias Peak on the Mac and the Shockwave converter Xtra in Director on Windows. You can choose from a range of bit rates between 8Kbps and 128Kbps. The following list will help you decide which to use:

- **8Kbps**—Limited use for voice-only sounds when you need maximum compression.

- **16Kbps**—The only real choice for any type of audio that needs to stream over 28.8 modems. Sound quality supports voice, music, and sound effects.

- **32Kbps**—Should be used only when users are using 56Kbps modems or better. Good quality, although still mono.

- **48Kbps**—Enables you to use stereo sounds, but at a relative 24Kbps per channel rate. Users must have fast connections. This rate and higher can also be used for streaming sounds from the hard drive or CD-ROM.

- **64Kbps**—At this rate, you can do good-quality stereo sound.

- **96 and 128Kbps**—Accommodates excellent-quality audio. 128Kbps is a typical rate used for the popular MP3 format because it sounds pretty close to CD-quality audio.

If you want to get an idea of which bit rate settings match which sample frequency settings, 8Kbps uses 8KHz output sample rate, 14 and 24Kbps use 16KHz output sample rate, and 32Kbps and above try to use the same sample rate as the original sound file. However, if the sound file was at 44.1KHz and the Shockwave audio compression is set to be less than 48Kbps for mono and 96Kbps for stereo, it is forced to use 22.050KHz.

You can import a Shockwave audio sound completely into Director as a cast member. You can also import it as a normal linked sound. Shockwave audio files can be streamed, however, only by linking to them as Shockwave audio files.

To link to an external Shockwave audio file, choose Insert, Media Element, Shockwave Audio. This brings up the SWA Cast Member Properties dialog box shown in Figure 5.2.

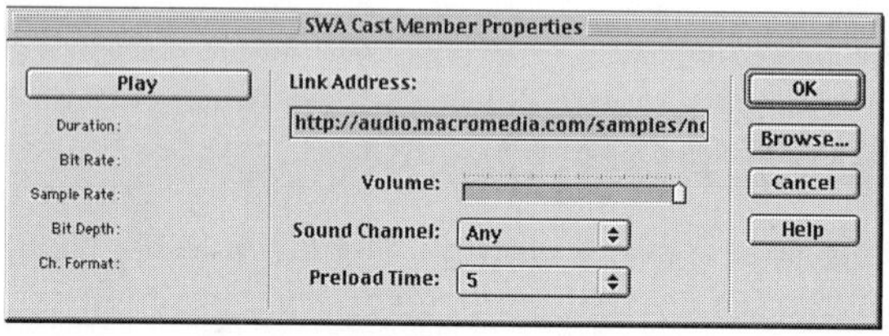

Figure 5.2
The SWA Cast Member Properties dialog box enables you to link to an external Shockwave audio file.

You can type a full or relative path for the SWA file. The path can be a file on your hard disk or CD-ROM, or a Web address. Use the browse button to quickly get the path of a local file.

You can also set the volume and Sound channel for the sound. Choosing Any for the Sound channel means the machine will attempt to play the sound in the first unused channel.

You can also set the preload time of the sound. The preload time determines how many seconds of sound have to load before the sound starts. Smaller numbers mean that the sound can begin sooner. However, a larger number reduces the chance that a streaming sound will be interrupted if the user has a bad connection. This occurs because Director buffers that many seconds of sound at the start. If Director buffers 5 seconds of sound, there needs to be only a 5-second interruption in the transmission for the Shockwave audio to need to pause and wait for more data. With a 10-second buffer, Director can take a 10-second interruption, or even two 5-second interruptions before it needs to pause the sound.

You can change all the Shockwave audio member settings later with the Property Inspector.

▷ *For more information on controlling Shockwave Audio,* ***see*** *"Using Shockwave Audio," **p. 370** (Chapter 17)*

USING SOUND IN DIRECTOR

Without using Lingo, there are four ways to make a sound play in Director: Use the Score, use a Play Sound Member behavior from the library, use a Play Sound File behavior from the library, or use another behavior that uses a sound effect. A button behavior, for instance, may ask for a sound that plays when the user clicks. In Chapter 11, "Advanced Techniques," you see how to construct behaviors that use sound in a variety of ways. In Chapter 17, you get the full rundown on what is possible with sounds and Lingo.

Using the Score to Play Sound

Using the Score is the simplest method to produce sound. Just drag and drop a sound cast member, either internal or linked, onto one of the two Sound channels in the Score. The sound starts playing when the playback head reaches the first frame with this sound. The sound continues to play while it exists on the current frame or until it is done playing. If the sound is set to loop, the sound continues to play until you get to a frame that is out of the sound's current sprite span.

You can play two sounds at once in the Score by using the two Sound channels. However, to play a streaming Shockwave audio file, you need to add the Shockwave audio member as a regular sprite, even though it has no visible element.

Using Library Behaviors to Produce Sound

A second way to play sounds is to use some Lingo commands. Fortunately, the Play Sound behavior in the library enables you to do this without writing code. You just attach the behavior to a sprite or frame and choose when you want it to play.

In the Play Sound behaviors, you get to choose the Sound channel where the sound should play. You can type any number you want, although you should stick to numbers 1 through 8 to ensure compatibility with all machines. Actually, it's a good idea to use channels higher than channel 2 to ensure that the Sound channel never interferes with channels 1 and 2, which can be used by the Score.

WAITING FOR SOUNDS AND CUE POINTS

You can also make your movie wait for a sound to complete. To do this, use the Tempo channel in the Score. First, place a sound in either Sound channel. Then, double-click the Tempo channel to bring up the Frame Properties: Tempo dialog box. Select the last option, Wait for Cue Point, and then use the two pop-up menus to set its parameters.

If you already have another behavior attached to a sprite, you will want to experiment when the sound plays. If a button behavior uses the "on mouseUp" message to do an action, it might interfere with the *on mouseUp* that the sound behavior expects to get to play the sound. Sometimes, swapping the order of the behaviors for that sprite in the Behavior Inspector fixes the problem.

First, select the Sound channel that this tempo command should be watching. Then, select the cue point that it should be looking for. Always present here are the {Next} and {End} options. Choose {End} to make the movie wait on that frame until the sound ends.

If you want, you can set cue points in a sound file with SoundEdit 16 or Bias Peak on the Mac. Similar functionality is possible with SoundForge 4.0 in Windows. Figure 5.3 shows a sound file opened in SoundEdit 16 with some cue points placed. Save the file as an AIFF file when you are finished.

Figure 5.3

SoundEdit 16 enables you to place cue points in sound files. These cue points can then be used in Director.

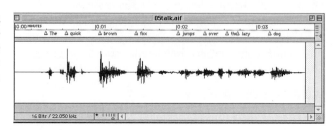

After you import a sound file that has some cue points, the second pop-up menu of the Wait for Sound option lists these cue points. You can then tell any frame to wait for a certain cue point before moving to the next frame. The {Next} option does not wait for any specific cue point, but the next one that the sound passes. With cue points, you can synchronize sound and animation.

TROUBLESHOOTING SOUNDS

- Although most PCs are still not capable of mixing more than one sound without a latency effect, Director 8 is capable of mixing sounds almost flawlessly. Director movies can use Microsoft DirectX technology or Apple QuickTime technology to mix sounds. This produces much better results. You need to use one Lingo line: either "the soundDevice = "DirectSound"" or "the soundDevice = "QT3Mix"". This should be done when the movie starts. See Chapter 17 for more information.

- If a sound created on the Mac does not work on Windows, make sure it is in a format that Windows can recognize, such as 16-bit and 22.050Khz, for instance. Using an odd setting can result in an unplayable sound in Windows.

- Does a sound seem to wait a while to start, even when no other sounds are playing? It could simply be that the sound has a second or so of silence at the start. Many sounds that come from CD-ROM sound collections have this. It is recommended that you check all your sounds in a sound-editing program before importing them.

- If a large internal sound does not work in a projector, it might simply mean that not enough memory is available to play it. Mac users can increase the amount of memory allocated to a Projector by choosing File, Get Info, and then changing the memory allocated to the application. Otherwise, you may want to consider downsampling large sounds to something that will take up less space, or use them as external sounds.

DID YOU KNOW?

* You can create Shockwave audio compressed files and then import them into Director as internal cast members. You can create sounds that are compressed all the way down to 8Kbps in this way. However, be sure you don't lose too much quality.

* You can't export sounds from Director normally, but you can copy a sound cast member and then paste it into another sound program. You can also choose an external editor by choosing File, Preferences, Editors and saving the sound that is referenced when you launch the editor.

* Just because a Shockwave audio file sits on an Internet server doesn't mean that the movie must sit there as well. A Director movie can be run as a Projector, or even in Director, and can still play Shockwave audio over the Internet as long as a connection exists.

6

DIGITAL VIDEO

Source movies for this chapter can be found on the CD-ROM in the "Book Movies" folder under folder 6.

Like animation, digital video presents successive frames of graphics to create a moving image. Video is typically real-life recordings, but can also be rendered animations. You can use various digital video formats with Director.

USING DIGITAL VIDEO FORMATS

Digital video has many aspects to consider, such as file type and compression. Because digital video files tend to be huge, uncompressed video is almost unheard of. Whatever type of file you choose to store and play back the video, you should also choose a video compression algorithm to use with this file type.

> QuickTime underwent a major transformation in 1998 with the release of QuickTime 3. I do not recommend working with media using versions of QuickTime before version 3. With the release of QuickTime 4 in 1999, more improvements were made, including the addition of streaming video.

File Types

Director authors primarily use two digital video formats. The most common is QuickTime: a cross-platform multimedia format created by Apple. The other is the Video for Windows (AVI) format, which is built into Windows 95, 98, 2000, and NT.

QuickTime is more than just digital video, however. It actually consists of tracks of media, including video, sound, MIDI, text, controls, transitions, and even 3D objects. QuickTime deserves a book all to itself. This chapter discusses just Director's capability to use QuickTime.

Digital video files that are just video and sound include a variety of format and compression settings. You can use at least a dozen different types of compression with QuickTime Pro. Each one compresses in a different way, some better or worse for different types of video.

Digital video doesn't have to be video camera-recorded material. You can also render images, such as computer animations, as digital video. Plus, video footage of a basketball game differs greatly from video footage of a college professor lecturing. Therefore, the types of compression that work well with each vary as well.

Like sounds, digital video can use different sample rates and bit depths. It gets even more complex as you are trying to compress both images and sound.

⇨ For more information on digital video, **see** "Exporting Animations," **p. 45** (Ch 1, "Animation with Director")

Compression

You can think of a digital video as composed of a series of images. Like a child's flip-book, the images are shown in rapid succession to give the illusion of animation.

If you have an image that is 320×240 pixels and in 32-bit, that image will be 300KB in size (320×240×32 bits/8 bits per pixel/1,024 bytes per kilobyte = 300KB). Imagine if you have some digital video that runs at 24 frames per second. Five seconds of it will contain 120 images. That's 36,000KB, or about 35MB. All for five seconds of quarter-screen video!

The secret to digital video is that it compresses each image to bring this file size down. It also compares consecutive images to determine whether it really needs to store all the data for each image. If one image is 90% the same as the preceding image, only the 10% that is different should be needed.

This type of compression is called *temporal compression*, or *delta change compression*. This technique records the changes between images, rather than the images themselves. It works well for some situations, such as when you have a talking head with a static background, but doesn't work well at all in cases such as a panning image in which the whole scene is changing constantly.

Spatial compression is a technique that looks at the images themselves. It tries to recognize "runs" of colors. For instance, it scans an image from left to right and recognizes lines of pixels that are the same color as a single piece of data. So, an image that has a solid white background compresses well using this algorithm. This is how JPEG compression works.

To really get digital video down to sizes that make sense, *lossy* compression needs to be applied. Lossy compression includes algorithms that attempt to summarize the images rather than represent them exactly as they are. Some of these compression techniques average the colors of adjacent pixels. Others apply mathematical formulae to a series of pixels to estimate the appearance. It is called lossy compression because the original image can never be restored from the compressed video. After it has lost some of its quality to become smaller, the file can never show details that were once there. For that reason, you should save your original files before compressing them when you use this technique.

With lossy compression, you can usually specify how much compression you want. A video compressed to 2:1 might not lose enough detail to be noticeable. However, a video compressed 100:1 might barely be recognizable.

Almost all compression algorithms that you will use are lossy compression algorithms. As you might expect, there are also *lossless* video compression techniques used for archiving and storage. Here, there is no loss of quality at all, and the original video file can be re-created from the compressed one. However, the compression is not as dramatic as with lossy compression. Sometimes the compression is only 2:1 and it is rarely as high as 10:1.

Data Rate

Another important factor in digital files is the data rate. The *data rate* is the amount of data that exists for each second of video. Because digital video needs to play in real-time, and the files tend to be huge, the data streams off the hard drive, CD-ROM, or the Internet. Because each of these storage methods can transfer data at only a certain rate, the digital video data rate must be less than the originating media. A single-speed CD-ROM drive can stream video at only 150Kbps. And because CD-ROM drives are not perfect, it is reasonable to expect only 90Kbps.

If you are streaming video from the Internet, your options are limited. Even with a poor-quality 90Kbps data rate, you are exceeding what a standard 28.8 modem can be expected to handle. However, if your access is across a reliable T1 line or local network, streaming video becomes possible.

> Few people have single-speed CD-ROM drives, but many still have double-speed CD-ROMs. They can read data at a theoretical 300Kbps, but you should assume that 180Kbps is the actual speed in practice.

IMPORTING DIGITAL VIDEO

Both QuickTime and Video for Windows can be imported into Director as cast members. In Windows, you can have either a QuickTime member or a digital video cast member. On Macintosh computers, QuickTime is the only option. In both cases, the cast members are linked to the external video file. Unfortunately, there is no way to import a video file completely in Director; you always have to rely on the external file.

To import a digital video file, just choose File, Import and select a digital video file in the same way you select an image file or a sound. You can import QuickTime files on the Mac, and both QuickTime and AVI files in Windows.

➪ *For more information about importing,* **see** *"Importing Bitmaps,"* **p. 74** *(Chapter 3, "Bitmap Members")*

UNDERSTANDING DIGITAL VIDEO SETTINGS

After a QuickTime or AVI member is in the Cast, you can set a variety of important settings in the Property Inspector. You can bring the Property Inspector up with the digital video member's properties by pressing the "*i*" button at the top of the Cast window while the member is selected. The Property Inspector is shown in Figure 6.1.

Figure 6.1
The Property Inspector dialog box enables you to set a number of QuickTime video options.

The first option is the playback mode of the video. If set to Sync to Sound, the video plays normally. However, setting it to Play Every Frame (No Sound) tells Director to ignore the video timing in the digital video movie, and instead display each frame at a constant frame rate. When you do this, the sound for the video is disabled. This is useful for digital video files that contain simple, silent animation. You can present this video at a speed different than intended in the original file.

You can use the Framing options to determine what happens when you stretch the sprite on the Stage. Because the size of the sprite will no longer equal the original size of the digital video, Director needs to know what to do in this case. The first option is to crop the video. Of course, if you are stretching the sprite, a crop will not occur, but neither will the video stretch to fill the space. If you choose Crop, the Center option tells Director whether it should automatically center the video in the sprite rectangle.

If you select the Scale option, Director forces the video to fill the sprite rectangle, even if it's larger or smaller than the original digital video. You can distort the video this way. Note that a digital video member that's playing back in a stretched sprite requires more processor power than one playing back at the original size.

You can even move and change the size of the digital video sprite over time with the same tweening effects mentioned in Chapter 1, "Animation with Director." The digital video adjusts while it is playing!

The lower portion of the Property Inspector shows a number of options that you can turn on or off. The first two items enable you to specify whether you want to hide or show the video or sound portions of the video. In case you are using video that does not have one of these two elements, you can turn it off. For instance, if you have a QuickTime movie that contains only a MIDI track, you can turn off the video portion. Or, if you have a video that has both video and sound, you might want to turn off the sound in a situation where it isn't needed.

With the Paused option, you can specify whether you want the movie to begin playing automatically, as soon as it appears on the Stage. If you want it to show up paused on the first frame, be sure to include the controller so that the user can start the video. Alternatively, you can use some Lingo to kick off the video.

With the Loop option, you can tell the movie whether it should automatically loop. If set, this causes the movie to start at the beginning again as soon as it is finished.

The Direct to Stage option enables the video to be placed over all other sprites in the frame. This means that Director is telling the QuickTime or Video for Windows portion of the operating system to ignore other sprites. The result is a faster, smoother playback. If you are not trying to blend the video in with any other sprites or perform any special effects with the sprites, use this option.

The Show Controller setting tells Director to place the standard video controller bar under the digital video. This controller is not a part of Director, but a part of QuickTime and Video for Windows.

The Streaming option is new to both Director 8 and QuickTime 4. It tells the member to take advantage of the streaming capabilities in QuickTime and stream the movie from the hard drive or the Internet.

The last option is the Preload option, which tells Director to load as much of the video into memory as it can before it starts playing. Although this might cause a pause at the start of the video, it allows for smoother playback because Director continues to load and store sections of the video in memory while the video plays. Otherwise, the entire video will be played from disk.

WORKING WITH DIGITAL VIDEO

To use a digital video member, just drag it to the Score or Stage. A sprite contains the video member and automatically sizes itself to the proportions of the video. If you selected the video controller option, it displays below the sprite.

If you are using the video in a presentation, you are likely to want it to appear on a frame that has a "Hold On Current Frame" behavior placed on it. This keeps the playback head steady and enables the video to be played back.

You can use the same "Wait for Cue Point" tempo setting with QuickTime movies that you can with sounds. Many editing tools enable you to place cue points in video and export the video as QuickTime. You can use the {End} setting to have the movie pause on a frame and wait for the video to end. You use this feature, of course, when you are not using the video controller and when you have the movie set so that it is not paused when it appears.

QuickTime videos are cross-platform, so the same files work on both Macintosh computers and Windows, provided that the computer has QuickTime installed. If you create a QuickTime movie on the Mac, be sure to save it following your video software's instructions on how to make a cross-platform video file. Otherwise, your Mac file might not work on Windows machines.

⮕ *For more information about controlling video,* ***see*** *"Using Video Commands," **p. 394** (Chapter 19)*

MAKING CUSTOM VIDEO CONTROLS

If you prefer not to use the video controller that QuickTime or Video for Windows uses, you can make your own. Simply select the option to not have this controller appear in the Digital Video Member Settings dialog box. Then, you need to create your own buttons. Figure 6.2 shows a video sprite and some sample buttons.

You can create the bitmaps to have any appearance that you want. To make them control something about the video, look in the Library palette for some digital video control behaviors. QuickTime control buttons will take care of most of your needs. Attach these to the sprites and choose the function you want them to perform. You will also have to specify which sprite the video is in.

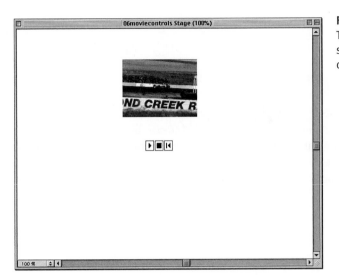

Figure 6.2
The Stage has a video sprite and several bitmaps that act as video controls.

TROUBLESHOOTING DIGITAL VIDEO

* Just because Director supports QuickTime doesn't mean that QuickTime movies will play on any machine. It is a common mistake for developers to assume that the users have QuickTime installed. You can point the users to the Apple Web site (http://www.apple.com/quicktime/) to download and install QuickTime 4 free.

* Digital video is a processor-intensive medium. Newer computers handle it with ease, but older machines may just not have the power to display video of any decent quality.

* If you are having a problem playing digital video in Director, the first place to look is always the member's properties in the Property Inspector. Is the member set to Paused? Are both the sound and video tracks enabled? You might try the Direct to Stage option if all else fails.

* In the past, QuickTime movies with sound have not relinquished the Sound channels to Director immediately after playing on Windows. If sound doesn't seem to work immediately after a QuickTime movie plays, try having the movie jump to a frame without either QuickTime or a Director sound. Then, have it proceed to the frame with sound. If that fails, try using the Lingo sound stop command from Chapter 17, "Controlling Sound."

DID YOU KNOW?

- Using QuickTime movies that contain only a MIDI track is an easy way to use MIDI inside Director. You can convert any standard MIDI file to a QuickTime movie with the QuickTime MoviePlayer application. Simply open a MIDI file with the QuickTime MoviePlayer, and it prompts you to convert the MIDI file to QuickTime format.

- You can use cue points in QuickTime movies in Director in the same way that you can use sound cue points. If a QuickTime movie is present in a frame, you can double-click the Tempo channel and select Wait for Cue Point. In addition to any Sound channels, you can see any QuickTime sprites listed. You can choose a cue point as well as {Next} or {End}.

7

VECTOR MEMBERS

IN THIS CHAPTER

Source movies for this chapter can be found on the CD-ROM in the "Book Movies" folder under folder 7.

You can divide still-image computer formats into two groups: bitmaps and vectors. A *bitmap* is a collection of colored pixels that stores an image. A *vector* is a description of lines, curves, fills, colors, and other information that can be used to construct an image.

Bitmaps can be used for all sorts of images, but have one main drawback: They are already set to a certain size. You can shrink bitmaps without much trouble, but enlarging them results in a loss of quality. With vector graphics, on the other hand, you can stretch the image to any size without changing the level of detail. Vector graphics are not useful for complex images, such as photographs, however. The descriptions of such images would make the file huge and a burden for the computer to interpret.

Although bitmap images are stored pixel for pixel, with color data recorded for each pixel, vector graphics are stored as a description. This description typically states positions, colors, and curves of lines, rather than information on specific pixels.

For those of you familiar with graphics programs, bitmaps are typically created with such applications as PhotoShop, Fireworks, Painter, and other image-editing software. Vector graphics are typically created with applications such as Macromedia Freehand and Adobe Illustrator.

In Director, you can use three types of vector graphics. The first is a group of simple shapes, such as circles and lines, which are built into Director as special cast members. Second, you can create simple vector graphics as vector shape cast members. Third, you can import and use images and animations created with Macromedia's Flash tool.

USING SHAPE MEMBERS

There are eight kinds of shape members: two kinds of lines, and filled and unfilled ovals, rectangles, and rounded rectangles. You can create all these shape members with the Tool palette shown in Figure 7.1. If this Tool palette is not already present, choose Window, Tool Palette, and then select the tool and draw on the Stage. This creates a cast member with the shape as well as a sprite that contains the member. After you have a cast member for a shape, you can drag that member from the Cast window to the Stage or Score to reuse it in another sprite. You can even stretch or shrink it differently in different sprites.

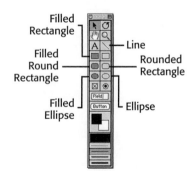

Figure 7.1
The Tool palette enables you to create all eight types of shape members using just seven different buttons.

The ovals, rectangles, and rounded rectangles are fairly straightforward. You can set their colors by selecting the forecolor chip in the Tool palette. This changes the color of the entire shape in the case of filled shapes. However, it changes the color of only the outline in the case of non-filled shapes. The background color chip has no effect.

Director sometimes refers to round shape members as "ellipses" and sometimes as "ovals." They are, in fact, the same thing.

If you want to create an area that is both filled with a color and uses an outline of a different color, you need to create both shapes, filled and nonfilled, and change their colors separately. The shapes cannot share the same cast member, either, because one cast member must be filled and the other not.

Most properties of shapes are properties of the shape member, not the sprite. The shape type and filled property, for instance, can be changed in the Property Inspector, but these changes affect all the sprites that use the same shape member. The location, rectangle, and color of the shape are sprite properties and can be set to different values for different sprites that use the same shape member. In addition, normal sprite properties, such as ink and blend, can also be set on a sprite-by-sprite basis.

You can, therefore, have four different sprites—a small blue oval outline, a small black oval outline, a large green oval outline, and a large green oval outline with a thick border—that all use one single cast member. However, if you want an oval outline and a filled oval, you need two separate cast members.

The type of shape and filled property can be changed in the Property Inspector. Figure 7.2 shows the Property Inspector with the shape properties visible. To get to this, select the member in the Cast and click the Info button in the Cast window. Within this dialog box you can actually change the type of member to another shape type. Although it doesn't make sense to change a line into an oval, having the capability to change a rectangle into a rounded rectangle might be useful at some point.

Figure 7.2
The Property Inspector enables you to change the shape type and whether it is filled or outlined.

Line shapes don't have a filled and nonfilled version, of course. The filled property of a line member must always be turned on for the line to be visible. However, there are still two types of line members: lines that draw from the upper-left to the lower-right, and lines that draw from the upper-right to the lower-left.

If you think about it, you can see why these two types are needed. A sprite is placed on the screen at a certain position and with a certain rectangular area. This is all that is needed for a rectangle shape to be drawn, but a line shape does not automatically sense which diagonal direction to use to fill the sprite's shape. When you first draw a line, it uses your drawing motion to determine which type of line to create.

The danger is not immediately apparent. If you draw a line on the Stage from upper-left to bottom-right, and then use that same cast member in another sprite for a second line, you will have one cast member and two sprites. If you then alter one of the sprites to draw from the upper-right to the lower-left, the change is made to the cast member itself. This means that your first sprite will also flip! The solution is to use two different cast members, one for each type of line. Or, you can simply use a new line member each time if you don't mind the extra members.

Most uses for lines are not sensitive to this problem, however. If you draw a straight horizontal or vertical line, as you might use in a presentation screen layout to separate elements, it doesn't matter which line type is used.

Lines can be set to be different widths as well. You won't find this setting in the Property Inspector until you switch it to List view. You can do this by clicking the List icon at the upper-right corner of the Property Inspector. Figure 7.3 shows this view. Using the list view, you can now set the line width and the line direction.

List View button

Figure 7.3
In List view, the Property Inspector enables you to also change the line width and direction.

USING VECTOR MEMBERS

Vector members are a powerful feature introduced in Director 7. You can create common lines and shapes that can be scaled, anti-aliased, and modified on-the-fly. These shapes also take up a relatively small amount of file space, making them ideal for Internet delivery.

Vector Shape Editing Window

To create a vector member, choose Insert, Media Element, Vector Shape to bring up the Vector Shape editing window shown in Figure 7.4. You can also choose Window, Vector Shape. Like the Paint window, it includes two toolbars. Most of the tools are on the left, whereas you use the top toolbar to set fills.

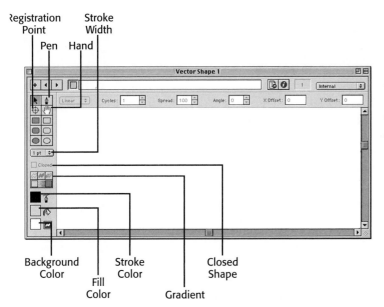

Figure 7.4
The Vector Shape editing window enables you to create and edit vector members.

A vector shape is essentially one or more long curves built around two or more points each. Some points also contain curvature information. If the image is set to be closed, the first and last points of each curve are connected and a fill can be applied to the enclosed area.

To create a vector shape, choose the Pen tool. Click in the window to create the first point of the vector shape. If you click and hold the mouse button down, you can set the curvature amount, or handles, of the point. You can then place other points in different locations. A quick click adds a point with no handles; a prolonged click and hold enable you to set the curve of the line.

An improvement in Director 8 is that you can have more than one curve in a vector shape member. However, the closed property and the fill type are set for the entire member, not for each individual curve.

Figure 7.5 shows a vector shape in the middle of its creation. The user has clicked to create several points. You can see the two handles of the last point created. You can also see the second handle of the next-to-last point because that handle affects the curve drawn between the two points. Any of these handles shown can be grabbed and moved to change the curve of the line.

Figure 7.5
While you create a vector graphic, you see not only the points you have created so far, but also the handles of your current point and the second handle of the preceding point. The handles define the amount of curve from one point to the next.

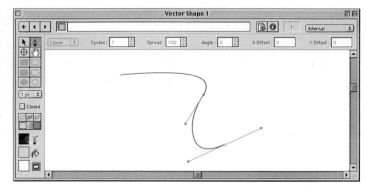

The last point in any curve is very important. If you match that last point up to the first point in the vector shape, you then have the option to set the vector to filled. If the two points do not match, the shape can still be used filled, but a line segment is added to complete the loop.

After you finish drawing, you can edit any point by selecting it with the Arrow tool. The arrow turns white when it is positioned over an editable point. After you select one point, you can edit its location and the locations of its handles. You can also continue the curve by selecting the Pen tool again and clicking to create another point. To insert a new point between two points that already exist, use the Pen tool with the Option key held down on the Mac or the Alt key held down in Windows.

Curves defined by points and handles are also known as *Bézier curves*. The first handle of any point determines how the line curves into the point, whereas the second handle determines how the line curves away from a point. So, any section of the curved line will curve depending on the second handle of the preceding point and the first handle of the next point. If neither point has these handles, the line is drawn straight from one to the other.

Six shapes are also shown in the toolbar. You can use them to make some standard shapes. Because these shapes all exist in Director as regular shape members, there is little point to using them here to create plain shapes. Instead, you can use them to create a starting point for a shape that still needs to be edited to get the result you want. For instance, you can use the rectangle shape to create a rectangle that you will edit and to which you will add other points.

Another reason to use these standard shapes is that you might want to take advantage of the fill techniques available to vector shapes but not standard shapes. By having a closed shape and turning on the Closed setting, you can apply a fill. Select the type of fill from the toolbar on the left side of the screen. You can have no fill, a solid fill, or a gradient.

If you select a solid fill, you must also select the fill color from the collection of color chips on the left toolbar. The first is the color of the line. The line color does not matter if you set the line to be 0 pixels wide. The second is the color of a solid fill. Having these as two separate colors means that you can have a vector graphic that has one color for the outline and another for the fill. The last color chip enables you to set the color of the background. This color comes into play only if you set the sprite that uses the vector member to Copy ink.

If you set the fill type to be a gradient, you can also set the destination color with a color chip arrangement that is similar to what is used in the Paint window. A host of settings in the top toolbar defines the type of gradients.

You can use a linear or radial gradient and set the number of *cycles*, or the number of times that the gradient is to travel between the initial and destination colors. The Spread setting enables you to restrict the fill to only a small portion of the image, or enlarge it so that only a portion of the gradient fits into the shape. You can also change the angle and offset location of the gradient. This gives you an incredible amount of control over where the gradient is placed and how it looks.

⇨ *For more information about creating vector shape members,* ***see*** *"Building Vectors with Lingo,"* **p. 412** *(Chapter 20, "Controlling Vector Graphics")*

Vector Shape Properties

In addition to the vector shape editing window, the Property Inspector, shown in Figure 7.6, has a few other settings you can establish. You can access the Property Inspector when you are editing the vector shape by clicking the Info button.

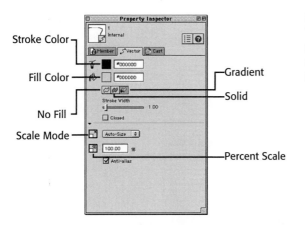

Stroke Color
Fill Color
No Fill
Scale Mode
Gradient
Solid
Percent Scale

Figure 7.6
The Property Inspector enables you to define what happens when a sprite containing this member is stretched.

One of the settings on the Property Inspector determines whether the shape is drawn using anti-aliasing. Anti-aliasing uses shading to smooth out the line. This type of line is slower to draw, of course, but looks much better than a ragged line of pixels.

The Scale Mode pop-up menu enables you to choose what happens when the member is stretched on the Stage. Here are the options:

- **Show All**—The vector shape keeps the same dimensions, stretching only when it can still fit the entire shape in the sprite.

- **No Border**—The vector shape keeps the same dimensions, but scales to fill the sprite area, even if it means cutting off some of the shape horizontally or vertically.

- **Exact Fit**—The vector scales to the new dimensions of the sprite, stretching horizontally and vertically as needed.

- **Auto Size**—The sprite's rectangle changes its shape to fit the entire member as you rotate, skew, or flip it.

- **No Scale**—The vector does not scale when the sprite is stretched. This keeps the vector looking the same size, even if it means that the shape is cropped if the sprite is shrunk.

Unfortunately, you cannot import vectors from other programs, such as Freehand and Illustrator. Vectors created with these programs are usually much more complex than vector cast members. Chapter 20, "Controlling Vector Graphics," however, teaches you how to import some vector graphics files.

The last setting in the Vector Shape Properties dialog box enables you to scale the cast member. This is independent of any scaling on the Stage. Sprite scaling affects each sprite individually, whereas member scaling affects all instances of the member in a sprite.

Vector Shape Techniques

The number of uses for vector shapes grows every day as developers experiment with this relatively new member type. You can now create everything from little arrows to vector maps. Because they can be rotated and resized on the Stage, a single vector member can be used over and over in different ways. Figure 7.7 shows a single vector shape member that has been used in a variety of ways in different sprites. Some of the sprites are rotated, some are skewed, and others are stretched.

Figure 7.7
The Vector Shape editing window shows a single vector shape member. The Stage shows this member used in a variety of sprites.

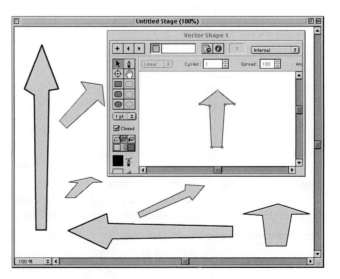

You can use fills to perform a variety of effects. If, for instance, you want to place a gradient over the entire Stage as a background, you can make a simple rectangular vector shape, apply a gradient fill, and place it in sprite 1. Figure 7.8 shows this technique. The vector shape editing window shows a small, simple member, and the Stage shows that member in sprite 1, stretched to encompass the whole Stage. Before Director 7, you had to create a huge bitmap member to get the same result.

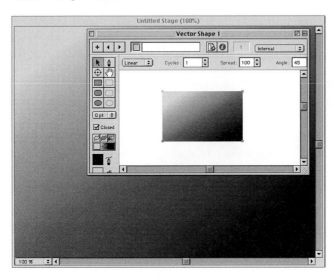

Figure 7.8
A simple vector shape can be used to create a gradient background.

The most powerful thing about this type of background gradient is that you can change your mind about the colors as often as you want. To change the colors, all you have to do is double-click the sprite, which brings up the Vector Shape editing window, and then use the color chips.

Another technique enables you to create some areas that are filled and others that are not. If you cross a line while drawing the curve in your vector shape, the crossover area is treated as a nonfilled area. Figure 7.9 demonstrates this technique. The star is created by overlapping five lines. The center area is then covered more than once by the area made by the lines. Therefore, the center area is blank, rather than filled.

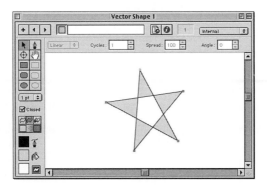

Figure 7.9
The vector's lines cross each other and create an area that is transparent rather than filled.

➪ *For more information about vector shape properties, **see** "Using Vector Shape Lingo," p. 409 (Chapter 20)*

USING FLASH MEMBERS

Another type of vector graphic is the Flash member. Macromedia Flash is a standalone tool for creating vector graphics and animations for Web pages. It uses vectors, rather than bitmaps, to create very small files that can do a lot.

Starting with Director 6.5, developers have had the capability to import Flash members into Director as cast members. A Flash movie can be as simple as a single frame with a vector drawing on it. In this case, you can use Flash members like vector shape members. The advantage is that you can have much more in a Flash member, such as text and bitmap elements.

Flash movies can also be animations, so you can use Flash members as you use digital video. The movie can play once, loop, or even contain interactivity tools, such as simple buttons.

You can also import bitmaps and sounds into Flash movies, but because Director can already use bitmaps and sounds as members, there is little point. However, if you have graphic artists who are accustomed to working in Flash, you can easily import their animations.

After you import a Flash movie, the Property Inspector gives you many options that you can alter for the member, as you can see in Figure 7.10. You can bring up the Property Inspector by selecting the Flash member in the Cast window and clicking the Info button.

Figure 7.10
The Property Inspector offers many settings for Flash members.

The Scale Mode option enables you to set the scale mode of the member. This determines how the member reacts when a sprite that uses it is stretched. Here are the options available:

- **Show All**—As you stretch, the smaller of the horizontal or vertical scale is used to size the image. The result is that the Flash member will always fit in any rectangle.

- **No Border**—As you stretch, the larger of the horizontal or vertical scale is used to size the image.

- **Exact Fit**—As you stretch, the image is stretched horizontally and vertically according to the rectangle of the sprite.

- **No Scale**—The image is never stretched, but is instead shown at 100% in the center of the sprite.

- **Auto Size**—Similar to Exact Fit, but if you rotate the sprite, the bounding box of the sprite expands so that the image is not clipped.

You might also want to set a Flash member to start paused if the Flash movie is a one-frame static graphic, and not meant to be an animated element. This will speed up performance of the rest of the Director movie's elements.

Next to the Scale Mode setting is a space for you to type a scale percentage. Unlike sprite stretching, this percentage will affect every sprite that uses the member.

Next, you can choose High, Low, Auto-High, or Auto-Low for the Quality setting. The High setting shows vector line and text in the Flash member with smooth edges as opposed to jagged edges. If you choose Auto-High, the Flash movie starts by using high quality, but reverts to low quality if it has trouble on a slower computer. Auto-Low does the opposite, starting at low quality, but then switching to high if the computer can handle drawing the graphics quickly.

The Rate setting enables you to alter the rate that the Flash movie plays back by setting it to either Normal, Lock Step, or Fixed. Normal plays the Flash movie at the speed in which it was created. Lock Step sets its tempo so that it plays one frame of Flash animation for every one frame that the Director movie moves. The Fixed setting enables you to specify a frame rate for the Flash member.

In the lower part of the Property Inspector, you can turn on or off certain features of the Flash member. You can turn off the sound, or the image if your Flash movie needs to have only one or the other. You can have the movie be paused, rather than playing, when it appears on the Stage. This is useful when you want to use Lingo to start the movie. You can also set a Flash animation to loop. Otherwise, it will play through once and then stop.

The Preload option is useful only when the Flash movie is a linked external file rather than an imported member.

The last option is Direct to Stage, which will play the Flash movie on top of everything else on the screen. It may give you a performance boost if you need it.

At the time of this writing, the More Options button in the Property Inspector leads to a dialog box that shows the same options available in the Property Inspector. Because Flash members are handled by an Xtra, and not really native to Director, the Flash Xtra could see an update before the next version of Director appears. This dialog box, then, could be the way to access new options.

Many Lingo commands can also be used to control Flash movies. Chapter 20 shows you how to control Flash movie playback.

➡ *For more information about Flash member properties,* ***see*** *"Using Flash Member Lingo," **p. 406** (Chapter 20)*

TROUBLESHOOTING VECTOR MEMBERS

- If you make a mistake when you are creating a vector shape member in the editing window, you can just delete the whole thing and start again, rather than try to adjust everything.

- If you are trying to create a very small or very large circle with the vector shape editor, it's better to create a medium-sized one and scale it on the Stage. Small ones, fewer than 50 pixels in diameter, and large ones, more than 300 pixels in diameter, start to look distorted because they are drawn with just four points. Drawing one about 100 pixels in diameter and then stretching it on the Stage produces a near-perfect circle.

- Remember that there are two types of line shapes: lines that draw from the upper-left to lower-right and lines that draw from the upper-right to lower-left. If you use one line member on the Stage and try to make it go in different directions for different sprites, all the sprites that use that line will turn out to be the same type.

DID YOU KNOW?

- You can change the fill color of a vector shape member as a sprite on the Stage. Just take a filled vector shape, place it on the Stage, and use the foreground color chip in the Tool palette. You can also tween the fill color over a series of frames. You cannot, however, change the line color.

- You can greatly improve the performance of Director movies that use large Flash members by setting Flash sprites to Copy ink, rather than Background Transparent. Try as hard as you can to use other inks besides Copy only when absolutely necessary.

- You can apply patterns to standard shape members but not to bitmaps or vector shapes. Just select the shape sprite and use the pattern chip in the Director Tool palette to set a pattern.

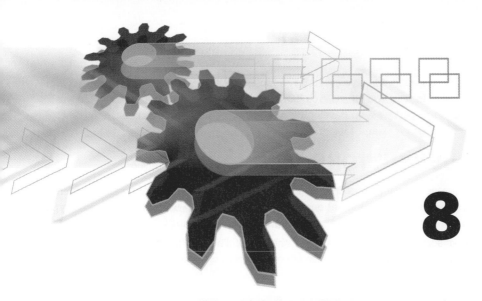

8

OTHER MEMBER TYPES

IN THIS CHAPTER

Source movies for this chapter can be found on the CD-ROM in the "Book Movies" folder under folder 8.

Although the last few chapters have covered the most common cast member types, there are actually many more. In fact, with Xtras, you can keep adding cast member types as long as Macromedia and third parties keep developing more Xtras. This chapter summarizes some of the minor cast member types and their uses.

CREATING PUSHBUTTONS

Director pushbuttons are easy to create and use, but lack a professional appearance, which makes them useless in real-world situations. However, they can be useful for quick prototypes or as placeholders until you get around to making the final buttons.

Figure 8.1 shows some typical pushbuttons on the Stage. These buttons all are black-bordered, rounded rectangles with text in them. They are reminiscent of buttons used in Hypercard on the Mac.

Figure 8.1
Examples of Director's standard pushbutton cast member.

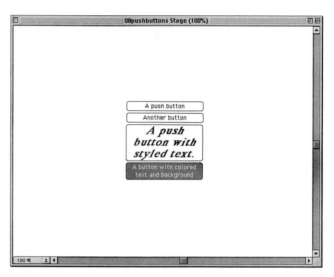

To place a pushbutton on the Stage, use the Tool palette, select the Pushbutton tool, and then draw the pushbutton on the Stage. After you finish, you can adjust the size of the pushbutton by grabbing the corners. You can also double-click and type text into the pushbutton.

You can do a few things to get away from the standardized look of the pushbutton. For one, you can change the font and style of the text inside it. As a matter of fact, if you double-click the member, you can edit it directly on the Stage. If you choose to edit it from the Cast, you do so in an editing window that looks just like the field-editing window. You can select any font and style, and even right-, left-, or center-justify the text.

Pushbuttons are similar to fields with regard to how they handle text. They use the system's installed fonts, so make sure that any font you use in pushbuttons is available on all machines that are expected to run the movie. The text is not anti-aliased.

You can customize pushbuttons by setting the foreground and background colors of the text. To do this, you must be editing the text, not just the sprite. Then, use the color chips to set the background color of the button and the foreground color of the text.

The behavior of the pushbutton is similar to the behavior of a bitmap member with the Hilite When Clicked option turned on. When the users press the button, the colors reverse. When the users release the mouse, the action usually occurs. You can use any standard library behavior that reacts to a mouse click.

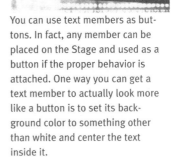

You can use text members as buttons. In fact, any member can be placed on the Stage and used as a button if the proper behavior is attached. One way you can get a text member to actually look more like a button is to set its background color to something other than white and center the text inside it.

For more information on creating buttons, *see* "Creating Simple Button Behavior," **p. 265** (Chapter 14, "Creating Behaviors")

CREATING CHECK BOXES

If you examine a pushbutton's member properties, you can see that you can change its type. You can examine the properties by selecting the member in the Cast and clicking the Info button. You can choose either a pushbutton, check box, or radio button. All three of these button types are the same cast member, but with different settings. You can choose the other two types from the Tool palette as well.

The check box is a small square that users can click to signify a true or false value. You see them all the time in other software programs and even in Director's own dialog boxes.

The check box cast member, however, is like the pushbutton cast member in that it shows a fairly old-fashioned version of a check box that is not used in either Mac or Windows operating systems anymore. Figure 8.2 shows some Director check boxes.

Rather than use Director's built-in check boxes, it is better to use a series of bitmaps to represent a multiple-state button, such as a check box. However, using the built-in check box member provides an ease-of-use benefit. See Chapter 15, "Graphic Interface Elements," for more advanced check boxes that use bitmaps.

For more information on using check boxes, *see* "Using Check Boxes," **p. 292** (Chapter 15)

The check box also uses a text editor similar to that of the field member. Adding a background color, however, is fairly useless because the color wraps around the check box area and you are not offered any option for setting a margin or border.

After a check box member is on the Stage as a sprite and the movie is running, you can click it to turn the check on or off. This value is then available for Lingo commands to interpret.

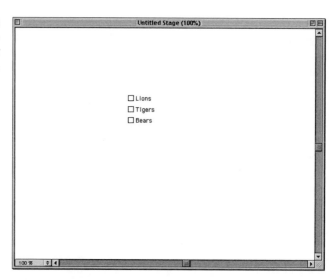

Figure 8.2

Director's built-in check box member is a bit old-fashioned for today's applications.

CREATING RADIO BUTTONS

Radio buttons are similar to check boxes. They have some text next to an on/off switch. The visible difference is the type of switch. Whereas check boxes have a box with an x in them to signify whether the switch is on or off, radio buttons are circles that have a dot in them to signify whether they are on or off. Figure 8.3 shows some radio buttons on the Stage.

The term radio button comes from the old-style car radios that had a row of pushbuttons on the front. If you pressed down one button, the others would automatically pop up. In fact, you could have only one button down at a time. This made sense, because you could listen to only one radio station at a time.

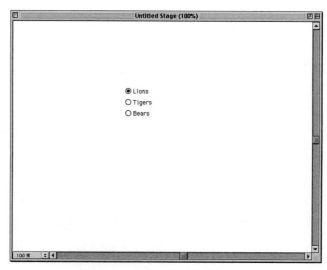

Figure 8.3

Director radio buttons.

The same is true for computer radio buttons. In any group of radio buttons, only one should be selected at any time. They are usually used to offer a choice between many options. If you want users to choose one color from three, for instance, clicking the button for one color immediately turns off any other selection.

For this reason, radio buttons are grouped together. In any one group, only one can be selected at any time. Another rule is that one *must* be selected. So, you have to start users with a default setting.

Both radio buttons and check boxes rely on the cast member to determine whether the button is on or off. For this reason, you cannot reuse a cast member, even if it appears exactly the same, in two sprites. Clicking one of the sprites affects any others that use the same member.

You need Lingo to interpret radio button selections, and to make them work properly. A behavior that enables you to group radio buttons together is included in the Macromedia Director library.

To make this behavior work, first create two or more radio buttons and place them on the Stage. Then, drag the behavior to the first radio button. You are prompted to assign a group name to the button. The group name should be exactly the same for the other buttons you want to group together. You also need to select the Initially Selected option for one of the radio buttons. Drag the behavior and set the parameters for each of the other buttons.

Now when you run the movie, each of these buttons controls how the others are set. Only one can be selected at a time. You can always add more radio buttons to a group, or start another group on the same frame.

Chapter 16, "Controlling Text," explains how to interpret the results of a radio button group with Lingo. You also learn how to make radio buttons from bitmap members, so you can customize them in many ways.

For more information on using radio buttons, **see** *"Using Radio Buttons," **p. 294** (Chapter 15)*

USING PALETTE MEMBERS

Typically, a palette is a set of 256 colors. Palettes are used in situations in which the computer does not have enough power to display the thousands of colors visible to the eye. Instead, the computer is instructed to use 256 colors.

Palettes can also be applied to bitmaps to make them smaller. Rather than having each pixel of a bitmap represent one of thousands or millions of colors, it can represent just one of 256 colors from a palette. This means the image might not look as nice, but it takes up less file space.

If a computer is using a 256-color palette, it must define those colors. Macintosh computers and Windows machines have a different idea about what these colors should be. The result is two standard palettes: the Mac system palette and the Windows system palette.

Because these palettes were designed for a wide range of uses and are used by the operating systems, they are the most common palettes. They contain a variety of colors that can be used for almost any image.

Another common palette is the Web palette. This palette actually contains only 216 colors. The rest of the color slots are empty. The 216 colors used are found in both the Mac and Windows system palettes. The other 40 colors change depending on the system. This means that a graphic created using the Web palette can be displayed on either system without having to swap out colors. Web browsers are built to handle this special Web palette.

You can also build your own custom palettes. You might want to do this for a variety of reasons. Suppose, for instance, that you are doing a project about Mars. All the images you have use a lot of reds and oranges, but few other colors. The space in the palette used by greens, blues, and other colors is never used. You can make a palette that is mostly reds, thus giving your images the capability to show a wide range of reds. The other colors are not missed because no images use them.

You can make your own palette in Director by choosing Insert, Media Element, Color Palette. This brings up the Color Palettes editing window shown in Figure 8.4.

A variety of tools are in this window, some above the color chart and some below. The pop-up menu enables you to select the palette you are working on. All of Director's built-in palettes are displayed, as well as any cast member palettes you have created. If you select a built-in palette and then edit it, Director automatically creates a new cast member with the new palette.

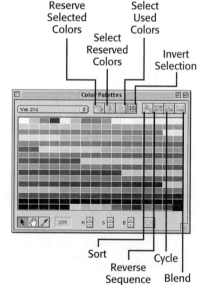

Figure 8.4
The Color Palettes editing window allows you to examine palettes or build your own.

The tools across the top are used to reserve, select, and move colors in the palette. The first button, Reserve Selected Colors, enables you to reserve colors. First, select some colors in the palette. Use the Shift key to select multiple consecutive colors and use the ⌘ key on the Mac or the Ctrl key in Windows to add to the selection. Then, click the Reserve Selected Colors button to reserve colors. These colors now cannot be used by any bitmaps being converted to this palette. They are reserved for use for things such as color cycling, which you learn about in Chapter 11, "Advanced Techniques."

Another button on the toolbar, called the Select Used Colors button, enables you to select all the colors used by the currently selected member in the Cast. This member must be set to 8-bit color. This is useful if you want to alter a palette but do not want to edit any colors used by a certain member. You can also select several members in the Cast and use this button to determine which colors are used by any of the members. This can help you develop new palettes based on which colors are most important.

To convert any bitmap to use a palette you create, select the member and choose Modify, Transform Bitmap. You can choose whether you want to dither the colors or remap them color for color.

The Sort, Reverse Sequence, Cycle, and Blend buttons enable you to alter the color values of a series of colors that you have selected. The Sort button sorts them by color. The Reverse Sequence button reverses the color positions. The Cycle button moves them all by one position and places the last color as the first. The Blend button creates a new series of colors based on the first and last color selected.

You can choose from three tools on the lower-left side of the Color palette. The first is the standard Selection tool (Arrow tool). The second, the Hand tool, enables you to drag colors around the chart. The third, the Eyedropper tool, enables you to select a color based on where the cursor is located on the Stage. To use the Eyedropper tool, first select it. Then, click and hold down on any color in the chart. While holding, drag the cursor over to the Stage. The selection in the color palette then reflects the closest one to the color that the cursor is over.

The rest of the Color Palette's editing window enables you to specify the exact color of the selected color. You can either play with the hue, saturation, and brightness of the color, or you can click the Color Picker button to bring up your computer system's color options.

Color palettes give you more control over what your movie is doing. Complex movies can be made without any special color palettes. However, learning how to use them might enable you to do things more easily and make your movies look better.

⇨ For more information on developing cross-platform movies, **see** "Developing for the Mac and Windows," **p. 700** (Chapter 35, "Cross-Platform Development")

ADDING CURSORS

Three types of custom cursors are available in Director: built-in cursors, custom bitmap cursors, and animated cursors. Each of these cursor types is discussed in the following sections.

Built-In Cursors

The Director's built-in cursors include the arrow, the hand, the crosshairs, and the clock. The following is a list of some of the most common built-in cast members and their numbers. Use their numbers to refer to them in behaviors that ask for a cursor type.

- **0**—Revert to system default.
- **-1**—Arrow cursor.

- **1**—I-beam cursor.
- **2**—Thin crosshair cursor.
- **3**—Thick crossbar cursor.
- **4**—Watch cursor.
- **200**—Blank cursor.
- **280**—Finger cursor.

To use these cursors, you will either need to write some Lingo code, or use a prebuilt behavior. One such behavior is the "Rollover Cursor Change" behavior from Director's built-in library. With this behavior, you don't even have to remember the number of the cursor. Instead, you can choose from a list of names that the Behavior Parameters dialog box provides.

Custom Bitmap Cursors

You can also build your own cursors. The easiest way to do this is to create a single bitmap member that contains a 1-bit image that is no larger than 16 pixels wide and 16 pixels high. Figure 8.5 shows the Paint window with a bitmap member that is destined to be used as a cursor. The zoom is turned on to show detail.

Figure 8.5
The Paint window can be used to create 1-bit bitmaps to be used as custom cursors.

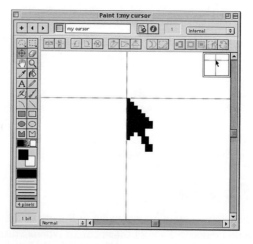

Notice the registration point in Figure 8.5. This point is used to determine the control point of the cursor. Even though cursors can be 16×16, only one point (the control point) is the actual clicking area. In an arrow cursor, it is usually the tip of the arrow; in a paint bucket cursor, it is usually the bottom tip of the falling paint.

You can use cursors such as this in the "Rollover Change Pointer" behavior of the library. Just select the member as the Custom Image for the effect. Note that you can also provide a mask image for the cursor. This is another 1-bit image that shows the cursor where it should be opaque.

Animated Cursors

A third way to create a custom cursor is to use the special cursor Xtra. Choose Insert, Media Element, Cursor to add one of these cast members to your movie. The Cursor Properties Editor, shown in Figure 8.6, appears.

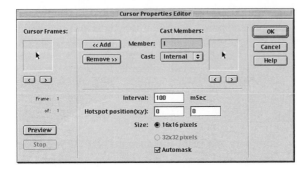

Figure 8.6
The Cursor Properties Editor window enables you to create color and animated cursors.

You can add and remove bitmap members from the animated cursor sequence. The members must use 8-bit color. You can add only one bitmap to the cursor if you want it to remain a static cursor. Adding more than one bitmap makes the cursor animate between the two or more members that make it up. You can set the interval time between the frames of the animation.

The Automask option in the Cursor Properties Editor window enables you to determine whether the cursor should use a mask that fits around the cursor, just as the matte ink fits around sprites. Turning this off masks the entire cursor rectangle. You cannot make custom masks for animated cursors.

Like the other custom cursor type, you set the control point of the cursor by setting the registration point of the members involved.

For more information on using cursors, **see** *"Using Cursors,"* **p. 430** *(Chapter 21, "Controlling the Director Environment")*

USING ANIMATED GIFS

Director 8 comes complete with an Xtra that enables you to add animated GIFs as cast members. When you import a file that is in GIF format, Director prompts you as to whether you want to import it as a bitmap or an animated GIF member.

As you can imagine, animated GIF members have a special dialog box (see Figure 8.7) to handle their properties. You can access it by selecting the member in the Cast window and clicking the Info button. You then need to click the Options button in the dialog box that appears.

You can choose to have the animated GIF file embedded in the Cast, or to have it linked to an external file. You can also choose Direct to Stage for faster playback when you don't need to use special inks.

Figure 8.7
The Property Inspector enables
you to determine how an animated GIF member is played on
the Stage.

You have three Rate choices as to how you want the animated GIF to keep pace. The first
option (Normal) uses the same tempo that it would if it were presented on the Web. The second option (Fixed) throws away its built-in tempo information and makes the GIF move at a
consistent rate, which you can define. The third method (Lock Step) ties the tempo of the GIF
to the tempo of the movie.

USING QUICKTIME VR

QuickTime virtual reality (VR) files are often considered another media type. In fact, with
QuickTime 3, they are treated in Director just like any other QuickTime media file. The main
difference is that the control strip for a QuickTime VR movie has different controls.

There are two types of QuickTime VR. The first is a *panoramic image*. Here, the users can use
the cursor to swing the image left, right, up, and down, and enjoy a 360-degree view. Users
can even zoom in and out of such images. Real-life images must be captured with a special
camera and stitched together with special software. Some 3D rendering tools enable you to
create modeled panoramic scenes.

The second type of QuickTime VR file is an *object file*. This is a series of pictures or renderings of an object from every direction. Using controls, the users can view the object from any
angle.

QuickTime VRs can contain one or more panoramic objects. Quite often, several scenes are
combined into one file and linked together with hotspots that the users can click to go from
scene to scene. These combined scenes are called QuickTime VR tours.

Before QuickTime 3, you needed a special Xtra and a lot of Lingo code to use QuickTime VR
files in Director. Now, you can simply import them as QuickTime media and place them on the
Stage.

ADDING NEW CAST MEMBER TYPES WITH XTRAS

Xtras enable third-party companies to develop programs that add to the functionality of Director. Sometimes they add new Lingo commands. Other times they add the possibilities for new types of cast members. Many times they add both.

Xtras that enable you to use new types of cast members are called *asset Xtras*. Some of the cast members that you might think are built in to Director are actually made possible by asset Xtras that come preinstalled with Director. Examples are QuickTime 3 members, Flash members, cursor members, and even vector shape members.

Other Xtras enable you to add even more types of members. You just need to download or purchase them from the companies that make them and then follow their installation instructions. For instance, the AlphaMania Xtra from Media Lab enables you to import anti-aliased images and perform special effects on them. See Appendix H, "Guide to Xtras," for a listing of where you can find some asset Xtras.

TROUBLESHOOTING OTHER MEMBER TYPES

- Because the vertical size of pushbuttons is determined by the type, size, and amount of text in them, the size can differ from platform to platform. Be sure to test these, or use more advanced types of buttons, such as the ones described in Chapter 15.

- Both radio buttons and check boxes also have text associated with them. Not only can the size of the text differ across platforms, but the text usually doesn't line up with the check box or radio button graphic. Use more advanced radio buttons, such as the ones in Chapter 15, for more precise results.

- Custom cursors that refer to members that are not 1-bit do not work. This is the first thing to check when you are having problems. Also, animated cursors need to use 8-bit members. You need to create members of these bit depths to use them as cursors, or convert them by choosing Modify, Transform Bitmap.

- With Shockwave versions 7 and 8, as of this writing, the Animated GIF Xtra, which is required to have animated GIFs in your movies, is not included with Shockwave. This means that many Shockwave users on the Web won't be able to see your animated GIFs in your Director movies. In fact, they might be hit with an error message. An alternative is to save your original animation as bitmaps that you can easily animate in Director, thus avoiding animated GIFs altogether.

- Check box and radio button members actually change when you click them while the movie is running. Be sure you reset them to their starting values before you save the movie.

DID YOU KNOW?

- You can change the background color of a pushbutton by selecting the text in it and then using the background color chip in the Tool palette. This creates more interesting buttons.

- Even if you are working in 16-, 24-, or 32-bit color, palettes are still useful. If you have a large image of trees, for instance, you can save it from PhotoShop as an 8-bit image with an *adaptive* palette. This palette contains the 256 colors that best represent the colors in the image. When you import the image, you also import that palette in another member. This makes the image more compact in the file, but ensures that it still looks good on the Stage. Plus, you can have many images using many different palettes on the Stage at the same time when you are above 8-bit color.

AUTHORING IN DIRECTOR

IN THIS PART

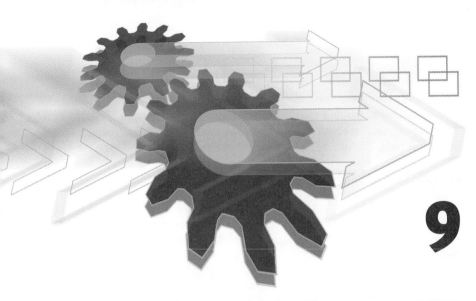

9

THE DIRECTOR ENVIRONMENT

IN THIS CHAPTER

Director is a customizable working environment. This means that there are many ways to display and position windows and many ways that the contents of these windows can look. Understanding all the options is the first step to customizing your work environment. In addition, there are many ways to organize your work. An entire book can be written on the subject, but this chapter presents a brief summary of ways to work.

WAYS TO WORK IN DIRECTOR

If you are creating a small project, one in which only you are involved and you expect to finish the work in a few days, it probably doesn't matter how you organize your work. However, if the project takes months and involves many people with different talents, a systematic approach will help.

Such a system should involve careful planning, documentation, division of labor, a hardware network, and a lot of teamwork.

Planning Your Attack

Diving into a project might be okay for small programs, but does not work for large projects when more than one person is involved. Sometimes the most important work is done before the first image is generated or the first line of code is written. Planning your strategy can include creating an outline, determining your specifications, and setting up a schedule.

The Outline

There are many ways to plan a project. One is to outline. Creating a list of contents and ordering it can reveal the true scope of the project and act as a checklist later on. For a presentation, each line in the outline can represent a screen. For an animation, each line can represent a different scene. For larger projects, the outline should also represent a hierarchy with small parts of the project organized under larger headings.

The outline doesn't necessarily have to present the project in a linear fashion. It can divide the project into media types or production deadlines. However, the outline should include everything in the project: art, sounds, code, and the like.

The Flowchart

Similar to an outline, a flowchart is a step closer to describing exactly how the project should work. Arrows and lines define the possible flow of navigation from screen to screen or function to function.

Storyboarding

Similar to a flowchart, a screen-by-screen plan of your project works well for presentation-style Director projects. Typically, you may incorporate some basic artwork as well. Although not as functional as a flowchat, a storyboard is an ideal technique when you need to show your boss or a client what the project will look like.

Your Specifications

A specification document, or spec, tells you exactly how the project should look when it is finished. If you are working for a client, it's always a good idea to have the client write up a detailed spec so that you know what is expected of you. The same goes for management within your own company. It is best that all parties agree on the project's specifications before you start.

The Schedule

After you know what the project needs to look like, the next step is to determine when everything needs to be done. You need to think about early steps, such as research, as well as later steps, such as testing. Try to build some extra time into the schedule to allow for unforeseen events or difficulties. Also, consider what would happen if a critical piece of content were not delivered on time by the client or someone outside of your control.

Creating Documentation

After work begins, you need to take into account more than just the work itself. When a task is done, it might not necessarily be done. Three months later, you might have to go back into your code and change something. If you take the time to document what you are doing while you are doing it, the editing process becomes easier.

Also, take into account that one day someone else might have to open your movie and alter it. If all the markers are named "marker01" and the cast members have names such as "a button," it will be very difficult to make changes later.

Your Naming Scheme

Name your cast members and movies intelligently. There is no excuse for an unnamed cast member. Because Director 8 doesn't work on Windows 3.1, you have no reason to ever use filenames such as cfr99.dir. Use real names, such as Corporate Financial Report.dir.

Name media files with the same amount of detail. Image, sound, video, and text files should all have names that make their contents obvious, without requiring you to check inside the files. It's a hassle to launch PhotoShop just to see whether a file is what you think it is.

You should also come up with a naming convention for all your files. This way, different people will name files in a way that everyone can understand. If your project has chapters and sections, a naming convention could be to include the chapter and section numbers in the filename: 6[nd]2 golden gate bridge, for example, for a picture of the Golden Gate Bridge in Chapter 6, Section 2.

Documents

All users who are responsible for a portion of the project should take the time to document their procedures. For instance, if the people in charge of sounds are running all the sounds through a filter and downsampling them to 22KHz, they should prepare a document that says just that. If another team needs to take over that job or later alter those files, they have everything they need to know in that document. It could save a temporary employee a few hours of work in the morning; it could help if the person doing the work leaves the position; or if that same person returns to the project after months away from it.

Code Comments

When writing Lingo code, it is important to comment as much as necessary to make the text readable by another programmer who might come along later. More frequently, you'll find that comments help you remember what a line or handler was supposed to do. That first line of code might seem obvious when you write it, but three months and 100,000 lines of code later, it might look like a foreign language.

To add comments in Lingo, just use a double dash, - -. You can place a comment on a line by itself, or on the same line as code by using the double dash to signify that everything on that line that follows it is a comment.

Division of Labor

If more than one person is on your team, it's important to decide who does what before anyone starts working. The biggest mistake is letting one person do too much. That mistake creates a bottleneck and others can waste time waiting for the overworked individual to finish his or her job.

Are all team members doing things suited to their skill sets? Are they all enthusiastic about what they are doing? Does anyone have too much to do, or feel that way? Too little? Address all these issues up front and continually as the project progresses.

Hardware Network

An integral part of the work environment for multimedia production is the hardware network. What computers are people using? Are peripherals, such as scanners and printers, accessible by the people who need them? Do all team members have the types of computers they need?

Look at your equipment and determine whether you have everything you need to finish the job. If you are developing a cross-platform project, do you have both Mac and Windows machines available to use for creation and testing? How will people working together share files: on a network, over the Internet, or by swapping disks?

Software is also an important part of the network. Do the team members have what they need to complete their work? How about what they need to do a really good job and beat the competition?

Teamwork

The underlying theme for any team project should be teamwork. If people are not working well together, their efforts will cancel each other, work will suffer, and deadlines will be missed.

Consider the structure of the project. Is there a clear project leader? Who has the final say over decisions? Who runs the project from day to day? Do these responsibilities belong to the same person? If not, how do these people work together?

SETTING PREFERENCES

After all the organizational details of a project have been ironed out, you can get down to work. If your job is working in Director 8 all day, you're the lucky one. Now you just have to organize your working environment.

Director has several preferences dialog boxes that you can use to change the Director environment. There are no correct or incorrect ways to set these preferences; it's all a matter of personal taste. The best approach is experimentation to find what suits you best.

General Preferences

You can bring up most of the preferences dialog boxes by choosing File, Preferences, and then the appropriate category. The General Preferences dialog box is shown in Figure 9.1. It contains some settings similar to those seen when creating a projector.

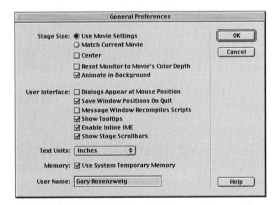

Figure 9.1
The General Preferences dialog box enables you to specify a few general options. Some options are not necessary in Windows.

The Stage Size set of options has to do with the Stage size and position. You can set the Stage to either use the settings of each movie that is opened (Use Movie Settings option), or match only the current movie (Match Current Movie option). You can use the Center option to set the Stage to automatically center when a new movie is opened and force the monitor to change color depths for each movie with the Reset Monitor to Movie's Color Depth option. You can also use the Animate in Background option to tell Director to keep playing the movie even when Director is not the frontmost application.

The next set of options in the dialog box are the User Interface options:

- **Dialogs Appear at Mouse Position**—Determines whether dialog boxes appear at the mouse position or centered on the monitor.

- **Save Window Positions On Quit**—Tells Director to remember the window positions when you quit, so when you return to Director the next time, they are in the same places.

- **Message Window Recompiles Scripts**—Automatically recompiles all scripts when you enter something in the message window. Although it makes sense to always do this, if you are working on a movie that is filled with errors, you cannot use the message window for much until you fix the errors.

- **Show Tooltips**—Turns Tooltips on or off. Tooltips are the little yellow boxes that appear as you hover the mouse over buttons in the interface. They can be useful, but you might find them annoying.

- **Enable Inline IME**—An IME is an Input Method Editor. Turning this option on allows you to use special hardware or software to enter characters in some languages, such as Japanese.

- **Show Stage Scrollbars**—You can turn this option off to make the Stage look more like it did in Director 7. You can still zoom in and out with the Magnifying Glass tool and move the Stage inside the Stage window with the Hand tool.

The Text Units list in the General Preferences dialog box also enables you to set the ruler measurement for windows that use a ruler. You can select inches, centimeters, or pixels.

The Use System Temporary Memory check box enables Mac users to tell Director to use memory outside its normal memory block. It doesn't work with virtual memory turned on, however.

At the bottom of the dialog box is a space to change the username. It starts off with the username entered when Director was installed. However, you can change this here. When you modify a cast member, the name of the user is recorded in the Modified By property of that member.

Network Preferences

The Network Preferences dialog box enables you to set the network preferences for Director. Figure 9.2 shows this dialog box. It has settings similar to those found in a Web browser.

Figure 9.2
The Network Preferences dialog box enables you to set the default browser and cache options.

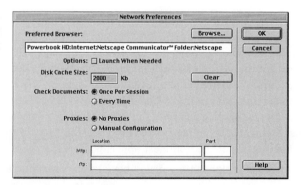

The Preferred Browser option sets the default browser used by Director. Primarily, this comes into play only when you use a *gotoNetPage* Lingo command. It is also used when you choose File, Preview in Browser to check how your movie works in Shockwave.

The Launch When Needed option specifies whether Director should automatically launch the browser when it is required by the movie, such as a *gotoNetPage* command. If you turn it off, the browser will not launch.

The Disk Cache Size text box enables you to define the size of the disk cache. Like browsers, Director movies can access files from the Internet and store them in a cache for later retrieval. You can set Director to check the file on the Internet for new versions Every Time or only Once per Session. Choosing Once per Session, means that if a document on the Internet is updated after you access it once, you might get the older copy of it when accessing it the second time during the same session.

For those who have to work inside a firewall of some sort, the Proxies set of options enable you to set proxies to get files through the firewall. Consult your network administrator about these settings if you need them.

Editors Preferences

If you double-click a bitmap member, it brings up the Paint window to enable you to edit the bitmap. However, you can have it launch PhotoShop instead by associating bitmaps with PhotoShop. You can edit that member in PhotoShop and then save the changes back into the cast member.

The Editors Preferences dialog box, shown in Figure 9.3, enables you to select different editors for different cast types. You can access this dialog box by choosing File, Preferences, Editors. You can also choose some options for some Director-only member data.

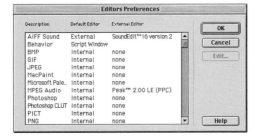

Figure 9.3
The Editors Preferences dialog box enables you to choose external editors for some cast member types.

For example, a common setting is to use SoundEdit 16 to handle sound members. You can point Director to your copy of that application using this window. Then, when you double-click a sound member, you will launch SoundEdit 16.

Certain member types have special settings. Behaviors, for instance, enable you to pick between opening the behavior inspector or the script window.

You can even tell Director to scan your computer for applications that can be used to edit a type of file. You will be presented with a list and asked to choose your preferred editor.

Script Window Preferences

The last preference dialog box listed in the File menu enables you to set a few options for the script-editing window. Figure 9.4 shows the Script Window Preferences dialog box.

Figure 9.4
The primary use of the Script
Window Preferences dialog box is
to control coloring.

With the Default Text option, you pick a default font for the script window. You are still able to change the font of any script; this option just establishes the font to be used when a new script is created.

The rest of the settings are for script colorization. Director 8 automatically colors your scripts to make them easier to read. These settings determine what colors you want Director to use. You can also turn this option off and color the scripts on your own.

Movie Properties

Each movie has some global properties that can be altered. To access these, choose Modify, Movie, Properties. The Property Inspector appears showing the movie's properties. The settings here affect only the current movie. Figure 9.5 shows the Property Inspector.

Figure 9.5
In the Property Inspector dialog
box, you can change the size,
location, and color of the Stage.

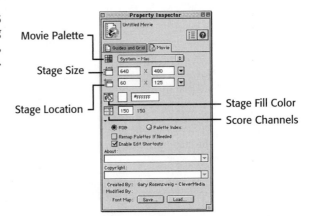

The first group of settings lets you change the palette, size, and location of the Stage. You can also set the background color of the Stage.

The palette is simply the default palette that the movie will use to display itself on an 8-bit monitor. The palette setting is not very important anymore because most computers have monitors set to a higher bit depth.

The only reason to set the number of Sprite channels to less than 1,000 is because movies will play slightly faster with fewer channels to examine.

The last item in the top portion of the Property Inspector enables you to change the number of Sprite channels in the movie. The default is 150, but you can set it as high as 1,000.

The color selection option is very important. If you select RGB, the movie does not use a specific color palette, but instead displays with thousands or millions of colors. If you select Palette Index, however, you can specify a default movie palette. These settings affect mostly Lingo commands that need to specify color numbers.

The Remap Palettes If Needed setting enables Director to display a bitmap image on the Stage with the best possible colors even when the bitmap's palette and the Stage's palette are different.

 The Enable Edit Shortcuts option allows the user to use standard cut, copy, and paste functions in editable text members on the Stage. This is a new feature of Director 8.

You can use the About and Copyright options to set an information message and a copyright line in the Director movie. This will be embedded in the file and seen by people looking for more information about the movie from within some playback methods. The Created By and Modified By information is set by Director according to the registration of the Director application.

The buttons at the bottom of the dialog box enable you to define a font map for the movie. A *font map* is a small text file that you can save out from this dialog box and edit. After it is edited, it can be loaded into the movie with this same dialog box.

The font map was once very important. It tells Director, Shockwave, or a projector, exactly how to deal with fonts when the movie is played back on a different platform: Mac or Windows. The file is well commented and easy to edit. The font map is no longer very important because text members can use fonts that are embedded into the movie as cast members.

For more information on developing cross-platform movies, **see** "Developing for the Mac and Windows," **p. 700** (Chapter 35, "Cross-Platform Development")

Movie Playback Properties

The Movie Playback Properties dialog box, shown in Figure 9.6, offers even more movie settings.

Figure 9.6
The Movie Playback Properties dialog box gives you control over streaming and Shockwave menu settings of a movie.

The first setting, Lock Frame Durations, enables the movie to remember the speed at which it played back on your machine. Every frame that is played remembers how long it was on the screen. When the movie is on another computer, it plays back at the same speed, no matter how much the speed ight differ from frame to frame. This setting enables you to prevent faster computers from playing your movie back too fast, but it does not enable your movie to gain any extra speed on slower machines.

The next setting, Pause When Window Inactive, determines whether the movie keeps playing when it is a movie in a window (MIAW) and it is not the frontmost MIAW. A *MIAW* is a Director movie that is run in a separate window rather than on the Stage. You can read more about them in Chapter 24, "Movies in a Window and Alternatives."

The next set of options has to do with streaming movies over the Internet. Play While Downloading Movie enables streaming. Download X Frames Before Playing enables the machine to download a specified number of frames before the movie begins playing. Show Placeholders enables you to show placeholders, usually boxes, in place of media that has not yet been loaded. When the graphics arrive, the boxes are replaced with the graphics.

➪ *For more information on movie settings, **see** "Making Projectors," **p. 710** (in Chapter 36, "Delivering the Goods")*

Memory Inspector

Although not really a settings dialog box, the Memory Inspector is an important part of the Director environment. Choose Window, Inspectors, Memory to display the Memory Inspector dialog box (see Figure 9.7). It tells you how much memory each part of Director is using and enables you to purge memory when things are tight.

Figure 9.7
The Mac version of the Memory Inspector, shown here, looks different from the Windows version, but they both perform the same service.

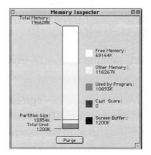

Although purging memory when there are problems might seem like just what you need, in practice only quitting and restarting Director really gets you back to square one.

PUBLISH SETTINGS

A new feature of Director 8 is the Publish command. You can find this command on the File menu. Publish quickly and easily saves your Director movie as a Shockwave-compressed file. It also performs a number of other tasks depending on how you have your Publish Settings set.

The Formats Tab

To access the Publish Settings dialog box (see Figure 9.8), choose File, Publish Settings. This multi-tabbed dialog box has many options, starting with the options on the Formats tab.

Figure 9.8
The Publish Settings dialog box starts off in the Formats tab. Here, you can set the HTML template that Director uses to create a sample HTML page.

In the Formats tab, you can choose from a number of different HTML templates. Director uses these templates to create a sample HTML page every time you use the Publish command. The following list describes these template options:

- **No HTML Template**—No HTML sample file is created. Use this when you just want Publish to output a compressed movie, nothing more.

- **Shockwave Default**—Makes an HTML page with both an <OBJECT> tag for Internet Explorer and an <EMBED> tag for Netscape Navigator.

- **Detect Shockwave**—Uses browser scripting to make sure the users have Shockwave, and tells the users to get it if they don't have it.

- **Fill Browser Window**—Takes the Shockwave movie and makes it fill the entire browser window, regardless of the size of the window. Use this if you plan to have a scalable Shockwave movie that acts as the entire interface on the page.

- **Java**—Use only to make HTML pages for Director movies that are to be converted to Java applets.

- **Loader Game**—Loads a small Macromedia-created game that the users can play while they wait for your movie to download.

- **Progress Bar with Image**—With this option, you can specify an image to be shown that appears in place of the Shockwave movie while the movie loads. A progress bar appears with the image. You can specify the image in a new field that appears at the bottom of the Publish Settings dialog box when you select this option.

- **Shockwave with Image**—If the users don't have Shockwave installed, a JPG image is displayed instead. You can specify the image.

- **Simple Progress Bar**—Displays a simple progress bar, without any special image, while your movie loads.

- **Center Shockwave**—Contains HTML code to center your Shockwave movie in the browser window.

⇨ *For more information on creating Java applets from Director movies, **see p. 709** (Chapter 36, "Delivering the Goods")*

After you choose your HTML format, you can specify the name of both the Shockwave movie and the HTML page. If you have selected an HTML template that uses an image, you can also specify an image filename.

If you select the No HTML Template option, all the tabs in the Publish Settings dialog box that are not needed disappear. The only tabs that will be left are Formats and Compression.

The General Tab

The General tab in the Publish Settings dialog box enables you to alter the dimensions of the movie according to the HTML generated. In other words, the General settings affect only the HTML page, not the movie itself. Figure 9.9 shows the General settings.

Figure 9.9
The General settings portion of the Publish Settings dialog box enables you to alter several parameters in the sample HTML page generated.

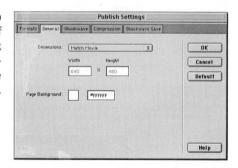

You can change the dimensions of the movie to match the movie, to fit into a percentage of the size of the browser window, or to match a specific pixel size. This changes the numbers used in the <EMBED> and <OBJECT> tags; it doesn't change anything about your Shockwave movie. You can also set the background color of the HTML page created in the Page Background text box.

The Shockwave Tab

The Shockwave tab in the Publish Settings dialog box has a lot of options that affect how Shockwave allows the users to access your movie. You can see this set of settings in Figure 9.10.

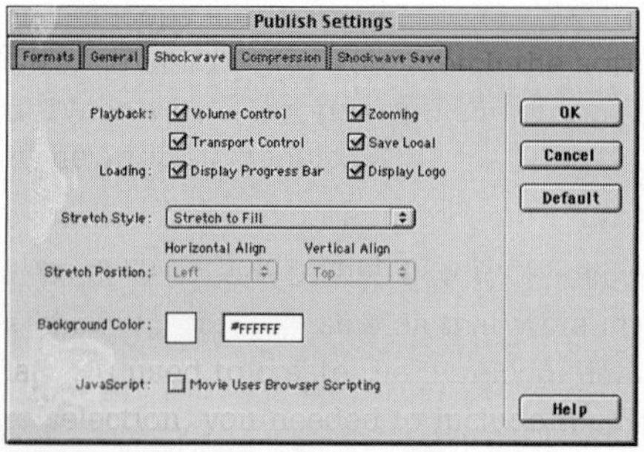

Figure 9.10
The Shockwave settings portion of the Publish Settings dialog box enables you to set how much access the users have to your movie.

The first four options, Volume Control to Save Local, set parameters in the <OBJECT> and <EMBED> tags of the sample HTML. They each restrict what users can do by right-clicking in Windows or Ctrl+clicking on the Mac. With all the options on, users can change the volume of the movie, step through frames of the movie, zoom in and out, and save the movie as a local file to be used in Macromedia's ShockMachine product.

ShockMachine is a standalone Shockwave player that Macromedia has developed and now offers free on the Web. You can find out more about it at `http://www.shockwave.com`.

The two loading options allow you to turn off the default logo and progress bar that appear in place of your Shockwave movie as it loads. The options here add "progress" and "logo" parameters to your <OBJECT> and <EMBED> tags.Shockwave tab in the Publish Settings dialog box has a lot of options.

The Stretch Style options also result in parameters being added to the <OBJECT> and <EMBED> tags. These options determine exactly how the movie fits into the rectangle created by the use of the <OBJECT> and <EMBED> tags. The four Stretch Style options are as follows:

- **No Stretching**—Shows the movie at 100%, no matter what.

- **Default (Preserve Proportions)**—Stretches the movie to fit, but does not change its dimensions.

- **Stretch to Fill**—Stretches the movie to fit in the rectangle exactly.

- **Expand Stage Size**—Keeps the movie at 100%, but allows users to see more of the Stage if the rectangle is larger than the movie.

With the Expand Stage Size option selected, the Stretch Position settings come in handy so that you can decide how the movie is positioned within the larger rectangular space.

The Background Color option enables you to set the background color of the Shockwave rectangle before the movie loads. After the movie loads, the background color of the Stage is the color specified by the movie's properties and not the color specified here.

If the last option, JavaScript, is selected, the proper tags are added to the <OBJECT> and <EMBED> tags to ensure the browser knows that the Shockwave movie will attempt to communicate with JavaScript.Shockwave tab in the Publish Settings dialog box has a lot of options.

The Compression Tab

The Compression tab contains items that actually change properties of your movie, as opposed to just something on the sample HTML page.

Figure 9.11 shows this portion of the Publish Settings dialog box. The Image Compression settings enable you to determine the default compression technique used by images in the movie. Each image can be set to use standard or JPEG compression, or it can be set to use the movie's default compression, which is this setting here in the Compression Tab. If you choose JPEG, you can set the quality percentage.

Figure 9.11
The Compression tab of the Publish Settings dialog box enables you to control image and sound compression.

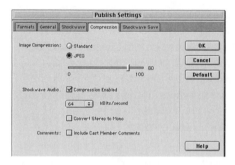

You can also set the compression amount for Shockwave audio. Like JPEG compression, Shockwave audio compression trades quality for file size. You also have the option to not use any sound compression, which guarantees large Shockwave files. Use at least 128Kbps compression to save some file size. A 32Kbps setting will give you much smaller Shockwave movies and will still sound pretty good for most purposes.

Using standard compression means that the image will look exactly the same as your original cast member. However, JPEG compression sacrifices quality for file size.

The last option on the Compression tab falls under the Comments setting. The Include Cast Member Comments option enables you to keep the cast member comment fields that you added to organize your media. Use this option only when you have written some Lingo code to access this information.

The Shockwave Save Tab

The last tab in the Publish Settings dialog box is Shockwave Save. Here, you find places to include information about your Shockwave movie should you be interested in having users download the file for their ShockMachine program. Figure 9.12 shows this tab of the dialog box.

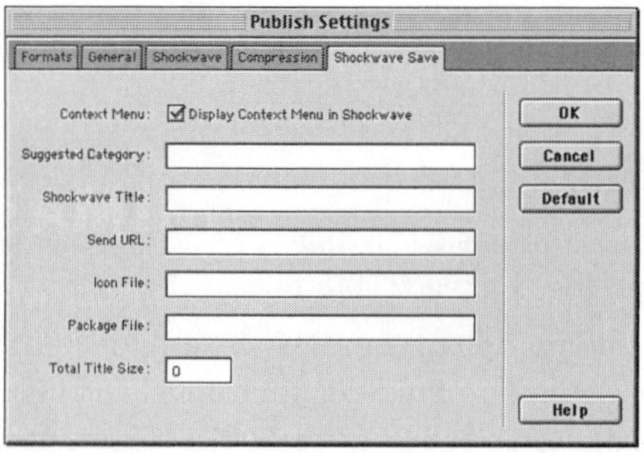

Figure 9.12
The Shockwave Save tab of the Publish Settings dialog box enables you to specify information about your movie for use by ShockMachine.

The Display Context Menu in Shockwave option enables you to control whether users can bring up a pop-up menu by right-clicking in Windows or Ctrl+clicking on the Mac. If users can bring up a pop-up menu, they can choose to save the movie locally, providing the Save Local setting has been turned on in the Shockwave tab of the Publish Settings dialog box.

If users try to save your movie, Shockwave uses the information in this part of the Publish Settings dialog box to categorize it. You can also specify an icon for the movie, which ShockMachine uses to display the movie. The Package file enables you to create a complex download, such as one that includes external casts and other media. The use of all this information is subject to change as Macromedia continues to develop ShockMachine. Your best bet is to check the Macromedia site to find the latest developer guidelines for creating ShockMachine-compatible movies.

Publishing

After you select all the settings under each tab of the Publish Settings dialog box, you are ready to use the Publish command. Just choose File, Publish, to save your movie as a Shockwave file. The HTML page, if you have selected a template, is saved as well.

USING THE DIRECTOR LIBRARY PALETTE

The Library Palette is actually a direct connection to a folder in your Director folder named Libs. The Libs folder holds external cast files that contain behaviors and other media. You can drag items from the library into your current movie or Cast.

Figure 9.13 shows the Library palette. You can select from many categories of behaviors here. After you find the right category, you can drag and drop any behavior into your open movie.

Figure 9.13
The Library palette contains a pop-up menu that appears when you click a button in the upper-left corner. This menu enables you to select the category of behavior you want to use.

Although Director comes with a nice selection of behaviors in the library, you can add and edit Casts in the folder to include your own behaviors or media. A collection of commonly used graphics or sounds can make a fine library. In addition, you might be able to download or purchase third-party library files that enable you to use new behaviors or media.

To add a library, just place the library file, which is really just a plain external cast file, in the Libs folder of your Director folder. That library then becomes available in the Library palette. You can access your libraries by choosing Window, Library Palette.

➪ *For more information on using the behavior library, **see** "Using Behavior Libraries," p. 520 (Chapter 26, "Developing for Developers")*

USING XTRAS

Like the library, Xtras have their own special folder named Xtras. Xtras add functionality to Director, such as a new type of cast member or some new Lingo commands.

A large number of Xtras already come with Director, but even more can be added. To add one, follow the Xtra's specific installation instructions. Installation usually results in the Xtra just being placed in the Xtras folder.

The following list includes some Xtras that are included with Director 8 in its final release. Some are included when you install Director, and others elsewhere on the CD-ROM. For a more complete list, see Chapter 25, "Xtras."

* **Photocaster**—This Xtra enables you to import a single layer of a PhotoShop document rather than the entire image. If you buy the full version, you can actually import all the layers of the document with matching registration points.

* **Print-o-Matic Lite**—The lite version of Print-o-Matic enables you to print out text or many types of cast members, such as bitmaps. You can bring up the Page Setup and Print dialog boxes and specify many print options.

* **Beatnik**—Plays specially formatted music files.

* **Flash Asset**—Enables you to include entire Macromedia Flash movies as single cast members in Director.

* **PowerPoint Importer**—You can import Microsoft PowerPoint presentations. This Xtra places all the elements into the Cast and builds a Score that resembles the original presentation.

* **XML Parser**—Allows you to use Lingo to interpret data from an XML-formatted file.

* **Save As Java**—You can export some of your Director movies to cross-platform Java applets.

For more information about using Xtras, **see** Chapter 25, "Xtras," **p. 493**

GETTING HELP

Director comes with a full-featured online help application. Although the manuals and this book contain just about everything you need to know, sometimes the online help is the quickest way to find the details of a feature. The Director help files are informative and comprehensive.

To access help, use the Help menu. Or, on most computers, you can press Alt+H or the Help key.

In addition, a lot of information is available in the support section of Macromedia's Web site (http://www.macromedia.com). The Web site has a Tech Notes section that includes a variety of helpful tips and tricks. When you are having a problem and you think, "I bet I'm not the first one to run into this!," check the Tech Notes. They are compiled by Macromedia tech support from common and interesting support calls.

Also, many other Web sites offer information, tips, and developer forums. See Appendix C, "Online Resources," for more information and a list of places to start.

TROUBLESHOOTING THE DIRECTOR ENVIRONMENT

- Some preferences, such as Cast window thumbnail sizes, do not persist across movies. If you change this preference, and then open an old movie, the Cast window reflects the preferences set for that movie.

- If you get an error when you start Director that claims a duplicate Xtra is in the Xtras folder, the only way to determine which Xtra is a duplicate is to make an educated guess. If you don't find two of the same name, it might be two of similar names, such as "sound xtra" and "sounds xtra." You might have to use trial and error to find the culprit.

- When you use an item from the library, a copy is made and placed in your current Cast. If you need to use that item again, use the version from your Cast, not the library, to avoid a chance that a second instance of the library item might be added. This is especially true if you change the library item after it is in your Cast. Even if you change the name of the item, Director does not recognize that the item already exists in your Cast.

DID YOU KNOW?

- If you ever want to reset your preferences to the default settings, and you are using a Mac, just throw away the "Director 8.0 Preferences" file in the Preferences folder in your system folder. In the past, this has been the only way to retrieve a window that is lost from sight.

- You can also set the font type, size, and style of text in the Message window. This is not a preference, but you can select the text in the Message window and change it. New text placed in the Message window picks up the font used where the cursor in the Message window is located.

- You can modify the HTML templates used by the Publish command to suit your own needs. You will find these files in the Publish Templates folder in your Director folder. You can even find the loader movies there. Be careful when messing with these, however, they contain special tags and code that are required if the templates are to work correctly.

- You can also find files in a folder called Props that describe the way the Property Inspector creates its property options. They are interesting to look at, but fool around with these at your own risk.

- You can place any cast library in the Libs folder to create a library. It can include members of any type, including scripts, bitmaps, sounds, and so on.

- Mac users can also set how much memory is available in Director. Select the Director application in the Finder and choose File, Get Info. Under the Memory category, you can set the Preferred Size much larger. I prefer at least 20MB. This helps when you are working with large images or importing many images at a time.

10

PROPERTIES OF SPRITES AND FRAMES

IN THIS CHAPTER

Source movies for this chapter can be found on the CD-ROM in the "Book Movies" folder under folder 10.

Simple animations and presentations can be created with plain sprites and ordinary frames. However, a large number of special settings can do everything from change the speed of the movie to determine the color of a bitmap. Some of these properties are part of the special channels in the Score. Other properties are applied directly to individual sprites. This chapter covers all these types of settings.

CONTROLLING FRAME TEMPO

The special Tempo channel in the Score enables you to control the forward flow of the movie. All settings are performed through the Frame Properties: Tempo dialog box shown in Figure 10.1. To access it, just double-click the Tempo channel in the Score.

Figure 10.1
The Frame Properties: Tempo dialog box is the only place to control the Tempo channel in the Score.

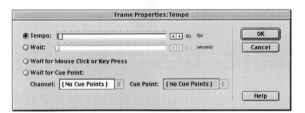

The Tempo button determines how long the movie waits on a frame. You can set this to one of four options. The first is the most common, and causes the movie to wait for a fraction of a second on a frame.

This standard tempo is measured in frames per second (fps). You can set the movie to run from one to 999 frames per second. The movie attempts to run at this speed, but is restricted by the speed of the computer on which it is running. Director displays every single frame, never skipping any. So, if a frame contains a lot of graphic changes, and the computer takes a full half a second to draw it, the relative fps is 2fps, even if you are set to run at 15fps.

Instead of using the Wait tempo or the Wait for Mouse Click or Key Press tempo setting, use the "Loop for X Seconds" and "Wait for Mouse Click or Key Press" behaviors that come with Director 8. Both of these behaviors differ from using the Tempo channel in that any frame animation will continue to play.

The Wait button enables you to make the frame wait for between 1 and 60 seconds. This is sort of an extension of the last option. Rates such as these are too slow for real animation. However, for an automatic slideshow that changes images every few seconds, this is perfect. It's also commonly used at the end of an animation to pause the movie on the last frame for a few seconds before continuing to whatever is next.

The Wait for Mouse Click or Key Press button was discussed in Chapter 2, "Presentations with Director." It pauses the frame until the mouse is clicked or the keyboard is used. This is a simple, nonbehavior, and non-Lingo way to make presentations.

The Wait for Cue Point setting ties the tempo of the movie to a sound or QuickTime sprite. You can make the movie wait on a frame until a point in the sound is reached. To use it, you need to have one of these two sprites in the Score on that frame. The names of all the channels with cue points appear in the Channel pop-up menu. Select which one you want to use. Then, select the cue point in the next pop-up menu.

In addition to the cue points in sounds and QuickTime sprites, you always have the standard {Next} and {End} choices. They enable you to have the frame end when the next cue point is hit, or when the sound or video is done playing.

The {End} choice is very useful, because you can have any frame wait until a sound or video clip is done playing. Chapter 5, "Sound Members," has information about how to add cue points to sounds.

> ➪ For more information on sound cue points, **see** "Waiting for Sounds and Cue Points," **p. 115** (Chapter 5)

> ➪ For more information about using library behaviors, **see** "Using the Behavior Library," **p. 188** (Chapter 11, "Advanced Techniques")

USING FRAME PALETTES

Under the Tempo channel is the Palette channel. The Palette channel enables you to set the palette for each frame in a movie. To access the Frame Palette dialog box, double-click the Palette channel in the Score. Although some developers can go their entire lives without this feature, others use it constantly.

Suppose you are making an educational CD-ROM about the planets in our solar system. You want to display the best possible images of each planet, but the movie must run on machines that use 256-color monitors. You can display a nice image of Mars by using a palette with a lot of reds. However, an image of Saturn should have a lot of yellows. You can make custom palettes for each of these and then display them in frames that use these palettes. The palette should be assigned to both the bitmap and the frame it is on.

When you use multiple palettes in a movie, one of the problems you are faced with is how to switch between them. Performing a simple switch shows only one or more images in the old palette before switching to the new one. It looks like a screen flash.

The simple solution is to go to a frame that is all black or all white before switching palettes. Because all palettes contain both black and white, the screen will not appear to change. Then, you can go to the new frame knowing that the movie has already switched palettes. The Frame Properties: Palette dialog box, shown in Figure 10.2, enables you to perform even more complex palette transitions.

Unless you actually like complicating your work by using Frame palettes, it is best to avoid them. Because all consumer machines sold in the last few years are capable of handling millions of colors or better, using 8-bit, 16-bit, and 32-bit graphics together without worrying about palettes is your best option. Even if the users have their monitors set down to 256 colors, Director can handle most situations and adjust the colors appropriately.

Figure 10.2
Access the Frame Properties dialog box for palettes by double-clicking the Palette channel in the Score.

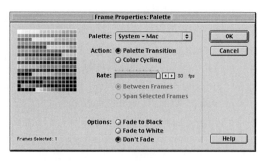

You can choose three types of transitions: one that gradually takes the movie from one palette to another (Don't Fade), one that fades to black between changes (Fade to Black), and one that fades to white between changes (Fade to White). You can choose which option you prefer at the bottom of the dialog box. To choose any of them, you must have the Palette Transition button selected. Color Cycling is another palette technique that you learn about in the next chapter.

For more information on color cycling, **see** *"Color Cycling,"* **p. 197** *(Chapter 11, "Advanced Techniques")*

Using the fade option turns the entire monitor black or white, even the area outside the Stage. The actual palette change takes place as soon as the screen is completely blank. You can control the speed of the fade with the Rate setting in the dialog box.

If you choose the Don't Fade option, one palette transitions into the other. You can also use the rate setting to control the speed of this change. If you select Between Frames, the movie pauses between the last frame and the first frame with the new palette. During this pause, the palette transition occurs. Every color gradually changes to the new color used in that position in the palette. If you select Span Selected Frames, you can actually have this transition occur while the movie is going forward and sprites are animating.

For more information on color palettes, **see** *"Types of Bitmaps,"* **p. 72** *(Chapter 3, "Bitmap Members")*

ADDING FRAME TRANSITIONS

Frame transitions are effects that help usher in a new frame. When placed in the Transitions Frame channel, they control the change from the preceding frame to the current one.

Figure 10.3 shows the Frame Properties: Transition dialog box. Most of the dialog box is used to select the type of transition. You can also control the duration, smoothness, and changing area of a transition.

Palette changes and transitions have no real effect when the monitor is set to thousands or millions of colors. In that case, the computer is not using palettes at all. Therefore, make sure the playback monitor is set to 256 colors before you begin your presentation or your palette transitions will not appear.

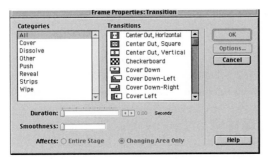

Figure 10.3
The Frame Properties dialog box for transitions comes up when you double-click the Transitions channel in the Score.

Seven transition categories are listed. If you were to add an Xtra that adds some new transitions, those categories would appear as well. Selecting All in the Categories list on the left shows all the available transitions in the Transitions list on the right.

Not all the transitions enable you to set the duration, smoothness, and change area. For those that do, the Duration setting is self-explanatory. Note that a transition might actually take longer to complete than the set time if the computer is having trouble making it happen.

The Smoothness setting can be used to help in situations where the transition is taking too long to complete. Moving the smoothness slider to the right makes the steps in the transition more dramatic. Keeping the slider all the way to the left ensures that the transition uses the smallest steps possible. You should move the slider as far left as possible while ensuring that the transition is still occurring quickly enough for you.

The Affects radio buttons at the bottom of the Frame Properties: Transition dialog box enable you to decide whether the transition affects the whole Stage (Entire Stage option) or just the changing area (Changing Area Only option). It makes no difference for dissolve-like transitions. However, for any transition that actually moves images around the Stage, such as the Push category, it matters. If you have changed only one area of the Stage between frames and use a Push transition with Changing Area Only turned on, the push happens only in that rectangle of the Stage that was changed.

After you have set a transition in the Score, Director creates a transition cast member in the Cast. You can access the properties of this transition through the Score again, or by double-clicking the cast member. Any changes are applied to the member, which in turn affects how the transition plays in the Score.

You can create a new cast member for every frame transition by double-clicking in empty Transition channel cells in the Score. Or, you can reuse transitions by dragging the member from the Cast onto the Score, or by copying and pasting it around in the Score. If you use a transition member in more than one place in the Score, remember that the transition in each frame is affected by any changes to that one cast member.

This can be a great timesaving technique. If you use a certain transition in several places in the Score, having it

Setting a transition on a frame that loops is a bad idea. The transition will occur every time the frame loops, even if this does not make a visible change after the first time. The result will be sluggish performance and maybe a blinking cursor.

as one member enables you to adjust the duration, smoothness, and even the transition type itself in one place and have it affect the whole movie.

⇨ *For more information on the Score, **see** "The Score," **p. 25** (Chapter 1, "Animation with Director")*

⇨ *For more information on transitions, **see** "Advanced Presentations," **p. 58** (Chapter 2)*

SETTING SPRITE INKS

Any sprite is drawn on the Stage according to the rules set by the sprite's ink. The ink takes into account the image itself, often the images and Stage color behind it, and sometimes the sprite's foreground and background colors.

The most common inks are Copy, Matte, and Background Transparent. Anything else can be considered a special effect. However, sometimes a special effect is just what you need to make things work the way you want them to.

You can set the ink of a sprite in many ways. The Score and Sprite Inspector windows have pop-up menus for setting inks. You can also use ⌘+click on the Mac or Ctrl+click in Windows directly on the Stage to bring up an instant pop-up menu.

To help you understand how inks change the appearance of sprites, Figure 10.4 shows the same pair of sprites 20 times. One sprite is in front of the other. The sprite in front is a black circle that is half filled with a light shade of gray and half filled with white. The second sprite is behind that one and is half dark gray and half light gray. Each of the 20 pairs shows what happens when an ink is applied to the first sprite.

Figure 10.4
Twenty pairs of sprites show how each ink changes the appearance of sprites on the Stage. Note that the Mask ink is shown when no mask bitmap has been provided for Director.

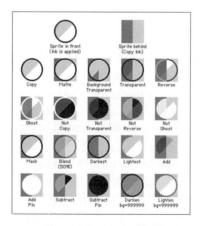

Figure 10.4 does not give the complete picture, however. To do so first requires a color image. But even then, many inks behave differently depending on the color combinations between the sprite and the background image, and the color and background color of the sprite. The figure does give you a basic guide, however.

The following list includes descriptions of all the inks. The list describes what happens to a single pixel in the image. This description is applied to every pixel in your sprite to create the complete effect. The descriptions also assume that white is being used as the background color of the sprite, which is the default setting for all new sprites.

- **Copy**—Each pixel, including all white pixels, completely overrides the pixels under the sprite.

- **Matte**—A mask is created for the sprite that makes white pixels on the outside of the image transparent. All other pixels, including white ones completely enclosed in the image, are shown as Copy ink.

- **Background Transparent**—All pixels, except for white pixels, are shown as Copy ink. The rest are transparent.

- **Transparent**—A pixel's red, green, and blue values are compared to the pixel behind it. The darkest value of each color is used. So, a light red on a dark red shows up as dark red.

- **Reverse**—Performs a logical "exclusive or" between each red, green, and blue color value of the pixel and the one under it. The resulting value is then reversed. This transforms colors in all sorts of odd ways that are hard to predict.

- **Ghost**—Like Reverse, this performs a complex mathematical transformation of the color values. In this case, a logical "or" is performed between the color under the pixel and the opposite of the pixel's color.

- **Not Inks**—These ink effects are based on the immediately preceding four ink effects. First, the color values of the sprite are reversed. Then, the Copy, Transparent, Reverse, or Ghost ink effect is reapplied to the selected sprite.

- **Mask**—Uses the next cast member in the Cast window to block or unblock background colors. Rules for a Mask are as follows: must be the same size as the masked cast member, must be the next cast member position in the Cast window, and must be 1-bit. If there is a black pixel in the mask, the same pixel position of the sprite will be the color of the sprite. Otherwise, it will be completely transparent.

- **Blend**—Applies a blend to the sprite. The amount used in the blend is set in Sprite Properties from the Modify menu or in the Score or Property Inspector. The blend percentage determines the amount of each color used from the sprite and the pixels under it.

- **Darkest**—Takes the darkest color values from the pixel and the pixel behind it.

- **Lightest**—Takes the lightest color values from the pixel and the pixel behind it.

- **Add**—Takes the red, green, and blue color values of the pixel and the pixel under it and adds them. If this is greater than 255, the number wraps back around starting at 0.

- **Add Pin**—The same as Add with the exception that if the color value exceeds 255, 255 is used.

- **Subtract**—Takes the red, green, and blue color values of the pixel and subtracts them from the pixel under it. If this is less than 0, the number wraps back around from 255.

- **Lighten**—This ink uses the foreground and background colors of the sprite. It does not use color information from the pixels under the sprite. In addition to the color translation, it behaves like the Matte ink by making exterior white pixels transparent. It takes the red, green, and blue values of each pixel and multiplies it by the red, green, and blue values of the sprite's background color. Then it adds the color values from the foreground color.

- **Darken**—The same as Lighten, but in addition, the red, green, and blue values of the background color are reversed and then added to the color for each pixel.

Ink descriptions are quite complex and hard to understand unless you are a mathematician. Almost all Director users stick to the Copy, Matte, and Background Transparent inks.

The real power of the other inks can only be appreciated by experimentation. Figure 10.5, for instance, shows a creative use of the Lightest ink. In this example, a member is placed on the Stage in two places. The sprite on the left uses Copy ink. The sprite on the right uses Lightest ink. Under the sprite on the right is a black circle. Because the image is lighter than the black circle, it shows over it. However, the rest of the image is over only the white Stage, which is lighter than the sprite.

Figure 10.5
A member is placed on the Stage in two places. The placement on the right uses the Lightest ink and is positioned over a black circle. The result is that only the pixels over the circle are visible.

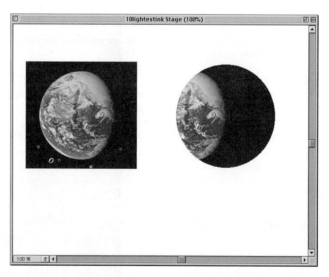

*For more information on using inks, **see** "Controlling Sprite Properties," **p. 244** (Chapter 13, "Essential Lingo Syntax")*

USING THE SPRITE BLEND

In addition to inks, you can use blends to modify the appearance of a sprite. Blends enable you to mix the sprite with whatever is behind it. You control the percent of the blend, with 100% being totally opaque.

To use blends, you should set the ink of the sprite to Blend. Director enables you to use other inks, but the use of a Blend overrides them. The Blend ink is similar to Matte in that Director creates a mask to fit the shape of the image. You can also use Copy ink if you want no mask, or use Background Transparent ink if you want all the white pixels to be transparent. Both these inks work as expected in addition to having the blend.

One effective use of blends is to use images in both the normal way and as background images. You can do this by stretching an image to the size of the Stage, while at the same time reducing its blend to somewhere around 50%. Figure 10.6 shows this type of effect.

Figure 10.6
Two sprites are used to show the same image. One is stretched and faded with a blend.

The Stage in Figure 10.6 shows two sprites. The first one is selected and then stretched on the Stage to cover the whole Stage area. Then its ink is set to Blend. Finally, the blend of that sprite is set to 50%. Both the ink and blend settings can be controlled in the Score or the Sprite Inspector. The second sprite is at normal size with Copy ink.

⇨ *For more information on using blends,* ***see*** *"Controlling Sprite Properties," **p. 244** (Chapter 13)*

SETTING SPRITE COLORS

You can also set the foreground and background colors of your sprites. You can change these colors by selecting the color chips in the Score window, Sprite Inspector, or Tool palette. The defaults are to have the foreground black and the background white.

By changing the colors of sprite, you ask Director to perform a type of tint. Changing the foreground color causes all pixels to be tinted to that color, except for black. All black pixels simply become that color. With the background color, all pixels are tinted except for white, which then becomes that color.

One way to use this color is to set 1-bit bitmap colors. Because 1-bit bitmaps contain only black and white pixels, you are essentially changing the two colors from black and white to whatever you want. The display of the sprite also depends on the ink used.

➡️ *For more information on altering sprite colors,* ***see*** *"Controlling Sprite Properties," **p. 244** (Chapter 13)*

ADJUSTING THE SPRITE SHAPE

In addition to changing the appearance and color of pixels in a sprite, you can also distort the sprite in a variety of ways. You can stretch, shrink, rotate, and skew many types of sprites.

To stretch a sprite, select it on the Stage and pull one of the four corners or four sides. You can make the sprite wider or taller, or hold down the Shift key and drag one of the corners to maintain proportions. You can always reset the sprite by choosing Modify, Sprite, Properties, and clicking the Restore button.

You can also set the rectangle of a sprite through the number fields at the top of the Score or in the Sprite Inspector.

Sprites can be resized over time with the same tweening techniques used in Chapter 1. You can reuse cast members for sprites that need the same image, but at a different size.

➡️ *For more information on stretching sprites,* ***see*** *"Animating with the Cast, Stage, and Score," **p. 36** (Chapter 1)*

You can also rotate bitmap sprites. Choose the Rotate tool in the tool palette and then click and drag a sprite to pull it around its registration point. Some member types, such as fields and simple shapes, cannot be rotated.

You can also set the rotation of a sprite, a group of sprites, or a single frame in a sprite animation with the toolbar at the top of the Score or with the Sprite Inspector.

Figure 10.7 shows two sprites that use the same cast member, but one is presented normally, whereas the other is rotated.

Figure 10.7
Both sprites use the same cast member, but the second has been rotated.

You can also rotate with tweening. You can have a sprite that rotates a full 360 degrees. The result is that the sprite spins around its registration point.

You can also use the Rotation tool to grab the sides of sprites to skew them. You can pull one side of the sprite rectangle independent of the other three sides. Figure 10.8 shows the same sprite skewed in a number of ways.

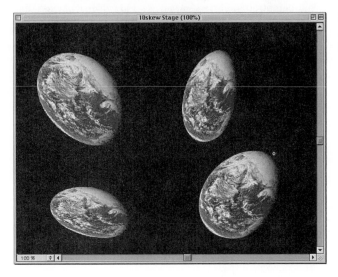

Figure 10.8
A single member is used in several sprites with different skewing.

While you are using the Rotate tool, you can also pull on the four corners or four sides. You can use this method to stretch the sprite just as you can with the Selection tool, but you can go even further. If you pull the left side of the sprite past the right side of the sprite with the Rotation tool, the new image is flipped. The same is true for all four sides, in fact.

Flipping can be accomplished this way, or by simply using the Flip buttons in the toolbar portion of the Score or in the Sprite Inspector. With flipping, you can cut down on the number of images you need. For instance, if you want to have a spaceship in a game fly both left and right, you can use a "fly right" member for flying right and then flip that member horizontally to show it flying left.

Figure 10.9 brings together the concepts of flipping and rotating to create a whole series of sprites. All these sprites use just one cast member. With earlier versions of Director, you would have had to create a separate cast member of each image.

➡️ *For more information on rotating sprites, **see** "Distorting Sprites," **p. 374** (Chapter 18, "Controlling Bitmaps")*

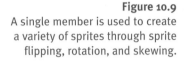

Figure 10.9
A single member is used to create a variety of sprites through sprite flipping, rotation, and skewing.

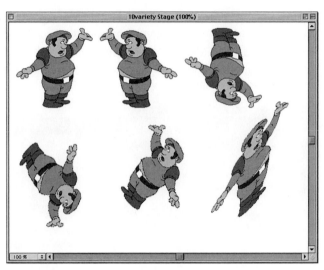

OTHER SPRITE PROPERTIES

Several other sprite properties are used to control how a sprite looks or acts. You can find them all at the top-right side of the Score window.

Editable Property

This property determines whether a text or field member can be edited by the users. Both types of members also have a cast member property of the same name.

If you turn on the Editable property for the members, they are editable even if the sprite property is not switched on. Otherwise, you can make a noneditable sprite editable in the Score with this switch.

The sprite property enables you to make a field or text member editable in some instances and not others. If you ask the users to enter their names at the start of a movie, you can still display that field later without worrying about them editing it.

Moveable Property

The Moveable property allows the users to click and drag the sprite from the position recorded in the Score. You can add interactivity to the movie this way without programming a line of Lingo.

The behavior library includes some behaviors that enable you to do similar, but more complex, functions. The main behavior is called "Draggable", but there are also behaviors that enable the users to drag multiple sprites at once, rotate a sprite, stretch it, and even pick a sprite up and toss it. Further behaviors can be applied that constrain the sprite to an area of the Stage. Check out the Animation, Interactive category of the Library palette to see these behaviors.

It's better to use Lingo or library behaviors rather than the Moveable property. The latter provides only limited functionality. Lingo, however, enables you to control when and where the sprite is moveable and also enables you to relate that movement to other sprites.

⇨ *For more information on using library behaviors*, **see** *"Using the Behaviors Library ," **p. 188** (Chapter 11, "Advanced Techniques")*

Trails Property

Not all visible elements on the Stage have to be sprites. With the Trails option turned on, the sprite leaves a copy of itself on the Stage wherever it is placed. To demonstrate, use both the Trails and Moveable property at the same time. As you drag the sprite around the Stage, it leaves a visible trail. Figure 10.10 demonstrates this effect.

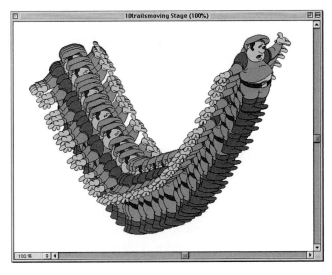

Figure 10.10
You can use the Moveable and Trails properties together to enable someone to draw on the Stage.

You can even use trails with regular animation. If you move the sprite from left to right across the Stage, and Trails is turned on for that sprite, the sprite leaves an image with each step. Figure 10.11 shows an animation that uses both trails and a blend.

Figure 10.11
The sprite is animated with tweening from left to right. The blend is
also tweened from 0%–100%.
Trails is turned on so that the animation leaves pieces behind.

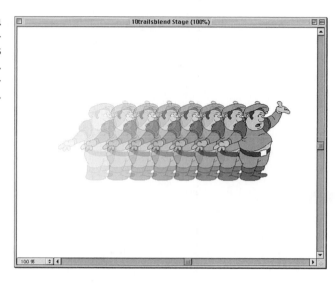

Lock Property

New to Director 8 is the capability to lock a sprite in the Score. This doesn't affect movie playback in any way, it simply stops anyone from editing or moving that sprite. The main purpose
for this is to allow developers to create movies that can then be altered by others without the
risk of moving sprites that should not be altered. It is strictly a development feature.

The trailing images are only temporary. They are erased by the first sprite that crosses their
path.

TROUBLESHOOTING PROPERTIES OF SPRITES AND FRAMES

- Setting the frame tempo below four frames per second is not recommended. Doing so
  means that some behaviors and other Lingo will react very slowly. Instead, keep the frame
  rate higher and increase the length of your animation. After all, a 30-second animation
  can be 30 1fps frames or 240 4fps frames.

- Switching from one palette to the next without a palette transition might cause the users'
  monitors to flicker.

- Some transitions, such as dissolves, are processor intensive. A fast machine, like the one
  on which you may be developing, might handle it fine, but even a slightly slower computer might take far longer. Decrease the Smoothness property as much as you can to
  counteract this.

- Transitions lock out animation and user interaction. They actually freeze the whole movie
  while the transition occurs. Keep this in mind, especially for longer transitions.

- Background Transparent inks and Matte inks look great for some images, and not so great for others. Try using a 32-bit image with an Alpha channel for more control over transparency.

- If you are developing for both Mac and Windows, it is important that you check your images to see how they look on both platforms. PC monitors show colors much darker than Mac monitors. Unfortunately, you need to have both types of machines to test on, regardless of which one you use to develop.

- When you change a bitmap sprite's shape, you make it much harder for Director to draw it. This can slow down animation considerably.

DID YOU KNOW?

- If you play your movie and watch the Control Strip as the movie plays, you can see the tempo at which your movie is actually playing, directly under the number showing how fast your movie should be playing. If your movie is playing slower than it should, adjust your tempo lower. Otherwise, a faster computer than yours will end up playing the animation at a faster frame rate.

- In addition to frame transitions, you can also have transitions on sprites. This is provided through the use of a set of behaviors in the Library palette found in the Animation, Sprite Transitions category.

- You can use the Darken ink—combined with applying a color other than black or white as the foreground color—to simulate color saturation in an image. PhotoShop users can do this with the Hue, Saturation, and Brightness tool. However, in Director you can tween color values to animate the color change!

11

ADVANCED TECHNIQUES

IN THIS CHAPTER

Source movies for this chapter can be found on the CD-ROM in the "Book Movies" folder under folder 11.

The previous 10 chapters have covered just about all the basic elements of Director. To perform most of the more advanced operations, you need Lingo. However, some advanced techniques don't require Lingo knowledge. This chapter examines these techniques, and the next chapter introduces Lingo.

USING THE BEHAVIORS LIBRARY

Chapter 2, "Presentations with Director," showed you how to use some behaviors that come with Director 8. These behaviors can be taken from the behaviors library, accessed by choosing Windows, Library Palette.

A behavior is a piece of Lingo code that will control either a sprite or an entire frame. It tells the sprite or frame how to behave. They are either written by typing Lingo, or using the Behavior Inspector, which produces the Lingo code automatically. This chapter shows you how to use the behaviors in the library that comes with Director 8 and how to make your own using the Behavior Inspector. In Chapter 14, "Creating Behaviors," you learn how to write behaviors with Lingo.

There are seven main categories of behaviors in the Library palette. Some of these categories include several subcategories. Let's take a look at some of the more useful behaviors. A full listing of all the behaviors appears in Appendix F, "Behavior Library Quick Reference." Let's look at them in order, starting with the Automatic subcategory of the Animation behaviors subcategory. You can see the Library palette with these behaviors showing in Figure 11.1.

Figure 11.1
The Library palette shows the first category of behaviors: automatic animation behaviors.

Animation Behaviors

There are three subcategories of Animation behaviors: automatic, interactive, and sprite transitions. They mostly deal with moving or somehow changing single sprites on the Stage.

The automatic behaviors allow you to set a sprite so that it continuously loops through a series of members, colors, or blends. There are several behaviors for making the sprite rotate.

The Cycle Graphics automatic behavior is one that you should make yourself familiar with. It allows you to define a set of members and have the sprite use these members as an animation. For instance, you could have a set of three members that show a bird flapping its wings. The sprite would then cycle through these images. The Waft automatic behavior is a nice effect when you are trying to show a leaf or snowflake drifting to the ground. There are several other behaviors that you can experiment with and find uses for in your animations.

The interactive animation behaviors allow you to set up sprites so that users can drag them around the Stage in a variety of ways. You can use the Draggable behavior for simple dragging, or the Drag to Rotate, Drag to Scale, and Drag to Stretch and Flip for other types of dragging. You can also confine users to an area with the Constrain to Sprite and Constrain to Line behaviors.

There are two behaviors in the interactive animation category that enable you to create *rollovers*, which indicate any type of feedback given to users when they move the mouse over a sprite. The first is Rollover Member Change, which causes the sprite to use a different member when the cursor is over it. The second is Rollover Cursor Change, which simply changes the cursor.

The third category for animation behaviors is sprite transitions. These are new to Director 8, and they use Director 8's capability to alter bitmap images during runtime. They imitate standard transitions such as slide and wipe, but on a single sprite rather than the whole Stage or an area of the Stage.

Controls Behaviors

The "Controls" behaviors allow you to add complex interface elements without having to write your own Lingo scripts to handle the interaction. The Radio Button Group and the Multi-State Button behaviors allow you to use bitmap images as radio buttons and check boxes, respectively. The Dropdown List behavior allows you to create pop-up menus. A variety of other behaviors enable you to make simple buttons to jump to other frames or movies.

Internet Behaviors

This category of behaviors relates to Shockwave movies, or Projectors that access the Internet. The first subcategory, Forms, gives you four behaviors that imitate the various types of elements usually found in an HTML form. You can use these to create a form-like interface in your Shockwave movie that would then submit the data to a server in an identical way to how an HTML form submits it.

The next subcategory, Multiuser, enables you to quickly create a chat room using some simple elements and a Macromedia Multiuser Server.

The third category is Streaming. This category contains several behaviors that help you deal with movies that are set to stream over the Internet. You can use these behaviors to hold the movie at a location in the Score until a piece or pieces of media have been downloaded. These behaviors are particularly useful when you want to create a simple animation that streams onto a Web page. In this case, you would want the animation to pause if it reaches a point in which it doesn't have some of the images ready to display.

Media Behaviors

There are three categories of media behaviors. Each handles a separate type of member. The Flash category sets several properties of Flash members. The QuickTime category allows you to create some custom QuickTime controls. We used one of these in Chapter 6, "Digital Video."

The Sound category allows you to control sound. Particularly useful is the Channel Volume Slider behavior, which lets you create a volume control.

Navigation Behaviors

Chapter 2 used several behaviors from the Navigation category. By applying these behaviors to buttons and frames, you can control the playback of a movie. You can create buttons that send users back and forth in a presentation, jump users to another movie, or even take users to another Web page.

Paintbox Behaviors

 The Paintbox set of behaviors uses Director 8's capability to edit images on-the-fly. To use these behaviors, first drop the Canvas behavior onto a 32-bit bitmap image. Then, use the other behaviors to create tools that users can use to edit the image.

Text Behaviors

The Text behaviors enable you to do some fairly complex things with text members. You can create a variety of special effects, such as a ticker tape or a typewriter effect. But perhaps the most useful behavior here is the "Custom Scrollbar" behavior. It enables you to forget about the standard text scrollbar, which has a fixed appearance, and use your own bitmap images as the scrollbar elements.

BUILDING YOUR OWN BEHAVIORS

Until now, you have been using behaviors that were part of the ones included with Director. You will soon be able to make your own behaviors by writing Lingo. However, you can also create your own behaviors by simply using the Behavior Inspector. To access the Behavior Inspector, choose Window, Inspector, Behavior.

The Behavior Inspector window, shown in Figure 11.2, contains three text lists and some buttons above each. In the top list, you can add and remove behaviors to/from a sprite. You can use the behavior pop-up menu button at the upper-left to create a new behavior.

If you already have behaviors assigned to a sprite, you can see them listed here. You can select and remove any behavior with the Delete key. You can also change the order in which the behaviors execute by selecting one behavior and using the up- and down-arrow buttons.

When you create a new behavior, Director asks you to name it. When you create a behavior in this way, all you are doing is creating a new cast member. Therefore, you can easily edit this name later in the Cast window.

Under the top text list is a set of two thinner text lists. If you don't see them, it might be because you have closed that section of the window. You can expand the window using the tiny expand buttons on the left side.

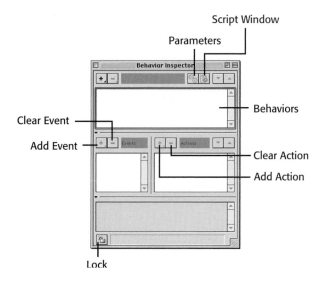

Script Window
Parameters
Behaviors
Clear Event
Add Event
Clear Action
Add Action
Lock

Figure 11.2
The Behavior Inspector enables you to build custom behaviors without using Lingo.

The left text list is for events and the right list is for actions. An *event* is something that happens, such as a mouse click. An *action* is something that you create to react to an event.

Start by selecting one event from the event pop-up menu. You can choose from a number of events, but for now choose Mouse Up. This event corresponds to the completion of a mouse click by the users. It is typically used as the primary way to have a button perform an action.

After you have selected at least one event, you can apply an action to it. Use the action pop-up button to select an action. A number of categories appear in the menu list. Under Sound, choose the Beep action.

Why not use the Mouse Down event? User interface standards for Mac and Windows machines specify that actions take place only after users click down and then lift up again. Otherwise, users can click and hold and the action can happen while they are still holding. It's an important user interface standard that most users will be familiar with, so it's best to use it.

Figure 11.3 shows the Behavior Inspector window with the event and action added. You now have a cast member that is a behavior. After you place it on a sprite, this behavior will play a system beep when the sprite is clicked.

Not only can you rename the behavior now, but you can also edit it. Just open the cast member and the Behavior Inspector appears again. You can add, alter, and delete events and actions.

Creating More Complex Behaviors

These behaviors, of course, can get a lot more complex. Suppose you want to create a button behavior. The goal is to have a button that changes when users roll over it, and also changes when users press down. When users lift the button up, it should return to its rollover state, because the mouse is still over the sprite. It should also then perform an action, such as going to another frame.

Figure 11.3
The Behavior Inspector window shows a simple behavior that plays a system beep when users click it.

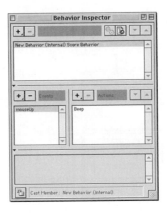

To do this, first create some bitmaps that you can use. You need a normal state of the button, a rollover state, and a down state. Figure 11.4 shows the Cast window with these three members.

Figure 11.4
The Cast window shows three states of the same button.

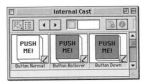

Create a new behavior with the Sprite Inspector. The first event you need to handle is a Mouse Enter event. This is the event that occurs when the users move the cursor into the rectangle or shape of the sprite. The rectangle of the sprite is used if the sprite is set to Copy ink. The shape of the sprite is used if the ink is set to Matte.

Now, assign the Change Cast Member action to the Mouse Enter event. You can find this action under the Sprite category. Director asks you for a cast member name. Assign the rollover state cast member to this action.

The sprite now changes to a rollover bitmap when users move the mouse over it. To turn this off when users leave the sprite, add a "Mouse Leave" event. To this event, add another "Change Cast Member" action. This time, assign the original, normal state of the button.

The next event is the "Mouse Down" event. Add this one and assign yet another "Change Cast Member" action. This is where you use the down state of the button. This bitmap appears on the Stage briefly, in between the user pressing down and lifting up.

The last event is the Mouse Up event. First, add a Change Cast Member action that uses the rollover bitmap member. When the user lifts up, the cursor is still over the sprite, so you don't want to change to the normal bitmap. In addition to this action, also add a second action. This is the action that corresponds to the actual function of the button. If the behavior reaches this point, it means that the user has rolled over the sprite, clicked down, and then lifted up.

Add the Go To Marker action with the Next option selected. You can find this action under the Navigation category. The result of this button is that the movie then moves forward to the next marker, just as one of the examples in Chapter 1, "Animation with Director," showed.

Figure 11.5 shows a Behavior Inspector window with this behavior set. You can see all four events listed, plus the actions for the Mouse Up event.

Figure 11.5
The Behavior Inspector shows a typical custom button behavior.

Adding Events to Behaviors

You can choose from many more actions and events when you create behaviors with the Behavior Inspector. The following is a list of all the events and when they are triggered:

- **Mouse Up**—Occurs when users release the mouse button while the cursor is positioned over the sprite.

- **Mouse Down**—Occurs when users click down on the mouse button while the cursor is positioned over the sprite.

- **Mouse Enter**—Occurs when users bring the cursor over the sprite from some position outside the sprite's area.

- **Mouse Within**—Occurs once per frame or frame loop as long as the cursor is within the sprite's rectangle or shape.

- **Mouse Leave**—Occurs when users bring the cursor to a position away from the sprite after it has just been inside the sprite. For each Mouse Leave event, there must have been a Mouse Enter.

- **Key Up**—Used for fields and text members; this event occurs when users lift up from pressing a key on the keyboard.

- **Key Down**—Used for fields and text members; this event occurs when users press down on a key on the keyboard.

- **Right Mouse Up**—Like Mouse Up, but with the right mouse button in Windows or a ⌘+click on the Mac.

- **Right Mouse Down**—Like Mouse Down, but with the right mouse button in Windows or a ⌘+click on the Mac.

- **Prepare Frame**—Occurs every frame or frame loop. It happens before the sprite is actually drawn on the Stage, so you can use it to change the appearance of a sprite before it is shown.

- **Exit Frame**—Occurs every frame or frame loop. It happens after the sprite is drawn and all other events have taken place.

- **Begin Sprite**—Occurs exactly once before the sprite is even drawn on the Stage.

- **End Sprite**—Occurs just before the movie jumps from a frame that contains the sprite to a frame that does not contain the sprite.

Adding Actions to Behaviors

You can also choose from plenty of actions. The following is a complete list of actions:

- **Navigation, Go To Frame**—You must enter a frame number. This action makes the movie jump to that frame.

- **Navigation, Go To Marker**—You must choose Next, Previous, or Loop. Next and Previous move the movie forward or backward one marker. Loop causes the movie to loop back to the current marker.

- **Navigation, Go To Movie**—You must enter a movie filename. Director takes users to the first frame in that movie.

- **Navigation, Go To Net Page**—With Shockwave, this causes the user's browser to jump to a specific Web page. While in Director or a projector, this causes the user's default browser to launch and go to that page.

- **Navigation, Exit**—This causes projectors to quit and Shockwave movies to stop playing. While in Director, it simply stops the movie.

- **Wait, On Current Frame**—The movie loops on the current frame. This is different from using the Go To Marker action with the Loop option, because that action loops back to the frame with the current marker.

- **Wait, Until Click or Keypress**—This is the same as setting the Tempo channel to the equivalent setting.

- **Wait, For Time Duration**—This is similar to setting the Tempo channel to wait for a number of seconds.

- **Sound, Play Cast Member**—The behavior plays a cast member sound.

- **Sound, Play External File**—The behavior plays an external sound file.

- **Sound, Beep**—This action plays the system beep.

- **Sound, Set Volume**—You must choose a sound level between zero and seven. The action then sets the volume to that level. You can make a series of buttons to set the volume to all different levels, or just one to set the volume to zero.

- **Frame, Change Tempo**—This enables you to set a new tempo. If you are animating at 30fps (frames per second), for instance, a button can be created to jump up the rate to 60fps.

- **Frame, Perform Transition**—This enables you to select a transition to be performed during the next frame change. Add this action before a navigation action to create transitions into the next screen.

- **Frame, Change Palette**—You can select a new palette to which the movie should change.

- **Sprite, Change Location**—You can specify a new location for the sprite. Use the format *point(x,y)* where x and y are numbers that represent the horizontal and vertical position.

- **Sprite, Change Cast Member**—You can pick a new cast member to be used by the sprite.

- **Sprite, Change Ink**—You can choose a new ink to be used by the sprite.

- **Cursor, Change Cursor**—You can pick a new cursor from a standard list. Useful for rollovers.

- **Cursor, Restore Cursor**—This releases control of the cursor so that it again appears as a standard arrow, or whatever cursor is appropriate.

Note that in addition to the events and actions listed here, you can also define your own actions with the New Action and New Event choices. However, you have to learn about Lingo programming to do that.

USING FILM LOOPS AND LINKED MOVIES

Although you already know about many different types of bitmap members, did you know that you can have a member that contains an entire Director movie?

Such members are called *film loops*. When a film loop cast member links to an external file, it is sometimes called a *linked movie*.

The simplest use of a film loop member is when it captures an entire animated sequence and places it in one sprite. Doing this is literally as easy as copying and pasting it.

First, create an animation in the Score. You can use as many different sprites and members as you want. Place them across as many different frames as needed. Use any area on the Stage, but be sure there is nothing else on the Stage in those frames.

To create a film loop of this sequence, first select the entire sequence, every sprite and every frame, in the Score. Then, copy it. Now, open the Cast window, select an empty slot, and paste it. The new film loop member appears after you give it a name.

Now you can go back to the Score and erase the entire animation sequence. In place of it, put the single film loop member. The result on the Stage is the same as your original animation even though the Score shows something much simpler.

Another way to create a film loop is to drag and drop the Score selection from the Score window to the Cast window. A third way is to save the animation all by itself in a separate movie. Then, you can import the movie the same way you import any other media. The result is a film loop member.

A film loop member relies on any other members that were used in constructing the animation. If you copy and paste or drag and drop to create the film loop, you already have the members. However, if you import a Director movie, it also brings the cast members from that movie that are needed in the film loop. Members that are not used in the Score are not imported.

Essentially, a film loop is an entire Director Score stored as a member. Even scripts and markers are included in a film loop.

If you import a movie and select Link To External File, only a single film loop member is created. All the other members are accessed directly from the linked file. This way, you can section off your project into smaller movies that appear in the main one. If your project contains three main animations, an animator can work on these as three separate files, and you can import them as linked movies into the main movie file later on.

You can choose several options for film loop members. They are accessed from the Property Inspector shown in Figure 11.6.

Figure 11.6
The Property Inspector enables you to determine what happens when the sprite is stretched and enables you to turn sound and looping on or off.

The two framing options for film loops are Crop and Scale. The Crop option keeps the film loop's images at the same size, no matter how you stretch the sprite. If you shrink the sprite, the images may be cropped. When you select this option, you can also check Center to have the film loop center itself in the sprite rectangle.

The Scale option scales the film loop, including bitmaps in it, to fit the sprite rectangle. Elements that are not scalable, such as fields, change position as the sprite is stretched.

You can choose to have the film loop play any sounds that were in the Sound channels of the movie or Score selection that was used to create the film loop. If you created the film loop by copying and pasting a Score selection, you needed to include the Sound channels to have them be a part of the film loop. You can also decide whether a film loop is to loop or play only once.

In addition to these options, a linked movie has the Enabled Scripts option. This option enables any behaviors attached to sprites inside the film loop to operate. It also includes any frame scripts. With this functionality, you can really include entire Director movies, with scripts and all, as a single sprite in the Score.

Although each bitmap image uses a palette, the actual palette used to display all the sprites on the Stage can be set with the Palette channel in the Score. This works only when the monitor is set to 8-bit or 256 colors.

➪ *For more information about linked movies, **see** "Using Linked Movies," p. 485 (Chapter 24, "Movies in a Window and Alternatives")*

COLOR CYCLING

Color cycling is an old technique that relies on palettes to shift the colors of an image. A *palette* is a list of 256 colors that an image uses to display its pixels.

➪ *To learn how to create and modify palettes, **see** "Using Palette Members," p. 143 (Chapter 8, "Other Member Types")*

Because each pixel in an image is assigned a color from the palette, Director remembers only the number assignment of that color, not what the actual color is. In other words, if a pixel uses color 57 from the palette, Director doesn't care what color 57 is: red, yellow, green, whatever. Instead, when it comes time to draw that pixel on the Stage, it looks up the actual color that position 57 represents and uses it to draw the pixel.

This means that you have the opportunity to tell Director that color 57 is actually something different than what was originally used in the image. When you do this, all the pixels that use that color from the palette will change. So if color 57 was originally a yellow, and you change it to green, all the yellow pixels in the image will change to green pixels.

One way to do this is to prepare two palettes, each with different colors in different positions. When you want to switch colors, simply switch palettes. The images on the Stage obey the color settings for the new palette.

Color cycling provides a way to alter the palette used. You can select a range of colors in the palette and make them move through a cycle. To demonstrate, bring up the Frame Properties: Palette dialog box (see Figure 11.7) by double-clicking the Palette channel in the Score.

First, choose Color Cycling. Then, you can select a range of colors in the small palette on the left side of the dialog box. It also includes options for the rate of the cycle, how many cycles occur on one frame, and whether the cycle loops back to the beginning or reverses direction when it reaches the end of the cycle.

The way the color cycle proceeds is that each color moves down one position. If you select colors 11 to 19 to cycle, Director's first step is to take the color in position 12 and place it in position 11, the color in position 13 is placed in 12, and so on. The color in position 11, meanwhile, is placed in position 19. The colors move through the selected range until they are back in their original positions.

Figure 11.7
The Frame Properties: Palette dialog box enables you to select a range of colors to use in a color cycle.

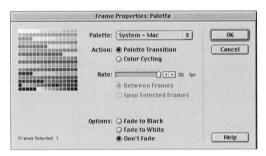

One way to use this unusual technique is to create all your images with this effect in mind. Decide that you don't want to use a group of colors in the palette, such as colors 11 to 19. Then, make all your images with these colors set to "reserved" in your custom palette.

The one image that you want to be affected by color cycling then uses these colors. The result is that when the cycle happens, all the other sprites show no change because they don't use these color positions. Meanwhile, the one sprite that does use them shows the cycle.

A good example is an image that has a flying saucer. You have one or more sprites that make up a background. These sprites use bitmaps that don't include the colors in the palette that you want to cycle. The one sprite that has the saucer uses these colors, and perhaps only these colors. Then, when the cycle occurs, the saucer changes colors and the background stays the same.

Using color cycling requires you to be an expert in using Director's color palettes and creating images with palettes. Director 8 gives you a number of options that make most color effects much easier to accomplish and give you more control over them than earlier versions did. For example, you can use the Lighten or Darken inks with a gradual change to the foreground or background colors.

The number one mistake made when trying to use color cycling is doing so with a monitor set to something other than 8-bit or 256 colors. Be sure to adjust this setting before you begin working with color cycling.

Changing the palette through color cycling affects the entire screen, not just the Stage. So, if the desktop shows through in your movie, users might see some of those colors change as well.

SHOCKWAVE STREAMING

With the introduction of cable modems, digital subscriber lines, and other modes of fast Internet access, people are able to download and view larger and larger pieces of media over the Internet. However, even at these high speeds, the loading process is still much slower than from a hard drive or CD-ROM drive. Plus, many people will continue to use 33.6Kbps or 56Kbps modems for a long time to come.

For these reasons, you may want to consider streaming your Shockwave movies rather than asking the users to download the entire movie before it begins playing. This is especially useful for linear animations, where the first frames of animation need only a few images.

Streaming is the process whereby a movie begins before all the media is loaded through the network. The movie starts with a minimum amount of media, and then adds more as it continues. This enables the movie to start sooner, rather than requiring users to wait for the entire movie to download.

However, you do not want to use streaming unless you have a good reason. If you expect the whole movie to load quickly, for instance, there is no advantage to streaming and it may cause an undesirable effect because images appear at random on the first few frames as they are being loaded. In my experience, streaming also increases nonreproducible bug reports from your users, including crashes and such, especially if you are using a lot of Lingo.

Streaming your Director movies is as easy as selecting the streaming option in the Movie Playback Properties dialog box, shown in Figure 11.8. You can access this dialog box by choosing Modify, Movie, Playback. From there, just choose Play While Downloading Movie.

Figure 11.8
The Movie Playback Properties dialog box provides the main streaming settings.

You can also choose to have the movie wait until a certain number of frames are downloaded before the animation begins by entering the number in the Download Frames Before Playing text box. This helps the movie play more smoothly. If you have a one-minute movie at 15fps, you might decide that you want 300 frames (one third of the movie) to download before playing. Shockwave makes sure that all the members it needs for those frames are present before it begins playing.

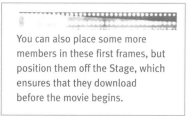

You can also place some more members in these first frames, but position them off the Stage, which ensures that they download before the movie begins.

When the movie needs to display a member that has not yet been loaded, it will simply not show that member. However, if you choose Show Placeholders, Director places a rectangle in place of the not-yet-loaded members.

You can also use a number of behaviors to control streaming. Director's built-in library has a whole set of streaming behaviors. Most of them wait on the frame until some other media is ready. You can specify a certain frame or a specific piece of media that you want to make sure has been loaded before continuing.

A typical way to use these behaviors is to have an opening animation sequence. Set the movie to start playing only when that many frames have been loaded. Then, at the end of this loop, use a behavior to have the movie wait until all the members used by the last frame in the next sequence have been loaded. Because Director loads members in the order in which they are used in the Score, you can be sure that the whole animation sequence is available when the last frame in the sequence has been loaded.

⇨ *For more information about Shockwave file size and streaming, **see** "Improving Performance," p. 692 (Chapter 34, "Performance Issues")*

TROUBLESHOOTING ADVANCED TECHNIQUES

- In the Behavior Inspector, you can use the little padlock button at the bottom-left corner to lock the contents of the window to the currently selected sprite. Then, you can use the Score and Stage to look at other sprites without changing the Behavior Inspector.

- It is easy to add multiple behaviors to a sprite by accident. Keep that in mind and check for it if you see strange things happening to a sprite.

- If you want film loops to be Background Transparent, you must set the individual sprites to use Background Transparent ink before you copy and paste or drag them to the Cast to create a film loop. The same is true for other inks, such as Matte.

- Most developers who attempt to use color cycling are really not looking for the effect that it provides. A much more useful effect is the one provided by the Color Cycling behavior in the Animation category.

- Is your streaming movie not working correctly after it is on the Internet? The first thing you should do is try to upload the movie with streaming turned off, just as a test. If it works, you know it is the streaming that is causing you problems. Now try to determine which elements are not loading in time and use the library behaviors to have the movie wait for them.

DID YOU KNOW?

- If you want to use streaming and you want to make sure that some members get loaded before the movie starts, just place these members in frame 1, but position them offscreen. Then set the movie to begin playing only after frame 1 has been loaded.

- Film loops can include multiple sprites. They can even include other film loops!

- When you use a behavior from the library, it is imported into your Cast. You can use the Behavior Inspector to edit these behaviors, although some are too complex for you to alter without knowing Lingo.

- You can see the behaviors from the Library palette in the Libs folder inside your Director folder. Each category is just an external cast library. You can open these and alter their contents, adding your own behaviors if you want.

USING BASIC LINGO

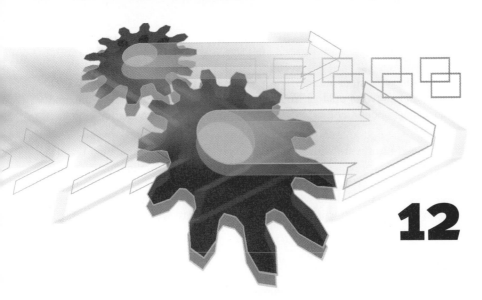

12

LEARNING LINGO

IN THIS CHAPTER

Director is much, much more than an animation or presentation tool. You can make full applications, Web applets, and software utilities. You can build games, educational software, and business applications. Just about anything that can be done with software can be done in Director.

The key to writing powerful software with Director is *Lingo*, Director's programming language. Lingo started out as a simple set of scripting commands used to control animation. Now it is a complete object-oriented language rivaling traditional ones, such as C and Pascal, as well as new languages, such as Java. Chapter 13, "Essential Lingo Syntax," continues this discussion with a more complete list of all the important Lingo commands with which you should be familiar.

WHAT IS LINGO?

Lingo is a programming language. It's a way of speaking to the computer by giving it commands and asking it questions. In Director, you can speak to the Director environment: the Score, the Cast, and the Stage.

Lingo is an English-like programming language. All the commands, functions, and other keywords in Director are English words, groups of words, or abbreviations. This makes Lingo easier to learn than other languages.

Lingo is a cast member type, which means that when you create the Lingo code that controls your movie, it is stored in cast members called *scripts*. Scripts are cast members that contain a piece of text that is valid Lingo code. They exist alongside the bitmaps, sounds, and shapes of your Director movie in the Cast. In some cases, they are also placed in the Score.

Lingo is power. Out of all the possible things that Director can do, only a handful can be done without using Lingo. Almost any project that has been done with software can be accomplished using Lingo and Director. In some cases, it isn't the best tool for the job, but in other cases Lingo can be used to program a piece of software with less effort than traditional methods.

Learning Lingo is the key to using Director fully. Unless you stick to bare bones, PowerPoint-like presentations or linear animations, you need to learn Lingo to use Director.

Fortunately, Lingo is easy to learn. Hundreds of Lingo keywords are in the language, but you need only a few to get started. You can start with the Lingo Message window.

FIRST STEPS WITH THE MESSAGE WINDOW

Although Lingo scripts are usually stored in cast members, you can also run short, one-line programs in something called the Message window. Open the Message window by choosing Windows, Message, or by pressing ⌘+M on the Mac or Ctrl+M in Windows.

The Message window is plain, with just a large area to type and view text. When you type while the Message window is open, the characters appear there. It is doing more than just echoing text, however. The Message window is, in fact, a Lingo interpreter. It takes Lingo commands and evaluates them in the same way as the scripts you will soon learn how to write.

Type **put** **42** into the Message window. When you press Return/Enter, the Message window interprets what you just typed and returns **-- 42** on the next line. Figure 12.1 shows how the Message window now looks.

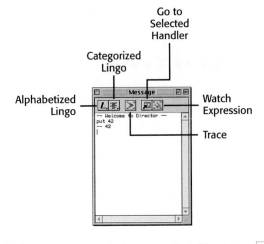

Go to
Selected
Handler

Categorized
Lingo

Alphabetized
Lingo

Watch
Expression

Trace

Figure 12.1
The Message window enables you to type single lines of Lingo code and see the results.

The double dash, a - -, appears before lines that Director returns to you in the Message window. Later, you will learn how to use the double dash to comment your code.

Now you know your first Lingo command: *put*. The *put* command is used to place text into the Message window. It has some other uses that you will learn much later.

You asked Director to put the number 42 into the Message window. It did just that. But it did more than just echo a number back at you. It actually understood what you meant by 42. To prove it, try this:

```
put 42+1
-- 43
```

There are two pop-up menus at the top of the Message window. The Alphabetize Lingo button looks like an *L* and the Categorized Lingo button is next to it (refer to Figure 12.1). By using these two pop-up menus, you can browse through all the Lingo commands, functions, and properties. The first pop-up menu shows you an alphabetical list, and the second a category list.

Now you see that Director can add. It doesn't merely spit back *42+1*, but instead understands that these are numbers and that the plus symbol means that they should be added together.

You can do other things with Lingo besides math. Try this in the Message window:

```
beep
```

You should hear your computer's default system beep. If you don't, it is probably because your volume is turned down or your system beep is turned off.

Notice that the Message window does not return anything in the next line, because you didn't ask it to. The command *beep* simply plays the system beep. It does not place anything in the Message window as the *put* command does.

The Message window is nice for taking your first Lingo steps, and it continues to be useful as you learn new Lingo commands. Even expert Lingo programmers use the Message window constantly to program in Lingo.

➪ *For more information about using numbers in Lingo,* **see** *"Integers and Floats,"* **p. 220** *(Chapter 13, "Essential Lingo Syntax")*

UNDERSTANDING SCRIPT TYPES

The Message window enables you to type and interpret one line of Lingo code at a time, but you need to string together many lines of Lingo code to make programs. You store these lines of Lingo code in cast members called *scripts*. There are three different types of script members: movie scripts, behavior scripts, and parent scripts. In addition, other cast members, such as bitmaps, can have scripts embedded inside them. These are usually referred to as *cast scripts*.

The difference between all these script types is not in what they look like or how they behave, but it is in *when* they act. Here is a summary:

- **Movie script**—Contains handlers that can be accessed by any other script. Cannot be assigned to specific sprites or frames.

- **Behavior script**—Assigned to sprites or frames. Controls the sprite or frame that it is assigned to.

- **Parent script**—Can be used only by object-oriented programming techniques.

- **Cast script**—Exists inside a cast member. Only affects that one cast member, but affects every sprite instance of the cast member.

A movie script is a global presence in a movie. If a movie script produces a system beep whenever the mouse is clicked, this script sounds the beep whenever the mouse is clicked anywhere in the movie. Thus the name "movie" script: It acts on the entire movie.

A behavior script is similar in concept to the behaviors that you read about in Chapter 2, "Presentations with Director." It does nothing until it is placed on a sprite or in a Frame Script channel. When a behavior script is placed on a sprite, the Lingo commands inside the script are active only as far as the sprite is concerned. If you have a behavior that plays a beep when the mouse is clicked, for example, and you apply that behavior to a sprite, the beep sounds only when users click that sprite. Behavior scripts are sometimes called sprite or Score scripts for this reason. They act only on a sprite in the Score to which they are assigned.

Behavior scripts can also be assigned to the Frame Script channel of the Score. When they are, they act like movie scripts, but only for the frame or frames to which they are assigned. Behaviors used this way are sometimes called Score scripts.

Parent scripts are a different type of script. They actually don't do anything until you use some object-oriented programming Lingo commands to tell them how and when they are to be used.

Cast scripts, on the other hand, are easy to use. You can create one by selecting a member, such as a bitmap, and clicking the Script button at the top of the Cast window. This opens the Script window and enables you to add a script to that particular member.

Cast scripts act only on that one cast member. If you place a script with a cast member that makes the system beep when users click the mouse, that action affects only that one cast member when it is on the Stage. If you use that cast member more than once in the Score, the script that is a part of that cast member is active in all those places.

Cast scripts are not used much with modern Lingo programming. Behaviors can accomplish the same tasks and are much more flexible. However, they do come in useful when you want to create some quick buttons without crowding a Cast with both the button members and the scripts that are assigned to them.

To create a script, select an empty location in the Cast window and press ⌘+0 (zero) on the Mac or Ctrl+0 in Windows. The Script window appears. It is a fairly simple window, but has a few tricks hidden in the buttons at the top. The Script window also appears when you edit the script of another type of cast member. Figure 12.2 shows the Script window.

Jump to Selected
Handler   Uncomment

                  Toggle
        Comment   Breakpoint

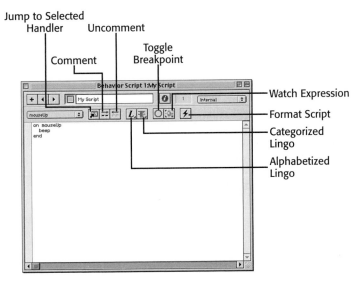

Watch Expression

Format Script

Categorized Lingo

Alphabetized Lingo

Figure 12.2
The Script window enables you to edit movie scripts, behaviors, and parent scripts.

The top of the Script window has the typical Director cast member buttons that take you forward and backward in the Cast, enable you to add a new cast member, and enable you to switch cast libraries. The rest of the buttons deal with more advanced Lingo functions, such as handlers and debugging. You will learn about them as you learn about those functions.

The two buttons called Alphabetized Lingo and Categorized Lingo enable you to hunt for and automatically insert any Lingo keywords into your script. They come in handy when you just can't remember the name of a command, but you have a good idea of how it starts or under which category it falls. They are also handy in refreshing your memory as to the proper syntax for using Lingo commands.

A script cast member's properties can be changed with the Property Inspector, shown in Figure 12.3. Script cast members have one script-related property: the type of script. The three options, of course, are Movie, Behavior, and Parent. You can also use the Link Script As button to use an external file, rather than an internal member, as the script text.

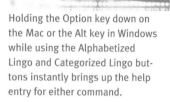

Holding the Option key down on the Mac or the Alt key in Windows while using the Alphabetized Lingo and Categorized Lingo buttons instantly brings up the help entry for either command.

Figure 12.3
The Property Inspector enables you to change the script's type.

Linked scripts, which are new to Director 8, can be used to allow several movies to share a single script. The code resides in an external text file that you can edit with any text editor. Linked scripts also permit what is called *source control*—you can check your scripts into a source database, keep track of changes to scripts, perform backups, and so on.

USING MESSAGES AND HANDLERS

The Script window shown earlier in Figure 12.2 contains a very small, very simple script. It states

```
on mouseUp
    beep
end
```

You might recognize the "mouseUp" message from your work with behaviors in Chapter 11, "Advanced Techniques."

A message is a signal sent by an event. When users click the mouse button and then release it, a "mouseUp" message is sent. Similarly, the initial click down sends a "mouseDown" message.

Messages such as these get sent to any Director object that is related to the action. A "mouseUp" message, for instance, is sent to the sprite that was clicked. If users click a bitmap that happens to be sprite three on the Stage, that sprite gets a "mouseUp" message. If a behavior happens to be attached to that sprite, Director checks to see whether that behavior handles a "mouseUp" message.

A behavior, or any script, handles a message such as this by defining a handler. Handlers start with the word *on*. In the preceding example, the first line of the handler is *on mouseUp*. This simply means that the handler is to handle any "mouseUp" messages sent to that sprite.

Many times, programmers like to place the name of the handler after the end. So, the last line of Figure 12.3 would read "end mouseUp". Lingo doesn't require this, but some programmers use it anyway.

The contents of the handler—in this case, the lone command *beep*—are the Lingo commands that are executed when the handler is triggered by the message. The series of commands ends with *end*, which signifies the end of the handler.

You can place more than one handler in a script. So, for instance, you can have an *on mouseUp* and an *on mouseDown* handler both in one behavior. They are triggered by different messages, so they won't get in each other's way.

➪ *For more information about creating behaviors,* **see** *"Creating Simple Behaviors,"* **p. 259** *(Chapter 14, "Creating Behaviors")*

Types of Messages

There are many more types of messages besides "mouseUp" and "mouseDown". They all correspond to some event that takes place in Director. The following list includes some of the most common events and messages:

- **mouseDown**—The user clicks the mouse button. In Windows, this corresponds to the left mouse button.

- **mouseUp**—The user releases the mouse button after clicking. Every "mouseUp" message is preceded by a "mouseDown" message, although they don't necessarily have to be on the same sprite.

- **mouseEnter**—The cursor enters the area of a sprite.

- **mouseLeave**—The cursor leaves the area of a sprite.

- **mouseWithin**—A message sent continuously, once per frame, as long as the cursor is over a sprite.

- **mouseUpOutside**—A message sent when users click in a sprite, but move the cursor away and then release the mouse button.

- **beginSprite**—A message sent once when the sprite is first encountered by the playback head in the Score.

- **prepareFrame**—A message sent when each new frame starts, before the frame is drawn on the Stage.

- **enterFrame**—A message sent when each new frame starts, after the frame is drawn on the Stage.

- **exitFrame**—A message sent when a frame is done and the movie is about to move on to the next frame.

- **prepareMovie**—A message sent before the first frame of the movie is drawn.

- **startMovie**—A message sent immediately after the first frame of a movie is drawn.

- **stopMovie**—A message sent when the movie ends.

- **idle**—A message sent continuously while the movie is advancing from the start of a frame to the end of a frame. The number of times it is sent depends on how slow the tempo is and how fast the computer is.

- **keyDown**—A message sent when users press a key on the keyboard.

- **keyUp**—A message sent when users release a key on the keyboard.

Message Hierarchy

In addition to the many messages that events in Director can send, it is important to understand where these messages go. A "mouseUp" message, for instance, can be received by a behavior attached to the sprite that was clicked. However, if the sprite has no behavior with an *on mouseUp* handler in it, the message continues to look for a receiving handler.

The next place it looks is in the cast member. It checks to see whether an *on mouseUp* handler has been placed in the cast script. If not, it checks the behavior in the Frame Script channel. Finally, if that fails, it looks for an *on mouseUp* in a movie script member.

If it still cannot find a handler to receive the message, the message is simply not used.

Messages look for handlers in

- A behavior attached to the sprite acted upon. If there is more than one behavior, it looks at them in the order that they appear in the Behavior Inspector.

- The cast script.

- A behavior in the Frame Script channel.

- Any movie script cast member.

In some cases, one or more of these steps is skipped because the object does not respond to a certain message. A "startMovie" message, for instance, looks only in movie scripts because sprites and frames are not meant to respond to it.

Creating Your Own Handlers

The preceding list of messages shows you some of the events messages that are built in to Director; you can actually create and send your own messages, too. In addition, you can create handlers to receive these messages.

Create a movie script and place a simple handler inside it:

```
on playBeep
  beep
end
```

Be sure it's a movie script, and close the Script window. Now go to the Message window.

Another function of the Message window is to enable you to send messages to the movie. Do this by typing the name of the message. If a movie script has a handler that deals with this message, the handler runs. Otherwise, an error message tells you that no handler is defined to receive the message.

When you type "playBeep" in the message window, your "on playBeep" handler is executed and you will hear a system beep.

A Lingo convention is to use several words, such as "my number" or "play beep" to define a handler or a variable. But a handler name cannot contain spaces. To make these names easier to read, capitalize the first letter of each word after the first word. So "my number" becomes "myNumber" and "play beep" becomes "playBeep". Lingo does not actually care about capitalization, so this is merely for readability. ("myNumber" and "mynumber" are exactly the same to Lingo.)

USING VARIABLES

Another key element in Lingo, and every programming language, is the variable. Variables are storage areas for values.

For instance, you can store the number 42 in a variable named "myNumber". To do this, assign this value with the = symbol. Try it in the Message window:

```
myNumber = 42
```

The syntax "myNumber" meant absolutely nothing to Director and Lingo before you typed this line. This line, however, told Director to create a variable called "myNumber" and store the numerical value 42 in it. You can now get this value back by using the *put* command to place it in the Message window.

```
put myNumber
-- 42
```

Director remembered that you stored the value 42 in a variable called "myNumber". When you asked it to place "myNumber" in the Message window, it looked into its memory and found a variable called "myNumber" and placed its value in the Message window. You can do even more complex things with variables. Try this:

In Director 6 and before, you had to use the Lingo command *set* to assign values to variables. Director 8 does not require this, but can accommodate this old syntax for simple commands such as this one.

```
myNumber = 42+1
put myNumber
-- 43
```

Director performed the arithmetic before placing the value in the variable. You can even do arithmetic with variables that already have a value.

```
myNumber = 5
myOtherNumber = 3
put myNumber+myOtherNumber
-- 8
```

You can also change the value of a variable that already exists.

```
myNumber = 42
put myNumber
-- 42
myNumber = myNumber+1
put myNumber
-- 43
```

Numbers are not the only items that variables can store. They can also store characters. Try this:

```
myName = "Gary"
put myName
-- "Gary"
```

A series of characters is called a *string*. Strings are usually shown with quotation marks around them. Lingo, in fact, insists that these quotation marks be present. So, a number, such as 42, can just be written as 42, but a string, such as my name, must be written with quotes: "Gary".

Variables can be used in handlers as well. For instance:

```
on playWithVariables
  myNumber = 5
  myNumber = myNumber+4
  myNumber = myNumber-2
  put myNumber
end
```

If you place this handler in a movie script, and then type **playWithVariables** in the Message window, you will see the number 7 placed in the Message window.

A variable used in this way is called a *local variable*. That means it is used inside only one handler. It exists only when the handler is being used, and is disposed of when the handler ends. If the handler is called again, the variable is re-created from scratch.

If you created another handler that also used a variable named "myNumber", it would in fact be a different variable altogether. Each handler is like a little world all to itself. A local variable inside it belongs to it and no other handler.

> A string can be only one character long, or even zero characters long (""). There is no limit to how long a string can be, except your computer's memory.

You can create another type of variable, called a *global variable*, which is shared by more than one handler. Here is an example of a global variable. The following is the complete text of a movie script. It contains three handlers:

```
on initNumber
  global myNumber
  myNumber = 42
end

on addOneToNumber
  global myNumber
  myNumber = myNumber+1
end

on putNumberInMessageWindow
  global myNumber
  put myNumber
end
```

Rather than declare the global variable with *global* commands in each and every handler, you can place one *global* command outside all the handlers, perhaps in the first line of the script. This declares the global variable for every handler in that script member.

You can use the *clearGlobals* command in the Message window or in a handler to erase all global variables. You can also use the *showGlobals* command in the Message window to see a list of all current globals and their values.

Because all three handlers use the command *global* to state that the variable "myNumber" is a global variable, they all share that variable. So, you can now do the following in the Message window:

```
initNumber
putNumberInMessageWindow
-- 42
addOneToNumber
putNumberInMessageWindow
-- 43
```

This code demonstrates how each of the handlers is actually referring to the same variable. Try it without the *global* declarations inside or outside of each script and see what happens.

WRITING LINGO CODE

There are many ways to go about creating a Director movie with Lingo. Over time, you will adopt your own method.

For instance, some programmers create one movie script member to hold all their movie handlers. Others break them up into several script members by category. Some people even create one script member per handler.

If you do a lot of programming, you will find that your style adjusts over time. There is no right or wrong way to go about doing it. However, some basic programming guidelines can help you get started.

The Lingo Programmer

Lingo programmers are really of two types. The first type is someone who has a background in computer science or engineering. These programmers probably know languages such as C or Pascal, and took courses such as "Data Structures" and "Linear Algebra" in college.

The second type is far more common. This is the graphic artist or multimedia producer. These programmers may have used presentation tools before, even Director, but have never used a programming language before. They have explored the basic range of Director and want to go beyond the basics. They are now ready to start learning Lingo.

For both types of programmers, starting to learn Lingo can be difficult. For experienced programmers, Lingo takes care of much of the tedious work that they were used to in the past, but gives them control over graphics elements and the user interface. For graphic artists, Lingo can seem like lines and lines of text that stand between them and their end products.

The important point to remember is that programming is an art. Programming languages, such as Lingo, provide a wide canvas for programmers to express themselves. Two programmers given the same task are almost certain to write two different programs. Each one shows the programmer's own style.

For experienced programmers, this means that programming in Lingo provides another type of canvas on which they can create. As an experienced programmer myself, I will even venture to say that Lingo will enable them to be more creative than before.

For graphic artists, this means that Lingo is a new brush with which they can paint. I know many artists who have become Lingo programmers and used it as a way to create the art they envision.

Programming As Problem Solving

Programming is just problem solving. If you want to make a Director movie that is a matching game, think of it as a problem. Your goal is to find a solution.

As with all problems, more than one step is usually needed to solve the problem. You have to examine the problem, take it apart, and find out what you know and what you don't. Then, you need to come up with a plan for solving it.

To solve a programming problem, first define it. What, exactly, do you want to have happen? Saying "I want to animate a sprite" is not a well-defined problem. Saying "I want to move a sprite from the left side of the Stage to the right side" is better. What you really should be going for is something like "I want to move a sprite from position 50,200 to position 550,200 over the period of 5 seconds at the rate of 10fps."

After a problem has been defined, you can start to see how it can be solved. Imagine that your goal is to move a sprite 500 pixels in 5 seconds at 10fps. At 10fps, 5 seconds will be 50 frame loops. So, you want to move the sprite 10 pixels per frame loop.

Only by clearly defining the problem can you start to envision a solution.

Solving Smaller Problems

The key to writing a program in any language is being able to break it down. You start off with a large concept, such as "A quiz that teaches children about geography." That's a fairly tall order. You can bet that Lingo has no *quizKidsOnGeography* command.

So, you break it into smaller parts. Maybe you want to have each question of the quiz show a map of the world with one country lit up. Then, three choices are presented as to what the country might be. So, now forget about the whole program and start to concentrate on just asking one question.

Did you read the last paragraph? It just might be the most important one in the book. Check it out again even if you have. Make it your personal mantra while using Lingo.

But this part is also too big to tackle all at once. However, it has smaller parts. How does the map display a country? How do the three choices appear? How do you make sure one of the three choices is correct?

A very small part of this might be just having a Lingo program that selects a random country out of a list of 100 names. Now that you have broken the problem down this far, you might begin to program. The result is a handler that selects a random country and outputs it to the Message window. You build it and test it and you've solved your first small problem.

Then, you continue to identify and solve other small problems in this way. Before you know it, you have a working program.

The concept of breaking big problems into smaller ones is the most important aspect of programming. If you ever get stuck while programming in Lingo, it is likely to be because you have not broken the problem down into small enough pieces. Take a step back from what you are doing and decide how you can break it down before continuing.

Setting Up Your Script Members

If you are creating a small applet or projector, a useful way to organize your scripts is to have one movie script member and several behavior members.

In fact, you might not need to have any movie scripts at all. Well-written behaviors can eliminate the need for movie scripts.

If your movie requires mostly buttons, some behavior scripts can handle it all. Each behavior can be attached to a button and tell the movie what to do when it is clicked.

A larger Lingo project might require a few movie scripts. Movie scripts are needed for items placed in the *on startMovie* handler, for instance, where commands need to be executed when the movie is initially run.

Movie scripts can also hold handlers that are used by more than one behavior. If you want various behaviors to play a random sound, for instance, you might want them all to call your "on playRandomSound" handler that is stored in a movie script member. This saves you from having to include a similar handler in many different behavior scripts.

It is always a good idea to keep movie scripts together in the Cast. The same goes for behaviors. There are exceptions, of course. Sometimes, you might want to place behaviors near the bitmap members that they usually control.

Writing Your Code

Director 8 is equipped with an automatic script color function. This function adds color to different types of words in your scripts. The goal is to make it easier for you to read. You can also turn this function off in the Script Preferences dialog box. If you do, you can use the Text Inspector to color and style your code manually.

The most important task to complete when writing code is to remember to add comments. Comments are words, phrases, and even sentences that you can sprinkle throughout your code to help clarify what the code is doing. You can place comments on a new line, or at the end of a line with code. Use a double dash to tell Director that everything after it is a comment and should be ignored when the Lingo runs. Here is an example:

```
-- This handler output powers of 2 to the Message Window
on powersOfTwo
  n = 2 -- start with 2
  repeat with i = 1 to 100 -- output 100 numbers
    put n -- send to the Message window
    n = n*2 -- multiply by 2 to get the next number
  end repeat
end
```

Now compare that with the same exact handler that is not commented:

```
on powersOfTwo
  n = 2
  repeat with i = 1 to 100
    put n
    n = n*2
  end repeat
end
```

The first can be understood immediately. If you wrote the second one and then saved the file and came back to it a year later, would you be able to remember what it did immediately? Now imagine a 100-line handler that picks random geography quiz questions and modifies a map on the Stage.

In addition to straightforward commenting, you can also accomplish a lot by using sensible names for handlers and variables. You could name a handler "convTemp", for instance, but it would be better if it were named "convertTemperature". You could have variables in it called "f" and "c", but it would be much more readable code if they were named "fahrenheitTemp" and "centigradeTemp".

Because you can use long variable names in Lingo, take advantage of it to make your code more readable. Because you can copy, cut, and paste in the Lingo scripting window, there's really no reason to use short, one-character names.

Using colors, styles, comments, and realistic handler and variable names will save you time and frustration. Get used to using them now, from the beginning, and your work will go much more smoothly.

⇨ *For more information about code-writing practices,* **see** *"Writing Good Code," **p. 660** (Chapter 33, "Debugging")*

TROUBLESHOOTING LINGO

- Remember that the concept of breaking big problems into smaller ones is the most important aspect of programming. If you get stuck while programming in Lingo, it is likely to be because you have not broken the problem down into small enough pieces. Take a step back and decide how you can break the problem down before continuing.

- Remember that a local variable is destroyed when a handler is done. The next time that handler begins, it will not have a value. If you want a variable to retain its value, you should use a global or a behavior property variable, which is introduced in Chapter 14, "Creating Behaviors."

- Even if you don't plan on using them all, you should familiarize yourself with the different messages and event handlers. You should not try to use an event handler name as a custom handler or a variable name. You should also avoid using any other Lingo syntax as handler names or variable names.

- Every Lingo programmer eventually runs into the problem of a movie script not working when it should. The code might seem perfect—the Score, Cast, and Stage are all set up as they should be—yet the script acts as if it weren't even there. Sure enough, the simple solution is that the movie script is set to be a behavior script by mistake. Keep this in mind, because it will happen to you one day. To fix it, just use the member's Script Cast Member Properties dialog box to change it to the proper script type.

DID YOU KNOW?

- You can change the font in the Message window by selecting text and using the Text Inspector. This is especially useful when you are teaching Lingo and need to show a class the Message window on a projection screen.

- Because the Message window can do math for you by using the *put* command, consider using it rather than launching a separate calculator program. I find it useful for computing data, such as the midpoint between two locations on the screen.

- You can use the Lingo *scriptText* property to get the text of a script cast member. You can also set the text of a script with this property.

- You can use the Script Preferences dialog box to change the default font of the script window. You can also turn the auto-coloring function on or off. If you turn the auto-coloring function off, you can color in the text manually with the Text Inspector.

- Handler names can contain some symbols and punctuation marks. You can use a question mark or an exclamation point, for example. You can even have a handler called "on !". You can also use symbols in handler names or as variable names.

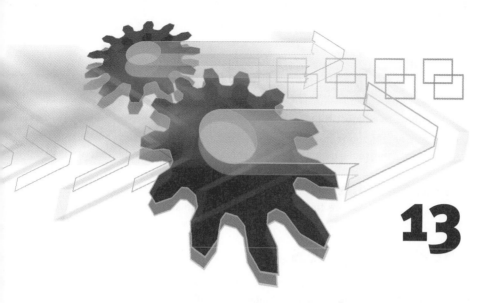

13

ESSENTIAL LINGO SYNTAX

Source movies for this chapter can be found on the CD-ROM in the "Book Movies" folder under folder 13.

Although there are hundreds of Lingo keywords, few of them are used in day-to-day programming. Most have to deal with specific properties of cast members or events; the essential syntax is all you need to know to do most things.

The essential commands enable the program to make decisions, repeat actions, and manipulate variables. After you master those commands, you have mastered Lingo. The rest are just details.

This chapter goes through these essential commands, functions, and properties quickly, with the simplest of examples. When you are finished, you will have the knowledge to start building useful Lingo scripts.

USING NUMBER VARIABLES

You learned how Lingo performs simple math functions in the last chapter. However, there are many more ways to work with number variables. Lingo has a full set of commands and functions that work with numbers just as any other programming language does.

Performing Operations

You can add, subtract, multiply, and divide numbers and variables. The symbols you use to do this are the +, -, *, and /. The first symbol, the plus sign, is the only one that makes complete sense, because a plus sign is standard notation used for addition.

The dash is used as a substitute for the minus symbol. An asterisk is used as a multiplication symbol. It is used in just about every programming language for this purpose. The forward slash is used in place of the division symbol, because a standard keyboard does not include a division character.

To use these operators, apply them to numbers as you would write them on paper. Here are some examples in the message window:

```
put 4+5
-- 9
put 7-3
-- 4
put 6*9
-- 54
put 8/2
-- 4
put 9/2
-- 4
```

Integers and Floats

Notice that the last operation, 9 divided by 2, returned a 4. This is because Director is dealing here in integers only. An integer is a number, positive or negative, with no fractional value. Four is an integer. However, 4 1/2, or 4.5, is not.

Numbers that have fractional parts are called floating point numbers. This name refers to the way in which the computer stores these values, using a more complex method than how it stores integers. The number 4.5 is a floating point number, or a float.

Be aware that floating point numbers include integers. A 4 is an integer and a floating point number. However, 4.5 is a floating point number, although not an integer, because it has a fractional component.

> Director does not round when dividing two integers such as these. Instead, the decimal portion is dropped. So, 7/4 returns a 1, not a 2.

In Lingo, floating point numbers are always shown with a decimal point. This way, Director can tell the difference between the two types of numbers.

If Director is asked to interpret an operation such as 9/2, it looks at all the numbers involved and determines whether the result should be an integer or a float. In this case, because you are asking it to perform an operation on two integers, it returns an integer. To do this, it drops the fractional component of the number and returns only the integer component. So, 9/2 returns a 4, not a 4.5.

You can force Director to return a floating point value by making one of the numbers in the calculation a floating point number. Try this in the Message window:

```
put 7/4
-- 1
put 7.0/4
-- 1.7500
put 7/4.0
-- 1.7500
put 7.0/4.0
-- 1.7500
```

You can also use two functions to convert back and forth between integers and floats. A function is a piece of Lingo syntax that usually takes one or more values and returns a value. Try this in the Message window:

```
put 7
-- 7
put float(7)
-- 7.0000
put 7.75
-- 7.7500
put integer(7.25)
-- 7
put integer(7)
-- 7
put integer(7.75)
-- 8
```

These two functions, *integer* and *float*, convert any number value, either integer or floating point, to the type you want. Notice in the example that applying the *integer* function to an integer value does not change it. Also, notice that the integer function rounds numbers. So, a value of 7.75 produces an integer of 8.

You can use these commands on functions inside operations. Try this in the Message window:

```
put 8/5
-- 1
put float(8)/5
-- 1.6000
put float(8/5)
-- 1.0000
put integer(float(8)/5)
-- 2
```

Notice that the line "put float(8)/5" behaves in the same way as "put 8.0/5" would. Also notice that the third example returns what appears to be a wrong answer. It says that the floating point result of 8/5 is 1.000. This is because you are asking it to evaluate 8/5 first, before converting it to a floating point number. As the first example shows, the value of 8/5 is 1. So, the line is simply converting a 1 to a 1.000.

The last example shows how you can use the two functions together to perform an operation and get a rounded result. The division returns a floating point number, which is then rounded to an integer with the integer function.

Precedence

These last two examples bring up an interesting topic: order of operations, also called *precedence*. When more than one operation is performed, or a combination of operations and functions, which operation is performed first? Try this in the Message window:

```
put 5+3
-- 8
put 8*6
-- 48
put 5+3*6
-- 23
```

Add 5 plus 3 and you get 8. Multiply 8 times 6 and you get 48. However, if you try to do that all at once on the same line, you get 23. Why? Well, some multiplication and division operators take precedence over addition and subtraction. So, in the statement 5+3*6, multiplication is evaluated first, and then the addition. Most programming languages work this way.

However, you can override precedence by specifying which operations you want to perform first. To do this, use parentheses to group together operations. Try this in the Message window:

```
put 5+3*6
-- 23
put (5+3)*6
-- 48
```

The use of parentheses ensures that the addition is performed first, and then the sum is multiplied by 6. You can use multiple layers of parentheses if you need to.

```
put ((5+3)*6+(7-3)*4)*8
-- 512
```

Operations and Variables

Now that you have all the basic functions for math, the next step is to combine this knowledge with the use of variables. Variables used in mathematical operations are interpreted just as numbers were in the preceding examples.

```
myNumber = 5
put myNumber
-- 5
put myNumber+1
-- 6
put myNumber*7
-- 35
put (myNumber+2)*3
-- 21
```

You can also set a variable to be equal to the result of an operation.

```
myNumber = 7+4
put myNumber
-- 11
myNumber = (7+4)*2
put myNumber
-- 22
myNumber = 5
myOtherNumber = 6
mySum = myNumber + myOtherNumber
put mySum
-- 11
```

The last example shows you how one variable can be set to the result of an operation that involves two other variables. Performing operations on variables and storing the results in other variables is common in Lingo and other programming languages. In this case, it's so obvious what the variable contains, that it almost makes more sense to just use the numbers instead. However, in a real program, the variable holds values that change, such as the score of a game or the age of the user.

Functions

In addition to the integer and float functions, many other functions manipulate numbers. Table 13.1 lists these functions and what they do.

Table 13.1 Lingo Math Functions

Function	Description	Example
abs	Returns the absolute value of the number. It basically strips off the negative sign from numbers less than 0.	abs(-7) = 7
atan	Returns the arctangent of the number. It uses the radians system rather than degrees.	atan(1.0) = 0.7854
cos	Returns the cosine of the number. It uses the radians system rather than degrees.	cos(3.14) = -1.000
exp	Returns the natural logarithm base (2.7183) to the the power of the number provided.	exp(3) = 20.0855
float	Converts the number to a floating point number.	float(4) = 4.000
integer	Converts a floating point number to an integer using rounding. Leaves integers the same.	integer(7.8) = 8
mod	Used to perform modulus arithmetic. It will limit a number to a range. The limit always starts with 0, and goes up to the specified number.	4 mod 3 = 1
sqrt	Returns the square root of the number. If given an integer, it rounds the result to the nearest integer. If given a float, it returns a float.	sqrt(4) = 2
sin	Returns the sine of the number. It uses the radians system rather than degrees.	sin(3.14/2) = 1.000

Many of these functions are based on trigonometry. Trig functions are useful for defining curved and circular animation paths with Lingo, but are rarely used by anyone but advanced Lingo programmers. Don't worry if you can't remember your high school math class; you probably won't need it for most things.

⇨ *For more information about using trigonometry functions, **see** "Adding 3D Effects," **p. 380** (Chapter 18, "Controlling Bitmaps")*

USING STRING VARIABLES

The other basic type of variable is the *string*, which stores a series of characters. Strings can be as simple as a single character, as complex as words, lines, or pages of text, or can even contain no characters at all. The following examples demonstrate different types of strings in the Message window:

```
myString = "A"
put myString
-- "A"
myString = "Hello"
```

```
put myString
-- "Hello"
myString = "Hello World."
put myString
-- "Hello World."
myString = ""
put myString
-- ""
```

Chunk Expressions

You can use Lingo to take strings apart and get single characters or groups of characters from them. A subset of a string is called a *chunk*. To define chunks, use keywords such as *char* and *word*. Try this in the Message window:

```
myString = "Hello World."
put char 1 of myString
-- "H"
put word 1 of myString
-- "Hello"
put char 2 to 4 of myString
-- "ell"
```

Using a chunk expression such as *char* in conjunction with the keyword *of* and the string is actually old-fashioned Lingo syntax. Director 8 enables you to do the same thing with the new dot syntax. It is called dot syntax because it uses dots, or periods, to formulate expressions.

```
myString = "Hello World."
put myString
-- "Hello World."
put myString.char[1]
-- "H"
put myString.word[1]
-- "Hello"
put myString.char[2..4]
-- "ell"
```

There are more chunk expressions than just *char* and *word*. There are also *line* and *paragraph*. *Paragraph* means the same thing as line. Although word returns items based on where spaces are in the string, a *line* or *paragraph* returns whole lines, based on return characters in the string.

In addition, there is the *item* chunk expression. This returns segments of a string based on the location of commas in a string. Try this in the Message window:

```
myString = "apples,oranges,pears,peaches,bananas"
put item 2 of myString
```

```
-- "oranges"
put myString.item[3]
-- "pears"
```

As you can see, the *item* expression can be used with both the old syntax and the new dot syntax. In addition, you can change the character that the item expression uses as its delimiter. To do this, you need to set a value for a special variable called *the itemDelimiter*. The keyword *the* signifies that this is a special property in Director. Try this in the Message window:

```
myString = "walnuts;peanuts;sunflower seeds"
the itemDelimiter = ";"
put item 2 of myString
-- "peanuts"
put myString.item[3]
-- "sunflower seeds"
```

The best thing about chunk expressions is that they can all be used together. You can get a character of a word of a line, for instance. Try this in the Message window:

```
the itemDelimiter = ","
myString = "red,yellow,blue,green,light brown"
put myString.item[5]
-- "light brown"
put myString.item[5].word[2]
-- "brown"
put myString.item[5].word[2].char[4]
-- "w"
put char 4 of word 2 of item 5 of myString
-- "w"
```

Table 13.2 shows a summary of all the chunk expressions in Lingo.

Table 13.2   Lingo Chunk Expressions

Function	Description	Example
char	A single character or range of characters.	myString.char[1] myString.char[2..4]
word	A single group of characters broken up by whitespace.	myString.word[1] myString.word[2..4]
item	broken up by *the itemDelimiter*.	myString.item[2..4]
line	A single group of characters broken up by a Return.	myString.line[1] myString.line[2..4]
paragraph	A single group of line characters broken up by a Return.	myString.paragraph[1] myString.paragraph[2..4]

Manipulating Strings

In addition to getting pieces of strings, you can also add to or delete pieces of strings. To concatenate strings, use the & (ampersand) character. Try this in the Message window:

```
myString = "Hello"
put myString&"World."
-- "HelloWorld."
myOtherString = "World."
put myString&myOtherString
-- "HelloWorld."
put myString&&myOtherString
-- "Hello World."
```

The first example used a string variable and a string literal, which describes values such as numbers and strings. When you use the ampersand (&) to concatenate the string variable with the word "Hello" and the literal string "World.", you get a result of "HelloWorld.". When you use two variables instead, it returns the same thing. Finally, when you use two ampersands (&&), it inserts an extra space in the new string. The double ampersand is used for exactly that purpose: to concatenate two strings with an extra space. You can see how it comes in handy in the final line.

You can also use concatenation to create a new string and store it in a variable. Try this in the Message window:

```
myString = "Hello"
myOtherString = "World."
myNewString = myString&&myOtherString
put myNewString
-- "Hello World."
```

You can alter the contents of a string in still another way, which involves using the *put* command. When you use the *put* command by itself, it places something in the Message window. However, if you use the *put* command along with the keywords *after*, *before*, or *into*, it becomes something very different. It actually assigns a new value to a variable. Try this in the Message window:

```
myString = "Hello"
put "World." after myString
put myString
-- "HelloWorld."
put "I said " before myString
put myString
-- "I said HelloWorld."
```

You see that you can use the *put* command to add text to strings. You could have done the same thing by concatenating strings together and assigning them to a new (or the same) variable. However, the *put* command technique is something you should know about.

One special way to use this is to combine the *put* command with chunk expressions. You can actually insert text into a string.

```
myString = "HelloWorld."
put " " after myString.char[5]
put myString
-- "Hello World."
```

The *into* keyword can also be used with the *put* command. It would replace the string. However, that would be the same as just stating the variable name followed by an = and the new value. But you can use *put* and *into* to surgically replace characters in the middle of a string.

```
myString = "Hello World."
put "Earth" into myString.char[7..11]
put myString
-- "Hello Earth."
```

In addition to the *put* command, there is also a *delete* command. This command removes a chunk from a string variable. Try this in the Message window:

```
myString = "Hello World."
delete myString.char[2]
put myString
-- "Hllo World."
```

Delete works with character spans, words, lines, and items as well.

For more information about strings, **see** *"Using Strings and Chunks," **p. 322** (Chapter 16, "Controlling Text")*

COMPARING VARIABLES

One of the tasks that you will want Lingo to do for you is to make decisions. For the computer to make decisions, it needs to have information. Information, to a computer, is binary: 1 or 0, on or off, *TRUE* or *FALSE*.

Lingo uses the idea of true or false in cases where it needs to make decisions. When you compare variables, for instance, you are asking, "Are they equal?" The answer can either be yes or no, which the computer shows as *TRUE* or *FALSE*.

Use the Message window to try an example. The operator = is the most common comparison operator. Try it out:

```
put 1 = 1
-- 1
put 1 = 2
-- 0
put "abc" = "def"
```

```
-- 0
put "abc" = "abc"
-- 1
```

You can see that when a comparison is true, Director returns a value of 1. When it is false, it returns a value of 0. The use of 1 and 0 as true and false is used so much that Director even recognizes the words *TRUE* and *FALSE* as those numbers.

```
put TRUE
-- 1
put FALSE
-- 0
```

The words *TRUE* and *FALSE* are capitalized in the preceding example because they are constants. Constants are Lingo terms that always define the same thing, such as *TRUE* being 1. Because Lingo is not case sensitive, you don't have to capitalize these terms, but it is a common convention that this book follows.

Variables and literals can be compared in a lot of ways besides using the = operator. Table 13.3 shows all of Lingo's comparison operators.

Table 13.3 Lingo Comparison Operators

Operator	Comparing Numbers	Comparing Strings
=	Are the two numbers equal?	Are the two strings the same?
<	Is the first number less than the second?	Does the first string come before the second alphabetically?
>	Is the first number greater than the second?	Does the first string come after the second alphabetically?
<=	Is the first number less than or equal to the second?	Does the first string come before the secondalphabetically or match up exactly?
>=	Is the first number greater than or equal to the second?	Does the first string come after the second alphabetically or match up exactly?
<>	Is the first number different from the second? In other words, are they not equal?	Are the two strings

Here are some examples from the Message window:

```
put 1 < 2
-- 1
put 2 < 1
-- 0
put 2 <= 1
-- 0
put 2 <= 2
-- 1
put 2 <=3
-- 1
put 2 >= 2
-- 1
```

```
put 2 >= 1
-- 1
put 2 <> 1
-- 1
put "this" > "that"
-- 1
```

One important point to note is that when strings are compared with the equals operator, Director rules out capitalization. So, "abc" and "Abc" are seen as equal. However, when using other comparison operators, case is used to break ties. Uppercase letters are seen as coming before lowercase ones. So "Abc" and "abc" are equal when using =, but "Abc" is less than "abc" when using < or >.

USING HANDLERS

In the last chapter, you saw how to create handlers. Handlers are collections of Lingo statements brought together to perform a task. Handlers can be named with specific keywords to react to Director events. Handlers can also have custom names and can be called from other handlers you write. Sometimes, handlers can even return a value.

For more information about creating handlers, **see** *"Writing Your Code," **p. 216** (Chapter 12, "Learning Lingo")*

Event Handlers

A handler, such as *on mouseUp* or *on exitFrame,* is an event handler. It is built to respond to a message sent by a specific event in Director. Chapter 12, "Learning Lingo," lists many types of events and gives some examples, such as when the users click the mouse or when a frame is done playing.

It is important to know which types of scripts use which types of handlers. An *on mouseUp* handler is typically found in a behavior script that is meant to be attached to a sprite that users can click. An *on exitFrame* handler is usually meant for a frame script where an action is to be performed after the frame is drawn. These are typical locations for these handlers in scripts written by beginner Lingo programmers.

Most handlers can actually be placed anywhere. An *on mouseUp* behavior can be in a frame script or a movie script, as long as you want that handler to be called every time users click and no other object is there to get the message. An *on exitFrame* script can be used on a sprite behavior script, as long as you want the handler to run every time a frame ends while the sprite is present.

Some handlers don't belong in some places. An *on keyDown* handler gets a message when users press a key on the keyboard. It can be used on an editable text member or field, in the frame script, or even in the movie script. However, if *on keyDown* is used in a behavior assigned to a bitmap sprite, it will never be called. This occurs because bitmaps, unlike editable text members or fields, do not accept or react to keystrokes. Table 13.4 lists the most common event messages and where the event travels to first.

Table 13.4   Lingo Event Messages

Message	Sent	Travels to First
mouseDown	When mouse button clicked	Sprite behavior
mouseUp	When mouse button clicked	Sprite behavior
mouseEnter	When mouse moved	Sprite behavior
mouseLeave	When mouse moved	Sprite behavior
mouseWithin	Constantly, from mouse	Sprite behavior
beginSprite	When sprite first appears	Sprite/Frame behavior
endSprite	When sprite is removed	Sprite/Frame behavior
prepareFrame	Before each frame is drawn	Sprite/Frame behavior
enterFrame	After each frame is drawn	Sprite/Frame behavior
idle	Once or more while frame is waiting to end	Sprite/Frame behavior
exitFrame	Just before frame ends	Sprite/Frame behavior
keyDown	When key pressed	Text Sprite or Frame
keyUp	When key pressed	Text Sprite or Frame
prepareMovie	Before first frame drawn	Movie Script
startMovie	After first frame drawn	Movie Script
stopMovie	When movie stopped	Movie Script

Any Lingo code must always be called from an event handler. Even if you write your own custom handler to do something, that handler must be called from some event handler; otherwise, custom handlers sit idle until called. There are a few exceptions, such as typing a custom handler's name in the Message window, which will run the handler although no event handler was involved.

Custom Handlers

When you write your own handler, it can have any name you want, as long as it is not the name of an event. You would typically place it in a movie script. That way, the handler is available to be called from any behavior or other movie script. A custom handler can be placed in a behavior, but then it can be used only by other handlers in that behavior. When you learn to write complex behaviors, you will be adding custom handlers to them, but they will all be called by other event handlers in that behavior.

The following example is a movie script. An *on startMovie* handler is called by an event message when the movie starts. It, in turn, calls a custom handler named "on initScore". The word "score" refers to a game score, in this case, rather than the Director Score. This handler sets a few global variables:

```
on startMovie
  initScore
  go to frame "intro"
end
```

```
on initScore
  global gScore, gLevel
  set gScore = 0
  set gLevel = 0
end
```

You could have all the lines of the "on initScore" handler included in the *on startMovie* handler. However, creating your own custom handler does a couple of things. First, it makes the code neater. The "on initScore" handler takes care of one task and one task only. Second, it makes it so that the "on initScore" handler can be called again later in the program. In this case, you might need to reset the score when users start a new game. If you were to place the same lines in *on startMovie*, you would be stuck executing unwanted lines, such as "go to frame "intro"" again, even though that might not be required the next time you want to reset the score.

Functions

One type of custom handler is sometimes called a function. What makes this type of handler different is that it returns a value. It works in the same way as the math functions shown earlier in this chapter. The difference, of course, is that you can define what the function does.

Two elements of a function are different from a simple handler: input and output. A function handler usually accepts one or more values as input, and sends one value back. The inputs are called *parameters* and the output is simply called the *returned value.*

For a handler to accept parameters, all you need to do is add the variable names to the handler declaration line. This is the line that begins with the word on. Here is an example:

```
on myHandler myNumber
  put myNumber
end
```

This example is not showing a real function, because it does not return a value. However, it is a valid handler. After you begin writing your own programs, you will commonly write handlers that accept one or more parameters even if they do not return a value.

By placing the variable name "myNumber" in the declaration line of a handler, you are preparing the handler to receive its value when it is called. If you place this handler in a movie script and then type the following in the Message window, the handler executes:

```
myHandler(7)
-- 7
```

You can see that the number 7 was sent back to the Message window. The line "put myNumber" is responsible for placing it there. When you called the handler "on myHandler" with the number 7 as the parameter, the handler executed. Before any Lingo commands were performed, it placed the number 7 into the local variable "myNumber".

You can also have more than one variable as a parameter. Just use commas to separate them in the declaration line as well as when you are calling the handler. Here is an example:

If a function handler expects a value to be passed into it, and none is, the parameter variables start off with a value of *VOID*.

```
on myHandler myNumber, myOtherNumber
  mySum = myNumber + myOtherNumber
  put mySum
end
```

When you call this handler from the Message window, place two numbers after the handler name in the parentheses. The handler places both those numbers in the variables specified by the declaration line. In the case of our handler, it then adds them to create a new variable and then outputs that variable to the Message window.

```
myHandler(7,4)
-- 11
```

You are actually only one step away from turning this example into a real function. You need to have the handler return a value to do that. For this, simply use the *return* command. Here is the same handler without the *put* command, but with a *return* command:

```
on myHandler myNumber, myOtherNumber
  mySum = myNumber + myOtherNumber
  return mySum
end
```

Now, you can call this handler from the Message window in the same way that you called functions, such as integer, earlier in the chapter. Try this in the Message window:

```
myNumber = myHandler(7,4)
put myNumber
-- 11
```

The handler "on myHandler" is now a self-contained unit that takes two numbers and returns their sum. It would probably be more appropriate to assign names to the handler and the variables in it that are more suitable to their functions:

```
on addTwoNumbers num1, num2
  sum = num1 + num2
  return sum
end
```

This function can now be used in the Message window, as well as other handlers.

```
put addTwoNumbers(5,24)
-- 29
put addTwoNumbers(-7,2)
-- -5
put addTwoNumbers(4.5,2.1)
-- 6.6000
```

You can also use functions to compare variables. Rather than returning a new value, it can return a *TRUE* or *FALSE* value:

```
on isOneGreaterThan num1, num2
  return (num1 - 1) = num2
end
```

This function takes two numbers and compares them. It actually subtracts one from the first number and compares it to the value of the second. It returns a 1 if this is true and a 0 if it is not.

```
put isOneGreaterThan(5,4)
-- 1
put isOneGreaterThan(7,2)
-- 0
```

USING *IF...THEN* STATEMENTS

Now that you know how to compare variables and get a true or false value, it would be useful to have some additional syntax to enable you to process these comparisons.

Simple *If* Statements

The *if* and *then* keywords can be used to process comparisons. Here is an example:

```
on testIf num
  if num = 7 then
    put "You entered the number 7"
  end if
end
```

You can probably guess what the result of trying this in the message window is:

```
testIf(7)
-- "You entered the number 7"
```

Any commands that you place between the line starting *if* and the line *end if* are executed if the value of the statement between the *if* and the *then* is true.

A natural extension of the *if* statement is the *else* keyword. You can use this keyword to specify commands to be performed when the *if* statement is not true. Here is an example:

```
on testElse num
  if num = 7 then
    put "You entered the number 7"
  else
```

You can also place the entire *if* statement on one line:

```
if num = 7 then put "You
entered the number 7"
```

This works only when you have one line of commands that needs to be inside the *if* statement.

```
    put "You entered a number that is not 7"
  end if
end
```

Here is what happens when you test this function in the Message window:

```
put testElse(7)
-- "You entered the number 7"
put testIf(9)
-- "You entered a number that is not 7"
```

Case Statements

If statements can actually get a little more complex. You can use the *else* keyword to look for other specific situations. For example:

```
on testElse2 num
  if num = 7 then
    put "You entered the number 7"
  else if num = 9 then
    put "You entered the number 9"
  else
    put "You entered another number"
  end if
end
```

Now you have a handler that deals with all sorts of different cases. In fact, Director has some special syntax that handles multiple condition statements like those in this handler. Here is a handler that does exactly the same thing:

```
on testCase num
  case num of
    7:
      put "You entered the number 7"
    9:
      put "You entered the number 9"
    otherwise:
      put "You entered another number"
  end case
end
```

The *case* statement is simply a neater way of writing multiple condition statements. It provides no extra functionality over the *if* statement.

In the *case* statement, you enclose the condition between the word *case* and the word *of* in the first line. Then, you order your commands under each value, followed by a colon. The *otherwise* keyword acts as a final *else* in an *if* sequence.

Nested *If* Statements

It is important to understand how dynamic commands in Lingo are. An *if* statement, for instance, can exist inside another *if* statement. Check out this example:

```
on nestedIf num
  if num < 0 then
    if num = -1 then
      put "You entered a -1"
    else
      put "You entered a negative number other than -1"
    end if
  else
    if num = 7 then
      put "You entered a 7"
    else
      put "You entered a positive number other than 7"
    end if
  end if
end
```

The preceding example first determines whether the number is less than 0. If it is, it does one of two things depending on whether the number is -1 or another negative number. If the number is not less than 0, it does another one of two things—one if the number is 7 and something else otherwise.

Although this nesting is not really necessary to achieve the desired result, it demonstrates using the *if* statement in a nested fashion. You could do this to make your code better fit the logic you have in mind, or you could do this because the logic requires nested *if* statements. You will encounter situations like this as you gain more programming experience.

The nests can even go further. You can go as many levels deep as you want. You can even embed *if* statements inside *case* statements and vice versa.

Logical Operators

But what if you want to test more than one item at a time? Suppose you have a function that tests two numbers rather than one. Such a function would look like this:

```
on testTwoNumbers num1, num2
  if num1 = 7 then
    if num2 = 7 then
      put "You entered two 7s"
    end if
  end if
end
```

An easier way to do this is to use the logical operator *and*. It enables you to check multiple conditions in one *if* statement:

```
on testTwoNumbers2 num1, num2
  if num1 = 7 and num2 = 7 then
    put "You entered two 7s"
  end if
end
```

The second handler is much more compact and readable. You could also use the *or* operator to determine whether either of two conditions is true rather than both.

```
on testEither num1, num2
  if num1 = 7 or num2 = 7 then
    put "You entered at least one 7"
  end if
end
```

Another logical operator that you should know about is the *not* operator. This operator reverses the result of a comparison. A true value becomes false and a false value becomes true. This simple example shows you how one is used:

```
on testNot num
  if not (num = 7) then
    put "You did not enter a 7"
  end if
end
```

These simple examples of logical operators only scratch the surface of their real uses. You can construct complex logical statements by using *and*, *or*, *not*, and parentheses.

USING *REPEAT* LOOPS

Computers are great at doing repetitive tasks. To ask a set of Lingo commands to repeat, you use the *repeat* command. You can have commands repeat a certain number of times, until a certain condition is met, or forever.

Repeat With

If you want to make a Lingo program count to 100, all you need are a few simple lines. Here is an example:

```
on countTo100
  repeat with i = 1 to 100
    put i
  end repeat
end
```

The *repeat with* loop creates a new variable—in this case, "i"—and tells it where to start and where to end. Everything in between the *repeat* line and the *end repeat* is executed that many times. In addition, the variable "i" contains the number of the current loop.

The result of this handler is to count from 1 to 100 and place each value in the Message window.

> You can also have *repeat* loops count backward from a specific number by using *down to* rather than just *to*.

Repeat While

Another type of *repeat* loop is the *repeat while* loop. This operator repeats until a certain statement is true. Here is a handler that does exactly the same thing as the last example:

```
on repeatTo100
  i = 1
  repeat while i <= 100
    put i
    i = i + 1
  end repeat
end
```

This handler starts the variable "i" out as one, and then repeats over and over, each time outputting the number to the Message window and increasing it by 1. Each time, before the *repeat* loop begins, the statement "i <= 100" is checked to see whether it is true. When it is, the *repeat* loop ends.

This example is, of course, very simple. If you wanted to do this in real life, you would use the *repeat with* loop in the earlier example. The *repeat with* syntax is good for counting and the *repeat while* syntax is good for a lot of other things, such as in the following simple example. In this case, you are writing a handler that counts until the user presses and holds the Shift key to stop it:

```
on countWhileNoShift
  i = 1
  repeat while not the shiftDown
    put i
    i = i + 1
  end repeat
end
```

This example uses a new property called *the shiftDown*. It returns a 1 when the Shift key is held down, and a 0 when it is not. When you run this handler in the Message window, the "i" variable starts counting. Press and hold the Shift key and it stops. The Message window contains the history of the count.

Other *Repeat* Commands

Suppose you want a handler that counts to 100, but can also be interrupted by the Shift key. The following is one way to do that:

```
on countTo100orShift1
  i = 1
  repeat while (i <= 100) and (not the shiftDown)
    put i
    i = i + 1
  end repeat
end
```

This handler uses a *repeat while* loop that checks to make sure two conditions are true: "i" is still less than or equal to 100 and the Shift key is not down. Another way to do this is to use the *exit repeat* command:

```
on countTo100orShift2
  repeat with i = 1 to 100
    put i
    if the shiftDown then exit repeat
  end repeat
end
```

This second handler is much neater. It uses a *repeat with* loop, which makes more sense for a loop that counts. One line of the loop checks whether the Shift key is down, and then the *exit repeat* command breaks Director out of that loop.

The *exit repeat* command works in both *repeat with* and *repeat while* loops. It acts as essentially a second way for the loop to end. The loops you are writing now are only a few lines long, but advanced Lingo programmers write loops that are much more involved. Sometimes an *exit repeat* command is the best way to break out of a loop when needed.

There is also a *next repeat* command that doesn't go quite as far as the *exit repeat*. Rather than end the loop, the *next repeat* prevents all the rest of the lines in that loop from executing and goes immediately back to the beginning of the loop. Here is an example:

```
on countTo100WithShift
  repeat with i = 1 to 100
    put "Counting..."
    if the shiftDown then next repeat
    put i
  end repeat
end
```

The preceding handler counts from 1 to 100 like a lot of the previous examples. Each time through the loop it sends a "Counting..." to the Message window. It then sends the number to the Message window. However, if you hold the Shift key down while it is running, the *next repeat* command prevents Director from continuing to the "put i" line. The result is that only "Counting..." goes to the Message window those times.

Repeating Forever

Sometimes, it might be necessary to construct a *repeat* loop that keeps going until an *exit repeat* command is executed. In that case, you don't want to use *repeat with*, because that command causes the loop to repeat only a certain number of times. Using *repeat while* demands that you also place a condition on when the *repeat* loop stops.

> Lingo is fast—so fast, in fact, that it might be impossible to interrupt the previous handlers with the Shift key before they get the chance to finish. You might want to try them with 10,000 or an even higher number, instead of 100.

However, there is a tricky way to use *repeat while* without a condition, but instead basically tell it to repeat forever. Here is an example:

```
on repeatForever
  repeat while TRUE
    put "repeating..."
    if the shiftDown then exit repeat
  end repeat
end
```

This handler doesn't really repeat forever; it just repeats until the Shift key is pressed. However, an *exit repeat* and only an *exit repeat* can terminate the loop, because you have placed a *TRUE* as the condition on the *repeat while* loop. Because *TRUE* is always true, it repeats forever, or at least until the *exit repeat* command executes.

You need this kind of *repeat* loop when you don't want the conditions that determine when the *repeat* loop ends to be after the *repeat while* statement. You might want to have a loop like this when the condition is long and involved, or because several conditions exit the *repeat* loop and no one condition is more important than the other.

USING LINGO NAVIGATION COMMANDS

Repeat loops, *if* statements, and handlers are ways to organize and control Lingo commands. But what about commands that actually *do* something?

The simplest commands in Director are the ones that move the playback head around the Score. You have total control over where the playback head goes next. You can jump to a frame number or marker, or even to another movie.

Go

You can make the movie jump to a frame number by simply telling it to *go*. Open the Score window and the Message window. The playback head should be on frame 1. Now, in the Message window, type **go 5**.

The playback head should proceed to frame 5. A more common form of this command is to use the full statement "go to frame 5". This is a little more readable.

> If you ever set up a repeat loop to repeat forever and don't give Director a way to get out of it, you can always press [cmd]+. (period) on the Mac or Ctrl+. (period) in Windows to halt Director and Lingo. If you don't, Director might eventually crash.

You can also tell the movie to go to the next marker. Create a marker label for frame 7 simply called "intro". Then, in the Message window type **go to frame "intro"**.

Table 13.5 shows all the variations of the *go* command.

Table 13.5   The Many Versions of the go Command

Version	Description	Example
go to frame X	The movie goes to frame number X.	go to frame 7
go to frame "X"	The movie goes to the frame labeled X.	go to frame "credits"
go to the frame	The movie begins the same frame over again.	go to the frame
go to the frame + X	The movie jumps ahead X frames.	go to the frame + 1
go to the frame - X	The movie jumps back X frames.	go to the frame - 1
go next	The movie jumps to the next labeled frame.	go next
go previous	The movie jumps to the labeled frame immediately before the currently labeled frame.	go previous
go loop	The movie jumps back to the currently labeled frame.	go loop
go marker(X)	The movie jumps forward X labeled frames.	go marker(2)
go marker(-X)	The movie jumps back X labeled frames.	go marker(-2)

The most confusing concept is the difference between the current label and the previous label. Figure 13.1 shows the Score with some labeled frames. The playback head is between two of them in frame 7. Frame 5 is labeled "that", frame 1 is labeled "this", and frame 10 is labeled "other". If you were to execute a *go loop*, the movie would jump back to "that", because it is the closest marker just before the playback head. However, a *go previous* command takes the movie back to "this", which is considered the previous label.

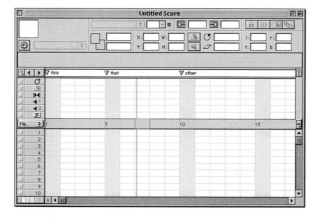

Figure 13.1
The playback head is between two labeled frames. "that" is considered the current label and "this" is the previous one.

Some other Lingo elements are introduced in Table 13.5. The first is the property *the frame*. This property returns the current frame number. If you set the Score up as it is in Figure 13.1, you could do this in the Message window:

```
put the frame
-- 7
```

The function *marker* also gets information from the Score. It takes one number as a parameter. If that number is a 0, it returns the name of the current label marker. If it is a -1, it returns the name of the previous marker. A 1 returns the name of the next marker. Try this in the Message window with a Score like that shown in Figure 13.1:

```
put marker(0)
-- "that"
put marker(1)
-- "other"
put marker(-1)
-- "this"
```

So, the Lingo command *go previous* is the same as saying "go to marker(-1)". Also, *go next* and *go loop* match the other two lines in the preceding example.

You can even use the *marker* function to get or go to markers that are several markers after or before the current one. Just use a higher number, such as 2 or -2, to go to markers more than one away from the current marker.

Using *Go*

To use the *go* command to actually do something, all you need to do is place it in a simple behavior script. Here is an example:

```
on mouseUp
  go to frame 8
end
```

Be sure that you create this as a behavior script, not a movie script. Check this option using the Script Cast Member Properties dialog box. Use the Info button in the script window to access this dialog box.

After you have this behavior script, you can drag and drop it on any sprite to create a simple button. The script acts in the same way as a behavior created with the Behavior Inspector would act.

A more useful behavior would go to a frame label rather than a number. You can also use *go next* and *go previous* to create forward and backward buttons.

Another way to use the *go* command is in a frame script. This example is probably the most commonly written script in Lingo:

```
on exitFrame
  go to the frame
end
```

All that this frame script does is hold the movie on the current frame. Every time the frame ends, it simply starts over again. A behavior in the library called "Hold on Current Frame" does this as well. You use this script to hold the movie on a frame while the user selects buttons and performs actions.

You can also use the *go loop* command in this way to have the movie loop back to the current frame marker. While "go to the frame" loops on one frame, *go loop* can loop on a whole series of frames. This enables you to have looping animation present while still keeping elements, such as buttons, around for the users to select.

Play

A second way to navigate around a movie is to use the *play* command. The basic command works just like a *go*, but there is a major difference. *Play* actually remembers which frame the movie was on when the command was issued. That way, the *play done* command can be used to return the playback head to the original frame.

Suppose you have three labels named "menu", "chapter1", and "chapter2" in the Score. A button on the frame labeled "menu" can issue this command:

```
play frame "chapter1"
```

Then, another button on the frame labeled "chapter1" can issue a *play done* to have the playback head return to the frame "menu". The same *play done* button and behavior can be reused in the frame labeled "chapter2".

You could, in fact, issue the initial *play* command anywhere in the movie and Director remembers that frame and uses it with the *play done* command.

Leaving the Movie

Both *go* and *play* can be used to jump to another movie as well as a frame in the current movie. The syntax is simply an extension of what you have already read about.

Here is a behavior that opens another movie and starts playing it from frame 1:

```
on mouseUp
  go to movie "nextMovie.dir"
end
```

If you don't want to have the movie start playing on frame 1, you can specify the frame by extending the command a bit:

```
on mouseUp
  go to frame "intro" of movie "nextMovie.dir"
end
```

You can use the same format with the *play* command. The power of the *play* command really shines here. You can have a button that takes users to a completely separate movie and enables them to navigate there. When they are finished, they can press a button that executes a *play done* command and they will return to the previous movie. The *play done* command even returns users to the correct frame in that movie.

Director is actually smart enough to assume the correct extension at the end of a movie name if you leave it off. This way, you don't have to worry about having a .dir extension on a Windows file and not on a Mac. It also solves the problem of changing the movie's filename to have a .dxr or a .dcr when you protect or compress it later.

⇨ *For more information about movies and navigation,* **see** *"Nonlinear Presentations,"* **p. 55** *(Chapter 2, "Presentations with Director")*

CONTROLLING SPRITE PROPERTIES

Besides navigation, the next most important task that a Lingo command can perform is to change the properties of a sprite. Properties are attributes of sprites that describe anything from their positions on the Stage to their ink types. Changing the sprites' properties is how you use Lingo to animate your sprites.

You will usually set sprite properties in the behavior scripts attached to the sprites, but for now you can examine some sprite properties in the Message window.

Sprite Location

For these examples, create a bitmap member and place it on the Stage and in the Score at Sprite channel 1. Then, open the Message window. Try this:

```
sprite(1).locH = 50
updateStage
```

You should see your sprite jump so that its registration point (usually the center) is 50 pixels from the left side of the Stage. It was the first line of the example that actually did this. It set the property *locH* of sprite 1 to the number 50. The *locH* property is the horizontal location of the sprite.

However, you didn't see any change on the Stage until the second command, *updateStage*. This is a special command that shows changes to sprite properties on the Stage while the movie is not playing. If the movie had been playing, and the change to the property had been inside a behavior script, the Stage would have updated automatically the next time a frame began. But for all the examples here, you need to use *updateStage* to see the sprite properties change.

The syntax "sprite(1).locH" uses dot syntax. Had you been programming in Director 6.5 or earlier, you would have actually typed this:

```
set the locH of sprite 1 = 50
updateStage
```

This older syntax still works for simple examples such as this one. However, it is best to get used to the new dot syntax. It's not only easier to type, but also required for features of Director that are new to this version.

You can also set the vertical location of a sprite. To do this, use the *locV* property.

```
sprite(1).locV = 100
updateStage
```

There is also a way to set both the horizontal and vertical locations of a sprite. This property is just called the *loc* of the sprite. However, it doesn't take a number value, but rather a *point.*

A *point* is a special Lingo object that looks like this: "point(x,y)". The two numbers in the parentheses represent a horizontal and vertical location. Here it is in use:

```
sprite(1).loc = point(200,225)
updateStage
```

You can also set many other sprite properties. Table 13.6 shows a partial list of them.

Table 13.6 Partial List of Sprite Properties

Property	Description	Example Value
member	The member used by the sprite	member"myButton"
locH	The horizontal position of the sprite	50
locV	The vertical position of the sprite	50
loc	The position of the sprite	point(50,50)
rect	The rectangle of the sprite	rect(25,25,75,75)
ink	The sprite's ink	8
blend	The sprite's blend	100
trails	Whether the trails property is on or off	FALSE
color	The foreground color of a sprite	rgb("#000000")
bgcolor	The background color of a sprite	rgb("#FFFFFF")

Sprite Member

Setting the *member* of the sprite to something different from the original member is quite common. This way, rollover and down states for buttons can be different cast members from the normal state of the button, and animations can use different images.

To change the member that a sprite is using, just set the *member* property of that sprite. You cannot simply set it to the name or number of a member, but to an actual *member* object.

Member objects are simply ways of referring to a member that Lingo can understand. If there is a member called "button down state", you need to refer to it as "member("button down state")". If that member is member number 7, you could also refer to it as "member(7)".

Create a movie with two bitmaps. They can be anything, even just scribbles in the Paint window. Name them "bitmap1" and "bitmap2". Place the first bitmap on the Stage, as sprite 1. Try this in the Message window:

```
sprite(1).member = member("bitmap2")
updateStage
sprite(1).member = member("bitmap1")
updateStage
```

You will see the sprite change and then change back with each *updateStage*. You could have also referred to the members by their numbers.

Sprite Rectangle

The *rect* property also has a special Lingo object associated with it. In Table 13.6, the example "rect(25,25,75,75)" was used. This represents the position of the left, top, right, and bottom of the sprite, respectively.

You can set the *rect* of a sprite to any size, regardless of how well this corresponds to the dimensions of the actual member. In cases in which the member can be stretched, such as bitmaps, the member is distorted on the Stage to correspond to the sprite's rectangle. Try this in the Message window:

```
sprite(1).rect = rect(50,50,175,75)
updateStage
```

Sprite Ink

The *ink* property takes a number as its value. Unfortunately, you cannot set it to values such as "Background Transparent". Refer to Table 13.7 for corresponding ink numbers.

Table 13.7   Lingo Ink Numbers

Number	Corresponding Ink
0	Copy
1	Transparent
2	Reverse
3	Ghost
4	Not Copy
5	Not Transparent
6	Not Reverse
7	Not Ghost
8	Matte
9	Mask
32	Blend
33	Add Pin
34	Add
35	Subtract Pin
36	Background Transparent
37	Lightest
38	Subtract
39	Darkest
40	Lighten
41	Darken

Sprite Color

Changing the *color* and *bgColor* of a sprite has an effect only some of the time. It depends on the type of sprite and which ink it is using. A 1-bit bitmap uses these two colors to set the color of the black and white pixels of the bitmap. Color bitmaps that use the Lighten and Darken inks use these colors to alter the appearance of the bitmap.

There are several ways to define colors. The first is to set them to the red, green, and blue values for the *color*. To do this, you need to use the *rgb* structure. Like the point and *rect* structure, *rgb* helps you define an item that cannot be represented by a single number.

For these examples, create a 1-bit bitmap and place it on the Stage. It should be in sprite 1. It should appear black on the Stage as a default. Try this in the Message window:

```
sprite(1).color = rgb(0,0,255)
updateStage
```

The color of the black pixels in the bitmap should change to blue. The three numbers in the *rgb* structure represent red, green, and blue colors. The results of them being set to 0, 0, and 255 is that the color becomes pure blue. When defining *rgb* like this, keep in mind that the minimum value is 0 and the maximum value is 255.

Another way to define a color with *rgb* is to use the hexadecimal string value for the color. This corresponds to the color values used in HTML. Here is an example:

```
sprite(1).color = rgb("#0000FF")
updateStage
```

This sets the *color* to pure blue just as the previous example did. The six digits in the string represent the three colors: a "00" is a 0 and an "FF" is a 255. If you are familiar with hexadecimal values, you can use this system. It also comes in handy if you are used to working with HTML colors. Otherwise, stick to the other version of the *rgb* structure.

To refer to a color based on the color palette of the movie, use the *paletteIndex* structure. This enables you to use a palette color number rather than an *rgb* value:

```
sprite(1).color = paletteIndex(35)
updateStage
```

With both the Mac System palette and the Windows System palette, the color 35 is a red.

⇨ *For more information about sprite properties,* **see** *"Controlling a Single Sprite,"* **p. 256** *(Chapter 14, "Creating Behaviors")*

Before Director 7, you could define colors only according to the movie's color palette. These 256 colors were used for the *foreColor* and *backColor* properties. Both of these properties are now obsolete, but they still work in Director 8 if you really want to use them.

CONTROLLING MEMBER PROPERTIES

As well as setting sprite properties, you can also set member properties. These properties depend on the member type.

One example is the shape member. It has a property of *shapeType*. You can set this to be *#rect*, *#roundRect*, *#oval*, or *#line*. Create a shape member on the Stage and make sure it is in cast member slot 1. Then try this:

```
member(1).shapeType = #rect
member(1).shapeType = #oval
member(1).shapeType = #roundRect
member(1).shapeType = #line
```

Notice that the shape changes without an *updateStage* command. This happens because this command usually updates sprite properties. Member properties, on the other hand, update as soon as the property changes. There are exceptions to this, as you'll discover later with more advanced Lingo.

USING LIST VARIABLES

Every major programming language has the capability to store a series of variables. In some languages, these are called arrays. In Lingo, they are called *lists*. There are two types of lists: linear lists and property lists.

Linear Lists

A linear list is a series of numbers, strings, or data of some other type that is contained in a single variable. Try this in the Message window:

```
myList = [4,7,8,42,245]
put myList
-- [4, 7, 8, 42, 245]
```

Now that you have created a list, you need a way to access each of the items in it. This is done with some special syntax:

```
put myList[1]
-- 4
put myList[4]
-- 42
```

Lists can also hold strings. In fact, they can hold a combination of numbers and strings. They can even hold structures such as *points*, *rects*, and *rgb* values. Here are some examples of valid lists:

In Director 6 and before, you needed to use the function *getAt* to accomplish this task. This function still works, but the new syntax makes it unnecessary.

```
myList = ["apples", "oranges", "peaches"]
myList = [1, 2, 3, "other"]
myList = [point(50,50), point(100,100), point(100,125)]
myList = [[1,2,3,4,5], [1,2,3,5,7,9], [345,725]]
```

The last example shows a list that actually contains other lists. These come in handy in advanced Lingo. Here is an example of a list that holds a small database of names and phone numbers:

```
myList = [["Gary", "555-1234"], ["William", "555-9876"], ["John", "555-1928"]]
```

Here is a handler that shows a somewhat practical use for lists. The list contains a series of member names. When the handler is called, it uses the list to rapidly change sprite 1's member to these members:

```
on animateWithList
  myList = ["arrow1", "arrow2", "arrow3"]
  repeat with i = 1 to 3
    sprite(1).member = member myList[1]
    updateStage
  end repeat
end
```

The handler uses a *repeat* loop to take the variable "i" from 1 to 3. It then sets the member of sprite 1 to the member with the name used in each location of the list. An *updateStage* is used to make the change visible on the Stage.

Another way to create lists is to use commands that add or remove an item from them, rather than create the list all at once. The *add* command places an item in a list that already exists. A *deleteAt* command removes an item from a list. Try this in the Message window:

```
myList = []
add myList, 5
add myList, 7
add myList, 9
put myList
-- [5, 7, 9]
add myList, 242
put myList
-- [5, 7, 9, 242]
deleteAt myList, 3
put myList
-- [5, 7, 242]
```

The first line in this example creates an empty list. Then, you added three items to it. After taking a look at the contents, you added a fourth item. Finally, you deleted item number 3, which was the number 9, from the list.

Another command you should know about is the *count* property of a list. It tells you how many items are currently in the list. Try this in the Message window:

```
myList = [5,7,9,12]
put myList.count
-- 4
```

In the preceding handler example, instead of having "i" go from 1 to 3, you could have had "i" go from 1 to "myList.count". This would have made it possible to add or remove items from the list later, without having to worry about changing the hard-coded number "3" in the script as well.

Property Lists

One of the problems with linear lists is that you can refer to the items in the list only by position. A different type of list, called a *property list*, enables you to define a name for each item in the list. Here is a typical property list:

```
myList = [#name: "Gary", #phone: "555-1234", #employedSince: 1996]
```

Each item in a property list contains both a property name and a property value. For instance, the first item in the preceding list is the property *#name*, and its value is "Gary". The property name and the property value are separated by a colon.

To refer to a property in a list such as this, you can use the property name rather than the position. Try this in the Message window:

```
myList = [#name: "Gary", #phone: "555-1234", #employedSince: 1996]
put myList.name
-- "Gary"
put myList[#name]
-- "Gary"
```

You can add items to a property list with the *addProp* command, and you can also delete an item in a property list with a *deleteProp* command.

```
myList = [:]
addProp myList, #name, "Gary"
addProp myList, #phone, "555-1234"
put myList
-- [#name: "Gary", #phone: "555-1234"]
deleteProp myList, #phone
put myList
-- [#name: "Gary"]
```

Notice that you use a [:] rather than a [ ] to create an empty property list. You cannot use *addProp* with a linear list and you cannot use *add* with a property list.

To get values from a property list, you can use dot syntax, or the function *getProp*.

The properties in this list are called *symbols*. In Lingo, anything prefaced by a # character is a symbol. Anything referred to with a symbol can be accessed by Lingo very quickly. Symbols are ideal for property lists for this reason. However, you can use numbers and strings as property names in property lists as well.

```
myList = [#name: "Gary", #phone: "555-1234"]
put myList.name
-- "Gary"
put getProp(myList,#name)
-- "Gary"
```

USING FRAME SCRIPTS

Frame scripts are behaviors that occupy the Frame Script channel of a frame in the Score. This chapter already had one example of a frame script. It looked like this:

```
on exitFrame
  go to the frame
end
```

This simple frame script is very important. It holds the movie on a single frame and enables your other scripts to receive many "prepareFrame", "enterFrame", and "exitFrame" messages while users can explore the screen.

Without this type of frame script, the movie is obliged to move on to the next frame in the Score. For straight animation, this is fine, but for actually creating real programs, you need the movie to loop on the frame.

Just about all the scripts in this book from this point on rely on an on "exitFrame" handler that loops on the frame.

TROUBLESHOOTING LINGO SYNTAX

- Any time you place something inside quotes, it represents a string. So, "4+2" is just 4+2, whereas 4+2 is 6.

- Remember that rounding works two different ways in Lingo. If you perform an operation on integers, such as 3/4, the fractional remainder is dropped, giving you a 3/4 = 0. However, if you use the integer function, the result is rounded. So, integer(.75) = 1.

- A function that does not use a *return* command at the end, or instead uses an *exit* command to leave the handler, returns a value of *VOID*, which is interpreted by Lingo to be equal to *FALSE*. You can test for *VOID* with the *voidP()* function.

- If you use *getProp* to get the property value in a property list, and for some reason the property does not exist, you get an error message. This halts the program for users. However, if you use *getAProp* instead of *getProp*, you will get a *VOID* value rather than an error message. You can test for this and handle it in your code.

DID YOU KNOW?

- You can set the default number of decimal places that Lingo is to use in floating point values with *the floatPrecision* system property. It starts with a value of 4.

- Using a function called *chars* is another way to extract a piece of a string. If you try *chars*("abcdefgh",3,5), you get the value "cde". Because chunk expressions cannot be used if you plan to export to a Java applet, *chars* is the only option for extracting characters from strings or fields.

- If you use an *if* statement on a single line, Director expects there to be an *else* statement on the very next line. If there isn't, or if there is a blank line, Director assumes that there is no *else* statement to match the *if* statement. However, it is very easy to accidentally nest a one-line *if* statement inside another *if* statement that has an *else*. In that case, Director assumes that the *else* goes with the second *if*, not the first. This example shows how to fix this problem with a blank line:

```
if a = 1 then
  if b = 1 then c = 1
  -- need comment or blank line here
else
  c = 2
end if
```

- You can include more than one possible value as a condition of a *case* statement by simply placing a list of values before the colon separated by commas.

- Rectangles can be a series of four numbers, such as "rect(10,20,50,60)" or a series of two points, such as "rect(point(10,20),point(50,60))".

- You can also use the function *list* to create a list. So, list (4, 7, 8) is the same as [4, 7. 8].

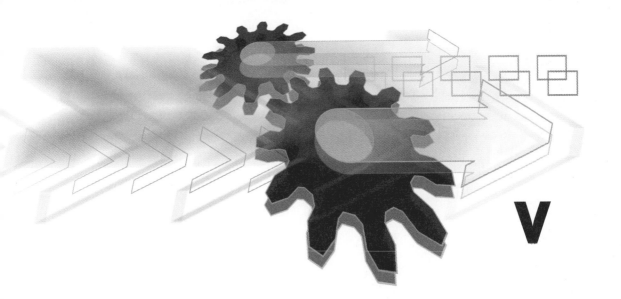

USING BEHAVIORS

IN THIS PART

V

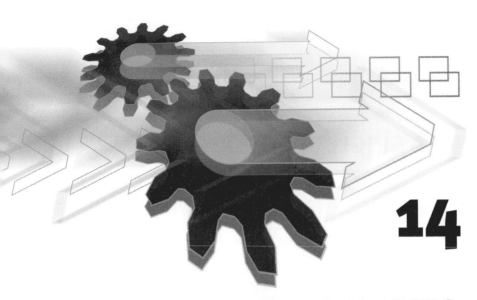

14

CREATING BEHAVIORS

Behaviors have become the standard way of getting things done with Lingo. Understanding behaviors—how to write them, how they work, and how to use them—is the key to powerful Lingo scripting.

CONTROLLING A SINGLE SPRITE

All that most behaviors essentially do is control a single sprite. You write them, and then attach them to one or more sprites in the Score to have them take control of that sprite.

As the name suggests, a behavior tells a sprite how to behave. For instance, an *on mouseUp* handler in a behavior tells the sprite how to behave when users click the sprite.

Sprite Messages

Many messages are sent to behaviors from different Director events. A "mouseUp" is a common example. A behavior script is the first script to get such messages and so it has the capability to use them before frame or movie scripts do.

Here is a complete list of messages that can be sent to behaviors. It is similar to the list in Chapter 12, "Learning Lingo," but only messages that behaviors can receive are included here:

- **mouseDown**—The user has pressed down the mouse button while the cursor is over the sprite.

- **mouseUp**—The user pressed down the mouse button while the cursor was over the sprite and has now lifted the mouse button up while still over the sprite.

- **mouseUpOutside**—The user pressed down the mouse button while the cursor was over the sprite and has now lifted the mouse button up while no longer over the sprite.

- **mouseEnter**—The cursor enters the sprite's area. In the case of an ink, such as Copy, the sprite area is the rectangle that bounds it. In the case of an ink, such as Matte, the sprite is the masked area of the sprite.

- **mouseLeave**—The mouse leaves the sprite's area.

- **mouseWithin**—This message is sent with every frame loop if the cursor is within the sprite's area.

- **prepareFrame**—This message is sent with every frame loop just before the frame is drawn on the Stage.

- **enterFrame**—This message is sent with every frame loop just after the frame is drawn on the Stage.

- **exitFrame**—This message is sent with every frame loop just before the next frame begins.

- **beginSprite**—This message is sent when the sprite first appears or reappears on the Stage.

- **endSprite**—This message is sent just before the sprite leaves the Stage.

- **keyDown**—This message is sent when the user first presses a key on the keyboard. It is sent for editable text members or fields only.

- **keyUp**—The user pressed down on a keyboard key and has now lifted it up. It is sent for editable text members or fields only.

Each one of these messages can be handled in a behavior with a handler of the same name. In addition to these event handlers, several special functions, listed next, can be added to behaviors. Each enables you to customize the behavior further.

- **getBehaviorDescription**—This gives you a chance to define a text description of a behavior. This is the text that appears in the bottom area of the Behavior Inspector window. It's a simple function; you are expected to create a string and use *return* to send it along.

- **getPropertyDescriptionList**—This function enables you to create a property list that contains the parameters for the behavior. This function enables the library behaviors to show a dialog box containing parameter settings when the behavior is dragged to a sprite.

- **runPropertyDialog**—With this function, you can use Lingo to automatically set the parameters of a behavior when it is dragged to a sprite.

- **getBehaviorToolTip**—ToolTips are those little yellow boxes of help text that appear when you roll over some screen elements. You can add this text to a behavior so that, if it is added to your Library palette, it displays that text as the ToolTip.

Properties

A behavior is an object-oriented programming method. Object-oriented in this context means that both the program and its data are stored in the same place. In the case of behaviors, the program is composed of the handlers of the behavior. The data is composed of the variables used by the behavior. These variables are called *properties*.

A property is something in between a local and a global variable. A local variable exists only inside a single handler, whereas a global variable exists throughout the entire movie. A property, however, exists throughout the entire behavior script, accessible to all the handlers in the behavior, but not normally accessible outside of it.

You create properties the way you create global variables. Rather than use a *global* command, you use a *property* command. The best place for this is in the first lines at the top of a behavior script.

Properties hold the data that is important to the behavior. For instance, if a behavior needs to move a sprite horizontally across the Stage, two properties might be "horizLoc" and "horizSpeed". They would correspond to the current horizontal location of the sprite and the number of pixels that the sprite moves each frame, respectively.

Although the first property, "horizLoc", might just start off from wherever the sprite begins, the second property, "horizSpeed", might be something that can be set when you drag the behavior to a sprite. In that case, "horizSpeed" might be referred to as a parameter as well as a property.

Using *me*

Because behaviors are object-oriented, each handler in a behavior must have a reference to the object it is a part of as its first parameter. Sound confusing? It can be.

A behavior script by itself is just a bunch of text in a cast member. When you attach it to a sprite, it's still just a bunch of text with which the sprite knows it has a relationship. However, when you run the movie and the sprite appears on the Stage, an object is created.

The object, called an *instance of the behavior*, is sort of a copy of the behavior. The Lingo code is loaded into a new location of memory and the property variables are created. This instance is now attached to and controlling the sprite.

If the same behavior is attached to two different sprites, and they both appear on the Stage at the same time, they actually have two different instances of the behavior. Both instances have copies of the same handlers, and both have properties of the same names, but the values of these properties are stored in different locations and can have different values.

The idea of an instance needs to be present in your behavior code. Each handler needs to know that it is part of a behavior. To signify this in your code, you should place the *me* parameter as the first parameter of all handlers in the behavior.

Create a new script member and set its type to be "Behavior". Now, add this simple script to it:

```
on mouseUp me
  put me
end
```

Name this behavior "Test Behavior" and attach it to any sprite on the Stage. A simple shape will do. Run the movie and click the sprite. You should see something like this appear in the Message window:

```
-- <offspring "Test Behavior" 4 33b1e64>
```

The actual numbers at the end of this line will vary. They are the memory locations of the instance of the behavior and are not important to your programming. However, the special variable *me* is important. Because it points to the actual instance of the object, having it as the first parameter of all the handlers in a behavior indicates that the handlers are all meant to be a part of the behavior.

If you are still confused, think of it this way: The common first parameter *me* of the handlers in a behavior ties all those handlers together. *me* is a reference to the instance of the behavior where all the handlers and properties exist.

me itself has some properties, the most useful of which is *spriteNum*. You can use *spriteNum* to get the Sprite channel number of the sprite to which the behavior is currently attached:

```
on mouseUp me
  put me.spriteNum
end
```

If you don't place *me* after the handler name, the script doesn't work. As a matter of fact, it gives you an error message when you try to close the script window because Director doesn't even know what *me* is supposed to refer to if it isn't included after the handler name.

For more information about object-oriented programming, **see** "Creating an Object in Lingo," **p. 466** (Chapter 23, "Object-Oriented Programming")

CREATING SIMPLE BEHAVIORS

Simple behaviors can consist of no more than one handler with one Lingo command. Complex behaviors, on the other hand, can be hundreds of lines long with just about every known event handler and many custom handlers.

Navigation Behaviors

A simple navigation handler is usually applied to a button or bitmap sprite. It uses the *on mouseUp* event to trigger a navigation command. Here is an example:

```
on mouseUp me
  go to frame 7
end
```

This handler is no more useful than one created with the Behavior Inspector. However, using a single property, you can create a behavior that can be used on many different buttons.

```
property pTargetFrame

on getPropertyDescriptionList me
  return [#pTargetFrame: [#comment: "Target
Frame:",\
        #format: #integer, #default: 1]]
end

on mouseUp me
  go to frame pTargetFrame
end
```

This behavior uses a property "pTargetFrame" to determine to which frame the button will cause the movie to jump. This property is used in the *on getPropertyDescriptionList* function to set things up so that the Parameters dialog box for this behavior will enable you to select the frame number.

Notice the continuation character (\) at the end of the first part of a long line in the first handler. Lines of Lingo can be as long as you like, whereas lines in a printed book cannot. So, feel free to leave out this character and just type one long line. To use the continuation character in Lingo, hold down the Option key and press Return on the Mac or hold down the Alt key and press Enter in Windows. If you simply press Return or Enter, the line actually becomes two lines and generates errors.

Also know that the backslash (\) continuation character is new to Director 8. In earlier versions of Director, the continuation character looks like a lazy L (➡). This old character works in Director 8 as well.

The list in the *on getPropertyDescriptionList* function is a property list that contains one or more other property lists. The property name for the first (and only, in this case) item of the list is the name of the property, turned into a symbol by adding a # in front of it.

The list that is its property value contains three items. The first is the #comment property. This is the string that the Parameters dialog box will show for this parameter. The second item, the #format, tells the Parameters dialog box which types of values to accept for this parameter. The last item is a default value for this parameter.

When you drag and drop this behavior onto the Stage or Score, the Parameters dialog box appears with a field labeled "Target Frame:". You can see this dialog box in Figure 14.1. This field takes any number as a value. At first, it shows the default value of 1.

The property "pTargetFrame" can also easily be named just "targetFrame". However, sometimes it is useful to have your variable names provide a hint as to which type they are. Some programmers like to place a "p" as the first letter of property variables. "g" is a common prefix for global variables. Some developers prefer to place an "i" in front of property variables, to stand for *instance*. These are not really part of Lingo, but just convenient conventions.

Figure 14.1
The Parameters dialog box appears when you drop a behavior on a sprite and that behavior needs custom parameters set.

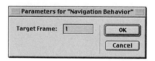

This behavior can now be attached to many sprites, but with a different target frame each time. This reusability is one of the powerful features of behaviors. You can have a movie filled with navigation buttons, but you need only this one behavior.

To complete this behavior, you should add an *on getBehaviorDescription* function to it. This function displays some informative text in the Behavior Inspector when the script is added to a sprite:

```
on getBehaviorDescription me
  return "Jumps to a frame number on mouseUp."
end
```

Figure 14.2 shows the Behavior Inspector when a sprite with this behavior is attached. Notice the description in the bottom area.

Rollover Behaviors

A common behavior in Director is one that has a button or other graphic that changes appearance when the cursor is over it. This is commonly referred to as a *rollover*.

Rollover behaviors are easy to do with the *on mouseEnter* and *on mouseLeave* events. The bitmap should change when the cursor enters the sprite's area, and then change back when it leaves it. The behavior can be as simple as this:

```
on mouseEnter me
  sprite(1).member = member("button rollover")
end

on mouseLeave me
  sprite(1).member = member("button normal")
end
```

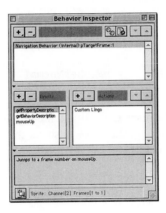

Figure 14.2
The Behavior Inspector shows a custom behavior with a description.

This behavior works fine as long as you use it only on a sprite in Channel 1, and you use only the two members, "button rollover" and "button normal," as the bitmaps. So, it is not much of a behavior because it can be used only in one specific instance.

The first thing that you can do to improve this behavior is to have it automatically figure out in which sprite it is used. The sprite number is a property of the behavior instance, which you know better as *me*. Rather than hard-coding the number 1 as the sprite, you can use the syntax *me.spriteNum*. This works as a variable that contains the number of the Sprite channel that this sprite is using. If it happens to be in sprite 1, it will contain a 1; otherwise, it will contain whatever Sprite channel number it is in.

```
on mouseEnter me
  sprite(me.spriteNum).member = member("button rollover")
end

on mouseLeave me
  sprite(me.spriteNum).member = member("button normal")
end
```

Now you have a behavior that can be attached to any sprite in any channel. However, it still uses two hard-coded members as the normal and rollover states. You can easily figure out the normal state of a button because it is probably the member with which that button is initially set. You can get that member and store it in a property in the *on beginSprite* handler.

```
property pMemberNormal

on beginSprite me
  pMemberNormal = sprite(me.spriteNum).member
end

on mouseEnter me
  sprite(me.spriteNum).member = member("button rollover")
end

on mouseLeave me
  sprite(me.spriteNum).member = pMemberNormal
end
```

The *on beginSprite* handler uses the sprite number, through *me.spriteNum*, to get the member that is assigned to the sprite in the Score. It stores this member in the property variable "pMemberNormal" and then uses it in the *on mouseLeave* handler as the member of the normal state.

Now you have only one hard-coded element left: the member of the rollover state. It is set to always be the member named "button rollover" no matter which sprite and which normal state member are used.

Three techniques for completing this behavior are most commonly used. The first is to assume that the rollover member for the button is always in the very next cast slot over from the normal member. So, if the normal member is number 67, the rollover member is 68.

```
property pMemberNormal, pMemberRollover

on beginSprite me
  pMemberNormal = sprite(me.spriteNum).member
  pMemberRollover = member(pMemberNormal.number + 1)
end

on mouseEnter me
  sprite(me.spriteNum).member = pMemberRollover
end

on mouseLeave me
  sprite(me.spriteNum).member = pMemberNormal
end
```

The *on beginSprite* handler gets the current member and places it in "pMemberNormal" as before. It also gets the number of that member and adds one to it to create a new member object. This member would always be the very next member in the Cast. It stores that in "pMemberRollover".

This behavior works only when the normal and rollover states of the sprite are placed in consecutive member slots. It's far more flexible than the previous script. However, you can use the member names to make it even more flexible. You can get the name of the normal member and append something to it, such as "rollover", for instance.

```
property pMemberNormal, pMemberRollover

on beginSprite me
  pMemberNormal = sprite(me.spriteNum).member
  pMemberRollover = member(pMemberNormal.name&&"rollover")
end

on mouseEnter me
  sprite(me.spriteNum).member = pMemberRollover
end

on mouseLeave me
  sprite(me.spriteNum).member = pMemberNormal
end
```

The only difference between the last two behaviors is how they set the "pMemberRollover" property. In the last example, the name of the normal state is taken and the word "rollover" is appended to it. The double ampersand is used to insert a space between the two. So, if the normal member is named "button1", the rollover member must be named "button1 rollover". It doesn't need to be placed anywhere in particular in the Score as long as it is named appropriately.

Another way to determine which member is used in the rollover state is to set the property in the Parameters dialog box each time the behavior is applied. Use the *on getPropertyDescriptionList* handler to do this.

```
property pMemberNormal, pMemberRollover

on getPropertyDescriptionList me
return [#pMemberRollover: [#comment: "Rollover Member:", \
        #format: #member, #default: VOID]]
end

on beginSprite me
  pMemberNormal = sprite(me.spriteNum).member
end

on mouseEnter me
  sprite(me.spriteNum).member = pMemberRollover
end

on mouseLeave me
```

```
  sprite(me.spriteNum).member = pMemberNormal
end
```

In the *on getPropertyDescriptionList* function, the format #member is used. This presents a pop-up menu list of all the current members in the Parameters dialog box for the behavior. You could have also used #string to enable yourself to enter a member name manually. Or, the value of #bitmap could have been used to restrict the pop-up to bitmap members only. Because no default makes sense here, a value of *VOID* is used.

Animation Behaviors

Now that you know how to change the location of a sprite on the Stage, you can apply that technique to a behavior and have it animate a sprite without tweening it in the Score.

Three events occur regularly and send messages to sprite behaviors: "prepareFrame", "enterFrame", and "exitFrame". The "exitFrame" is the best general-purpose animation handler, because it enables you to show the sprite untouched at first, and then altered by the commands in the *on exitFrame* handler the second time the frame loops. Here is a simple example:

```
on exitFrame me
  sprite(me.spriteNum).locH = sprite(me.spriteNum).locH + 1
end
```

This behavior simply takes the horizontal position of the sprite and adds one to it each time the frame loops. If you have a *go to the frame* command in the *on exitFrame* handler of the frame script, the playback head holds on the current frame and this behavior makes the sprite move one pixel every frame loop.

Instead of hard-coding a 1 as the number of pixels that the sprite moves every frame, you can create a property. You can use the *on getPropertyDescriptionList* function to have this property set when you drag the behavior to the sprite.

```
property pSpeed


on getPropertyDescriptionList me
  return [#pSpeed: [#comment: "Speed:", \
          #format: #integer, #default: 1]]
end


on exitFrame me
  sprite(me.spriteNum).locH = sprite(me.spriteNum).locH + pSpeed
end
```

This behavior now prompts you to enter a number for the speed of movement when you drop it on a sprite. The default is set to 1. Nothing is in the code that would prevent you from entering a negative number and making the sprite move to the left.

You can use another technique in the *on getPropertyDescriptionList* function that enables you to place a sliding bar in the Parameters dialog box rather than a plain typing field. All you need to do is add the property #range to #pSpeed's property list and add a small list with #min and #max properties in it. These properties determine the bounds of the sliding bar.

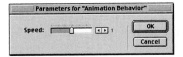

You can use this same behavior to make a sprite move from right to left instead of left to right. All you need to do is use a negative number for "pSpeed" instead of a positive number.

```
property pSpeed

on getPropertyDescriptionList me
   return [#pSpeed: [#comment: "Speed:", #format: #integer, \
         #default: 1, #range: [#min:-50, #max:50]]]
end


on exitFrame me
   sprite(me.spriteNum).locH = sprite(me.spriteNum).locH + pSpeed
end
```

Figure 14.3 shows the Parameters dialog box with this slider in it. Sliders such as this are great tools for controlling the range of values that a parameter can contain. You can also make it a pop-up menu rather than a slider by placing a linear list, such as [1,5,10,15,-5,-10] as the *#range* property. Those values would then be the ones available in the pop-up menu for the "pSpeed" property.

Figure 14.3
The Parameters dialog box can contain interface elements, such as as sliders, rather than plain text boxes.

CREATING A SIMPLE BUTTON BEHAVIOR

A simple button behavior should do several things. First, it should make the sprite switch members when users press it. This "pressed" version of the sprite is called the *down state*. Second, it should recognize the difference between the mouse being released above the sprite and it being released outside the sprite. This enables the users to click down, but then move the mouse so that it doesn't activate the button when it's released. Third, the button should perform a task, such as simple navigation, when there is a successful button press.

A behavior such as this should have two parameters. The first is a property that determines the down state of the button. The second defines what the navigation function of the behavior should be. Here is the *on getPropertyDescriptionList* handler for this behavior:

```
property pMemberNormal, pMemberDown, pTargetFrame

on getPropertyDescriptionList me
  list = [:]
  addProp list, #pMemberDown, [#comment: "Down State Member:", \
     #format: #member, #default: VOID]
  addProp list, #pTargetFrame, [#comment: "Target Frame Label:", \
     #format: #marker, #default: VOID]
  return list
end
```

First, notice that the variable "list" is built, property by property, and then returned. This makes the code easier to read than a one-line *return* command does.

Two special formats are used for the properties in the list. The first is #member, which presents a pop-up menu of all the available members. The second is #format, which presents a pop-up menu of available Score markers. It also adds the markers #next, #previous, and #loop, which can be used along with the go to *frame* command to go to the next, preceding, or current marker.

The *on beginSprite* handler gets just the starting member of the sprite, which is used for the normal button state member.

```
on beginSprite me
  pMemberNormal = sprite(me.spriteNum).member
end
```

The next three handlers refer to the three mouse button actions that are possible: "mouseDown", "mouseUp", and "mouseUpOutside". The difference between the *on mouseUp* and *on mouseUpOutside* handlers is that the first also performs the action that the button is meant to do. The second just sets the member of the sprite back to the normal state.

```
on mouseDown me
  sprite(me.spriteNum).member = pMemberDown
end

on mouseUp me
  sprite(me.spriteNum).member = pMemberNormal
  action(me)
end

on mouseUpOutside me
  sprite(me.spriteNum).member = pMemberNormal
end
```

Rather than just perform the action in the *on mouseUp* handler, the handler calls another handler called "action". This is a custom handler that you create specifically for this behavior. It does not need to be called "action", but it seems like a sensible choice.

```
on action me
  go to frame pTargetFrame
end
```

This custom handler simply needs to execute the command "go to frame pTargetFrame". The property must contain either the name of a frame marker, or one of the special symbols that can be used by *go to frame*: #next, #previous, or #loop.

This completes the simple button behavior. Later in this chapter, you will see how to add a lot more functionality to it, including rollover states, actions other than navigation, sounds, and even different ways of deciding among the members for the down and rollover states.

USING COMPLETE BEHAVIORS

A behavior script has many parts. However, they are all optional. When you are writing quick behaviors to take care of a single action for a single sprite, you might use only one handler with one command. However, for complete behaviors, you will want to include all the optional functions.

Behavior Descriptions

The only use for a behavior description is to have something to appear in the bottom area of the Behavior Inspector. However, because it is in your script as the *on getBehaviorDescription* function, it can also act as commentary in your script.

All that the *on getBehaviorDescription* does to accomplish this task is return a string. You can do this with one line:

```
on getBehaviorDescription me
  return "This behavior plays a sound when clicked."
end
```

Chances are, however, that you want to present more information than just seven words. You could expand that line to include as much information as you want, but a better way might be to construct the string in a variable first, and then return its value.

```
on getBehaviorDescription me
  desc = ""
  put "This behavior plays a sound when clicked."&RETURN after desc
  put "Choose a sound to play as the Sound parameter."&RETURN after desc
  put "Choose an action as the Action parameter." after desc
  return desc
end
```

This example is easier to write and edit, and will also be easier to read for someone editing the script.

The behavior description is also a good place to include your name or your company's name if the behavior is to be distributed in any way.

Behavior Property Description List

Although the behavior description is cosmetic, the behavior property description list is an essential element for behaviors that require customization. You can use the *on getPropertyDescriptionList* function to create a Parameters dialog box for any behavior. The Parameters dialog box can contain a wide array of interface elements.

The property list that the *on getPropertyDescriptionList* returns contains a series of smaller lists. Each smaller list defines a single parameter. It does this through the use of four properties: #comment, #format, #default, and #range. Here is an example from earlier in the chapter:

```
on getPropertyDescriptionList me
    return [#pSpeed: [#comment: "Speed:", #format: #integer, \
            #default: 1, #range: [#min:-50, #max:50]]]
end
```

The main list contains the definition of one property: "pSpeed". In this list, you can see each of the four properties needed to define the way the parameter should appear in the Parameters dialog box.

The #comment property is a short string that is used to label the parameter in the Behavior Parameters dialog box. It's nice to place a colon as the last character if you like that style.

The #format property can be set to one of many things. Many settings place a specific type of pop-up menu in the Parameters dialog box. The #member setting, for instance, places a pop-up menu that enables you to select any member used by the movie. Table 14.1 shows the different #format property settings.

Table 14.1   Settings Used by the #format Property

Setting	Parameter Dialog Result	Possible Values
#integer	A text entry area	The value is converted to an integer
#float	A text entry area	The value is converted to a floating point number
#string	A text entry area	A string
#boolean	A check box	TRUE or FALSE (1 or 0)
#symbol	A text entry area	A symbol
#member	A pop-up menu with a list of all members	A member name
#bitmap	A pop-up menu with a list of bitmap members	A member name
#filmloop	A pop-up menu with a list of film loop members	A member name
#field	A pop-up menu with a list of field members	A member name
#palette	A pop-up menu with a list of palette members and built-in Director palettes	A string with the name of the palette
#sound	A pop-up menu with a list of sound members	A member name
#button	A pop-up menu with a list of pushbutton, radio button, and check box members	A member name

Table 14.1   Continued

Setting	Parameter Dialog Result	Possible Values
#shape	A pop-up menu with a list of shape members	A member name
#vectorShape	A pop-up menu with a list of vector graphic members	A member name
#font	A pop-up menu with a list of font members	A member name
#digitalVideo	A pop-up menu with a list of digital video members	A member name
#script	A pop-up menu with a list of script members	A member name
#text	A pop-up menu with a list of text members	A member name
#transition	A pop-up menu with a list of built-in transitions	A transition member name
#frame	A text field	A frame number
#marker	A list of markers in the Score, plus "next", "previous", and "loop"	A string or the symbol #next, #previous, or #loop
#ink	A list of inks	An ink number

Most of the #format types result in a pop-up menu being placed in the Parameters dialog box. When there are absolutely no values that can be used there, a text field appears instead. For instance, if one parameter is set to #sound and there are no sound members in the movie yet, a text field replaces the pop-up menu.

The #range property is optional at all times, but can be useful for narrowing choices. There are two ways to use it: as a pop-up menu list of items or as a slider with minimum and maximum values.

A slider is created in the Parameters dialog box with the format [#min: a, #max: b]. The values of the slider go from a to b. When used with a linear list, such as ["a", "b", "c"], the values of that list are used as choices in the pop-up.

The #default property is required for any parameter. However, you can use values such as VOID, "", and 0 in cases where you really don't plan on using a default.

Automatic Property Setting

In rare cases, you will want to create a behavior that sets its parameters semiautomatically, rather than requiring you to set them each time you apply the behavior. The *on runPropertyDialog* handler enables you to intercept the message that triggers the Parameters dialog box when you apply a behavior. You can use it to examine the properties and even change them. You can also decide whether the Parameters dialog box ever appears.

Here is an example behavior. It has both *on getPropertyDescriptionList* and *on runPropertyDialog* handlers. When the behavior is applied to a sprite, the *on runPropertyDialog* runs and sends a message using the *alert* command. It takes the property list for the behavior, which is passed in as a second parameter to the handler, and resets one of the properties. It then uses the *pass* command to signify that the "runPropertyDialog" message should pass on to open the Parameters dialog box as usual.

```
property pFrame, pBoolean

on getPropertyDescriptionList me
  list = [:]
  addProp list, #pFrame, [#comment: "Frame:", \
      #format: #integer, #default: 0]
  addProp list, #pBoolean, [#comment: "Boolean:", \
      #format: #boolean, #default: TRUE]
  return list
end

on runPropertyDialog me, list
  setProp list, #pFrame, the frame + 1
  alert "I will now set the pFrame property to the next frame."
  pass
  return list
end
```

> The *alert* command generates a plain dialog box with a string message and an "OK" button. It is a quick and easy way to show some information.

The properties in the behavior are passed to the *on runPropertyDialog* handler through the second parameter, which is the variable "list". The variable should contain something like this: [#pFrame: 0, #pBoolean: 1].

Because this is just a plain property list, the *setProp* command can be used to change the value of one of the properties in it. The "pBoolean" property is used only to color up the example a bit. The only property affected by the *setProp* command is "pFrame".

After the variable "list" holds a new value, you need to remember to return this value with the *return* command so that the changes can be applied to the behavior. The *pass* command can be placed anywhere in the handler, because it just tells Director that when the handler is done, the message that called it (in this case, a "runPropertyDialog" message) should continue to be used. The result is that the message triggers the normal Parameters dialog box.

Without *pass*, the Parameters dialog box never appears. This is sometimes desired when the *on runPropertyDialog* handler is meant to set all the parameters and override any use of the Parameters dialog box.

Controlling Where Behaviors Are Used

A new feature of behaviors in Director 8 is their capability to allow themselves not to be used. The handler *on isOKToAttach* enables you to execute some Lingo when the Director author first adds a behavior to a sprite. You can then determine whether the behavior really belongs with that sprite. If it does, the handler returns a *TRUE*. If a *FALSE* is returned instead, the behavior will not attach itself to the sprite.

The reason you would want to do this is to prevent a behavior from being attached where it doesn't make sense. For instance, if a behavior controls the text in a text member, it would make no sense to attach it to a bitmap sprite.

There are two parameters in addition to the *me* that are passed into the handler. The first is the sprite's type: either #script for the Script channel, or #graphic for a normal Sprite channel. The second parameter is the sprite number. You can then use the sprite number to determine whether the sprite is appropriate for the behavior.

Here is a handler that restricts the use of a behavior to only the Script channel:

```
on isOKToAttach me, spriteType
  if spriteType = #script then return TRUE
  else return FALSE
end
```

Here is a handler that restricts the use of a behavior to only a text member:

```
on isOKToAttach me, spriteType, spriteNum
  if spriteType = #script then return FALSE
  else if sprite(spriteNum).member.type= #text then return TRUE
  else return FALSE
end
```

If you do not use the *on isOKToAttach* handler at all, the behavior is able to attach to any sprite or the Script channel.

ToolTips

The only use for the *on getBehaviorTooltip* function is if you plan to use the behavior in the Library palette. If so, placing this function there enables you to define what text appears in that little yellow box called a *ToolTip*.

Here is an example. It basically works the same way as the *on getBehaviorDescription* handler. You need to simply return a string. In the case of ToolTips, these should be as short as possible so that they fit on the screen nicely and don't cover up too much when they appear.

```
on getBehaviorTooltip me
  return "Button Behavior"
end
```

BUILDING A COMPLETE BUTTON BEHAVIOR

Now you know enough to build a complex button behavior. This behavior needs to perform many tasks, such as the following:

- Changing state when users press down on the button. There should be a choice of how the down state member is chosen: as the next member in the Cast, as a member with the same name as the original member, but with the word "down" appended, or as a specific member name.

- Changing state when users roll over the button. There should be a choice of how the rollover state member is chosen: as two members from the original in the Cast, as a member with the same name as the original member, but with the word "rollover" appended, or as a specific member name.

- Playing a sound when users press down on the button. The sound name is chosen from the current sound members in the Cast.

- Playing a sound when users roll over the button. The sound name is chosen from the current sound members in the Cast.

- Changing the cursor when users roll over the button. The cursor is chosen from the built-in cursors.

- Playing a sound when the button is successfully clicked.

- Taking the movie to another frame with a *go* or *play* command when the button is successfully clicked. Also, a *play done* command can be executed.

- Calling a specific Lingo command or handler when the button is successfully clicked.

A behavior such as this is typical of what you need in a large movie. It takes care of all the different buttons that you may use. It even enables you to create nonbutton rollover sprites.

Creating the Parameters

To begin, create the *on getPropertyDescriptionList* handler. By making this handler, property by property, you can see how many properties are used and name them appropriately. You can then return to the beginning of the script and add the property declarations.

Start by creating the property list:

```
on getPropertyDescriptionList me
  list = [:]
```

Now, take care of the first course of action: creating a down state for the sprite.

In addition to the three choices previously listed in the bullet item, you should have a fourth choice: no down state. Here is the line of code that adds this property. The name of the property will be "pDownState" and a pop-up list will be used to let you choose the type of down state. You need to list these choices with the #range property.

```
addProp list, #pDownState, \
    [#comment: "Down State", #format: #string, \
     #range: ["No Down State", "Member + 1",\
             "Append 'down'", "Name Down State"],\
     #default: "No Down State"]
```

Notice that the default state is set to "No Down State". You need to set default states for all the properties.

One of the down state options is to name a down state member. You then need a pop-up menu for the name of this member as a parameter.

```
addProp list, #pDownMemberName, \
    [#comment: "Down Member", #format: #bitmap, #default: ""]
```

You need to provide similar functionality for a rollover state as you did for the down state. However, because you already have a way for the down state to be the next member in the Cast, it makes sense that the rollover state should be the second member after the current one. This way, you can line up normal, down, and rollover bitmaps in the Cast if you want.

```
addProp list, #pRolloverState, \
    [#comment: "Rollover State", #format: #string, \
    #range: ["No Rollover", "Member + 2", "Append 'rollover'",\
            "Name Rollover", "Cursor Change"],\
    #default: "No Rollover"]
```

As with the down state, you need to provide a pop-up menu of bitmaps for use in case the "Name Rollover" choice is selected.

```
addProp list, #pRolloverMemberName, \
    [#comment: "Rollover Member", #format: #bitmap, #default: ""]
```

There is an extra option for rollovers: the cursor change. If that option is selected, you want to know which cursor has been chosen as the rollover cursor.

```
addProp list, #pRolloverCursor, \
    [#comment: "Rollover Cursor", #format: #cursor, #default: ""]
```

You also need to provide a way for sounds to play when the button is clicked down and when the button is rolled over. You need to provide a check box for whether the sound is played, and then a pop-up menu with a list of sounds.

```
addProp list, #pPlayDownSound, \
    [#comment: "Play Down Sound", #format: #boolean, #default: FALSE]

  addProp list, #pDownSound, \
    [#comment: "Down Sound", #format: #sound, #default: ""]
```

The same properties need to be present for the rollover action:

```
addProp list, #pPlayRolloverSound, \
    [#comment: "Play Rollover Sound", #format: #boolean, #default: FALSE]

  addProp list, #pRolloverSound, \
    [#comment: "Rollover Sound", #format: #sound, #default: ""]
```

All that is left now is to define what happens when the button is successfully clicked. The first option is to have some navigation. This could be either a *go to* frame, a *play* frame, or a *play done*. There should also be an option for no navigation, and that should be the default.

```
addProp list, #pActionNavigation, \
    [#comment: "Action Navigation", #format: #string, \
    #range: ["None", "go to frame", "play frame", "play done"],\
    #default: "None"]
```

If either a *go* frame or *play* frame is selected, there needs to be a property that holds the name of that frame. A *play done* does not need a frame name.

```
addProp list, #pActionFrame,\
    [#comment: "Action Frame", #format: #frame, #default: ""]
```

There should also be an option for a sound to be played when the button is successfully clicked. This requires two more properties, similar to the sound properties for down states and rollovers.

```
addProp list, #pPlayActionSound, \
    [#comment: "Play Action Sound", #format: #boolean, #default: FALSE]

  addProp list, #pActionSound, \
    [#comment: "Action Sound", #format: #sound, #default: ""]
```

The last property is another action that takes place when there is a successful click. It is the name of a Lingo command or a custom handler. Using a special command named *do*, you can execute this command when users press the button. It can be something as simple as a beep or as complex as the name of a custom movie handler that does a variety of things. For the *on getPropertyDescriptionList* purposes, it just needs to be a string.

```
addProp list, #pActionLingo, \
    [#comment: "Action Lingo", #format: #string, #default: ""]
```

The *on getPropertyDescriptionList* is now complete. Just top it off with a return list. You should now go back and figure out what the property declarations for the behavior should be. Figure 14.4 shows the Parameters dialog box that results from all of this code. You can see each property listed in the *on getPropertyDescriptionList*.

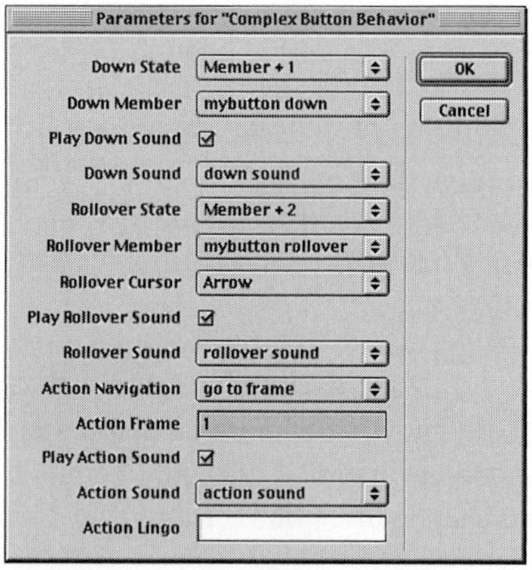

Figure 14.4

The Parameters dialog box for the complex button behavior shows the properties grouped together by function rather than in the order discussed in the text.

All the properties used in the *on getPropertyDescriptionList* handler should be present, as well as other properties that you can predict you will need. You should have properties to hold the normal, down, and rollover state member references. You will also need a property called "pPressed" that is *TRUE* when a button press is in progress and *FALSE* at all other times.

> You can use the property declaration on several different lines (as shown in the preceding example) or one long line. The same is true of the global declaration.

```
property pNormalMember, pDownMember, pRolloverMember, pPressed
property pDownState, pDownMemberName
property pPlayDownSound, pDownSound
property pRolloverState, pRolloverMemberName, pRolloverCursor
property pPlayRolloverSound, pRolloverSound
property pActionNavigation, pActionFrame
property pPlayActionSound, pActionSound, pActionLingo
```

Writing the Event Handlers

Now that all the preliminary steps have been taken to create the behavior, you can actually start writing the event handlers. A logical place to start is with the *on beginSprite* handler.

This handler should be used to set the properties that contain references to the three members used: "pNormalMember", "pDownMember", and "pRolloverMember". Their settings depend on the parameter properties. For instance, if the "pDownState" is set to "Member + 1", you need to get the member number of the original member, add one to it, and get that member.

Here is the *on beginSprite* handler. It first gets the member currently used by the sprite, and stores it as the "pNormalMember". Then, it looks at the "pDownState" property to determine what to place in the "pDownMember" property. The same thing is done for the "pRolloverState" and "pRolloverMember" properties.

```
on beginSprite me
  pNormalMember = sprite(me.spriteNum).member

  case pDownState of
    "No Down State":
      pDownMember = member pNormalMember
    "Append 'Down'":
      pDownMember = member(pNormalMember.name&&"Down")
    "Member + 1":
      pDownMember = member(pNormalMember.number + 1)
    "Name Down State":
      pDownMember = member pDownMemberName
  end case
```

```
  case pRolloverState of
    "No Rollover":
      pRolloverMember = pNormalMember
    "Cursor Change":
      pRolloverMember = pNormalMember
    "Append 'Rollover'":
      pRolloverMember = member (pNormalMember.name&&"Rollover")
    "Member + 2":
      pRolloverMember = member (pNormalMember.number + 2)
    "Name Rollover":
      pRolloverMember = member pRolloverMemberName
  end case

  pPressed = FALSE
end
```

The last thing that the *on beginSprite* handler does is set the "pPressed" property to *FALSE*. Note that properties such as "pDownState", "pDownMemberName", and "pRolloverMemberName" are no longer needed in the behavior. Their purpose was to determine what "pDownMember" and "pRolloverMember" are supposed to be.

A comprehensive behavior such as this one requires you to use most of the basic event handlers: *on mouseDown, on mouseUp, on mouseUpOutside, on mouseEnter,* and *on mouseLeave.* The last two are used to determine when the sprite is being rolled over.

In the *on mouseDown* handler, you need to place the commands that get executed when the sprite is first clicked. Specifically, you need to set the member to the down state, play a sound if needed, and set the "pPressed" property.

```
on mouseDown me
  pPressed = TRUE
  sprite(me.spriteNum).member = pDownMember

  if pPlayDownSound then
    puppetSound pDownSound
  end if
end
```

The *on mouseUp* handler is the other end of the click. Here you need to call a custom handler that performs the button's actions. You also need to set the "pPressed" property to *FALSE*. Because you can't assume that the action of the button will be to leave the current frame entirely, it's a good idea to set the member of the sprite back to a nonpressed state. Because the cursor must still be over the sprite when the button is released to get an *on mouseUp* message, you should set the sprite not to the normal state, but to the rollover state.

```
on mouseUp me
  pPressed = FALSE
```

```
  sprite(me.spriteNum).member = pRolloverMember
  doAction(me)
end
```

The companion to *on mouseUp* is *on mouseUpOutside*. If this handler is executed, it means that the user clicked the button when the cursor was over the sprite at first, but then moved off it before lifting up. This is a standard user interface way of backing out of an action. The user clearly does not want the action to take place, so you should not call the "on doAction" handler as in the *on mouseUp* handler. In addition, you know that the cursor is not over the sprite, so you can set the member back to the normal state.

```
on mouseUpOutside me
  pPressed = FALSE
  sprite(me.spriteNum).member = pNormalMember
end
```

The two rollover handlers, *on mouseEnter* and *on mouseLeave*, actually have a lot more to do. The first handler needs to set the member to the rollover member. However, if the user has already clicked and is holding down the mouse button, the down state member should be used instead.

In addition, the *on mouseEnter* handler needs to play a sound if required. If the "pRolloverState" property is set to "Cursor Change", the cursor command should be used to change the cursor.

```
on mouseEnter me
  if pPressed then
    sprite(me.spriteNum).member = pDownMember
  else
    sprite(me.spriteNum).member = pRolloverMember
  end if

  if pPlayRolloverSound then
    puppetSound pRolloverSound
  end if

  if pRolloverState = "Cursor Change" then
    cursor(pRolloverCursor)
  end if
end
```

The companion *on mouseLeave* handler has to undo what the *on mouseEnter* handler does. This is fairly simple. It needs to set the member back to the normal state, and change the cursor back if needed.

The *cursor* command changes the cursor to one of many special built-in cursors. In this case, it gets the setting from the Parameters pop-up. You can also use numbers, such as 280 for a hand or 4 for a clock/watch. The number -1 resets the cursor.

```
on mouseLeave me
  sprite(me.spriteNum).member = pNormalMember

  if pRolloverState = "Cursor Change" then
    cursor(0)
  end if
end
```

That takes care of all the event handlers needed. Only the custom "doAction" handler is left. This handler needs to look at three possible values for "pActionNavigation" that need processing. In each case, it performs the necessary commands. Because a navigation command takes the movie immediately away from the current frame where the sprite is, you should use "cursor(0)" to reset the cursor before that happens.

In addition to navigation, the "on doAction" handler figures out when a sound is needed. It also determines whether any Lingo command was entered as the "pActionLingo" property. It uses the *do* command to run that command or handler.

Also notice that rather than just using the "pActionFrame" as a marker name, the code checks to see whether it can be considered a number. It uses the *integer* function to do this. This function tries to convert the string to a number. If it is successful, it uses the number as a frame to jump to, rather than as a marker label string. The same can be done for the "play frame" option if you want.

```
on doAction me
  if pActionNavigation = "go to frame" then
    cursor(0)
    if integer(pActionFrame) > 0 then
      go to frame integer(pActionFrame)
    else
      go to frame pActionFrame
    end if
  else if pActionNavigation = "play frame" then
    cursor(0)
    play frame pActionFrame
  else if pActionNavigation = "play done" then
    cursor(0)
    play done
  end if

  if pPlayActionSound then
    puppetSound pActionSound
  end if

  if pActionLingo <> "" then
    do pActionLingo
  end if
end
```

This behavior is now a powerful multipurpose script that can be used over and over in your current movie and others. Gather any general-purpose behaviors such as this and store them in your own behavior library for future use.

CREATING ANIMATION BEHAVIORS

With Lingo, animation does not have to take place over several frames anymore. Instead, it can exist on a single frame as the movie loops on that frame. The possibilities are limitless, but the following two examples show some of them.

Bouncing off Walls

Changing the position of a sprite is easy enough to do. Moving one in a straight line is no great feat, because the Score and tweening already enable you to do this easily. With Lingo, however, you can create a behavior that makes a sprite react to its environment. For example, it can bounce off walls.

A behavior to do this is relatively simple. As usual, first create the on getPropertyDescriptionList handler. Three properties should be sufficient: the speed of movement in horizontal and vertical directions, plus a rectangle to bound the object.

```
property pMoveX, pMoveY, pLimit

on getPropertyDescriptionList me
  list = [:]
  addProp list, #pMoveX, [#Comment: "Horizontal Movement",\
    #format: #integer, #range: [#min:-10,#max:10], #default: 0]
  addProp list, #pMoveY, [#Comment: "Vertical Movement",\
    #format: #integer, #range: [#min:-10,#max:10], #default: 0]
  addProp list, #pLimit, [#Comment: "Limit Rectangle",\
    #format: #rect, #default: rect(0,0,640,480)]
  return list
end
```

Using sliders for the horizontal and vertical movement is a good idea, because you probably don't want to be using far-out values anyway. In this case, the properties are limited to plus or minus 10 pixels at a time.

The "pLimit" property is supposed to be a *rect* structure. Using the format type #rect forces the value of the text entered for this property into a *rect*.

Figure 14.5 shows the Parameters dialog box that results when this behavior is dropped onto a sprite.

The use of X and Y in variable names is common in Lingo and other languages. The X value is commonly used to denote horizontal positions and movement, whereas Y is commonly used to denote vertical positions and movement.

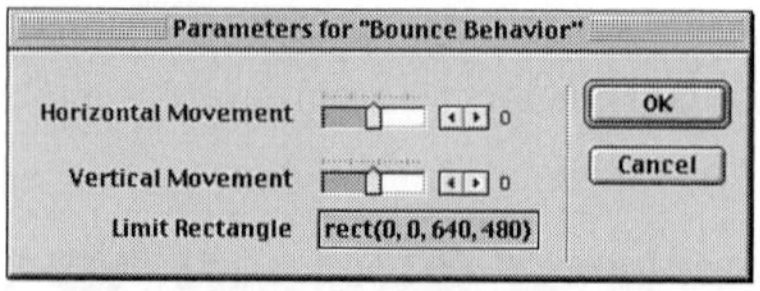

Figure 14.5
The Parameters dialog box for the bouncing behavior.

To make this behavior work, you need only one event handler. The *on exitFrame* handler is commonly used for animation such as this. You can take the current location of a sprite and add a point to it. Points and rects can be added and subtracted like other variables. Try this in the message window:

```
p = point(100,150)
p = p + point(40,20)
put p
-- point(140, 170)
```

This technique makes the coding easy. You don't have to break the location of the sprite into horizontal and vertical components. Here is the handler:

```
on exitFrame me
  -- get the old location
  currentLoc = sprite(me.spriteNum).loc

  -- set the new location
  newLoc = currentLoc + point(pMoveX, pMoveY)

  -- set the sprite location
  sprite(me.spriteNum).loc = sprite(me.spriteNum).loc + \
     point(pMoveX, pMoveY)
end
```

You will also need to check the "pLimit" property to figure out whether the sprite has hit a side and should turn around. A *rect* structure, like the "pLimit" property, can be broken into four properties: left, right, top, and bottom. You must check the left and right to see whether a side was hit, and the top and bottom to see whether they were hit.

After a hit is determined, the movement in that direction, represented by either the "pMoveX" or "pMoveY" property, should be reversed. That is, a positive value becomes negative and vice versa.

To make sure the handler works correctly when the limiting rectangle is tight or the sprite starts outside the limit, each case is handled individually. When the sprite hits the right wall, the "pMoveX" property is taken as an absolute value and made a negative. When it hits the left wall, the absolute value is taken and kept positive. The result in most cases is that the sign of the property changes when a wall is hit.

```
on exitFrame me
  -- get the old location
  currentLoc = sprite(me.spriteNum).loc
```

```
-- set the new location
newLoc = currentLoc + point(pMoveX, pMoveY)

-- check to see if it has hit a side of the limit
if newLoc.locH > pLimit.right then
  pMoveX = -abs(pMoveX)
else if newLoc.locH < pLimit.left then
  pMoveX = abs(pMoveX)
end if

-- check to see if it has hit top or bottom of the limit
if newLoc.locV > pLimit.bottom then
  pMoveY = -abs(pMoveY)
else if newLoc.locV < pLimit.top then
  pMoveY = abs(pMoveY)
end if

-- set the sprite location
sprite(me.spriteNum).loc = sprite(me.spriteNum).loc + \
    point(pMoveX, pMoveY)
end
```

You now have a behavior that causes a sprite to move at a constant rate and bounce off walls when necessary. The animation does not stop as long as the sprite is present on the Stage.

Adding Gravity

The "bounce" behavior seems to act on a sprite as if it were in outer space in a perfect universe. When the sprite hits the side of the screen, it bounces back without losing any speed or being pulled down by gravity.

To create convincing animation, you sometimes need to include elements such as energy loss and gravity. After all, in real life a ball thrown against a wall will hit the wall, fall down to the ground, and bounce back with less energy.

Adding gravity is easy, but it always takes two properties. The first is the amount of force that you want gravity to exert on the sprite. The second is the speed at which the sprite is traveling downward.

When you release an object in real life, it begins falling down slowly at first, and then picks up speed as it continues, because gravity accelerates the object's speed toward the ground. Acceleration is a change in speed, rather than the speed itself.

This acceleration is your first property: "pGravity". In addition, there needs to be a "pSpeedDown" property that keeps track of how fast the sprite travels downward. For the energy-loss feature of the behavior, all that is needed is a "pLoseEnergy" property that can be either *TRUE* or *FALSE*.

To create this behavior, you can start with the "bounce" behavior just described. You need to add a few properties to the property declaration:

```
property pGravity, pSpeedDown, pMoveX, pMoveY, pLimit, pLoseEnergy
```

Now, you need to add two new parameters in the *on getPropertyDescriptionList* handler:

```
addProp list, #pGravity, [#Comment: "Gravity",\
    #format: #integer, #range: [#min:0,#max:3], #default: 0]
  addProp list, #pLoseEnergy, [#Comment: "Lose Energy",\
    #format: #boolean, #default: FALSE]
```

The "pGravity" property works best when it is set to 1, but the slider accommodates values up to 3. The 0 is used as the default, which results in no gravity effect. You can see the resulting parameters dialog box in Figure 14.6.

Figure 14.6
The Parameters dialog box for the gravity behavior.

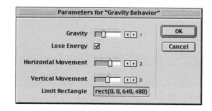

The "pSpeedDown" property needs to be set when the sprite starts, so you need to create an *on beginSprite* handler.

```
on beginSprite me
  pSpeedDown = 0
end
```

Then, each time the *on exitFrame* handler runs, you increase the downward speed by the force of gravity.

```
pSpeedDown = pSpeedDown + pGravity
```

Also, this property must be reversed when the sprite hits the ground, according to Isaac Newton. You can add one line after the line in the *on exitFrame* handler that reverses the "pMoveY" property.

```
pSpeedDown = -abs(pSpeedDown)-1
```

The -1 is added to the resulting speed to fix an inconsistency. When the sprite hits the ground and the "pSpeedDown" changed to negative, the location of the sprite is not changed again until the next time through the *on exitFrame* handler. At that point, a 1 is added to it before the location is changed again. So, if the "pSpeedDown" is 22, and it hits bottom, it changes to a -22. Then, it goes through the handler again and gets 1 added, so now it is a -21.

The result is that the sprite moves 22 one time, and then -21 the next. It gains one pixel because of this. But, by adding a -1 to the "pSpeedDown", it evens out.

To create the energy loss, first check to see whether "pEnergyLoss" is *TRUE*. Then, you add 1 to the "pSpeedDown" when the sprite hits the ground. However, be careful not to do this when the speed of the sprite is near 0, because it will slowly suck the sprite under the ground.

```
if pSpeedDown < -1 then pSpeedDown = pSpeedDown + 1
```

Here is the final behavior. Notice that the code that handles the ceiling hit has been taken out. This is because a ceiling hit is less likely now that gravity is involved. Plus, it would further complicate the code that handles the gravity. So, this behavior acts as if there were walls on the sides and ground below, but only sky above.

```
property pGravity, pSpeedDown, pMoveX, pMoveY, pLimit, pLoseEnergy

on getPropertyDescriptionList me
  list = [:]
  addProp list, #pGravity, [#Comment: "Gravity",\
    #format: #integer, #range: [#min:0,#max:3], #default: 0]
  addProp list, #pLoseEnergy, [#Comment: "Lose Energy",\
    #format: #boolean, #default: FALSE]
  addProp list, #pMoveX, [#Comment: "Horizontal Movement",\
    #format: #integer, #range: [#min:-10,#max:10], #default: 0]
  addProp list, #pMoveY, [#Comment: "Vertical Movement",\
    #format: #integer, #range: [#min:-10,#max:10], #default: 0]
  addProp list, #pLimit, [#Comment: "Limit Rectangle",\
    #format: #rect, #default: rect(0,0,640,480)]
  return list
end

on beginSprite me
  pSpeedDown = 0
end

on exitFrame me
  -- Accelerate due to gravity
  pSpeedDown = pSpeedDown + pGravity

  -- get the old location
  currentLoc = sprite(me.spriteNum).loc

  -- set the new location
  newLoc = currentLoc + point(pMoveX, pMoveY+pSpeedDown)

  -- check to see if it has hit a side of the limit
  if newLoc.locH > pLimit.right then
    pMoveX = -abs(pMoveX)
```

```
  else if newLoc.locH < pLimit.left then
    pMoveX = abs(pMoveX)
  end if

  -- check to see if it has hit top or bottom of the limit
  if newLoc.locV > pLimit.bottom then
    pMoveY = -abs(pMoveY)
    pSpeedDown = -abs(pSpeedDown)-1
    if pLoseEnergy then
      if pSpeedDown < -1 then pSpeedDown = pSpeedDown + 1
    end if
  end if

  -- set the sprite location
  sprite (me.spriteNum).loc = newLoc
end
```

COMMUNICATING BETWEEN BEHAVIORS

Behaviors do not have to control only their own sprites; they can actually send instructions and information to other sprites and behaviors as well. Three special commands are used for doing this—*sendSprite*, *sendAllSprites,* and *call.*

Sending a Message to a Sprite

The first command in question is *sendSprite*, which sends a message to a specific sprite, along with additional information. For example:

```
sendSpritesprite(sprite 1, #myHandler, 5)
```

This line sends the message "myHandler" to sprite 1. If that sprite has an "on myHandler" handler, it runs. In addition, the number 5 is passed to it as the first parameter after *me.* It might look like this:

```
on myHandler me, num
  put "I got your message:"&&num
end
```

A more useful example might be to tie two sprites together so that when one is dragged by the mouse, the other follows in sync. The first sprite's behavior might look like this:

```
property pPressed

on beginSprite me
  pPressed = FALSE
end
```

```
on mouseDown me
  pPressed = TRUE
end

on mouseUp me
  pPressed = FALSE
end

on mouseUpOutside me
  pPressed = FALSE
end

on exitFrame me
  if pPressed then
    -- calculate move amount
    moveAmount = the mouseLoc - sprite(me.spriteNum).loc

    -- move this sprite
    sprite(me.spriteNum).loc =  sprite(me.spriteNum).loc + moveAmount

    -- move another sprite
    sendSprite (sprite 2,#move,moveAmount)
  end if
end
```

This is a fairly basic drag behavior. When users click it, the "pPressed" variable is set to *TRUE*. This enables three lines to run in the *on exitFrame* handler. Those three lines calculate the difference between the current location of the cursor and the current location of the sprite, move the sprite that amount so that it matches the cursor, and then send that movement amount to sprite number 2.

The second behavior should be attached to sprite 2 and it can simply be

```
-- get message from another sprite to move
on move me, moveAmount
  sprite(me.spriteNum).loc = sprite(me.spriteNum).loc + moveAmount
end
```

This handler receives a message from the first sprite and uses the point included with the message to change its location. The result is that the two sprites move together when the first one is dragged.

Sending a Message to All Sprites

Another way for behaviors to communicate is to use the *sendAllSprites* command. This is essentially the same as *sendSprite*, but it does not require the first parameter:

```
sendAllSprites(#myHandler, 5)
```

As you can probably guess, this command sends the message and information to all the sprites in the current frame. Any of them that have an "on myHandler" handler receive the message and use it. If a behavior does not have this handler, the message is ignored.

The *scriptInstanceList* of a sprite does not exist until the movie is running and the sprite appears in the frame. Until then, the sprite and behavior are just Score information waiting for their chance to appear. When they appear, that is when the script instances are actually created.

Sending a Message to Specific Behaviors

Another way to send messages between behaviors is by using the *call* command. The difference between *sendSprite* and *call* is that *call* sends the message to a specific behavior attached to a sprite. This is handy when more than one behavior is attached to a sprite.

To use *call*, you need to specify both the sprite number and the behavior. You specify the behavior by using a script instance. You get this special value by using the *scriptInstanceList* of a sprite. Here is how you call the second behavior attached to a sprite:

```
scriptInstance = sprite(7).scriptInstanceList[2]
call(#myHandler,scriptInstance)
```

Instead of using *call* with a single script instance, you can pass a whole list of script instances. You can also include handler parameters after the script instance in the *call* command.

TROUBLESHOOTING CREATING BEHAVIORS

- Make sure that if you are creating a behavior, the script type is set to "Behavior". Otherwise, you won't even be able to attach the member to a sprite.

- Remember to use return at the end of the on *getPropertDescriptionList* handler. Without returning the property list defined within, Director cannot make the Parameters dialog box.

- When you refer to a sprite with the "sprite(x)" syntax, the sprite number needs to be totally contained in the parentheses. The code "sprite(x)+1_ is wrong, but "sprite(x+1)" is correct.

- When you build a list for an on *getPropertyDescription* handler, each item must have a #comment, #format, and #default property. Even in cases where there is no logical #default, you need to put something there, such as a 0, *VOID*, or an empty string.

DID YOU KNOW?

- You can set a #min and #max to a range of values in a behavior parameter description, and also can include an #increment property that determines how much one click of the arrow keys next to the slider will change the value.

- The continuation character was more useful in Director 6 and earlier, when lines in script could only be a finite length before a wrap was forced. A line is considered continued when the last character is a backslash (\).

- If you have overlapping sprites and you want to make sure your rollover behaviors work only when you roll over a visible portion of the sprite, check to make sure that *the rollover* is the same as the behavior's sprite number (*me.spriteNum*) before you set the member in the *on mouseEnter* handler.

- When you are determining the wall, floor, and ceiling positions for the bounce behavior, you might want to compute them relative to the Stage size. Use *(the stage).sourceRect* to get a rectangle with the Stage size. Use *(the stage).sourceRect.width* and *(the stage).sourceRect.height* to get the right wall and floor positions.

15

GRAPHIC INTERFACE ELEMENTS

IN THIS CHAPTER

Source movies for this chapter can be found on the CD-ROM in the "Book Movies" folder under folder 15.

Whether you are creating a simple presentation or a complex piece of software, it is primarily through user interface elements that the Director movie and the user interact. These elements can be as plain as pushbuttons, or as complex as slider bars. This chapter looks at the most common user interface elements and the behaviors that you use to create them.

CREATING DISPLAY ROLLOVERS

Chapter 14, "Creating Behaviors," contained a script that showed a simple rollover behavior. Typically, a rollover is a sprite that changes members when the cursor is "rolled" over it. However, there is another type of rollover as well, one that leaves the rolled-over sprite alone, but instead changes another sprite.

A typical use for this interface element is to present a list of items and then show more information about them in another part of the screen when users roll over it. Figure 15.1 shows a screen that does this. Rolling over the three items on the left brings up three different text members in the sprite to the right.

Figure 15.1
The screen shows three sprites on the left and one on the right. The one on the right changes depending on which sprite on the left the cursor is over.

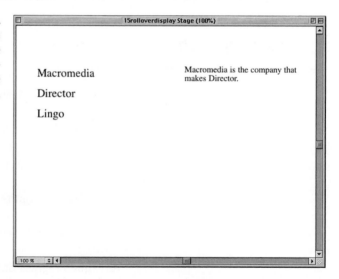

The behavior to do this is similar to the rollover behavior discussed in Chapter 14. Rather than change the same sprite, it must change a different one. It also needs to know which member to use. One last parameter should be a default member that is displayed when the cursor is not over one of the rollover sprites. Here is the start of a behavior:

```
property pRolloverMember, pRolloverSprite, pDefaultMember

on getPropertyDescriptionList me
    list = [:]
    addProp list, #pRolloverMember, [#comment: "Rollover Member",\
```

```
        #format: #member, #default: ""]
    addProp list, #pRolloverSprite, [#comment: "Rollover Sprite",\
        #format: #integer, #default: 0]
    addProp list, #pDefaultMember, [#comment: "Default Member",\
        #format: #member, #default: ""]
    return list
end
```

The "pRolloverSprite" parameter defines which sprite is changed. The actual sprite that the users must roll over is the one that the behavior is attached to. The "pRolloverMember" parameter is the member that the "pRolloverSprite" changes to. The "pDefaultMember" is the member that "pRolloverSprite" will show when the cursor is not rolled over the behavior's sprite anymore.

The default member should be the one in the rollover sprite on the Score. You can use *on mouseEnter* to change this sprite to the desired member. Then, when the cursor leaves the sprite, the *on mouseLeave* handler can switch it back to the default member.

```
on mouseEnter me
    sprite(pRolloverSprite).member = pRolloverMember
end


on mouseLeave me
    sprite(pRolloverSprite).member = pDefaultMember
end
```

As the cursor moves between the sprites, the "mouseEnter" and "mouseLeave" messages control which member the rollover sprite displays. Make sure that the sprites do not overlap; otherwise, the order of the messages can create undesired results. For instance, if sprites 1 and 2 overlap, the cursor can enter sprite 2 before it leaves sprite 1. The result would be that the default member would be displayed rather than the member specified by sprite 2.

To set this up in the Score, you need to attach this behavior to the sprites that are active and initiate the change in the nonactive sprite. Then, assign the same "pRolloverSprite" and "pDefaultMember" parameters to each, but a different "pRolloverMember" to each. This creates the basic effect discussed in this section. However, you can create more complex interfaces with different values of "pRolloverSprite" and "pDefaultMember" for each rollover.

Because you can attach multiple behaviors to a sprite, you can add a button behavior to these same sprites. That way, the rollovers are handled by the rollover display behavior here, but a click is handled by the button behavior. You can have sprites that display preview information, such as "Click this button to go to the index" in one sprite, but also react to the click to go to another frame.

➯ *For more information about creating rollover behaviors, **see** "Creating Simple Behaviors," **p. 259** (Chapter 14, "Creating Behaviors")*

USING CHECK BOXES

A check box is a button that has two states: on and off. Director has a check box member type that is a variant on the button member. You can use this built-in member as a check box, or build your own check boxes with two members per selection.

A behavior for the built-in check box member is almost not needed. The member reacts to a mouse click by itself, placing a mark in the box when clicked and then removing it on a second click. Figure 15.2 shows a small group of check box members.

Figure 15.2
A group of three check box members.

☐ Apples
☒ Oranges
☐ Bananas

One thing that a behavior can do is make it easier to determine which check boxes are checked. You can get this as a simple Lingo property of the member. For instance, in this example

```
member("apple check box").hilite
```

the *hilite* property returns *TRUE* or *FALSE*.

A behavior can use similar syntax, but because behaviors are assigned to sprites, not members, you can get the state of a check box according to the sprite number. Here is a simple behavior to do this:

```
on isChecked me
  return sprite(me.spriteNum).member.hilite
end
```

You can check the state of any check box by asking "isChecked(sprite *X*)", where *X* is the number of the sprite. Or you can do the same thing with "sendSprite(sprite *X*, #isChecked)". A value of *TRUE* indicates that the check box has a mark in it, and a value of *FALSE* indicates that the box is empty.

Because the built-in check boxes are rather limited in appearance, it is usually a good idea to create your own multistate buttons with bitmaps. Figure 15.3 shows three such buttons, with the middle one being checked.

Figure 15.3
Three sprites are used to hold bitmap representations of check boxes. Behaviors control these sprites.

Each sprite can contain one of two members: the on state and the off state. So, Figure 15.3 has a total of six members. In this example, the on states look the same as the off states, except for the addition of a check mark next to them.

A behavior to handle these states needs to know what the on and off state members are. It also needs to know whether the sprite should start out in the on or off state. Three properties and parameters take care of this, as follows:

```
property pOnMember, pOffMember, pState

on getPropertyDescriptionList me
  list = [:]
  addProp list, #pOnMember, [#comment: "On Member",\
    #format: #member, #default: ""]
  addProp list, #pOffMember, [#comment: "Off Member",\
    #format: #member, #default: ""]
  addProp list, #pState, [#comment: "Initial State",\
    #format: #boolean, #default: FALSE]
  return list
end
```

When the sprite begins, it should adjust itself to be the proper state, regardless of what is in the Score. This can be done by the *on beginSprite* handler. Because you need to reuse the code that changes the member of the sprite according to the "pState" property, it is a good idea to create a custom handler to do that. The *on beginSprite* handler needs to call that custom handler.

```
on beginSprite me
  setMember(me)
end

on setMember me
  if pState = TRUE then
    sprite(me.spriteNum).member = pOnMember
  else
    sprite(me.spriteNum).member = pOffMember
  end if
end
```

The sprite needs to change state when users click it. If it's on, it needs to go off, and vice versa. This can be done with one line using the *not* operator.

```
on mouseUp me
  pState = not pState
  setMember(me)
end
```

The *on mouseUp* handler calls the "on setMember" handler to change the member after the state changes.

One final handler can be a function that returns the state of the check box. This can be used by other Lingo handlers in movie scripts or other behaviors.

```
on isChecked me
   return pState
end
```

Note that you can also ask for this property directly in this manner:

```
sprite(X).pState
```

➡️ *For more information about using check boxes, see "Creating Questionnaires," p. 564 (Chapter 28, "Business Applications")*

USING RADIO BUTTONS

The topic of check boxes naturally leads into the topic of radio buttons. They are similar to each other. Whereas check boxes enable users to select one or more items from a list, radio buttons enable users to select only one item from a list.

Director also has a built-in radio button member in the form of a button member variant. It works the same way as the check box in that it already accepts mouse clicks and turns itself on and off accordingly. Figure 15.4 shows a small group of radio buttons.

Figure 15.4
A group of three radio buttons.

○ Apples
◉ Oranges
○ Bananas

Whereas check boxes don't really need any Lingo to work, radio buttons definitely require some. The reason is that at this point the radio buttons don't know of one another's existence. In the example in Figure 15.4, the "Apples" button and the "Oranges" button do not interact in any way. This means that the users can select both buttons, which goes against the whole point of radio buttons. The users should be able to select only one of the buttons at a time.

A simple behavior works to restrict the three buttons and get them to work together. To start, the behavior needs to know what other sprites are in its group. It also needs to know whether it begins as selected, which is the equivalent of *TRUE*.

```
property pState, pGroupList

on getPropertyDescriptionList me
   list = [:]
   addProp list, #pState, [#comment: "Initial State",\
     #format: #boolean, #default: FALSE]
   addProp list, #pGroupList, [#comment: "Group List",\
```

```
      #format: #list, #default: []]
   return list
end
```

The property "pGroupList" should contain a linear list of sprites in the group. For instance, if the example's three radio buttons are in sprites 1 to 3, "pGroupList" should be [1,2,3].

The "pState" property should also be set with care. One and only one of the radio buttons in the group should be set to *TRUE*. Then, in the *on beginSprite* handler, the sprite needs to be set to the on member if its initial "pState" is set to *TRUE*.

```
on beginSprite me
   if pState then turnMeOn(me)
end
```

The custom handler "on turnMeOn" is used to set the member of the sprite. Because these are radio buttons, this handler also has to make sure that the other sprites in this group are turned off.

```
on turnMeOn me
   pState = TRUE
   sprite(me.spriteNum).member.hilite = TRUE
   repeat with i in pGroupList
     if i <> me.spriteNum then
       sendSprite(sprite i,#turnMeOff)
     end if
   end repeat
end
```

The *repeat* command in this handler uses the form *repeat with i in*. This special form of the repeat command can be used only with lists. Instead of the variable "i" counting from one number to the next, it moves through the values of the list. If the list is [5,8,14], the loop runs three times and the value of "i" is set to 5, 8, and 14 for those times through the loop.

The *sendSprite* command is used to send the message "#turnMeOff" to each of the sprites in the list. An if statement makes sure that this message isn't sent back to the current sprite. The "on turnMeOff" handler is a simple one:

```
on turnMeOff me
   pState = FALSE
   sprite(me.spriteNum).member.hilite = FALSE
end
```

Now that there is a handler to turn on the current radio button, a mouse click is easily handled. It just calls the "on turnMeOn" handler, which turns on the current sprite and turns off all the others.

```
on mouseUp me
   turnMeOn(me)
end
```

One last handler can be used to determine which sprite in the group is currently selected. This handler uses the same repeat loop as the "on turnMeOn" handler, but rather than change the sprite, it just finds one that is on and returns that value.

```
on selected me
  repeat with i in pGroupList
    if sprite(i).pState = TRUE then return i
  end repeat
end
```

This handler relies on the fact that one and only one sprite is turned on. There should never be a time when none, or more than one, are on. The handler also has the unusual capability to return the same answer no matter which sprite in the group is used to call it. If a radio button group is in sprites one to three, a "sendSprite(1,#selected)" and a "sendSprite(2,#selected)" should return the same answer because they should have the same "pGroupList" property value.

Although this behavior takes care of the complexity of the radio button group, it does not offer the opportunity to use custom bitmaps as radio buttons rather than the boring built-in radio button member. However, it can be easily modified to do so.

The first step is to add two new properties to represent the on and off state bitmaps. These look the same as they do in the check box behavior:

```
property pOnMember, pOffMember, pState, pGroupList


on getPropertyDescriptionList me
  list = [:]
  addProp list, #pOnMember, [#comment: "On Member",\
    #format: #member, #default: ""]
  addProp list, #pOffMember, [#comment: "Off Member",\
    #format: #member, #default: ""]
  addProp list, #pState, [#comment: "Initial State",\
    #format: #boolean, #default: FALSE]
  addProp list, #pGroupList, [#comment: "Group List",\
    #format: #list, #default: []]
  return list
end
```

Then, the "on turnMeOn" and "on turnMeOff" handlers need to be modified to set the member of the sprite, rather than the *hilite* property of the member:

```
on turnMeOn me
  pState = TRUE
  sprite(me.spriteNum).member = pOnMember
  repeat with i in pGroupList
    if i <> me.spriteNum then
      sendSprite(sprite i,#turnMeOff)
```

```
      end if
   end repeat
end

on turnMeOff me
   pState = FALSE
   sprite(me.spriteNum).member = pOffMember
end
```

The rest of the behavior can stay the same. Figure 15.5 shows what this screen might look like. The off members and the on member differ only in that the on member includes an arrow to the right of the picture to signify that it is selected.

➥ For more examples of using radio buttons, **see** "Creating Standardized Tests," **p. 544** (Chapter 27, "Educational Applications")

Figure 15.5
A set of custom-built radio buttons. A behavior controls which member is used depending on which item is selected.

DRAGGING SPRITES

Although dragging sprites is possible without Lingo (by setting the *movable* property of a sprite in the Score), Lingo enables you to add all sorts of functionality to dragging. Learning how to drag a sprite with Lingo is the first step, and then you will be ready to try some dragging applications.

Dragging is a very useful interface action that all computer users are familiar with. The operating systems on modern computers require you to drag and drop files and folders all the time. Using them in Director movies is a good way to allow the users to manipulate items on the screen.

Simple Drag Script

A drag script can be as simple as setting the sprite to constantly follow the cursor. However, a real drag behavior waits until the user clicks the sprite, and then follows the cursor around until the user releases the mouse button.

To do this type of drag, you don't even need any parameters. However, you do need one property to tell the behavior when the dragging is taking place. This should be set to *FALSE* when the sprite begins.

```
property pPressed

on beginSprite me
  pPressed = FALSE
end
```

When the user clicks the sprite, the behavior needs to change this "pPressed" property to *TRUE*. When the user lifts up, it needs to be set to *FALSE*.

```
on mouseDown me
  pPressed = TRUE
end

on mouseUp me
  pPressed = FALSE
end
```

It's possible for the user to lift up the mouse button while the cursor is not over the sprite. The mouse location is updated in real time, whereas you will be setting the location of the sprite only every frame loop. To make sure that dragging stops whenever the mouse button is lifted, you need to also use the *on mouseUpOutside* handler.

```
on mouseUpOutside me
  pPressed = FALSE
end
```

Finally, the *on exitFrame* handler does all the heavy lifting. It checks to see whether the "pPressed" property is *TRUE*, and moves the sprite to the mouse location if it is

```
on exitFrame me
  if pPressed then
    sprite(me.spriteNum).loc = the mouseLoc
  end if
end
```

A Better Drag Behavior

The main problem with the simple drag script is a cosmetic one. The sprite appears to snap to center itself on the cursor no matter where users click. So, if you click the upper-right side of the sprite, the sprite immediately shifts so that the center, or actually the registration point, is directly under the cursor.

Fixing this glitch is not a problem. When the initial click is made, the difference in location between the mouse and the center of the sprite can be recorded. This value can then be applied to every change in the sprite's location. The result is that the cursor and the sprite remain synchronized, no matter where the user grabs the sprite. If the user grabs the sprite by the upper-right corner, it then drags by the upper-right corner.

To make this change, first add the property "pClickDiff" to the property declaration. Then, alter the *on mouseDown* handler to record the difference between the click location and the sprite location, as follows:

```
on mouseDown me
  pPressed = TRUE
  pClickDiff = sprite(me.spriteNum).loc - the clickLoc
end
```

Now that the offset is stored in the "pClickDiff", it can be applied to the position of the sprite in the *on exitFrame* handler.

```
on exitFrame me
  if pPressed then
    sprite(me.spriteNum).loc = the mouseLoc +
pClickDiff
  end if
end
```

If this is still confusing, seeing it in action will help; check the example on the CD-ROM called 15dragging.dir.

The property *the clickLoc* is similar to *the mouseLoc*. They both return a point as their value. However, *the mouseLoc* might change if the mouse moves between the time the click was made and the time the line of Lingo code runs. *the clickLoc* gives the exact location of the last click in an *on mouseDown* or similar handler, whereas *the mouseLoc* is the current mouse position.

Click, Drag, and Lock

You can apply what you've learned about dragging by using it to build a matching game or quiz. You have elements of one type on one side of the screen and elements of another type on another side. The game is essentially made up of matching pairs. It's up to the user to drag the sprites on the left over to the sprites on the right. Figure 15.6 shows what this might look like.

Although this can be done with the drag scripts already described, these scripts have no capability to tell the user whether the match is correct. A better way to do it would be to have a script that locks a sprite into position if it is near the place it belongs.

This requires some parameters. The first is the number of the sprite to which that behavior's sprite should lock. The second should be the maximum distance that the dragged sprite can be from the destination sprite before it automatically locks.

Also, an option is needed to tell the behavior what to do in case the sprite is not close enough to its destination to lock. One option is for it to snap back to its original position. The other option is to leave it where it is.

Figure 15.6
The screen shows four pairs of matching items. The user's task is to drag the items on the right onto the correct ones on the left.

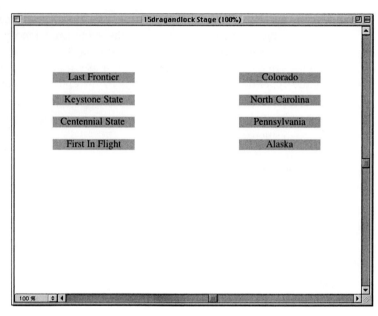

In addition to these new properties, you still need the old properties of "pPressed" and "pClickDiff". You also need a property to store the original location of the sprite in cases in which it needs to snap back.

```
property pPressed, pClickDiff, pLockToSprite, pOrigLoc, pLockDist, pSnapBack

on getPropertyDescriptionList me
  list = [:]
  addProp list, #pLockToSprite, [#comment: "Lock To Sprite",\
    #format: #integer, #default: 0]
  addProp list, #pLockDist, [#comment: "Maximum Lock Distance",\
    #format: #integer, #default: 25]
  addProp list, #pSnapBack, [#comment: "Snap Back If Not Locked",\
    #format: #boolean, #default: TRUE]
  return list
end
```

The "pLockDist" is a key property for this behavior. Without it, the user would be required to lock the sprite exactly into position over the destination sprite.

The behavior needs to start off by initializing "pPressed" and also setting the "pOrigLoc" property.

```
on beginSprite me
  pPressed = FALSE
  pOrigLoc = sprite(me.spriteNum).loc
end
```

The mouse click handlers are the same as before, except that a custom handler is called from the *on mouseUp* and *on mouseUpOutside* handlers. This behavior has more to do than just setting the "pPressed" back to *FALSE*, so it's best to place it all in a custom handler rather than attempt to duplicate the code between *on mouseUp* and *on mouseUpOutside*.

```
on mouseDown me
  pPressed = TRUE
  pClickDiff = sprite(me.spriteNum).loc - the clickLoc
end

on mouseUp me
  release(me)
end

on mouseUpOutside me
  release(me)
end
```

The *on exitFrame* script is exactly as before.

```
on exitFrame me
  if pPressed then
    sprite(me.spriteNum).loc = the mouseLoc + pClickDiff
  end if
end
```

The custom "on release" handler has to do several things. First, it sets the "pPressed" to *FALSE*. Then, it needs to determine whether the sprite is now close enough to its destination to lock into place. It calls yet another custom handler, "on distance", to do this. This function takes two points as parameters and returns the distance between them in pixels.

If the sprite is close enough, the new location of the sprite is set to exactly the location of the destination sprite. Otherwise, if the "pSnapBack" property is *TRUE*, the location snaps back to the original location. If not, the location remains where the user left it.

```
on release me
  pPressed = FALSE

  if distance(me,sprite(me.spriteNum).loc,sprite(pLockToSprite).loc) \
      < pLockDist then
    sprite(me.spriteNum).loc = sprite(pLockToSprite).loc
  else if pSnapBack then
    sprite(me.spriteNum).loc = pOrigLoc
  end if
end
```

The "on distance" function is a handy tool that is used in a lot of behaviors. It takes two points and uses the square root of the sum of the squares of the differences between horizontal and vertical locations. You might remember this formula from high school trigonometry:

$$\sqrt{((X_2 - X_1)^2 + (Y_2 - Y_1)^2)}$$

```
on distance me, point1, point2
  return sqrt(power(point1.locH-point2.locH,2)+ \
    power(point1.locV-point2.locV,2))
end
```

All that is left to do is apply the behavior to some sprites. In the example shown previously in Figure 15.6, the behavior should be applied to the sprites on the right. They are in higher Sprite channels and appear above the sprites on the left. The "pLockToSprite" of each one of these sprites should be set to the matching item's sprite.

If you were really making a game of this, you could use this movie script to determine whether all the sprites were locked in place.

```
on checkGameDone
  done = TRUE
  repeat with i = 5 to 8
    if (sprite i).loc <> sprite(sprite(i).pLockToSprite).loc then
      done = FALSE
    end if
  end repeat
  if done then beep()
end
```

This movie handler assumes the game is done by setting the local variable "done" to *TRUE*. It then looks at sprites 5 through 8, which is where the dragging sprites are located, and compares their locations to the locations of their designated destination sprites. If they all match, "done" is never set to *FALSE*. In this case, the result is a simple beep. However, you could also make it jump to another frame or play a sound.

The perfect place for a call to this handler is in the "on release" handler of the behavior. The movie needs to check this every time a sprite is locked, so place it after the "sprite(me.spriteNum).loc = sprite(pLockToSprite).loc" line.

⇨ For an example of click, drag, and lock behavior, **see** "Creating a Matching Game," **p. 526** (Chapter 27)

Drag and Throw

Another way to apply a drag behavior is to enable users to grab and throw a sprite. They click it and drag it around while the mouse is down, like the other drag behaviors, but then when they release it, the sprite keeps going with some amount of momentum.

This is much more complex than a simple drag behavior. First, you have more than just pressed and nonpressed states. A third state is the state of being thrown. So, the "pPressed" property should be replaced with a "pMode" property that is *#normal, #pressed,* or *#throw.*

In addition, you need to know how far and in which direction to throw the sprite when it is released. Measuring the distance between the position of the sprite upon release and the position of the sprite just before release provides the appropriate information. However, don't take the position of the sprite exactly one frame prior to release, because that can be too short a period of time: It is only one sixtieth of a second if the frame rate is 60fps. Instead, have a parameter that determines how many frames back to look to determine the momentum of the released sprite. A good default for this is five. So, if a sprite is clicked and dragged for 150 frame loops and then released, the position in frame 145 and the position in frame 150 are compared to set the throwing momentum. A list is needed to record the last five positions at any given time. Here is the property list *and on getPropertyDescriptionList* for this behavior:

```
property pThrowSpan, pMode, pCurrentLoc, pLocList, pMoveAmount

on getPropertyDescriptionList me
  list = [:]
  addProp list, #pThrowSpan, [#comment: "Frame Span of Throw",\
    #format: #integer, #range: [#min: 1, #max: 20], \
    #default: 5]
  return list
end
```

The sprite starts by setting the "pMode" to *#normal.*

```
on beginSprite me
  pMode = #normal
end
```

When the user clicks, the mode must change to *#pressed* and the list used to store the positions must be initialized:

```
on mouseDown me
  pMode = #pressed
  pLocList = []
end
```

Whenever the mouse button lifts, a custom handler called "on throw" runs. This handler calculates the momentum by taking the current mouse location and the first item in the "pLocList". It needs to divide that by "pThrowSpan" to get a relative per-frame movement amount. This way, if "pThrowSpan" is set to 5, the "pMoveAmount" is set to the current location of the sprite, minus the location of the sprite 5 frame loops ago, divided by 5:

```
on mouseUp me
  throw(me)
end
```

```
on mouseUpOutside me
  throw(me)
end

on throw me
  pMoveAmount = (the mouseLoc - pLocList[1])/pThrowSpan
  pMode = #throw
end
```

The *on exitFrame* handler must move the sprite whether it is being dragged or thrown. If being dragged, it needs to set the location of the sprite to the current mouse location. It also needs to record this location in "pLocList". If "pLocList" has more items than specified by "pThrowSpan", the oldest item is removed.

If the mode is *#throw*, the "pMoveAmount" is used to move the sprite. In addition, this property is multiplied by .9, thereby decreasing it by approximately 10%. This imitates a sort of friction that one would expect the sprite to exhibit when thrown. If you want, the .9 can be made into a property, say "pFriction", and altered using the behavior parameter dialog box.

```
on exitFrame me
  if pMode = #pressed then
    pCurrentLoc = the mouseLoc
    sprite(me.spriteNum).loc = pCurrentLoc
    pLocList.add(pCurrentLoc)
    if pLocList.count > pThrowSpan then pLocList.deleteAt(1)

  else if pMode = #throw then
    pCurrentLoc = pCurrentLoc + pMoveAmount
    sprite(me.spriteNum).loc = pCurrentLoc
    pMoveAmount = pMoveAmount * .9
  end if
end
```

Think of the possibilities of a behavior like this. Do you want to add code like that used in the bouncing behavior so that the sprite bounces off the sides of the screen? How about code that adds gravity? How about code that locks the sprite to the position of another if it's close enough? Combine all three and you get something that resembles a basketball free-throw video game.

CREATING SLIDERS

A slider is a familiar user interface element used in all major software programs. Sliders offer the best way to enable users to input a number within a small range. They are even used in behavior Parameter dialog boxes for this purpose.

Creating a slider with several bitmap members and a behavior can be fairly complex. A lot of actions must be taken into account, and more than one sprite is needed to form the elements of a slider.

Figure 15.7 shows what a slider should look like. This is just a straight imitation of the sliders used in the Director Preferences dialog boxes.

Figure 15.7
A typical slider enables users to pick a number from a range.

A full slider element contains six parts: a marker, a shadow, a background graphic, two buttons, and a text field. However, you can start by creating the main three parts: the marker, the shadow, and the background graphic. The shadow is the dark coloring to the left side of the marker. It is the only nonbitmap element in this case; it uses a shape sprite instead.

You actually will need only one behavior script, attached to the marker sprite. Like the button and drag behaviors, this behavior needs a property to tell whether it is in the process of being pressed. It also needs to know how far to the left and right it can move, and what range of values it represents, such as 1 to 3, 0 to 100, or -500 to 500. A relationship with the shadow sprite is needed, so one property should hold that sprite number. Another property needs to record the current value of the slider, as follows:

```
property pPressed -- whether the sprite is being pressed
property pBounds -- the rect of the shadow sprite at start
property pMinimumValue, pMaximumValue -- used by the marker sprite only
property pShadowSprite -- the number of the shadow sprite
property pValue -- actual value of the slider
on getPropertyDescriptionList me
  list = [:]
  addProp list, #pShadowSprite, [#comment: "Shadow Sprite",\
    #format: #integer, #default: 0]
addProp list, #pMinimumValue, [#comment: "Minimum Value",\
    #format: #integer, #default: 0]
  addProp list, #pMaximumValue, [#comment: "Maximum Value",\
    #format: #integer, #default: 100]
  addProp list, #pValue, [#comment: "Start Value",\
    #format: #integer, #default: 50]
  return list
end
```

The on *getPropertyDescriptionList* needs to use only four of the properties as parameters: the minimum, maximum, and starting value of the slider, as well as the shadow sprite's number.

Although the minimum and maximum values are set by the behavior's Parameter dialog box, the behavior also needs to know the physical screen locations of the minimum and maximum values. To determine these locations, a trick is used. The shadow sprite is set to mark the exact bounds of the marker sprite. Because the shadow sprite will be reset by the behavior when it starts anyway, using it to show the boundaries of the slider does not affect its future appearance. In the case of the slider shown previously in Figure 15.7, the shadow sprite is stretched all the way across the inner part of the background graphic. Its *rect* is recorded by the *on beginSprite* handler of the behavior. Then, it is set to display properly, as shown earlier in Figure 15.7:

```
on beginSprite me
  pBounds = sprite(pShadowSprite).rect
  setMarker(me)
  setShadow(me)
end
```

The left and right physical limits of the slider could have been added to the *on getPropertyDescriptionList* handler, but this would mean that you would have had to determine the exact screen locations and type them in. Worse than that, if the slider were moved, even by one pixel, you would have to re-enter these numbers. Using the shadow sprite as a "template" of sorts saves you the trouble, and it is easily adjusted on the Stage.

The *on beginSprite* handler includes calls to the custom "on setMarker" and "on setShadow" handlers. These take the current value of the slider and set the position of these two sprites.

The "on setMarker" handler first figures out the value range of the slider. If the slider goes from 0 to 100, the range is 100 (not 101). It computes the value of the slider as a number between 0 and 1, regardless of the real range. It then takes this percentage and applies it to the physical screen range to get the location of the marker:

```
-- this sets the marker sprite
on setMarker me
  -- compute the value as a number between 0 and 1
  valueRange = pMaximumValue - pMinimumValue
  sliderPos = float(pValue)/float(valueRange)

  -- translate to a screen position
  sliderRange = pBounds.right-pBounds.left
  x = sliderPos*sliderRange + pBounds.left

  -- set marker
  sprite(me.spriteNum).locH = x
end
```

The "on setShadow" handler sets the shadow to its original rectangle, but with the right side adjusted to fall under the marker.

```
-- this handler lets the marker sprite set the shadow sprite
on setShadow me
  x = sprite(me.spriteNum).locH
  r = rect(pBounds.left, pBounds.top, x, pBounds.bottom)
  sprite(pShadowSprite).rect = r
end
```

These handlers accomplish the task of setting the slider to its starting position. Now you need some handlers to enable users to click and drag the marker:

```
on mouseDown me
  pPressed = TRUE
end

on mouseUp me
  pPressed = FALSE
end

on mouseUpOutside me
  pPressed = FALSE
end

on exitFrame me
  if pPressed then
    moveMarker(me)
    setMarker(me)
    setShadow(me)
  end if
end
```

The *on exitFrame* handler checks to make sure that "pPressed" is true, and then calls other handlers to handle the work. The "on setMarker" and "on setShadow" handlers are there, but called after an "on moveMarker" handler. The "on moveMarker" handler does the opposite of what the "on setMarker" handler does: It determines the value of the slider based on the mouse location.

In addition, the "on moveMarker" handler translates the value to an integer. If you want the slider to show floating point numbers instead, just remove that line:

```
-- this handler takes the mouse position and figures the
-- value of the slider
on moveMarker me
  -- compute the position as a number between 0 and 1
  x = the mouseH - pBounds.left
  sliderRange = pBounds.right-pBounds.left
  pos = float(x)/sliderRange

  -- translate to a value
  valueRange = pMaximumValue - pMinimumValue
  pValue = pos*valueRange + pMinimumValue
  pValue = integer(pValue)
```

```
    -- check to make sure it is within bounds
    if pValue > pMaximumValue then
      pValue = pMaximumValue
    else if pValue < pMinimumValue then
      pValue = pMinimumValue
    end if
end
```

The "on moveMarker" also makes sure that the new value of the slider falls within its range. Note that this handler's sole purpose is to set the "pValue" property. After it is called in the *on exitFrame* handler, the "on setMarker" and "on setShadow" handlers update the sprites.

Because the value of the slider is held in the "pValue" property, a handler that returns the value of the slider is quite simple. You can call this handler with *sendSprite* from other behaviors or movie scripts to get the current value of the slider, even while it is being dragged.

```
-- this handler returns the value of the slider
on getValue me
  return pValue
end
```

Several elements can be added to a slider to make it as complete as sliders found in other software. For example, a text field can show the current value of the slider and two buttons can enable users to move the slider one value at a time.

Figure 15.8 shows all these elements. There are a total of eight cast members if you include down states for the buttons.

Figure 15.8
The Cast window shows the eight elements of the slider. The Score shows the sprite placement of each. The Stage shows the assembled slider.

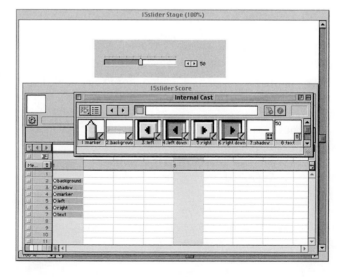

The first bit of extra functionality that you should add to a simple slider, such as this, is a text field that shows the value of the slider. To do this, create a text field and place it on the Stage. You need to tell the marker sprite where this text sprite is located. An extra parameter should do it. Add a "pTextSprite" property to the property declarations at the top of the behavior. Add this to the *on getPropertyDescriptionList* handler:

```
addProp list, #pTextSprite, [#comment: "Text Sprite",\
   #format: #integer, #default: 0]
```

An "on setText" handler places the current value of the slider in this text field. Just in case no text sprite is used, this handler makes sure that the "pTextSprite" property is not 0. If it is, the "on setText" handler assumes that there is no text sprite and does not place the text:

```
-- this handler sets the text of the text sprite
on setText me
   if pTextSprite <> 0 then -- is there a text sprite?
     sprite(pTextSprite).member.text = string(pValue)
   end if
end
```

Calls to "on setText" need to be added immediately after the calls to "on setShadow" in both the *on beginSprite* and *on exitFrame* handlers.

The next elements that the slider needs are the buttons that enable the users to move the slider one value in either direction. You need both normal and down states for these buttons, as shown previously in Figure 15.8.

These buttons need their own behavior, but before you create the behavior, a handler needs to be added to the marker behavior. This handler enables the marker to be moved one value in either direction. It should take one parameter that is either a #left or a #right depending on which direction the slider should move. It also needs to perform the same boundary check that the "on moveMarker" handler does to make sure that the slider doesn't go past its limits.

```
-- this handler moves the marker one value left or right
on moveMarkerOne me, direction
   if direction = #left then
     pValue = pValue - 1
   else if direction = #right then
     pValue = pValue + 1
   end if

   -- check to make sure it is within bounds
   if pValue > pMaximumValue then
     pValue = pMaximumValue
   else if pValue < pMinimumValue then
     pValue = pMinimumValue
   end if
```

```
    setMarker(me)
    setShadow(me)
    setText(me)
  end
```

The "on moveMarkerOne" handler ends by calling the three handlers needed to update the slider. This makes it possible to call this one handler and have the slider changed and updated by the other three automatically.

A handler to take care of the two buttons is similar to any simple button handler. It mostly controls normal and down states for the button sprite. It also has to know where the marker sprite is so that it can send the "moveMarkerOne" message to it. A key parameter is "pArrowDirection", which is set to *#left* or *#right* depending on which button is selected:

```
property pDownMember, pOrigMember -- down and normal states
property pPressed -- whether the sprite is being pressed
property pMarkerSprite -- the number of the marker sprite
property pArrowDirection -- 1 or -1 to add to slider

on getPropertyDescriptionList me
  list = [:]
  addProp list, #pMarkerSprite, [#comment: "Marker Sprite",\
    #format: #integer, #default: 0]
  addProp list, #pDownMember, [#comment: "Arrow Button Down Member",\
    #format: #bitmap, #default: ""]
  addProp list, #pArrowDirection, [#comment: "Arrow Direction",\
    #format: #symbol, #range: [#left,#right], #default: #right]
  return list
end
```

The rest of the slider button behavior handles the mouse clicking and calls the "moveMarkerOne" handler in the marker behavior once per frame loop while the button is pressed:

```
on beginSprite me
  pOrigMember = sprite(me.spriteNum).member
end

on mouseDown me
  pPressed = TRUE
  sprite(me.spriteNum).member = member pDownMember
end

on mouseUp me
  liftUp(me)
end
```

```
on mouseUpOutside me
  liftUp(me)
end

on liftUp me
  pPressed = FALSE
  sprite(me.spriteNum).member = member pOrigMember
end

on exitFrame me
  if pPressed then
    sendSprite(sprite pMarkerSprite, #moveMarkerOne, \
    pArrowDirection)
  end if
end
```

With eight members and two behaviors, you have all the functionality of the sliders used by other software programs. Even better, you can change the graphics used to anything you want to stylize your sliders to fit your design.

You have a lot of control over how the slider looks and behaves. You can alter your code to place an extra word behind the number in the text field. So, rather than reading "50", it can read "50%" or "50 widgets". You can tweak the slider screen boundaries if the shadow sprite isn't working the way you want. You can even remove the shadow sprite.

There is nothing to stop you from taking all the references to horizontal locations and boundaries and converting them to vertical locations and boundaries to make a vertical slider. This is a good example of how much control Lingo behaviors give you as opposed to the drag-and-drop interface elements in other authoring programs.

For an example of a slider, **see** "Creating Volume Controls," **p. 602** (Chapter 30, "Sound Applications")

CREATING PROGRESS BARS

Using some of the same techniques used to make the slider bar, you can create a progress bar behavior. A *progress bar* is a rectangle that enlarges to fill a space as a process is completed. An example is the progress bar the Director displays every time you choose File, Save.

If you have a Lingo process that takes more than a fraction of a second to complete, you might want to display a progress bar so that the users know that the computer is not frozen, but simply processing their requests.

Figure 15.9 shows a simple progress bar. It shows two sprites: a hollow rectangle shape and a filled rectangle. To make the progress bar look like others used in various pieces of software, the fill of the rectangle is set to a pattern, rather than a solid.

Figure 15.9
A simple progress bar showing a
task about one-half done.

To create a progress bar, you need a process to test it. Here are two movie handlers that work together to compute all the prime numbers between one and 1,000. (Recall that a prime number is a number divisible only by one and itself.)

```
on findPrimeNumbers
  list = []
  repeat with i = 1 to 1000
    if isPrime(i) then add list, i
  end repeat
  return list
end


on isPrime n
  repeat with i = 2 to integer(sqrt(n))
    div = float(n)/float(i)
    if div = integer(div) then return FALSE
  end repeat
  return TRUE
end
```

The "on isPrime" function tries every number between two and the square root of the number to see whether it can find a case where there is no fractional remainder to the division. It compares the number to itself converted to an integer to see whether there is a remainder.

This process takes about a second to run on a PowerMac G3 with a 400MHz processor. It also does this calculation in 1,000 steps, so it's a prime candidate for a progress bar.

Of the two sprites involved in the progress bar, only the filled portion needs a behavior. The other sprite is there for merely cosmetic purposes.

Like the slider marker behavior, this sprite needs to know the size of its final, full rectangle. To make that easy to determine, set the sprite up on the Stage to already be its full size. That way, the *on beginSprite* handler can get the full rectangle size by simply looking at the *rect* of the sprite when the behavior starts.

```
property pFullRect


on beginSprite me
  pFullRect = sprite(me.spriteNum).rect
end
```

The only other handler needed is the one that sets the progress bar when needed. It will be a custom handler that a process, such as "on findPrimeNumbers", calls when it can.

```
on setProgress me, currentVal, highestVal
  -- get amount filled as a value between 0 and 1
  percentFilled = float(currentVal)/float(highestVal)

  -- convert to a pixel width
  pixelRange = pFullRect.right-pFullRect.left
  x = percentFilled*pixelRange

  -- set the rect of the sprite
  r = rect(pFullRect.left, pFullRect.top, \
      pFullRect.left + x, pFullRect.bottom)
  sprite(me.spriteNum).rect = r
end
```

The "on setProgress" handler takes two parameters. The first is the current value of the progress bar, and the second is the maximum value of the progress bar. It takes these two values and divides them to get the percentage of fill needed. It then determines the physical width of the progress bar area and determines the point to which the sprite should stretch. Finally, it builds a rectangle from this information and sets the sprite.

To use this behavior, you need to call it from the process taking place. In this case, the "on findPrimeNumbers" handler will use it.

```
on findPrimeNumbers
  list = []
  repeat with i = 1 to 1000
    sendSprite(sprite 2,#setProgress,i,1000)
    updateStage
    if isPrime(i) then add list, i
  end repeat
  return list
end
```

Notice that an *updateStage* is needed because the frame is not looping here. Director is caught inside the *repeat* loop and does not know to update the Stage without you telling it.

Check out the sample movie, 15progressbar.dir, which activates the "on findPrimeNumbers" handler with a button, shows the progress bar as the prime numbers are calculated, and then displays the list of prime numbers when it is done.

You can easily change the color and dimensions of a progress bar such as this. If you prefer a more stylized progress bar, you may want to convert this behavior to use three elements: a left end, a right end, and a stretchable middle piece. Doing so would require the same behavior to control two other sprites, possibly specified as parameters.

CREATING GRAPHICAL POP-UP MENUS

Like the check boxes, radio buttons, sliders, and progress bars, another item that can be created with bitmaps and a behavior is the pop-up menu.

Pop-up menus are the little menus that appear in windows and dialog boxes, as opposed to the main menu bar that appears at the top of a screen or window. In the Director authoring environment, you can see examples of these in the Score window and Sprite Inspector. As a matter of fact, just about every window in Director includes some type of pop-up menu.

Pop-up menus are useful when you want the users to choose from a list of items, but don't have the space in your interface to show all the choices. The users click to reveal the list of items, select one, and then the list goes away, leaving their choice in that space.

Creating pop-up menus as interface elements in your movies is possible with a behavior. First, create a series of bitmaps in the Cast to be used. Figure 15.10 shows the Cast window with some example bitmaps. A single bitmap represents the pop-up menu when it is not active, and then five other bitmaps that appear under it when it is pressed. All five of these bitmaps have a corresponding hilite state.

To create the pop-up on the Stage, place the sprites as you would want to see them when the pop-up is pressed and active. Never mind that the list under the "Choose One" graphic should not be present when the user first comes to the frame; the behavior will handle that.

For the behavior to do that, it needs to know where these sprites are. So, one property of this behavior must be a list of sprites. Another property will be the members that are initially in these sprites. The behavior itself will be attached to the pop-up menu button, which is the "Choose One" graphic in this case:

```
property pSpriteList, pMemberList, pPressed

on getPropertyDescriptionList me
  list = [:]
  addProp list, #pSpriteList, [#comment: "Sprite List", \
    #format: #list, #default: []]
  return list
end
```

To start, the behavior needs to record the members used by each of the sprites that are part of the pop-up. This example does not include the pop-up button.

```
on beginSprite me
  pMemberList = [:]
  repeat with i in pSpriteList
    addProp pMemberList, i, sprite(i).member.name
  end repeat
  hidePopup(me)
end
```

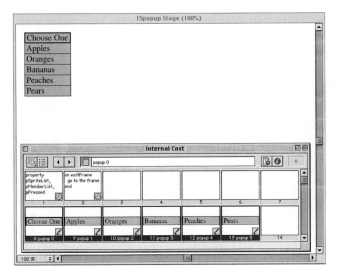

Figure 15.10
The Stage shows a pop-up menu as it appears during creation of the movie. The Cast window shows these members, as well as the hilite states.

The call to "on hidePopUp" removes the pop-up items before the user sees them. The best way to do this is to set the *memberNum* property of the sprites to 0:

```
on hidePopup me
  repeat with i = 1 to pSpriteList.count
    sprite(pSpriteList[i]).memberNum = 0
  end repeat
end
```

The mouse click handlers look similar to those used in earlier behaviors. Both *on mouseUp* and *on mouseUpOutside* call a custom handler that calls the "on hidePopup" again, as well as an "on select" handler:

```
on mouseDown me
  pPressed = TRUE
end

on mouseUp me
  liftUp(me)
end

on mouseUpOutSide me
  liftUp(me)
end

on liftUp me
  pPressed = FALSE
  hidePopup(me)
  select(me)
end
```

The *getOne* property of a list enables you to find the position of an item in a list. If the item is there, it returns the number of the item, which can also be interpreted as *TRUE*. If the item is not in the list, a 0 is returned, which is always seen as *FALSE*.

In the *on exitFrame* handler, a variety of tasks are performed when the pop-up is pressed. First, it calls "on showPopup", which returns the sprites to the members they used when you set up the movie. Then, it uses *the rollover* property to determine over which sprite the mouse is currently hovering. It uses *getOne* on the "pSpriteList" property to determine whether this is one of the pop-up items.

If the mouse is over a sprite in the list, it then changes the member of that sprite to a member of the same name, except with the word "hilite" appended. This is just a convention that this behavior uses to figure out which highlighted members belong to which normal members. You could just as easily have placed all the highlighted members in the next member over from the normal members, and recorded the member numbers of the sprites, using a +1 to find the highlight member, which will be the very next member in the Cast.

```
on exitFrame me
  if pPressed then
    showPopup(me)
    s = the rollover
    if (pSpriteList.getOne(s)) then
      sprite(s).member = member (pMemberList.getProp(s)&&"hilite")
    end if
  end if
end
```

The result of this handler is that the pop-up items will be shown if the "pPressed" property is *TRUE*, and any item that the cursor is currently over will show up as the highlighted member. Figure 15.11 shows this in action.

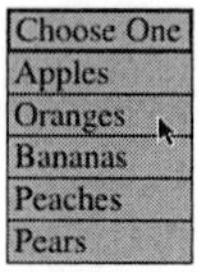

Figure 15.11
The pop-up menu has been selected and the cursor is over the second item.

The "on showPopup" handler is similar to the "on hidePopup" handler except that the "pMemberList" is used to assign the correct member to each sprite:

```
on showPopup me
  repeat with i in pSpriteList
    sprite(i).member = member pMemberList.getProp(i)
  end repeat
end
```

Finally, the "on select" handler is called when the user releases the mouse button. This handler cannot assume that the cursor is over an item in the pop-up list, so it must check in the same way that the *on exitFrame* handler checks:

```
on select me
  s = the rollover
```

```
if (pSpriteList.getOne(s)) then
  alert pMemberList.getProp(s)
end if
end
```

In this case, a simple *alert* box appears to signify that a choice has been made. However, in your program you will want to set a global, go to a frame, or perform some other action.

This pop-up menu behavior can be customized in a lot of ways. With a little more work, you can even have the selected item appear to replace the "Choose One" graphic, or have sounds play as the pop-up is used.

Notice that nothing in the script specifies that the items must be positioned directly below the original sprite. Why not have them line up to the right of the sprite? Or, have them appear above it? There are many possibilities.

➡ *For another way to make pop-up menus, **see** "Creating Text Pop-Up Menus," **p. 338** (Chapter 16, "Controlling Text")*

TROUBLESHOOTING GRAPHIC INTERFACE ELEMENTS

- Be sure you understand the difference between *the clickLoc* and *the mouseLoc*. The first is the exact location of the mouse when the user clicked. The second is the current location of the mouse, which might have changed since the user clicked.

- When performing calculations in which the result will be a number between 0 and 1, as in the slider behavior or the progress bar behavior, it is important to convert the numbers to floats before doing division. Otherwise, a calculation such as 3/6 will return a 0, rather than a 0.5.

- If you are using floating point numbers in a parameter and assigning a range to that parameter, you can control the number of decimal places used by setting *the floatPrecision* system property. The default is four digits after the decimal point.

- The *memberNum* property of a sprite enables you to set the member of a sprite by just referring to it by number. This property is good for setting a sprite to the next member or something similar, but should not be used otherwise. You should use the member property instead and set the sprite to a specific member by name.

DID YOU KNOW?

- In the *sendSprite* command, the word "sprite" is optional. So, you can write "sendSprite(7,#myHandler)" instead of "sendSprite(sprite 7, #myHandler)".

- There are two forms of syntax for the keyword "rollover". The function *rollover*(x) returns a *TRUE* if the cursor is over sprite *x*. The property *the rollover* returns the number of the sprite directly under the cursor.

- The *memberNum* property does not enable you to set the sprite to a member in another cast library. However, you can change the *castLibNum* to do that.

- The obsolete property *castNum* can still be used. It returns the same value as *memberNum* for members in the first cast library, but returns much higher values for members in other cast libraries. For instance, the first member in cast library 2 would have a *castNum* of 131073.

VI

USING LINGO TO CONTROL MEDIA

IN THIS PART

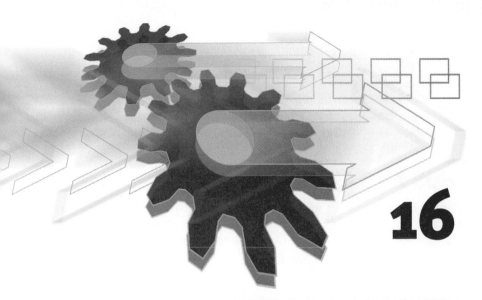

16

CONTROLLING TEXT

Although text might seem primitive compared to images, sounds, and digital video, it's still the primary way in which most computer programs communicate information to users. Director 8 has two primary cast members that handle text, plus dozens of Lingo commands and functions used to manipulate these members and strings. Using these cast members, commands, and functions is the topic of this chapter.

USING STRINGS AND CHUNKS

Strings—whether in variables or as text inside members, such as fields and text members—are controlled with string commands, chunk expressions, and string functions. A group of string constants also enables you to refer to common characters such as returns and tabs.

Building Strings

Chapter 13, "Essential Lingo Syntax," provided a brief summary of string commands and functions. Here is a more detailed list of commands and operators used to build strings:

- **&**—Concatenates two strings.

- **&&**—Concatenates two strings and inserts a space in between them.

- **put … after**—Appends a string onto another string. Can be used with chunk expressions to insert characters into the middle of a string.

- **put … before**—Puts a string into another string, before the characters that are already there. Can be used with chunk expressions to insert characters into the middle of a string.

- **put … into**—Puts a string into another variable. Can be used with chunk expressions to replace characters in one string with characters from another.

- **delete**—Removes a chunk from a string.

All the preceding commands can use chunk expressions to modify their functions. Chunk expressions are elements such as *char*, *word*, *line*, and *item*.

For example, if you have a simple string that looks like this: "abcdefg", and you want to insert "xyz" in between the "c" and the "d", here's what you can do:

```
s = "abcdefg"
put "xyz" after s.char[3]
put s
-- "abcxyzdefg"
However, you could have also done this:
s = "abcdefg"
put "xyz" before s.char[4]
put s
-- "abcxyzdefg"
```

Suppose you want to replace the letter "c" with an "x". That's easy:

```
s = "abcdefg"
put "x" into s.char[3]
put s
-- "abxdefg"
```

But what if you wanted to replace the letter "c" with more than one character? The *put* command does not require that the replacement string and the original chunk be the same size.

```
s = "abcdefg"
put "xyz" into s.char[3]
put s
-- "abxyzdefg"
```

You can also replace a larger chunk with a smaller string:

```
s = "abcdefg"
put "xyz" into s.char[2..6]
put s
-- "axyzg"
```

Using Chunk Expressions

Notice in the preceding section that the *char* chunk can accept a single number parameter to refer to one character, but can also use the "a..b" notation to refer to a series of characters. The same is true of all chunk expressions.

Chunk expressions were also introduced in Chapter 13. Here is a more detailed list and description of the chunk expressions:

- **char**—Enables you to specify a single character or group of consecutive characters in a string.

- **word**—Enables you to specify a word or group of words in a string. Words are delimited by spaces or any nonvisible character, such as a tab or return. A request for a single word does not include these delimiters, but a request for a group of words includes the delimiters between them.

- **item**—Enables you to specify an item or group of items in a string. Items are delimited by the character that corresponds to the *itemDelimiter* property. This property is initially set to a comma, but can be changed. A request for a single item does not include the delimiter, but a request for a group of items includes the delimiters between them.

- **line**—Enables you to specify a line or group of lines in a string. Lines are delimited by returns. Any soft wrapping in fields is ignored. A request for a single line does not include the returns, but a request for a group of lines includes the returns between them.

- **paragraph**—Acts the same as *line*.

Chunk expressions can be combined to create specific descriptions of the position of chunks in a string. For instance: "myString.line[1].word[1..2].char[3..4]".

You can also use old Director 6 syntax to refer to strings. The preceding example could have been stated: "char 3 to 4 of word 1 to 2 of line 1 of myString."

Comparing Strings

You need to compare strings in complex programs frequently. You can use the plain old = operator to see whether strings match exactly, but you can also use a variety of operators and functions to perform other types of comparisons:

- = —Compares two strings and returns *TRUE* if they are equal.

- < —Compares two strings and returns *TRUE* if the first one comes before the second alphabetically.

- <= —Compares two strings and returns *TRUE* if the first one comes before the second alphabetically, or if they are equal.

- > —Compares two strings and returns *TRUE* if the first one comes after the second alphabetically.

- >= —Compares two strings and returns *TRUE* if the first one comes after the second alphabetically, or if they are equal.

- <> —Compares two strings and returns *TRUE* if they are not the same.

- **contains**—Compares two strings and returns *TRUE* if the first one contains the second.

- **starts**—Compares two strings and returns *TRUE* if the first one starts with the same characters as the second.

- **offset**—This is not really an operator, but is a function that can be used like *contains*. It returns the character position of one string inside another, or a 0 if the one string is not in the other string.

The *contains* and *starts* operators are used in the same way as the = syntax. Here are some examples:

```
s = "Hello World."
put (s contains "World")
-- 1
put (s contains "Earth")
-- 0
put (s starts "World")
-- 0
put (s starts "Hello")
-- 1
```

Lingo string-comparison functions handle case in a sensible, but sometimes hard to follow, way. When comparing two strings, such as "ABC" and "abc," Lingo sees them as equal. However, when using < or >, Lingo considers "ABC" to come before "abc." However, they are still seen as equal as well!

The *contains* function works fairly fast even on large strings or fields. It can be used to quickly search hundreds or even thousands of field members for a phrase or keyword. This makes it very useful for database programs.

The *contains* function is also more forgiving than =, which requires an exact match, except for case. If you need to know whether a cast member name has the word "button" in it, *contains* finds members named "button normal," "button down," "button rollover," and so on, whereas = finds only an exact match.

String Functions

In addition to commands and operators, a variety of functions can be used to get information from strings, convert strings to other variable types, or convert other variable types to strings. Here is a detailed list of these string functions:

- **chars**—An old function from early versions of Director that enables you to get a series of characters from a string. For example, "chars(myString,3,5)" is the same as "myString.char[3..5]".

- **charToNum**—This function converts a single character to its ASCII code number. This is the number that the computer uses to store the character.

- **count**—This function can be used as a property of a chunk, such as *char* or *word*, to return the total number of such chunks in a string. For example, "myString.count."

- **float**—This function, when given a string, tries to convert the string to a floating point number. A "4.5" returns a 4.5000.

- **integer**—This function, when given a string, tries to convert the string to an integer number. A "4" returns a 4.

- **length**—This function returns the length of a string in characters. It can also be used as a property of the string.

- **numToChar**—The opposite of *charToNum*, this function takes an integer that represents the ASCII value of a character and converts it into a single-character string.

- **offset**—This function takes two strings as parameters. It returns a number that corresponds to the character position of the first time the first string appears in the second. If the first string does not appear at all, it returns a 0.

- **stringP**—This function tests a variable to see whether it is a string. It returns *TRUE* if it is.

- **string**—This function takes any other type of variable (*integer*, *float*, *list*, and so on) and returns a string representation of it.

- **value**—This function takes a string and tries to evaluate it as a Lingo expression. For instance, "4" returns 4, and "4.0" returns 4.0000. You can even evaluate mathematical operations, such as "4+1" using this function.

The *charToNum* and *numToChar* functions can be incredibly useful. Every character maps to a corresponding number, called an ASCII code. A list of these numbers appears in Appendix D, "Tables and Charts."

The number that corresponds to a capital "A" is 65, "B" is 66, and so on. The number that corresponds to a lowercase "a" is 97, lowercase "b" is 98, and so on. Knowing this, you can create a simple handler that converts a mixed-capitalization string to one that is all capitals.

```
on allCaps text
  repeat with i = 1 to text.length
    thischar = charToNum(text.char[i])

    -- check to see if it is a lowercase letter
    if thischar >= charToNum("a") and \
        thischar <= charToNum("z")  then

      -- subtract 32, to make it uppercase
      thischar = thischar - 32

      -- replace the character
      put numToChar(thischar) into text.char[i]
    end if
  end repeat
  return text
end
```

Any string passed into this handler returns the same string, but with capital letters replacing the lowercase ones:

```
put allCaps("This is a test.")
-- "THIS IS A TEST."
```

You can easily write a handler that reverses this process and converts a string to all lowercase.

The preceding handler also uses the *length* property. This keyword can be used as either a property or a function. It returns the number of characters in a string:

```
s = "Hello World."
put s.length
-- 12
put length(s)
-- 12
```

You can also use the *count* property to get the number of chunks in a string:

```
s = "Hello World."
put s.word.count
-- 2
```

```
put s.line.count
-- 1
```

The *length* property can be combined with chunk expressions to return the number of characters in a chunk as well:

```
s = "Hello World."
put s.word[1].length
-- 5
```

The *offset* function doesn't offer anything that can't be done with a *repeat* loop and some = comparisons. However, it is very fast. If you need to find the first instance of a string in another very long string, *offset* is the way to go.

It might seem like finding only the first instance of a string inside a string is a little limiting. However, you can use the *offset* function to find all the instances of the string inside the string. Here is a handler that does it for you:

```
on findStringInString substring, text

  -- initialize list and character position
  list = []
  currentChar = 1

  repeat while TRUE
    -- find in remaining string
    loc = offset(substring,text.char[currentChar..text.length])

    -- see if none left
    if loc = 0 then exit repeat

    -- add char pos to list
    add list, currentChar+loc-1

    -- move char pointer forward
    currentChar = currentChar+loc
  end repeat
  return list
end
```

In the Message window, the function works in this way:

```
s = "Hello World."
put findStringInString("o",s)
-- [5, 8]
```

The last string function in the preceding list is the *value* function. Even from its short description, you can see how powerful it is.

If you want to convert a string to a number, *value* is often better than *integer* and *float* because it converts the string to whichever of the two is appropriate, rather than forcing it into one type or the other. Also, the capability of *value* to perform math functions on strings, such as returning 2 for the string "1+1", is very powerful.

You can even call Lingo functions with *value*. Suppose you have the following handler in a movie script:

```
on test
  return "testing!"
end
```

Now try this in the Message window:

```
put value("test()")
-- "testing!"
```

You can make an entire "calculator" movie using just value to determine the result. Figure 16.1 shows such a calculator. The first field is editable so that users can alter the equation.

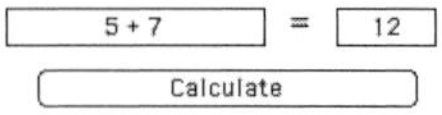

Figure 16.1

Four sprites make up a simple calculator: two text fields, an "=" graphic, and a "calculate" button.

The only Lingo scripting needed is a simple, two-line handler in a behavior attached to the button. This can even be shortened to one line if you prefer:

```
on mouseUp
  answer = value(member("question").text)
  member("answer").text = string(answer)
end
```

String Constants

Although characters such as a space are easy enough to represent, some characters, such as tabs and returns, are not. You could figure out which ASCII numbers they correspond to, and use *numToChar*, but Lingo has some built-in constants that you can use for some characters.

- **SPACE**—The same as a " ". The main purpose of this is that it looks neater in your code.

- **TAB**—This corresponds to ASCII character 9, which is the character generated by the Tab key on the keyboard. It comes in handy when you import some text from a spreadsheet that uses tabs as item delimiters.

- **RETURN**—This corresponds to ASCII character 13, which is generated by the Return key on Macintosh computers and the main Enter key in Windows. It is also the character used to separate the line chunks from a string.

- **QUOTE**—Because the quotation mark character is used in Lingo to define strings, you need this character to add actual quotation marks into your strings.

- **EMPTY**—This corresponds to `""`, or a string with zero length.

- **BACKSPACE**—This corresponds to ASCII character 8, which is generated by the Delete key on Mac or the Backspace key in Windows. It is handy for interpreting keyboard input by users.

- **ENTER**—This corresponds to ASCII character 3, which is generated by the Enter key on the numeric keypad if the keyboard is set to use it properly.

The *QUOTE* constant is the one that comes in the handiest in day-to-day Lingo programming. If you want to create a string that uses quotes, combine the use of *QUOTE* with the use of &, as follows:

```
s = "The computer replied, "&QUOTE&"Hello World."&QUOTE
put s
-- "The computer replied, "Hello World.""
```

Text References

Director has a variable structure called *ref*. This variable enables you to reuse a reference to a chunk in a text member. For instance, you can use

```
put member("myText").line[2].word[2]
-- "is"
put member("myText").line[2].word[2].font
-- "Times"
```

Or, you could use the *ref* property to set a variable to be a reference to this chunk. Then, you can use that reference to get other properties.

```
r = member("myText").line[2].word[2].ref
put r.text
-- "is"
put r.font
-- "Times"
```

Only the *text*, *font*, *fontStyle*, and *fontSize* properties are available to *ref* references. All those except the *text* property can be set to new values, and that change is related in the text member.

➡️ *For more information about using strings, **see** "Using String Variables," **p. 224** in Chapter 13*

USING TEXT MEMBERS AND FIELDS

Although text members and fields essentially hold just text, they also have many other properties that affect how the text appears on the Stage. Text formatting, such as styles, fonts, and sizes, is not a part of strings, but plays a major part in the text used in these members.

Fields

A field member's primary property is the text it contains. You can get this text in Lingo with the text property of the member. You can also use the Lingo syntax field to refer to any field's text as if it were a string.

Using *field*, you can use the *put* commands and chunk expressions directly on the field contents without having to first store them in a string variable. For instance, if a field holds the text "Hello World," you can perform this command:

```
put "-" into char 6 of field 1
```

Notice that you cannot use dot syntax with this type of functionality. You cannot write "put "i" into field(1).char[6]", for instance. However, you can write "put "i" into member(1).char[6]". This is true because *field* is considered antiquated syntax, so the dot syntax was not implemented for it after Director 6.

Some things can still be done to field members only using the old syntax, such as setting the font of characters inside the field. If you want to set the font of the entire member, you can do that with dot syntax:

```
member(1).font = "Times"
```

However, if you want to set the font of just a few characters, words, or lines in the field, you need to use the field syntax:

```
set the font of word 6 to 9 of field 1 = "Geneva"
```

You can set many properties in a field like this one. Here is a detailed list of such properties:

- **font**—The typeface of the characters. You should specify the font as you would a string, as in Times or Arial, for example.

- **fontSize**—The size of the font of the characters. Should be an integer, such as 9, 12, or 72.

- **fontStyle**—The style of the font. Should be a comma-delimited string that contains all the styles requested. For instance, "bold", or "bold, underline". You can use the styles "plain", "bold", "italic", "underline", "shadow", and "outline". The last two are Mac only. To turn off all styles, use "plain".

- **foreColor**—The color of the characters. You can set the color of any chunk in the field to a color in the movie's color palette.

In addition to these properties that can be applied to chunks in the field, a variety of properties can be applied to the entire field member. Here is a detailed list:

- **alignment**—This can be set to either "left", "right", or "center" to change the alignment of the field.

- **autotab**—Use *TRUE* or *FALSE* to change the member property of the same name. When *TRUE*, and the field is editable, the user can use the Tab key to move quickly between fields.

- **bgColor**—Enables you to set the background color of the field member. You can use the new *rgb* and *paletteIndex* structures.

- **border**—Enables you to set or change the border width around the field. A value of 0 removes the border.

- **boxDropShadow**—Enables you to set or change the drop shadow around the box of the field. A value of 0 removes the drop shadow.

- **boxType**—Enables you to change the type of field member. The options are *#adjust*, *#scroll*, *#fixed*, and *#limit*, just as they are in the field member's Properties dialog box.

- **color**—The same as *foreColor*, but you can use the new *rgb* and *paletteIndex* structures. The entire field has to be set at once.

- **dropShadow**—Enables you to set or change the drop shadow around the text of the field. A value of 0 removes the drop shadow.

- **editable**—Enables you to change the editable property of the member. Can be either *TRUE* or *FALSE*. When *TRUE*, and the movie is playing, users can click and edit the text in the field.

- **lineHeight**—Enables you to set the line height, in pixels, of the entire text field. Typically, line heights are set to be a few points above the font size.

- **margin**—Enables you to change the inside margin property of the text field.

- **wordWrap**—Enables you to turn automatic word wrapping on or off by setting this to *TRUE* or *FALSE*.

If a field is set to be a scrolling type, several commands and properties enable you to control the field, as follows:

- **scrollByLine**—A command that forces the field to scroll up or down a number of lines. For instance, "scrollByLine member(1), 2", scrolls down two lines. Use a negative number to scroll up.

- **scrollByPage**—The same as *scrollByLine*, except that it scrolls by pages. A page is the number of lines in the field visible on the Stage. Use a negative number to scroll up.

- **scrollTop**—This property corresponds to the number of pixels that the scrolling field is from the top. If a field uses the line height 12, and it is scrolled one line, the *scrollTop* is 12.

The powerful thing about these three scrolling field commands is that they also work on fields set to be a "fixed" type. This means you can use Lingo to scroll a field even if the scrolling bar elements are not on the screen.

Editable text fields have a special quality in that text can be selected inside them by users. Some Lingo code relates to this. You can get the position of the selection, the selection itself, and even set the selection:

- **hilite**—This command enables you to set the selection of an editable text field. For instance: "hilite word 2 of member "myField"".

- **the selection**—This property returns the text selected in the currently active editable text field. Do not place a member reference after this property; it stands on its own.

- **the selStart**—This returns the number of the first character in the current selection. You can use it to set the selection. Do not place a member reference after this property; it stands on its own.

- **the selEnd**—This returns the number of the last character in the current selection. You can use it to set the selection. Do not place a member reference after this property; it stands on its own.

Lastly, for fields, several functions enable you to find the correlation between a location on the screen and the characters in a field:

- **charPosToLoc**—Takes a field member and a number as parameters and returns a point that corresponds to where that character is located in the member. The point is relative to the upper-left corner of the member, regardless of any scrolling that is taking place.

- **linePosToLocV**—Takes a field member and a number as parameters and returns the distance, in pixels, from the top of the member to where the line is located.

- **locToCharPos**—Takes a member and a point as parameters and returns the number of the character located at that point in the field. The point should be relative to the upper-left corner of the member, regardless of any scrolling that is taking place.

- **locVtoLinePos**—Takes a member and a number as parameters and returns the line number indicating the distance from the top of the field.

- **the mouseChar**—Returns the number of the character that is under the cursor, regardless of what field it is.

- **the mouseWord**—Returns the number of the word that is under the cursor, regardless of what field it is.

- **the mouseLine**—Returns the number of the line that is under the cursor, regardless of what field it is.

- **the mouseItem**—Returns the number of the item that is under the cursor, regardless of what field it is.

Although *the mouseChar* and similar properties tell you what chunk number is under the cursor, they do not tell you to which field that chunk belongs. You can use the other functions to get a more accurate reading. Here is a function that tells you what field and chunk is under the cursor at any time, regardless of scrolling:

```
on underCursor
  s = the rollover
  loc = the mouseLoc

  -- is there a sprite under the cursor?
  if (s > 0) then

    -- is there a field attached to that sprite?
    if sprite(s).member.type = #field then

      -- subtract the loc of the sprite to get relative loc
      loc = loc - sprite(s).loc

      -- add any field scrolling
      loc.locV = loc.locV + sprite(s).member.scrollTop

      -- get the character number
      c = locToCharPos(sprite(s).member,loc)

      -- figure out the character
      ch = (sprite(s).member.text.char[c])
      put "The cursor is over character"&&c&&"("&ch&")"
    end if
  end if
end
```

Text Members

Text members have a similar set of properties and functions as fields. However, sometimes the syntax varies.

For instance, you can still set the font, size, style, and color of any chunk in a text member, but you must use the new dot syntax. *Font* and *fontSize* work much as you would expect. For example:

```
member("myText").char[2..5].font = "Times"
member("myText").char[2..5].fontSize = 18
```

However, *fontStyle* works a little differently. Rather than giving it a string, such as "bold, underline", you need to give it a list, such as "[#bold, #underline]". As is the case elsewhere, using "[#plain]" removes all styles.

Coloring text is also a little different. You can use the *color* property to set the color of the whole text member or just a chunk inside it. Here are some examples:

```
member("myText").color = rgb(40,120,0)
member("myText").char[2..5] = rgb("#6699CC")
member("myText").word[7].color = paletteIndex(35)
```

The text members do not have any border, margin, or drop shadows. However, they do share some of the other properties of fields. Most of these, however, use different values. They also have some new properties, as follows:

- **alignment**—This can be set to either #left, #right, or #center to change the alignment of the member. Text members also have a #full setting that justifies text.

- **autotab**—Use *TRUE* or *FALSE* to change the member property of the same name. When *TRUE*, and the member is editable, users can press the Tab key to move quickly between text members.

- **boxType**—Enables you to change the type of text member. The options are #adjust, #scroll, and #fixed, just as they are in the text member's Properties dialog box.

- **editable**—Enables you to change the editable property of the member. Can be *TRUE* or *FALSE*. When *TRUE*, and the movie is playing, users can click and edit the text in the member.

- **fixedLineSpace**—The same as the *lineHeight* property of fields, but you can set different lines to different amounts.

- **charSpacing**—The number of extra pixels to place between characters. The default is 0.

- **kerning**—Set this to *FALSE* if you do not want Director to automatically adjust the character spacing in the text member if the text changes.

- **kerningThreshold**—Set this to the minimum font size that you think the kerning property should default to within that cast member.

- **leftIndent**—The number of pixels away from the edge that the text should start at the left side of the member.

- **rightIndent**—The number of pixels away from the edge that the text should start at the right side of the member.

- **firstIndent**—The number of pixels away from the left edge that the first line of text in a paragraph should start.

- **wordWrap**—Being able to turn off word wrapping by setting this to *FALSE* in text members, as well as fields, is new to Director 8.

- **tabs**—A list containing the tab types and pixel positions. For example: "[[#type: #left, #position: 72]]". You can create your own list of tabs and set the *tabs* property of a text member.

- **antiAlias**—Set to *TRUE* or *FALSE*, depending on whether you want the text in the member to display with a smooth, anti-aliased effect.

- **antiAliasThreshold**—A point size at which the member should display text as anti-aliased. Any characters under this point size are displayed normally.

Text members, when set to be editable, can also have a selected area. The Lingo functions to deal with this are different from those that deal with fields.

To get the selected text, use *the selectedText* property. This returns a *ref* structure. From that, you can get the text string of the selected area, and some font information:

```
r = member("myText").selectedText
put r.text
-- "the"
put r.font
-- "Times"
put r.fontSize
-- 12
put r.fontStyle
[#plain]
```

The selection property returns a list with the first and last character number of the selected area. You can also set the selected area of a text member, as long as the member is editable, the movie is playing, and the text member has focus. This means you cannot use the Message window to successfully set the selection.

```
on preselectText
  member("myText").selection = [6,9]
end
```

Text members also have the capability to tell you which character is at a certain spot. The functions for this are quite different than with fields. The basic function is *pointToChar* and it tells you which character is under a point. It looks like this:

```
pointToChar(sprite 1, point(x,y))
```

This function has several companions: *pointToWord*, *pointToItem*, *pointToLine*, and *pointToParagraph*. They perform basically the same way, but with different chunk expressions.

Unlike the field functions, these text member functions figure things out according to the actual Stage location, calculating differences caused by the sprite location and scrolling automatically.

Text members also differ from fields in how they are represented in memory. Text members can be either rich text or HTML text. Fields have a text property that holds the plain, unformatted text of the member. So do text

Notice that this function uses the sprite reference, rather than the member reference. To determine which character is under the cursor, use *the mouseLoc* as the point.

members. However, they also have rich text and HTML properties named *rtf* and *html*. Here is what happens if you create a simple text member, place the word "Testing" in it, and then try to access these properties in the Message window:

```
put member(1).text
-- "Testing"

put member(1).rtf
-- "{\rtf1\mac\deff3 {\fonttbl{\f3\fswiss Geneva;}{\f20\froman Times;}}{\col-
ortbl\red0\green0\blue0;}{\stylesheet{\s0\fs24 Normal Text;}
}\pard \f3\fs24{\plain\f20\fs24 Testing\par}}"

put member(1).html
-- "<html>
<head>
<title>Untitled</title>
</head>
<body bgcolor="#FFFFFF">
<font face="Times, Times New Roman" size=5>Testing</font></body>
</html>
"
```

The *rtf* and *html* properties are constantly updated to reflect changes in the text member. Even better, you can directly set either of these properties, and the text member re-creates itself to match.

Few people are familiar with rich text format, but many know HTML. The capability to create custom HTML text in Lingo and then have it applied to a text member *was* possibly the most powerful and underused feature of Director 7, and might continue to be underused in Director 8.

CREATING TEXT LISTS

A few interface elements use fields and text members. One of these is sometimes called a *text list*. It is similar to a group of radio buttons, but only one sprite is needed. This sprite contains a text field on which users can click to select a line of text from a list. Figure 16.2 shows an example of such a text list.

Figure 16.2
A small text list that highlights the text line selected by the user.

To create one of these text lists, first create the field member. The field in Figure 16.2 has several lines of text, uses a 2-pixel margin, and a 1-pixel border. It is not editable, despite the fact that selecting text does highlight it.

The behavior is short and simple. Only one property is needed, and that is one of convenience. You need to reference the member of the sprite several times, so placing it as a property makes it easily available:

```
property pMember

on beginSprite me
  pMember = sprite(me.spriteNum).member
end
```

The selection action can take place on either an *on mouseUp* or an *on mouseDown* handler. It calls one custom handler to determine the line clicked, and then one to select the line:

```
on mouseDown me
  -- get the number of the line clicked
  clickedLine = computeLine(me,the clickLoc)

  -- select that line
  selectLine(me,clickedLine)
end
```

The next handler calculates the line clicked from the click location, the sprite location, and the scrolling position of the field. The field in this example isn't a scrolling one, but this extra line ensures that the behavior will be ready to go in the future if you want to have a scrolling text list:

```
on computeLine me, loc
  -- get the vertical location minus the top of the sprite
  verticalLoc = loc.locV - sprite(me.spriteNum).locV

  -- add any amount that the field has been scrolled
  verticalLoc = verticalLoc + pMember.scrollTop

  -- return the results of locVtoLinePos
  return locVtoLinePos(pMember,verticalLoc)
end
```

You could replace the entire "on computeLine" function with the use of *the mouseLine*, but this can be considered sloppy. If users click one line and then move the mouse quickly away before Director executes the line that includes *the mouseLine*, the actual line clicked and the line selected differ.

The "on selectLine" handler can be as simple as one line. If you use the command *hilite*, and refer to the member as a field, nothing more is needed.

```
on selectLine me, clickedLine
  -- use a simple hilite command to highlight the line
  hilite line clickedLine of field pMember
end
```

If you take another look at the image in Figure 16.2, you can see that the results do not look as nice as they could. Most importantly, the highlight does not go all the way across the line. It just stops with the last character in the line. It would be nicer to have the highlight go from left margin to right margin. This can be accomplished by using *char* references rather than line references with the *hilite* command. All that is needed is for the invisible Return character at the end of each line to be included in the *hilite*, as follows:

```
on selectLine me, clickedLine
  --figure out the first and last chars for hilite
  if clickedLine = 1 then
    -- first line, start with char 1
    startChar = 1
  else
    -- not first line, count chars before line
    -- and add 2 to go past return to the next line
    startChar = (pMember.text.line[1..clickedLine-1]).length + 2
  end if

  -- for last char, count chars including line,
  -- and then add 1 for the RETURN character
  endChar = (pMember.text.line[1..clickedLine]).length + 1

  hilite char startChar to endChar of field pMember
end
```

The text list can also be accomplished by just using the radio button behaviors and some members that contain one line of text each. Or, you could use text members rather than field members and place a rectangle shape behind the text to act as the highlight. By doing so, you could even add more code and allow for multiple selections in the text list, so the items in the list act like a group of check boxes. You cannot do this using *hilite*, because it allows only for a continuous selection area.

CREATING TEXT POP-UP MENUS

Pop-up menus are a natural extension of text lists. These types of pop-ups are one of those tricks that developers have learned over the years. Because fields can be set to "Adjust to Fit" and can be updated on-the-fly, you can make them imitate pop-ups fairly convincingly.

Take a look at Figure 16.3. It shows a single text field with one line of text. The field has been set to have a 1-pixel border, a 2-pixel margin, and a 2-pixel box drop shadow to make it look like something that can be clicked.

Figure 16.3
A simple field can be made to look like an inactive pop-up menu.

The behavior attached to the field changes its appearance by simply placing more lines of text in it. Because the field is set to "Adjust to Fit," it grows when that happens. Figure 16.4 shows what the field will look like when clicked. Not only is more text added, but a *hilite* command is used to show which item would be selected if the mouse were released at the moment.

Figure 16.4
The field pop-up expands as more text is placed in it.

To accomplish this neat trick, the behavior first needs to get the list of items to place in the field when the field is active. This can be done a number of ways. For this sample behavior, the field starts with all the items present. All the lines but the first are hidden from view when the sprite begins. The field should be set to a frame type of "fixed" and contain an extra Return at the end of the last line. Here is the start of the behavior:

```
property pMember -- the field used in the pop-up
property pText -- the complete text of the pop-up
property pSelection -- the selected text
property pPressed -- whether the user is making a selection
property pLastHilite -- the last line highlighted


on beginSprite me
  -- get some properties
  pMember = sprite(me.spriteNum).member.name
  pText = member(pMember).text
  pSelected = pText.line[1] -- assume first line is default
  pPressed = FALSE

  -- set the field to the selected item
  member(pMember).text = pSelected

  -- set the field rectangle
  setMemberRect(me)

  -- remove any highlight
  hilite member(pMember).char[the maxInteger]
end
```

The action starts when the user clicks the field. Then, the pop-up menu needs to appear. Here are the handlers for that action:

```
on mouseDown me
  pPressed = TRUE
  openPopup(me)
end


on openPopup me
  member(pMember).text = pText
  setMemberRect(me)
  pLastHilite = 0
end


-- This handler will adjust the field to be the size
-- of the text contained in it
on setMemberRect me
  memRect = member(pMember).rect
  numLines = member(pMember).text.lines.count
  if member(pMember).text.line[numLines] = "" then numLines = numLines - 1
  memRect.bottom = memRect.top + (numLines * member(pMember).lineHeight)
  member(pMember).rect = memRect
end
```

The *on exitFrame* handler now needs to keep checking the mouse location to ensure that the correct item is highlighted:

```
on exitFrame me
  if pPressed then
    -- What line is the cursor over?
    thisLine = the mouseLine

    -- is it over a different line than before?
    if (thisLine <> pLastHilite) and (thisLine > 0) then
      selectLine(me,thisLine)
      pLastHilite = thisLine
      pSelection = pText.line[thisline]
    end if
  end if
end
```

When the mouse button is released, the pop-up text needs to go away and the field should be restored to its former self. In addition, if the mouse is released over the sprite, it probably means that a selection has been made:

```
on mouseUp me
  pPressed = FALSE
  closePopup(me)
  makeSelection(me)
end
```

```
on mouseUpOutside me
  mouseUp(me)
end

-- set the pop-up to the current selection
on closePopup me
  member(pMember).text = pSelection
  setMemberRect(me)
end
```

The "on selectLine" handler is the same one used for the text list behavior:

```
on selectLine me, clickedLine
  --figure out the first and last chars for highlight
  if clickedLine = 1 then
    -- first line, start with char 1
    startChar = 1
  else
    -- not first line, count chars before line
    -- and add 2 to go past return to the next line
    startChar = (member(pMember).text.line[1..clickedLine-1]).length + 2
  end if

  -- for last char, count chars including line,
  -- and then add 1 for the RETURN character
  endChar = (member(pMember).text.line[1..clickedLine]).length + 1

  hilite member(pMember).char[startChar..endChar]
end
```

Finally, the "on makeSelection" handler is the one that actually does something. In this case, just an alert is shown. Note, however, that it must subtract one from the line number to get a corresponding choice number. This subtraction is necessary because the choices start at line two of the field. There is also an *updateStage* just before the *alert* command. If the *updateStage* were not there, the alert dialog box would appear and freeze the Director movie with the pop-up menu still open.

```
on makeSelection me
  if pLastHilite > 0 then
    updateStage -- update stage before alert
    alert "You picked number"&&(pLastHilite-1)
  end if
end
```

One last handler needed is the *on endSprite* handler, which is called when the movie leaves the frame with the sprite. This handler ensures that the original text gets replaced inside the field:

```
on endSprite me
  -- restore the contents of the field
  pMember.text = pText
end
```

Pop-up menus such as this are not as pretty as those created with bitmaps. However, they are easy to create and customize. If you need dozens of different pop-up menus and appearance is not critical, this is the way to go.

➪ *For another way to create pop-up menus,* ***see*** *"Creating Graphical Pop-Up Menus," **p. 314** (Chapter 15, "Graphic Interface Elements")*

➪ *For an example of using pop-up menus,* ***see*** *"Creating Questionnaires," **p. 564** (Chapter 28, "Business Applications")*

USING KEYBOARD INPUT

Although great multimedia presentations and games that use only the mouse can be made, sooner or later users will need to use the keyboard, either to enter text or perhaps use the arrow keys to control a game.

Keyboard Lingo

Lingo has quite a few functions and events that handle keyboard input. Here is a detailed list:

- **the commandDown**—Returns a *TRUE* only if the [cmd] key on the Mac or the Ctrl key in Windows is pressed.

- **the controlDown**—Returns a *TRUE* only if the Control key on the Mac or the Ctrl key in Windows is pressed. In Windows, this is the same as the *commandDown*.

- **the optionDown**—Returns a *TRUE* only if the Option key on the Mac or the Alt key in Windows is pressed.

- **the shiftDown**—Returns a *TRUE* only if the Shift key is pressed.

- **on keyDown**—An event handler that can be used in editable field or text member sprites, or in the frame or movie script. The message is sent when users first press the key. If users hold down the key, it keeps sending "keyDown"s according to the keyboard repeat settings of the user's computer. When called, the properties *the key* and *the keyCode* are set.

- **on keyUp**—An event handler that can be used in editable field or text member sprites, or in the frame or movie script. The message is sent when a user lifts his or her finger off a key. It does not repeat if the key is held down. When called, *the key* and *the keyCode* properties are set.

- **keyPressed**—A function that tests to see whether a character key is pressed. For instance, "keyPressed("a")" returns *TRUE* if the "a" key is being held down at the moment.

- **the keyPressed**—Returns the character of the last key pressed, as long as that key is currently down.

- **the key**—Exists inside an *on keyDown* or *on keyUp* handler and holds the character that was pressed and thus activated the handler.

- **the keyCode**—Exists inside an *on keyDown* or *on keyUp* handler and holds the keyboard number of the key that was pressed and thus activated the handler. It is reliable for only arrow keys and function keys.

- **the keyboardFocusSprite**—Enables you to change which sprite has text entry focus in case more than one editable field or text member is on the Stage.

The *on keyDown* and *on keyUp* event handlers are used to modify the text input in fields and text members. The *keyPressed* function is primarily used for direct access to the keyboard in games and other real-time applications.

Recognizing the Return

A simple first step to using keyboard Lingo is to build a behavior that recognizes when users press the Return key while typing. The purpose would be to "steal" the Return, so users cannot type a second line of text, and also to use the Return as a trigger for performing some event.

For instance, if you have a screen in which you want to have users enter their names, capturing the Return key might be a good idea. First, it prevents users from starting a second line of text, something not ordinarily done when typing a name. Second, it signals the end of the entry, and does not require users to click a special "I have finished typing" button.

Here is a behavior that captures the Return key. You can attach it to an editable field or text member sprite:

The Return key is actually labeled "Enter" on most Windows keyboards. This may be confusing because there is also an "Enter" key on the numeric keypad of most keyboards. Macintosh computers use a Return key on the main keyboard and an Enter key on the numeric keypad. When this text refers to a Return key, it means the Return key on Mac and the primary Enter key in Windows.

```
on keyDown me
  if the key = RETURN then
    alert "You typed:"&&sprite(me.spriteNum).mem-
ber.text
    dontpassevent
  else
    pass
  end if
end
```

The behavior uses only an *on keyDown* handler. It checks the key to see whether it is equal to the constant *RETURN*. If it is, it performs an action. It also uses the command *dontpassevent*, which prevents the "keyDown" message from traveling any farther than this handler. Its next stop would have been to tell the editable member itself that a key was pressed, and the member would have added that key—in this case, a Return—to the text in the member.

When the key is not a Return, the *pass* command sends the message on its way, and the character is then added to the text. The use of the *dontpassevent* command is implied in this handler, actually, and only the *pass* command is needed. However, using the *dontpassevent* command doesn't hurt, and it makes the handler code a little clearer.

This simple behavior uses only an *alert* command to signify that the Return key has been pressed. In a real program, you would want to do something such as record the text in a global and go to another frame. If there is more than one editable text field on the Stage, you might want to use *the keyboardFocusSprite* to move the text entry insertion point to another sprite.

Restricting Input

Because the *on keyDown* handler can capture any keystroke, you can also use it to restrict the characters that are allowed to pass to the member. Suppose you want users to enter only digits into a field. You can write a behavior that accepts only digits.

Such a behavior needs to know which characters are allowed. This work is best performed by a parameter:

```
property pAllowed

on getPropertyDescriptionList me
  list = [:]
  addProp list, #pAllowed, [#comment: "Allowed Chars",\
    #format: #string, #default: ""]
  return list
end
```

The rest of the behavior is an *on keyDown* handler that tests to see whether the character typed is acceptable:

```
on keyDown me
  if pAllowed contains the key then
    pass
  else
    dontpassevent
  end if
end
```

This behavior is not very restrictive. As a matter of fact, even the Backspace key has no effect on it. Creating a behavior that accepts the Backspace key is easy. Plus, the handler can also look for the Return key and process it as well.

```
on keyDown me
  if the key = RETURN then
    alert "You typed:"&&sprite(me.spriteNum).member.text
    dontpassevent
  else if the key = BACKSPACE then
    pass
  else if pAllowed contains the key then
    pass
  else
    dontpassevent
  end if
end
```

This same handler can be used to restrict the text to only letters, or both letters and digits, excluding all symbols. Using the same basic idea, you can even restrict the number of characters accepted in an editable member. Here is a handler that does this:

```
property pMaxChars

on getPropertyDescriptionList me
  list = [:]
  addProp list, #pMaxChars, [#comment: "Maximum Number of Chars",\
    #format: #integer, #default: 10]
  return list
end

on keyDown me
  if the key = RETURN then
    alert "You typed:"&&sprite(me.spriteNum).member.text
    dontpassevent
  else if the key = BACKSPACE then
    pass
  else if sprite(me.spriteNum).member.text.length < pMaxChars then
    pass
  else
    dontpassevent
  end if
end
```

This handler makes sure there are fewer than the maximum number of accepted characters present before enabling users to add another character. Note that the *BACKSPACE* check is handled separately, so it can still be used even when the maximum length of the member has been reached.

Capturing Keystrokes

Text entry in editable field and text members is fine for soliciting information from users. However, if you just want to capture single keystrokes to enable users to control something else in the movie, you don't need these members.

If an editable member is not present, the keyboard events pass on to the frame, where they can be captured by the frame script. You use the same handlers, *on keyDown* and *on keyUp*, to do this.

The following handler in a frame script captures keystrokes and places a message in the field in sprite 1. The message contains *the key*, *the keyCode*, and also the key converted to its ASCII number:

```
on exitFrame
  go to the frame
end


on keyUp me
  sprite(1).member.text = \
    "You pressed:"&& \
    the key&& \
    "("&chartonum(the key)&"," \
    &the keyCode&")"
end
```

The purpose of this behavior is not only to demonstrate how you can capture keystrokes with a frame script, but also how you can test different keys and determine their corresponding key codes. A little playing around with this script reveals that the key codes for the arrow keys are 123, 124, 125, and 126, which correspond to left, right, down, and up, respectively.

With this knowledge, you can write a behavior that captures these keystrokes and then tells a sprite to move relative to them. Here is a frame script that does this:

```
on exitFrame
  go to the frame
end


on keyDown
  case the keyCode of
    123: sendSprite(sprite 1, #move, point(-5,0))
    124: sendSprite(sprite 1, #move, point(5,0))
    125: sendSprite(sprite 1, #move, point(0,5))
    126: sendSprite(sprite 1, #move, point(0,-5))
  end case
end
```

Each arrow key sends a "move" message to sprite 1. It also sends along a point structure that tells it how much to change the position of that sprite. Here is a behavior that can be used to capture these "move" messages for sprite 1:

```
on move me, dist
  loc = sprite(me.spriteNum).loc
  loc = loc + dist
  sprite(me.spriteNum).loc = loc
end
```

The *on keyDown* and *on keyUp* event handlers require that the Stage has focus. This means that it is the active window and receives keyboard events. This may require users to click the Stage after playing the movie and before using the arrow keys.

Because the frame script uses *on keyDown* to capture the keys, users can hold down the arrow keys to keep the sprite moving. This works only because the computer itself sends multiple "keyDown" messages when users hold down a key. The result is the same as when users press the key down repeatedly.

This sort of movement might work for very basic onscreen activity, but you can create a more fluid movement. Use the *keyPressed* function to constantly check the keyboard to determine whether a key is being pressed.

Here is a frame script that uses *keyPressed* to check the keyboard and send "move" messages to sprite 1:

```
on exitFrame
  if (keyPressed(123)) then sendSprite(sprite 1, #move, point(-5,0))
  if (keyPressed(124)) then sendSprite(sprite 1, #move, point(5,0))
  if (keyPressed(125)) then sendSprite(sprite 1, #move, point(0,5))
  if (keyPressed(126)) then sendSprite(sprite 1, #move, point(0,-5))
  go to the frame
end
```

The difference is remarkable. The *on keyDown* method creates a jerky, slow movement, whereas *the keyPressed* method creates the type of movement that you expect in an arcade game. In fact, the faster the frame rate, the more fluid the movement.

Although *the keyPressed* works great for arrow keys and alphanumeric keys, it can't be used to check keys such as the Shift key or Command key. For these, you must use the special properties for each that are described previously in the "Keyboard Lingo" section.

USING RICH TEXT FORMAT

By using the *rtf* property of a text member, you have access to its rich text format version. This is an entire language unto itself and is now maintained by Microsoft. Here are the results of creating a text member with the word "Testing" in 18-point Times New Roman font, and using the Message window to get the *rtf*:

```
put member(1).rtf
-- "{\rtf1\mac\deff3 {\fonttbl{\f3\fswiss Geneva;}{\f20\froman Times;}}{\col-
ortbl\red0\green0\blue0;}{\stylesheet{\s0\fs24 Normal Text;}}\pard
\f3\fs24{\pard \f20\fs36\sl360 Testing\par}}"
```

Rich text format, as you can see, requires a lot of control structures to define styles and colors. Detailing the meanings of each of these structures would take a whole book. Because RTF is so rarely used nowadays, and is being replaced by HTML as a text standard, it is hardly worth going into.

However, you should know that you do have the power to create your own rich text formatted code and replace the text in a member by setting the *rtf* property. If you took the messy line shown previously and replaced Times New Roman with Courier, for instance, you could set the text member to look the same, but with Courier font instead.

USING HTML AND TABLES

The *html* property of text members is much easier to use. You can actually create your own HTML code with Lingo and apply it to the member. The following example illustrates how easy this property is to use.

A Simple HTML Application

Here is the same "Testing" member's *html* property:

```
put member(1).html

    -- "<html>
    <head>
    <title>Untitled</title>
    </head>
    <body bgcolor="#FFFFFF">
    <font face="Times, Times New Roman" size=5>Testing<br>
    </font></body>
    </html>
    "
```

You can see that Director likes to make sure the proper "<html>", "<head>", "<body>", and "<title>" are present. The title is always given as "Untitled", but the "bgcolor" actually reflects the background color of the member.

The *html* property is easy to edit, especially if you already know HTML. You can even ignore some of the tags and Director will fill them in for you. Try this in the Message window with a text member in cast member position one:

```
member(1).html = "Testing"
put member(1).html
-- "<html>
<head>
<title>Untitled</title>
</head>
<body bgcolor="#FFFFFF">
Testing</body>
</html>
"
```

You can see that most of the proper tags were added by Director. However, these tags are required if you want to use some of your own HTML tags to modify the text. Try this:

```
member(1).html = "<B>Testing</B>"
put member(1).html
-- "<html>
<head>
<title>Untitled</title>
</head>
<body bgcolor="#FFFFFF">
&lt;B&gt;Testing&lt;&#47;B&gt;</body>
</html>
"
```

You can see that Director did not correctly interpret your bold tag to make the text bold. Instead, it took it as a literal. The resulting text on the Stage would look like "<B>Testing</B>". For Director to recognize the bold tag, it needs to see the "<body>" tag.

```
member(1).html = "<HTML><B>Testing</B></HTML>"
put member(1).html
-- "<html>
<head>
<title>Untitled</title>
</head>
<body bgcolor="#CCCCCC">
<b>Testing</body>
</html>
"
```

Now Director correctly identifies the bold tags as tags. However, the background color of the member has been set to gray, which is meant to imitate the default gray background of browsers. To make it something other than gray, you have to set your own body tag as well:

```
member(1).html = "HTML><BODY BGCOLOR=#FFFFFF><B>Testing</B></BODY></HTML>"
put member(1).html
-- "<html>
```

```
<head>
<title>Untitled</title>
</head>
<body bgcolor="#FFFFFF">
<b>Testing</body>
</html>
"
```

Now the text member appears as you want it to. You can add font tags with sizes and faces to set the font of the text. You can even add table tags to create tables.

Applying Tables

Creating tables with HTML is an extremely powerful function of Director. It enables you to create highly formatted text in a way that was nearly impossible before Director 7.

To create a table, all you need to do is construct it in HTML and then apply that to the *html* property of the text member. Here is a simple example. Create a text field, name it "html text", and then place the following text in it:

```
<html>
<body bgcolor="#FFFFFF">
<table border=1>
<TR><TD>
Test1
</TD><TD>
Test2
</TD></TR>
<TR><TD>
Test3
</TD><TD>
Test4
</TD></TR>
</table>
</body>
</html>
```

Now, create an empty text member and place it on the Stage. Name it "html member". Using the Message window, you can apply the HTML text to the text member.

```
member("html member").html = field "html text"
```

The text member on the Stage should appear as shown in Figure 16.5.

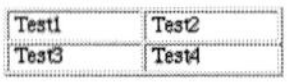

Figure 16.5
A text member that contains some simple HTML has constructed a table with a border.

Just about all the special features of HTML tables are available to the text member. Using a movie handler, you can create tables to suit any need. Here is a handler that takes a few lists and creates a table from them:

```
on makeTable memberName, headings, widths, data
  -- start with <HTML> and <BODY> tags
  htmlText = "<HTML><BODY BGCOLOR=FFFFFF>"

  -- beginning of table
  put "<TABLE BORDER=0><TR>" after htmlText

  -- place headings as TH tags
  repeat with i = 1 to count(headings)
    put "<TH WIDTH="&widths[i]&">" after htmlText
    put "<B>"&headings[i]&"</B></TD>" after htmlText
  end repeat
  put "</TR>" after htmlText

  -- add each row
  repeat with i = 1 to count(data)
    put "<TR>" after htmlText

    -- add a row
    repeat with j = 1 to count(data[i])
      put "<TD>" after htmlText
      put data[i][j]&"</TD>" after htmlText
    end repeat

    put "</TR>" after htmlText
  end repeat

  -- close table and html
  put "</TABLE></BODY></HTML>" after htmlText

  member(memberName).html = htmlText
end
```

This handler takes a member name and three linear lists as parameters. The first list contains the column heading text. The second list contains the widths of the columns in HTML-based pixels. The third list contains a series of smaller lists, each representing a row in the table.

The number of items in these smaller lists should be the same as the number of items in the other two lists. Here is an example handler that uses this "on makeTable" handler:

```
on testTable
  headings = ["Name","Address","Phone","Birthday","City"]
  widths = [100,150,60,60,80]
  data = []
  add data, ["John Doe", "123 Street Road", "555-3456", \
    "7/28/65", "Seattle"]
  add data, ["Betty Deer", "654 Avenue Blvd", "555-1234", \
    "9/11/68", "Los Angeles"]
  add data, ["Robert Roberts", "9346 Dead End Pl.", \
    "555-9999", "1/8/67", "New York"]
  makeTable("html table",headings, widths, data)
end
```

The result of using these two handlers is shown in Figure 16.6.

Figure 16.6

This table was generated with Lingo and applied to a text member.

Name	Address	Phone	Birthday	City
John Doe	123 Street Road	555-3456	7/28/65	Seattle
Betty Deer	654 Avenue Blvd.	555-1234	9/11/68	Los Angeles
Robert Roberts	9346 Dead End Pl.	555-9999	1/8/67	New York

One of the strengths of tables such as this is that text can wrap inside a column. This is far superior to using multiple lines with tabs to form a table. You can even place tables such as this into scrolling text members when they are too long to fit on the screen all at once.

USING HTML AND HYPERTEXT

Director also has the capability to easily add hypertext to text members. In fact, it's so simple, you hardly need any Lingo at all.

Setting and Using Hyperlinks

Indicating that some text represents a link only requires the use of the member and the Text Inspector. You can edit the text on the Stage or in the Text Cast Member editing window. Just select some text, and then type the hyperlink data in the bottom text field of the Text Inspector.

Figure 16.7 shows this process in action. The Stage contains a text member, with the word "dog" selected. The Text Inspector has been used to place "man's best friend" as the hyperlink data for that text. The result is that the word "dog" in the text member is now underlined and colored blue, as hypertext in Web browsers is typically styled. The word "quick" has already been set as hypertext.

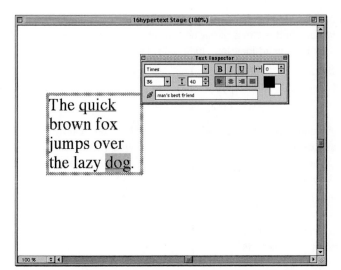

After the hypertext has been set, the hyperlink data is accessible through Lingo whenever the text is clicked. The styling of the text is automatic. Also, the cursor automatically changes into a finger cursor.

You can turn off the automatic styling and cursor change by setting the member property *useHyperlinkStyles*. Then, you can color and style the text independently.

For hypertext to actually do anything, you need to create a simple behavior to capture the messages sent when users click a hyperlink. An *on hyperlinkClicked* handler gets this message as well as the hyperlink data stored for that specific link. Here is an example:

```
on hyperlinkClicked me, data
  put data
end
```

This simple handler places the hyperlink data in the Message window. That line of code is not very useful by itself, but can be used instead to place the data in another field. A handler like this can be used to create a simple glossary function. Users can click a hyperlinked word, and the definition appears at the bottom of the Stage.

```
on hyperlinkClicked me, data
  member("Glossary").text = data
end
```

You can also have this script do something, such as make the movie jump to another frame. The frame name would be the *data* parameter.

```
on hyperlinkClicked me, data
  go to frame data
end
```

If you were creating a Shockwave movie, the hypertext could be used to make the browser go to another location. This would then act just like a normal hyperlink on a Web page. The hyperlink data would have to be a valid location, such as `http://clevermedia.com`.

```
on hyperlinkClicked me, data
  gotoNetPage(data)
end
```

One more parameter can be used with the *on hyperlinkClicked* handler. It returns a small list with the first and last character positions of the hyperlink that was clicked. You can use this to get the actual text of the hyperlink by using a normal chunk expression. Here is a modified version of the hyperlink glossary script:

```
on hyperlinkClicked me, data, pos
  definition = data
  hyperword = sprite(me.spriteNum).member.char[pos[1]..pos[2]]
  member("Glossary").text = hyperword&":"&&definition
end
```

Modifying Hyperlinks with Lingo

In addition to setting hyperlinks with the Text Inspector, you can also set them with Lingo. The *hyperlinks* and *hyperlink* properties of text members enable you to add, modify, and delete hyperlinks and their data.

The *hyperlinks* property returns a list of small lists that contains the first and last character positions of each link. For instance, the example in Figure 16.7 shows two hyperlinks. If you use the Message window to get the hyperlinks, this is the result:

```
put member(1).hyperlinks
-- [[5, 9], [41, 43]]
```

Although this property is useful for determining what hyperlinks are present in the text, you cannot actually set hyperlinks this way. Instead, use the *hyperlink* property. Here is an example:

```
put member(1).char[5..9].hyperlink
-- "fast, speedy"
```

You can set the hyperlink data to something new in a similar manner.

```
member(1).char[5..9].hyperlink = "no definition"
put member(1).char[5..9].hyperlink
-- "no definition"
```

Setting the hyperlinks in this manner without specifying the exact character positions of the hypertext is not a good idea. However, Director does behave in a logical

You can also set hyperlinks simply by setting the entire contents of the text member using the *html* property. You can include <A HREF=""> tags in that HTML code. These tags will be interpreted to add hyperlinks to the text member, just as they add hyperlinks in Web browsers.

way when this happens. If you try to set a subset of the hyperlink, such as characters 6 to 8 of the previous example, the entire hyperlink is changed.

To remove a hyperlink, set its hyperlink data to " ", or the empty string.

```
member(1).char[5..9].hyperlink = EMPTY
```

Setting the hyperlink on a set of characters that does not already have a hyperlink applied to it creates one. Here is a script that searches for a word in a text member and sets all instances of it to act as hyperlinks:

```
on makeHyper memberName, hyperword, hyperdata
  text = member(memberName).text
  repeat with i = 1 to text.word.count
    if text.word[i] = hyperword then
      member(memberName).word[i].hyperlink = hyperdata
    end if
  end repeat
end
```

USING TEXT FILES AND THE FILEIO XTRA

Using text files has always been more difficult in Director than it should be. Director 8 is no different. It requires you to use the FileIO Xtra. This is an Xtra that adds Lingo commands to handle reading and writing files.

Using an Xtra such as this is like using a behavior, except that the Xtra is referenced through a variable, not a sprite. Here is an example. To read a text file, use the following series of commands:

```
fileObj = new(xtra "FileIO")
openFile(fileObj, "myfile.txt", 1)
text = readfile(fileObj)
closeFile(fileObj)
```

The variable "fileObj" is used to store an instance of the Xtra. The new command in the first line creates this instance, and a pointer to it is placed in the variable "fileObj". You can think of "fileObj" as the *me* in a behavior. It is now needed to refer to this instance of FileIO.

An instance of FileIO is capable of opening, creating, writing, reading, and deleting files. In the preceding example, the object is used to open a file with the *openFile* command, read the contents of the file with the *readFile* command, and then close the file with the *closeFile* command. The 1 at the end of the *openFile* command signifies that the file is being opened for reading. A 2 would mean that it is opened for writing.

Here is a complete list of commands used with the FileIO Xtra:

- **new**—Creates a new instance of the Xtra.

- **fileName**—Returns the name of the file currently being controlled by this instance of the Xtra.

- **status**—Returns the error code of the last command used on the Xtra. A 0 means that there was no error.

- **error**—Takes the object and an integer as parameters. It returns a string with the description of the error number passed in as the integer.

- **setFilterMask**—Takes the object and a string as parameters. The string defines the type of files to be shown in the Open and Save dialog boxes. On the Mac, pass a string that contains one or more four-letter file types, such as "TEXT" or "JPEGGIFF". In Windows, the string should be a comma-delimited list alternating file descriptions and types, such as "Text Files,*.txt,GIF Files,#.gif".

- **openFile**—Opens the file for reading, writing, or both. You need to call this function before performing most other file functions. It takes an additional parameter, which should be a 1 to read, a 2 to write, or a 0 for both.

- **closeFile**—Closes the file associated with the file object. You must call this when you are finished with the file.

- **displayOpen**—Displays a Mac or Windows Open dialog box and enables users to browse and select a file. It returns that file path.

- **displaySave**—Displays a Mac or Windows Save dialog box and enables users to browse and select the destination of that file. It returns that file path.

- **createFile**—Give this command the object and a string that represents the filename or full path of the file. You must call this before *openFile* in cases where the file does not yet exist.

- **setPosition**—Takes an integer as an extra parameter. It sets the position in the file where the next read will take place.

- **getPosition**—Returns the current reading position in the file.

- **getLength**—Returns the length of the currently opened file.

- **writeChar**—Writes a single character to the file.

- **writeString**—Writes a complete string into the file.

- **readChar**—Reads a single character from the file.

- **readLine**—Reads from the current position in the file to the next return character. It includes the return character in the returned value.

- **readFile**—FileReads from the current position in the file until the end.

- **readWord**—Reads from the current position in the file until the next space or nonvisible character.

- **readToken**—Takes three parameters: the object, a skip character, and a break character. It reads from the current position in the file until the break character, and it skips the skip characters whenever it encounters them.

- **getFinderInfo**—Gets the file type and creator of the currently opened file. It returns it as a nine-character string with a space between the file type and creator. For example: "TEXT ttxt". Mac-only function.

- **setFinderInfo**—Enables you to set the file type and creator of the currently open file. You must use a nine-character string, such as "TEXT ttxt". Mac-only command.

- **delete**—Removes the currently opened file.

- **version**—Returns the version of the Xtra. Use it in this manner: "put version(xtra "FileIO")".

- **getOSDirectory**—Part of the Xtra, but does not require a reference to it. Use it in this manner: "put getOSDirectory()". It returns the path to the Mac system folder or the Windows directory.

Reading and writing files take many lines of code. However, a handler that does this can be reused many times. Here is a handler that prompts users for a text file to read, and then returns that text file's contents:

```
on openAndReadText
  -- create the FileIO instance
  fileObj = new(xtra "FileIO")

  -- set the filter mask to text files
  if the platform contains "mac" then
    setFilterMask(fileObj,"TEXT")
  else
    setFilterMask(fileObj,"Text Files,*.txt,All Files,*.*")
  end if

  -- open dialog box
  filename = displayOpen(fileObj)

  -- check to see if cancel was hit
  if filename = "" then return ""

  -- open the file
  openFile(fileObj,filename,1)

  -- check to see if file opened ok
  if status(fileObj) <> 0 then
    err = error(fileObj,status(fileObj))
    alert "Error:"&&err
    return ""
  end if
```

```
-- read the file
text = readFile(fileObj)

-- close the file
closeFile(fileObj)

--return the text
return text
end
```

Oddly, when writing out a new file, you must first open the file, and then use the *delete* command to delete it. Then, you can use *createFile* and *openFile* to create and write a new file. If you do not do this, the new file overwrites any file of the same name that already exists, and there might be some parts of the old file left in the new one.

If you want to use this handler to read a file that you already know the name of, just pass in the "filename" variable as a parameter to the handler, and remove the references to the *setFilterMask* and *displayOpen* commands.

The opposite of this handler is one that saves any text to a file. This handler takes care of it all, down to setting the file type of the new file to a SimpleText file for the Mac. The text placed in the file is passed in as a parameter.

```
on saveText text
  -- create the FileIO instance
  fileObj = new(xtra "FileIO")

  -- set the filter mask to text files
  if the platform contains "mac" then
    setFilterMask(fileObj,"TEXT")
  else
    setFilterMask(fileObj,"Text Files,*.txt,All Files,*.*")
  end if

  -- save dialog box
  filename = displaySave(fileObj,"","")

  -- check to see if cancel was hit
  if filename = "" then return FALSE

  -- delete existing file, if any
  openFile (fileObj,filename,2)
  delete(fileObj)

  -- create and open the file
  createFile(fileObj,filename)
  openFile(fileObj,filename,2)

  -- check to see if file opened ok
```

```
if status(fileObj) <> 0 then
  err = error(fileObj,status(fileObj))
  alert "Error:"&&err
  return FALSE
end if

-- write the file
writeString(fileObj,text)

-- set the file type
if the platform contains "Mac" then
  setFinderInfo(fileObj, "TEXT ttxt")
end if

-- close the file
closeFile(fileObj)
return TRUE
end
```

The "on saveText" and "on openAndReadText" handlers can be customized in many ways to suit many purposes. You can use *getOSDirectory( )*, for instance, to find the path to the operating system and store files in the preferences folder. You can also use the Lingo property *the pathname* to get the path of the Director application or Projector to store files there.

USING 3D TEXT

3D text, covered in Chapter 4, "Text and Field Members," can be controlled to some extent with Lingo. There are properties to match everything you can change in the property inspector.

The *displayMode* property allows you to change a text member into a 3D text member. Set this property to *#mode3d* for that and reset it to a normal text member with *#modeNormal*.

Once you have switched to 3D mode, you can use a whole bunch of other properties to control the appearance of the text. Details of what each property does were given in Chapter 4. Here is some more information that will help you manipulate them with Lingo.

- **displayFace**—This is actually a combination of the three checkboxes, "Front Face", "Back Face" and "Tunnel", as seen in the property inspector. However, with Lingo, this is represented as a list. If all three are turned on, then the list is [#front, #back, #tunnel].

- **cameraPosition**—This is a vector that represents the x, y, and z values of the position of the camera. Chapters 38, "Using 3D Media," and 39, "3D Lingo," explain vectors.

- **cameraRotation**—This is also a vector.

- **tunnelDepth**—This should be a number from 1.0 to 100.0.

- **bevelDepth**—This should be a number from 0.0 to 10.0.

- **bevelType**—This can be either *#none, #miter,* or *#round.*

- **smoothness**—This should be an integer from 1 to 10. A value of 1 creates very distorted text.

- **diffuseColor, reflectiveColor**—These two shade properties take *rgb* values like "rgb("FFFFFF")" or "rgb(255,255,255)".

- **reflectivity**—This should be a value from 0 to 100. A value of 0 doesn't reflect any of the directional light, while a value of 100 makes the text very shiny.

- **textureType**—This can be set to *#none, #default,* or *#member.*

- **textureMember**—This is actually not a member, but a string representing the name of the member.

- **directionalColor, ambientColor** —These are *rgb* colors that represent the color of the directional light and the ambient light.

- **directionalPreset**—This setting determines where the directional light comes from. It can be any one of these values: *#none, #topLeft, #topCenter, #topRight, #middleLeft, #middleCenter, #middleRight, #bottomLeft, #bottomCenter, #bottomRight.*

- **bgColor** This is an rgb color that represents the background of the member. It is not seen if the sprite is set to Background Transparent ink.

While you have these new 3D properties for text members that have been changed to 3D text members, you lose almost all of the normal text members. For instance, don't try using hypertext.

However, you also gain hundreds of new properties and commands, as all of the new 3D Lingo works with the 3D text members just like they were normal 3D members. In Chapter 39, we'll look at a lot of these new properties and apply them to both 3D models and 3D text.

So what is the relationship between a 3D text member and a normal 3D member? Well, a 3D text member sits in the Cast like a normal text member, but with some extra properties. When it is displayed on the Stage, however, it appears like a 3D member would. Director generates a 3D member on the fly and places it on the Stage instead of the text member.

If you wish, you can turn the text member completely in to a 3D member. To do this, create some text member. You don't have to set its mode to 3D or anything. Then, choose Insert, Media Element, Shockwave 3D to create a new 3D member. Name it right away or it may disappear.

The following two lines of Lingo demonstrate how to make a 3D model from a text member. The first line creates a model resource from the text. The second line creates a model from the model resource. Models and model resources are covered in detail in Chapter 39.

```
myTextResource = member("myTextMember").extrude3d(member("my3Dmember"))
member("my3Dmember").newModel("My Text Model",myTextResource)
```

Note that the 3D member will have the text in it, but the camera and the texture of the text will not be set up automatically like they are with a normal 3D text member. You'll have to set them yourself like we will be doing in Chapters 38 and 39.

TROUBLESHOOTING TEXT AND STRINGS

- ASCII codes for normal letters and numbers are exactly the same for all nonsymbol fonts on both Mac and Windows. As a matter of fact, almost all ASCII characters between 32 and 127 are the same for all fonts. However, characters above 127 can be very different in different fonts and be different even on the same fonts from different platforms. These are special symbols, such as currency symbols and accent marks. See "Fonts" in Chapter 35, "Cross-Platform Issues," for information on font mapping.

- If you are restricting the input of an editable field or a text member, remember to allow the *BACKSPACE* character. Otherwise, users might not be able to erase what they are typing when they make mistakes.

DID YOU KNOW?

- You can force Director to be your own RTF-to-HTML converter by importing RTF files and then getting the *html* property of that member. The same would work in reverse.

- Use "put interface(xtra "FileIO")" in the Message window to get a list of all the FileIO commands and functions. The same function works with most Xtras.

- Rather than using *put* to place text before, after, or into a text member, you can use some undocumented Lingo: *setContentsBefore*, *setContentsAfter*, and *setContents*. For instance, you can write

```
member("myText").setContentsBefore("abc")
```

  to place "abc" before the text in the member, or

```
member("myText").char[7].setContentsAfter("abc")
```

  to place "abc" after character 7 of the member, or just plain member("myText"). setContents("abc") to replace the contents of the member completely.

- If you import a text file that was created in Windows, you might see extra block characters at the start of each line. These are newline characters. Director and most modern word processors do not use them. To get rid of them, write a repeat look that checks each character against "numToChar(10)" and deletes it if it matches. Or, you can use the *offset* function in a repeat look to quickly hunt down and remove them.

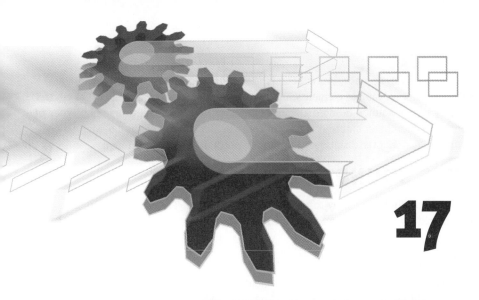

17

CONTROLLING SOUND

Although the Score can handle background sounds, and behaviors from the library can add sounds to buttons and other simple elements, understanding the Lingo commands that control sound is necessary to use sounds in more advanced Director programs. All three main types of sounds—internal cast members, external files, and compressed Shockwave audio—can be controlled using Lingo. This chapter discusses the ways to control sound using Lingo.

USING LINGO'S SOUND COMMANDS

Director 8 introduces a whole new way to play sounds with Lingo. These new sound commands replace the old *puppetSound* command, which still works.

Old Sound Lingo

It's important to understand the *puppetSound* command, even though it is technically obsolete. Chances are that it will be around in old source code and Lingo programmers' heads for years to come. A typical *puppetSound* command looks like this:

```
puppetSound 1, "mySoundMember"
```

The number 1 represents the first Sound channel. The word "mySoundMember" represents a cast member. If a sound is already being played in Sound channel 1 of the Score, it is replaced by the sound in that member. The sound plays immediately; it doesn't wait for the frame to loop or for an *updateStage* command to begin.

You can also play sounds in Sound channel 1 with a plain *puppetSound* command:

```
puppetSound "mySoundMember"
```

Using this command differs in two ways from using the *puppetSound* command with a channel number. First, the sound does not begin playing until the next frame starts, or an *updateStage* command is used. The second difference is that the first available Sound channel is used. Therefore, if Sound channels 1 and 2 are busy, Channel 3 will be used.

To stop a sound from playing and to return control of the Sound channel to the Score, just issue a *puppetSound* command with a 0 as the member, as follows:

```
puppetSound 1, 0
```

New Sound Commands

The new way that Director 8 plays sounds revolves around the *sound* object. This is much like the *sprite* object, which relates to a Sprite channel in the Score. The *sound* object relates to a Sound channel. There is a total of eight Sound channels that you can use. Here is a quick way to play a sound:

You can use Sound channels 1 through 8, even though only the first two are available in the Score.

```
sound(1).play(member("mySound"))
```

The *play* function takes a sound member as its only parameter. It begins to load the sound and then plays it when it has enough of the sound loaded. You might experience some delay as the sound loads, but not usually.

You can also queue a sound for playing, and then trigger it with a *play*. Here is an example:

```
sound(1).queue(member("mySound"))
sound(1).play()
```

Instead of passing a plain member to the *queue* or *play* function, you can send it a property list with several other pieces of information. For instance, you could include the *#preloadTime* property to specify how much of the sound should load before it begins playing. The time is in milliseconds.

```
sound(1).queue([#member: member("mySound"), #preloadTime: 1000])
```

You can use multiple *queue* functions to set up several sounds to play one after the other. When the *play* command is used, all the sounds play, without any break in between.

```
sound(1).queue(member("ragtime"))
sound(1).queue(member("wacky"))
sound(1).play()
```

Using the #startTime and #endTime properties, you can play only a segment of a sound. The time is in milliseconds.

```
sound(1).SetPlayList([ \
   [#member: member("ragtime"), \
   #startTime: 7604, \
   #endTime: 10105]])
sound(1).play()
```

You can also make the sound loop for a finite number of times with the #loopCount property.

```
sound(1).queue( \
   [#member: member("ragtime"), \
   #startTime: 10105, \
   #loopCount: 3, \
   #endTime: 15017])
sound(1).play()
```

The property list used in a *queue* or *play* can get complex. Not only can you specify the start and end times of a sound, but you can also have different start and end times for a loop inside the sound. For instance, suppose you wanted to have the sound start at the beginning, play until millisecond 10105, loop back to 7604, do that three times, and then continue to the end of the sound. This code would accomplish this:

```
sound(1).queue( \
   [#member: member("ragtime"), \
   #loopStartTime: 7604, \
```

```
    #loopCount: 3, \
    #loopEndTime: 10105])
sound(1).play()
```

Other Sound Commands

There are many other sound properties, functions, and commands that can alter the way a sound is played. All the commands in the following list can be used after a *sound* object with dot syntax, in the same way that the *play* and *queue* commands were used.

- **breakLoop()**—When a sound is inside a looping area, this command enables the sound to travel past the end of the loop and continue to play the rest of the sound.

- **isBusy()**—Returns a *TRUE* if the Sound channel is currently being used to play a sound.

- **fadeIn(s)**—Sets the volume of the sound to 0, and then increases the volume over *s* milliseconds until the full volume is reached.

- **fadeOut(s)**—Same as *fadeIn*, but in reverse.

- **fadeTo(v,s)**—Moves the volume of the sound to *v* (a number between 0 and 255) over *s* milliseconds.

- **getPlayList()**—Returns the play list for the Sound channel.

- **setPlayList()**—Instead of using multiple *queue* commands, you can set the entire play list of a Sound channel by sending it a list of sound members or property lists.

- **pause()**—Stops the sound, allowing you to use the *play()* command to resume it at the same spot.

- **playNext()**—Immediately advances the sound to the next one queued.

- **rewind()**—Brings the current sound back to the beginning.

- **stop()**—Stops the sound. Any sound members still queued in the sound's buffer remain there, ready for the next *play()* command.

- **showProps()**—Spits out all the Sound channel's properties to the Message window.

In addition to these commands, there are also a number of sound properties. The following is a complete list:

- **channelCount**—Returns the number of Sound channels in a sound member. For instance, a value of 2 tells you that the sound is in stereo.

- **currentTime**—The current time, in milliseconds, of a sound. This property can now be set in Director 8.

- **elapsedTime**—The number of milliseconds that the sound has been playing. This number continues to increase, regardless of looping or changes made to *currentTime*.

- **endTime**—The ending time, in milliseconds, of the sound currently playing.

- **loop**—A member property. This is the equivalent to the *loop* property in the Sound Cast Member dialog box. You can change its value with this Lingo property.

- **loopCount**—How many times the current sound is set to loop. A value of 0 means that the sound will loop forever.

- **loopEndTime**—The ending time of the loop in the current sound.

- **loopStartTime**—The starting time of the loop in the current sound.

- **loopsRemaining**—If the sound is currently looping, this property returns the number of loops still to go.

- **member**—The member reference of the currently playing sound.

- **pan**—Enables you to change the balance of a sound. -100 means that all the sound comes out of the left speaker and 100 means it all comes out of the right.

- **preloadTime**—The number of milliseconds of sound that is loaded before playing begins. 1,500 is the default.

- **sampleCount**—The bit rate of the sound, taking into account whether the sound is mono or stereo.

- **sampleRate**—Returns the sample frequency rate of the sound member.

- **sampleSize**—Returns the sample size, in bits, of the sound member. Typical values are 8 or 16.

- **startTime**—The starting time of the currently playing sound in the channel.

- **status**—Returns either 0 for nothing, 1 for loading, 2 for queued, 3 for playing, or 4 for paused.

- **volume**—Enables you to set the volume, from 0 to 255, of a Sound channel.

The *pan* property is particularly fun to use. Here is a behavior that plays a sound in Channel 1 with a *pan* based on the location of the sprite. As the sprite moves around the Stage, the *pan* makes the sound come more from the left or right speaker to reflect the location of the sprite.

```
property pSound

on getPropertyDescriptionList me
   list = [:]
   addProp list, #pSound, \
```

```
    [#comment: "Sound",\
     #format: #sound,\
     #default: ""]
  return list
end

on beginSprite me
  sound(1).queue(pSound)
  sound(1).play()
end

on exitFrame me
  x = sprite(me.spriteNum).locH
  stageWidth = (the stage).drawRect.width
  p = 200*x/stageWidth-100
  sound(1).pan = p
end

on endSprite me
  sound(1).stop()
end
```

There are also several properties for determining the computer's capability to play sounds, as follows:

- **the multiSound**—This is *TRUE* if the computer supports playing more than one sound at a time.

- **the soundDevice**—This property tells you which system device is being used to play sounds. The property can currently have three values: "MacSoundManager," "Macromix," and "QT3Mix." The first is available only on the Mac, and it works quite well. "Macromix" is available only on a Windows machine without QuickTime 3, and it is very slow. If the movie is playing back on Windows and QuickTime 3 is present, you should set this property to "QT3Mix" for best performance.

- **the soundDeviceList**—This property returns a list of the sound devices currently available.

- **the soundEnabled**—This property provides you with a mute function. If you set it to *FALSE*, the sound shuts off, but the value of the volume property does not change, so the same volume level is used when the *soundEnabled* property is reset to *TRUE*.

⇨ *For more information about using sounds, **see** "Using Sound in Director," p. 115 (Chapter 5, "Sound Members")*

⇨ *For more information about using sounds, **see** Chapter 30, "Sound Applications," p. 595*

USING CUE POINTS

Accessing cue point information in Lingo is easy. There are a variety of commands and functions that you can use, as described here:

- **cuePointNames**—A sound member property that returns a list of cue points in the sound.

- **cuePointTimes**—A sound member property that returns a list of times, in milliseconds, when cue points appear.

- **mostRecentCuePoint**—Returns the number of the most recently passed cue point from a sound member or a Sound channel.

- **isPastCuePoint()**—Tells you whether the sound has already passed a cue point number.

- **on cuePassed**—A handler that responds to the event of a cue point in a sound being passed.

All the cue point syntax can also be used for digital video. Simply specify the Sprite channel number that the digital video is in, rather than the Sound channel number.

By using *cuePointNames* and *cuePointTimes* together, you can have lists of both the names of the cue points and the exact times when they occur.

Adding cue points to a sound is something that is done in your sound-editing software. The method varies for each piece of software, so consult your documentation to see how to do it. It is usually fairly simple.

To synchronize a presentation or animation to a sound, you can use a basic *on cuePassed* handler in a frame behavior. Here is an example. The following behavior holds the movie on the current frame while the sound plays. Then, when a cue point arrives, it jumps the movie to a frame labeled exactly the same name as the cue point.

```
on exitFrame me
  go to the frame
end

on cuePassed me, whichChannel, cuePointNumber, cuePointName
  member("cue").text = cuePointName
  go to frame cuePointName
end
```

In addition, this behavior places the name of the cue point into a text member. You can use a technique like this to display song lyrics for a singalong. Just place the lyrics in the sound file as cue points. Then, use the *on cuePassed* handler to dump the cue points to a text member.

➡ *For more information about cue points, see "Waiting for Sounds and Cue Points," p. 115 (Chapter 5, "Sound Members")*

PLAYING EXTERNAL SOUNDS

Playing most external sounds is actually exactly like playing Internet sound members. All you need to do is import them as linked files. The sound member refers to this external file for the sound data, but all the Lingo commands treat it as an internal sound.

>
> The main advantage to playing external sound files is that Director streams them off the hard drive or CD-ROM. This means that the entire sound does not have to be loaded into memory before being played.

However, you can also play a sound file that is not linked as a cast member. Just one two-word command performs this action: *sound playFile*. Here is an example:

```
sound playFile 1, "mySound.aif"
```

This sound plays the file specified in Channel 1. If the file is not in the same folder as the movie, you should specify a full pathname.

The *sound playFile* command can play AIFF or wave sounds, the most common formats for Mac and Windows, respectively. It can also play Shockwave audio files. "AU" formatted sounds can be played as long as the "Sun AU Import Export" Xtra is present.

To stop a sound that was started with the *sound playFile* command, you can use the *puppetSound* command, with the Sound channel and a 0 for the sound name, such as

```
puppetSound 1, 0
```

There is also the obsolete sound *stop* command that does the same thing, but which may not be supported in the future.

➡ *For more information about using external sounds, **see** "External Sounds," p. 113 (Chapter 5)*

USING SHOCKWAVE AUDIO

Playing Shockwave audio is a little different from playing regular sounds. To play Shockwave audio, you need to create a Shockwave audio cast member. You can do this by choosing Insert, Media Element, Shockwave Audio.

The result is a new member that has a Properties dialog box like the one shown in Figure 17.1. The most important part of this dialog box is the Link Address, which specifies the full or relative path of the Shockwave audio file. If the path is relative and the movie is playing in Director or a projector, the path can specify a file on the hard drive or CD-ROM rather than on the Internet.

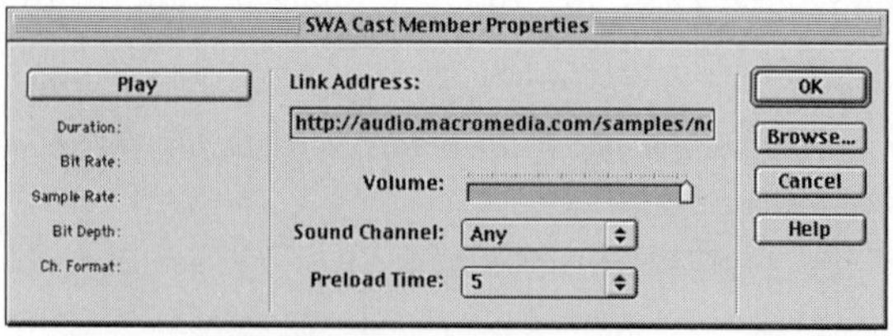

Figure 17.1
The SWA Cast Member Properties dialog box enables you to set the location of the Shockwave audio file.

After a Shockwave audio member has been created, you can also use the *url* property to change the location of the file in Lingo. This means that only one member is needed to play multiple files, as long as the files play at separate times.

To start a Shockwave audio member playing, just use the *play* command, as follows:

```
play member "mySound.swa"
```

The *stop* command halts playback, as follows:

```
stop member "mySound.swa"
```

It is just that simple. The *pause* command enables you to halt a sound, but then use the *play* command to resume playing it again at that same point, rather than at the beginning of the sound.

If you want to get more information from a playing Shockwave audio member, there are many properties that you can access. Here is a complete list of member properties:

> You can use the Import dialog box to completely import a SWA sound so that it is contained in the internal Cast. However, this defeats the purpose of streaming, which is to play very large sounds without requiring that they be loaded completely into memory first. Internal SWA sounds also do not work in Shockwave.

- **bitRate**—returns the bit rate, in Kbps, of the file.

- **bitsPerSample**—Returns the size, in bits, of each sample. Typical values are 8 and 16.

- **copyrightInfo**—Returns the copyright information set when the Shockwave audio file was created.

- **duration**—Returns the length of the sound in ticks (1/60 of a second).

- **numChannels**—Returns the number of channels in the sound. For example, 2 means it is in stereo.

- **percentStreamed**—Returns a value between 0 and 100 that corresponds to how much of the file has been read from the Internet.

- **percentPlayed**—Returns a value between 0 and 100 that corresponds to how much of the file has been played.

- **preloadTime**—The amount of the file that should be loaded into memory before playback begins, displayed in seconds.

- **sampleRate**—The frequency rate of the sound.

- **soundChannel**—The member property that determines which Sound channel is used to play back the sound. If the value 0 is given, Director chooses the first available Sound channel.

- **state**—Returns a value that tells you what the member is doing at any given time. A list of values is given in Table 17.1.

- **streamName**—Same as the *url* property.

- **url**—The location of the Shockwave audio file. You can set and reset this many times to use one member over and over. This way, you can play different audio files but only use one member.
- **volume**—The volume of the sound. A value between 0 and 255.

Table 17.1 Values for the State of a Shockwave Audio Member

State	Definition
0	Cast streaming has stopped.
1	The cast member is reloading.
2	Preloading ended successfully.
3	The cast member is playing.
4	The cast member has paused.
5	The cast member has finished streaming.
9	An error occurred.
10	There is insufficient CPU speed.

The *percentStreamed* and *percentPlayed* properties are prime candidates for the progress bar behavior described in Chapter 15, "Graphic Interface Elements." The *volume* property can be set with the slider behavior discussed in that same chapter.

For more information about making Shockwave audio files, **see** "Shockwave Audio," **p. 113** (Chapter 5)

TROUBLESHOOTING SOUND

- Remember that when you use Lingo to take control of a Sound channel, it cuts off any sound being played in the Score using that channel. It is often a good idea to use Channel 3 and above for Lingo commands if you are using Score sounds, also.
- Using a relative path to a Shockwave audio file can be tricky. It does not work until the movie is located on a server and running from Shockwave. Instead, use the pathname and the relative path to construct a string for the *url* if *the runMode* is "Author". Also, remember that you need to use different pathnames for Mac and Windows, because Mac uses a colon (:) as a path delimiter and Windows uses a backslash (\).

DID YOU KNOW?

- There is no need to create more than one SWA cast member unless you are planning to play more than one sound at a time. Instead, just create one SWA member and use Lingo to set the *url* property to the sound you want to play.
- Shockwave audio file format is very similar to the popular MP3 format. In fact, you can link to MP3 files as Shockwave audio and they will play. MP3 formatted files are usually compressed at too high of a bit rate to be successfully streamed over the Internet, but it is potentially possible.

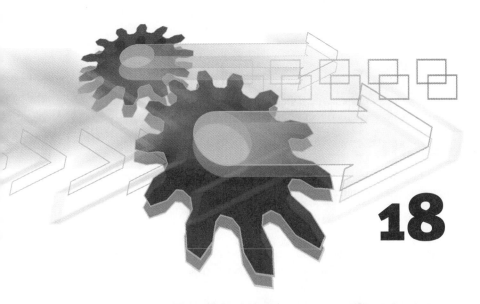

18

CONTROLLING BITMAPS

IN THIS CHAPTER

Director offers many commands, functions, and properties that enable you to modify the appearance of bitmap sprites on the Stage. Director 8, in fact, has many new features not available in its predecessors, such as direct editing of bitmap members.

DISTORTING SPRITES

So far, you have used the *loc*, *locH*, and *locV* properties to change the location of a sprite. Many additional properties determine the appearance of bitmaps.

The *rect* Property

The *rect* property was used in the slider and progress bar behaviors in Chapter 15, "Graphic Interface Elements," to redefine the shape of rectangles. This same property can be used to stretch or shrink sprites.

For instance, if you place a sprite on the Stage and use the Message window, you can check its initial *rect*. Here is an example:

```
put (sprite 1).rect
-- rect(200, 150, 400, 400)
```

You can then set the *rect* to something else. It doesn't even have to have the same relative dimensions. For instance, you can squeeze the sprite horizontally by moving only the left and right portions of the *rect*. Try this:

```
(sprite 1).rect = rect(250,150,350,400)
updateStage
```

The *rect* gives you all the power of the *loc* property, plus much more. You are essentially controlling the locations of all four sides of the sprite, so you can move it, stretch it, or shrink it. This works for all bitmap sprites, plus shapes and vector graphics. It even works for text and field members to a limited extent; these are truly adjustable only if the frame property of the member is not set to "Adjust to Fit". You can adjust this property by selecting the member and using the Property Inspector.

The *rotation* Property

The *rotation* property gives you complete Lingo control over the orientation of the sprite. Bitmaps and text sprites can be rotated, but shapes cannot.

The value of *rotation* is in degrees. It can range from 0 to 360, but you can use numbers outside of that range and Director can translate them to a number in that range. A new sprite is always set to a rotation value of 0.0.

The first number in *rect* represents the position of the left side of the rectangle. The second is the top of the rectangle. The third is the right-side location. The last is the bottom location. So, it goes: left, top, right, bottom.

```
put (sprite 1).rotation
-- 0.0000
```

You can set the rotation just as easily, as follows:

```
(sprite 1).rotation = 45
updateStage
```

The following shows a one-line behavior that makes a sprite rotate around its center. It rotates one degree every frame:

```
on exitFrame me
  (sprite 1).rotation = (sprite 1).rotation + 1
end
```

A more complex behavior is one that aligns the *rotation* of the sprite to always point to the cursor. The behavior assumes that the "point" of the bitmap is normally pointing to the right side of the Stage. It reorients it to point toward the cursor, as follows:

```
on exitFrame me
  -- get the mouse location
  p = the mouseLoc
  x1 = p.locH
  y1 = p.locV

  -- get the sprite location
  x2 = (sprite me.spriteNum).locH
  y2 =  (sprite me.spriteNum).locV

  -- use atan to compute the angle
  if x2 = x1 then exit
  angle = atan(float(y2-y1)/float(x2-x1))

  -- correct the angle
  if x1 < x2 then angle = pi()+angle

  -- convert the angle to degrees
  angle = angle*360.0/(2.0*pi())

  -- set the sprite
  (sprite me.spriteNum).rotation = angle
end
```

You can use this behavior just as easily with other points, as well. For instance, it can align a sprite to the location of another sprite. As that sprite moves, either through user interaction or animation, the controlled sprite follows.

The *atan* function is at the heart of this behavior. Its purpose is to convert a slope, made by two points, into an angle. The results are limited to only one half of a circle, so an adjustment is made to deal with angles on the left side of the circle. The angle resulting from this is in radians, so there needs to be a conversion into degrees before the angle can be applied to the *rotation* property.

Radians, if you remember your high school trigonometry, are another way to measure the size of an angle. Whereas there are 360° in a circle, there are 2∏, or 6.2832, radians in a circle. In other words, 360° is equal to 2∏.

The *flipH* and *flipV* Properties

Bitmap sprites can also be flipped along either the horizontal or vertical axis. Flipping takes place around the registration point of the member. Lingo controls this feature through the *flipH* and *flipV* properties. They can be set to either *TRUE* or *FALSE*. If the setting is *TRUE*, the sprite is displayed flipped.

Here is an example. This example flips a sprite horizontally:

```
(sprite 1).flipH = TRUE
updateStage
```

However, if the sprite is already flipped, this last example does nothing. Here is an example that reverses the horizontal flip of a sprite:

```
(sprite 1).flipH = not (sprite 1).flipH
updateStage
```

Here is a behavior that controls a sprite's flip properties according to where the cursor is located relative to the sprite. It flips whenever the cursor crosses one of the sprite's axes:

```
on exitFrame me
  -- get the cursor location
  cLoc = the mouseLoc

  -- get the sprite location
  sLoc = (sprite me.spriteNum).loc

  -- flip horizontally if needed
  if cLoc.locH > sLoc.locH then
    (sprite me.spriteNum).flipH = TRUE
  else
    (sprite me.spriteNum).flipH = FALSE
  end if

  -- flip vertically if needed
  if cLoc.locV > sLoc.locV then
    (sprite me.spriteNum).flipV = TRUE
  else
```

```
      (sprite me.spriteNum) .flipV = FALSE
   end if
end if
```

The *skew* Property

The *skew* property can also be set with Lingo. The result is a change in the angle of the vertical sides of the sprite's rectangle. Angles from 0° to 90° tilt the vertical sides to the right, whereas angles from 0° to -90° tilt it to the left. Angles between 90° and 180° and -90° and -180° appear to flip the sprite. Any change of 360° places the *skew* back where it started, which is the same as a *skew* of 0.

Here is a simple behavior that repeatedly adds 10° to the *skew* of a sprite:

```
on exitFrame me
   (sprite 1).skew = (sprite 1).skew + 10
end
```

The results of the behavior are shown in Figure 18.1.

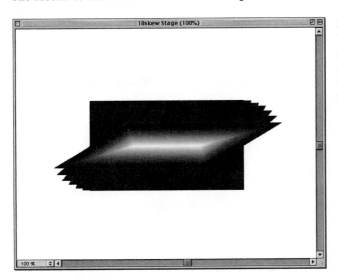

Figure 18.1
The result of changing the skew of a sprite by 10° several times, and having trails turned on to record each step.

The *quad* Property

The last and greatest of the sprite-manipulation properties is the *quad* property of the sprite. This property contains a list of four items, like *rect*, but it contains points, not numbers. Each of these points represents one of the corners of a sprite. Here is an example:

```
put (sprite 1).quad
-- [point(184.0000, 126.0000), point(463.0000, 126.0000), point(463.0000, \
302.0000), point(184.0000, 302.0000)]
```

The beauty of the *quad* property is that you can set the four points to whatever you want. You can essentially "pull" on any of the corners using Lingo.

For instance, if you take a rectangular image, and then push the upper-left corner of the sprite down and to the right, and the upper-right corner of the sprite down and to the left, you can imitate perspective on the Stage and create the illusion of 3D. Figure 18.2 shows this effect.

Figure 18.2
The Stage shows two sprites, both with the same bitmap member. However, one sprite's quad has been changed to imitate 3D perspective.

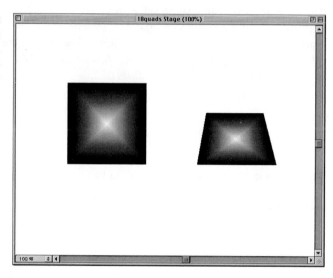

The difference between using *quad* and *skew* is that with *quad* you have total control over the four corners of a sprite. With *skew*, you control just the angle of the sides of the sprite's rectangle.

You have no way of altering a sprite's *quads* on the Stage, but this handler enables you to do it while the movie is playing. It enables you to click and grab any corner of the sprite and drag the corner:

```
property pCorner

on beginSprite me
  pCorner = 0
end

on mouseDown me
  pCorner = 0
  repeat with i = 1 to 4
    if distance(me,the clickLoc,sprite(me.spriteNum).quad[i]) < 10 then
      pCorner = i
      exit repeat
    end if
```

```
    end repeat
    put pCorner
end

on mouseUp me
    pCorner = 0
end

on mouseUpOutside me
    pCorner = 0
end

on exitFrame me
    if pCorner > 0 then
        q = sprite(me.spriteNum).quad
        q[pCorner] = the mouseLoc
        sprite(me.spriteNum).quad = q
    end if
end

on distance me, p1, p2
    return sqrt (power(p1.locH-p2.locH,2)+power(p1.locV-p2.locV,2))
end
```

Other Distortion Properties

Many other properties affect bitmap sprites at a less dramatic level than the properties previously discussed. Here is a complete list:

- **useAlpha**—Determines whether Alpha channel information included with 32-bit bitmaps is used in displaying the member. When *TRUE*, the Alpha channel is used to vary the level of transparency of the bitmap.

- **alphaThreshold**—If an Alpha channel is present, this property can be set to a value between 0 and 255. 0 means that all pixels in the sprite can respond to mouse clicks. Any other setting determines the degree of nontransparency required for a pixel to register a click.

- **blend**—This corresponds to the "blend" property in the Score. You can set it to values between 0 and 100, but the ink of the sprite must be one that supports blends.

- **color**—The foreground color of the sprite. This property can be set to either a *paletteIndex* structure, such as "paletteIndex(255)", or a *color* structure, such as "color(255,255,255)" or "color("#FFFFFF")". The difference is most dramatic with 1-bit members that use their *color* property for all used pixels. It is also used by sprites set to Lighten or Darken inks.

- **bgColor**—The background color of the sprite. This can be set to either a *paletteIndex* structure, such as "paletteIndex(255)", or a *color* structure, such as "color(255,255,255)" or "color("#FFFFFF")". The difference is most dramatic with 1-bit members that use their *bgColor* property for all unused pixels. Results vary according to ink. The *bgColor* property is also used by sprites set to Lighten or Darken inks.

- **locZ**—Sprites normally appear on the Stage with sprite in higher-numbered channels on top of sprites in lower-numbered channels. However, you can change this with the *locZ* property. You can use any integer, even negative numbers, to define which order the sprites should be drawn. For instance, setting a sprite to have a *locZ* of 500 means that it appears on top of sprites 1 to 499.

⇨ *For more information about bitmaps, **see** "Bitmap Member Properties," p. 86 Chapter 3, "Bitmap Members"*

⇨ *For more information about inks, **see** "Setting Sprite Inks," p. 176 Chapter 10, "Properties of Sprites and Frames"*

⇨ *For more information about sprite blends, **see** "Using the Sprite Blend," p. 178 in Chapter 10*

⇨ *For more information about sprite color, **see** "Setting Sprite Colors," p. 179 in Chapter 10*

⇨ *For more information about sprite shapes, **see** "Adjusting the Sprite Shape," p. 180 in Chapter 10*

ADDING 3D EFFECTS

Computer screens are flat. By nature, 3D computer graphics are just illusions that trick the users into seeing 3D on what is really only a flat screen. This section discusses how to use Lingo to make those illusions as realistic as possible.

Shrinking Sprites

The shrinking sprite illusion is a special effect that Director and Lingo can easily handle. The basic idea is that real-life objects that are farther away look smaller to the eye. So, if you have two objects that are the same size, but one is twice as far away, the farther one appears to be half as big.

Figure 18.3 shows a Stage with two sprites. The sprite on the left is shown at 100%, whereas the sprite on the right is shown at 50%. The result is that the bigger one appears closer than the other.

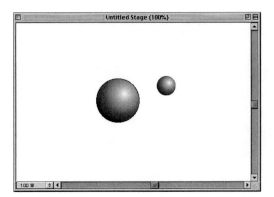

Figure 18.3
Setting the sizes of sprites
can create the illusion of
depth.

The illusion becomes even stronger when used with animation. Imagine, for instance, an object that appears as a small dot at first, and then grows to full size. It looks as if the object is moving toward the viewer.

The following code shows a behavior that does just that. It assumes that the center of the screen is 320, 240, and that it is the origination point for the sprite. It gets the *quad* of the sprite and manipulates all four points according to the scale and the center of the screen. It stops when the scale reaches 1.0, as follows:

```
property pOrigQuad, pScale

on beginSprite me
  pOrigQuad = sprite(me.spriteNum).quad
  pScale = 0.0
end

on exitFrame me
  if pScale < 1.0 then
    -- increase scale 1%
    pScale = pScale + .01

    -- copy the quad
    newQuad = duplicate(pOrigQuad)

    -- set new quad points
    repeat with i = 1 to 4
      newQuad[i] = newPoint(me,newQuad[i],pScale)
    end repeat

    -- set the sprite
    sprite(me.spriteNum).quad = newQuad
  end if
end
```

```
-- this handler will take a point and a scale
-- and return a new point based on the
-- center of 320, 240
on newPoint me, p, scale
  centerPoint = point(320,240)

  -- find relative location
  p = p - centerPoint

  -- multiply by the scale
  p = p*scale

  -- add back center point
  p = p + centerPoint

  return p
end
```

A script such as this can be used to make objects come from a distance to their positions on the screen. It can also be a good effect for creating text that flies "toward" users, rather than just moving left, right, up, or down.

Shrinking Sprites with Movement

Another way to create a feeling of depth is to resize the sprite as it moves around the Stage. If, for instance, the left side of the Stage is supposed to be farther back than the right side, you can shrink the object depending on how far from the left side of the Stage it is.

The following code shows a behavior that has the center of a sprite follow the mouse. The closer users bring the sprite to the left side of the Stage, the smaller the scale gets:

```
property pWidth, pHeight

on beginSprite me
  pWidth = sprite(me.spriteNum).rect.width
  pHeight = sprite(me.spriteNum).rect.height
end

on exitFrame me
  -- get the new location
  x = the mouseH
  y = the mouseV

  -- figure the size as a number between 0 and 1
```

```
    if x = 0 then  percent = the maxInteger
    else percent = 640.0/x

    -- figure the new height and width
    w = pWidth/percent
    h = pHeight/percent

    -- make a rectangle with the point at the center
    newRect = rect(x-w/2,y-h/2,x+w/2,y+w/2)

    -- set the sprite
    sprite(me.spriteNum).rect = newRect
end
```

An illusion such as this becomes even easier to see when the background graphic hints toward it. In the preceding example, you might want to include a background graphic of a wall that recedes back toward the left.

Using the *quad* Property to Create Illusions

Yet another way to create 3D illusions is to play with the *quad* of sprites to form 2D representations of 3D shapes. A cube is a good example. Figure 18.4 shows a cube on the Stage. It is actually drawn with six sprites, one for each side. It uses 3D trigonometry and *quads* to figure out where each side goes.

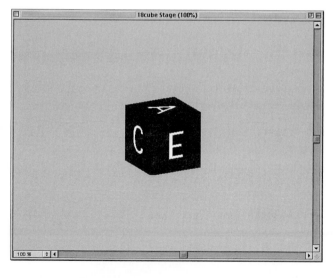

Figure 18.4
Six sprites are used to draw this 3D cube.

Here is the code that makes this 3D cube. There are actually many different ways to pull this off, but this example uses the following movie script:

```
global gCorners, gCenter, gRectList, gRotate,
gPlane

on startMovie
  -- initialize lists for a cube
  initBox
end

on frameScript
  -- add to rotation based on mouse location
  gRotate = gRotate - (float(the mouseH-
320)/30)*pi()/100

  -- calc plane tilt based on mouse location
  gPlane = - (float(the mouseV-240)/30)*pi()/20
  drawSides
end

on initBox
  -- list of corners with x, y and z coordinates
  gCorners = [[-60,-60,-60],[60,-60,-60],[60,60,-60],\
              [-60,60,-60],[-60,-60,60],[60,-60,60],\
              [60,60,60],[-60,60,60]]

  -- the screen center
  gCenter = point(320,240)

  -- list of sides
  -- each side has four corners
  gRectList = [[1,2,3,4],[1,2,6,5],[3,4,8,7],\
               [2,3,7,6],[8,5,1,4],[5,6,7,8]]
end

on drawSides
  -- generate a list of screen points and depths based on the
  -- gCorners list and the transformation to 2d screen coordinates
  list = []
  repeat with i = 1 to gCorners.count
    temp = plotPoint(gCorners[i])
    add list,temp
  end repeat

  -- create a quad list that takes four points to display a side of the cube
  repeat with i = 1 to gRectList.count
```

This code can be considered very complex. If you don't understand exactly what is going on, don't worry. Try the demo file on the CD-ROM called 18cube.dir to get a better understanding of this example.

```
      -- get the four corners that make this side
      thisRect = gRectList[i]

      -- get the four screen points to draw
      q = [list[thisRect[1]][2],list[thisRect[2]][2],\
          list[thisRect[3]][2],list[thisRect[4]][2]]

      -- get the closest (depth) screen point
      z = min(list[thisRect[1]][1],list[thisRect[2]][1],\
            list[thisRect[3]][1],list[thisRect[4]][1])

      -- draw the side
      sprite(i).quad = q
      sprite(i).locZ = z
    end repeat
end

on plotPoint objectInfo
  -- get x, y, and z from objectInfo list
  x = getAt(objectInfo,1)
  y = getAt(objectInfo,2)
  z = getAt(objectInfo,3)

  -- TRANSFORM BY ROTATION AROUND Z

  -- compute the radius
  radius = sqrt(x*x+y*y)

  -- compute the angle
  if x = 0.0 then angle = atan(the maxInteger)
  else angle = atan(float(y)/x)
  if y < 0 then angle = angle + pi()

  -- rotate
  set angle = angle+gRotate

  -- compute new x, y, and z
  realX = radius*cos(angle)
  realZ = radius*sin(angle)
  realY = z

  -- TRANSFORM BY ROTATION AROUND X
```

```
      -- compute the radius
  radius = sqrt(realY*realY+realZ*realZ)

      -- compute the angle
    if realZ = 0 then angle = atan(the maxInteger)
    else angle = (atan(realY/realZ))
    if realZ < 0 then angle = angle + pi()

      -- rotate
    angle = angle - gPlane

      -- compute the new x, y and z
  screenX = realX
    screenY = radius*sin(angle)
    screenZ = radius*cos(angle)

      -- return both z, and the x and y point
    return  [screenZ,point(screenX,screenY)+gCenter]
  end
```

The code uses the mouse position to determine the plane and rotation of the cube. However, you can remove this code and include buttons that enable users to move the cube. You could even have the cube rotate at a constant rate.

Mapping Sprites

When you use the *quad* property to distort a sprite, Director still keeps track of the original member's appearance. In fact, you can use two special functions in Lingo to convert between screen locations and the relative locations of pixels in the original bitmap.

Figure 18.5 shows a good example of why you need to do this conversion. The chessboard has been distorted with *quads* to appear as if it has depth. In reality, the board is a simple 160×160 square with 64 spaces.

Figure 18.5
The chessboard bitmap is actually a straight-down image that has been altered using quads to appear to have depth.

Here is the *on beginSprite* handler that takes the plain, square board and turns it into the 3D one you see in Figure 18.5. It simply moves the top two *quad* points. No special math is used—just estimated, hard-coded points for simplicity in this example:

```
on beginSprite me
  q = sprite(me.spriteNum).quad
  q[1] = q[1]+point(-30,100)
  q[2] = q[2]+point(30,100)
  sprite(me.spriteNum).quad = q
end
```

When the movie runs, this sprite appears as it does in Figure 18.5. When it was just a plain rectangle, it would have been easy to get the column and row of a mouse click. Each space on the board is 20[ts]20, so you could just divide the horizontal and vertical location by 20, and add one to get a number between one and eight. However, with the board distorted as shown in Figure 18.5, you need to map the click location with Lingo.

The function needed to map the click location is *mapStageToMember*. It takes a sprite number and a Stage location and then converts these to a location relative to the bitmap member.

So, if users click the upper-left corner of the distorted sprite, the function returns point (0,0). Here is an *on mouseUp* handler that uses the *mapStageToMember* function to calculate where users clicked:

```
on mouseUp me
  p = mapStageToMember(sprite 1, the clickLoc)
  x = 1+p.locH/20
  y = 1+p.locV/20
  put "Row:"&&x&&"Column:"&&y
end
```

The flip side of the *mapStageToMember* function is the *mapMemberToStage* function. You can use it to find any Stage location based on a location in the member. Here is a handler that returns the Stage location when given a space on the chessboard:

```
on getPos me, x, y
  p = point(x*20-10,y*20-10)
  return mapMemberToStage(sprite 1, p)
end
```

To position the queen as seen previously on Figure 18.5, you can use this behavior. It assumes that the board is in Sprite channel 1.

```
on beginSprite me
  p = getPos(sprite 1, 4, 5)
  sprite(me.spriteNum).loc = p
end
```

Mapping sprites in this way enables you to distort one sprite and then position other sprites relative to this distortion. It can be used along with the cube example to place an object on the face of a cube. Or, it can be used with the shrinking sprite example to map one sprite onto another, or provide valid clicks on the sprite as it changes size.

⇨ *For an example that uses the 3D cube script, see "Creating Shockwave Ads," p. 614 (Chapter 31, "Shockwave Applets")*

MANIPULATING BITMAP MEMBERS

Director 8 offers an entirely new set of commands for editing bitmap images. Direct control of bitmaps has never been present before in Director and developers are sure to find all sorts of useful new applications for it. Already, the "Sprite Transitions" category of the Behavior Library has been created to take advantage of them, as well as the "Paint Box" category.

All the new image functionality revolves around the *image* property of a bitmap member. You can affect the *image* of a member directly, or store *images* in variables, and then assign them back to members later.

The main command used to alter images is *copyPixels*. This command has three main parameters: the source image, the destination rectangle, and the source rectangle. The fact that they can specify each rectangle separately means that you can copy small areas into larger ones and vice versa.

If you had two bitmap members and you wanted to copy a section of one bitmap into a section of the other, here's how you would do it:

```
member("bitmap2").image.copyPixels(member("bitmap1").image, \
rect(50,50,70,70),rect(30,30,50,50)
```

You can also use a fourth parameter of *copyPixels* to specify a whole bunch of options. List parameter should be a property list that can contain #color, #bgColor, #ink, #blendLevel, #dither, #useFastQuads, #maskImage, and #maskOffset. Most of these behave in the same way that the sprite property of the same name acts. The #maskImage enables you to specify a bitmap image to be used as a mask or matte for copying the pixels.

You can also use a *quad* rather than a *rect* for the second parameter. This enables you to take a rectangular section from one *image*, and place it in an odd-shaped (nonrectangular) area of another *image*.

In addition to the wholesale movement of pixels with *copyPixels*, you can change an *image* one pixel at a time. The *setPixel* command enables you to set a specific pixel to a specific color. Here is an example:

```
setPixel(50,75,rgb("FFFFFF"))
```

You can also use *setPixel* with a *point* as the first parameter and a *color* as the second instead of using three parameters. The opposite of this command is the function *getPixel*, which enables you to retrieve the color value of a pixel.

In addition to being able to get the *image* of a bitmap member, you can get the *image* of the Stage. The code "(the stage).image" enables you, with the use of *getPixel*, to determine the color of any pixel on the Stage. You can also place the *image* of the Stage in a bitmap member.

There are several other functions and commands that help you manipulate bitmap images, as follows:

- **crop**—Enables you to crop an *image* or a bitmap member to a size given by a *rect*.

- **draw**—Draws a line from one point in an *image* to another. It can take either two *points* and a *color* as parameters, or the horizontal and vertical locations of each point (four numbers) and a *color*. To draw a rectangle or oval, you can use a property list as the last parameter with a #shapeType (#oval, #rect, #roundRect, or #line), #lineSize, and #color. This property list would replace the color property.

- **fill**—Takes two parameters, a *rect* and a *color*, and fills that area of the *image*. You can also add a property list as a third parameter with a #shapeType (#oval, #rect, #roundRect, or #line), #lineSize, #color, and #bgColor. This third parameter makes the *fill* command work like the *draw* command, but with a filled area rather than just an outline.

- **createMask**—From an image, returns a special object that can be used with *copyPixels* to simulate the Mask ink when copying.

- **createMatte**—From an image, returns a special object that can be used with *copyPixels* to simulate the Matte ink when copying.

- **trimWhiteSpace**—Removes white pixels outside of the minimum rectangle of the *image*. It returns a new image, which you can then apply back to the original if that is your intention.

- **duplicate**—If you assign the *image* of a member to a variable, you simply are creating a reference to that member's *image*. This function enables you to create a true duplicate of that *image* instead of a reference.

- **extractAlpha**—Returns a grayscale *image* taken from the Alpha channel of a 32-bit *image*.

- **setAlpha**—Sets the Alpha channel of a 32-bit image to a grayscale *image*, or to a single number that will be applied evenly throughout the *image*.

You can also use standard Lingo properties such as *width*, *height*, *rect*, and *depth* to get information about an *image* object, although you cannot set these properties.

Playing with these new commands and functions is the best way to learn about them. Here is a handler that fills a bitmap member.

```
on fillMemberImage memName, fillColor
  myImage = member(memName).image.duplicate()
  myImage.fill(myImage.rect,rgb(fillColor))
  member(memName).image = myImage
end
```

There is an undocumented way to use the *fill* command to fill odd shapes. If you feed the fill command only two parameters, a single point, and a color, Director will perform a paint-bucket fill starting at that point and extending as far as a paint-bucket fill would normally go. This is great for filling in circles or odd shapes or changing the color of an odd-shaped area of a bitmap. You can also use the undocumented command *floodFill* to do the same thing with the same parameters.

Here is a handler that draws a random line from one point in the *image* to another.

```
on drawRandomLine memName
  myImage = member(memName).image.duplicate()
  x1 = random(myImage.width)
  y1 = random(myImage.height)
  x2 = random(myImage.width)
  y2 = random(myImage.height)
  myImage.draw(point(x1,y1),point(x2,y2),rgb("000000"))
  member(memName).image = myImage
end
```

Here is a handler that takes the *image* from one member and draws it, vertical line by vertical line, onto another member. If that second member is on the Stage, the handler appears to create a horizontal wipe transition for that one member. It assumes that both members are exactly the same size.

```
on wipeRight sourceMem, destMem
  sourceImage = member(sourceMem).image
  destImage = member(destMem).image.duplicate()
  repeat with x = 0 to destImage.width-1
    destImage.copyPixels(sourceImage,\
        rect(x,0,x+1,destImage.height),\
        rect(x,0,x+1,sourceImage.height))
    member(destMem).image = destImage
    updateStage
  end repeat
end
```

➡️ *For an example that uses bitmap manipulation,* **see** *"Making a Drawing Activity," p. 531 in Chapter 27, "Educational Applications"*

TROUBLESHOOTING BITMAPS

- Nothing is free. When you rotate, skew, or stretch sprites, you take a speed hit. You cannot expect to have dozens of constantly rotating sprites on the Stage and others stretched with *quad* and still have your animation running as fast as an animation without all that. Keep this in mind when designing.

- If a 32-bit image is displayed incorrectly, or it looks different in the Paint window than on the Stage, try turning off the "Use Alpha" property. Sometimes bad Alpha channels creep into 32-bit images.

It's important to understand the difference between an *image* reference to a member, and an *image* stored in a variable. To create the latter, use the *duplicate* function on an *image* reference. Macromedia recommends that you don't try to edit the *image* of a member directly, but instead store a copy of it in a variable and edit that *image* before applying it back to the member. The three examples in this section do exactly this.

- Using straight PhotoShop documents with an Alpha channel produces a "premultiplied" Alpha channel. This just means a white halo appears around the images. One easy way to correct this is to open the file in Macromedia Fireworks first, save it as a PNG file, and then import that file.

DID YOU KNOW?

- The *useFastQuads* property, set to *TRUE*, allows sprites stretched with the *quad* property to draw more quickly, but they are not stretched in quite the same way. The result is not as good for simulating 3D.

- To convert degrees to radians, divide the number by 360.0 and multiply by 2.0∏ (or 6.2832). To convert radians to degrees, divide by 2.0∏ and then multiply by 360.0. Make sure your original number is a floating point number, not an integer.

- You can make a bitmap semitransparent by using the *setAlpha* command on its image. If you set it to an integer midway between 0 and 255, you will get a similar effect as to having the *blend* of the sprite set to 50%.

19

CONTROLLING VIDEO

Source movies for this chapter can be found on the CD-ROM in the "Book Movies" folder under folder 19.

Whereas most digital video used in Director is simply placed on the Stage with the default control bar, sometimes it's necessary to control video with Lingo. Digital video is not as easy to manipulate as bitmaps are, but a variety of properties can be used to affect how video is displayed. These properties are the subject of this chapter.

USING VIDEO COMMANDS

There are more member and sprite properties for digital video than for any other media type. Because some of the properties are for the member and others for the sprite, it can get confusing. There are even functions involving QuickTime tracks that act like properties. For the sake of clarity, this section separates the properties for the members from the properties for the sprites.

Member Properties

Two groups of member properties are for digital video members: member properties and sprite properties. The first group corresponds exactly to the properties shown in the Property Inspector when you have a video member selected. The following is a brief list of the most common digital video member properties:

- **center**—A *TRUE* or *FALSE* value that determines whether the video is centered in the sprite's rectangle. This works only if the *crop* property is set to *TRUE*.

- **controller**—A *TRUE* or *FALSE* value that determines whether the default QuickTime or AVI controller is shown.

- **crop**—If this value is set to *TRUE*, the movie remains the same scale, even if the sprite's rectangle is changed. If it's set to *FALSE*, the movie adjusts to fit in the sprite's rectangle.

- **directToStage**—This property determines whether the video is drawn directly to the screen, covering and ignoring other sprites. If the video is drawn directly to the screen, you get a smoother display, but you do not have the capability to use as many special effects.

- **frameRate**—This property can be set to a number that becomes the playback frame rate of the video. Using the special value -2 causes the video to play back as fast as it can, whereas the value -1 causes it to play back at normal speed. Playing a video with this property set disables the sound for the video. Set the *frameRate* to 0 to return the video member to the "Sync to Soundtrack" normal state.

- **loop**—This property determines whether the video is to automatically loop back to the beginning when it reaches the end.

- **pausedAtStart**—This property determines whether the movie starts playing as soon as it appears on the Stage, or whether it waits for the controller or Lingo to tell it to play.

- **sound**—This property determines whether the sound is played.

- **video**—This property determines whether the video is displayed.

In addition to these member properties that can be controlled with or without Lingo, a few properties can be accessed, but not set, with Lingo:

- **digitalVideoType**—Returns either #quickTime or #videoForWindows.

- **duration**—Returns the length in ticks (1/60 of a second) of the video.

- **isVRMovie**—Returns a *TRUE* if the video is a QuickTime VR movie.

To determine whether QuickTime is present, use the *quickTimeVersion()* function. If QuickTime is not present, it will return a 0.0; otherwise, it will return the version number.

Sprite Properties

Several sprite properties also can be set with Lingo. These properties are useful for creating video controls and effects:

- **loopBounds**—This property enables you to set the start and end times of a looping video. Use a short, two-item list, such as [0,240].

- **movieRate**—This property represents the speed of forward movement of the video. A value of 0 means the video has stopped. A value of 1 means it is playing normally. A value of 2 means it is going at double speed. You can also use negative values to make the video go backward.

- **movieTime**—This property represents the current time, in ticks, of the video. You can set this to 0 to go to the start, or to the member's duration to go to the end.

- **rotation**—Believe it or not, you can rotate a QuickTime video. Set this property to the angle, in degrees, of rotation. This property works best when the video member is not set to "Direct to Stage".

- **scale**—You can also scale the video by setting this property to a small list with the horizontal and vertical scale values, such as [1.5,1.5].

- **volume**—This property works just as it does for sound members, enabling you to change the sound level of the video.

Masks

Digital video members can also have masks. A mask is a 1-bit bitmap that tells Director which pixels of the video to show and which pixels to throw away. Figure 19.1 shows three images: a video (left), a 1-bit bitmap (middle), and the same video with the 1-bit bitmap applied as a mask (right).

Figure 19.1
A 1-bit bitmap can be used as a mask for a digital video member.

The best part about masks is that they can be used when the video is in "Direct to Stage" mode. This means that the video is not slowed by the mask effect.

To apply a mask, create the 1-bit bitmap and name it. Then use the mask property to apply it to the member. You can even do it in the Message window to test it. The *mask* property is a member property, but this command uses the sprite to figure out the member:

```
sprite(1).member.mask = member("myMask")
```

You can also use the *invertMask* property to have white pixels, rather than black, represent visible pixels in the movie. Keep in mind that the registration point for the mask should be set to the upper-left corner rather than the center.

> Setting a video *mask* works best when you do it before the sprite appears on Stage. An *on beginSprite* handler is a good place for it. To remove a video mask, set the *mask* property of the member to *VOID*.

➡ *For some background on using digital video in Director, see "Understanding Digital Video Settings," p. 122 (Chapter 6, "Digital Video")*

BUILDING VIDEO CONTROLS

Using the video properties explained previously, it's easy to build your own custom controls. As a matter of fact, one behavior can handle 10 types of controls.

The following behavior needs to know which sprite contains the digital video. It also needs to know for what type of control is being used.

```
property pControlType, pVideoSprite

on getPropertyDescriptionList me
  list = [:]
  addProp list, #pControlType, [#comment: "Control",\
    #format: #symbol,\
    #range: [#play, #stop, #pause, #stepForward, #stepBackward,\
      #start, #reverse, #fastForward, #fastReverse, #end, #loop],\
    #default: #stop]
  addProp list, #pVideoSprite, [#comment: "Video Sprite",\
    #format: #sprite, #default: 1]
  return list
end
```

Although a more complex behavior might also include button handler[nd]like effects, such as down states and rollovers, this behavior sticks to doing only what is necessary to control the video sprite.

In the case of a "play" button, all that is needed is for the *movieRate* to be set to 1.

```
on mouseUp me
  case pControlType of
    #play:
      sprite(pVideoSprite).movieRate = 1
```

A stop button does the opposite, setting the *movieRate* to 0. The same can be done for the "pause" button. To make the "play" button different, it can also set the *movieTime* back to 0, which stops and rewinds the video, rather than just stopping it.

```
    #stop:
      sprite(pVideoSprite).movieRate = 0
      sprite(pVideoSprite).movieTime = 0
    #pause:
      sprite(pVideoSprite).movieRate = 0
```

A "start" or "end" will take the video to the beginning or end and pause it. Note that this means the "start" button and "stop" button actually do the same thing!

```
    #start:
      sprite(pVideoSprite).movieRate = 0
      sprite(pVideoSprite).movieTime = 0
    #end:
      sprite(pVideoSprite).movieRate = 0
      sprite(pVideoSprite).movieTime = sprite(pVideoSprite).duration
```

A "reverse" button plays the video at normal speed, but backward.

```
    #reverse:
      sprite(pVideoSprite).movieRate = -1
```

There are two types of "step" buttons: forward and reverse. If the digital video is set to play at a typical 15 frames per second, that means there is one frame every 4/60 of a second, or 4 ticks.

```
    #stepForward:
      sprite(pVideoSprite).movieTime = sprite(pVideoSprite).movieTime + 4
    #stepBackward:
      sprite(pVideoSprite).movieTime = sprite(pVideoSprite).movieTime - 4
```

A "fast forward" or "fast reverse" button can make the video travel at speeds greater than 1 or less than -1. In this case, 3 is used.

```
    #fastForward:
      sprite(pVideoSprite).movieRate = 3
    #fastReverse:
      sprite(pVideoSprite).movieRate = -3
```

One last button type is the loop switch. This determines whether the movie loops at the end. Make this a separate behavior and use some of the same code from the check box behaviors so that the button can change from a looping to nonlooping state. However, to simplify the coding, this button just toggles the *loop* property and does not give any feedback to the users.

```
  #loop:
    sprite(pVideoSprite).member.loop = \
        not sprite(pVideoSprite).member.loop
end case
end
```

Other video buttons can be made as well. For instance, you can use *loopBounds* to switch between different loops within the same video. A slider can be used as a volume control. Or, you can even use a slider to set the *movieTime* property. Such a slider is just like the one used by QuickTime's default controller, but you can use your own custom graphics.

⇨ *For more information on digital video properties, see "Understanding Digital Video Settings," p. 122 (Chapter 6)*

USING OTHER VIDEO TECHNIQUES

These video properties can also be used to make video sprites perform tricks. For instance, the following behavior uses the blend property of the sprite to cause a video sprite to fade in:

```
property pSpeed

on getPropertyDescriptionList me
  list = [:]
  addProp list, #pSpeed, [#comment: "Speed", #format: #integer,\
      #range: [#min: 1, #max: 20], #default: 7]
  return list
end

on beginSprite me
  sprite(me.spriteNum).member.directToStage = FALSE
  sprite(me.spriteNum).member.crop = TRUE

  sprite(me.spriteNum).blend = 0
end

on exitFrame me
  if sprite(me.spriteNum).blend < 100 then
    sprite(me.spriteNum).blend = \
        min(sprite(me.spriteNum).blend+pSpeed,100)
  end if
end
```

Notice that the handler also sets the *directToStage* and *crop* properties of the video sprite. Although this is usually not necessary, it ensures that any changes to these properties from other behaviors are not still in effect.

The same things can be done in reverse. Here is a behavior that fades a video sprite to a blend of 0:

```
property pSpeed

on getPropertyDescriptionList me
  list = [:]
  addProp list, #pSpeed, [#comment: "Speed", #format: #integer,\
    #range: [#min: 1, #max: 20], #default: 7]
  return list
end

on beginSprite me
  sprite(me.spriteNum).member.directToStage = FALSE
  sprite(me.spriteNum).member.crop = TRUE

  sprite(me.spriteNum) .blend = 100
end

on exitFrame me
  if sprite(me.spriteNum).blend > 0 then
    sprite(me.spriteNum).blend = \
       max(sprite(me.spriteNum).blend-pSpeed,0)
  end if
end
```

These behaviors can, of course, be combined into one that provides either function. Note that they can be used for bitmaps and even text members, too.

For a more complex effect, the following behavior causes the video to start off as a small point. It then grows lengthwise until it is a line. Then, it grows up and down until it is the original shape of the video. The result looks something like an old-fashioned television warming up.

```
property pOrigRect, pSpeed

on getPropertyDescriptionList me
  list = [:]
  addProp list, #pSpeed, [#comment: "Speed", #format: #integer,\
    #range: [#min: 1, #max: 20], #default: 7]
  return list
end

on beginSprite me
```

```
    sprite(me.spriteNum).member.directToStage = TRUE
    sprite(me.spriteNum).member.crop = FALSE

    pOrigRect = sprite(me.spriteNum).rect

    -- set rect to center point
    x = pOrigRect.left+(pOrigRect.width/2)
    y = pOrigRect.top+(pOrigRect.height/2)
    r = rect(x,y,x,y+1)
    sprite(me.spriteNum).rect = r
end

on exitFrame me
  if sprite(me.spriteNum).rect.width < pOrigRect.width then
    r = sprite(me.spriteNum).rect
    r.left = max(r.left-pSpeed, pOrigRect.left)
    r.right = min(r.right+pSpeed, pOrigRect.right)
    sprite(me.spriteNum).rect = r

  else if sprite(me.spriteNum).rect.height < pOrigRect.height then
    r = sprite(me.spriteNum).rect
    r.top = max(r.top-pSpeed, pOrigRect.top)
    r.bottom = min(r.bottom+pSpeed, pOrigRect.bottom)
    sprite(me.spriteNum).rect = r

  end if
end
```

Digital video can also be rotated. This next behavior probably has no real use, but is a good demonstration. It will take a digital video sprite and rotate it continuously.

```
property pSpeed

on getPropertyDescriptionList me
  list = [:]
  addProp list, #pSpeed, [#comment: "Speed", #format: #integer,\
    #range: [#min: 1, #max: 20], #default: 7]
  return list
end

on beginSprite me
  sprite(me.spriteNum).member.directToStage = TRUE
  sprite(me.spriteNum).member.crop = TRUE
end
```

```
on endSprite me
  sprite(me.spriteNum).rotation = 0
end

on exitFrame me
  sprite(me.spriteNum).rotation = \
        sprite(me.spriteNum).rotation + pSpeed
end
```

Here is a very different effect. The following behavior takes the video, shrinks it, and then places it on the left side of the screen. It turns on the *trails* property of the sprite so that the image is left behind. It then moves over to the right and leaves another image. It continues to do this, leaving behind what looks like a filmstrip. When it gets to the right side of the screen, it starts replacing the images to the left.

```
property pOrigRect, pSize, pSpacing, pStart, pDirect

on getPropertyDescriptionList me
  list = [:]
  addProp list, #pSize, [#comment: "Size (%)", #format: #integer,\
    #range: [#min: 5, #max: 100], #default: 25]
  addProp list, #pSpacing, [#comment: "Spacing", #format: #integer,\
    #range: [#min: 0, #max: 25], #default: 5]
  addProp list, #pStart, [#comment: "Start X", #format: #integer,\
    #default: 0]
  addProp list, #pDirect,  [#comment: "Direct To Stage", #format: #boolean,\
    #default: TRUE]
  return list
end

on beginSprite me
  sprite(me.spriteNum).member.directToStage = pDirect
  sprite(me.spriteNum).member.crop = FALSE
  sprite(me.spriteNum).trails = FALSE

  pOrigRect = sprite(me.spriteNum).rect
  r = sprite(me.spriteNum).rect
  r = (r*pSize)/100.0
  sprite(me.spriteNum).rect = r
  sprite(me.spriteNum).locH = pStart
  sprite(me.spriteNum).trails = TRUE
end

on endSprite me
  sprite(me.spriteNum).trails = FALSE
```

```
    sprite(me.spriteNum).rect = pOrigRect
end

on exitFrame me
  x = sprite(me.spriteNum).locH
  x = x + sprite(me.spriteNum).rect.width + pSpacing
  if x > the stageRight then x = pStart

  sprite(me.spriteNum).locH = x
end
```

Figure 19.2 shows the effects of this code in action.

Figure 19.2

The Film Strip behavior places images of the video in different positions on the Stage.

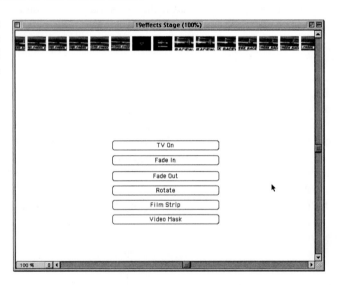

These are only simple examples of what can be accomplished with the digital video member and sprite properties. You can combine and expand on them depending on your needs. Experimentation is the best way to find what works best for you.

⇨ *For more information on using digital video, see "Working with Digital Video," p. 124 (Chapter 6)*

TROUBLESHOOTING VIDEO

- If you are using the built-in QuickTime controller, check the size on both Mac and Windows; they might be slightly different. It depends on the version of QuickTime. The Windows controller was slightly taller than the Mac in QuickTime 2.1.

DID YOU KNOW?

- You can use the video control scripts to control MIDI-only or sound-only QuickTime video. This way, you can build a jukebox that uses MIDI or supercompressed QuickTime audio.
- When you set the *movieRate* property to a negative number, not only does the movie play backward, but so does the sound!

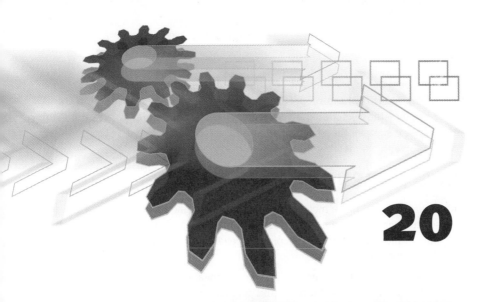

CONTROLLING VECTOR GRAPHICS

IN THIS CHAPTER

Source movies for this chapter can be found on the CD-ROM in the "Book Movies" folder under folder 20.

Vector shape cast members have an entire set of Lingo properties and commands that you can use to manipulate them. Many of these properties and commands were borrowed from the Flash cast member because the vector shape cast member uses the Flash engine in the Flash Asset Xtra. This chapter discusses the Flash member and vector shape member Lingo you need to understand to use these members.

USING FLASH MEMBER LINGO

Flash cast members are, no doubt, the most complex type of cast member. After all, they are created in Macromedia Flash, a program all to itself. Flash creates mostly vector-based animations that are streamlined for the Internet. The program even warrants a few books all to itself and there are several to choose from.

Flash members are made up of frames, just like Director movies. Each frame can contain different elements, such as shapes, bitmaps, buttons, and sounds. Rather than being a still media like bitmaps, Flash members are a time-based media like digital video. Most of the Lingo for Flash movies reflects that fact.

The following is a list of properties that control the speed at which the Flash movie plays while it is on the Stage:

- **playBackMode**—You have three options: #normal, #lockstep, and #fixed. The #normal option tells the Flash movie to rely on the settings established when it was created in Flash. The #lockstep setting causes one frame of the Flash movie to play for every one frame of the Director movie. The #fixed setting uses the *fixedRate* property of the member to determine the Flash movie's frame rate.

- **fixedRate**—Set this only when you are using the #fixed setting for the *playBackMode*. It enables you to specify the frame rate for the Flash movie. You can even change it during playback.

- **frameRate**—This property tells you the Flash movie's original frame rate.

- **frameCount**—This property tells you the number of frames in the Flash movie.

You can also use Lingo to navigate within the Flash movie, as follows:

- **goToFrame**—This command enables you to specify a frame number or frame label in the Flash movie. An example looks like this: "goToFrame(sprite 5, "intro")". The sprite must contain a Flash member.

- **findLabel**—This function takes a sprite number and a frame label as parameters. It tries to return the frame number that corresponds to the frame in the Flash movie that contains that label. If a frame is not found, a 0 is returned.

- **pausedAtStart**—This *TRUE* or *FALSE* property determines whether the Flash movie automatically starts playing when it appears on the Stage.

- **playing**—This property tells you whether the Flash movie is currently playing.

- **rewind**—This command takes the sprite number as its only parameter. It takes the Flash movie back to its first frame.

- **stop**—This command stops the Flash movie in the sprite specified.

- **play**—This command enables the Flash movie in the specified sprite to continue playing.

You can also control how much like a Flash movie a Flash member should act. Because Flash movies have their own buttons and actions, you will sometimes want to disable those elements in the Flash member when using it in Director.

- **actionsEnabled**—Determines whether any of the actions in a Flash sprite or member work.

- **buttonsEnabled**—Determines whether buttons in the Flash sprite or member work.

You can also establish when you want to have mouse events, such as clicks and rollovers, passed to your Lingo behaviors attached to the sprite.

- **clickMode**—This property of a sprite or member can be set to one of three options: #boundingBox, #opaque, or #object. The #boundingBox option enables clicks and other mouse events to be detected over the entire sprite's rectangle. The #opaque option enables clicks to be detected only when the cursor is over an opaque portion of the Flash member. The #object option detects mouse events only when the cursor is over a filled shape in the Flash member. The #opaque option works only when the sprite is set to the Background Transparent ink.

- **eventPassMode**—Determines whether clicks are passed to Lingo behaviors. The four modes are #passAlways, #passButton, #passNotButton, and #passNever. The #passAlways setting is the default.

An additional two functions tell you when a point is over something in a Flash movie sprite:

- **hitTest**—This function takes two parameters: the sprite and a point. The point should be relative to the sprite's location. It returns *#background*, *#normal*, or *#button*, depending on what the point is over. *#normal* means that it's over a shape in the Flash movie.

- **mouseOverButton**—Returns a *TRUE* if the cursor is over a button in the specified Flash movie sprite.

There is also a way to call Flash ActionScript code directly with Lingo. Unfortunately, while the Flash Xtra that comes with Director 8.5 will work with Flash 5 movies, this new command seems more suited for Flash 4 movies. It is the *callFrame* command and it works just like the old Flash 4 *call* command. It will trigger ActionScript that I stored as the frame script in a specific frame. You can use *callFrame* like this:

```
sprite(1).callFrame("frameWithScriptInIt")
```

You can use the frame label or the frame number. Unfortunately, there doesn't seem to be a way to directly call a Flash 5 function yet; however, there are other ways to affect a Flash movie.

One method is to use the *setVariable* command. This will change the value of a variable in the Flash movie from Lingo. Here is an example:

```
sprite(1).setVariable("myFlashVariable",7)
```

You can also get a variable value with the *getVariable* function.

```
myLingoVariable = sprite(1).getVariable("myFlashVariable")
```

There is also a *getFlashProperty* function that allows you to get the value of a property of a movie clip in Flash. For instance, if you have a movie clip identified as "myClip" and you wanted to find its _alpha property, you would use this:

```
a = sprite(1).getFlashProperty("myClip",#alpha)
```

It would be nice if you could use the real names of the Flash properties in your Lingo code. However, for some reason some of the names are different. For instance, instead of _x and _y, you would need to use *#posX* and *#posY*. Most of the other properties are the same, except you need to remove the underscore character and replace it with a #.

The same is true for the *setFlashProperty* command. So here is how you would move a movie clip to be at horizontal pixel 50.

```
sprite(1).setFlashProperty("myClip",#posX,50)
```

New to Director 8.5 is the ability to indicate that a set of commands is meant for a specific movie clip. You can do this with the *tellTarget* and *endTellTarget* commands. For instance, you could set a property and then issue a command to the movie clip "myClip" like this:

```
sprite(1).tellTarget("\myClip")
sprite(1).setFlashProperty(#alpha,50)
sprite(1).goToFrame(7)
sprite(1).endTellTarget()
```

Director 8.5 can also print Flash graphics. This matches the printing capability of Flash itself, which has actually been around since Flash 4. You can either *print* or *printAsBitmap*. Both commands work the same way, but *printAsBitmap* works in some cases where *print* might not, such as if there are semi-transparent graphics present. *printAsBitmap* might not print as nicely, however, depending on the situation.

The *print* command can work with no parameters at all. Frames in the Flash movie must be labeled with a "#p" as the frame label. However, if the "#p" label is not present, then every frame is printed. You can also include one argument to specify a movie clip to be printed. A second argument can be *#bframe* or *#bmax*. The first will print each frame as large as it can. The second will find a common size between all the frames and print each at the same scale.

Here is an example of how the *print* command might be used. A lot more detail about Flash printing can be found in the Flash 5 documentation. It pretty much all applies to the Lingo *print* command as well.

```
sprite(1).print()
```

➪ *For some background on using Flash members in Director, see "Using Flash Members," p. 136 (Chapter 7, "Vector Members")*

For some background on using Flash members in Director, see "Using Flash Members," p. 136 (Chapter 7, "Vector Members")

Because vector shape members use the Flash engine in Director to draw themselves, many of the properties of Flash members are available to vector shapes and vice versa.

USING VECTOR SHAPE LINGO

Vector shape members have one major difference from Flash members: They are static images, rather than time-based media. However, unlike Flash members, they can be completely controlled with Lingo. You can even create a vector shape from scratch in Lingo and design it to look however you want.

The combined vector shape properties enable you to change every aspect of a vector shape. Here is a complete list:

- **antiAlias**—Determines whether the member is drawn anti-aliased. When off, the member may draw a little faster, but the lines do not look as smooth.

- **backgroundColor**—The member's (not the sprite's) background color.

- **broadcastProps**—Determines whether changes to the member are immediately reflected on the Stage. If not, the sprite shows changes to the member only after it leaves and then reappears on the Stage.

- **centerRegPoint**—If set to *TRUE*, the registration point of the member changes automatically when the sprite is resized. If you are changing the vector shape with Lingo while the member is visible on the Stage, you should set this property to *FALSE* to prevent the sprite from jumping around.

- **closed**—Determines whether the first and last point in the vector shape are joined. It must be set to *TRUE* for the shape to be filled.

- **defaultRect**—A property that can be used, in conjunction with *defaultRectMode*, to change the default rectangle for new sprites that use the vector shape member.

- **defaultRectMode**—This property can be set to either #flash or #fixed. The #flash setting sets all new sprites that use the member to the normal rectangle of the member. The #fixed mode instead uses the *defaultRect* property to set the initial rectangle of the sprite. This setting also affects any existing sprites that have not yet been stretched.

- **directToStage**—Determines whether the member is drawn on top of all other sprites, ignoring the sprite's ink effects. Drawing members in this manner improves performance.

- **endColor**—The destination color of a gradient fill in a vector shape member. Use an *rgb* or *paletteIndex* structure to set this. The *fillMode* must be set to gradient and the *closed* property must be *TRUE*.

- **fillColor**—The color of the interior of a vector shape member if the *fillMode* is set to #solid, or the starting color if the *fillMode* is set to #gradient. Use an *rgb* or *paletteIndex* structure to set this. The *closed* property must be *TRUE*.

- **fillCycles**—The number of fill cycles in a vector shape member that have the *fillMode* set to #gradient. Should be a number from 1 to 7.

- **fillDirection**—The direction of the fill, in degrees. The *fillMode* must be set to #gradient and the *gradientType* should be set to #linear.

- **fillMode**—This can be set to #none, #solid, or #gradient. Only when this is set to #solid will the property *fillColor* be useful. When it is set to #gradient, other properties, such as *fillCycles, fillDirection, fillOffset, fillScale,* and *endColor,* will determine the way the fill is drawn.

- **fillOffset**—This property is a point that corresponds to the horizontal and vertical offsets for the fill. This works only when the *fillType* is set to #gradient.

- **fillScale**—This corresponds to the "spread" in the vector shape editing window. The *fillMode* must be set to #gradient for this to work.

- **flashRect**—The original size of the vector member as a member, not as a sprite.

- **gradientType**—Can be set to #linear or #radial. Works only when the *fillMode* is #gradient.

- **originMode**—This is the relationship between the vertex points and the center of the sprite. It can be set to #center, #topLeft, or #point. The #center option makes the vertex points relative to the center of the member, whereas the #topLeft option makes them relative to the top-left corner. The #point option uses the *originPoint* property. Set the *originMode* to #center if you plan to adjust a vertex while the movie is playing.

- **originPoint**—A point indicating the relationship between the vertex points and the member's location. This is used only when *originMode* is set to #point. You can also use the *originH* and *originV* properties.

- **regPointVertex**—If 0, the *regPoint* and *centerRegPoint* properties are used to determine the registration point. Otherwise, the *regPointVertex* specifies the number of the vertex to use as the registration point for the member.

- **scale**—Enables you to scale the member, using a list such as [1.000,1.000], where the first item is the horizontal scale and the second is the vertical scale. This is an alternative to simply stretching the sprite.

- **scaleMode**—This is the equivalent to the *member* property in the vector shape's Properties dialog box. It can be set to #showAll, #noBorder, #exactFit, #noScale, and #autoSize. You can also use this as a property of a sprite that contains a vector shape.

- **strokeColor**—The color of the line used by the vector shape. The *strokeWidth* must be greater than 0 for this to work.

- **strokeWidth**—The width of the line used by the vector member.

- **vertexList**—The main property of a vector shape. It is a list of all the points that make up the shape.

- **viewPoint**—This point enables you to change the point of the vector shape that appears at the center of the sprite.

- **viewScale**—Another way to scale the size of the vector shape on the Stage.

There are a lot of vector shape properties, as you can see. These don't even include the many sprite properties that also work on vector shapes, such as *rotation*, *flipH*, *flipV*, and *skew*. You can always refer to the list view of the Property Inspector to see all the properties of any member.

The key property of any vector shape member is the *vertexList*. Taking a look at one using the Message window will help you understand how it works. Create a new vector shape and draw a rectangle in it. Then, use the Message window to view the *vertexList*.

```
put member(1).vertexList
-- [[#vertex: point(-104.0000, -40.0000)], [#vertex: point(104.0000, -
40.0000)],\
   [#vertex: point(104.0000, 41.0000)], [#vertex: point(-104.0000, 41.0000)]]
```

The *vertexList* is a list of lists. Each small list is a property list with one property: #vertex. The value of #vertex is a point. Each point corresponds to a corner of the vector shape.

You can alter the *vertexList* in a few ways. The *addVertex*, *deleteVertex*, and *moveVertex* commands enable you to do so without dealing with the member's properties directly. For instance, to add a new vertex, just use a command like this:

```
addVertex(member(1),3,point(0,0))
```

This command adds a point at 0,0 after the second vertex point and before the third. You can move an existing vertex by using a relative point and the *moveVertex* command:

```
moveVertex(member(1),3,100,10)
```

This command moves the third vertex point over to the right by 10 pixels. You can also delete a vertex, as follows:

```
deleteVertex(member(1),3)
```

Rather than using these commands, you can replace the entire *vertexList*. This next series of commands moves the third vertex over to the right 10 pixels:

```
vl = member(1).vertexList
v = vl[3].vertex
v = v + point(10,0)
vl[3].vertex = v
member(1).vertexList = vl
```

This is a lot more involved than just using *moveVertex*. However, resetting the entire vertex list actually makes sense in many cases. If you are using Lingo to create a vector shape from scratch, and then you want to replace it with another, slightly different, shape, you can use the same handler to create both shapes. This handler uses parameters to make the two shapes different, by simply replacing the entire vertex list each time, rather than trying to figure out which points differ. Tests show that there is no difference in drawing speed either way.

☞ *For some background on using vector members in Director, see "Using Vector Members," p. 131 in Chapter 7*

BUILDING VECTORS WITH LINGO

By setting the *vertexList* property of a vector member, you can create all sorts of interesting things with Lingo. For instance, here is a short behavior that creates a new, simple line and replaces the sprite's vector shape member with this line:

The *vertexList* items actually have two elements other than the #vertex: #handle1 and #handle2. They are points as well. However, they correspond to the curve handles of the point. These are the same handles that you can see when you edit a point in the vector shape editing window. The values in the *vertexList* are points that are relative to the actual #vertex point.

```
on beginSprite me
  sprite(me.spriteNum).member.vertexList = \
    [[#vertex: point(0,0)], [#vertex:
point(200,100)]]
end
```

This handler sets the sprite's *vertexList* to two simple points. You can also use *strokeWidth* and *strokeColor* to set the line's thickness and color.

In Director 7, all vector shape members were limited to only one continuous line. However, in Director 8, you can have multiple lines. The way to do this is to insert a [#newCurve] element into the *vertexList*. Here is a behavior that creates a grid using 11 vertical and 11 horizontal lines:

```
on beginSprite me
  mem = sprite(me.spriteNum).member

  vlist = []

  repeat with x = 0 to 10
    add vlist, [#vertex: point(x*10,0)]
    add vlist, [#vertex: point(x*10,100)]
    add vlist, [#newCurve]
  end repeat

  repeat with y = 0 to 10
    add vlist, [#vertex: point(0,y*10)]
    add vlist, [#vertex: point(100,y*10)]
    add vlist, [#newCurve]
  end repeat

  mem.vertexList = vlist
end
```

Here is a behavior that creates a curve using the *sin* function. Figure 20.1 shows the results of this handler, placed on the Stage.

```
on beginSprite me
  mem = sprite(me.spriteNum).member

  list = []
  repeat with x = -100*pi() to 100*pi()
    y = sin(float(x)/100.0)*100
    add list, [#vertex: point(x,y)]
  end repeat
  mem.vertexList = list
end
```

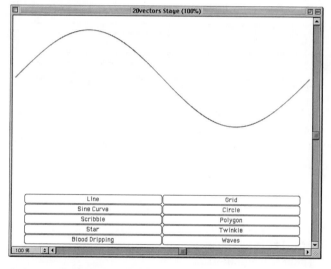

Figure 20.1
This sine curve is a single vector shape member created with Lingo.

Only a little more work is needed to create a circle. Unlike the circle created with the vector shape editing window, this circle consists of 64 individual points with lines attaching them. The result actually looks very round, despite being made up of little lines. Figure 20.2 shows the result.

```
on beginSprite me
  mem = sprite(me.spriteNum).member

  radius = 50

  list = []
  repeat with angle = 0 to 63
    x = cos(float(angle)/10.0)*radius
    y = sin(float(angle)/10.0)*radius
    add list, [#vertex: point(x,y)]
  end repeat
  mem.vertexList = list
end
```

Figure 20.2
This circle is made up of 64 small lines in a single vector shape member created by Lingo.

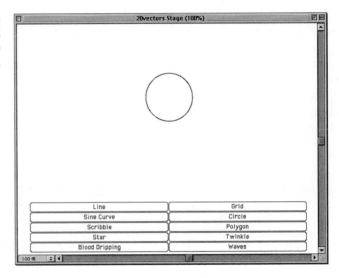

Simple shapes are not where Lingo vector creation shines. Complex ones, such as polygons, really show off the power of creating vectors with Lingo. Here is a behavior that sets a vector graphic in a sprite to a polygon. You can even choose the number of sides in the polygon.

```
property pNumPoints, pRadius

on getPropertyDescriptionList me
  list = [:]
  addProp list, #pNumPoints, [#comment: "Number of Points",\
    #format: #integer, #default: 5]
  addProp list, #pRadius, [#comment: "Radius",\
    #format: #integer, #default: 100]
  return list
end

on beginSprite me
  mem = sprite(me.spriteNum).member

  -- how many degrees apart is each point
  angleDiff = 360/pNumPoints

  -- build vertex list
  list = []
  repeat with angle = 0 to pNumPoints
    p = circlePoint(angle*angleDiff,pRadius)
    add list, [#vertex: p]
  end repeat
```

```
  -- set the member
  mem.vertexList = list
end

-- the following handler returns the point on any circle
-- given the angle and radius
on circlePoint angle, radius
  a = (float(angle-90)/360.0)*2.0*pi()
  x = cos(a)*radius
  y = sin(a)*radius
  return point(x,y)
end
```

Figure 20.3 shows the use of this behavior. It resets the member used by the sprite as a polygon. If the same member is used in more than one sprite, the behaviors interfere with each other. Instead, create multiple copies of a vector shape and place each one on the Stage only once. The initial vector shapes can be anything, such as small rectangles or circles. The behavior resets the *vertexList* of the sprite, and makes sure it is closed. However, the fill color and type remain as they were before. A more complex behavior can set these, too.

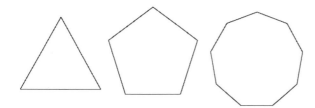

Figure 20.3
These polygons were created with a polygon behavior that takes any vector shape and molds it into a polygon.

A little modification to this behavior gives you a handler that creates a star rather than a polygon. It just needs to set alternative outer and inner points. Figure 20.4 shows the result of this behavior.

```
property pNumPoints, pRadius

on getPropertyDescriptionList me
  list = [:]
  addProp list, #pNumPoints, [#comment: "Number of Points",\
    #format: #integer, #default: 5]
  addProp list, #pRadius, [#comment: "Radius",\
    #format: #integer, #default: 100]
  return list
end

on beginSprite me
  mem = sprite(me.spriteNum).member

  -- how many degrees apart is each point
```

```
  angleDiff = 360/pNumPoints

  -- build vertex list
  list = []
  repeat with starPoint = 0 to pNumPoints-1

    -- outer point location
    p = circlePoint (starPoint*angleDiff,pRadius)
    add list, [#vertex: p]

    -- inner point location
    p = circlePoint((starPoint+.5)*angleDiff,pRadius*.5)
    add list, [#vertex: p]
  end repeat

  -- set the member
  mem.vertexList = list
  mem.closed = TRUE
end


-- the following handler returns the point on any circle
-- given the angle and radius
on circlePoint angle, radius
  a = (float(angle-90)/360.0)*2.0*pi()
  x = cos(a)*radius
  y = sin(a)*radius
  return point(x,y)
end
```

Figure 20.4
This star was created with a star behavior, which takes any vector shape and molds it into a star.

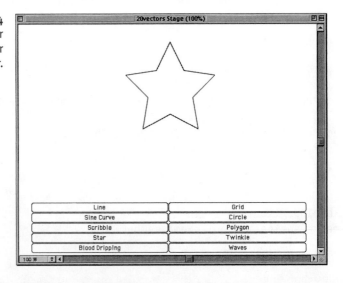

All the previous handlers and behaviors draw a shape once, usually *on beginSprite*, and leave the vector shape alone. However, Lingo can just as easily redraw the vector shape each and every frame to create animated vector shapes.

A simple example draws a random shape. The following behavior draws a vector between 20 random points. The result is a messy scribble. However, it re-creates itself on each frame to create a unusual animated effect. Check the movie on the CD-ROM (20vectors.dir) to see it in action.

Notice that the closed property of the vector shape member is set to *TRUE*. This enables you to also set the *fillMode* property to #solid and set the *fillColor* property to the color you want to use. You can also use a gradient by setting the *fillMode* to #gradient and then setting the entire collection of fill properties to specify the color, type, direction, scale, and type of gradient fill.

```
on exitFrame me
  mem = sprite(me.spriteNum).member

  list = []
  repeat with i = 1 to 20
    x = random(100)
    y = random(100)
    add list, [#vertex: point(x,y)]
  end repeat
  mem.vertexList = list
end
```

The same idea can be applied to the star shape behavior. Stars are sometimes known to twinkle. The following behavior redraws the star every frame, but with a different random point stretched slightly. The result, if done with the right color and size, is an animated twinkling star:

```
property pNumPoints, pRadius, pPointToMove, pPointMoveDiff,\pPointMoveAmount,
pTwinkleSpeed, pTwinkleAmount

on getPropertyDescriptionList me
  list = [:]
  addProp list, #pNumPoints, [#comment: "Number of Points",\
    #format: #integer, #default: 5]
  addProp list, #pRadius, [#comment: "Radius",\
    #format: #integer, #default: 25]
  addProp list, #pTwinkleSpeed, [#comment: "Twinkle Speed",\
    #format: #integer, #default: 1]
  addProp list, #pTwinkleAmount, [#comment: "Twinkle Amount",\
    #format: #integer, #default: 3]
  return list
end

on beginSprite me
```

```
  moveNewPoint(me)
  mem = sprite(me.spriteNum).member
  mem.centerRegPoint = FALSE
  mem.originMode = #center
end


-- this handler decides which new point of the star
-- to twinkle
on moveNewPoint me
  repeat while TRUE
    r = random(pNumPoints)
    if r <> pPointToMove then exit repeat
  end repeat
  pPointToMove = r
  pPointMoveDiff = 0
  pPointMoveAmount = pTwinkleSpeed
end


on exitFrame me
  mem = sprite(me.spriteNum).member

  -- how many degrees apart is each point
  angleDiff = 360/pNumPoints

  -- build vertex list
  list = []
  repeat with starPoint = 1 to pNumPoints

    -- move twinkling point in or out
    if starPoint = pPointToMove then
      pPointMoveDiff = pPointMoveDiff + pPointMoveAmount
      if pPointMoveDiff > pTwinkleAmount then pPointMoveDiff = -pTwinkleSpeed
      if pPointMoveDiff <= 0 then moveNewPoint
      p = circlePoint(starPoint*angleDiff,pRadius+pPointMoveDiff)
    else

      -- keep non-twinkling point normal
      p = circlePoint(starPoint*angleDiff,pRadius)
    end if

    add list, [#vertex: p]
    p = circlePoint((starPoint+.5)*angleDiff,pRadius*.5)
    add list, [#vertex: p]
  end repeat
```

```
  -- set the member
  mem.vertexList = list
end
```

```
-- the following handler returns the point on any circle
-- given the angle and radius
on circlePoint angle, radius
  a = (float(angle-90)/360.0)*2.0*pi()
  x = cos(a)*radius
  y = sin(a)*radius
  return point(x,y)
end
```

The result looks just like the previous star shape behavior, but one point at a time is animating. First it moves a little bit out from the center, and then it moves back into place.

A more dramatic behavior is one that uses the handles of each vertex point. Because these handles measure the curve of the line coming into and going out of the vertex, they are very difficult to use. Changing the handles is easy enough, but getting them to do what you want is another matter. Even illustrators who have used vector editing programs for years can sometimes be at a loss to explain exactly how to use handles. They simply use them intuitively. There are mathematics behind these handles, but the complexities are beyond the scope of this book.

The following code shows a behavior that uses #handle1 to create a curved look to many points along the bottom of a vector shape. The behavior then moves the vertex points downward to create a "curtain" or "dripping blood" effect. Figure 20.5 shows the result in midanimation.

```
property pNumPoints, pRadius, pVlist

on getPropertyDescriptionList me
  list = [:]
  addProp list, #pNumPoints, [#comment: "Number of Points",\
    #format: #integer, #default: 25]
  addProp list, #pRadius, [#comment: "Radius",\
    #format: #integer, #default: 12]
  return list
end

on beginSprite me
  pVlist = []

  -- space between drips
  spacing = 640/pNumPoints

  -- add top and sides
```

```
  add pVlist, [#vertex: point(640+spacing,0)]
  add pVlist, [#vertex: point(640+spacing,0)]
  add pVlist, [#vertex: point(0-spacing,0)]

  -- add drip spots along bottom
  repeat with i = 0 to pNumPoints
    add pVlist, [#vertex: point(i*spacing,0), \
#handle1: point(spacing/2,spacing)]
  end repeat

  -- set member
  mem = sprite(me.spriteNum).member
  mem.vertexList = pVlist
  mem.centerRegPoint = FALSE
  mem.originMode = #center
  mem.closed = TRUE
end

on exitFrame me
  -- change 20 vertex points at a time
  repeat with i = 1 to 20
    r = random(pNumPoints+1)+3
    pVlist[r][#vertex] = pVlist[r][#vertex] + \
      point(0,random(pRadius))
  end repeat
  sprite(me.spriteNum).member.vertexList = pVlist
end
```

Figure 20.5
The dripping blood effect was created with a vector shape and a Lingo behavior that move the vertex points down over time.

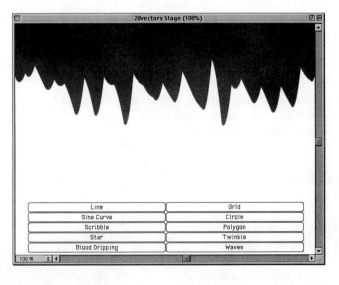

Another effect uses both the #handle1 and #handle2 properties to direct the curve of many points along a line. With each frame, the angle of the curve changes to make the point appear to roll over, like a wave. The final result, seen in Figure 20.6, is a sea-like graphic.

```
property pNumPoints, pRadius, pList, pOffset, pAngle

on getPropertyDescriptionList me
  list = [:]
  addProp list, #pNumPoints, [#comment: "Number of Points",\
    #format: #integer, #default: 25]
  addProp list, #pRadius, [#comment: "Radius",\
    #format: #integer, #default: 12]
  return list
end

on beginSprite me
  pOffset = 0
  pAngle = 0
end

on exitFrame me
  pList = []
  spacing = 680/pNumPoints
  pOffset = pOffset + 2
  if pOffset > spacing then pOffset = 0

  -- create bottom and sides
  add pList, [#vertex: point(680+spacing,0)]
  add pList, [#vertex: point(680+spacing,100)]
  add pList, [#vertex: point(0-spacing,100)]

  -- add wave points
  repeat with i = 0 to pNumPoints

    -- move the waves
    pAngle = pAngle - 1
    if pAngle < -90 then pAngle = 90

    -- get the handle
    h = circlePoint(pAngle,pRadius)
    h2 = circlePoint(pAngle+180,pRadius)

    add pList, [#vertex: point(i*spacing-pOffset,0), \
#handle1: h, #handle2: h2]
  end repeat
```

```
-- set the member
mem = sprite(me.spriteNum).member
mem.vertexList = pList
mem.centerRegPoint = FALSE
mem.originMode = #center
mem.closed = TRUE
end


-- the following handler returns the point on any circle
-- given the angle and radius
on circlePoint angle, radius
  a = (float(angle-90)/360.0)*2.0*pi()
  x = cos(a)*radius
  y = sin(a)*radius
  return point(x,y)
end
```

Figure 20.6
The changing locations of the handles for each vertex point create animated waves.

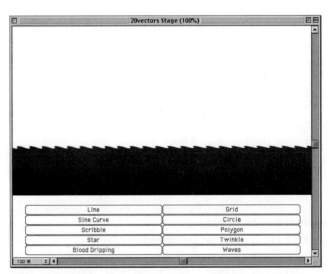

USING VECTORS FOR COLLISION DETECTION

One of the ways in which vector shape members are different from bitmaps is that, with vector shapes, you can actually tell whether a point is inside or outside a vector shape. You can do this with bitmaps and the *rollover* property, but only when the ink is set to matte and the mouse is at the location you are trying to detect.

The function *hitTest* enables you to specify a sprite and a Stage location. The returned value is either #background, #normal, or #button. The last value can be returned by only a Flash movie, not a vector shape. However, the other two values can be used to determine whether any point is inside or outside a shape, no matter how complex that shape is.

The following code shows a behavior that takes advantage of this feature. It assumes there is a shape in sprite 1 that the behavior cannot move its sprite over. It looks for key presses and then moves its sprite accordingly. If the behavior finds that the new location is inside the shape in that sprite, it doesn't allow the move to take place.

```
property px, py

on beginSprite me
  -- get initial location
  px = sprite(me.spriteNum).locH
  py = sprite(me.spriteNum).locV
end

on exitFrame me

  -- assume x doesn't change
  newx = px

  -- see if it does
  if keyPressed(123) then newx = px - 1
  if keyPressed(124) then newx = px + 1

  -- see if new x will hit the shape
  if hitTest(sprite(1),point(newx,py)) <> #normal then
    px = newx
  end if

  -- assume y doesn't change
  newy = py

  -- see if it does
  if keyPressed(125) then newy = py + 1
  if keyPressed(126) then newy = py - 1

  -- see if new y will hit the stage
  if hitTest(sprite(1),point(px,newy)) <> #normal then
    py = newy
  end if

  -- new location for the sprite
  sprite(me.spriteNum).loc = point(px,py)
end
```

A more complex behavior might have a parameter that specifies which sprite the behavior should be looking at. Or, perhaps the behavior can specify an entire range of sprites.

TROUBLESHOOTING VECTOR LINGO

- When setting the *vertexList* with Lingo, be sure that it is a valid vertex list, with all the properties spelled correctly and the values in the proper format.

- If you are animating by using Lingo to change the *vertexList* while the movie is playing, the *centerRegPoint* should be set to *FALSE*, the *originMode* set to "center", and the vector's scale mode set to "auto-size". Otherwise, the sprite appears to move around the Stage as the shape changes.

- If you are trying to apply a fill color to a vector shape, make sure that the *closed* property is set to *TRUE*. Otherwise, there is no area to fill.

- The more vertex points in a vector shape, the more slowly it draws. Anti-aliased vector shapes also draw more slowly than non[nd]anti-aliased shapes.

- You usually want to set a vector shape's sprite *ink* to Background Transparent. Leaving it as Copy applies the background color of the member to the whole rectangle on the Stage.

DID YOU KNOW?

- Although vector shape members have only one fill type, color, stroke width, and other properties, you can create more complex Freehand or Illustrator[nd]like images by using several vector shapes on top of each other.

- EPS files are actually lists of vertex points and handles. If you get to know the EPS file format well enough, you can write a Lingo script that reads these files and creates vector shape members based on the data.

- Vector shapes and Flash members, when placed in a sprite, can be rotated, skewed, and scaled like bitmaps. However, because they are made of curved lines, enlarging them does not degrade the image resolution.

- You can use the Lingo command to put "showProps(member x)" in the Message window, where *x* is a vector shape member, to get a complete list of all its properties. The same is true for Flash members.

VII

USING ADVANCED LINGO

IN THIS PART

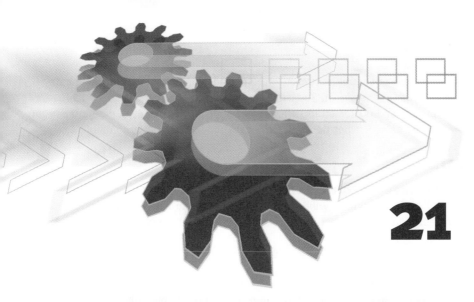

21

CONTROLLING THE DIRECTOR ENVIRONMENT

IN THIS CHAPTER

Source movies for this chapter can be found on the CD-ROM in the "Book Movies" folder under folder 21.

Lingo provides many ways to control and react to the playback environment. You can create your own menus and change the cursor. You can detect when the computer has been left alone for a period of time and do something when that happens. You can even determine what type of computers users have or what time it is, and have the movie react accordingly.

USING MENUS

When you create a projector, it runs inside a plain window. On the Mac, it's a simple rectangle. In Windows, it looks like a typical window, but without a menu bar. To make your projector look and act more like a normal program, you have to add a menu bar.

Creating Menus

You can add a menu bar to any projector with the *installMenu* command. This command places the standard Mac menu bar at the top of the screen on Macs, but only with the items you specify. In Windows, it places a standard menu bar at the top of the projector's window.

While you are authoring, the *installMenu* command replaces Director's menu bar from the time the command is issued until the movie stops. This makes it very easy to test. In Shockwave, *installMenu* has no effect.

To use *installMenu*, you first need to create a field cast member that contains the menu description. Here are the typical contents of such a field:

```
menu: @
menu: File
Open/O|myOpenHandler
(-
Quit/Q|halt
menu: Edit
Cut(
Copy(
Paste(
Clear(
menu: Navigation
Main Menu/M|go to frame "main"
Chapter 1/1|go to frame "one"
Chapter 2/2|go to frame "two"
Chapter 3/3|go to frame "three"
```

The first line of this text, "menu: @", tells Director to place the Apple menu, with all its contents, in the menu bar. This is for Macs only. In Windows, this command results in a small menu labeled with a block character.

The second line creates a menu labeled "File". The next three lines place three items in this menu. The first is the item "Open". The character after the forward slash is the command key shortcut. So, a ⌘+O on the Mac or a Ctrl+O in Windows acts as a shortcut for selecting this menu item. After the vertical bar, created while holding down the Shift and the backslash (\) key, is the Lingo command that will execute. In this case, it's a custom movie handler called "on myOpenHandler". The next line, a simple "(-", places a dividing line in the menu. The third item in the menu is "Quit", which uses "Q" as a shortcut and executes the Lingo *halt* command.

The next menu is the "Edit" menu. All the items in this menu are grayed out, or inactive, and made so by the "(" added to the end of each line.

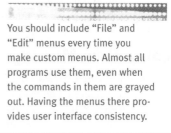

You should include "File" and "Edit" menus every time you make custom menus. Almost all programs use them, even when the commands in them are grayed out. Having the menus there provides user interface consistency.

The last menu is called "Navigation" and contains four lines that take users to four different frames. The resulting menu looks like the one shown in Figure 21.1.

Figure 21.1
This custom menu was created with a field member and the *installMenu* command.

To actually use this menu, you must specify its member in the *installMenu* command. A likely place for this is the *on startMovie* handler:

```
on startMovie
   installMenu member("menu")
end
```

All the special characters in the menu field can be quite confusing. There are actually a lot more of them. Table 21.1 lists them all and describes what each one does.

Table 21.1   Menu Definition Symbols

Symbol	Example	Description
@	menu: @	Creates the Apple menu on the Mac, complete with the existing Apple menu items.
!v	!vMusic	Places a check mark next to an item.
<B	Copy<B	Sets the item to bold.
<I	Copy<I	Sets the item to italic.
<U	Copy<U	Sets the item to underlined.
<O	Copy<O	Sets the item to outlined.
<S	Shadow	Sets the item to shadow styled.
|	Quit|halt	Associates a Lingo handler or command with the item.
/	Quit/Q	Adds a ©/Ctrl key shortcut.
(	Copy(	Grays out the item and makes it unselectable.
(-	(-	Creates a dividing line in the menu.

The styling items listed in Table 21.1 (such as bold, italic, and so on) are available on the Mac only. Windows menus do not accommodate this sort of styling.

Controlling Menus

You can also use Lingo commands to control the custom menu after it has been created by the *installMenu* command. The menu bar itself is treated like an object, and is referred to by the keyword menu and the name or number of the menu. For instance, to get the name of the second menu from the left:

```
put the name of menu 2
-- "File"
```

Note that you must use the old syntax with a *the* rather than dot syntax. The menu functionality in Director was not updated with the new version, so the dot syntax is not recognized.

To get the total number of menus in the menu bar, use *the number of menus*:

```
put the number of menus
-- 4
```

You can also get the name of any menu item in a menu by using the *menuitem* keyword:

```
put the name of menuitem 1 of menu 4
-- "Main Menu"
```

As you might expect, you can use *the number of menuitems* to get the total number of items of any menu. The next example also demonstrates how you can refer to a menu by its name:

```
put the number of menuitems in menu "Navigation"
-- 4
```

You can also set the name of a menu item. However, you cannot set the name of a menu:

```
the name of menuitem 3 of menu 2 = "Exit"
```

Three more properties—*the checkMark*, *the enabled*, and *the script*—enable you to change three other aspects of individual menu items. The *the checkMark* property enables you to place a check mark next to the item. The *the enabled* property enables you to dim an item and make it unusable. The *the script property* enables you to alter the script for an item.

Another method for changing the menu is to update your menu description field by using Lingo string and text member commands and then reapplying *installMenu*.

➪ *For more information on using fields, see "Using Text Members and Fields," p. 330 (Chapter 16, "Controlling Text")*

USING CURSORS

There are three ways to change the cursor in Director 8. The first is to use the *cursor* command with a built-in cursor. The second way is to use the *cursor* command with one or two bitmaps that represent a black-and-white cursor. The third way is to use the Cursor Xtra to make colored or animated cursors.

Using Built-In Cursors

Using one of the 30 built-in cursors is simple with the *cursor* command. All you need to do is give the *cursor* command one of the cursor numbers to use. For instance, to change the cursor to a watch on the Mac or an hourglass in Windows, use the following:

```
cursor(4)
```

A simple behavior that changes the cursor to a finger when users roll over a sprite looks like this:

```
on mouseEnter me
  cursor(280)
end

on mouseLeave me
  cursor(0)
end
```

Use the cursor number -1 to return control of the cursor to normal. Usually this means that the cursor returns to an arrow.

Table 21.2 shows all the available cursors. Figure 21.2 shows what these cursors look like on the Mac. Windows cursors appear slightly different. For instance, the watch cursor appears as an hourglass cursor in Windows. You should test your cursors in a cross-platform environment if consistency is important.

Table 21.2 Cursor Numbers

Cursor Name	Cursor Number
Arrow	-1
I-Beam	1
Crosshair	2
Crossbar	3
Watch/Hourglass	4
Blank	200
Help	254
Finger	280
Hand	260
Closed Hand	290
No Drop Hand	291
Copy Closed Hand	292

Table 21.2   Continued

Cursor Name	Cursor Number
Pencil	256
Eraser	257
Select	258
Bucket	259
Lasso	272
Dropper	281
Air Brush	301
Zoom In	302
Zoom Out	303
Vertical Size	284
Horizontal Size	285
Diagonal Size	286
White Arrow (Mac)	293
Black Arrow with white outline (Windows)	293
Magnify	304
Wait Mouse 1 (Mac)	282
Wait Mouse 2 (Mac)	283

Figure 21.2
Some of the cursors Director uses, taken from the Director resource file using ResEdit.

Using Custom Bitmap Cursors

The second way to create cursors is to use bitmaps. With bitmaps you can define the cursor any way you want, as long as it is black-and-white and static.

The key to doing this is to create two bitmap members. Each member should be no more than 16 by 16 pixels in size, and be 1 bit in bit depth. The first member is the actual cursor. The second member is the mask for the cursor. In that second member, the black pixels are the mask for the cursor, whereas the white pixels are transparent.

The two bitmaps should line up with each other according to their registration points. The location of the registration point is the actual hot spot of the cursor, so be careful where you place it. Figure 21.3 shows two Paint windows, one with the cursor and one with the mask.

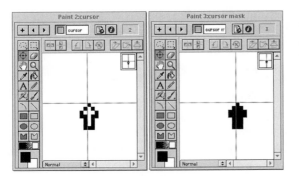

Figure 21.3
Two Paint windows show each of
the two parts of a custom cursor.
The registration points show the
hotspot for the cursor.

After you have these two members, you can use the *cursor* command, as before, but with a
list as the parameter:

```
cursor([member "cursor", member "cursor mask"])
```

If the bitmaps are not 1 bit, or a member name is wrong, the cursor command simply does
nothing.

Using the Cursor Xtra

The Cursor Xtra enables you to build custom cursors from one or more 8-bit color bitmaps. The
way you create this type of cursor is by using the Cursor Properties Editor, shown in Figure
21.4. You can get this dialog box by double-clicking a cursor member in the Cast.

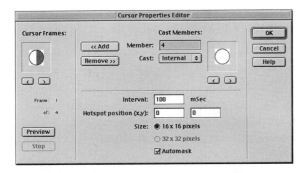

Figure 21.4
The Cursor Properties Editor
enables you to create and modify
animated cursors.

Adding cast members to a cursor is easy. Just use the Cast Members section of the dialog box
to find the right member, and then use the Add button to add it. You can also set the speed of
the animation and the hotspot location. Check the Automask feature if you do not want the
cursor to be transparent.

After you have created the cursor, you can use the *cursor* command, but this time with a single cast member as the parameter:

```
cursor(member("Custom Cursor"))
```

➡️ *For some background on creating custom cursors, **see** "Adding Cursors," p. 145 (Chapter 8, "Other
Member Types")*

USING TIMEOUTS

Suppose you are making a kiosk that sits in a public place. Users are meant to walk up to the kiosk and start on screen one. However, it is impossible to get users to press an "I'm Done!" button when they are finished using the kiosk. You just can't rely on it. The result usually is that the next user walks up and sees the middle of the presentation.

> The *on timeOut* handler needs to be placed in a movie script. It does not work if it's in a behavior.

One way to handle this is for the movie to detect when the computer has been idle for some time, and then automatically return to the beginning of the movie or perform some other task. A traditional timeout is when some function is performed after a specified amount of time has passed with no action taken by the user. The new *timeout* objects, however, perform a task after a specific amount of time regardless of what the user does.

Traditional Timeouts

Director has some Lingo commands to handle the timeout request. The primary command is the handler *on timeOut*. This handler is called after three minutes of inaction. If the handler does not exist, nothing happens. A typical *on timeOut* handler:

```
on timeOut
  go to frame "intro"
end
```

Some movie properties can be used to alter how the *on timeout* script is called. For instance, if you want the timeout to happen after two minutes rather than three, use *the timeoutLength* property. Its value is in ticks, or 1/60s of a second:

```
the timeOutLength = 60*60*2
```

The timeout timer can be accessed with *the timeoutLapsed* property. It tells you how much time has passed since the last action. This timer is reset whenever the mouse is moved or a key on the keyboard is pressed. However, you can turn either or both of these conditions off by setting *the timeoutMouse* or *the timeoutKeyDown* to *FALSE*.

You can also further modify your timeouts by choosing which handler is called. Usually it's the *on timeout* handler. However, you can set it to something else with *the timeoutScript* property. Just set it to a string that is the name of a movie script handler:

```
the timeOutScript = "myTimeOutHandler"
```

For most uses, you won't need to set *the timeOutScript* and can just use *on timeOut*. However, you can use it if you have several different ways in which you want to handle timeouts, depending on where in the program the user left the computer.

Timeout Objects

Director 8 contains a new type of object called a *timeout object*. These are little timers that you can set to call a handler after a period of time goes by. They can go off on a regular basis.

The *new* command is used to create a *timeout* object. You can specify a time delay and a handler name:

```
myTimer = timeout("myTimeoutName").new(5000,#myTimeoutHandler)
```

This example creates a *timeout* object that is pointed to by the variable "myTimer". The object will trigger the handler "on myTimeoutHandler" after 5,000 milliseconds go by.

After you create a *timeout* handler, you can see it in the system property *the timeOutList*. The handler will have the name you gave it—for instance, "myTimeoutName" as specified previously.

Timeout objects also have properties. The #period property is the number of milliseconds between times that the object is set off. The #time is the number of milliseconds before the next time the object is set off. The #timeoutHandler is the name of the handler that the object sets off.

LEARNING ABOUT THE COMPUTER

Many other movie properties can be accessed to tell you something about the computer on which Director, a projector, or a Shockwave applet is currently running. The following is a list of these properties:

- **the platform**—Returns either "Macintosh,PowerPC" or "Windows,32" depending on which platform the movie is running on.

- **the runMode**—Returns either "Author", "Projector", "Plugin", or "Java Applet". The first tells you that the movie is running in Director, the second tells you when it is running as a projector, the third option refers to Shockwave, and the fourth tells you when it is running as a Java applet.

- **the colorDepth**—Returns the bit depth of the current monitor being used by the movie. Examples are 8, 16, 24, or 32.

- **the environment**—Returns a list of the values for the three preceding properties and many more.

- **the desktopRectList**—Returns a list of rectangles that correspond to the one or more monitors connected to the computer.

- **quickTimeVersion( )**—Not a property, but a function that returns the version of QuickTime on the computer. It returns only "2.1.2" if the version is before version 3.0.

> You can also assign a third parameter when using *new* to create a *timeout* object. This third parameter can specify a script object created from a parent script. If this parameter is used, the handler called will be in that object, not in a movie script.

- **version**—Not a property either, but actually a persistent global variable automatically created when Director starts. It contains the version number of the Director engine, whether it is Director, a projector, or Shockwave. An example is "8.0".

You can use these properties to make decisions about what the movie should do if users do not have a computer capable of performing the tasks you want it to. For instance, to test whether the computer is set to 16-bit color or better, you might do this:

```
on startMovie
  if the colorDepth < 16 then
    alert "Please set your monitor to 16-bit."
    halt
  end if
end
```

Or, if you want to make sure that the user's monitor is at least 800 pixels wide, you can test the *width* of the first item in *the deskTopRectList*. Because most users have only one monitor, and those with two rarely have their primary monitor set smaller than 800 pixels across, this is a good test.

```
on startMovie
  if (the deskTopRectList)[1].width < 800 then
    alert "Please set your monitor to 800 pixels across."
    halt
  end if
end
```

The system property *the environment* is a list filled with properties that can describe the playback environment. The following properties can be found in this list:

- **#shockMachine**—*TRUE* if the movie is running in Macromedia's ShockMachine program.

- **#shockMachineVersion**—Contains a string with the version number of ShockMachine. It is an empty string if the movie is not being played in ShockMachine.

- **#platform**—Same as *the platform* property. Either "Macintosh,PPC" or "Windows,32".

- **#runMode**—Same as *the runMode*. Either "Author", "Projector", "Plugin", or "Java Applet".

- **#colorDepth**—Same as *the colorDepth*. Either 1, 2, 4, 8, 16, or 32.

- **#internetConnected**—The value of this is #online if the computer is currently connected to the Internet, and #offline if not.

- **#uiLanguage**—The language being used to display the operating system's user interface.

- **#osLanguage**—The native language of the computer's operating system.

- **#productBuildVersion**—The number of the Director engine build that is being used. This can be used to determine the exact version of Director's engine used in Shockwave or projectors, even if Macromedia releases several versions with the same version number.

- **#productVersion**—This returns a string like "8.5" that lets you know what version of Shockwave the user is running.

- **#osVersion**—This returns a string that corresponds to the official operating system version. For MacOS 9.1, you get "Macintosh OS 9.1.0"; for one version of Windows 98, you get "Windows 98,4,10,148,1, A ".

Look for more properties to be added to *the environment* in updates of Director 8. Several of the previous elements were not present in Director 7.0, but were added in 7.0.2 and Shockwave version 7.0.3.

⮕ For examples that use machine information, **see** *"Designing for a Target Machine," **p. 682*** (Chapter 34, "Performance Issues")

⮕ For Lingo functions that relay information about the computer's graphic capabilities, **see** Chapter 39, "3D Lingo"

TELLING TIME

Lingo has several ways to tell the date and time. First, there is the *date* property. This system property is a little different, in that you can preface it with the terms *short*, *long*, or *abbr*.

```
put the date
-- "12/9/98"
put the short date
-- "12/9/98"
put the long date
-- "Wednesday, December 9, 1998"
put the abbr date
-- "Wed, Dec 9, 1998"
```

The *abbr* prefix can also be spelled *abbrev* or *abbreviated*. You can use the returned strings as they are, or use chunk expressions to get pieces of them:

```
put (the long date).item[1]
-- "Wednesday"
put (the long date).item[2].word[1]
-- "December"
the itemDelimiter = "/"
put integer((the date).item[2])
-- 9
```

Another property, called *the time,* works in a similar way. However, only the long prefix makes any difference in the result:

> The string format of the date depends on your computer's settings. If you check in the control panels in both Mac and Windows, you can see that users have many options as to how dates are displayed. Director reflects these preferences in the date.

```
put the time
-- "9:18 PM"
put the short time
-- "9:18 PM"
put the long time
-- "9:18:43 PM"
put the abbrev time
-- "9:18 PM"
```

You can also use chunk expressions to get interesting parts of *the time:*

```
put (the time).word[1]
-- "9:20"
the itemDelimiter = ":"
put integer((the time).word[1].item[2])
-- 20
put integer((the long time).word[1].item[3])
-- 57
```

Although the time and the date are great for getting ready-to-use strings and occasionally an integer, there is a better way to work with dates. The property *the systemDate* returns a *date* object.

```
put the systemDate
-- date( 1998, 12, 9 )
```

As you might expect, you can extract the year, the month, and the day properties from this *date* object:

```
d = the systemDate
put d.day
-- 9
put d.year
-- 1998
put d.month
-- 12
```

What is even more impressive about the *date* object is that you can add integers to it and it does all the calculations for you. Here are some examples:

```
put the systemDate
-- date( 1998, 12, 9 )
put the systemDate + 1
-- date( 1998, 12, 10 )
d = the systemDate
```

```
put d + 10
-- date( 1998, 12, 19 )
put d + 30
-- date( 1999, 1, 8 )
put d + 365*3
-- date( 2001, 12, 8 )
put d - 365
-- date( 1997, 12, 9 )
```

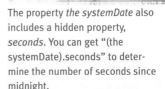

The property *the systemDate* also includes a hidden property, *seconds*. You can get "(the systemDate).seconds" to determine the number of seconds since midnight.

Using the *date* object, you can perform all sorts of interesting calculations. The following handler computes the number of days since a certain date. Give it your birth date, as a *date* object, and it computes the number of days you have been alive:

```
on daysAlive birthDate
  t = 0
  repeat while TRUE
    birthDate = birthDate + 1
    t = t + 1
    if birthDate = the systemDate then
      return t
    end if
  end repeat
end
```

In addition to dates and times, *the ticks* property is very important. This is the amount of time, in 1/60s of a second, since Director, the projector, or the Shockwave applet started.

Although it isn't useful information to display to users, it's useful for timing animation. This short handler creates a pause for two seconds:

```
on pauseForTwo
  t = the ticks + 120
  repeat while (the ticks < t)
  end repeat
end
```

The property *the milliseconds* is a more accurate companion of *the ticks*. This measures the same amount of time, but with thousandths of a second instead.

The newer timed features of Director 8, such as sound queuing and timeout objects, use milliseconds to measure time, rather than ticks. Many digital video properties use milliseconds as well. Because there is no advantage to using *the ticks* over *the milliseconds*, it's better to start using *the milliseconds* even if you have used *the ticks* in the past.

Another property, called *the timer*, also uses *ticks*. The difference between this property and *the ticks* is that you can use *startTimer* at any time to reset the timer. This is more of a convenience, rather than an added feature. There's nothing you can do with the timer that you can't do with a variable, some math, and *the ticks*. The following handler pauses for two seconds, but uses *the timer*:

```
on pauseForTwo
  startTimer
  repeat while (the timer < 120)
  end repeat
end
```

MEMORY MANAGEMENT

Several Lingo commands and properties enable you to see and control how memory is used. Controlling memory mostly has to do with loading and unloading cast members from memory.

Member Loading

All cast members are present in either the Director movie's internal Cast, an external Cast, or an external file that is linked in a Cast. Simply put, they are in a file on the hard drive or CD-ROM. For cast members to be displayed on the Stage, they first have to be loaded into the computer's memory.

Director takes care of this automatically. If a sprite needs a cast member, Director checks to see whether it is present in memory, and if not, loads it into memory. As Director uses up more and more memory, it occasionally removes a cast member from memory if it's no longer present on the Stage. This clears room for other members to be loaded.

Although this is automatic, you do have a set of Lingo commands and properties that gives you control over this loading and unloading. This control can come in handy when speed is critical. After all, it takes time for Director to load and unload. If you know you will need a cast member soon, and have the time to load it now, a Lingo command forces the load and the member will be ready to go when needed.

Before looking at the Lingo commands, take a look at a typical Property Inspector display for a member, as shown in Figure 21.5.

Figure 21.5
The Property Inspector for almost all member types includes an Unload setting as a pop-up menu.

There are four Unload options: 3-Normal, 2-Next, 1-Last, or 0-Never. The last option, 0-Never, keeps the member in memory, after it's loaded the first time, and ensures that it's never unloaded. The 1-Last setting keeps the member in memory as long as possible. The 2-Next setting flags the member for removal as soon as it isn't needed. The 3-Normal setting removes the member after all 2-Next members are removed, but before 1-Last members are removed.

It's almost never worthwhile to use any setting other than 3-Normal. However, if you have a member that is constantly being put on and pulled off the Stage, and the speed of the movie seems to be affected by the loading and unloading, setting this member to 1-Last might be a good idea.

You can set this property with the Lingo *purgePriority* property. Just use the number, such as 0, 1, 2, or 3:

```
member("large image").purgePriority = 2
```

The Lingo commands to control loading and unloading are fairly straightforward. To load a member into memory, issue a *preLoadMember* command:

```
preLoadMember "large image"
```

You can also specify a range of members to preload. This command loads both members specified by the range numbers, plus any members that are in between them in the Cast:

```
preLoadMember "large image 1", "large image 7"
```

You can even use the *preLoadMember* command by itself. In this case, Director attempts to load all members in the Cast until it runs out of memory.

There is also a *preLoad* command. This takes frame numbers rather than member names. By itself, it tries to load all the members used in the current frame of the movie to the last frame of the movie. This includes only members actually in the Score. Any members not in the Score but used by Lingo (such as button state images) are not loaded.

You can also specify two frames in the *preLoad* command, and it loads all the members used in those two frames and any in between. Specifying only one frame loads all the members from the current frame to the one specified.

But what if you are about to jump to another movie with the *go* or *play* command? Because those members are not in the current movie, you cannot use the *preLoadMember* or *preLoad* commands. However, you can use the *preLoadMovie* command. This command loads all the members in the first frame of the new movie.

The commands *unLoad*, *unLoadMember*, and *unLoadMovie* work the opposite of the previous commands by unloading members from memory.

A good rule of thumb with manually loading and unloading members is to experiment. Try running the movie with no special memory management commands, and then try it with your commands. See whether it really makes a difference.

Memory Information

Several functions can tell you how much memory is available. The simple *freeBytes()* function returns the number of available bytes in Director or the projector's memory space.

A more useful function is *freeblock()*, which returns the size of the largest contiguous block of memory. Because cast members need to be loaded in a continuous block of memory, you can use this function to make sure that such a block exists.

The *size* property of a member returns the size, in bytes, of a member. You can combine this with *freeblock()* to determine whether there is enough room for the member in memory. For instance, if you find that a huge sound member is having trouble playing on a machine with low memory, you can also have a smaller sound ready to play in its place. The following bit of code can decide which sound to use:

```
if freeBytes() > member("large sound").size then
  puppetSound "large sound"
else
  puppetSound "small sound"
end
```

You can also use the *ramNeeded* function to determine how much memory is needed for a series of frames. This handler measures how much memory is available to determine whether the movie will jump over a set of frames:

```
if ramNeeded(10,14) > the freeBytes then
  go to frame 15
else
  go to frame 10
end
```

A system property, *the memorySize*, returns the number of total bytes available to Director or the projector. You can use this to test that the program is running with enough memory to perform a memory-intense function.

You can also get the movie's file size using the *movieFileSize* property. Another property, the *movieFileFreeSize*, returns the amount of space in the file that is not in use. This extra space is thrown away when you choose File, Save And Compact.

➪ For examples of loading and unloading cast members, *see* "Performance Issues," *p. 681 (Chapter 34)*

LAUNCHING OTHER APPLICATIONS

You can use Director to launch other applications on the user's computer system. All you need to do is use the *open* command:

```
open "Macintosh HD:Applications:SimpleText"
```

It seems simple enough, but note that you have to give the full pathname of the application. This can be inconvenient, even if you are trying to run something as simple as Mac SimpleText or Windows NotePad. Sometimes simple Windows applications, such as NotePad, can be launched without a pathname, but you can't count on that.

You can use *open* to launch an application with a predefined starting document. For instance, you can launch SimpleText with the document "text file" in this manner:

```
open "Macintosh HD:text file" with "Macintosh HD:Applications:SimpleText"
```

However, there are problems with this form of the *open* command as well. On the Mac, if SimpleText is already running and you try to use the *open* command to open a file with SimpleText, SimpleText ignores the command. SimpleText appears, but the document does not open. In Windows, this is not a problem because you can't have NotePad running with no windows open.

Many users report problems on Director lists when trying to open Adobe Acrobat files, PowerPoint files, and even Word documents. It appears that *open* is a far from perfect command. However, for professional projects, several Xtras are available that will help you open certain applications. Some of these Xtras even enable you to open documents inside Director using ActiveX components. Check out Appendix H, "Guide to Xtras," for a list of Xtras that can help.

The news is better when it comes to Web browsers, because the *gotoNetPage* command actually launches the user's default browser and goes to a predefined Web location. You can read more about this command in Chapter 22, "Shockwave and Internet Access."

For more information about launching browsers, **see** "Controlling the Web Browser with Lingo," p. 448 in Chapter 22

QUITTING AND SHUTTING DOWN

Director also has the capability to turn itself off. As a matter of fact, on Macs, it can even turn the computer off. The *quit* command does just what you would expect: It acts just like choosing File, Quit or Exit from a typical application. The projector instantly quits. In Shockwave, the movie stops.

The *quit* command works very well; in fact, it works too well. If you issue a *quit* command while in Director, the command tries to quit Director. This can be annoying while you are authoring.

Instead, the *halt* command should be used in place of *quit*. In Director, the halt command stops the movie. In projectors, the *halt* command acts just like the *quit* command and quits the projector.

If you are building a kiosk on a Mac, you might also want to use the *restart* or *shutDown* commands. They perform the same actions as the menu items in the Mac Finder's Special menu. You can use these commands to enable a store owner or museum curator to shut down the computer at night, or restart it. This way, users don't have to exit the projector and then use the Finder.

You can also use these commands in association with code that reads the time. This way, you can automatically shut down or restart the computer at a certain time, or after a period of inaction. For example, the following handler shuts the computer down at 9:00 p.m. It can be called periodically from an *on exitFrame* handler:

```
on checkTimeShutDown
  if the time = "9:00 PM" then
    shutDown
  end if
end
```

TROUBLESHOOTING ENVIRONMENT LINGO

- Don't rely on the playback computer using the same time settings as your computer does. Months and days can easily be reversed in the date and different item delimiters can easily be set by users. Even if the target machines are in the same country, users sometimes play with the settings. Use *the systemDate* property when you can.

- Developers waste a lot of time loading and unloading Lingo. Determine whether and precisely where you are having a speed problem before trying to solve it with one of the loading commands. Director is probably already performing optimally.

- Make sure any custom cursor cast members conform to the required bit depths. Plain custom cursors need to be 1 bit and animated cursor members need to be 8 bits. They won't work otherwise.

- Double-check the text in your menu description fields if you are having trouble. The *installMenu* command is literal and does not forgive many mistakes.

- Don't forget that adding an Apple menu on the Mac means that a Windows projector will have a strange menu added as well. You might want to keep separate Mac and Windows menu description fields. In Windows, place any "About" menu item in the traditional "Help" menu, rather than in the Apple menu.

DID YOU KNOW?

- You can build the menu description field with Lingo. Just use string commands and other string Lingo to create or alter the field, and then use *installMenu* to make the changes take effect. This way, you can have a dynamically changing menu bar.

- If you want a cursor of unusual size, you can simply use cursor number 200 to turn off the cursor, and then a sprite in the highest channel can be set to follow the mouse around. Users won't be able to tell that the sprite is not a cursor; it will behave just like one.

- You can use the global version with Shockwave to redirect users who have various versions of Shockwave. For instance, you can make a Director 5 Shockwave movie that checks the version and uses *gotoNetMovie* to run a Director 5, Director 6, Director 7, or Director 8 movie.

- Many more functions exist in the Buddy API Xtra that tell you about the user's system, and even control parts of it. See Chapter 25, "Xtras," for details.

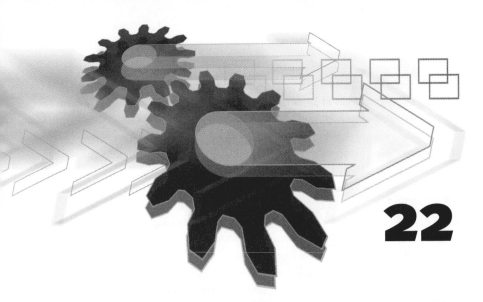

SHOCKWAVE AND INTERNET ACCESS

IN THIS CHAPTER

Source movies for this chapter can be found on the CD-ROM in the "Book Movies" folder under folder 22.

When Shockwave was introduced in 1995, it was simply a plug-in for Netscape Navigator that enabled the browser to play compressed Director movies. Since then, the term "Shockwave" has grown to encompass just about anything that has to do with both Director and the Internet.

At the same time, Director has grown to incorporate all aspects of Shockwave into the authoring environment and projectors. Early on, only movies running under a Web browser had capabilities such as accessing Internet information or controlling browser locations. Now, anything made with Director can do this.

This means that all Shockwave commands work while you are authoring in Director and in projectors. In cases where commands are supposed to control the Web browser, a projector even launches the user's default Web browser automatically.

Shockwave Lingo can be divided into many parts. There is Lingo for controlling the Web browser, getting and sending information over the Internet, saving preference files, and streaming in media over the Internet. There is also Lingo for communicating directly with the server and other Shockwave clients, something that we will deal with in Chapter 38, "Creating Multiuser Applications."

CONTROLLING THE WEB BROWSER WITH LINGO

The primary command for forcing the Web browser to go to another Web page is *gotoNetPage*. This command can be used with a relative location, or with an absolute location if the location starts with http://. For instance, if the user is already at http://clevermedia.com, the two commands are identical:

```
gotoNetPage("http://clevermedia.com/resources/")
gotoNetPage("resources/")
```

You can also use a target frame or window with *gotoNetPage*. Web developers are familiar with how to use targets. Basically, every browser window, and every frame inside a window, has a name. A target tag modifier can specify which of these targets should receive the *gotoNetPage* signal.

If you have developed your own set of windows or frames with HTML, you already know the names of these targets. However, there are a few target names, such as "_blank" and "_top" that are reserved for special purposes. Table 22.1 shows their usage.

Table 22.1   Reserved http Target Names

Name	Action
_blank	Creates a new, blank window without a name.
_self	The new page loads in the current frame. This works even if the HTML pages use the BASE structure.
_parent	Loads the new page one level up in the frame set, replacing the current frame and all its siblings.
_top	Loads in the current window, replacing all frames there.

The following are examples of *gotoNetPage* commands that use a target:

```
gotoNetPage("mypage.html","_blank")
gotoNetPage("http://clevermedia.com","_top")
gotoNetPage("http://clevermedia.com","mainframe")
```

If you are planning to use the *gotoNetPage* command in a projector, you might want to have more control over which browser is launched. Director uses the browser specified in the network preferences, or the system's default browser if none is specified. You can check the path of the browser with the *browserName( )* function:

```
put browserName()
-- "Macintosh HD:Netscape Communicator
Folder:Netscape Communicator"
```

You can also set this path with the *browserName* command:

```
browserName "Macintosh HD:Other Browser"
```

If, for some reason, you want to disable the projector's capability to launch a browser, use the *browserName* command with this odd syntax:

```
browserName(#enabled, FALSE)
```

Use a *TRUE* in place of the *FALSE* to enable browser launching.

In addition to telling the browser which page to display, you can replace the current Shockwave movie with a new one. The *gotoNetMovie* command is the network equivalent to *go to movie*. It loads a new movie from the network and replaces the current one directly in the page:

```
gotoNetMovie("newmovie.dcr")
gotoNetMovie("http://clevermedia.com/newmovie.dcr")
```

You can use both relative and absolute pathnames, as you can see. You can even specify a frame in the new movie to jump to. Just place a "#" after the filename and then the name of the frame label.

```
gotoNetMovie("newmovie.dcr#intro")
```

When the *gotoNetMovie* command is used, the current movie continues to play until the new movie has been loaded. If you issue another *gotoNetMovie* command, it cancels the first command and replaces the current movie.

As with any HTML, you should test targets in all browsers that you plan to support. Many browsers, especially the Mac version of Internet Explorer, will behave differently, even for simple HTML-like commands such as *gotoNetPage* with a target specified.

You can let users select the browser application if you use the *displayOpen* function of the FileIO Xtra, and then use the *browserName* command with the results.

If you want to determine whether the user has a connection to the Internet before using a *gotoNetPage* in a projector, you can access the #internetConnected property of *the environment*. If the user is connected, its value is #online.

⇨ *For information on saving and reading files from the hard drive, **see** "Using Text Files and the FileIO Xtra," p. 355 (Chapter 16, "Controlling Text")*

GETTING TEXT OVER THE INTERNET

Shockwave Lingo enables you to get many forms of media over the Internet or an intranet. For bitmaps, getting an external image is as easy as specifying its location. Getting text, however, is a little more complex.

You might get text from another file on the Internet to store textual data in an external file so that non-Director users in your company can update this data. This technique would work with the numbers that make up a chart, for example. You might also import text data from another source, such as a weather report or a small text database.

The primary command for getting text over the Internet is *getNetText*. But this command cannot stand alone. It simply initiates the call to the network. You have to use a series of commands and functions to perform the whole operation.

After *getNetText* is issued, a *netDone* function tells you when the text has been received. Then, you use *netTextResult* to get the text and store it in a variable or member.

However, you can't use *getNetText* and then simply lock the movie in a repeat loop until *netDone* returns *TRUE*. A repeat loop monopolizes the computer and limits its capability to actually get the text. The computer will be so busy running the repeat loop that it will never have the time to do the network functions.

The proper way to get text is to issue the *getNetText* call, and then let the movie run. The movie can even loop on a frame to appear paused. Remember, looping on a frame is completely different from using a repeat loop inside a handler. While looping, the movie enables the network functions to complete and the text to be received.

The following example is in two frames. Each frame has an *on exitFrame* script placed in the Frame Script channel. The first frame initiates the network call:

```
on exitFrame
  global gNetID
  gNetID = getNetText("http://clevermedia.com")
end
```

As you can see, *getNetText* is actually a function. It returns a number that corresponds to the network identification number for this network function. Because Director can perform more than one network function—such as *getNetText*—at a time, these ID numbers are needed to refer to them in the future. This number is likely to be 1 in this case, unless you have already performed a network function.

The next frame contains code that checks to see whether the network function corresponding to the variable "gNetID" is complete. If so, it gets the text, and then moves on. If not, it keeps looping on the frame:

```
on exitFrame
  global gNetID
```

```
-- check to see if text has arrived
if netDone(gNetID) then

    -- it has, so get it
    text = netTextResult(gNetID)
    put text

    -- move the movie forward
    go to the frame + 1
  else

    -- text is not here yet, keep looping
    go to the frame
  end if
end
```

It might also be a good idea to make sure that the system did not experience any problems in getting the text. You can use the *netError* function immediately after confirming that the operation has been completed with *netDone*. For instance, you can add this code:

```
if netError(gNetID) <> 0 then
  alert "An error occurred trying to get the text."
  halt
end if
```

A 0, obviously, means there is no error. However, any other number means there is a problem. Table 22.2 shows all the possible errors.

Table 22.2 The *netError* Codes

Code	Meaning
0	Operation completed successfully.
4	The required network Xtras are not installed.
5	Bad MOA Interface. Probably same as 4.
6	Bad location. Or, could be same as 4.
20	Browser detected an error.
4146	Connection could not be established with the remote host.
4149	Data supplied by the server was in an unexpected format.
4150	Unexpected early closing of connection.
4154	Operation could not be completed due to timeout.
4155	Not enough memory available to complete the transaction.
4156	Protocol reply to request indicates an error in the reply.
4157	Transaction failed to be authenticated.

Table 22.2 Continued

Code	Meaning
4159	Invalid URL.
4164	Could not create a socket.
4165	Requested object could not be found.
4166	Generic proxy failure.
4167	Transfer was intentionally interrupted by client.
4242	Download stopped by a *netAbort* command.
4836	Download stopped for an unknown reason, possibly a network error, or the download was abandoned.

⇨ *For an example that uses text on the Internet, see "Information Processing and Displaying," p. 615 (Chapter 31, "Shockwave Applets,")*

SENDING TEXT

Since the introduction of Shockwave in 1995, movies have been able to send text over the Internet. However, until Director 7, there were no commands to do this in Director. Instead, a trick was used to send information to server CGI scripts using *getNetText*. This trick is still a great way to communicate with the server. Director 8 also includes the *postNetText* command, which enables the movie to post information to a server in the same manner as an HTML page form.

Using *getNetText* to Send Text

It seems confusing, but you can send text by getting text. The *getNetText* command is used to get text information from a server. However, in doing so, you can give information to the server. It is similar to the way that Lingo functions work. A function returns information, but it can also accept information as a parameter.

The following is a typical *getNetText* call asking for an HTML page on a Web server:

```
getNetText("http://clevermedia.com/test.txt")
```

You can also use *getNetText* to call a CGI program. A CGI program is a small computer program, usually written in a language called Perl, which resides on the server. The output of a Perl program is usually text, such as an HTML page:

```
getNetText("http://clevermedia.com/cgibin/echo.cgi")
```

In this case, the CGI program returns text, just as the call to "test.txt" did previously. Neither the browser nor Director cares that the server had to run a program rather than just serve up a text file.

CGI programs can do much more than just serve up static text. They can actually take some data and then use it. For instance, they can store data in a file on the server. Information can be given to a CGI program by simply placing a "?" after the Web location, followed by text:

```
getNetText("http://clevermedia.com/cgibin/echo.cgi?gary")
```

In this case, the information "gary" was sent to the server. The Perl program on the other end just needs to look for it, get it, and then do something with it. The following Perl program sits on the server:

```
#!/usr/bin/perl
$invar = $ENV{'QUERY_STRING'};
print "Content-type: text/html\n\n";
print "Input: $invar <BR>\n";
```

Although it is beyond the scope of this book to go into Perl, which has many books of its own, this script works like this:

1. The first line tells the server that this is a Perl program, so when it is called, the server knows to run Perl and use this file as the source code.

2. The second line gets the data from after the question mark in the server call. In this case, that information is "gary".

3. The third line starts the output. It places the line "Content-type: text/html" plus two new-line characters into the output stream. This is needed to tell the server and the Web browser what type of output is coming. This line and the extra newline character never appear in the text you get back. However, everything after the newline character does.

4. The last line outputs the word "Input:" followed by the text. So, the result is an echo of what was sent. It is a good test and shows that the server can get information as well as send it. In this case, the server got "gary", processed it, and sent it back. It could also have opened a file and stored the information. It could have even opened another file, such as a database, and used this information to look up other information.

Usually, when you call a CGI program on a server, you want to send a specific piece of information to the server. You can easily construct a URL that reflects this piece of information. For instance, if your CGI script is at http://clevermedia.com/cgibin/submit.cgi and you want to send the contents of variable "myVariable" to the script, you do something like this:

```
submitText = "http://clevermedia.com/cgibin/submit.cgi?"&myVariable
getNetText(submitText)
```

As explained earlier in the chapter, after the call to *getNetText*, you need to make periodic checks to *netDone* to see whether the operation was successful. Note that the GET method of sending information has a length limit. It should be roughly 4,000 characters, but this limit is imposed by the browser when the movie is running in Shockwave. So, if the browser has a limit of 250 characters, Shockwave cannot send a longer string. In addition, a 250-character limit on *getNetText* string lengths was a bug that plagued earlier versions of Shockwave and could easily be a problem again in the future.

Using *postNetText* to Send Text

The *postNetText* command enables you to perform the same function as an HTML form with "METHOD=POST". The main advantage of using this command is that it can send much more information than the *getNetText* method, which is limited to about 4,000 characters in most situations. The information also arrives in a different format than the *getNetText* method, which many CGI programmers prefer.

> Even if no text is meant to be returned, or you don't need the text, you should go through the steps of using *netDone* and *netTextResult*. Otherwise, the call to the server is never ended and you can have only so many open-ended calls before network calls stop working.

The two required arguments of a *postNetText* command are the location of the CGI script and the data. The data, in this case, is a list. Here is an example:

```
postNetText("http://clevermedia.com/echopost.cgi", ["name": "Gary", "ID":
1])
```

The list should be a property list. Each property corresponds to the name of an item, whereas each value is the value of the item. All properties should be strings, but Director translates them to strings if they are not.

After a *postNetText* call, the same process as used for the *getNetText* function has to be followed. You must use the function's return value as an ID number, check *netDone*, and then use *netTextResult* to get the returned text.

Getting *postNetText* to work in Lingo is the easy part. Getting a CGI program that receives and deals with the data is a little more difficult. Hopefully, if you do not know about server programming, you will have the opportunity to work with someone who does. Otherwise, a good book on Perl or maybe some Web research into the subject will help.

WORKING WITH BROWSERS

Shockwave movies placed in Web pages have the capability to communicate with the HTML page and the Web browser. They can read information from the <EMBED> and <OBJECT> tags of which they are a part, and also talk to JavaScript and VBScript.

<EMBED> and <OBJECT> Tag Parameters

Movies shown in Netscape Navigator are part of the <EMBED> tag in the HTML. Movies shown in Microsoft Internet Explorer are part of the <OBJECT> tag. Both these tags are explained in full detail in Chapter 36, "Delivering the Goods."

These tags look different, but have a lot in common. For one, they accommodate the use of extra parameters. These parameters can be used to pass information into the Shockwave movie.

The following is an <EMBED>/<OBJECT> tag that uses the extra parameter "sw1". Notice that the <EMBED> tag is actually inside the <OBJECT> tag. Microsoft Internet Explorer uses the <OBJECT> tag and ignores the <EMBED> tag inside it, whereas Netscape Navigator ignores the <OBJECT> tag and uses the <EMBED> tag:

```
<OBJECT classid="clsid:166B1BCA-3F9C-11CF-8075-444553540000"
codebase="http://download.macromedia.com/pub/shockwave/cabs/director/
sw.cab#version=8,0,0,0" WIDTH=512 HEIGHT=384 ID="shock">
<PARAM NAME=src VALUE="mymovie.dcr">
<PARAM NAME=sw1 VALUE="testing! ">
<EMBED SRC="mymovie.dcr" NAME="shock" WIDTH=512 HEIGHT=384 sw1="testing!">
</OBJECT>
```

Notice that the "sw1" parameter needed to be added to the code twice: once for Explorer and once for Navigator. This is an unfortunate necessity. The <WIDTH> and <HEIGHT> tags should match the movie's Stage exactly to ensure that the movie is displayed properly.

The Shockwave movie can get the parameters from this tag by using the *externalParamValue* function. The function takes either a name, such as "sw1", or a number. You can use the *externalParamName* function to get the name of a parameter, given its number. You can also use the *externalParamCount( )* function to get the total number of parameters.

Although you can name parameters anything you want with Navigator, Explorer demands that parameter names come from a preset list. The following is a complete list:

> sw1, sw2, sw3, sw4, sw5, sw6, sw7, sw8, sw9, swURL, swText, swForeColor, swBackColor, swFrame, swColor, swName, swPassword, swBanner, swSound, swVolume, swPreloadTime, swAUdio, swList

None of these parameter names need to be used for any particular purpose. This collection is just a convenient list of names that the Macromedia engineers came up with, faced with the task of having to decide what sort of parameters developers would want. You could pass a sound name in with the "swURL" parameter, for instance. It doesn't really matter.

Because Explorer requires that you use one of these preset parameter names, you should stick to them if you are on the Navigator side as well. This way, you won't have to read one parameter for one platform and a different one for another.

➡ *For more information on using Shockwave and built <EMBED> and <OBJECT> tags, **see** "Making Shockwave Movies," p. 712 (Chapter 36)*

JavaScript to Shockwave

JavaScript is the programming language of Netscape Navigator. It is also available on Microsoft Internet Explorer, in addition to Explorer's own language, VBScript. These languages are embedded into the HTML page. They are both complex, object-oriented programming languages. Learning these languages is a task for an entire book, and indeed there are many more JavaScript books than Director and Lingo books in existence.

However, the commands used to enable these languages to talk to a Shockwave movie are fairly simple. They just basically send a message to the movie.

Showing examples of JavaScript-to-Shockwave communication is difficult because browsers are constantly changing. At the time of this writing, Netscape Navigator 4.7 and Microsoft Internet

Explorer 5.0 are the primary browsers being used. However, Internet Explorer 5.5 is being tested as well as Netscape 5.0.

Be prepared to use these examples as a guide to help you formulate your code, not as verbatim code samples. Also keep in mind that some users will still be working with older browsers. With browser differences and the lack of good documentation for JavaScript, using JavaScript with Director or alone is something you might want to avoid if at all possible.

To send a message to Shockwave, you first need to name your Shockwave object in the <OBJECT>/<EMBED> tag. In the example earlier in this chapter, the object was named "shock" by using the ID parameter in the <OBJECT> tag and the <NAME> parameter in the <EMBED> tag.

Now you need to assign the object to a JavaScript variable. This is also different for each browser. This JavaScript code takes care of this difference and stores the object reference in *myMovie*:

```
if (navigator.appName == "Netscape") {
  myMovie = document.shock;
} else {
  myMovie = shock;
}
```

Now, to send a message to the applet, you just need to use the object, followed by the message. For example:

```
myMovie.GotoFrame(42)
```

This code issues a command to the Shockwave movie to jump to frame number 42. You can use eight different message types. The following list includes them all. Remember that these commands are for use in the HTML code of the browser, not in the Director movie.

- **Stop( )**—Halts the movie.

- **Play( )**—Starts the movie from the current position.

- **AutoStart( )**—If *TRUE*, the movie starts playing after it is loaded or after a *Rewind( )*.

- **Rewind( )**—Takes the movie back to frame 1.

- **GotoFrame(*x*)**—Jumps the movie to frame number x.

- **GotoMovie(*location*)**—Loads another movie in place of the current one.

- **GetCurrentFrame( )**—Returns the number of the current frame.

- **EvalScript(*string*)**—Sends a text string into a movie to be used by the Lingo *on EvalScript* handler.

EvalScript( ) is the most useful of all of these commands. It can pass any string into the movie. At the other end should be an *on EvalScript* handler. Here is a simple example:

```
on EvalScript text
  alert("Message From JavaScript:"&&text)
end
```

Of course, a handler that actually takes the text and does something with it is far more useful. You can even have the movie execute any Lingo command or handler call by using the *do* command:

```
on EvalScript text
  do text
end
```

> The *do* command takes a text string and runs it as if the text string were typed into the Message window. You can call handlers, set globals, or even issue direct commands.

Shockwave to JavaScript

The opposite of the *EvalScript* handler is the *externalEvent* command. It sends a string that represents a command to JavaScript. Here is an example:

```
externalEvent("myJavaScriptFunction('param')")
```

If the user has Netscape Navigator, this command simply runs the JavaScript function named, with the parameter included. However, Microsoft Internet Explorer attempts to send the command to VBScript, not to JavaScript. If you know how to use VBScript, you can write a function that does the same thing as the Netscape JavaScript, or even calls out to the same JavaScript handler, passing the parameter information along. The following script assumes that the <OBJECT> tag set the ID of the applet to "shock":

```
<script language="vbscript">
sub shock_ExternalEvent(byVal aMessage)
  call myJavaScriptFunction(aMessage)
end sub
</script>
```

USING SHOCKWAVE PREFERENCE FILES (COOKIES)

Suppose that a Shockwave movie were to ask users for their names and then use their names throughout the presentation. It would be nice if, when a particular user returns to the page later, the movie remembered the user's name. This sort of thing can be done with preference files.

A preference file is just a small text file that can be stored on the user's computer. It is actually placed in the user's browser's file space, separate from the user's other files for security reasons.

You can create a preference file with the *setPref* command. For instance, to store a user's name, you can do this:

```
setPref("cmprefname.txt", gUserName)
```

In this example, "cmprefname.txt" is the preference filename, and the text of the variable "gUserName" is the contents of that file. The reason that such a complex name is given for the file is that the preference file area must be shared by all Shockwave movies. If you simply named the file "name.txt", and some other developer made a Shockwave applet with "name.txt", one file would overwrite the other.

You should pick a file prefix that another developer is unlikely to use. "cmpref" seems to be a good one if your company is "CleverMedia". If you are working for "Joe's Multimedia and Burgers," you might want to start the name of the preference file "jmb" or something similar. You should also use ".txt" as the suffix for the file, because Windows requires this sort of suffix and at least some, if not most, of your users will be using Windows. If you try to use a suffix other than ".txt", you get an error message.

The contents of the preference file can be anything, as long as it is a string. If you need to store a lot of information, you might want to consider converting a property list to a string, and then converting it back with the *value* command when you read the file.

To read a preference file, use the *getPref* command:

```
text = getPref("cmprefname.txt")
```

If the preference file does not exist, you get a *VOID* as a value. You can test for this to see whether a user has ever used that particular movie before.

One use for the preference file is to store a local high score for a game. If your movie is a game that uses a scoring system, you can simply have it write the user's score after a game, and then retrieve it when the user returns. It can be displayed as "Your best score" or something similar. This score is in no way compared to other users' on other computers, but that is also how home and mall arcade games work because they are not connected to each other.

You can also use *getPref* and *setPref* in Director and projectors. Doing so creates a preference folder in the same location as the application. Any preference files are stored there. This folder is primarily for testing purposes, but if it's used correctly, it can replace simple uses of the FileIO Xtra for storing some text and information.

➡️ *For another way to save and read text, **see** "Using Text Files and the FileIO Xtra," p. 355 (Chapter 16)*

CONTROLLING STREAMING MEDIA

Lingo also contains a variety of commands for checking on the status of a streaming movie, or loading in new members from the Internet.

Checking Streaming Status

When you set your Shockwave movie to stream by choosing Modify, Movie, Playback, "Play While Downloading Movie", you might want to use Lingo to determine whether a particular piece of media is ready before advancing in the movie.

For example, consider an interactive presentation. Users start on the first frame, where there is a menu of choices. They can choose from screens one to six on that menu. When the user clicks one of the buttons, the movie normally goes to the frame where the screen is located. However, you might want to ensure that all necessary media has been loaded on that frame first. If the media elements are not ready, you might want to take the user to a "wait" screen instead.

To determine whether all the media on a frame is ready, use the *frameReady* function. You can pass it a single frame number, a range between two frames, or no parameters. If no parameters are used, the function determines whether all the frames in the movie are ready. The following is an example:

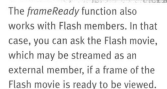

The *frameReady* function also works with Flash members. In that case, you can ask the Flash movie, which may be streamed as an external member, if a frame of the Flash movie is ready to be viewed.

```
on mouseUp me
  if frameReady(7) then
    go to frame 7
  else
    go to frame 6
  end if
end
```

This handler could be useful if frame six were a looping frame that had a "try again" button on it, along with a message explaining that the frame had not yet been downloaded.

You can use *frameReady* in an animation as well. Suppose you have an animation that spans frames 1 to 100. On frame 50, a whole bunch of new members are used. You might place the following script on frame 49. It would loop back to the last market until frame 50 is ready. It assumes that the frames from the previous marker to frame 49 make a nice holding-pattern animation.

```
on exitFrame me
  if frameReady(the frame+1) then
    go to the frame + 1
  else
    go loop
  end if
end
```

You can also find out if a particular member is ready. This is useful when you are using Lingo to change members on the screen. In that case, *frameReady* will not know about the members not in the Score, and so might return a *TRUE*, even though the members you need for your Lingo handlers are not ready.

To do this, use the *mediaReady* function. It can be used with either a member or a sprite. It also comes in handy for determining whether a very important member of an animation is ready, even if the rest of the members in a frame are not. This handler will loop on the current frame until the member "myMember" has been loaded.

```
on exitFrame me
  if member("myMember").mediaReady then
    go to frame "myFrame"
  else
    go to the frame
  end if
end
```

Loading in New Media

You can access media over the Internet in several ways. The easiest way is to use external linked members. For instance, when you import a bitmap, you can make it an external file, and the media will really reside in the original image file, not the Cast.

In this case, the movie becomes dependent on the external file. If the external file exists in the same directory as your movie, a copy of it must be in the same directory as the Shockwave movie in order for the media to be available. If you place the file in a subfolder, Shockwave expects the same subfolder to be available on the Web site.

After a linked member is in the Cast, you can set the *filename* property of the member to something different from the original file. The new media replaces the old media in the member.

Before you do this, however, you need to use the *preloadNetThing* command. This command tells the browser to load the file into the user's local cache. You can use *netDone* to determine when the item has been loaded. After that, you can safely set the *filename* property.

TROUBLESHOOTING SHOCKWAVE LINGO

- When you upload a Director movie, make sure you are using the binary setting on your FTP program. Using the ASCII setting results in an invalid file at the other end.

- If you upload a Shockwave file to a server for the first time, test it with Netscape. The server may not have the proper MIME types set to allow Netscape to know that a .dcr is a Shockwave movie. A MIME type is an identifier for a file on a server. If there is a problem, search the Macromedia site for "MIME" to find information that you can send to your server's administrator to add the Shockwave MIME type.

- If you are trying to use JavaScript communication, be sure to test your movie on all browsers and versions that you expect your audience to use. It is a lot of work, but there is no other way to ensure that all browsers will handle your commands correctly.

- When using preference files, you should always use the .txt suffix. Using another suffix is considered a security problem by Shockwave and an error message will be shown to users.

- When a movie attempts to get text from a different server with *getNetText*, a security alert appears. To avoid this alert, place both text and the movie on the same server and use a relative pathname.

- In the past, using a target with *gotoNetPage* sometimes did not work in Microsoft Internet Explorer if the *gotoNetPage* command was issued by an *on exitFrame* handler or a handler called by an *on exitFrame* handler. Test to make sure your targets work in Internet Explorer; if they don't, use *on mouseUp* handlers instead.

- For most developers, using Perl scripts means either controlling your own Web server so that you can create any type of Perl scripts you want, or contacting the Internet service provider who hosts your site/domain to find out what you are allowed to do.

- Using Perl scripts can be frustrating if you have never used them before. You can test your Perl scripts by typing the CGI calls in your browser. Do this to confirm that they work before trying to use Shockwave movies to call them.

- Make sure you preload external media files into the user's cache with *preloadNetThing* before setting the *filename* property of a member to a new file. If the file is not ready in the user's cache, the new media will probably not replace the old.

DID YOU KNOW?

- You can place multiple lines of text in a preference file. Store as much information as you want.

- You can use a second parameter with *getNetText* to specify a different server character set: "JIS" or "EUC". The default for this parameter is "ASCII" and the setting "AUTO" attempts to automatically determine the server character set.

- The *netMIME* function can be used to determine the file's MIME type after the *netDone* command returns *TRUE*.

- The function *netLastModDate* can be used to determine the server's time stamp for the file after the *netDone* returns *TRUE*.

- You can use network Lingo over HTTPS (secure servers).

- An *on EvalScript* handler can use *return* to send information back to JavaScript.

- Global variables persist from movie to movie when you use the *gotoNetMovie* command.

- Another network function is *downloadNetThing*. This function downloads an entire file from the Internet and places it on a user's hard drive. For security reasons, it is not available in Shockwave. However, it is a powerful feature of projectors.

- A powerful feature of Shockwave is that you can switch the *filename* property of a linked member to point to a new file. Even more powerful, however, is that you can do the same thing with entire external cast libraries. Remember to use *preloadNetThing* first!

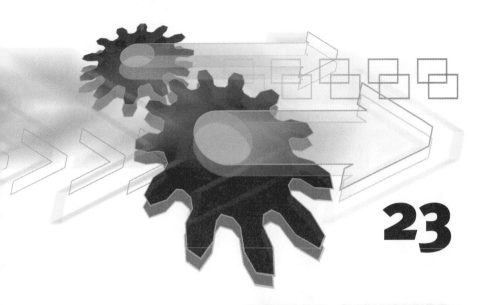

23

OBJECT-ORIENTED PROGRAMMING

Source movies for this chapter can be found on the CD-ROM in the "Book Movies" folder under folder 23.

Object-oriented programming, also known as OOP, is a term that might scare some nonprogrammers. It sounds mysterious and complex. In reality, it is what you have been doing all along in Director. OOP is simply programming that marries code to data. A behavior, attached to a sprite, is OOP. The code is the Lingo in the behavior, and the data is the properties of the sprite: the member, location, and custom properties of the behavior.

OOP enables you to write one piece of code, and then reuse that code for different objects. In Director, those objects are usually sprites, but they don't have to be. An object can be just an invisible set of data, such as an entry in a database or an enemy ship in a game.

A *code object* is a self-contained unit of code in memory that keeps track of its own internal data. Code objects have internal variables called *properties* and they respond to messages just as behaviors do. But unlike behaviors, you can't just drop them into the Score to use them.

WHAT IS AN OBJECT?

Behaviors are object-oriented scripts customized to fit Director's sprite-oriented nature. You can use parent scripts to create non–sprite-oriented objects, sometimes called *code objects*.

In Lingo, you define an object template by writing a parent script. Parent scripts are like templates for code objects. You then create an object from that parent script by sending a "new" message to the parent script. You can create as many objects as you want from the same parent script. The Director manuals call the objects created from a parent object *child objects*.

You get a Lingo object to respond by sending it a message. The object's handler determines which messages it responds to. An object can have a handler for just about anything you can program in Lingo. Director objects also have a built-in data management system, similar to structures in more traditional programming languages. Other than the messages sent to and from an object, the objects are completely isolated from each other.

If you are coming to Lingo with experience in an OOP language, such as C++, it might take you some time to get your bearings. Lingo does not have a ready-made class library, nor does it impose many rules about object structure, but it uses its own unique terminology. Table 23.1 shows the OOP terms and their Lingo equivalents.

Table 23.1 Object-Oriented Programming Versus Lingo Terms

OOP Term	Lingo Equivalent
Base class	Ancestor script
Class	Parent script
Instance variable	Property variable
Class instance/object	Child object
Method/member function	Method

*For more information about behaviors as objects, **see** "Controlling a Single Sprite," p. 256 (Chapter 14, "Creating Behaviors")*

REASONS TO USE OBJECTS

Almost everything you can do with objects in Lingo can be done without much difficulty using Director's Score-based environment. So, why use objects? Objects offer advantages of efficiency, flexibility, and optimal use of processing and memory resources. The following sections give five reasons to use objects.

Objects Organize Your Code

Better organization is achieved with objects because the parent contains both the code and the variables on which the code relies. If all your code and variables related to printing a report or playing digital video are in the same place, it's easier to maintain them using objects.

Objects Persist over Time

Like globals, an object's property variables maintain their state over time; unlike globals, the properties are known only to the object maintaining them. This helps you keep the number of gloabls used in your program down.

Suppose you wanted to make a program to keep track of employees. Each employee had a name, a home phone number, and other personal information. These are properties that they all have in common. That is, they have the same properties, even though they have different values from employee to employee. All these variables must be globals, or part of a global list, to be capable of maintaining their contents over time. In this case, you would end up with a lot of global variables all named with some variation of a product section name and counter or timer, all available everywhere in the movie. How long before you accidentally use the same global name twice for two different purposes?

Alternatively, you could make an object for each employee from the same parent script template. They would each have the same properties, but with different values.

If you had some salary employees that get paid monthly, and some hourly employees that get paid weekly, you could create a different parent script for each. Both parent scripts would have properties, such as the employee's name and number, but one would have salary information and the other hourly wage information.

None of these variables are part of the global pool because its scope is restricted to the object to which it belongs. This way, you don't have to worry about using a variable name multiple times for different purposes; instead, you can reference the properties of each object.

Objects Are Easy to Test

An object is self-contained. Because it isn't dependent on any code outside of itself, an object can be tested before other parts of the project are finished. After an object is coded, you should be able to test it by sending messages to all its handlers. If the handlers set the correct property variables or return the correct values, you know that the object is functioning properly and can be integrated into the larger project. While in Director, you can even send messages to an object after the movie has been stopped, which can come in handy to test variable names and handler functionality.

Objects Make Coding Easier and More Efficient

Using objects makes coding easier and more efficient through the use of inheritance. *Inheritance* is an OOP term that refers to the capability of one script to incorporate the handlers and properties of another script. Inheritance is a way of reusing existing code for similar programming problems, rather than writing code completely from scratch every time.

In Lingo, inheritance works in this manner: A parent script defines the handlers and properties that any object created from it will have. The created object inherits the handlers and properties of the parent. Multiple objects can be created from the same parent, and if appropriate, individualized with their own additional properties and handlers.

An *ancestor script* is another level of script in Lingo that uses inheritance. A parent script can link to an ancestor script. In this way, all the ancestor script's handlers and properties become part of the parent script and are, in turn, passed on to the child object. The child object inherits the ancestor's handlers and properties, plus any of the parent's handlers and properties that are also needed. Ancestor scripts are discussed in more detail in the "Using Ancestors" section later in this chapter.

Objects Can Be Reused

If you create objects with reuse in mind, eventually you will have a library of objects that you can put together to handle much of your routine coding. Director has the capability to link a movie to more than one Cast. This capability enables you to maintain a code library containing library objects that you can easily link to any movie. Almost any object you create has the potential to be reused, and if it's an external cast library, reuse is easy. If you create an object to handle grading a quiz, for example, the same object can be used in any quiz by simply changing a few of the properties.

CREATING AN OBJECT IN LINGO

To create an object, you must first create a parent script. As mentioned in the previous section, a parent script defines the methods and properties of objects created from it. The programming problem you are trying to solve determines the handlers and properties that you should include in your parent script. The basic method required by all parent scripts is the *on new* handler.

The *on new* handler creates a new object from a parent script. A parent script is like a template document in a word processing program. Just as you can create any number of identical documents from one template, you can create any number of identical objects by calling the *new* method of a parent script. Each time you send a parent script a new message, it creates a new object from that parent script.

The syntax for the *new* method is as follows:

```
on new me
    return me
end
```

It's important to use the word *me* in the line beginning with *on*. The word *me* holds a pointer to the location in memory of the object created from the parent script. It is also important to include the *return* line inside the *on new* method. This line returns a pointer to the object. If you don't include this *return*, you have no way of communicating with the object after you create it.

Director has a parent script type, available through the Script window, which is the proper place for creating parent scripts. If you accidentally create an object from a movie script and send it a message, Director looks through all the movie scripts for a handler for that message. If you have a movie script handler with the same name as one of your object methods, the movie script handler, rather than your object, gets the message.

When you create objects from a parent script, it's a good idea to store them in global variables so that the objects are available to code anywhere in the movie that you want to use them.

Global objects, like any other global variable, persist across movies. After an object is created from a parent script, it exists independently in memory. The object no longer references the parent script. If you go to another movie that does not contain the object's parent script, the object still works. The object is using its own copy of the code defined in the parent script that it has stored in memory.

If you change a parent script's code after you have created an object from it, you do not change the object already in memory. You must create a new object from the edited parent script; if you want to update multiple objects created from the same parent script, you must create new objects to replace each of the older ones.

With these background facts in mind, we can build an object. Create a new, empty parent by first creating a script cast member. Click the Info button in the Script window and use the Type pull-down menu in the Property Inspector to change the script's type property to Parent. Enter the name **minimal** in the script's Name field. A name is not optional for a parent script; it is required because you need to refer to it in other Lingo code.

Enter the following code into your minimalist parent script and name the script member minimal:

```
on new me
    return me
end
```

Create a new object by typing the following Lingo into the Message window:

```
minimalObj = new(script "minimal")
```

The code line you entered created a new object from the minimal script and put it in the global "minimalObj". You should store your objects in globals so that they will be available to code anywhere in your movie that they are needed.

Enter the following in the Message window and press Return or Enter to see whether you created an object. Director returns the contents of the object variable, which confirms that the object was successfully created:

```
put minimalObj
-- <offspring "minimal" 2 8daa90>
```

The object "minimalObj" was created successfully, but it can't really do anything yet. It cannot receive any messages other than *new*, and it has no property variables to store data.

Add a script so that you can create a new object with the click of a button. This way, you don't have to create a new object by typing commands in the Message window every time you play the movie. Make an *on mouseUp* handler that handles creating the object, as follows:

```
on mouseUp
  global gObj
  set gObj = new(script "minimal")
end
```

Rewind and play your movie and create a new object by clicking the button on the Stage. Check to see whether the object was properly created by typing **put gObj** in the Message window and pressing Return or Enter.

Create an "on hello" method for the object that makes the object beep. Edit the parent script to contain the following code:

```
on new me
    return me
end

on hello me
    beep
end
```

Rewind and play your movie and create a new instance of the object by clicking the button you created on the Stage. You should now be able to type the following code into the Message window. If everything worked correctly, your computer should beep.

```
hello(gObj)
```

⇨ *For more information about behaviors,* **see** *"Creating Simple Behaviors," p. 259 (Chapter 14)*

CREATING OBJECT PROPERTIES

So far, you have created a simple object that beeps if you send it the hello message. This object isn't terribly useful, however. To add greater functionality to an object, it needs more than methods. The minimal object is missing the second component of truly functional objects in Director: properties. The property variables of an object can be used to hold any type of data and are unique to each instance of the object.

You declare an object's property variables at the top of the parent script in the same manner as you declare globals and properties in behaviors:

```
property pProp1, pProp2, pProp3...
```

You can refer to the property inside the parent script by just its name. Outside the parent script, you can refer to it using the dot syntax. For instance, if an object is referenced by the variable "gObj" and you want to get the value of its property "pProp1", "gObj.pProp1" gives you that value.

The following is a simple parent script that sets a property during the new handler. You can then use the "on test" handler to see that the property is there.

```
property pTest


on new me
  pTest = "Hello World."
  return me
end


on test me
  put pTest
end
```

You can try it out in the Message window:

```
gObj = new(script "Test Object")
test(gObj)
-- "Hello World."
```

As noted earlier in this chapter, you can produce multiple identical objects from the same parent script. You can then individualize the objects by giving them different properties. In this way, you can enjoy the efficiency of not rewriting code for methods and properties that are the same from object to object. Yet, you still have the flexibility to create unique objects as your programming problem demands.

The following is a script parent similar to the last one. In this case, however, it sets the property "pTest" in the new handler according to a parameter:

```
property pTest


on new me, val
  pTest = val
  return me
end


on test me
  put pTest
end
```

Now, try this in the Message window. It demonstrates the creation of two separate objects from one parent script and how the values of the properties inside each object can be different:

```
gObj1 = new(script "Test Object 2", "Hello World.")
gObj2 = new(script "Test Object 2", "Testing...")
put gObj1
-- <offspring "Test Object 2" 2 4abfdac>
put gObj2
-- <offspring "Test Object 2" 2 4abfe24>
test(gObj1)
-- "Hello World."
test(gObj2)
-- "Testing..."
```

➪ *For more information about properties, see "Controlling a Single Sprite," p. 256 (Chapter 14)*

USING OOP

In Director 8, using OOP is so automatic that you can hardly avoid doing it. Every behavior is OOP code that controls a sprite or frame.

In the past, parent scripts were created to take control of sprites and make them behave in certain ways. Behaviors have taken over this responsibility. As a result, the usefulness of parent scripts has decreased.

You can still use parent scripts for nonvisually oriented tasks. For instance, if you want to create a vocabulary program, you can store words as objects. After all, a word can have many properties: spelling, definition, synonyms, and so on. Here is a simple parent script that can be used to create a word object:

```
property pWord
property pDefinition

on new me, theword
  pWord = theword
  return me
end

on setDefinition me, def
  pDefinition = def
end

on define me
  return pDefinition
end
```

Using the Message window, you can see how this can be applied:

```
gWord = new(script "Word Object", "Clever")
put gWord.pWord
-- "Clever"
setDefinition(gWord, "Skillful in thinking. ")
put define(gWord)
-- "Skillful in thinking. "
```

Now you can add more properties, such as synonyms, antonyms, homonyms, anagrams, common misspellings, and so on. You can add more handlers to accept and process these properties, or create universal ones that accept and return any property.

This same sort of OOP logic can be applied to any type of data. You can have a database of employees, for instance. Each object can have properties such as the employee's name, address, phone number, date of birth, Social Security number, and so on.

In turn, the handlers in the parent script would be custom built to work with this data.

⇨ For more information about behaviors, see "Creating Simple Behaviors," p. 259 (Chapter 14)

USING ANCESTORS

Parent scripts can use a special property, called an *ancestor*, which is a reference to another parent script.

When you define and use the *ancestor* property, you give the object access to all the handlers and properties in that ancestor parent script. In this way, you can have objects created with different parent scripts, but that use the same *ancestor* script. In other words, they can share some handlers, but not others.

Suppose you want to use objects to track items in a store. One of the problems with items in a store is that they have different properties. A piece of fruit, for instance, has an expiration date. A can of food, on the other hand, might not have an expiration date, but does have a size property: It can fit on some shelves but not others. The following is an *ancestor* script that has all the properties shared by both types of items. It also has a handler that does something with them:

```
property pProductName
property pAisleNumber

on new me
  return me
end

on whereIs me
  return pProductName&&"is in aisle"&&pIsleNumber
end
```

The shared item is the aisle number. This is the way the store keeps track of where things are. In addition, all products have a name. An "on whereIs" handler returns a string that contains both.

The first type of product that the store stocks is fruit. It is a product, so it uses the ancestor script, and from that gets the use of the "pProductName" and "pAisleNumber" properties, as well as the "on whereIs" handler. In addition, it has an expiration date. Here is a parent script for a piece of fruit:

```
property ancestor
property pExpires


on new me
  ancestor = new(script "Product Ancestor")
  return me
end


on expiration me
  return me.pProductName&&"expires"&&pExpires
end
```

The first property in the fruit parent script is the *ancestor*. In the *on new* handler, this is set to be a new instance of the ancestor script. In addition, this parent script has a "pExpires" property and a handler that uses it. This handler also accesses the "pProductName" property from the ancestor script by using the *me* property and dot syntax.

You can see how all this works in the Message window. When an object is created from the fruit parent script, the ancestor is attached to it. You can then assign the object with properties from both its own parent script and its ancestor script. Then you can access handlers from both as well.

```
gApple = new(script "Fruit Parent")
gApple.pProductName = "Apple"
gApple.pAisleNumber = 14
gApple.pExpires = "12/31/98"
put expiration(gApple)
-- "Apple expires 12/31/98"
put whereIs(gApple)
-- "Apple is in aisle 14"
```

The power of this technique comes when you need to create another type of product, such as canned food, for instance. The following is a parent script for cans:

```
property ancestor
property pSize


on new me
  ancestor = new(script "Product Ancestor")
```

```
    return me
end

on size me
  return me.pProductName&&"is size"&&pSize
end
```

This script looks similar to the fruit parent script, but has a different property. Things such as product name and aisle number are already taken care of because you used the same *ancestor* script.

```
gYams = new(script "Can Parent")
gYams.pProductName = "Canned Yams"
gYams.pAisleNumber = 9
gYams.pSize = "Medium"
put size(gYams)
-- "Canned Yams is size Medium"
put whereIs(gYams)
-- "Canned Yams is in aisle 9"
```

You can now go on to create dozens or hundreds of types of parent scripts that all use the same *ancestor* script. If you then want to add another shared property, such as an order number, you can add it to the ancestor script. All the objects that use that ancestor script inherit the property when you run the movie again.

TROUBLESHOOTING OOP

* A common error is to forget the "return me" at the end of the *on new* handler.

* When you use the *new* command to create an object, it takes the code as it currently exists. If you change the script member, you have to re-create the object with the new command before the change takes effect.

* If you use a handler name in a parent script, be sure not to use that same handler name somewhere else.

* Creating parent scripts might seem natural to OOP programmers, but in many cases a behavior is really what is needed. A good rule of thumb is to use parent scripts only when there is no visual component to the object, or possibly when more than one sprite needs to be controlled by an object.

DID YOU KNOW?

- When you create an object and then examine it in the Message window, the strange-looking result is actually the name of the script, the number of references to the script, and the member location of the object. It might look like this: "<offspring "Can Parent" 2 4abfeec>".

- There is a system property called *the actorList*. If you use *add* to add objects to this list, the objects begin to receive *on stepFrame* handler calls exactly once per frame.

- You can assign any object, such as a member, or *the systemDate* to a script object as its *ancestor*. For instance, if you assign a sprite as the *ancestor* of a script object, you can treat properties such as *locH* and *ink* as properties of that script object.

- If you assign a sprite as the *ancestor* of a script object, all the behaviors attached to that sprite also become ancestors of the script object. You can access normal properties in the sprite, as well as properties of the behaviors.

- You can use parent scripts to store handlers in memory to be used when the projector or Shockwave changes movies. Because the code resides in a global variable, it persists beyond the movie. You can use that global to call the handlers that existed in the parent script, even though the script is not present in the current movie.

MOVIES IN A WINDOW AND ALTERNATIVES

IN THIS CHAPTER

Source movies for this chapter can be found on the CD-ROM in the "Book Movies" folder under folder 24.

Movies in a window, usually referred to as MIAWs (often pronounced "meow," as in the sound a cat makes), are an unusual part of Director. They enable you to open other windows, besides the Stage, that contain Director movies.

MIAWs have many uses. Because they play independently of each other and of the Stage, they are useful for functions that don't fit into the Stage's window. You can create your own custom dialog boxes or message windows with MIAWs. You can even create your own application using several different windows, just as Director and almost every other professional computer application does.

USING MIAWS

MIAW Lingo can be simple or complex. If you just want to open a window to display some information, only a few lines of code are needed. On the other hand, an entire set of commands, functions, properties, and special event handlers exist to support further use of MIAWs. In any case, you first need to create a MIAW, which is covered in the following section.

Creating a MIAW

To use MIAWs, you first need to have another movie file besides your main movie. When you want to create a small window, the Stage size for the MIAW movie should be set accordingly. Save that file as miaw.dir and open another new movie. You can actually use the Message window to show the MIAW.

```
miaw = window("Test MIAW")
miaw.filename = "miaw.dir"
miaw.visible = TRUE
```

The new window appears over the Stage. It shows a title of "Test MIAW". The global variable that is created, "MIAW", holds the reference to that window. You can get its value:

```
put miaw
-- (window "Test MIAW")
```

You can refer to this MIAW using both the global variable and the structure "window("Test MIAW")". To close and remove that MIAW, you can also use the Message window:

```
close(miaw)
forget(miaw)
```

A handler that opens a MIAW for you looks similar to the preceding Message window code. Here is that handler, and one that closes the MIAW:

```
on startMIAW
  global gTestMIAW
  gTestMIAW = window("Test MIAW")
  gTestMIAW.filename = "miaw.dir"
  gTestMIAW.visible = TRUE
end
```

```
on endMIAW
  global gTestMIAW
  close(gTestMIAW)
  forget(gTestMIAW)
end
```

Notice that closing a MIAW takes two commands. The first, *close*, actually just makes the window invisible. The second command, *forget*, erases it from memory. If you issue only the first command, the MIAW is still there, taking up memory. It can also cause potential problems if you plan on using more MIAWs later.

MIAW Properties

The simple example described in the preceding section shows some of the basic properties of a MIAW. It has the *filename* and the *visible* property. You can also infer the *name* property from the previous example. The following is a complete list of the MIAW properties:

- **visible**—Determines whether the window is visible or hidden. Even hidden windows can execute Lingo code.

- **filename**—The filename that corresponds to the Director movie used for the MIAW. If the computer is connected to the Internet, a URL can be used.

- **name**—The name of the MIAW. This is used as a default title for the window, and used to refer to the MIAW with the window structure.

- **title**—Can be used to override the name of the window in the visible title bar.

- **titleVisible**—This determines whether the MIAW shows the title bar.

- **windowType**—You can set this to -1, 0, 1, 2, 3, 4, 5, 8, 12, 16, or 49. Tables 24.1 and 24.2 show what is included with each type.

- **drawRect**—This powerful property can be used to scale the MIAW, including bitmaps in it.

- **rect**—This property enables you to crop or expand the MIAW, with no scaling.

- **sourceRect**—Returns the original coordinates for the MIAW, before changes were made to the *drawRect* or the *rect*.

- **modal**—When this property of a window is set to *TRUE*, the window takes over all input and prevents other windows, including the Stage, from receiving clicks or key presses until the MIAW is gone or the modal is set to *FALSE*.

Tables 24.1 and 24.2 show you which elements are visible in which window types. Note the slight differences between windows on Macs and PCs. Windows on Macs have a maximize button. Windows in Windows have a stretch box and a resize box.

Table 24.1 MIAW Types for Windows

Type Number	Description	Movable	Close Box	Maximize	Minimize
0	Standard	Yes	Yes	No	No
1	Alert Box	No	No	No	No
2	Rectangle	No	No	No	No
3	Rectangle	No	No	No	No
4	Document	Yes	Yes	No	No
5	Document	Yes	No	No	No
8	Document	Yes	Yes	Yes	No
12	Document	Yes	Yes	Yes	No
16	Document	Yes	Yes	No	No
49	Palette (not in projectors)	Yes	Yes	No	No

Table 24.2 MIAW Types for Mac

Type Number	Description	Movable	Close Box	Stretch Box	Resize Box
0	Standard	Yes	Yes	Yes	No
1	Alert Box	No	No	No	No
2	Rectangle	No	No	No	No
3	Rectangle with Drop Shadow	No	No	No	No
4	Document	Yes	Yes	No	No
5	Document	Yes	No	No	No
8	Document	Yes	Yes	Yes	Yes
12	Document	Yes	Yes	No	Yes
16	Curved Border Box	Yes	Yes	No	No
49	Palette (not in projectors)	Yes	Yes	No	No

Although Tables 24.1 and 24.2 give you a good idea of what each window type should look like, keep in mind that the look is determined both by your Director version and the version of your operating system. A window type looks different in Mac OS 8.1 than it does in Mac OS 9.0 and different in Windows 98 than it does in Windows 2000.

Window Commands

The *open*, *close*, and *forget* are the primary commands used with MIAWs. Two others, *moveToFront* and *moveToBack*, however, are designed to work when more than one MIAW is open at once. Some additional commands enable MIAWs to talk to the Stage and to each other. The important window commands are described as follows:

- **open**—Creates a new MIAW and returns a reference to it.

- **close**—Makes a MIAW invisible, although the MIAW is actually still present.

- **forget**—Unloads the MIAW from memory.

- **moveToFront**—Takes the MIAW and makes it the frontmost window.

- **moveToBack**—Takes the MIAW and places it behind all others.

- **tell**—Sends a Lingo command or handler call to a MIAW. It can also be used to direct a set of Lingo commands to a MIAW.

MIAWs and the Stage use the *tell* command to communicate. You can use it to send a single command like this:

```
tell window("Test MIAW") to myHandler
```

You can also send a whole set of lines to the MIAW:

```
tell window("Test MIAW")
  myHandler
  myOtherHandler
  go to frame "x"
end tell
```

MIAW System Properties

In addition to the individual window properties available in Lingo, some system properties relate to windows. This is a complete list of properties that tell you which windows are present, which window is active, and which window is at the front:

- **the windowList**—Returns a list of all the current MIAWs, including ones that are invisible. If no windows are present, it returns an empty list.

- **the activeWindow**—Returns a reference to the currently active window. If the Stage is the active window, "(the stage)" is returned.

- **frontWindow**—Returns a reference to the frontmost window. If this is the Stage, "(the stage)" is returned.

- **windowPresent( )**—This function, when given a string with a window name, tells you whether a window with that name is present. It works only with window names, not window references in variables.

You can get good use out of *the windowList* property by creating a script that closes any and all MIAWs. It determines the number of windows from *the windowList* and then closes and forgets all the windows, as follows:

```
on closeAllMIAWs
  n = count(the windowList)
  repeat with i = 1 to n
    close window(1)
    forget window(1)
  end repeat
end
```

MIAW Event Handlers

MIAWs can also use many special event handlers. They involve typical window events, such as opening, closing, and moving the window.

Each of these handlers can be used in movie scripts in the MIAW's Director movie. The following is a complete list:

- **on activateWindow**—This handler is called when the window is not currently the active one and users click it to make it active.

- **on activateApplication**—If the projector is sent to the background or minimized, and then activated again, this handler is called in the main movie and in all the MIAWs.

- **on closeWindow**—This handler is called when users use the close box to close the window, or when the window is closed with the *close* command.

- **on deactivateWindow**—This handler is called when the window is the active one, and users click another window, thus making this one not active.

- **on deactivateApplication**—If the projector is sent to the background or minimized, this handler is called in the main movie and all MIAWs.

- **on moveWindow**—This handler is called every time the MIAW is dragged around the screen by users. The call comes when users release the mouse button.

- **on openWindow**—This handler is called immediately after the MIAW opens for the first time.

- **on resizeWindow**—This handler is called whenever users use the corner or sides of the window to resize it.

- **on zoomWindow**—This handler is called whenever users click a zoom, maximize, or minimize box.

*For some background about creating handlers, **see** "Using Handlers" p. 230 (Chapter 13, "Essential Lingo Syntax")*

CREATING DIALOG BOXES

With MIAWs, you don't have to be stuck with plain, ordinary alert boxes and dialog boxes. After all, if the artwork on your Stage is strange and unusual, why should your dialog boxes look like standard Mac and Windows interfaces? Instead, you can use the window properties and event handlers to construct your own custom dialog boxes and alert boxes. This section shows you how.

Confirmation Dialog Boxes

Confirmation dialog boxes usually ask a yes or no question. In most programs, yes or no is usually expressed as OK and Cancel. However, you can make them anything you want with MIAWs.

Figure 24.1 shows the Stage with a MIAW confirmation dialog box. It is simply a normal MIAW, like the one used in the example earlier in this chapter. The *windowType* has been set so that the window is a nonmovable rectangle. The modal property has been set to *TRUE* so that users must interact with it.

Figure 24.1
Out-of-the-ordinary dialog boxes can be easily created with MIAWs.

The following script opens this MIAW with the correct window type and modal:

```
on mouseUp
  global gFunkyDialog
  gFunkyDialog = window("Funky Dialog")
  gFunkyDialog.filename = "24funkydialog.dir"
  gFunkyDialog.windowType = 1
  gFunkyDialog.modal = TRUE
  gFunkyDialog.visible = TRUE
end
```

Inside the MIAW, the two buttons can be wired up with code that closes the dialog box and also tells the Stage what to do. For instance, here is the code for the Yes button:

```
on mouseUp
  close(the activeWindow)
  forget(the activeWindow)
  tell (the Stage) to continueYes
end
```

The handler "on continueYes" should be in the main movie. You can also have an "on continueNo" that is called by the No button.

In the preceding script, *the activeWindow* is used as a convenient way to determine which MIAW to close. After all, if the user is clicking it, it should be the active window. Using this function is more convenient than passing a global variable around.

Alert Dialog Boxes

Alert dialog boxes are as simple as MIAWs get. However, you might want to create a MIAW that can handle many types of alerts. To do this, you can use a command to place different pieces of text in a field in the MIAW so that it shows a different message each time. Figure 24.2 shows such a dialog box.

Figure 24.2
MIAWs can be used to create custom alert boxes.

A handler that creates such a MIAW could look like this:

```
on mouseUp
  global gAlertBox
  gAlertBox = window("Alert Box")
  gAlertBox.filename = "24alertbox.dir"
  gAlertBox.windowType = 4
  gAlertBox.modal = TRUE

  tell gAlertBox
    member("Text").text = "The Jundland wastes are not to be traveled lightly."
  end tell

  gAlertBox.visible = TRUE
end
```

This code is just like the other handlers that open MIAWs, but the *tell* command is used to change the text in a field in the MIAW. This is done just before the MIAW is made visible so that users don't see the change.

Text Input Dialog Boxes

Another type of MIAW dialog box is one that asks users for more information. You can have radio buttons, check boxes, and even text input fields in these input dialog boxes.

Following is an example of a MIAW that asks users to type their names. Figure 24.3 shows what this dialog box might look like. The field in the middle is a simple editable text field member.

Figure 24.3
MIAWs can gather information through text input and other interface devices.

The MIAW in the main movie is created in the same way as the other MIAWs. However, the code executed when users click the OK button is a little more complex. It takes the text in the field and passes it back to the Stage through a *tell* command:

```
on mouseUp
  text = member("Text Input").text
  close(the activeWindow)
  forget(the activeWindow)
  tell (the Stage) to textInputDone(text)
end
```

The code for the Cancel button is similar, but this button is intended to pass just a *VOID* constant back rather than text. Then, the main movie handles the input with something like this:

```
on textInputDone text
  if text = VOID then
    put "Cancelled."
  else
    put "Text Entered:"&&text
  end if
end
```

Of course, in real life, "on textInputDone" is likely to store the user's name in a variable or place it in a field. It probably also uses a *go* command to proceed to the next part of the movie.

 *For more information about creating buttons, see "Building a Complete Button Behavior," p. 271 (Chapter 14, "Creating Behaviors")*

For more information about text in dialog boxes, see "Using Keyboard Input," p. 342 (Chapter 16, "Controlling Text")

CREATING ODDLY SHAPED MIAWS

A hiddenfeature of Director 7 was its capability to create oddly shaped MIAWs. This was first revealed to developers at the 1999 Macromedia Conference in San Francisco, and then the information spread over the Internet.

Creating oddly shaped windows is an important feature because applications, such as MP3 players and games, use nonrectangular shapes for their windows. Director developers can do this easily.

To create an oddly shaped MIAW, simply set its *windowType* to a 1-bit bitmap member. This member will then be used as a mask to create the shape of the window.

```
gMyMIAW.windowType = member("MIAW Mask")
```

If you try this in Director, however, it won't work. This function works only in projectors. So, to test your oddly shaped MIAW, you need to build a projector first.

Figure 24.4 shows an oddly shaped MIAW. You can even shape the MIAW to have gaps and holes.

Figure 24.4

An oddly shaped MIAW can be used to create interesting inter-faces.

CREATING SELF-CONTAINED MIAWS

You don't actually need another movie file to create a MIAW. You can simply open a MIAW using the same file that the Stage is using.

To do this, use *the movie* instead of another filename when assigning the *filename* property of the MIAW. The idea is to hide the frame you want the MIAW to use in a frame near the end of the movie. Then, you can use *tell* to tell the MIAW to go to that frame before you make it visible. You can even resize the *rect* of the MIAW to make it fit a smaller size.

The only problems with this technique arise from the fact that the *on startMovie* handler and others like it are triggered in the MIAW as well as the Stage movie. You can either decide not to have these in the movie at all, or you can set a flag that tells the *on startMovie* handler to *exit* before doing anything.

This technique has only one advantage over using a separate movie for the MIAW—your project can be organized into a single file. You can also share media between the Stage movie and the MIAW, although that can be done with shared external casts as well.

One word of warning: When using this technique, you should save the movie often. When the MIAW is created, it is created from the saved movie file, not the current copy of the movie that Director has open. So, you can make a change in the Director movie and not see the change in the MIAW because you haven't saved recently.

OTHER USES FOR MIAWS

Confirmation dialog boxes, alert boxes, and input dialog boxes are just three of the many possible uses for MIAWs. Just about anything you can do in Director, you can do in MIAWs, so the sky's the limit.

Some developers use MIAWs as the primary screen in projectors. They make the Stage as small as possible, and even stick it out of the monitor's screen area, perhaps at a negative horizontal and vertical location. This way, you can have a movable window as the main screen, even in Mac projectors, which insist on a nonmovable rectangular window for the Stage.

Some other uses for MIAWs include

- **A Shockwave player**—Because you can use Internet locations as well as filenames for MIAWs, why not open up some Shockwave content in your projectors this way?

- **Hyperlinks**—In educational programs, MIAWs can be used as glossary windows or windows with additional information. Use hyperlinks in text members to activate them.

- **Multiple movies**—If you need to have more than one movie playing at a time, you can do so with a single projector that opens two MIAWs.

- **Debugging**—You can have a MIAW that contains extra information about the main movie that is meant for your eyes only. It can be updated with the *tell* command. When the project is done, just remove the MIAW or make it invisible.

- **Stage overlay**—If you create a plain rectangle MIAW, it can be placed on top of the Stage and users won't even know it's a separate window. You can use this to place animation or other external pieces in your movies.

USING LINKED MOVIES

An alternative to the "Stage Overlay" idea is to use linked movies rather than MIAWs. A *linked movie* is simply a cast member that has been imported into the main movie. The linked movie can be placed on the Stage and users won't know it's a separate movie. The Score and Cast for this linked movie still exist as independent files, but they are represented in your main movie as members.

After you have such a member, you can place it on the Stage and position it. You can even animate its position over a series of frames.

➡️ *For some basic information about film loops, see "Using Film Loops and Linked Movies," p. 195 (Chapter 11, "Advanced Techniques")*

The difference between a linked movie and a film loop is that all the scripts in the linked movie are still active and working. In a film loop, only behaviors and some other scripts work. Film loops are meant more for animation, whereas linked movies are for more complex interactive movies.

USING MUI XTRA DIALOG BOXES

The MUI Xtra (pronounced "moo-ee") that comes with Director is used by various parts of the authoring environment to create dialog boxes similar to the ones that behaviors bring up when dropped onto a sprite. MUI stands for *Macromedia User Interface*, which is a set of guidelines that Macromedia follows for all its software products.

Macromedia also provided a straight Lingo interface for this Xtra, which enables you to create some standard and custom dialog boxes. All the elements in the dialog boxes look like Macromedia standard interface elements, but that is not necessarily a bad thing. Macromedia has created a good set of cross-platform elements that look like standard dialog boxes.

There are actually five ways to call the MUI Xtra. The first four represent some standard dialog box types: file open, file save, get URL, and an alert. The alert box is very customizable. The fifth way to call the MUI Xtra is to create a custom dialog box from scratch.

Creating a File Open Dialog Box

Creating a file open dialog box is simple. All you need to do is create an instance of the Xtra, use its *FileOpen* method to generate the dialog box, and then retrieve its results. The following handler does just that:

```
on muiFileOpen
  gMUI = new(xtra "mui")
  filename = FileOpen(gMUI,the pathname)
  gMUI = 0
  return filename
end
```

The only other parameter for *FileOpen* is the default pathname of the file. The function returns the resulting filename. After that, you should dispose of the Xtra instance by setting it to *VOID* or *0*. Figure 24.5 shows an example of a file open dialog box created on the Mac.

Figure 24.5
The file open dialog box created with the MUI Xtra.

Creating a File Save Dialog Box

The *FileSave* method for the MUI Xtra works in a similar way. You need to give it two parameters: the default name for the file, and a piece of text to be displayed in the dialog box.

```
on muiFileSave
  gMUI = new(xtra "mui")
  filename = FileSave(gMUI,"myfile", "Save Game")
```

```
gMUI = 0
return filename
end
```

The *FileSave* command returns the pathname to the location of the file to be created. Figure 24.6 shows an example.

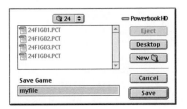

Figure 24.6
The file save dialog box created with the MUI Xtra.

Creating a Get URL Dialog Box

The *GetURL* method displays a dialog box with the name "Open URL". You can specify a default location, and whether the dialog box is movable, as shown in the following code. Figure 24.7 shows an example.

```
on muiGetURL
  gMUI = new(xtra "mui")
  default = "http://clevermedia.com"
  moveable = TRUE
  filename = GetURL(gMUI, default, moveable)
  gMUI = 0
  return filename
end
```

Figure 24.7
The Open URL dialog box created with the MUI Xtra.

Creating Alert Boxes

Creating alert boxes is much more complex because so many more options are available. This handler creates the alert box shown in Figure 24.8. It is a simple alert with a caution icon and an "OK" button:

```
on muiAlert
  gMUI = new(xtra "mui")
  list = [:]
  addProp list, #buttons, #Ok
  addProp list, #default, 1
  addProp list, #title, "Alert!"
  addProp list, #message, "The Jundland wastes are not to be traveled lightly."
```

```
    addProp list, #icon, #caution
    addProp list, #moveable, FALSE
    res = Alert(gMUI,list)
    gMUI = 0
    return res
  end
```

Figure 24.8
A simple alert dialog box created
with the MUI Xtra.

As you can see in the handler, a list is passed into the *Alert* function. This list contains various options that describe how the alert box is to look.

The first property, #buttons, can be set to #OK, #OKCancel, #AbortRetryIgnore, #YesNoCancel, #YesNo, or #RetryCancel. Each of these options determines how many buttons the alert box has, and what they are named.

The #default property determines which of the buttons is the default one. This button looks different from the others and also reacts to a Return or Enter key press.

The #title property enables you to customize the label in the title bar of the alert window. The #message and #icon properties enable you to determine the contents of the box. Additional options for #icon are #stop, #note, #caution, #question, or #error.

The #moveable property enables you to determine whether the alert box window is movable.

This type of dialog box returns the number of the button pressed. So, if the buttons are *#OKCancel*, it can return a 1 or a 2.

Creating Custom MUI Dialog Boxes

Custom MUI dialog boxes are even more complex than alert boxes because you can specify every aspect of the window as well as the interface elements inside it.

The best way to learn how to use the custom dialog boxes is to take a look at an example. But even a short example has a lot of Lingo lines associated with it. Figure 24.9 shows a simple custom dialog box that the following handler creates.

Figure 24.9
A custom handler dialog box created with the MUI Xtra.

```
on muiCustom
  global gMUI
  gMUI = new(xtra "mui")
```

Next, the properties for the window must be defined. Rather than requiring you to build the lengthy window properties list from scratch, the MUI Xtra enables you to get a copy of a default property list with the *getWindowPropList* function. This default list contains all the properties needed to define a window, plus their default settings. So, all you have to do is change the settings for the properties you want to alter:

```
windowProps = getWindowPropList(gMUI)
windowProps.type = #normal
windowProps.name = "Custom MUI Dialog"
windowProps.callback = "myCallbackHandler"
windowProps.width = 160
windowProps.height = 230
windowProps.mode = #pixel
```

In this case, the name, callback handler, width, height, and mode of the window were changed. The callback handler is the name of the movie handler that is called each time the dialog box is touched by users. The mode can be set to #data, #dialogUnit, or #pixel. The #data option attempts to do the layout of the dialog box for you, whereas #dialogUnit and #pixel enable you to specify locations for items.

After the window properties are set, you need to start creating interface elements to be added to the dialog box. Create a list to which these items should be added:

```
list = []
```

Now you can create your first element. Like the window properties, the element properties are so complex that the MUI Xtra includes a special function, *getItemPropList*, which returns a default item property list. Customize this list to become a specific interface element. The following is a label element:

```
element = getItemPropList(gMui)
element.type = #label
element.value = "What size burger do you want?"
element.locH = 10
element.locV = 10
element.width = 140
element.height = 40
add list, element
```

Next, you can add a pop-up menu. This element needs a special #attributes property that includes some information specific to that interface element type.

```
element = getItemPropList(gMui)
element.type = #popupList
element.locH = 10
```

```
element.locV = 45
element.width = 140
element.height = 20
element.attributes = \
  [#popupStyle: #tiny, #valueList: ["Small", "Medium", "Large"]]
add list, element
```

After another label, the three check boxes can be added.

```
element = getItemPropList(gMui)
element.type = #label
element.value = "What do you want with your burger?"
element.locH = 10
element.locV = 70
element.width = 140
element.height = 40
add list, element

element = getItemPropList(gMui)
element.type = #checkBox
element.title = "Fries"
element.locH = 10
element.locV = 110
element.width = 140
element.height = 20
add list, element

element = getItemPropList(gMui)
element.type = #checkBox
element.title = "Chips"
element.locH = 10
element.locV = 140
element.width = 140
element.height = 20
add list, element

element = getItemPropList(gMui)
element.type = #checkBox
element.title = "Onion Rings"
element.locH = 10
element.locV = 170
element.width = 140
element.height = 20
add list, element
```

The last element needed is the "OK" button.

```
element = getItemPropList(gMui)
element.type = #defaultPushButton
element.title = "OK"
element.locH = 40
element.locV = 200
element.width = 80
element.height = 20
add list, element
```

After all the elements are ready, a call to *Initialize* creates the dialog box. You need to pass it the window properties and the element properties. Then, use *Run* to create the dialog box.

```
Initialize(gMUI, [#windowPropList: windowProps, #windowItemList: list])
Run(gMUI)
end
```

Unlike the other MUI dialog boxes, a custom dialog box does not return a simple value. Instead, it uses the callback handler defined to send any activity information. It sends every click or item change. It passes this information back as three parameters: what happened, which item it affected, and the property list for that item.

The following handler receives these messages. It is a simple handler that just sends messages to the Message window:

```
on myCallbackHandler action, elementNumber, elementList
  global gMUI
  put "Action Reported:"&&action
  if action = #itemClicked and elementList.title = "OK" then
    put action, elementList.title
    put gMUI
    Stop(gMUI,0)
    gMUI = VOID

  else if action = #itemChanged then
    newval = elementList.value
    itemName = elementList.title
    put itemName&&"changed to"&&newval
  end if
end
```

In real life, you should record the information provided to this handler in global variables or fields. Each time an item is changed, you can record the change. Or, you can reference the values of all the interface elements through the "gMUI" global.

The scope of custom MUI dialog boxes does not end with pop-ups, labels, and check boxes. You can have radio buttons, sliders, bitmaps, editable text fields, dividers, and other types of buttons as well.

To see all the possibilities, try this in the Message window:

```
put interface(xtra "Mui")
```

You will see a huge listing of all the possibilities in the MUI dialog box. This listing is also the most up-to-date one. The MUI Xtra is constantly being updated by Macromedia to accommodate new needs in the software. Just about every update of Director has a slightly different MUI Xtra.

TROUBLESHOOTING MIAWS AND ALTERNATIVES

- Always make sure you *forget* MIAWs when you want to get rid of them. Closing them only makes them invisible.

- Be sure to test all your code in a MIAW. If a Lingo error occurs in the code in a MIAW while it is running as a MIAW, Director might return bad information about what is wrong and where the problem is.

- Test your MIAWs on both platforms, and in various versions of operating systems (Windows 95 and 98, for instance), to make sure they look okay.

- The MUI Dialog Xtra was not designed for developers to use. Instead, it was made for Macromedia to use for future Director and Xtra development. It's a very advanced technique and should not be attempted by beginners. This Xtra is also not fully supported by Macromedia.

- Errors in MUI Xtra property lists can cause Director to crash. The Xtra was not created with abuse in mind. Save your movies often when you are working with the MUI Xtra.

- MIAWs can position themselves differently for different screen sizes. Be sure to test your MIAWs with different monitor settings and adjust the *rect* property accordingly.

DID YOU KNOW?

- You can use one MIAW file to create many MIAWs. Just use the *tell* command to make the MIAW go to another frame in the MIAW movie file before making it visible.

- You can use the *drawRect* property to scale the MIAW, including all bitmaps and other scalable sprites. You can use this to display a MIAW as double-pixel size, for instance.

- You can change items in a custom MUI dialog box while the dialog box is on the screen so that you can have a bitmap in the MUI dialog box that changes in reaction to another interface element.

- You can take a picture of a MIAW just as you can take a picture of the Stage. Just use "(the stage).image" in a piece of code in the MIAW, or use the *tell* command. The MIAW doesn't even have to be visible.

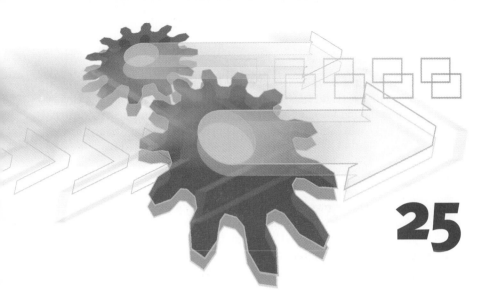

25

XTRAS

Source movies for this chapter can be found on the CD-ROM in the "Book Movies" folder under folder 25.

Even with all the features in Director 8, most developers, at one time or another, need to use an Xtra. Xtras are small files that extend Director capabilities, either by adding cast member types, Lingo commands, or authoring tools. In fact, many standard items in Director, such as vector members, network Lingo, and bitmap importing, are made possible by Xtras already installed in Director.

WHAT ARE XTRAS?

Xtras serve three purposes. First, they give Macromedia a way to develop pieces of Director independently, without requiring it to make a whole new version of Director. Features such as Java export, animated cursors, image filters, and vector graphics are all made possible by Xtras, not anything inside the Director program itself.

Xtras are also used by Macromedia to add features that not all developers may need in their finished products. Network Lingo, for instance, is not needed in a projector that does not communicate with the Internet. Because network Lingo is enabled through Xtras, these Xtras can be left out when a projector is created and the resulting projector is smaller.

Finally, Xtras can be developed by third parties to add functionality to Director that Macromedia has not provided. Many companies produce Xtras commercially, and you can purchase them. At other times, companies develop Xtras for their own use in a single product.

XTRAS THAT COME WITH DIRECTOR 8

Macromedia provides many Xtras that come installed with Director. You can find these in the Xtras folder inside the Director folder. Still more are on the Director 8.5 CD-ROM in the Xtra Partners folder. Most are Xtras that add functionality to the authoring environment, but some can be used in projectors as well.

The following list includes most of the Xtras that come with Director:

- **ActiveX**—Also known as the Control Xtra, this Windows-only Xtra enables you to access and use ActiveX controls, such as the Internet Explorer browser engine, or custom-built ActiveX programs.

- **Cursor Asset Xtra**—This Xtra allows you to use the animated cursors mentioned in Chapter 21, "Controlling the Director Environment."

- **MacroMix**—This Windows-only Xtra enables Director movies to play more than one sound at a time in Windows.

- **PhotoShop Filters**—This Xtra enables you to use PhotoShop-compatible filters on bitmap cast members. Many filters will not work in Director, and they must be compatible with PhotoShop 3.1.

- **Flash Asset**—This Xtra enables you to import Flash movies as cast members. It is also used as the engine for vector shape members.

- **Intel Effects**—This Windows-only Xtra enables you to perform a variety of processor-intensive special effects.

- **Animated GIF Asset**—This Xtra enables you to import and use animated GIFs.

- **FileIO**—This Xtra adds Lingo commands to enable you to open, save, and modify text files.

- **Font Asset Xtra and Font Xtra**—These Xtras enable you to import fonts as cast members and use these fonts in text members.

- **Import Xtra for PowerPoint**—This Xtra enables you to import Microsoft PowerPoint files. It converts the file to a Score and a Cast, complete with all the items in the original presentation.

- **MUI**—This Xtra contains code to generate many of the dialog boxes used in Director. You can also use it to create your own dialog boxes.

- **SWA Xtras**—These Xtras enable you to import and create Shockwave audio files and use them in your movies. They also enable you to compress internal sounds with Shockwave audio compression.

- **Text Asset**—This Xtra drives the text member, as well as all the text-based authoring windows, such as the script window.

- **XMLParser**—This Xtra contains additional Lingo commands for dealing with XML code, such as HTML.

- **Mix Xtras**—These Xtras enable you to import all sorts of different file types, including images and sounds.

- **Multiuser**—This Xtra enables you to communicate with the Director Multiuser server program. It also communicates with other Director projectors or Shockwave movies as long as they are networked.

- **Net Support Xtras**—These Xtras add the network Lingo commands and the protocols to support them.

- **Sound Control**—This new Xtra in Director 8 enables you to use new sound Lingo in Director 8.

- **QuickTime 4**—This Xtra enables you to use any QuickTime 4 movie, including QuickTime VR movies, as a cast member.

- **Shockwave 3D Asset Xtra**—This is the main engine behind Shockwave 3D.

- **RealMedia Asset**—This allows you to add RealMedia streams.

- **Havok**—The Havok physics Xtra works with the Shockwave 3D Xtra to allow you to easily make models in the 3D world. This gives your objects real physical properties like mass, momentum, and friction.

Many of the Xtras in the Director Xtras folder are not meant to be used in projectors. The Xtras simply extend the authoring environment. The Mix Xtras, for instance, are used only to import images and sounds. However, sometimes this Xtra is required when you are importing new images in your projector while it is running on the user's machine.

Some Xtras cannot be used in projectors at all. The QuickTime 4 Asset Options Xtra, for instance, supplies the Options dialog box that the author uses during authoring. There are also "options" Xtras for the Flash and Animated GIF Xtras. Including these with a projector results in an error message. These three Xtras are all named with the word "options," so you know not to include them.

➪ *For more information about using the FileIO Xtra,* **see** *"Using Text Files and the FileIO Xtra,"* **p. 355** *(Chapter 16, "Controlling Text")*

➪ *For more information about using the MUI Dialog Box Xtra,* **see** *"Using MUI Xtra Dialog Boxes,"* **p. 486** *(Chapter 24, "Movies in a Window and Alternatives")*

➪ *For more information about using the Shockwave 3D Asset Xtra,* **see** *Chapters 38 and 39.*

➪ *For more information about using the Havok Xtra,* **see** *"Havok Physics Engine,"* **p. 817** *(Chapter 39, "3D Lingo")*

➪ *For more information about including Xtras in your projector,* **see** *"Making Projectors,"* **p. 710** *(Chapter 36, "Delivering the Goods")*

THIRD-PARTY XTRAS

The Xtra Partners folder on the CD-ROM includes many Xtras that are not installed with Director initially. Many are only demos or restricted versions. To use these Xtras, you have to register or purchase the full product from the individual companies.

However, the versions on the CD-ROM are very useful in themselves. The Buddy API Xtra, for instance, enables you to use without cost any two functions that you choose at a time, and the Print-O-Matic Lite Xtra is very powerful in itself because it allows you to do most basic print functions.

Most of these Xtras work on both Mac and Windows platforms. However, different versions of the Xtras will be needed for each platform just as different versions of Projectors are needed for each platform.

AlphaMania and PhotoCaster

For some developers, PhotoCaster from As Is Software has been their best friend since Director 5. This Xtra enables you to import PhotoShop files. No big deal, right? After all, you can import PhotoShop files normally. However, PhotoCaster enables you to import layers from a PhotoShop file. It even preserves the Alpha channel.

With the unregistered version that comes with Director, you can import layers only one at a time, but with the full

> Some of the following Xtras are on the Director 8.0 CD, but not the 8.5 CD, and vice versa. If the Xtra is not on the CD, you can simply download it from the Web site indicated with each entry.

version, you can import an entire file with each layer as a separate cast member. Even better, the registration points in the members match up perfectly when you are finished.

Using this tool, an artist can create a many-layered document in PhotoShop, and a Director developer can import the file as layers. This means that these layers can all be placed on the Stage together. They can be made background transparent so that higher layers show through to lower ones. The result looks just like the original PhotoShop document, but each layer is still independent and can be moved or removed as the developer wants.

This technique is often used so that an artist can create an entire array of art—backgrounds, buttons, animated actors, and so on—all in one PhotoShop document. This makes the art easy for the artist to maintain, and also easy for the Director developer to import.

Figure 25.1 shows the PhotoCaster import dialog box. This is just to give you an idea of the options that are available. Try it out yourself to get more precise information about how it works.

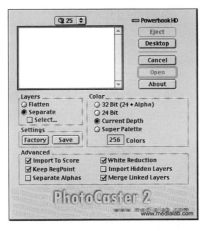

Figure 25.1
The PhotoCaster Xtra enables you to import individual layers of PhotoShop documents.

The AlphaMania Xtra from As Is Software also deals with images. It enables you to import high-quality 32-bit images with Alpha channels. Then, you can use *effector sets* to apply visual effects to the sprites. Such effects include ripple, blur, bevel, and drop shadow.

Web site: `http://www.medialab.com`

Audio Xtra

The Audio Xtra by Red Eye Software enables you to record sounds on Mac or PC, in Director or projectors. You can save these sounds as AIFF or WAV files. You can even examine the data in the sound. Figure 25.2 shows a part of the screen from the demo movie and you can see the data plotted.

PhotoCaster also takes 32-bit images and converts them to 8-bit images. It can actually take a set of images and convert them all to a new 8-bit color palette that is optimized for use across all the images.

Figure 25.2
The Audio Xtra enables you to record sound and analyze the data.

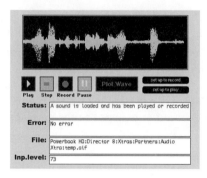

The Audio Xtra is full of Lingo options, such as setting the bit depth and frequency.

Web site: `http://www.updatestage.com/xtras/`

Autocomplete Xtra

This author-time Xtra works with the Script window. As you type a Lingo keyword, it will try to predict what you are typing and complete it for you. This is similar to how some browsers will try to complete the URL you are typing.

For Lingo programmers, this Xtra can save a lot of time and also help to avoid typos.

Web site: `http://www.peghole.com/xtras/`

Beatnik Xtra

The Beatnik Xtra is much more than just a MIDI player. It enables you to control and mix all sorts of music and sounds. Beatnik is also a plug-in for Internet browsers. It includes small files, similar to MIDI, that play music, plus a file that represents a bank of instruments.

The Beatnik Xtra with Director 8 comes with several demos. The sound quality is truly impressive. Plus, the Xtra is cross-platform, which is even more impressive.

You can use Beatnik to play simple MIDI files, if you like. The Lingo code is typical for an Xtra. First, you have to create an instance of the Xtra. Then, you have to give it some initial information. In this case, the Xtra needs to know the location of the instrument bank it is to use. This instrument bank is known as an .hsb file. You need to set the Xtra instance to look for an .hsb file. There is also a stub.hsb file that contains empty instruments. This file can be used if the Beatnik music file, called an .rmf file, has been created with its own set of internal instrument sounds.

When the Xtra instance is ready, a simple *play* command will kick off a MIDI file. To stop it, the *stop* command is used, and setting the Xtra instance to 0 clears memory.

The following code shows an example of how to get a basic MIDI file to play using Beatnik. Note that the pathnames of the .hsb file and the .mid file need to be set to something that matches the locations of these files on your computer.

```
global gBeatnik

-- This handler will initialize Beatnik
on startBeatnik
  -- create Xtra instance
  gBeatnik = new(xtra "beatnik")
  if not objectP(gBeatnik) then
    alert "Could not access Beatnik. "
    exit
  end if

  -- initialize it
  setSliceSize (gBeatnik,2)
  -- adjust the path below to match the location of the hsb file
  setSampleLibrary(gBeatnik, the applicationPath &\
      "Xtras:Beatnik:Patches020800.hsb")
  setReady(gBeatnik)

  -- check to make sure it is ready
  if not isReady(gBeatnik) then
    alert "Could not initialize Beatnik. "
    exit
  end if
end

on playMIDI
  play(gBeatnik,0,the pathname&"MYMIDI.MID")
end

on stopBeatnik
  stop(gBeatnik)
  gBeatnik = 0
end
```

Beatnik also includes Lingo commands, such as *noteOn* and *playNote*, which enable you to play one note at a time, even from different instruments.

In the preceding example, the location of the song bank is specified as the location of Director, plus the Patches020800.hsb file that should be included in the Beatnik folder in the Xtras folder. You need to change the path to use a backslash on Windows machines. You also need to modify the path of the MIDI file itself to match your MIDI file. To use this example, call "on startBeatnik" first and then "on playMIDI".

The documentation that comes with Beatnik is fairly comprehensive. Check it out for more information. This Xtra looks like it will finally bring high-quality music into Director.

Web site: http://www.beatnik.com/software/xtra_director.html

BinaryIO Xtra

This Xtra allows you to read and write binary files. The difference between a binary file and a text file (like the ones that the FileIO Xtra can handle), is that a binary file is not normally readable by word processors, or text editors. Binary files can contain values that would normally be used by text files for formatting or an end-of-file indicator.

You need the BinaryIO Xtra if you plan on reading or writing complex files that contain more than just text—for instance, if you want to create image files using an image file specification that states exactly what bytes should be present on the file.

Web site: http://www.updatestage.com/xtras/

Buddy API Xtra

The Buddy API Xtra adds a bunch of Lingo functions that deal with the computer operating system. Because the Mac and Windows operating systems differ so much, many of these functions work on only one platform or the other.

To be available for use, the Buddy API Xtra merely needs to be present in the Xtras folder. You don't have to create an instance of the Xtra or do anything else. Just use the functions as you would any other Lingo syntax.

A basic example uses this Xtra to get the operating system version. For instance, on a Mac, in the Message window, you can do this:

```
put baVersion("mac")
-- "8.5.1"
```

All functions of the Buddy API Xtra start with "ba" to distinguish them from other Lingo functions. Here are some more useful functions:

```
put baVersion("os")
-- "Mac8"
```

The other possible values for this function are "Win16", "Win95", "Win98", "WinNT", and "Mac7". The following function tests to see whether a font is installed:

```
put baFontInstalled("Arial","Plain")
-- 1
```

On Windows, you can even use Buddy API to install a font. You can also get Windows Registry information, INI files, or command-line arguments to Windows projectors, as well as restart Windows, set the default DOS directory, restrict the cursor to an area, and set screensaver information.

Buddy API can also create a folder and copy and rename files—tasks that are sadly missing from the FileIO Xtra.

Take a look at the Buddy API documentation on the CD-ROM to see a complete list of commands and functions. It is a truly impressive list. Here is a sampling:

- **SysFolder**—Returns the location of system folders.
- **CpuInfo**—Gets information about the processor installed.
- **DiskInfo**—Gets information about a disk.
- **DiskList**—Returns a list of mounted disks.
- **SoundCard**—Checks whether a sound card is installed.
- **FontInstalled**—Checks whether a font is installed.
- **FontList**—Returns a list of installed fonts.
- **FontStyleList**—Returns a list of available styles for a TrueType font.
- **CommandArgs**—Returns the command-line arguments the application was started with.
- **ScreenInfo**—Gets information about the screen.
- **MemoryInfo**—Returns information about the system memory.
- **DisableKeys**—Disables/enables key presses.
- **DisableMouse**—Disables/enables mouse clicks.
- **DisableSwitching**—Disables/enables task switching.
- **DisableScreenSaver**—Disables/enables the screensaver.
- **ScreenSaverTime**—Sets the screensaver timeout.
- **SetScreenSaver**—Sets the screensaver.
- **SetWallpaper**—Sets the desktop wallpaper.
- **SetPattern**—Sets the desktop pattern.
- **SetDisplay**—Sets the screen size and depth.
- **ExitWindows**—Exits or restarts Windows.
- **RunProgram**—Runs an external program, with command-line arguments.
- **WinHelp**—Shows a Windows help file.
- **HideTaskBar**—Shows/hides the Windows 95 taskbar.
- **PlaceCursor**—Positions the cursor.
- **RestrictCursor**—Restricts the cursor to a specific screen area.
- **FreeCursor**—Allows the cursor to move anywhere on the screen.
- **SetVolume**—Sets the volume of WAV files, MIDI files, and audio CDs.
- **GetVolume**—Gets the current volume of WAV files, MIDI files, and audio CDs.

- **InstallFont**—Installs TrueType or bitmap fonts.
- **SystemTime**—Returns the current system time/date.
- **SetSystemTime**—Sets the system time/date.
- **PrinterInfo**—Returns information about the installed printer.
- **SetPrinter**—Changes settings for the default printer.
- **RefreshDesktop**—Refreshes the desktop icons.
- **EjectDisk**—Unmounts and ejects a disk.
- **FileAge**—Returns the age of a file.
- **FileExists**—Checks whether a file exists.
- **FolderExists**—Checks whether a folder exists.
- **CreateFolder**—Creates a new folder.
- **DeleteFolder**—Deletes an empty folder.
- **RenameFile**—Renames a file.
- **DeleteFile**—Deletes a file.
- **DeleteXFiles**—Deletes files with wildcard matching.
- **XDelete**—Deletes files with wildcard matching, including subdirectories.
- **FileDate**—Returns the date of a file.
- **FileSize**—Returns the size of a file.
- **FileAttributes**—Returns the set attributes of a file.
- **SetFileAttributes**—Sets the attributes of a file.
- **RecycleFile**—Places a file in the Windows 95/NT Recycle Bin.
- **CopyFile**—Copies a file.
- **CopyXFiles**—Copies multiple files with wildcard matching.
- **XCopy**—Copies multiple files with wildcard matching, including subdirectories.
- **FileList**—Returns a list of files in a folder.
- **FolderList**—Returns a list of folders inside another folder.
- **FindFirstFile**—Searches a drive for a file.
- **FindDrive**—Searches all drives for a specified file.
- **GetFilename**—Displays a file selection dialog box.

- **GetFolder**—Displays a folder selection dialog box.

- **OpenFile**—Opens a file using its associated program.

- **PrintFile**—Prints a file using its associated program.

- **MakeShortcut**—Creates a shortcut/alias.

- **MakeShortcutEx**—Creates a Windows 95/NT shortcut.

- **FileCreator**—Returns the file creator type.

- **FileType**—Returns the file type.

- **SetFileInfo**—Sets the creator and type for a file.

- **WindowInfo**—Returns information about a window.

- **SendKeys**—Sends simulated key presses to the active window.

Web site: http://www.mods.com.au/budapi/

CD Pro Xtra

This Xtra from Penworks enables you to play music from the user's CD-ROM drive. You can re-create an entire CD player interface with commands such as Play, Stop, Loop, NumTracks, CurrentTrack, TotalTimeRemaining, and many more.

Web site: http://www.penworks.com

DirectOS Xtra

This Xtra is similar to the Buddy API Xtra. It enables you to get and set information about the user's operating system and hardware. Here's a list of what you can do according to the documentation:

- Retrieve the operating system type and exact version.

- Set and get screen resolution and color depth.

- Create, display, and operate a message box.

- Find an application associated with a specific file type.

- Create, display, and operate Open, Open Multiple, and Save file selection dialog boxes.

- Manipulate the external application's windows.

- Set cursor position or confine it to a rectangular area of the screen.

- Generate a mouse click for any of the three mouse buttons.

- Check whether any one or more keys are being held down.

- Change desktop wallpaper and pattern.

- Log off, shut down, or restart the system.

- Launch external applications at a specified state with command-line support.

- Retrieve information about disk drives, such as type, name, size, and free space.

- Check for existence of files and folders.

- Get and set file and folder attributes.

- Get file size, date, time, and version.

- Open or print a file using its associated application.

- Copy, move, delete, and recycle files.

- Retrieve a list of subfolders and files in a folder, with wildcard support.

- Create and delete folders.

- Create and resolve file or folder links and shortcuts.

- Retrieve a unique pathname to a nonexistent file that can be used as a temporary file.

- Retrieve the pathname of special system folders.

- Get and set the current working folder.

- Set the system date and time.

- Read from, write to, and delete from INI files.

- Easily read, write, and delete strings, integers, and binary data to and from the Windows Registry.

- Install screensavers; get and set their activity and time out.

- Disable/Enable Ctrl+Alt+Del, Alt+Tab, Microsoft key, and other system keys.

- Query for all available printers on the system; set the default printer and its properties.

- Retrieve the command-line string passed to your application.

- Convert long pathnames to short ones.

- Get a file's creator and type.

- Check whether a sound card is installed.

- Encrypt/decrypt text and string variables.

Web site: http://www.directxtras.com

DirectTransitions/DirectTransitions 3D Xtras

These two sets of Xtras give you several additional types of transitions. The first set, DirectTransitions, is similar to the sprite transitions included with Director 8's behavior library.

However, the second set, DirectTransitions 3D, has some unique and interesting transitions. Here is a list taken from the README file:

- **Bubbles**—Simulates the before image bubbling and popping to reveal the after image.

- **Flipboards**—Simulates boards with the before image on the front and the after image on the back flipping.

- **Fractal Fade**—Simulates the before image randomly and unevenly fading into the after image.

- **Fractal Morph I**—Simulates the before image randomly morphing into the after image with an unclearly defined center.

- **Fractal Morph II**—Simulates the before image randomly morphing into the after image with a clearly defined center.

- **Fracture**—Simulates the before image exploding into spinning fractures to reveal the after image.

- **Peel**—Simulates the before image peeling or unpeeling to reveal the after image.

Web site: `http://www.directxtras.com`

DirectXport Xtra

This Xtra allows you to export a bitmap member as a file. With Director 8's image Lingo enhancements, this Xtra is more valuable than ever. You can save a member as a BMP, DIB, EPS, GIF, JPEG, PICT, PSD, TIFF, or one of many other formats.

You can also use image effects such as Blur, OilPaint, AddNoise, Despeckle, Emboss, Sharpen, Flip, Flop, Magnify, Minify, Scale, Sample, Zoom, Roll, Edge, Implode, Solarize, Spread, Swirl, and Transparent.

There are other image export Xtras, but this is the only one I know of that is cross-platform. However, it does suffer from a very large file size, being more than 1MB.

Web site: `http://www.directxtras.com`

DM Tools

DM Tools is another set of transitions that can be easily added to Director. DM Tools is actually three sets of transitions and two Xtras that add additional effects.

> Take the time to check out other DirectXtras that come on the CD-ROM. They include Xtras that let you FTP files to and from servers, communicate with devices like joysticks, email directly from a Projector, and even turn text into computerized speech.

The first transition pack contains a fade, various transitions that fade with coloring, and many variations of wipe. The second pack contains close, cover, page turn, swap, twirl, and zoom in.

None of these transitions is overly spectacular, but the third pack, called DM Xtreme Transitions, contains glass, laser wipe, pixelate, ripple fade, roll, threshold, and wormhole. All of these are spectacular and interesting.

Web site: http://www.dmtools.com

File Xtra

The File Xtra comes on the Director 8.5 CD and is absolutely free to use. It picks up where the FileIO Xtra left off, giving you tons of commands to access all sorts of file functions. Here is a list of all of the commands in the version that ships on the CD.

- **fx_FileOpenDialog**—Presents an open dialog to the user and returns the file they select.
- **fx_FileSaveAsDialog**—Presents a save dialog to the user and returns the path and file-name they select.
- **fx_FileExists**—Checks to see if a file exists.
- **fx_FileIsLink**—Checks to see if a file is a Windows shortcut or a Mac alias.
- **fx_FileRename**—Renames a file.
- **fx_FileDelete**—Deletes a file.
- **fx_FileRecycle**—Places the file in the recycle bin or trash.
- **fx_FileCopy**—Makes a copy of a file to a new location.
- **fx_FileMove**—Moves a file to a new location.
- **fx_FileGetWriteState**—Checks to see if the file is read-only.
- **fx_FileSetWriteState**—Sets whether the file is read-only.
- **fx_FileGetModDate**—Returns the modification date of the file.
- **fx_FileGetSize**—Returns the size of a file.
- **fx_FileGetType**—Returns the Mac creator and file type or the Windows dot-three exten-sion.
- **fx_FileSetType**—Allows you to set the Mac creator and file type or the Windows dot-three extension.
- **fx_FileCompare**—Tells you if two files have the same size and modification date.
- **fx_FileOpenDocument**—Opens a file with the application that is associated with it.
- **fx_FilePrintDocument**—Prints a file using the application that is associated with it.
- **fx_FileGetAppPath**—Returns the path of the application that is associated with the docu-ment.

- **fx_FileRunApp**—Launches the application associated with the document.

- **fx_LinkCreate**—Creates a Mac alias or a Windows shortcut.

- **fx_LinkResolve**—Returns the actual file that an alias or shortcut links to.

- **fx_FolderSelectDialog**—Opens a dialog that lets the user select a folder.

- **fx_FolderGetSpecialPath**—Returns the path to special system folders, like the preferences folder, the favorites folder, the control panels folder, and so on.

- **fx_FolderExists**—Checks to see if a folder exists.

- **fx_FolderCreate**—Creates a new folder.

- **fx_FolderDelete**—Removes a folder.

- **fx_FolderRecycle**—Places a folder in the Windows recycle bin or the Mac trash folder.

- **fx_FolderCopy**—Copies a folder to a new path.

- **fx_FolderMove**—Moves a folder to a new path.

- **fx_FolderSyncOneWay**—Modifies the contents of one folder to match the contents of another.

- **fx_FolderSyncBothWays**—Modifies the contents of two folders to make them both match.

- **fx_FolderToList**—Creates a list of files and folders at a location.

- **fx_VolumeExists**—Checks to see if a hard drive or other volume exists.

- **fx_VolumeGetFreeBytes**—Checks to see how much space is left on a hard drive or other volume.

- **fx_VolumeGetTotalBytes**—Returns the size of a hard drive or other volume.

- **fx_VolumeIsCDROM**—Checks to see if a volume is a CD.

- **fx_VolumeIsRemovable**—Checks to see if a volume is removeable media like a Zip disk.

- **fx_VolumeEject**—Ejects a volume, such as a Zip disk or CD.

- **fx_VolumesToList**—Returns a list of all volumes.

- **fx_ErrorNumber**—Returns an error number for the last File Xtra operation.

- **fx_ErrorString**— Returns an error string for the last File Xtra operation.

Web site: `http://www.kblab.net/xtras`

LiveCD

This Xtra from Trevi Media enables you to embed HTML pages as single sprites. Although text members also enable you to do that, LiveCD actually enables you to embed images into these documents.

Not only that, but you can use Netscape plug-ins as well. This means you can embed things such as Adobe Acrobat files into your movies.

Web site: http://www.trevimedia.com/products/livecd/

MasterApp Xtra

This Xtra is a more reliable alternative to the *open* command in Director. With MasterApp, you can reliably open documents in applications without knowing the exact path of the application. You can even do things such as open documents in applications that are already running, or open documents in applications that did not create the document.

This Xtra also enables you to get information about running applications and to send messages to some applications.

Web site: http://www.updatestage.com/xtras/masterapp.html

OSControl Xtra

Want to add beveled button, progress bars, arrow button, sliders, radio buttons, and check-boxes to your Director movies? Sure you can do all of these with complex behaviors and lots of bitmaps, but the OSControl Xtra allows you to add them much more easily.

You can even add elements like buttons and have them change to reflect the user's operating system: Mac or Windows. This is the type of functionality that really should be part of Director, but isn't. This Xtra fills the gap.

Web site: http://www.peghole.com/xtras/

PDF Xtra

Adobe Acrobat files have been around for a while but are still gaining popularity. They present text in a highly formatted way on the screen, so they look more like printed pages than screen text.

Many online versions of documents are given in Acrobat format, also called PDF after the dot-three extension that the files use. Companies use them for reports and publications use them for articles and books.

With the PDF Xtra, you can embed Acrobat files right into Director. But it doesn't stop there. You can also control the presentation of the files via Lingo. This means you can build your own page-turning buttons and such.

Web site: http://www.integration.qc.ca/

PiMz Image Xtra

The PiMz Xtra enables you to import PhotoShop files. You can select from a variety of options, many of which you can see in Figure 25.3.

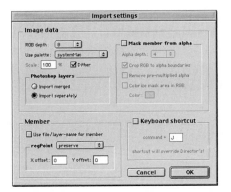

Figure 25.3
The PiMz Image Xtra enables you to import PhotoShop documents as individual layers.

I particularly like the idea that you can import many images with the registration point somewhere other than the center. For instance, you can set the registration point to the upper left for every image.

Web site: `http://pimz.com/xtras/ImageImport.html`

Print-O-Matic Lite

Director's printing functionality is restricted to the *printFrom* command. Although this is a nice feature for animators who want a frame of animation printed to help with development, it has little use in projectors.

All that the *printFrom* command can do is print a screenshot of the Stage. You can set a reduction amount, or choose to print one frame or a series of frames.

The Print-O-Matic Lite Xtra adds the *print* command to Lingo. You can use this command to print any cast member or text string.

Although this is already an improvement over the *printFrom* command, Print-O-Matic does a lot more when you create an instance of the Xtra and use more of its commands. A typical handler looks like this:

```
on printPage
  gPrintDoc = new(xtra "PrintOMatic_Lite")
  if not objectP(gPrintDoc) then
    alert "Unable to use Print-O-Matic"
    exit
  end if
  setDocumentName gPrintDoc, "My Document"
  setMargins gPrintDoc, Rect(36,36,36,36)
  setLandscapeMode gPrintDoc, TRUE
  append gPrintDoc, member "myMember"
  if doJobSetup(gPrintDoc) then print gPrintDoc
  gPrintDoc = 0
end
```

The handler first needs to create the Xtra instance. Then it checks to make sure that it was created. It then uses the *setDocumentName* command to name the print job. It uses the *setMargins* and *setLandscapeMode* commands to set the margins to about a half an inch and to print in landscape mode rather than vertically.

The *append* command is used to add items to the print job. In this case, just one member is added. However, you can add members, sprites, and even plain text.

Finally, the *doJobSetup* command is used to bring up the operating system's print dialog box. This function returns *TRUE* if the user clicks the OK button. Then, the *print* command sends the whole thing to the printer.

The full version of Print-O-Matic enables you to perform more functions and even draw lines directly to the print buffer.

Web site: `http://www.printomatic.com`

Relaunch Utility

You might have run across this situation before: You want Director to run a program, perhaps an installer, and then quit. The user then interacts with the other program for a while, until the user quits or the program ends. Then, it would be great if the Director projector would automatically relaunch.

The Relaunch Utility does just that. It can be particularly useful to get a user to run the QuickTime 4 installer, and then have them safely return to their projector.

Web site: `http://www.updatestage.com/xtras/`

TextCruncher Xtra

If you have ever had problems processing text with Lingo's string commands because they are too slow, TextCruncher is for you. When you drop it into your Xtras folder, it simply adds Lingo commands to your arsenal.

I tried the *FindFirst* command, which is a substitute for the Lingo *offset* command. In my tests, *FindFirst* was five times faster. In addition, TextCruncher also includes a host of other text-processing commands. Here is a partial list:

- **FindFirst**
- **FindNext**
- **FindAll**
- **GetWordOfCharPosition**
- **GetLineOfCharPosition**
- **GetItemOfCharPosition**
- **ReplaceFirst**

- ReplaceNext

- ReplaceAll

- GetListOfWords

- GetListOfLines

- GetListOfItems

- ToUpperCase

- ToLowerCase

- HardWrapText

- HardCenterText

- HardAlignTextRight

Web site: http://www.updatestage.com/xtras/

UIHelper Xtra

This mysterious little Xtra is on the CD with absolutely no documentation at all. By using "put xtra("UiHelper").interface()" in the Message window, you can see what functions are available.

The UIHelper is meant to be able to help you create tools that run inside Director. It can activate a Cast or window, get the parameters set for a behavior in the Score, and a variety of other odd functions useful to Xtra or tool developers.

V12-Database Engine Xtra

This Xtra is useful if you need to connect your Director movie to a large database. You can maintain and search the database, which can be local or across the Internet.

This Xtra is packed full of database features. There is a full version and a cheaper "light" version available.

Web site: http://www.integration.qc.ca

USING XTRA LINGO

A few Lingo properties and functions help you work with Xtras. You can, for instance, determine whether an Xtra is working simply by trying to use it. If the initial *new* command does not return a valid object, you know there has been an error. Use the *objectP* function to determine whether you have a valid object:

```
xObj = new(xtra "FileIO")
put objectP(xObj)
-- 1
```

If you want to determine whether an Xtra is present before you try to use it, you can take a look at each Xtra present by using the *name* property, as well as the *number* property, of the *xtras* object. Here is a handler that checks for the existence of an Xtra:

```
on checkForXtra xtraname
  repeat with i = 1 to the number of xtras
    if the name of xtra i = xtraname then
      return TRUE
    end if
  end repeat
  return FALSE
end
```

You can test this handler in the Message window:

```
put checkForXtra("FileIO")
-- 1
put checkForXtra("xxx")
-- 0
```

Two other properties also tell you about what Xtras are available. The *the xtraList* property returns a long list of what Xtras are available. Each item in the list contains a #name and #version property.

There is also a *the movieXtraList* property that corresponds to the dialog box you get when you choose Modify, Movie, Xtras. Each item is a list that contains either a name, a #packageFiles list, or both. The #packageFiles list contains a #name and a #version, which give the movie the information it needs to download the Xtra from the Internet for use in Shockwave.

For most Xtras, you can use the interface function to get a list of all the possible commands, properties, and usage guidelines. The results vary from Xtra to Xtra, depending on what the developer decided this function should return. You can use it in the Message window by typing something like this:

```
put interface(xtra "FileIO")
```

USING XTRAS IN SHOCKWAVE

It used to be nearly impossible to use Xtras in Shockwave. Shockwave itself worked fine with them. However, to use them it had to have a copy of the Xtra. This meant that the end users had to download the Xtra and place it in their Shockwave folders.

Easy enough for a developer, but impossible for the general public, who might not know about browser plug-ins and where to find their folders on their hard drives.

Starting with Director 7, you can use some Xtras through the automatic downloading function in Shockwave. This means that when a movie signals Shockwave that it needs an Xtra, Shockwave downloads it from the Internet and installs it.

For this to happen, the Xtra developer first has to go through the proper channels with Macromedia so that the Xtra is authorized to be downloadable. This is to prevent someone from making a viruslike Xtra that would cause harm.

Many of the Xtras mentioned earlier in this chapter are downloadable. Check with the Xtra manufacturer to find out whether the one you need is downloadable. Because this is a desirable feature, most Xtra developers note this on their Web pages and documentation.

To enable your movie to download Xtras, your first stop is choosing Modify, Movie, Xtras. This will bring up a dialog box with the names of Xtras that your movie needs. If the Xtra you need is not listed, click the Add button to add it.

After it's in the list of needed Xtras, select it and click the Download If Needed check box below the list. At this point Director calls out to the Internet to check the location of the Xtra. You will see a short-lived Downloading progress bar.

Now that your movie is set to download the Xtra if needed, you can check to see exactly what it will do. In the Message window, use *put the movieXtraList* to display a list of Xtras that the movie thinks it needs. This should be the same as the Modify, Movie, Xtras dialog box list, but with more information.

For instance, the item in the list that represents the QuickTime Xtra looks like this:

```
[#name: "QuickTime Asset", #packageUrl: "http://download.macromedia.com/pub/
shockwave8/xtras/QuickTime3Asset/QuickTime3Asset", #packageFiles: [[#fileName:
"QuickTime Asset", #version: "8.0"]]]
```

You can see that the Director movie knows which file to download and where it is located on the Internet. Other Xtras may include multiple files if they are needed by the Xtra.

When you run the movie for the first time in a browser, you will see a dialog box that asks whether you want the Xtra installed. Clicking OK causes the installation to proceed. Then the movie will run. It is as simple as that.

The Xtra install dialog box is necessary because of Internet security concerns. An Xtra developer can easily make an Xtra that would do harm to a user's machine. This is why Xtras must be certified by Macromedia before they can be made downloadable. The security dialog box is a second form of protection, allowing the user to abort the addition of the Xtra to Shockwave. You should put a warning about this on your Web pages so that users know to expect the Xtra install dialog box and do not feel that it will cause a security problem.

OTHER XTRAS

Appendix H, "Guide to Xtras," lists most, but not all, the Xtras available at the time of printing. Because Xtras are developed independently of versions of Director, new ones come out all the time. Xtras are also updated constantly.

It is possible, maybe even likely, that a new Xtra will be announced by some company the day after this book is published. Another developer will decide to retire an Xtra as well. For these reasons, trying to compile a list of available Xtras is difficult.

It is also unnecessary. Several online resources list the locations of Xtras on the Internet. These are usually updated fairly frequently, so they are always more up to date than a book. Check Appendix C, "Online Resources," for a list of Web locations.

TROUBLESHOOTING XTRAS

- Remember that Xtras require different files for different platforms. If you use the Buddy API Xtra, for instance, you have to bundle the Mac version with your Mac projectors and the Windows version with Windows projectors.

- After you decide to use an Xtra with a movie, you must include it with the projector when you are finished. You can do this in several ways. See Chapter 36, "Creating Java Applets," for detailed information.

- If you are thinking about making your own Xtra, beware of the trap into which many developers fall: They often assume that a task cannot be done with Lingo alone, when it can. Director 8 Lingo is so powerful that you should always carefully consider the option of using Lingo before commissioning an Xtra.

- If you ever get the message "A duplicate Xtra has been found…" when starting Director, this means that you have to go to your Xtras folder and find the duplicate. Unfortunately, Director does not point you in any direction. Because the same Xtra can have different filenames, it might be hard to find the culprit. Many times, you have to remove one Xtra at a time and restart Director until the mystery is solved.

DID YOU KNOW?

- The xtrainfo.txt file contains information that determines which Xtras are bundled with projectors by default. You can change this each time you make a projector, or edit this file to change the defaults.

- While authoring, you can use the *showXlib* command in the Message window to see a simple list of all the Xtras present. It isn't as detailed as *put the xtraList*, but most of the time it is what you need to see which Xtras are there.

- If you want to access an Xtra that is not in the Xtras folder, you can open it with the *openXlib* command, followed by the full or relative pathname. You can also use *closeXlib* to free up memory when you are finished with the Xtra.

26

DEVELOPING FOR DEVELOPERS

IN THIS CHAPTER

Source movies for this chapter can be found on the CD-ROM in the "Book Movies" folder under folder 26.

Many times, the Lingo programmer's job in a company is not to develop content directly, but to build templates and tools for others, usually referred to as "multimedia authors." These tools can take the form of Lingo-based Xtras, a behavior library, or even a set of Director movie templates. This chapter is all about creating those tools, either by Score recording, by creating Xtras, or by making behavior libraries.

SCORE RECORDING

Although behaviors can change the properties of a sprite while the movie is running, these properties all return to their default Score settings when the movie is done. Lingo does have the capability, however, to effect real changes in the Score.

To make changes in the Score, you need to use Score recording commands. You can define the beginning of a Score recording session, and then make changes to sprites. These changes then become "real," because the Score is permanently changed. You can even insert and delete frames.

Animators can use this technique to build Score-based animations, rather than just having Lingo control the animation during playback. This enables Lingo developers to make tools for animators that result in visible Score changes.

Writing to the Score

Creating or modifying sprites in the Score is fairly simple. First, you must use the *beginRecording* command. Every change to a sprite between the *beginRecording* and the *endRecording* command effects a change in the Score.

After a Score recording session begins, you can use regular Lingo commands, such as *go*, to jump around in the Score. When you start using sprite properties, you begin to make real changes.

The following is a handler that adds the member number 1 to the Score in sprite 7. It uses *go* to make sure that it is placing it in frame 1:

```
on simpleChange
  beginRecording
    go to frame 1
    sprite(7).member = member(1)
    sprite(7).loc = point(100,100)
    updateFrame
  endRecording
end
```

The command *updateFrame* is actually where the change is made. You need to issue either an *updateFrame* or an *insertFrame* command. The first command places all your changes in the current frame, and advances the movie to the next frame. The *insertFrame* command places the movie in the current frame, makes a copy of that frame, changes and all, and then inserts it after the current frame. The playback head is now in the inserted frame.

The following handler performs a more complex task. It inserts frames, beginning with the current one, and moves sprite 1 over to the right 10 pixels each time. It does this until the sprite reaches the horizontal location of 600:

```
on recordMove
  sNum = 1
  minX = 0
  maxX = 600
  stepSize = 10

  beginRecording
    x = minX
    repeat while TRUE
      sprite(sNum).locH = x
      insertFrame
      x = x + stepSize
      if x > maxX then exit repeat
    end repeat
  endRecording
end
```

Although this handler doesn't really do anything that a behavior can't do while the movie is running, it demonstrates creating animation in the Score with Score recording. A tool such as this can enable animators to easily add common animations to the Score, while also using traditional Score animation techniques in other sprites.

Score Recording Tools

A more useful Score recording handler takes existing sprites and manipulates them in a way that no other tool can. Director includes the Align tool, which enables you to lock horizontal and vertical positions of sprites to each other. However, what is missing is a tool that evenly spaces sprites.

The next handler does just that. It takes three or more sprites in the same frame, finds the minimum and maximum horizontal and vertical positions, and then uses that information to evenly space them. For simplicity, the handler assumes that the first sprite should be positioned first, the second should be positioned second, and so on. Therefore, it does not work in cases where you have the sprites out of order.

The first thing that this handler does is get the *scoreSelection*. This is a list of lists that tells you what the author has selected in the Score. For instance, if sprite 7 of frame 5 is selected, you get [[7,7,5,5]]. The first two numbers of each item are the sprite, and the third and fourth numbers represent the frame range. To get this handler to work, three sprites in the score need to be selected.

```
on evenlySpace
  set ss = the scoreSelection

  if ss.count < 3 then
    alert "You must select at least 3 items"
    exit
  end if

  -- find max and min locations
  minX = sprite(ss[1][1]).locH
  maxX = minX
  minY = sprite(ss[1][1]).locV
  maxY = minY
  repeat with i = 2 to ss.count
    x = sprite(ss[i][1]).locH
    y = sprite(ss[i][1]).locV

    if x < minX then minX = x
    if x > maxX then maxX = x
    if y < minY then minY = y
    if y > maxY then maxY = y
  end repeat

  -- figure out spacing
  spaceX = (maxX - minX)/(ss.count-1)
  spaceY = (maxY - minY)/(ss.count-1)

  -- record all changes
  beginRecording

    -- space in order of sprite number
    x = minX
    y = minY
    repeat with i = 1 to ss.count
      sprite(ss[i][1]).loc = point(x,y)
      x = x + spaceX
      y = y + spaceY
    end repeat

    -- set changes and end recording
    updateFrame
  endRecording

end
```

You can also use *the selection of castLib* to determine which members are selected in the Cast window. If the author has selected members 2 through 5 and member 8, for instance, you get this result:

```
put the selection of castLib 1
-- [[2, 5], [8, 8]]
```

Using *the selection of castLib* and *the scoreSelection,* you can determine which members and sprites the author is pointing to at any time. This property can be used to build tools that react to different author selections.

Setting Behaviors and Parameters Through Lingo

You can also set the behaviors attached to a sprite and the values of the parameters in them. This is represented as a list, which can be read with the *scriptList* property of a sprite.

```
put sprite(2).scriptList
-- [[(member 2 of castLib 1), "[#jumpframe: 7]"], [(member 3 of castLib 1), 0]]
```

You can set this entire list with the new *setScriptList* command. You can use the format returned with the *scriptList* property. Each behavior is a sublist of two elements: the behavior member and a property list of parameters and values. The parameters list has quotation marks around it for some strange reason.

```
sprite(2).setScriptList([[member("My Behavior"), "[#jumpframe: 12]",
[member("My Other Behavior"),0]]
```

Another strange fact about this command is that you cannot use it inside a score recording session. So, to truly create sprites in the Score with behaviors attached, you need to do some work within score recording, such as adding the sprites, and some after it, such as setting the script list.

CREATING MIAW XTRAS

After you have built a handy routine like the "on evenlySpace" handler described previously, it can be used to create an Xtra. These are not the sort of Xtras that were discussed in Chapter 25, "Xtras." Instead of creating an Xtra using C or some other programming language, you are simply creating a Director movie and then placing it in the Xtras folder.

After a Director movie is in the Xtras folder, it appears in the Xtras menu. When selected, it appears in a Movie in a Window (MIAW). It can then tell the Stage to do things, such as initiate Score recording.

The "on evenlySpace" handler can be turned into a simple Xtra by placing it in its own movie. Make the Stage size of that movie very small, maybe 240×160. Then, add a button that calls the "on evenlySpace" handler. This handler needs one change: The *tell the stage* command must be added before the first line, and an *end tell* must be added at the end. With this change, this handler directs all the commands at the Stage, not the MIAW Xtra itself.

All that is left is to place the Director movie in the Xtras folder. You can even compress it into a .dcr file before doing this. Doing so makes the Xtra available to be used, but makes the scripts unavailable to other developers. Therefore, you can produce Lingo-based Xtras for distribution without worrying about someone stealing your code.

⇨ *For more information on using MIAWs, see "Using MIAWs," p. 476 (Chapter 24, "Movies in a Window and Alternatives")*

USING BEHAVIOR LIBRARIES

Just as a Director movie can be placed in the Xtras folder, a Director cast library file can be placed in the Libs folder. This makes it available in the Library palette.

Director 8 already comes complete with a large set of behavior libraries that appear in this palette. Take a look at the Libs folder in the Director folder to see how these are arranged. Some cast libraries are just sitting in the folder, whereas others are in subfolders. This structure determines how the libraries appear in the Library palette pop-up menu.

You can use this structure by creating a new folder in the Libs folder for your own custom behaviors. The same structure relates the Xtras folder to the Xtras menu.

You are not restricted to just behaviors. You can also place any other type of cast member in a library Cast. You can store clip art, common sounds, and even movie scripts. Depending on the type of member, you can drag these members from the Library palette onto the Stage, Score, Cast, or all three.

You can even provide custom icons for cast members in a library. When you are building the members of the cast library to be used as a library, you can open the Property Inspector and Control-click on the Mac or right-click in Windows to bring up a pop-up menu, which enables you to copy, cut, and paste icons. The special icons with the behaviors in Director's built-in libraries were given their special icons in this way.

Many developers have a behavior library that they constantly update as needed. The Libs folder is the perfect place to keep this cast library so that the behaviors are always accessible.

If you want to prevent multimedia authors from using behaviors in places where they are not wanted, use the *on isOkToAttach* handler. It can analyze the sprite that the behavior is being dropped onto and prevent it from going on to one that it was not made for. See Chapter 14, "Creating Behaviors," for more details.

TROUBLESHOOTING DEVELOPING FOR DEVELOPERS

- Score recording always requires an *insertFrame* or *updateFrame* command to make the changes stick. Forgetting this is a common mistake.

- Score recording has been known to correctly update the Score, but to not show the changes in the Score window until the movie has been rewound and played again. Keep this in mind if it doesn't seem to work at first.

- MIAW Xtras are easy to create and open, but not so easy to eliminate. If you permit users to click the close box in the window to make the Xtra go away, the window is actually still there. You can even see it in *the windowList*. A good idea is to place a "forget(the activeWindow)" in the *on closeWindow* handler. This forces the window to be discarded when users click the close button.

DID YOU KNOW?

- If you don't want users to see each change in a Score recording session as it occurs, you can set *the updateLock* to *TRUE* at the beginning of the session. This causes the Stage to freeze while changes are made.

- You can set *the windowType* of a MIAW Xtra after it has been opened. The programmer will see this change occur, however.

- You can also set the MIAW Xtra's screen position after it has been opened.

VIII

USING DIRECTOR TO CREATE
PROFESSIONAL APPLICATIONS

IN THIS PART

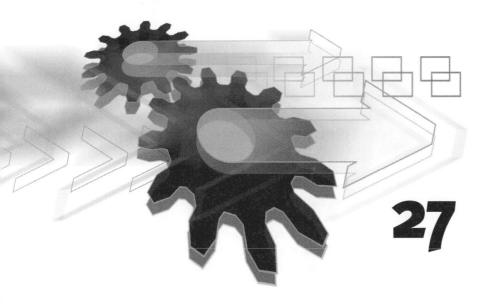

27

EDUCATIONAL APPLICATIONS

IN THIS CHAPTER

Source movies for this chapter can be found on the CD-ROM in the "Book Movies" folder under folder 27.

Using a single Director command, function, or property is easy for novice and advanced users alike. However, putting syntax together to make a useful program is a much harder task.

This chapter, and the chapters that follow, give examples of typical types of programs created with Director. An overview of each program is given, followed by the Lingo required to put it together. All this code, and in fact a complete demonstration movie, is included on the CD-ROM that accompanies this book. To get the most out of these chapters, look at the movie on the CD-ROM to see how the Lingo code, Score, Cast, and Stage all work together.

This first applications chapter focuses on educational programs. Five typical programs were selected. The first is a simple matching game in which users must click and drag items on the right to items on the left. The second is a drawing program that gives users the opportunity to create their own artwork. The third program is a simple example of using Lingo to turn on and off overlay sprites such as transparent overlays in a textbook. The fourth program is a geography quiz, in which users must answer questions by clicking a map. The last program simulates a standardized test.

CREATING A MATCHING GAME

A matching game is fairly common in most educational CD-ROMs. Users see two lists of words, names, or phrases. If they were working on paper, they would then draw lines between the two lists, matching up those items that are related.

For instance, users can be asked to match up inventors and their inventions. The two lists appear as this:

Benjamin Franklin	Cotton Gin
Thomas Edison	Telegraph
Eli Whitney	Electricity
Alfred Nobel	Light Bulb
Samuel Morse	Rocket Engine
Robert Goddard	Dynamite

The two lists do not match up directly, of course; such a game would be very simple.

When this type of activity is done as a computer program, drawing lines is no longer necessary. Instead, users can drag one item over to the other. Sometimes graphics are drawn to show that items fit together, like puzzle pieces.

Figure 27.1 shows a screen of a matching game program. It includes two columns of six words each. The items are drawn so that they appear to be pieces that have been ripped apart from each other. The user's task is to drag the pieces on the right over to match the pieces on the left.

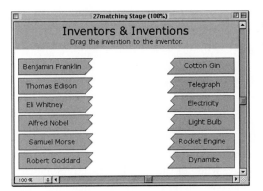

Figure 27.1
The matching game uses two columns of items. Users must drag items on the right over to their matches on the left.

To start a project like this, which requires many similar cast members, first come up with a logical naming scheme for the members. In this case, all the members on the left are named "left X", where the X stands for a number. All the members on the right are named "right X". The number assigned as the X signifies which left and right elements match up. So "Benjamin Franklin" is "left 1" and "Electricity" is "right 1".

The left elements do not move, so they do not need to have any behavior attached to them. The right elements, however, need a behavior. In fact, this behavior can take care of the entire game.

The behavior starts off with the declaration of the properties:

```
property pDrag -- is the sprite currently being dragged
property pOffset -- the cursor offset used in the drag
property pOrigLoc -- the starting location of the sprite
property pLocked -- is the sprite locked in place
```

When the behavior starts, it needs to record the original location of the sprite, plus set some other properties. The original location is needed so that when a user drags the item, but does not successfully match it to the correct item, it snaps back into place.

```
-- set all of the properties that need it
on beginSprite me
  pOrigLoc = sprite(me.spriteNum).loc
  pDrag = FALSE
  pLocked = FALSE
end
```

When the user clicks the sprite, the dragging begins. But first, the *on mouseDown* handler checks to see whether the sprite is already locked in place. If it is, dragging is not allowed any more. The *on mouseDown* handler also determines the offset between the mouse and the sprite location, so it can be used to make it possible to drag a sprite from any location on the sprite, not just the center.

```
on mouseDown me
  -- don't allow to drag if already in place
```

```
  if pLocked = TRUE then exit

  -- set to drag
  pDrag = TRUE

  -- record offset between cursor and sprite
  pOffset = sprite(me.spriteNum).loc - the mouseLoc
end
```

When the user releases the mouse button, the dragging comes to an end. It also means that the behavior must check to see whether the item has found its match. The *on mouseUpOutside* handler is also called, in case the user has moved so quickly that the mouse is not over the sprite when the mouse button is released.

```
-- turn off dragging and check for correct placement
on mouseUp me
  pDrag = FALSE
  checkLock(me)
end
on mouseUpOutside me
  pDrag = FALSE
  checkLock(me)
end
```

This behavior uses the *on prepareFrame* handler to reposition the sprite as it is being dragged. This keeps the sprite location as close as possible to the mouse location. However, handlers such as *on exitFrame* or *on enterFrame* produce virtually identical results.

```
-- reposition sprite if being dragged
on prepareFrame me
  if pDrag then
    sprite(me.spriteNum).loc = the mouseLoc + pOffset
  end if
end
```

The "on checkLock" handler takes the name of the member and determines which other member it should match. It then searches all the sprites for that matching member. When it finds it, it checks to determine whether the two sprites are close enough to be locked together. If a lock is called for, the sprites are set to be at the same location. Then, the "on checkForDone" handler is called to see whether the game is complete.

Because matching sprites are intended to lock together with their locations being equal, the two bitmaps need to be drawn so that their registration points determine how the two sprites appear on the Stage relative to each other. In the case of the images in Figure 27.1, the registration points for the left-side pieces are at the right side, and the registration points of the right-side pieces are on the left side. Therefore, when they are placed in the same location on the Stage, they appear to lock together, side by side. Check the movie on the CD-ROM to see exactly where the registration points are.

```
--check to see if there is a match
on checkLock me

  -- determine match member's name
  memName = sprite(me.spriteNum).member.name
  memNum = memName.word[2]
  matchName = "left"&&memNum

  -- check all the sprites
  repeat with i = 1 to the lastChannel

    -- is it the matching sprite?
    if sprite(i).member.name = matchName then

      -- is it close enough to lock in place?
      if closeEnough(me, sprite(i).loc,sprite(me.spriteNum).loc) then

        -- place sprite in exact location
        sprite(me.spriteNum).loc = sprite(i).loc

        -- set lock
        pLocked = TRUE

        -- change colors
        sprite(me.spriteNum).bgColor = rgb("#CCCCCC")
        sprite(i).bgColor = rgb("#CCCCCC")

        -- see if all sprites are locked in place
        checkForDone(me)

        -- leave this handler
        exit
      end if
    end if
  end repeat

  -- never found a matching member close enough
  -- return to original position
  sprite(me.spriteNum).loc = pOrigLoc
end
```

This next handler is used by the "on checkLock" handler to determine whether two pieces are close enough to each other to lock. It checks to see whether both the horizontal and vertical locations are within 10 pixels of each other:

```
-- determine if two locations are close
on closeEnough me, loc1, loc2
  maxdistance = 10 -- use 10 pixels as max distance
  if abs(loc1.locH - loc2.locH) < maxdistance then
    if abs(loc1.locV - loc2.locV) < maxdistance then
      -- close enough, return TRUE
      return TRUE
    end if
  end if
  return FALSE
end
```

This handler, which is called by the "on checkForDone" handler, returns a *TRUE* if the item has been locked in place:

```
-- simply report on condition of pLocked
on amIDone me
  return pLocked
end
```

To determine whether all the pieces have been locked in place, an "amIDone" message is sent to every sprite. Sprites that do not have this behavior attached to them return a simple *VOID*. The rest return a *TRUE* or *FALSE*. If a *FALSE* is encountered, the handler ends, because the game is not complete. If no *FALSE* is found in all the sprites, the movie jumps to the payoff, or final, frame:

```
-- check all sprites to see if all are locked
on checkForDone me
  repeat with i = 1 to the lastChannel

    -- ask a sprite if it is done
    done = sendSprite(sprite i,#amIDone)

    -- sprite did not know about #amIDone
    if voidP(done) then next repeat

    -- sprite returned that it was not locked
    if done = FALSE then exit
  end repeat

  -- if they got here, then all are done
  -- go to another frame
  go to frame "payoff"
end
```

The only other Lingo script needed to make this program work is a simple looping frame script. The rest is taken care of by one behavior. This means that you can easily add more items to the game. The trick is to create two matching members, both left and right items, and name them correctly. Then put them both on the Stage and drop this behavior onto the right-side item. You don't even have to worry about which sprites these members are in.

When this game is done, the movie moves to the "payoff" frame. Here, you can place any sort of sound or animation that you want. You can even have the matching items animate, because you already know exactly where they must be positioned for the game to end.

Another consideration is sound. Using the *puppetSound* command, you can add sounds that activate when the items lock in place and sounds that activate when there is a mismatch.

If you want to use text members, rather than bitmaps, there is only one thing to consider. Text members always have their registration points set to the upper left of the member. So, to match them up, you need to come up with a new way of determining when items "lock" and a new standard of how to position the items when they are locked. For instance, you might want to make the items lock to the upper-right corner of the rectangle of the sprite, instead of the location of the sprite, which is actually the upper-left corner.

⇨ For more information on behaviors that drag sprites, **see** "Dragging Sprites," **p. 297** (Chapter 15, "Graphic Interface Elements")

MAKING A DRAWING ACTIVITY

Drawing is a common activity in educational computer programs for younger kids. These programs are usually based on the early simple draw programs made for the computers in the '70s and '80s.

Users can click the screen and draw while moving the mouse. The example used in this section includes different colors that users can choose from, as well as different brushes.

With the new image Lingo in Director 8, drawing is actually fairly simple. All you have to do is store an *image* object in a behavior property. As users paint, you can use *copyPixels* to imprint another bitmap onto that *image*, and then apply it back to the member on the Stage.

If users move the mouse too quickly, subsequent impressions of the member can be far apart, leaving a gap in the drawing. This doesn't happen when you are drawing with a marker or crayon on paper. Therefore, this program must handle cases where the mouse is moved quickly, and place smooth lines between the two points.

Figure 27.2 shows the sample movie. On the left are some colors, with the current color outlined. Under that are some brushes with the current brush outlined. The main area starts off blank, and users can draw in it.

Figure 27.2
With this simple drawing applet,
users can change colors and
brushes. They can use the color
white, along with a larger brush,
to "erase."

This movie also has one large behavior driving it. However, it isn't on a sprite, but in the Frame Script channel. All the drawing is done in one large bitmap member, which is placed on the Stage in sprite 1.

The properties of the main behavior include one that determines whether drawing is happening at the moment, one that records the location of the last draw impression, the member to use for drawing (which can be considered the brush), and the color being used for drawing.

```
property pCanvas -- image of canvas
property pDraw -- drawing in progress
property pLastDrawLoc -- last spot drawn on
property pBrush -- member to use to paint
property pColor -- color to paint with
```

The behavior starts off by setting the last draw location to 0, which you can use as a sign that there is no last draw location. The property "pBrush" is set to the member "Brush 1". The "pCanvas" property holds the image being drawn to. The "pCanvas" property is initialized by getting the image of the existing canvas member. Then, "on clearImage" is called to fill the image with white.

```
on beginSprite me
  pLastDrawLoc = 0 -- no last drawing loc
  pBrush = member("brush 1")
  pCanvas = member("Canvas").image -- get starting image
  clearImage(me) -- start image empty
end

on clearImage me
  -- fill with white
  pCanvas.fill(member("Canvas").rect, [#color: rgb("FFFFFF")])
  member("Canvas").image = pCanvas
end
```

When users click the Stage, the drawing begins. All that is really needed is to set the "pDraw" property to *TRUE*. However, it is also useful to show users a representation of the brush currently in use. Because all the brushes are 1-bit members that are less than 16×16 in size, they can also be used as cursors with the *cursor* command:

```
on mouseDown me
  pDraw = TRUE
  cursor([member pBrush, member pBrush])
end
```

When users lift up the mouse button, drawing should end. The "pDraw" property needs to be reset. Because the next place users start to draw might be a different spot, "pLastDrawLoc" is reset so that a line is not drawn connecting the end point of this brush stroke with the starting point of the next. The cursor is also reset.

```
on mouseUp me
  pDraw = FALSE
  pLastDrawLoc = 0 -- forget last drawing loc
  cursor(-1)
end
```

The drawing is actually done with the *on exitFrame* handler. This means that the drawing is updated exactly once per frame. Because you want the program to run as smoothly as possible, you should turn the frame rate for the movie up to the maximum: 999fps.

This handler also checks to make sure that the mouse location is within a certain boundary. It then computes the point on the canvas that the cursor is currently over. It needs to take into account the location of the canvas sprite on the Stage, as well as the center of the brush's rectangle. After it does that, it calls either the "on drawPoint" or "on drawLine" handler to create either the starting point of a brush stroke or the continuation of one.

```
on exitFrame me
  if pDraw then

    -- restrict draw area
    mouseLocation = the mouseLoc
    if not inside(mouseLocation, sprite(1).rect) then exit

    -- get current location in image
    curLoc = mouseLocation
    -- subtract corner of image sprite
    curLoc = curLoc - point(sprite(1).rect.left,sprite(1).rect.top)
    -- subtract center of brush
    curLoc = curLoc - point(pBrush.width/2,pBrush.height/2)

    -- if there is a last location
    if (pLastDrawLoc <> 0) then
      drawLine(me,pLastDrawLoc,curLoc)
```

```
      -- if not, then just draw a point
    else
      drawPoint(me,curLoc)
    end if

    -- new last location
    pLastDrawLoc = curLoc
  end if

  go to the frame
end
```

When only a single application of the brush is needed, the following handler imprints that on the image. It uses ink number 36, "background transparent", so the white areas in the brush are transparent when drawing.

```
-- will draw a single point at a single location
on drawPoint me, loc
  rect = pBrush.rect + rect(loc,loc)
  (pCanvas).copyPixels(pBrush.image, rect, pBrush.rect, [#ink: 36, #color:
pColor])
  member("Canvas").image = pCanvas
end
```

The "on drawLine" handler is simple, but includes some scary-looking math. This handler uses the "distance" function to determine how many pixels apart the two points are. Then it loops over that distance amount divided by two, so it draws at every other point. If the brushes were only 1 pixel in size, this would create a dotted line, but because the brushes are all larger than that, covering only every other point makes little difference in the resulting line, but speeds up the drawing.

With every step of the loop, the location of the sprite is brought closer to the most recent mouse location and farther from the end of the previous location.

```
-- this handler will draw a line of dots from one point to the next
on drawLine me, loc1, loc2
  -- how many dots to draw
  numSteps = float(distance(me,loc1,loc2))/2+1

  -- repeat and place dots
  repeat with i = 1 to numSteps
    percent1 = float(numSteps-float(i))/numSteps
    percent2 = float(i)/numSteps
    loc = loc1*percent1 + loc2*percent2
    rect = pBrush.rect + rect(loc,loc)
    (pCanvas).copyPixels(pBrush.image, rect, pBrush.rect, \
            [#ink: 36, #color: pColor])
```

```
  end repeat

  -- apply changes to canvas
  member("Canvas").image = pCanvas
end
```

This simple distance function takes two points and returns the distance between them, in pixels. The handler is used in the "on drawLine" handler to determine the number of steps between brush points:

```
-- calculate the distance between two pixels
on distance me, loc1, loc2
  return sqrt(power(loc1.locH-loc2.locH,2)+power(loc1.locV-loc2.locV,2))
end
```

Because this frame script behavior seems to be in control of the functionality in this movie, it's a good idea to keep auxiliary operations in it as well. This next handler takes a color object as a parameter and sets the property "pColor" to that color. Because the brushes are all 1-bit members, they take on the color of the sprite when you apply a #color property to the copyPixels command. However, it's up to an external handler to call this handler and institute the color change. These external handlers will be the scripts that are attached to the color chips shown earlier in Figure 27.2.

```
-- accept a color and change to it
on changeColor me, color
  pColor = color
end
```

Using the same idea, this next handler accepts a new brush member from a script attached to one of the brushes on the left. It sets the "pBrush" property.

```
-- accept a brush member and change to it
on changeBrush me, brush
  pBrush = brush
end
```

This ends the main behavior for the movie. The whole thing works now, except that nothing will happen when users want to change colors or brushes. To change this, you need small behaviors on the color chips and brush icons. The following behavior is for the color chips. It takes the color assigned to that sprite and sends it to the main drawing behavior in the frame script, also known as sprite 0. It also issues a #changeColorSprite message to sprite 26. This message is used to reset the outline that shows users what color is currently in use.

```
on mouseDown me
  color = sprite(me.spriteNum).color
  sendSprite(0, #changeColor, color)
  sendSprite(26,#changeColorSprite,me.spriteNum)
end
```

The "on changeColorSprite" handler should be in a small behavior attached to the little outline box that surrounds the current color. When the message is sent to sprite 26, a handler there takes the rectangle of the current color chip and expands it by 3 pixels on all sides. The outline box is set to this new rectangle so that it surrounds the color chip:

```
on changeColorSprite me , colorSprite
  sprite(me.spriteNum).rect = \
    sprite(colorSprite).rect + rect(-3, -3, 3, 3)
end
```

The following behavior is meant for the brushes. It tells the main behavior that the brush has changed, and also sends a #changeBrushSprite message to sprite 33 so that the brush outline box sprite can recognize it and react:

```
on mouseDown me
  brush = sprite(me.spriteNum).member
  sendSprite(sprite 0, #changeBrush, brush)
  sendSprite(33,#changeBrushSprite,me.spriteNum)
end
```

The behavior for the brush outline box is almost the same as for the color outline box sprite:

```
on changeBrushSprite me , colorSprite
  sprite(me.spriteNum).rect = \
    sprite(colorSprite).rect + rect(-3, -3, 3, 3)
end
```

The CLEAR button is easily scripted. It just needs to send the "clearImage" message to the frame behavior so that the *fill* is reapplied.

```
on mouseDown
  sendSprite(0,#clearImage)
end
```

Lastly, there should be a way to prevent users from clicking the title bar or toolbar areas while drawing. Because the frame script behavior receives "mouseDown" messages only after a sprite has received the messages, all you need is a simple script that eats all "mouseDown" messages so that the main behavior never gets them:

```
on mouseDown
  -- no action
end
```

Assign this behavior to anything that should be considered inactive, such as the shaded boxes at the top and left sides of the screen.

Take a look at the example on the CD-ROM to see how all these pieces of code work together. You should be able to make modifications easily. You can change brushes by editing their bitmaps. Changing colors is even easier, because you can change the colors of the color chips on the Stage. You can also add more colors and brushes by adding more sprites and attaching the proper behaviors.

One major improvement to this program would be to add a way for users to save their work. You can use the *saveMovie* command to save this change to the movie file or the *save castLib* command to save an external cast library with the image and bring it back into the program later. You could also shop for an Xtra that enables you to export the canvas bitmap into a file of its own.

⇨ *For more information on Lingo commands that affect bitmap members,* **see** *"Manipulating Bitmap Members," p. 388 (Chapter 18, "Controlling Bitmaps")*

⇨ *For some background information on trails,* **see** *"Trails Property," p. 183 (Chapter 10, "Properties of Sprites and Frames")*

CREATING OVERLAYS

Remember your high school biology textbook? It had a lot of drawings of the human body with the organs and skeleton all exposed. Sometimes you could lift up transparent sheets to "remove" organs—one might have shown the skeleton, one the circulatory system, one the digestive system, and so on. This way, you were able to see where things were in relation to each other.

The same "overlay" technique can be used in other subjects as well. An astronomy book might show a picture of the night sky. Then an overlay can show the star names. Another can show drawings of the constellations, and so on.

Doing this in Director is fairly easy. After you create the layers of artwork as different bitmap images, you need to place them in the Score only in the order in which you want them to overlay each other. Then you can use the visibility switches on the left side of the Score to test them out.

Figure 27.3 shows such a screen. An outline of the human body is used as a background. On top of that are four other sprites, each showing a different organ.

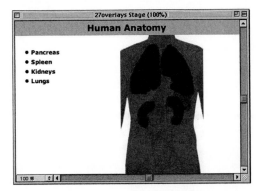

Figure 27.3
A simple overlay application has a background sprite, several overlays, and simple buttons to match each layer.

Only one simple behavior is needed to turn the overlay sprites on and off. This should be attached not to the overlays, but to the buttons that activate them. In this case, these buttons are the text members on the left side of the screen.

When users click one of these text member buttons, the overlay should appear or disappear, depending on its current state. The buttons should also reflect the change. In this case, the bullet character to the left of each word changes color when the word is clicked. A black color means that the layer is on, whereas white makes the layer invisible on the white background, signifying that the layer is off.

When the behavior begins, it tries to determine whether the bullet character should be black or white. It checks the corresponding overlay sprite. You can therefore set the sprites to be visible or invisible at startup, and the text buttons reflect that state:

```
on beginSprite me
  setDot(me)
end


-- takes the first character of the text member and makes
-- it either black or white to reflect the state
on setDot me
  if sprite(me.spriteNum+1).visible = TRUE then
    sprite(me.spriteNum).member.char[1].color = rgb("000000")
  else
    sprite(me.spriteNum).member.char[1].color = rgb("FFFFFF")
  end if
end
```

Notice that this behavior assumes that the next sprite "(me.spriteNum+1)" is the overlay sprite. By making this assumption, and then setting up the Score as shown in Figure 27.4, you can avoid any special behavior parameters that identify the overlay sprite manually.

Figure 27.4
The Score shows that each overlay sprite is in the next Sprite channel after its corresponding button sprite. This makes it easy for the button to know which sprite to affect.

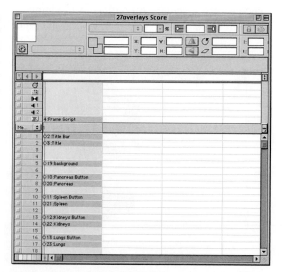

The last part of the behavior determines whether the sprite is visible or invisible. Because the "on setDot" handler is already able to change the state of the button according to the visibility of the overlay sprite, there is no need to write more code to do this here:

```
-- will change the visible property of the next sprite
on mouseUp me
  sprite(me.spriteNum+1).visible = \
    not sprite(me.spriteNum+1).visible
  setDot(me)
end
```

This behavior is simplified by the use of text member buttons. You can use bitmaps instead. In that case, you need members to represent on and off states. The check box behaviors in Chapter 15, "Graphic Interface Elements," can be adapted for this purpose.

Another thing to consider is the inks of the overlay sprites. Copy ink does not work because it hides anything under the sprite's rectangle with white. Background Transparent and Matte inks are obvious choices. They keep the overlay sprite's current colors, and enable white pixels to show through. In the preceding example, Transparent ink was used so that the edges would be smoother. However, this also altered the colors of the overlays.

One technique to consider is using 32-bit members with Alpha channels. You can then define the level of transparency throughout the image.

⇨ *For a review of the check box behavior,* **see** *"Using Check Boxes," p. 292 (Chapter 15)*

CREATING A GEOGRAPHY QUIZ

Although quizzes and tests in school are traditionally done with pencil and paper, with each question taking up a different space on the paper, computer quizzes can be far more interactive. A geography quiz, in fact, can present an interactive map that responds as students roll over it and click.

Figure 27.5 shows such a quiz using a map of the United States. The actual movie is made up of 51 sprites. The large, outlined map overlays the entire thing, and is always visible. Under that are 50 individual bitmap sprites, one for each state.

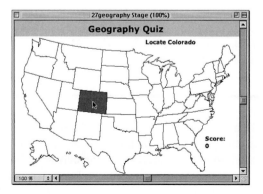

Figure 27.5
In this geography quiz, each state lights up as users roll over it so that they know what they are about to select.

As users move the cursor around the map, the state under the cursor lights up. It actually just changes color from white to blue. The simple behavior for this action uses the *on mouseEnter* handler to signify that the cursor has entered a state, and then changes its color. It also places the name of the state, which is the name of the cast member in the sprite, into a text member. Although this gives away the "answer" during the quiz, it is useful later on as a "payoff" screen activity. Therefore, the text member that shows the name of each state is not present on the quiz frame, and appears only after the student is finished with the quiz.

```
property pState

-- get the state name
on beginSprite me
  pState = sprite(me.spriteNum).member.name
end

on mouseEnter me
  -- on rollover, change state color
  sprite(me.spriteNum).color = rgb("336699")

  -- set the text member
  member("State Name").text = pState
end

on mouseLeave me
  -- change state color back to white
  sprite(me.spriteNum).color = rgb("#FFFFFF")

  -- reset text member
  member("State Name").text = " "
end

on mouseUp me
  -- see if answer is right
  answerQuestion(pState)
end
```

This behavior needs to be attached to all 50 state sprites. The state sprite behavior also calls the movie handler "on answerQuestion" when the state is clicked. Make sure the outlined map on top of the state sprites does not have a behavior attached to it that will eat these "mouseUp" messages and never let this behavior receive them.

Running the quiz is actually done via a movie script. This script uses several globals to keep track of all the questions, the number of the question the user is being asked, and the score. The scoring system in this quiz gives users 100 points for every correct answer. If the first answer is wrong, users are given another chance, but can only score 50 points. For a correct answer on the third try, the score is 25, and so on. The "gPoints" global keeps track of how many points users can score for a correct answer. The "gPoints" global is set to 100 at the start of each question, and then cut in half every time users answer incorrectly.

```
global gQuestionNum -- which question is being asked
global gQuestions -- list with all the questions
global gScore -- keep track of score
global gPoints -- keep track of potential points to be scored
```

To start the movie, the "on initQuiz" is called to determine the questions to be asked. Then some other globals are reset. The "on showScore" handler places the score, which starts at 0, in a text member. Finally, "on askQuestion" kicks off the quiz with question number 1:

```
on startMovie
  initQuiz
  gQuestionNum = 1
  gScore = 0
  showScore
  askQuestion
end
```

The "on initQuiz" handler's job is to come up with 10 random states to use in the quiz. It first gets a list of states by reading the member names of the "States" cast library, which holds all the state bitmaps. After the handler gets that list, it selects 10 states at random. Each time a state is selected, it's tested to see whether it is already used in the quiz. The result of this handler is that the "gQuestions" list is populated with 10 random and unique state names.

```
-- this handler will come up with 10 random and unique states
-- to make up the quiz
on initQuiz

  -- get a list of all states from the cast library member names
  listOfStates = []
  repeat with i = 1 to the number of members of castLib "States"
    add listOfStates, member(i,"States").name
  end repeat

  -- add 10 random names to quiz
  gQuestions = []
  repeat with i = 1 to 10

    repeat while TRUE

      -- get a random state
      r = random(listOfStates.count)
      state = listOfStates[r]

      -- see if the state is already in quiz
```

```
       if getOne(gQuestions,state) then next repeat

       -- add state, go on to add next
       add gQuestions, state
       exit repeat

    end repeat
  end repeat
end
```

This next handler places the text of the next question into a text member that is on the Stage. It also resets "gPoints" to 100:

```
on askQuestion
  -- set text member
  member("Question").text = "Locate"&&gQuestions[gQuestionNum]

  -- set potential points
  gPoints = 100 -- potential points to earn
end
```

When users click a state, the following handler is called to determine whether the state is correct. It compares the name of the member clicked to the name in the "gQuestions" list that corresponds to this question number. If they don't match, an alert box is used to send a message. You might want to use a sound or some other method to signify that the answer is wrong.

If the answer matches, "gScore" is changed, the new score is shown, and a beep is played. Again, you might want to develop a custom sound and use the *puppetSound* command. The question number is incremented, and if all 10 questions have been answered, the movie jumps to another frame. Otherwise, the next question is asked.

```
-- this handler will check to see if a state name matches
-- the expected answer
on answerQuestion state
  -- make sure we are not done
  if gQuestionNum > gQuestions.count then exit

  if state <> gQuestions[gQuestionNum] then
    alert "Wrong. Try Again."

    -- divide potential points in half when a wrong answer
    gPoints = gPoints/2

  else

    -- add to score
```

```
    gScore = gScore + gPoints
    showScore
    beep() -- replace with better sound

    -- next question
    gQuestionNum = gQuestionNum + 1

    -- are we done?
    if gQuestionNum > gQuestions.count then
      member("Question").text = "All done! Use the mouse to explore."
      go to frame "Done"
    else
      askQuestion
    end if
  end if
end
```

One last movie handler places the current score in a text member on the Stage:

```
-- this handler places the current score in a member
on showScore
  member("Score").text = "Score:"&RETURN&gScore
end
```

When the game is over, the movie jumps to the "Done" frame. This frame can be anything, such as a payoff animation. However, in this example, it is the same map used in the quiz, but this time users can explore at random. The state behavior is already placing the name of the state in a text member. This member is actually present on the "Done" frame and has another behavior attached to it so that it follows the cursor around.

```
on prepareFrame me
  -- determine sprite width
  textwidth = sprite(me.spriteNum).width

  -- set the location of the sprite to be just above the cursor
  sprite(me.spriteNum).loc = the mouseLoc+ \
      point(-textwidth/2,-16)
end
```

This "Done" frame can be used as a payoff, but it also can be used as an application all to itself. Rather than just display the state name in one member, it can also display information about the state elsewhere on the screen. Such information can come from text members or fields in another cast library. You can even wire the "on mouseUp" handlers to go to a frame specific to a state, or to a page on the Web with the *gotoNetPage* command.

⇨ *For more information about rollover behaviors,* **see** *"Creating Display Rollovers," **p. 290** (Chapter 15)*

CREATING STANDARDIZED TESTS

Although computer geography quizzes and matching games are much more interactive than old-fashioned paper and pencil tests, sometimes you just want users to answer questions. A lot of aspects of paper-and-pencil tests, however, are not easy to duplicate on the computer.

Tests usually have many questions, too many to fit on one sheet of paper. As you can imagine, it makes no sense to try to fit all the questions onto one computer screen, either. Instead, one question per screen is more appropriate. However, this brings up the issue of navigating between questions. After all, paper and pencil tests enable users to skip questions and go back to change answers on previous questions.

Figure 27.6 shows one screen of a standardized test program. It looks similar to the SAT, GRE, or ACT tests. The question is the focus of the screen, and under it are several possible answers. The top and left sides of the screen are reserved for the title and some navigation buttons.

Figure 27.6
One screen of a standardized test program.

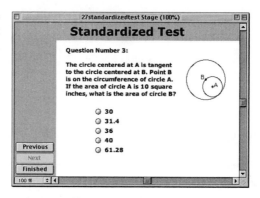

To create a test like this, you rely on two behaviors from earlier chapters. The first is the radio button behavior from Chapter 15. This behavior is applied to the small radio buttons that appear to the left of each possible answer. The navigation buttons use the complete button behavior from Chapter 14, "Creating Behaviors."

Like the geography quiz, this program relies on a movie script for all the important handlers. This movie script needs only one global: a list of answers that users have so far selected. The movie starts by resetting this global, and going to frame "question 1":

```
global gAnswerList

on startTest
  gAnswerList = []
  go to frame "question 1"
end
```

The movie relies on frame labels to determine on which question the user is currently working. So, frame "question 1" is question number 1, frame "question 2" is question number 2, and so on.

The three buttons on the left side of the screen—Previous, Next, and Finished—all have the complete button behavior attached. The sample movie on the CD-ROM has both normal and down states for the buttons. The behavior is set to execute the movie handlers "on previousQuestion", "on nextQuestion", and "on finishedTest" for each button.

The "on previousQuestion" and "on nextQuestion" buttons call the "on recordAnswer" handler, which stores the current radio button selection, the one the user has chosen, in the global. It then uses *go next* or *go previous* to go to the next or preceding question, and, if it is one the user has already answered, uses the "on setAnswer" to set the radio buttons.

```
on nextQuestion
  recordAnswer
  go next
  setAnswer
end

on previousQuestion
  recordAnswer
  go previous
  setAnswer
end
```

To record the answer, the program gets the question number from the frame label. Then, it takes the state of the radio buttons from the "on selected" handler in the radio button behavior. Because the radio buttons are in sprites 11 through 15, 10 is subtracted to get an answer between 1 and 5. This is then recorded in the global "AnswerList".

```
on recordAnswer
  -- get question number from frame label
  q = word 2 of the frameLabel
  q = value(q)

  -- get answer from radio buttons
  a = sendSprite(sprite 11, #selected)
  a = a - 10

  -- remember answer
  setAt gAnswerList, q, a
end
```

If users answer a question, move on, and then return to the already-answered question, you want to show the earlier choice. The "on setAnswer" handler takes care of this. It looks up the current value of the question in the "gAnswerList" and sets the radio buttons accordingly:

```
on setAnswer
  -- get question number from frame label
  q = word 2 of the frameLabel
  q = value(q)

  -- get answer from radio buttons
  if gAnswerList.count >= q then
    a = gAnswerList[q]
    sendSprite(sprite (a+10), #turnMeOn)
  end if
end
```

When a user clicks the Finished button, she is taken to the "finished" frame. Just before that, the program evaluates the user's results with the "on computeResults" handler. This handler relies on a field named "Correct Answers". This field should contain a line-by-line list of correct answers by number. Each correct answer is compared to the user's answers stored in "gAnswerList" and a total is calculated. The result is placed in a text member visible on the "finished" frame:

```
on finishedTest
  recordAnswer
  computeResults
  go to frame "finished"
end


on computeResults

  -- get list of correct answers
  correct = member("Correct Answers").text

  -- find the number that matches up correctly
  numright = 0
  repeat with i = 1 to correct.line.count
    if value(correct.line[i] = gAnswerList[i]) then
      numright = numright + 1
    end if
  end repeat

  -- put results in Results member
  member("Results").text = "Test complete."&RETURN&RETURN&\
    "You got"&&numright&& \
    "correct out of"&&correct.line.count&"."
end
```

The rest of the work you need to do is in setting the behaviors for the radio buttons and navigation buttons. Figure 27.7 shows a Score with a three-question test. The start frame has a "begin" button in it that executes the "on startTest" handler. There are then three frames with questions. The radio buttons are in sprites 11 through 15 in all cases. Therefore, the behavior for each of these radio buttons needs to be set to show that. Use the Behavior Inspector to check out these behavior properties.

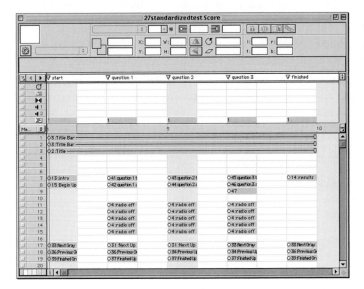

Figure 27.7
The Score is set up for a short standardized test with three questions.

The navigation buttons also have grayed-out states that are used when the buttons are not active. For instance, the Previous button is not active on the first question and the Next button is not active on the last question. These inactive buttons have no behavior attached, whereas the active buttons call one of the movie handlers: "on previousQuestion", "on nextQuestion", and "on finishedTest".

As shown earlier in Figure 27.6, you can also include other elements besides text on the screen. Some questions are likely to be just text, and others can use bitmaps, vectors, or even Flash members as additional material. You can even place film loops that animate on these frames. You can't do that with pencil-and-paper tests!

Another improvement that you can add is a more comprehensive scoring report. You can tell users what they answered incorrectly and what they answered correctly by keeping track of that information in a list. You might want to even allow users to walk through the questions again and show them explanations of how each problem is solved.

⇨ For more information about button behaviors, **see** "Building a Complete Button Behavior," p. 271 (Chapter 14)

⇨ For more information about radio button behaviors, **see** "Using Radio Buttons," p. 294 (Chapter 15)

TROUBLESHOOTING EDUCATIONAL APPLICATIONS

- A global is commonly used to record answers in quizzes and tests. To be sure that your program really works, use *clearGlobals* in the Message window often to make sure you are starting off fresh. You might even want to place it in your *on startMovie* handler.

- In the geography quiz program, make sure that the inks for the states are set to Matte and the behaviors are attached.

- All the aforementioned programs require that *go to the frame* be placed in the *on exitFrame* script on each frame. Forgetting to do so is a common mistake.

- Remember to test educational programs as much as you can. A student may click an area of the screen or perform an action that you may not think of. Make sure the program works even when it is misused.

DID YOU KNOW?

- You can combine all these educational applications to make one large test. One question can be matching, one geography, one can involve overlays, and a creative section can enable users to draw their own pictures.

- You can build a test that keeps questions and answers as a separate text file. At the start of the program, the text file is read from disk or over the Internet. Each question can be a single line in the file ("What is the fastest animal?;Duck,Pig,Cheetah;3"). This way, you can build a test that a nonprogrammer can change.

- The geography quiz doesn't have to use a map. You can have a periodic table of the elements, a diagram of the human body, or even a list of potential answers to questions. You can keep the "feel" of the application, without limiting your test to geography as the subject matter.

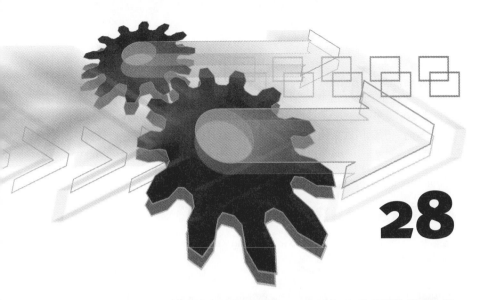

28

BUSINESS APPLICATIONS

IN THIS CHAPTER

Source movies for this chapter can be found on the CD-ROM in the "Book Movies" folder under folder 28.

Although they are not as fun as educational programs or games, many types of business applications can also be created in Director. Most presentations fall into this category, such as the example in Chapter 1, "Animation with Director," which showed a simple slideshow presentation.

Some higher-end movies can also handle or present data. This chapter shows you how to make a simple database program in Director, how to build graphs and charts, how to make a survey-like questionnaire, and how to develop training programs.

CREATING DATABASE APPLICATIONS

Building a database in Director is easy. However, creating an interface that a nonprogrammer can use to interact with the database is a tougher task.

You may have already noticed that property lists look like small databases. If you create a linear list that contains several property lists, you actually have a database. Look at this example:

```
[[#name: "Gary", #title: "Chief Engineer", #company: "CleverMedia"] \
, [#name: "Bill", #title: "CEO", #company: "Microsoft"]]
```

The property names in this list represent the field names, and the property values are the fields themselves. Each item in the linear list is then a record. This example contains a database with two records and three fields in each record.

The Main Menu Screen

Creating a database application is merely a matter of creating screens that manipulate a list database like the one shown previously. Such a program might use a global to store the database. A good name would be "gDatabase". It also needs to know which database record is currently being edited. That information can be a stored in a global called "gCurrentRecord".

A main menu screen enables users to perform various tasks. Figure 28.1 shows what this might look like.

Figure 28.1
The main menu screen contains buttons for all the functions of the database.

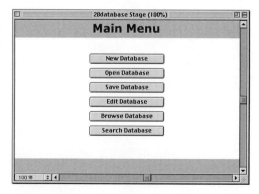

To begin, users need to create a new database. They do this by clicking the New Database button. This handler clears out the "gDatabase" global and goes to the data entry screen:

```
on newDatabase
  gDatabase = [newRecord()] -- database with one record
  go to frame "Entry"
  gCurrentRecord = 1
  showRecord
end
```

The function "on newRecord" returns a new, blank record. This function is handy for adding records to the database or replacing them.

```
on newRecord
  record = [:]
  addProp record, #item, ""
  addProp record, #id, ""
  addProp record, #category, ""
  addProp record, #number, ""
  addProp record, #price, 0.0
  addProp record, #description, ""
  return record
end
```

The "on newRecord" function defines the fields that the database is to contain. You can see that this database has six fields.

The Database Entry Screen

Next, you need a database entry screen so that users can enter new records and edit old records. The "on newDatabase" handler ends by calling the "on showRecord" handler. This handler populates the fields on the database entry screen:

```
on showRecord
  -- get current record
  record = gDatabase[gCurrentRecord]

  -- place fields into members on stage
  member("Entry - Item").text = record.item
  member("Entry - ID").text = record.id
  member("Entry - Category").text = record.category
  member("Entry - Number").text = record.number
  member("Entry - Price").text = string(record.price)
  member("Entry - Description").text = record.description

  -- show the record number
  member("Record Number").text = "Record"&&gCurrentRecord
end
```

Figure 28.2 shows what the database entry screen looks like.

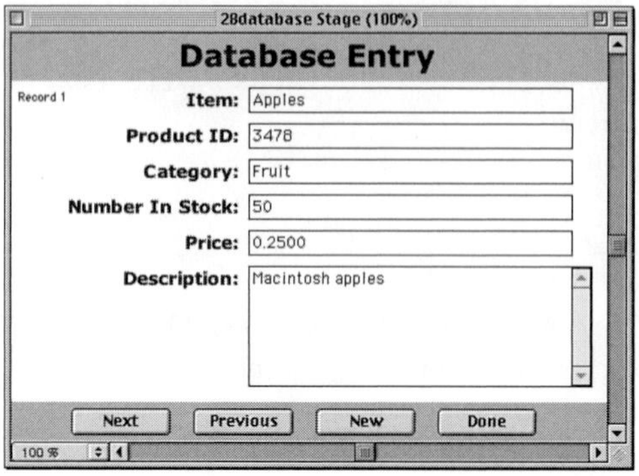

Figure 28.2
A database entry screen for a simple supermarket inventory database.

In the database entry screen, the six editable fields are the active elements. Most of the rest of the screen, such as the field labels to the left, are just static text. A record number field is in the upper-left corner. This is not editable, and displays the record number for the current entry.

Users can enter any text into any field on the screen. All fields are set to editable and "Tab to Next Editable Item" so that they respond to the Tab key as other programs do.

The buttons at the bottom of the screen use the complex button behavior described in Chapter 14, "Creating Behaviors." The Next and Previous buttons bring up the following or preceding record. The Done button brings up a main menu screen. The New button, of course, creates a new entry at the end of the database and makes that the current entry.

Whenever one of these buttons is clicked, the information in the fields on the screen needs to be recorded and placed in the database before the action is performed.

The "on recordRecord" handler takes the text from all fields and places it in a new, empty record. It then replaces the old record in the database global:

```
on recordRecord
  -- get empty record to use
  record = newRecord()

  -- change all fields of record to reflect screen data
  record.item = member("Entry - Item").text
  record.id = member("Entry - ID").text
  record.category = member("Entry - Category").text
  record.number = member("Entry - Number").text
  record.price = value(member("Entry - Price").text)
  record.description = member("Entry - Description").text

  -- replace record in database
  gDatabase[gCurrentRecord] = record
end
```

Navigating Through the Database

In addition to starting a new database, users should be able to return to the database entry screen to edit records. The "Edit Database" button calls the "on editDatabase" handler. This handler needs to make sure that a database exists before enabling the users to edit it. If a database is not present, it creates one rather than giving an error message:

```
on editDatabase
  -- check to see if any database exists
  if not listP(gDatabase) then
    nextDatabase
  else
    go to frame "Entry"
    gCurrentRecord = 1
    showRecord
  end if
end
```

The Next and Previous buttons also have movie handlers that take care of recording changes to the current item and moving forward or backward in the database:

```
-- move forward in the database
on nextRecord
  -- accept all changes in current record
  recordRecord

  -- go to the next record
  gCurrentRecord = gCurrentRecord + 1

  -- if past the end of the database, loop around
  if gCurrentRecord > gDatabase.count then
    gCurrentRecord = 1
  end if

  -- display the new record
  showRecord
end

-- move backward in the database
on previousRecord
  -- accept all changes in current record
  recordRecord

  -- go to the previous record
  gCurrentRecord = gCurrentRecord - 1
```

```
  -- if user tries to move back past 1, loop around
  if gCurrentRecord < 1 then
    gCurrentRecord = gDatabase.count
  end if


  -- display the new record
  showRecord
end
```

When users click the New button, a handler must find the last item in the database and add one past that:

```
-- create a new record in the database
on createRecord
  -- accept all changes in current record
  recordRecord

  -- go to the record one past the last in database
  gCurrentRecord = gDatabase.count + 1

  -- set this new record to a blank record
  gDatabase[gCurrentRecord] = newRecord()

  -- display the new record
  showRecord
end
```

The Done button enables users to exit the database entry screen and return to the main menu. Like the other handlers in this section, this button must first record changes to the current entry before performing its action:

```
-- finished entering data, return to main menu
on doneEntry
  recordRecord
  go to frame "Main"
end
```

The next two items to be dealt with are the Save Database and Open Database buttons. These both call handlers that use the FileIO Xtra to save or load the global database variable to a file.

The "on saveDatabase" handler creates a file and saves a string version of the list to it. In a more advanced application, this is known as a "Save As..." function. In that case, you would also need a handler that acts as a "Save" function, whereby the database would be saved to the same file each time, without prompting users for a file location. For simplicity, this program has only one handler:

```
-- save the current database to a text file
on saveDatabase
  -- ask user for a filename
  fileObj = new(Xtra "FileIO")
  filename = displaySave(fileObj, "Save Database", "database.txt")
  if filename = "" then exit

  -- create file and write to it
  createFile(fileObj,filename)
  openFile(fileObj,filename, 2)
  writeString(fileObj, string(gDatabase))
  closeFile(fileObj)
end
```

To open a file, you must make a handler similar to the one that writes a file. In addition, you must perform some verification on the type of file that the user has selected. Users can open any kind of file in this case, but the text in the file is tested to make sure it is a valid Lingo list. If so, the file is considered a valid database file.

You can perform a stricter test by making sure it is a linear list that contains only similar property lists if you like:

```
-- open an existing database file
on openDatabase
  -- ask user for a file
  fileObj = new(Xtra "FileIO")
  filename = displayOpen(fileObj)
  if filename = "" then exit

  -- open the file and read the text
  openFile(fileObj, filename, 1)
  text = readFile(fileObj)
  closeFile(fileObj)

  -- try to convert the text to a list
  database = value(text)
  if not listP(database) then
    -- not a list
    alert "Not a valid database file."
  else
    -- is a list, set database
    gDatabase = database
  end if
end
```

So, now you can create a database, add items to it, edit items, save it to your hard drive, and then load it back in at a later time. That takes care of building the database; now it would be nice to have the database actually do something.

Listing Records in the Database

The following handler creates a scrolling text field with all the items in the database. It uses HTML formatting to create a table in a text member. Figure 28.3 shows the screen with this list.

Figure 28.3
The browse database screen shows a list of all the items in the database in an HTML-formatted text member.

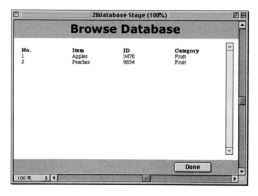

```
-- display a list of all the records using HTML
on browseDatabase

  -- html header
  htext = "<HTML><BODY BGCOLOR=#FFFFFF>"&RETURN

  -- put the table headings
  put "<TABLE><TR><TH>No.</TH><TH>Item</TH><TH>ID</TH><TH>Category</TH></TR>" \
     &RETURN after htext

  -- loop through database and create table rows
  repeat with i = 1 to gDatabase.count
    put "<TR>" after htext
    put "<TD>"&i&"</TD>" after htext
    put "<TD>"&gDatabase[i].item&"</TD>" after htext
    put "<TD>"&gDatabase[i].id&"</TD>" after htext
    put "<TD>"&gDatabase[i].category&"</TD>" after htext
    put "</TR>"&RETURN after htext
  end repeat

  -- close out table and HTML
  put "</TABLE></BODY></HTML>" after htext
```

```
  -- place HTML in text member
  member("Database List").html = htext

  go to frame "Browse"
end
```

Although it's nice to see each item of the database in one list, it's better to be able use some criteria to narrow the list. Here is a handler, similar to the preceding one, that performs a simple search on the database. The result is an HTML-formatted list.

This handler gets the search term from an editable text member. Users are first taken to a search screen and asked for a search term:

```
-- display a list of records that are found in search
on performSearch

  -- get search term from field
  searchText = member("Search Text").text

  -- HTML header
  htext = "<HTML><BODY BGCOLOR=#FFFFFF>"&RETURN

  -- put the table headings
  put "<TABLE><TR><TH>No.</TH><TH>Item</TH><TH>ID</TH><TH>Category</TH></TR>" \
    &RETURN after htext

  -- loop through all records
  repeat with i = 1 to gDatabase.count
    record = gDatabase[i]

    -- see if the record contains the search text
    -- search all properties for it
    if (record.item contains searchText) or \
       (record.id contains searchText) or \
       (record.category contains searchText) or \
       (record.number contains searchText) or \
       (record.price contains searchText) or \
       (record.description contains searchText) then

      -- a match was found, add a row to table
      put "<TR>" after htext
      put "<TD>"&i&"</TD>" after htext
      put "<TD>"&record.item&"</TD>" after htext
      put "<TD>"&record.id&"</TD>" after htext
      put "<TD>"&record.category&"</TD>" after htext
      put "</TR>"&RETURN after htext
```

```
    end if
  end repeat

  -- close out table and HTML
  put "</TABLE></BODY></HTML>" after htext

  -- put HTML into text member
  member("Database List").html = htext

  go to frame "Search Results"
end
```

Although every field in the database is searched for the search term, you might want to narrow the search a bit. You can search only the description and item name, for instance. You can also search only the category field and get lists of similar items, such as all fruits or all meats. You can even perform a search on the price field for items that are less than or greater than an amount, rather than those that are exactly the same.

It is these searches that make databases powerful. Another common database function is computation. You can have a function that reads through the whole database, multiplies price by quantity for each item, and then sums to get the total value of the inventory.

➯ *For an introduction to lists,* **see** *"Using List Variables," p. 248 (Chapter 13, "Essential Lingo Syntax")*

➯ *For more information about FileIO and using HTML in text members,* **see** *"Using Text Files and the FileIO Xtra," p. 355 and "Using HTML and Tables," p. 348 (Chapter 16, "Controlling Text")*

CREATING GRAPHS AND PIE CHARTS

Graphs and pie charts are often simply another type of bitmap image. You can easily create these with graphing programs, such as Microsoft Excel or Lotus, and then you can cut and paste bitmaps of these graphs into Director as cast members.

However, another option is to create these graphs in Director using various Director elements, such as shapes, text members, and lines.

Bar Graphs

Figure 28.4 shows a bar graph created in Director. It uses different shape sprites for all the bars, lines for the x- and y-axes, and text members for the x- and y-axis labels.

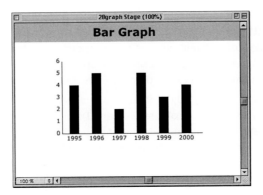

Figure 28.4
This graph was made with different Director elements, and then a Lingo handler was used to adjust the bars to the correct height.

Although you can easily lay out all the pieces of the graph shown in Figure 28.4 manually, the following Lingo handler is used to adjust the bars to the proper height:

```
-- adjust a 6-bar graph
on adjustGraph valueList
  repeat with i = 1 to 6

    -- bar sprites start at 6
    sNum = 5+i

    -- get the rectangle of the sprite
    r = sprite(sNum).rect

    -- reset the rectangle top
    r.top = r.bottom - valueList[i]*25

    -- set the sprite
    sprite(sNum).rect = r
  end repeat
end
```

This handler assumes that the bars are in sprites 6 through 11. It also uses 25 pixels as the measurement between one number and the next. You call the handler in this manner:

```
on startMovie
  adjustGraph([4,5,2,5,3,4])
end
```

This handler sets the bars to the heights that you see in Figure 28.4. You could call the same handler again, but with different numbers, to set the bars differently. Now you can develop a movie that contains several graphs, but uses Lingo to create them, instead of using different bitmap images each time.

For instance, the numbers on the left (the y-axis) can indicate sales in millions of dollars. The numbers on the bottom (the x-axis) are, of course, years. Then, you can have several different graphs that show the sales for different companies, or for different departments within the same company. Each frame with a graph has the same sprite elements used in the graph, but the "on adjustGraph" handler is called with different numbers each time.

A more complex handler can actually adjust the number of bars, the labels at the bottom and left of the graph, and maybe even add color to the bars. Doing this is far more complex, because creating the labels, and spacing them the proper distance apart, can be difficult. You may want to actually place each label in a separate text member and position it accordingly.

Pie Charts

Another type of visual aid is a pie chart. Before Director 7, these were difficult to do, because the pie slices had to be drawn pixel by pixel. However, with vector shape members, you can create a pie chart from a single member. Recall that these members enable you to create shapes from a curved line and optionally fill that shape with a color or gradient.

Figure 28.5 shows such a member on the Stage. The chart shown was generated from a single vector shape member with a behavior attached to it. The behavior shaped the member into the pie chart during the "on beginSprite" handler.

Figure 28.5
A pie chart made up of a single vector shape member.

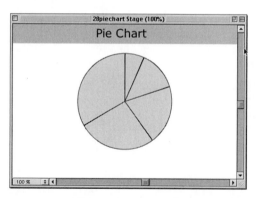

The behavior uses two parameters: the values of the pie slices and the radius of the pie. It then creates a pie chart, piece by piece, by drawing a circle and connecting a line to the center at the appropriate places.

```
property pValues, pRadius

on getPropertyDescriptionList me
  list = [:]
  addProp list, #pValues, [#comment: "Value List", \
    #default: [], #format: #list]
  addProp list, #pRadius, [#comment: "Radius", \
    #default: 100, #format: #integer]
  return list
end
```

```
on beginSprite me

  -- determine total value of pie
  total = 0.0
  repeat with i = 1 to pValues.count
    total = total + pValues[i]
  end repeat

  -- start new vertextList
  vlist = []

  -- start 1/4 circle, back
  oldAngle = -pi()/2

  -- start at 0
  swing = 0.0

  repeat with i = 1 to pValues.count

    -- begin slice at center
    add vlist, [#vertex: point(0,0)]

    -- calculate angle for end of piece
    swing = swing + pValues[i]
    newAngle = 2.0*pi()*(swing/total)-pi()/2

    -- move from start to end of piece
    repeat with a = 100*oldAngle to 100*newAngle

      -- add point on circumference
      x = pRadius*cos(a/100)
      y = pRadius*sin(a/100)
      add vlist, [#vertex: point(x,y)]
    end repeat

    -- set start for next piece
    oldAngle = newAngle
  end repeat

  -- use vertexList on this sprite
  sprite(me.spriteNum).member.vertexList = vlist
end
```

By dropping this behavior onto any vector shape member, you can create quick and easy pie charts. However, they don't look as nice as most pie charts because each slice is the same color. Because vector shape members can have only one fill color, it is impossible to create a multicolored pie chart from one vector shape. However, you can do so using multiple shapes.

The following behavior is similar to the last one, but it draws only one slice of the pie. You can attach this behavior to multiple shape members, all placed at the same location on the Stage, and thus create a pie chart that looks just like the last. However, each slice is actually a different vector shape member. Make sure that each sprite is using a different cast member. If the movie is using the same vector shape member for each sprite, this process won't work.

The behavior includes a new parameter, "pPiece". This parameter determines which piece of the pie the sprite should represent. When applying the behavior, you can drop it onto all six pie piece sprites at once, set the "pValues" and "pRadius" for all of them at once, and then go back and use the Behavior Inspector to reset the "pPiece" property for each one, as follows:

```
property pValues, pRadius, pPiece

on getPropertyDescriptionList me
  list = [:]
  addProp list, #pValues, [#comment: "Value List",  \
    #default: [], #format: #list]
  addProp list, #pRadius, [#comment: "Radius",  \
    #default: 100, #format: #integer]
  addProp list, #pPiece, [#comment: "Piece Number",  \
    #default: 1, #format: #integer]
  return list
end

on beginSprite me

  -- determine total value of pie
  total = 0.0
  repeat with i = 1 to pValues.count
    total = total + pValues[i]
  end repeat

  -- start new vertextList
  vlist = []

  -- start 1/4 circle, back
  oldAngle = -pi()/2

  -- start at 0
  swing = 0.0
```

```
repeat with i = 1 to pValues.count

  -- begin slice at center
  add vlist, [#vertex: point(0,0)]

  -- calculate angle for end of piece
  swing = swing + pValues[i]
  newAngle = 2.0*pi()*(swing/total)-pi()/2

  -- only draw my own piece
  if pPiece = i then
    -- move from start to end of piece
    repeat with a = 100*oldAngle to 100*newAngle

      -- add point on circumference
      x = pRadius*cos(a/100)
      y = pRadius*sin(a/100)
      add vlist, [#vertex: point(x,y)]
    end repeat
  end if

  -- set start for next piece
  oldAngle = newAngle
end repeat

-- use vertexList on this sprite
sprite(me.spriteNum).member.centerRegPoint = FALSE
sprite(me.spriteNum).member.originMode = #center
sprite(me.spriteNum).member.vertexList = vlist
end
```

After the pie chart has been created, you can edit each of the individual members and change its color. The result is a multicolored pie chart like the one shown in Figure 28.6. You can also add a "pPieceColor" parameter to the behavior and have it set the *fillColor* property of the member for you.

Like the bar graph, the pie chart behavior is only semiautomatic. You can easily change the values of the six pie pieces, without altering the Score or Stage by hand. However, if you want to add a seventh piece, you have to add another sprite and alert all the behavior properties.

A more complex pie chart behavior would create the pie pieces for you using a *new* command to create new members and then set up empty sprites with these members. That way, you could have pie charts created on-the-fly, with no pre-existing sprites or members.

➪ *For more information about building vector shape members, see "Building Vectors with Lingo," p. 412 (Chapter 20, "Controlling Vector Graphics")*

Figure 28.6
This multicolored pie chart was created with six vector members and a single behavior applied to each.

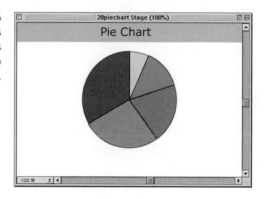

CREATING QUESTIONNAIRES

Surveys are rarely taken on paper anymore. Probably the most common way to take a survey is over the phone. Of course, on the other end of the phone is a person with a computer, entering the answers as you give them. Surveys are also taken on the Web and in standalone computer kiosks.

Creating a survey in Director is similar to creating the standardized test example shown in Chapter 27, "Educational Applications." The only real difference is that a survey might use more than just radio buttons to enable the respondent to provide answers. Check boxes and pop-up menus are also good options, as well as blank text fields in which users can type whatever they want. Another difference between a test and a survey is that a survey does not require any answer-checking because there are no "wrong" answers.

In the example on the CD-ROM, a simple survey with four questions is given. Users start by clicking a Begin button on the screen. This starts the survey by clearing out the global "gAnswers" and resetting any radio button or check box members in the Cast:

```
global gAnswers -- list to store all responses

on beginQuestions
  -- clear list
  gAnswers = []

  -- remove previous selections
  repeat with i = 1 to the number of members
    if member(i).type = #button then
      member(i).hilite = FALSE
    end if
  end repeat

  -- start
  go to frame "question 1"
end
```

The first question uses five radio buttons, just as the standardized test program did in Chapter 27. It looks like Figure 28.7.

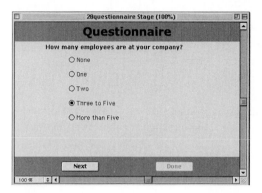

Figure 28.7
The first question in the survey uses radio buttons to ensure that the user picks one, and only one, item.

The code to control these radio buttons is similar to the radio button behavior described in Chapter 15, "Graphic Interface Elements." However, the behavior calls the following movie handler named "on addAnswer" each time a radio button is clicked:

```
property pState, pGroupList

on getPropertyDescriptionList me
  list = [:]
  addProp list, #pState, [#comment: "Initial State", \
    #format: #boolean, #default: FALSE]
  addProp list, #pGroupList, [#comment: "Group List", \
    #format: #list, #default: []]
  return list
end

on beginSprite me
  if pState then turnMeOn(me)
end

on turnMeOn me
  pState = TRUE
  sprite(me.spriteNum).member.hilite = TRUE
  repeat with i in pGroupList
    if i <> me.spriteNum then
      sendSprite(sprite i,#turnMeOff)
    end if
  end repeat
  addAnswer(sprite(me.spriteNum).member.text)
end
```

```
on turnMeOff me
  pState = FALSE
  sprite(me.spriteNum).member.hilite = FALSE
end

on mouseUp me
  turnMeOn(me)
end
```

In the movie script for this movie, "on addAnswer" takes a string and adds it to the "gAnswers" global. It figures out the question number from the frame label:

```
on addAnswer text
  -- get question number from frame label
  question = value((the frameLabel).word[2])

  -- set the item in the list
  setAt(gAnswers, question, text)
end
```

The second question in the movie uses check boxes. This enables users to select none, one, some, or all of the choices on the screen. Figure 28.8 shows this screen.

Figure 28.8
Check boxes are used to ask questions when multiple answers are possible.

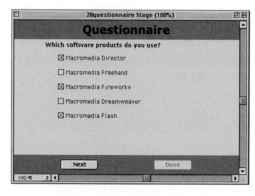

Check box buttons work on their own, switching on and off as users click them. However, a behavior is needed to alter the "gAnswers" global. This behavior calls the same "on addAnswer" handler that the radio button behavior did.

```
on mouseUp me
  text = ""
  repeat with i = 11 to 15
    if sprite(i).member.hilite = TRUE then
      if text <> "" then put "," after text
      put sprite(i).member.text after text
    end if
  end repeat
```

```
    addAnswer(text)
end
```

The third screen has another type of interface element. This one is a pop-up menu that enables users to select a single item from a list. Radio buttons can do this as well, but pop-up menus accommodate longer lists of items. Figure 28.9 shows this screen.

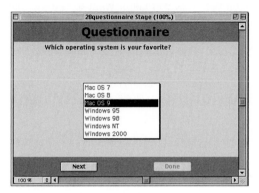

Figure 28.9
Pop-up menus are an alternative to radio buttons.

The pop-up menu can be run with the same script that was used in Chapter 16. The action to be performed by this script is to call "on addAnswer" with the behavior property "pSelected" as the parameter.

Finally, a questionnaire might also need an editable text field, such as the one shown in Figure 28.10.

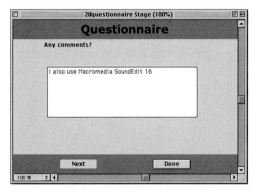

Figure 28.10
An editable text field enables users to enter comments and other information.

The editable field needs a behavior as well. The following simple behavior clears the text from the field when the sprite appears, and then sends the text to the "on addAnswers" handler when the frame is left.

```
on beginSprite me
    sprite(me.spriteNum).member.text = " "
end
```

```
on endSprite me
  addAnswer(sprite(me.spriteNum).member.text)
end
```

In the end, the list "gAnswers" can be converted to a string and saved to a file. You can even append it to the end of a file that already exists and thereby compile the results of multiple surveys. If this is an applet on the Web, you might want to take the data and use *postNetText* to send it back to a CGI program on your server.

▢⇨ *For more information about using radio buttons, **see** "Using Radio Buttons," p. 294 (Chapter 15)*

▢⇨ *For more information about using check boxes and making pop-up menus, **see** "Using Check Boxes," p. 292 and "Creating Graphical Pop-Up Menus," p. 314 (Chapter 15)*

▢⇨ *For more information about accepting keyboard input, **see** "Using Keyboard Input," p. 342 (Chapter 16)*

CREATING COMPUTER-BASED TRAINING PROGRAMS

Quizzes and tests are good for testing knowledge, but if done correctly, they can actually teach as well. Computer-based training programs are programs that teach concepts using a computer. They use human-computer interaction to reinforce ideas or processes.

As an example, computer-based training may be used to teach employees at a company how to use the new phone system. If the phone system has a lot of different codes that perform different tasks, a beginner can get confused easily and have to look up the codes in a book or on a reference chart. However, it would be far more efficient to have the employees memorize the codes so that they can use the phone system without a hassle.

A computer-based training program can show the users a picture of the phone and ask them questions such as, "How do you forward a call?" The users must then use the picture of the phone and press the buttons on it to type that code. If they get it wrong, they have to start again. If they are correct, they move on to the next code. Figure 28.11 shows what such a program could look like.

Figure 28.11
A computer-based training program screen that teaches users different telephone codes.

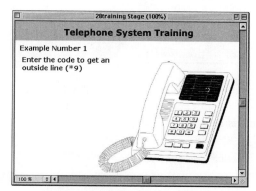

The idea is that people who use this program a few times a day will quickly get up to speed and memorize the codes. Plus, they can learn the codes before they actually need to use them.

The Lingo code for this movie is similar to the code used to create the questionnaire in this chapter. This program requires three globals: the current question number, the correct answer for the current question, and the answer the user has given so far.

```
global gQuestionNum -- which question number
global gCorrectAnswer -- correct for current question
global gAnswer -- the user's answer, so far
```

The movie starts by setting the "gQuestionNum" to 1 and then calling "on askQuestion". This handler grabs the question and correct answer from a text field, sets the question text on the Stage, and records the correct answer in "gCorrectAnswer".

```
-- reset questions and ask first
on startMovie
  gQuestionNum = 1
  askQuestion
end

-- get question info and ask it
on askQuestion
  -- data uses ; as separator
  the itemDelimiter = ";"

  -- get the data from a field
  text = member("Questions").text.line[gQuestionNum]

  -- set the question
  member("Question").text = text.item[1]

  -- get the answer
  gCorrectAnswer = text.item[2]

  -- reset user's answer
  gAnswer = ""

  -- set message
  member("Message").text = "Example Number"&&gQuestionNum
end
```

The text field that contains the questions and answers has to be carefully formatted. It uses a semicolon as the item separator:

```
Enter the code to get an outside line (*9);*9;
Enter the code to forward the current call (22#);22#;
Enter the code to turn auto answer on (#7);#7;
```

```
Enter the code to turn auto answer off (*3);*3;
Enter the code to get an operator (*072952#4);*072952#4;
```

The correct answers can use any of the 10 digits, plus the # and * characters. These characters correspond to the keys on a telephone. The picture of the telephone in Figure 28.11 actually contains small buttons that are hovering over the keypad. Each one has a cast member that is named appropriately. For example, the member over the 1 key is named "1". When one of these buttons is clicked, it sends a message to a movie handler.

```
on mouseUp me
  -- gets the character from the member name
  k = sprite(me.spriteNum).member.name

  -- send along to movie script
  addToAnswer(k)
end
```

The movie handler "addToAnswer" maintains the "gAnswer" string. It places the new character after all the characters already there. It then compares the whole string to the correct answer. If it matches, the program moves to the next question. If it doesn't match, but corresponds to the beginning characters of the correct answer, it means the user has not strayed from the correct answer—if the user has typed *6 so far, and the answer is *69, for instance.

However, if the answer is different in any way from the beginning of the correct one, a message is displayed and the user must try again.

```
on addToAnswer k

  -- add to answer
  put k after gAnswer

  put gAnswer, gCorrectAnswer

  if gAnswer = gCorrectAnswer then
    gotItRight
  else if gCorrectAnswer starts gAnswer then
    -- one step closer, nothing to do here
  else
    gotItWrong
  end if
end
```

The "on gotItRight" and "on gotItWrong" handlers take care of the messages and other post-question functions.

```
-- move on to next question
on gotItRight
```

```
-- next question
gQuestionNum = gQuestionNum + 1

-- all done?
if gQuestionNum > member("Questions").line.count then
  member("Message").text = "Finished."
  beep(3)
else
  beep()
  askQuestion
end if
end

-- wrong answer message
on gotItWrong
  member("Message").text =  "Wrong. Try again."
  gAnswer = ""
end
```

Notice that the questions in the program give the answers away. This is done simply to make the program easier to test. The real program will probably not give this information to users.

This program is simple. Real computer-based training programs can get much more complicated. You could ask the questions in a random order, for example. You could also record which questions were answered incorrectly and then retest users on questions they got wrong.

TROUBLESHOOTING BUSINESS APPLICATIONS

- When enabling users to type text, as shown in the database program and in the questionnaire, make sure that it isn't possible to type a *RETURN* character in the field. Doing so works, but you cannot convert the data list to a string and then back again. Solutions are to use an *on keyDown* script to not enable *RETURN*s to pass, convert *RETURN*s to another character before saving, or set the text member framing property to "Limit to Field Size".

- When you build pie charts, or any multiple vector shape-based image, make sure that the members are set to use "Auto-Size" in the member's Properties box. Also set the *centerRegPoint* to *FALSE* and the *originMode* to #center. If you don't, the members might not line up on the Stage.

DID YOU KNOW?

- When creating bar graphs, you can set the shape members to use a pattern as well as a color. Do this by selecting the member on the Stage and using the tool palette.

- When you save a database file on the Mac, you can use the FileIO *setFinderInfo* to set a file type for the database file. You can then use *setFilterMask* for both Mac and Windows to restrict users to opening only those files.

- If you write a short handler that saves the questionnaire data as a tab-delimited list, rather than as a Director list, you can import it into a spreadsheet or statistical analysis program to process the results of a survey.

29

GRAPHICS APPLICATIONS

IN THIS CHAPTER

Source movies for this chapter can be found on the CD-ROM in the "Book Movies" folder under folder 29.

Although graphics are almost always used in every Director movie, sometimes they are more than just a part of it. Sometimes, graphics are the whole point of the movie.

For instance, a slideshow presentation of different images places a set of graphics as the central focus of a movie. Sometimes the purpose of the movie is to display just one image. Often, this image exceeds the screen size, such as in a large map or diagram. In that case, users needs to pan, scroll, or zoom into the image.

Another possibility is a movie that continually changes an image or images, as in a montage. With inks and colors, Director can alter an image easily.

CREATING SLIDESHOWS

It's easy to make a slideshow movie like the one created in Chapter 1, "Animation with Director." A simple movie doesn't even require any Lingo. You can just import the images into the Cast, and then create frames in the Score to show each screen.

However, what if you don't know what images will be a part of the slideshow until the last minute? Or, what if the images are likely to change? Maybe the images need to be added by someone who does not even know how to use Director or doesn't have access to it.

You can make an intelligent Director movie that compiles a slideshow out of any collection of images in a folder. Users can even swap out the files in the folder with new ones to create a completely different slideshow.

Such a movie might look like Figure 29.1. The image is one cast member that is actually a linked member, not an imported one. To make the image a linked member, use the standard import method, but be sure to select "Link to File" in the Import dialog box before importing.

Figure 29.1
A simple slideshow presentation can import images one by one, rather than requiring them all to be present in the movie at the start.

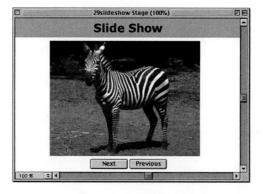

All the images for the slideshow should be placed in a folder named Images. This folder should appear in the same location as the movie itself, and eventually in the same folder as the projector. To make things simpler, link the initial image cast member to the first image of the slideshow inside this Images folder.

The movie first needs to read the contents of the Images folder and store the names of the files in a list. The *getNthFileNameInFolder* function performs this task.

The list of files is stored in a global. Also, the folder path is stored in a global. The folder path will be needed again when each image is imported. The folder path is determined by the location of the movie or projector, plus the word Images. In addition, an extra file separator is needed at the end. This file separator is a colon (:) on the Mac, but a forward slash (\) in Windows.

Here are the global declarations needed, as well as the *on startMovie* handler and the "on getImageList" handler that compiles the list of image files:

The *getNthFileNameInFolder* function takes a pathname and a number as its two parameters. It returns the name of the file that matches that number in the specified folder. If the number given is greater than the number of files in that folder, an empty string is returned. It has been known to be reliable only for folders with 255 or fewer files.

```
global gImageFolder -- where the images are
located
global gImageList -- a list of all image filenames
global gImageNum -- the number of the current image


on startMovie
  -- determine the location of the images
  gImageFolder = the pathname & "Images"
  if the platform contains "mac" then
    gImageFolder = gImageFolder & ":"
  else
    gImageFolder = gImageFolder & "\"
  end if

  -- set other globals
  getImageList
  gImageNum = 1

  -- show first image
  showImage
end


-- this handler looks at each file in the folder and gets the
-- filename of that image
on getImageList
  gImageList = []
  repeat with i = 1 to 255
    filename = getNthFileNameinFolder(gImageFolder,i)
    if filename = "" then exit repeat
    add gImageList, filename
  end repeat
end
```

After the filenames have been stored in a list, the task of importing the file into the cast member is simple. You just need to set the *filename* property of the member. The program will set it to the full path of the image, including the previously compiled "gImageFolder" global:

```
-- this handler resets the filename of the image to a new file
on showImage
  member("Image").filename = gImageFolder & gImageList[gImageNum]
end
```

Notice that no changes are needed to the sprites or Score. The Score does not change, it just keeps on displaying the same member. The member itself changes.

The example shown previously in Figure 29.1 showed Next and Previous buttons. Scripting these is not hard. You just have to make sure users do not go past the end or back up past the beginning of the slideshow.

```
on nextImage
  gImageNum = gImageNum + 1
  if gImageNum > gImageList.count then
    gImageNum = 1
  end if
  showImage
end

on previousImage
  gImageNum = gImageNum - 1
  if gImageNum < 1 then
    gImageNum = gImageList.count
  end if
  showImage
end
```

If the images being loaded are large, there will be a delay between the display of each image because the file needs to be read from the disk. You can minimize this by making the images smaller: Use GIFs or JPEGs rather than larger file formats.

The two buttons in the sample movie on the CD-ROM are wired up with the complex button behavior from Chapter 14, "Creating Behaviors." In addition, the frame has a simple *go to the frame* placed in the *on exitFrame* handler.

The images are shown in alphabetical order. Director actually has no say in the matter. The *getNthFileNameInFolder* function just returns the files in the order in which the operating system has them.

The *getNthFileNameInFolder* technique is restricted to Director and projectors. You cannot use this technique in quite the same way with Shockwave because you don't have access to the *getNthFileNameInFolder* function. However, you can still import images by resetting the *file-*

A simple way to get your images to appear in the order that you want is to place characters, such as numbers, at the beginning of each filename. For instance, you can have a file called 0010zebra.jpg that will appear before 0020elephant.jpg. By leaving some leading zeros, you ensure that you can represent at least 1,000 images and order them correctly. By adding the last zero, you ensure that you can easily insert images between others, such as 0015gorilla.

name property of a linked bitmap member. This property accepts Internet locations as readily as it accepts local disk locations.

The problem then becomes one of determining which files are present. You can maintain a separate list of image filenames in a text file on the server. This file can be read with the *getNetText* series of commands. You just have to update that file every time you add or remove an image.

Some servers even return a list of files in a directory as a simple HTML page, called an *index*. If your sever does this, you can get an up-to-date list by using "getNetText" with the path to the folder itself. However, the text returned is not a straight list and you might find it difficult to extract the filenames from it.

PANNING LARGE IMAGES

Sooner or later, every Director developer has to face the situation in which an image that needs to be displayed is larger than the Stage. Frequently, these are huge images of maps, diagrams, or even detailed photographs.

If the detail in the image needs to be preserved, shrinking the image to fit is not an option. The only solution is to display only a portion of the image at a time, and enable users to pan around the image to see whatever portions they need to examine.

Creating functionality like this can be as easy as turning on the sprite's movable option in the Score window. However, doing so enables users to move the image off the screen altogether. It also does not give you a way to provide additional functionality, such as special grab-and-drag cursors.

Figure 29.2 shows a movie that represents only a portion of an image. The entire image is actually there, in its single Sprite channel, but only the portion centered on the Stage can be seen. Some gray box-shape sprites cover the four edges of the screen as well. These box shapes can serve as places for additional buttons, instructions, or comments.

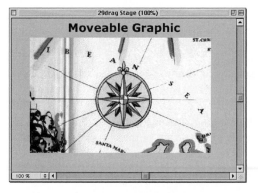

Figure 29.2
Only part of a large image can be seen in this movie. However, users can click and drag the image around to see any portions they want.

The desired functionality of this movie is to enable users to click the image and drag it around. Users should not, however, be able to drag the image past its edges. To prevent that, the script, which is a behavior in this case, needs to know the coordinates of the visible area.

It knows these coordinates by looking at a sprite that is one channel behind the image. Its dimensions fall directly behind the visible portion of the image. The behavior takes the *rect* of this sprite so that the sprite cannot be dragged past its limits.

The *on beginSprite* handler gets the *rect* of this underlying sprite and uses it to compute the "pBounds" property. This *rect* represents the limits within which the registration point of the image can be moved so that the image still fits inside the visible area. This math is tricky. Play around with the example on the CD-ROM to see it in action.

```
property pDrag, pOffset, pBounds, pCursor


on beginSprite me
  pDrag = FALSE

  -- get rectangle of display area
  spr = sprite(me.spriteNum)
  mem = sprite(me.spriteNum).member
  screen = sprite(me.spriteNum-1).rect
  pBounds = rect(0,0,0,0)
  pBounds.left = screen.right - (mem.width - mem.regPoint.locH)
  pBounds.right = screen.left + (mem.regPoint.locH)
  pBounds.top = screen.bottom - (mem.height - mem.regPoint.locV)
  pBounds.bottom = screen.top + (mem.regPoint.locV)
end
```

When users click the sprite, the "pDrag" property signals that dragging is taking place. In addition, the offset between the click location and the registration point of the sprite is recorded to enable users to drag the sprite from the point of the click, rather than the center.

```
-- when the image is clicked, enable dragging
on mouseDown me
  pDrag = TRUE
  pOffset = the clickLoc - sprite(me.spriteNum).loc
end
```

In addition to the dragging, this behavior also uses the cursor to show users what is happening. The *on mouseWithin* handler is called once per frame. It checks to see what is going on, and displays closed and opened hand cursors when appropriate. To make sure that the cursor command is not constantly being applied every frame, the "on changeCursor" handler first compares the desired cursor with its record of the cursor's last change. It uses the cursor command only when a change is necessary.

```
-- when the cursor is over the image, see if a cursor is needed
on mouseWithin me
  -- check to make sure the cursor is directly over sprite
  if the rollover = me.spriteNum then
    if pDrag = TRUE then
```

```
      -- closed hand for dragging
      changeCursor(me,290)
    else
      -- open hand if not dragging
      changeCursor(me,260)
    end if
  else
    -- normal cursor if not directly over sprite
    changeCursor(me,0)
  end if
end

-- if cursor leaves image area, reset it
on mouseLeave me
  changeCursor(me,0)
end

-- change the cursor only if not the same as last time
on changeCursor me, cursorNum
  if cursorNum <> pCursor then
    pCursor = cursorNum
    cursor(pCursor)
  end if
end
```

Dragging is stopped when the user releases the mouse button:

```
-- stop dragging
on mouseUp me
  pDrag = FALSE
end
on mouseUpOutside me
  pDrag = FALSE
end
```

The *on exitFrame* handler is where the action takes place. A new location is calculated, based on the mouse location. That location is then checked to make sure it doesn't place one of the edges of the image past a boundary. The code limits the location to this boundary if it does.

```
-- set the new location if dragging
on exitFrame me
  if pDrag then
    newloc = the mouseLoc - pOffset

    if newloc.locH < pBounds.left then newloc.locH = pBounds.left
    if newloc.locH > pBounds.right then newloc.locH = pBounds.right
```

```
    if newloc.locV < pBounds.top then newloc.locV = pBounds.top
    if newloc.locV > pBounds.bottom then newloc.locV = pBounds.bottom
    sprite(me.spriteNum).loc = newloc
  end if
end
```

You can use this behavior very easily by just dragging it on top of any sprite. However, you need to have a rectangle in the Sprite channel below it that determines the visible area. Check the example on the CD-ROM to see exactly how this is set up.

You can show images that are very wide or tall with this same behavior. If one dimension fits on the screen, but the other doesn't, set up the underlying rectangle to exactly match the smaller dimension. Users will not be able to drag in that direction at all, because there is nothing more to show. However, they will be able to drag in the longer dimension.

MAKING SCROLLBARS FOR LARGE IMAGES

Although panning enables users to see any part of a large image, there is no way for them to tell, at any particular time, where they are in the image. In addition, dragging with the cursor can be clumsy at times. If the image is very large, users might have to click and drag many times to get all the way across the image.

Scrollbars solve these problems. They are used so commonly throughout computer applications that even novices can use them without difficulty.

Figure 29.3 shows the movie from Figure 29.2. It has a large image that is only partially visible. The scrollbars at the right and bottom of the image enable users to get around inside the image. The marker in the middle of each scrollbar not only shows the relative position of the visible portion of the image, but it also can be dragged to move around inside the image.

Figure 29.3
Scrollbars enable users to decide which portion of a large image to view at any one time.

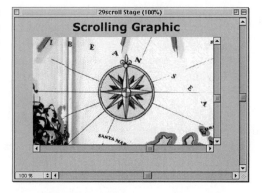

Scrollbars are similar to the slider interface element described in Chapter 15, "Graphic Interface Elements." Scrollbars include a marker, a background graphic, and two arrow buttons. However, there is really no need for the "shadow" used in the slider examples.

The behaviors that need to be developed for a program such as the one seen in Figure 29.3 need to work for both horizontal and vertical scrollbars. Whether a behavior controls a horizontal or vertical scrollbar can be decided by parameters. In addition, one parameter needs to link the marker to the background sprite and one parameter needs to link it to the image's sprite:

```
property pPressed -- whether the sprite is being pressed
property pBounds -- the rect of the shadow sprite at start
property pBGSprite -- the number of the shadow sprite
property pImageSprite -- the image to manipulate
property pValue -- actual value of the slider
property pOrientation -- horiz or vert scrollbar

on getPropertyDescriptionList me
  list = [:]
  addProp list, #pBGSprite, [#comment: "Scroll Background Sprite",\
    #format: #integer, #default: 0]
  addProp list, #pOrientation, [#comment: "Orientation",\
    #format: #symbol, #default: #horizontal,\
    #range: [#horizontal, #vertical]]
  addProp list, #pImageSprite, [#comment: "Image Sprite",\
    #format: #integer, #default: 0]
  return list
end
```

When the sprite starts, it needs to figure out some things. First, it uses the background sprite to determine the marker's movement limit. So, the background sprite acts in a fashion similar to that of the "shadow" sprite described in Chapter 15. It also sends the initial location of the scrollbar marker to the image's sprite, where a new handler called "on newImagePos" adjusts the position of the image accordingly.

```
on beginSprite me
  -- get the bounds on all four sides
  pBounds = sprite(pBGSprite).rect
  pBounds.right = pBounds.right - sprite(me.spriteNum).member.width/2
  pBounds.left = pBounds.left + sprite(me.spriteNum).member.width/2
  pBounds.bottom = pBounds.bottom - sprite(me.spriteNum).member.height/2
  pBounds.top = pBounds.top + sprite(me.spriteNum).member.height/2

  -- get initial value and send to image sprite also
  if pOrientation = #horizontal then
    pValue = sprite(me.spriteNum).locH - pBounds.left
    sendSprite(sprite pImageSprite,#newImagePos,getValue(me),VOID)
  else if pOrientation = #vertical then
    pValue = sprite(me.spriteNum).locV - pBounds.top
    sendSprite(sprite pImageSprite,#newImagePos,VOID,getValue(me))
  end if
```

```
    setMarker(me)
end
```

The movement of the marker is achieved through the typical handlers used for dragging behaviors.

```
on mouseDown me
  pPressed = TRUE
end

on mouseUp me
  pPressed = FALSE
end

on mouseUpOutside me
  pPressed = FALSE
end

on exitFrame me
  if pPressed then
    moveMarker(me)
  end if
end
```

When the marker is being dragged, the "on moveMarker" handler positions the marker to move with the mouse. The scrollbar boundaries are always checked to make sure that the marker is not moved too far. The "on newImagePos" handler in the image's sprite behavior is also called each frame so that the image's position is constantly updated to match the marker as it is being dragged.

```
on moveMarker me
  if pOrientation = #horizontal then
    pValue = the mouseH - pBounds.left
    -- check to make sure it is within bounds
    if pValue > pBounds.width then
      pValue = pBounds.width
    else if pValue < 0 then
      pValue = 0
    end if
    sendSprite(sprite pImageSprite,#newImagePos,getValue(me),VOID)
  else if pOrientation = #vertical then
    pValue = the mouseV - pBounds.top
    -- check to make sure it is within bounds
    if pValue > pBounds.height then
      pValue = pBounds.height
```

```
    else if pValue < 0 then
      pValue = 0
    end if
    sendSprite(sprite pImageSprite,#newImagePos,VOID,getValue(me))
  end if

  setMarker(me)
end
```

Like the slider behaviors in Chapter 15, the arrow buttons call a handler inside the marker's behavior. The handler moves the scrollbars one pixel at a time. It performs the same boundary checking as the preceding handler, and also sends a message to the image's sprite to update it.

```
-- this handler moves the marker one value left or right
on moveMarkerOne me, direction
  if direction = #left or direction = #up then
    pValue = pValue - 1
  else if direction = #right or direction = #down then
    pValue = pValue + 1
  end if

  -- check to make sure it is within bounds
  if pOrientation = #horizontal then
    if pValue > pBounds.width then
      pValue = pBounds.width
    else if pValue < 0 then
      pValue = 0
    end if
    sendSprite(sprite pImageSprite,#newImagePos,getValue(me),VOID)
  else
    if pValue > pBounds.height then
      pValue = pBounds.height
    else if pValue < 0 then
      pValue = 0
    end if
    sendSprite(sprite pImageSprite,#newImagePos,VOID,getValue(me))
  end if

  setMarker(me)
end
```

The behavior needs the supporting handler "on setMarker", which sets the marker according to the value of the scrollbar. This is used by the "on moveMarkerOne" handler so that the marker moves as users click the arrow buttons.

```
-- this sets the marker sprite
on setMarker me
  if pOrientation = #horizontal then
    sprite(me.spriteNum).locH = pBounds.left + pValue
  else
    sprite(me.spriteNum).locV = pBounds.top + pValue
  end if
end
```

The "on getValue" handler returns the value of the slider. This handler can be called by a movie handler or a handler in another behavior. Rather than returning the marker's pixel position, it returns a value between 0 and 1, representing the position of the marker in the scrollbar.

```
-- this handler returns the value of the slider between 0 and 1
on getValue me
  if pOrientation = #horizontal then
    return float(pValue)/float(pBounds.width)
  else
    return float(pValue)/float(pBounds.height)
  end if
end
```

Finally, the last handler in the scrollbar marker behavior enables an outside handler to set the position of the marker. It passes in a value between 0 and 1, and the handler figures out the pixel position of the marker from that. This handler enables users to drag the image around with the cursor, and the markers are updated as the image moves.

```
-- this sets the marker according to a number between 0 and 1
on setValue me, percent
  if pOrientation = #horizontal then
    pValue = percent*pBounds.width
  else
    pValue = percent*pBounds.height
  end if
  setMarker(me)
end
```

The scrollbar marker behavior is now complete, but it doesn't have the direct capability to move the image. It calls the handler "on newImagePos", which exists in the image sprite's behavior, several times. The following handler, which can be added to the same image sprite behavior used in the last section, repositions the image based on values from 0 to 1.

```
-- this handler receives messages from the scrollbars telling it
-- to change the position of the image
on newImagePos me, hPercent, vPercent
  if not voidP(hPercent) then
```

```
      -- message from horizontal scrollbar
      newH = pBounds.left + pBounds.width*(1.0-hPercent)
      sprite(me.spriteNum).locH = newH
    end if
    if not voidP(vPercent) then
      -- message from vertical scrollbar
      newV = pBounds.top + pBounds.height*(1.0-vPercent)
      sprite(me.spriteNum).locV = newV
    end if
end
```

The image sprite's behavior also needs to reciprocate by sending the scrollbars information any time users drag the image around. It does this with the "on sendPosition" handler. This handler needs to be called near the end of the "on exitFrame" script, immediately after the location of the sprite is set.

```
-- this handler sends the new position of the image to the scrollbars
-- so they can adjust their markers accordingly
on sendPosition me
  horizScrollSprite = 18
  vertScrollSprite = 25
  hPercent = 1.0-float(sprite(me.spriteNum).locV-pBounds.top)/pBounds.height
  sendSprite(sprite horizScrollSprite,#setValue,hPercent)
  vPercent = 1.0-float(sprite(me.spriteNum).locH-pBounds.left)/pBounds.width
  sendSprite(sprite vertScrollSprite,#setValue,vPercent)
end
```

The next items to work on are the scrollbar buttons. They use a script similar to the arrow buttons with the sliders described in Chapter 15. The behavior needs to know which direction each button represents and which marker it relates to. Each button also needs a down state.

```
property pDownMember, pOrigMember -- down and normal states
property pPressed -- whether the sprite is being pressed
property pMarkerSprite -- the number of the marker sprite
property pArrowDirection -- 1 or -1 to add to slider

on getPropertyDescriptionList me
  list = [:]
  addProp list, #pMarkerSprite, [#comment: "Marker Sprite",\
    #format: #integer, #default: 0]
  addProp list, #pDownMember, [#comment: "Arrow Button Down Member",\
    #format: #bitmap, #default: ""]
  addProp list, #pArrowDirection, [#comment: "Arrow Direction",\
    #format: #symbol, #range: [#left,#right,#up,#down], #default: #right]
  return list
end
```

```
on beginSprite me
  pOrigMember = (sprite me.spriteNum).member
end

on mouseDown me
  pPressed = TRUE
  (sprite me.spriteNum).member = member pDownMember
end

on mouseUp me
  liftUp(me)
end

on mouseUpOutside me
  liftUp(me)
end

on liftUp me
  pPressed = FALSE
  (sprite me.spriteNum).member = member pOrigMember
end

on exitFrame me
  if pPressed then
    sendSprite(sprite pMarkerSprite, #moveMarkerOne,\
    pArrowDirection)
  end if
end
```

This completes the scrolling image program. As you can see, it includes many complex handlers. Most of this complexity has to do with figuring out the moving boundaries of the scrollbar markers and of the image itself.

You can easily leave out one of the two scrollbars and create an image that scrolls in only one dimension. You can also remove the handlers that enable users to control the image by dragging it, leaving the scrollbars as the only option.

Also remember that the scrollbar graphics are totally up to you. The ones used in this example look very much like standard scrollbars. However, you can create colorful creative ones that fit your particular interface style.

ZOOMING IN ON LARGE IMAGES

A third way to enable users to view portions of a large image is to enable them to see the entire image at first, and then click a spot on the image to zoom in to full size. This is particularly useful for maps, where the shrunken, zoomed-out view of the map is still somewhat viewable.

A program that does this starts out looking like Figure 29.4. The entire image is visible on the screen. Users then click a spot and the result looks very much like Figure 29.2 (shown earlier). The only difference is that you need to use some extra cursors, such as a magnifying glass, to let users know what is going on.

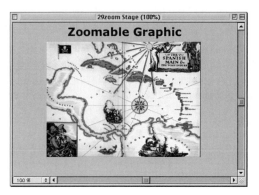

Figure 29.4
When users click the image, it enlarges to full size.

After the users click a spot on the image, the image is enlarged to full size. The spot where the users clicked is centered on the screen, unless it needs to be adjusted near the edges. Then, users can click and drag the image as before. To return to the zoomed-out image, users hold down the Shift key and click.

The behavior to do this is built from the panning image behavior discussed in the "Panning Large Images" section of this chapter. This time, the behavior needs to keep track of two modes. The first mode is the fully zoomed-out image, on which users can click to zoom in. The second mode is the full size image, which users can click to drag the image around, or press Shift+click to zoom back out.

```
property pMode, pDrag, pOffset, pBounds, pScreen, pOrigRect, pCursor

on beginSprite me
  pDrag = FALSE
  pMode = #zoom

  -- get rectangle of display area
  spr = sprite(me.spriteNum)
  mem = sprite(me.spriteNum).member
  pScreen = sprite(me.spriteNum-1).rect
  pBounds = rect(0,0,0,0)
```

```
    pBounds.left = pScreen.right - (mem.width - mem.regPoint.locH)
    pBounds.right = pScreen.left + (mem.regPoint.locH)
    pBounds.top = pScreen.bottom - (mem.height - mem.regPoint.locV)
    pBounds.bottom = pScreen.top + (mem.regPoint.locV)

    -- remember original "zoomed out" rect
    pOrigRect = sprite(me.spriteNum).rect
  end
```

The "gOrigRect" global is needed for the program to remember how the sprite looked on the Stage before the behavior started changing it. This original state is the "zoomed-out" view. You need to set the sprite up on the Stage by scaling it down and making it fit in the area to be used. You can even scale it differently horizontally and vertically if you want. This behavior works either way.

The next handler takes care of all mouse clicks. If the "pMode" property is #zoom, it uses the *mapStageToMember* function to determine the real point in the image that was clicked. It then centers this point on the Stage, using point (240,160) as the center of the Stage. The program checks to make sure the image is within the draggable boundaries, and then changes "pMode" to #drag.

If the "pMode" is set to #drag to begin with, the "pDrag" property is set to *TRUE* and the "pOffset" property is calculated. The "on exitFrame" handler takes care of the dragging until the mouse is lifted.

This handler also looks for the case in which the "pMode" is set to #drag when the user Shift+clicks the image. It then restores the sprite to its original size.

```
-- when the user clicks, perform one of three actions
on mouseDown me

  -- zoom in on location
  if pMode = #zoom then

    -- get real point clicked
    clickPoint = \
      mapStageToMember(sprite(me.spriteNum), the clickLoc)

    -- set sprite to full size
    mem = sprite(me.spriteNum).member
    sprite(me.spriteNum).rect = mem.rect

    -- center on the point clicked
    newloc = point(240,160) + \
        sprite(me.spriteNum).member.regPoint - clickPoint
    if newloc.locH < pBounds.left then newloc.locH = pBounds.left
    if newloc.locH > pBounds.right then newloc.locH = pBounds.right
```

```
    if newloc.locV < pBounds.top then newloc.locV = pBounds.top
    if newloc.locV > pBounds.bottom then newloc.locV = pBounds.bottom
    sprite(me.spriteNum).loc = newloc

    -- now enable dragging
    pMode = #drag

    -- zoom out to original view
  else if pMode = #drag and the shiftDown then

    -- set to original rect
    sprite(me.spriteNum).rect = pOrigRect

    -- ready for next zoom
    pMode = #zoom

    -- drag
  else if pMode = #drag then

    -- start drag
    pDrag = TRUE
    pOffset = the clickLoc - sprite(me.spriteNum).loc

  end if
end
```

The "on mouseWithin" handler, and the supporting "on changeCursor" handler, work the same way they did in the two preceding sections. However, two more cursors are needed. A magnifying glass with a plus (+) in it is used when users are over the image and the image is zoomed out. This means that users can click the image to zoom in. Also, a magnifying glass with a minus (-) in it is used when users are over the full-sized image and are holding down the Shift key. This cursor means that users can zoom out. Here is the code to take care of this:

```
-- when the cursor is over the image, see if a cursor is needed
on mouseWithin me
  if the rollover = me.spriteNum then
    if pMode = #zoom then
      changeCursor(me,302) -- magnifying glass with +
    else if pMode = #drag and the shiftDown then
      changeCursor(me,303) -- magnifying glass with -
    else if pMode = #drag and pDrag = TRUE then
      changeCursor(me,290) -- closed hand
    else if pMode = #drag then
      changeCursor(me,260) -- opened hand
    end if
```

```
    else
      changeCursor(me,0)
    end if
  end


  -- if cursor leaves image area, reset it
  on mouseLeave me
    changeCursor(me,0)
  end


  -- change the cursor only if not the same as last time
  on changeCursor me, cursorNum
    if cursorNum <> pCursor then
      pCursor = cursorNum
      cursor(pCursor)
    end if
  end
```

The "on mouseUp", "on mouseUpOutside", and "on exitFrame" handlers are identical to the ones used earlier.

```
  -- end dragging
  on mouseUp me
    pDrag = FALSE
  end
  on mouseUpOutside me
    pDrag = FALSE
  end


  -- set the new location if dragging
  on exitFrame me
    if pDrag then
      newloc = the mouseLoc - pOffset

      if newloc.locH < pBounds.left then newloc.locH = pBounds.left
      if newloc.locH > pBounds.right then newloc.locH = pBounds.right
      if newloc.locV < pBounds.top then newloc.locV = pBounds.top
      if newloc.locV > pBounds.bottom then newloc.locV = pBounds.bottom
      sprite(me.spriteNum).loc = newloc
    end if
  end
```

This zoom and pan behavior can be used without the panning action as well. You might just want to enable users to click and zoom in, and then click and zoom out. You might also want to use the "on changeCursor" handler to place some instructions in a text member on the

Stage. For instance, when users are in #zoom mode, it could say, "Click on the image to zoom in." When users are in #drag mode, it could say, "Click and drag the image to pan; Shift+click to zoom out."

⇨ *For more information on making sliders, **see** "Creating Sliders," p. 304 (Chapter 15)*

UTILIZING INK AND COLOR MANIPULATION

Most of the time, images in Director are displayed as is. However, with the wide variety of inks and the capability to change foreground and background colors, you can take an image and adjust its appearance in many ways.

Practical applications for this are not immediately apparent. The Lighten and Darken inks, for instance, can change the color of an image in all sorts of different ways. But why would you want to do that? One reason is to be able to reuse the same image several times and have it look different each time.

When you are manipulating the color of an image, it's sometimes hard to find the settings you are looking for. That is why a program such as the one shown in Figure 29.5 is useful. It enables you to change both the *color* and *bgColor* properties of the sprite by their red, green, and blue components. These color changes have a great effect on sprites that use the Lighten and Darken inks.

Figure 29.5
This program enables you to play with the colors used for the Lighten and Darken inks.

The program itself borrows a lot from behaviors earlier in the book. For instance, the sliders use the slider behaviors in Chapter 15. The two radio buttons also use behaviors from Chapter 15.

The image itself has a simple behavior that reads the values of the radio buttons and sliders and sets the ink and colors of the sprite accordingly. It does this constantly, so changes are shown as you make them.

```
on exitFrame me
  -- read radio buttons to set ink
  if selected(sprite 3) = 3 then
    ink = 40
```

```
   else
     ink = 41
   end if
   sprite(me.spriteNum).ink = ink

   -- read first set of sliders to set color
   c = rgb(0,0,0)
   c.red = sprite(7).pValue
   c.green = sprite(12).pValue
   c.blue = sprite(17).pValue
   sprite(me.spriteNum).color = c

   -- read second set of sliders to set bgcolor
   c = rgb(255,255,255)
   c.red = sprite(23).pValue
   c.green = sprite(28).pValue
   c.blue = sprite(33).pValue
   sprite(me.spriteNum).bgColor = c
end
```

You can expand a program such as this to test even more kinds of inks, although the color changes will not have quite as dramatic an effect on most. You can also include a button that enables you to import a new image into the member being shown. You can use the FileIO Xtra or the MUI Xtra to get the image filename, and then set the *filename* property of the image to import it. However, the member must start out as a linked image, not an internal one.

Another possibility for this program is to create your own Xtra with it. You can do this by placing the movie in your Director Xtras folder. You can add some interesting functionality, such as having it use the selection of *castLib* property to see whether users have selected a bitmap, and then take its picture property and replace the picture property of the image in the Xtra. This way, you can select an image in the Cast, and then launch the Xtra, which shows you a copy of the image you have selected and lets you play with its inks and colors.

For some background information about sprite inks, see "Setting Sprite Inks," p. 176, "Setting Sprite Colors," p. 179, and "Using the Sprite Blend," p. 178 (Chapter 10, "Properties of Sprites and Frames")

For some more information about making sliders, see "Creating Sliders," p. 304, and "Using Radio Buttons," p. 294 (Chapter 15)

TROUBLESHOOTING GRAPHICS APPLICATIONS

- If your slideshow can't seem to find the image files, it might be because the pathname is not being compiled correctly. Try placing the pathname in the Message with a *put* command each time the *filename* property is set. This way, you can check it.

- In a slideshow, you need to have the image member initially linked to some image. Make sure this image is present when you deliver your final product; otherwise, an error message comes up when the movie is launched. It's a good idea to make sure the filename is set to link to the first image in the slideshow, or to have it linked to some very small placeholder image file.

- When creating scrollbar graphics for the scrolling image behaviors, the placement of the background graphic determines the range of movement of the marker. So be sure to test it at both maximum and minimum values.

- Not all inks are affected by the *color* and *bgColor* properties of a sprite. If the image is 8-bit color or higher, these settings have little effect on the image for most inks.

DID YOU KNOW?

- Another way to create a slideshow is to simply have all the images in an external cast library. You can then swap out this library with a new one for a different slideshow. This works on the Web as well as in a projector, and makes the images harder to "steal" because they are not in plain image formats such as JPEG or GIF.

- To complete the scrollbar behavior, you might want to enable users to click the background bar itself. If they click above the marker, the scrolling area should page up, whereas if they click below the marker, it should page down. This is how most scrollbars work.

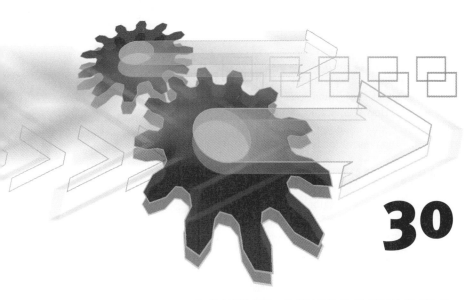

30

SOUND APPLICATIONS

IN THIS CHAPTER

Source movies for this chapter can be found on the CD-ROM in the "Book Movies" folder under folder 30.

Sound is the neglected medium in multimedia. Pictures and text are used in just about everything, and video and animation get all the glory. However, sound can be used to create compelling multimedia experiences as both the supporting media and as the central focus.

CREATING A PIANO KEYBOARD

Creating a musical note is an easy task for anyone familiar with computer sound programs. In fact, you can just record a piano or other instrument. Then, you can wire that sound up to a Director button.

It's as easy as that to create a one-note keyboard program. Adding additional notes, enough to enable users to play music, is the tricky part.

The first step is to get a sample sound. Make it a middle C note if possible. You can record this using a microphone and a musical instrument, an electronic instrument plugged directly into your computer, or a sound sample from a sound effects CD. Make this sample note as small as possible and save it to a file that you can import into Director.

An *undocumented feature*, such as the *rateShift* property, is something that the Macromedia engineers added to Director but is not officially supported by Macromedia. Many times, the features have not been tested well enough to ensure that they will work on all computers. Usually, undocumented features show up in later versions of Director as documented and supported features. However, Macromedia might also decide to remove such features from future versions altogether.

After you have your C note, you can create other notes from it from inside Director using the undocumented *rateShift* property of sounds that is new to Director 8. This will shift the sound up one musical note, also called a *semitone*.

So, using a *rateShift* of 1, the C becomes C sharp. Using a *rateShift* of 2 makes it a D.

With each shift, the sound gets shorter because you are essentially speeding up the sound. This means that by the time you get to the next octave, the sound is being played twice as fast as the original. The result is that the sound is very short and no longer contains much definition. An easy way to fix that is to use a new sound at that point of the scale. So, there will be a C3 sound for the first octave of notes, and then a C4 sound for the next. Each sound will then be shifted only slightly less than one octave up at most.

To create the simple keyboard shown in Figure 30.1, all you need is a single shape member. This rectangle is used for all the sprites. Some sprites are colored black and others, white. Because the black keys need to be in front of the whites, they should be in higher Sprite channels.

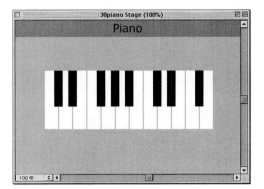

Figure 30.1
A simple keyboard contains keys made of rectangle shapes, colored white and black.

A behavior turns these rectangles into piano keys. The following behavior uses a parameter to determine which sound goes with which key. It also reacts to the key press by changing the color to red.

```
property pSound, pShift, pOrigColor, pChannel

on getPropertyDescriptionList me
  list = [:]
  addProp list, #pSound, [#comment: "Sound", #format: #sound, #default: VOID]
  addProp list, #pShift, [#comment: "Shift", #format: #integer, #default: 0]
  return list
end

on beginSprite me
  -- remember original color
  pOrigColor = sprite(me.spriteNum).color

  -- start with channel 1
  pChannel = 1
end

on mouseDown me
  press(me)
end

on mouseEnter me
  -- consider it a press when mouse button is down
  -- and the user rolls over to the key
  if the mouseDown then
    press(me)
  end if
end
```

```
on mouseUp me
  unpress(me)
end

on mouseUpOutside me
  unpress(me)
end

on mouseLeave me
  unpress(me)
end

on press me
  -- make key red
  sprite(me.spriteNum).color = rgb(255,0,0)
  updateStage

  -- play note
  sound(pChannel).play([#member: pSound, #rateShift: pShift])

  -- use next channel next time
  pChannel = pChannel + 1
  if pChannel > 8 then pChannel = 1
end

on unpress me
  -- restore key to black and white
  sprite(me.spriteNum).color = pOrigColor
end
```

This script takes into account some special behaviors that normal buttons don't use. If users press down on the mouse button outside of a key, and then roll over it, the note plays. This makes it possible to press down once and "roll" over the keys to play them all.

The script also rotates through the eight Sound channels as each note is played. If you stick to one Sound channel, playing the next note cuts off the previous note. Although this is not a problem if playing slowly, a quicker motion would sound awkward without using more Sound channels.

This keyboard works well, but it could use some graphical improvement. You can go ahead and create your own piano keys with a graphics program. Create up and down states for each. You can even place the keys at an angle to create a 3D effect.

⇨ *For more information on using sounds, **see** "Using Lingo's Sound Commands," **p. 364** (Chapter 17, "Controlling Sound")*

CREATING A PLAYER PIANO

Another possibility for a piano program is to have it play all by itself. You can provide it with a series of notes and durations, and feed them to the key behaviors at the proper time.

The first step is to come up with a simple notation scheme. Specifying the notes by their member names is a good start, but you also need to specify their duration. A good idea might be to measure this in one-tenths of a second, or six ticks.

Here is an example:

```
F3.3 0.1 G3#.3 0.1 C4.3
```

This notation uses spaces to separate notes. Each note contains a sound member name and duration, with a period in between. A 0 for a note simply means silence.

You can store notation such as this in a plain text field. Name it "Note List" or something similar.

To play this list of notes, a frame script behavior can be used. This behavior needs to keep track of the list of notes, the current note, the time to play the next note, and the sprite of the key being played.

```
property pNoteList -- a text list of notes and durations
property pNoteNumber -- the position of the current note
property pEndNoteTime -- when the current note is done
property pNoteSprite -- the sprite with the current note's key

on beginSprite me
  -- get the list of notes
  pNoteList = member("Note List").text

  -- start at the first note
  pNoteNumber = 1
  pEndNoteTime = the milliseconds
end
```

With every frame loop that goes by, the behavior checks "pEndNoteTicks". This is the time when the note currently being played is over, and another note needs to be played.

Before it does that, it needs to turn off the current key by sending an #unpress message to the key. This message calls the very same "on unpress" handler used in the preceding section.

```
on exitFrame me
  -- ready for next note?
  if the milliseconds >= pEndNoteTime then

    -- if there was a previous note, end it
    if not voidP(pNoteSprite) then
      sendSprite(pNoteSprite, #unpress)
    end if
```

```
        -- play new note
        playNote(me)
    end if

    go to the frame
end
```

The "on playNote" handler locates the note in the list and plays it. The part before the period is the sound member and the part after is the duration. It then uses the duration to set the new "pEndNoteTicks".

The handler then uses a list to map each note name to a sprite number. After it knows which sprite matches the note, it sends a message to that sprite to play.

```
on playNote me
  -- check to see if done
  if pNoteNumber > pNoteList.word.count then exit

  -- get new note and duration
  noteWord = pNoteList.word[pNoteNumber]
  the itemDelimiter = "."
  note = noteWord.item[1]
  duration = noteWord.item[2]

  -- set end time for note
  pEndNoteTime = pEndNoteTime + 200*integer(duration)

  -- if a "0", then just silence, else play note
  if note <> "0" then
    pNoteSprite = getProp(["C3":5, "D3":6, "E3":7 , "F3":8, "G3":9, "A3":10,\
        "B3":11, "C4":12, "D4":13, "E4":14, "F4":15, "G4":16,"C3#":17,\
        "D3#":18, "F3#":19, "G3#":20, "A3#":21, "C4#":22, "D4#":23,
"F4#":24],note)

    -- play it
    sendSprite(pNoteSprite, #press)
  end if

  -- next note
  pNoteNumber = pNoteNumber + 1
end
```

This behavior can now handle a string of notes as long as you want. The problem is converting your favorite song to this notation. The sample movie on the CD-ROM contains a relatively long song, just to give you an idea.

There is nothing to prevent you from going further with this movie. For instance, you can have two tracks running at once, one in Sound Channel 1 and one in Sound Channel 2. You can even have notes that are not represented by keys. Those notes can just play a sound rather than send a message along to a key sprite.

SIMULATING 3D SOUND

True 3D sound would mean a set of surround-sound speakers or some similar setup. However, you can easily simulate depth by setting the volume of a Sound channel.

Rather than using two different Sound channels as described in the preceding example, this example just uses one simple sound. The sound gets louder as the cursor approaches an object, and quieter as it moves away.

The behavior to do this is relatively simple. It uses the fact that the volume property ranges from 0 to 255. It computes the distance from the cursor to the sprite. If the distance is greater than 255, the volume is set to zero. If the distance is closer, it reverses it, so a distance of 0 plays the sound at full volume (255) and a distance of 254 plays the sound at a volume of 1.

```
on beginSprite me
  -- start sounds
  sound(1).play(member "static")
  setSoundVolume(me)
end


on setSoundVolume me

  -- calculate distance
  d = distance(me,sprite(me.spriteNum).loc,the mouseLoc)

  -- calculate volume
  vol = 255-d
  if d < 0 then d = 0

  -- set volumes
  sound(1).volume = vol
end


on exitFrame me
  -- change volumes
  setSoundVolume(me)
end

on distance me, p1, p2
  return sqrt(power(p1.locH-p2.locH,2)+power(p1.locV-p2.locV,2))
end
```

Notice that this behavior uses the member "Static" as the sound. If you want to use it with a different sound, you must change this name in the code to match your member's name.

Although the sample movie on the CD-ROM uses a television set and a static noise, you can find far more constructive ways to use this behavior. For instance, you can place several objects that have some sort of spoken narration on the Stage. As the cursor moves closer to an object, the looping audio gets louder.

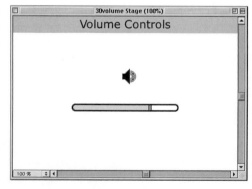

You can also use the *pan* property of a sound to make it play more in the left speaker when an object or the cursor is on the left side of the screen, and louder in the right speaker when the object or cursor is on the right. An example of the *pan* property is found in Chapter 17.

This simulates the experience that you might have at a museum, in which audio information is given at each exhibit. As you approach an exhibit, the audio become clearer, whereas the audio from the previous exhibit fades.

CREATING VOLUME CONTROLS

If your Director movie uses any sort of sound, it is usually a good idea to offer users a chance to control the overall volume. Although every operating system has a sound or volume control panel, you can imagine that plenty of people don't know that it exists. It's also unreasonable to expect people to have to leave your program to adjust the volume.

Adding a volume control is not hard. Using the *volume* property of a Sound channel, you can set the volume to a number from 0 to 255. If you are using more than one channel, you might want to set the volume of all the channels, 1 through 8, to the same number.

Volume Slider

The first step in adding a volume control is deciding which type of control you want. A slider is commonly used. Figure 30.2 shows a slider control and also a single-button control that you will learn more about later in this section.

Figure 30.2
Two different volume controls: a slider and a single-button control.

The slider control uses a behavior that is very similar to the slider behavior discussed in Chapter 15, "Graphic Interface Elements." The slider includes a marker, a shadow, and a background graphic. The behavior is attached to the marker. It tells the shadow's sprite to follow it.

You will recognize most of the code in this behavior from the slider behavior. However, some parameters are not present. The maximum and minimum values of the volume are always 0 and 255, so there is no need to make them parameters. This behavior also has no initial value parameter, because the behavior gets that from the current sound level to which the computer is set.

In fact, there's no need to store the current value of the slider at all. When users move the slider, the slider sets the *volume* property of all the Sound channels, which can be used in place of the "pValue" property.

```
property pPressed -- whether the sprite is being pressed
property pBounds -- the rect of the shadow sprite at start
property pShadowSprite -- the number of the shadow sprite
property pMinimumValue, pMaximumValue -- used by the marker sprite only

on getPropertyDescriptionList me
  list = [:]
  addProp list, #pShadowSprite, [#comment: "Shadow Sprite",\
    #format: #integer, #default: 0]
  return list
end

on beginSprite me
  pBounds = sprite(pShadowSprite).rect
  pMinimumValue = 0
  pMaximumValue = 255
  setMarker(me)
  setShadow(me)
end

on mouseDown me
  pPressed = TRUE
end

on mouseUp me
  pPressed = FALSE
end

on mouseUpOutside me
  pPressed = FALSE
end
```

```
on exitFrame me
  if pPressed then
    moveMarker(me)
  end if
  setMarker(me)
  setShadow(me)
end


-- this handler takes the mouse position and figures the
-- value of the slider
on moveMarker me
  -- compute the position as a number between 0 and 1
  x = the mouseH - pBounds.left
  sliderRange = pBounds.right-pBounds.left
  pos = float(x)/sliderRange

  -- translate to a value
  valueRange = pMaximumValue - pMinimumValue
  val = pos*valueRange + pMinimumValue
  val = integer(val)

  -- check to make sure it is within bounds
  if val > pMaximumValue then
    val = pMaximumValue
  else if val < pMinimumValue then
    val = pMinimumValue
  end if

  -- set volumes of all sounds
  repeat with i = 1 to 8
    sound(i).volume = val
  end repeat
end



-- this sets the marker sprite
on setMarker me
  -- compute the value as a number between 0 and 1
  valueRange = pMaximumValue - pMinimumValue
  sliderPos = float(sound(1).volume)/float(valueRange)

  -- translate to a screen position
  sliderRange = pBounds.right-pBounds.left
  x = sliderPos*sliderRange + pBounds.left
```

```
  -- set marker
  sprite(me.spriteNum).locH = x
end

-- this handler lets the marker sprite set the shadow sprite
on setShadow me
  x = (sprite me.spriteNum).locH
  r = rect(pBounds.left, pBounds.top, x, pBounds.bottom)
  sprite(pShadowSprite).rect = r
end
```

Note that the *on exitFrame* handler in this behavior sets the volume regardless of whether the slider is currently being moved. This means that the slider reacts to changes in the *volume*, even if the slider did not effect those changes. It cannot use all the channels, so channel 1 is used as an indicator of the current sound level.

You can test this by running the movie and using the Message window to set the *volume* of the first Sound channel. The slider reacts to the change. This also happens when users decide to change the volume manually with the computer's control panel. It ensures that the slider always displays the current sound setting.

⮕ *For more information about creating sliders, **see** "Creating Sliders," p. 304 (Chapter 15)*

Volume Button

Although a volume button does its job well, it's sometimes hard to implement. Perhaps you don't have the screen space, or a slider doesn't match your interface design.

I like to use a simpler option. You can place a single sprite on the Stage that users can click to change the volume. If the button is clicked once, the volume goes up one level. If the volume is at a maximum, it goes to 0.

Such a button can use a set of eight graphics to represent eight different volumes. Figure 30.2 showed this button just above the slider. Figure 30.3 shows the Cast that contains all eight variations of this button.

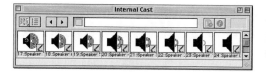

Figure 30.3
The Cast window shows eight images that represent the eight sound levels for a volume button.

The behavior that controls this button is much simpler than the slider behavior. But like it, it sets the member of the button every frame, regardless of whether the button was clicked. This ensures that the button reflects the current sound level even if users change it manually.

In fact, you can place both volume controls on the Stage at once, as shown previously in Figure 30.2. If you change the volume with one control, the other reflects the change. You can even wire up the button to be used to change the sound, whereas the slider just shows the change, but cannot be clicked.

```
on beginSprite me
  setIcon(me)
end

on setIcon me
  val = sound(1).volume / 36
  sprite(me.spriteNum).member = member("speaker"&&val)
end

on mouseDown me
  -- get sound level as value between 0 and 7
  val = sound(1).volume / 36

  -- increase sound level
  if val < 7 then val = val + 1
  else val = 0

  repeat with i = 1 to 8
    sound(i).volume = val*36
  end repeat

  setIcon(me)
end

on exitFrame me
  setIcon(me)
end
```

You can use any of the eight members to represent the eight sound states. You can get creative with this by using different size audio speakers or pictures of people whispering to pictures of them yelling.

TROUBLESHOOTING SOUND APPLICATIONS

- Does there seem to be a large delay in playing sounds when you are mixing more than one? Always check to see whether the movie is running on a Windows machine with *the platform* system property. If it is, try to set *the soundDevice* to "DirectSound" or "QT3Mix". If users have DirectX or QuickTime installed, this results in much better sound mixing. If they do not, *the soundDevice* reverts to "MacroMix".

- Windows machines have a history of difficulty in supporting good multichannel audio playback. It is especially important that developers test early and often on the machines they plan to support, and to document the system requirements for their users. Macromedia's Tech Support Web site is an important source of information in troubleshooting sound issues.

- If you are trying to use stereo sounds, and the sound ends up being mono after you make a Shockwave movie, check your Shockwave Audio Settings in the Xtras menu. It may be set to convert all stereo sounds to mono to make them smaller.

DID YOU KNOW?

- A better way to use *rateShift* is to have your original sample represent the middle of a set of notes, rather than the first note. So, a middle-C sound sample might use *rateShift* to represent the G below it, up to the F sharp above it. The next and previous octaves would use other samples. This way, you minimize the amount of *rateShift* used on any sample.

- If you don't like sliders or the single-button volume control, you have plenty of other options. You can use a text-based pop-up menu like the behavior described in Chapter 16, "Controlling Text." You can also use a set of radio buttons. Even a dial is possible: Just have eight dial graphics, one for each sound level, and have the volume increase when users click the right side of the dial, and decrease when they click the left side.

- Some developers prefer to use *the soundLevel* system property instead of the *volume* property of each Sound channel. This system property can be set to values from 0 to 7, and it changes the actual volume of the sound on the user's computer. This means that all sounds, including digital video and system beeps, are affected. However, *the soundLevel* has been known not to work on many Windows sound cards.

- You can create a mute button that uses some of the code from the check box behavior described in Chapter 15. Just have the behavior remember the current sound level and start in the "on" position. If users click the check box, set the *volume* property of the channel(s) to 0. When users click again, reset the *volume* to its original value, or better yet, use *the soundEnabled* property. This enables you to turn off sound without changing the *volume* of a specific channel.

- Sound placed in QuickTime 4 tracks offers you even more control over what is playing and what is not. You can have multiple tracks, all synchronized, and turn off and on individual tracks with *setTrackEnabled*.

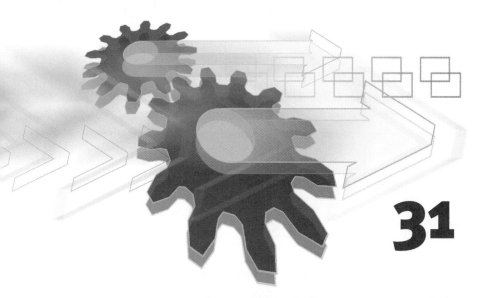

31

SHOCKWAVE APPLETS

IN THIS CHAPTER

Source movies for this chapter can be found on the CD-ROM in the "Book Movies" folder under folder 31.

Just about any Director movie can be a Shockwave applet. Most of the examples in the previous four chapters, plus the examples in the next chapter, can be placed on the Web or an intranet for viewing in a browser.

However, a few types of programs work only in the world of the Web. Navigation tools, such as navigation pages and navigation bars, are built specifically to enable users to navigate through a Web site. There are also Web advertisements, which can be made very interesting by creating them in Director. There are even programs that draw on other sources of information on the Web.

CREATING NAVIGATION PAGES

Just about every Web site has a front end. Although this can be a plain HTML page, you can also do something more complex, such as using a Shockwave applet.

Macromedia's site, for instance, uses Shockwave Flash to create an interactive experience right at the front door. Shockwave for Director is even better at producing interaction.

Although you can use any one of the many techniques discussed earlier in this book to make interactive movies, the basic difference between those movies and movies that are meant to be Shockwave navigation pages is the actual Web navigation.

Web navigation is achieved through the use of the *gotoNetPage* command. This command replaces the current HTML page with another one. It enables you to turn Shockwave buttons into links just like standard HTML <A HREF> tags.

Figure 31.1 shows a typical Shockwave applet navigation page in the Director Stage window. It contains six buttons, plus some extra text. The three-color swipes at the top animate from left to right.

Figure 31.1
A simple Director movie that can be used as the front end of a Web site.

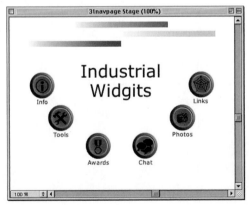

The behavior attached to each Web button is fairly simple. It takes one parameter: the Web location that the button will use. It doesn't even use the traditional "down" states like the complex button behavior discussed in Chapter 14, "Creating Behaviors."

```
property pURL

on getPropertyDescriptionList me
  list = [:]
  addProp list, #pURL, [#comment: "URL", #format: #string, #default: ""]
  return list
end

on mouseUp me
  gotoNetPage(pUrl)
end
```

The purpose of this behavior is to highlight what is needed to create a Web navigation button, which provides users with the capability to specify a URL and then use the *gotoNetPage* command to execute the jump.

You should use a behavior such as the complex button behavior described in Chapter 14. You can actually use that behavior as is by just placing a Lingo command such as "gotoNetPage("info.html")" in the parameter for "Lingo to Execute".

After the movie is done, it can be embedded in an HTML page and placed on your Web site. For more information on how to do this, see "Making Shockwave Movies" in Chapter 36, "Delivering the Goods." Figure 31.2 shows the Shockwave navigation movie embedded into a Web page so that it stretches to fit the browser window. This option is actually turned on in the HTML page. It isn't something you have to do while making the Shockwave movie itself.

Figure 31.2
What a movie embedded to fit the browser window might look like in Netscape Navigator.

In Director 8, you have the option to make a Shockwave movie stretch to fit the exact size of the browser window. This is both a good and bad thing. The good part is that you can create navigation pages like this example that resize to always encompass the entire browser window. The bad side is that bitmap images, like the ones used in the example, are stretched and might not look their best. You can see how Figure 31.2 shows the buttons slightly distorted. One way to get the best of both worlds is to use only scalable media, such as Flash and Vector Shape members.

The examples shown in Figures 31.1 and 31.2 are not all that they could be. Because you have so many power features in Director, it's a shame to use it only to display buttons and a simple animation. A more sensible use of the applet is to provide rollovers, as described in Chapter 15, "Graphic Interface Elements." Or, perhaps you can include sounds and sprites with behaviors that make them react to the mouse position. These are all things that are easy to do in Director, but much harder in HTML.

↪ *For more information about creating rollovers, **see** "Creating Display Rollovers," p. 290 (Chapter 15)*

↪ *For more information about using gotoNetPage, **see** "Controlling the Web Browser with Lingo," p. 448 (Chapter 22, "Shockwave and Internet Access")*

CREATING NAVIGATION BARS

Many Web sites use *frames*. Frames enable you to divide the browser's window into smaller parts, each of which contains a separate HTML page.

One use for frames is to have one large frame be a central area where information is displayed, while another small frame contains buttons that control what is in the large frame. Although you could place some plain HTML in this small frame, you could also make a Shockwave movie for it.

Such a movie might look like Figure 31.3. This is a narrow little applet that appears in a frame to the left of the main one.

Figure 31.3
A narrow navigation bar applet to control the HTML location of another frame in the browser.

The buttons in this applet are only a little more complex than the buttons in the previous program. This time, however, they need to specify the frame that the *gotoNetPage* command should affect. This is done with a second parameter:

```
property pURL, pTarget

on getPropertyDescriptionList me
  list = [:]
  addProp list, #pURL, \
    [#comment: "URL", #format: #string, #default: ""]
  addProp list, #pTarget, \
    [#comment: "Target", #format: #string, #default: "main"]
  return list
end

on mouseUp
  gotoNetPage(pUrl,pTarget)
end
```

The "pTarget" property should be set, for every button, to the name of the target frame. This name is determined by the HTML code in the parent page. Here is an example:

```
<HTML><HEAD>
<TITLE>Navigation Bar Demo</TITLE>
</HEAD>

<FRAMESET Cols="100,*">
<FRAME Name="bar" SRC="navbar.html" Scrolling="Auto">
<FRAME Name="main" SRC="info.html" Scrolling="Auto">
</FRAMESET>

</HTML>
```

The "navbar.html" page has the Shockwave applet on it. The other frame is called "main" and starts off with "info.html", the same content that might be displayed when users click the "Info" button in the applet.

Figure 31.4 shows the frames displayed in Netscape Navigator. The "info.html" page is shown, but there would obviously be more to it if this were not just a simple example.

Like the navigation page applet described earlier, this navigation bar is only an example. To make it worthwhile to use Shockwave, rather than just plain HTML images and links, you should add some animation or interaction.

⇨ *For more information about Web options,* **see** *"Controlling the Web Browser with Lingo," p. 448 (Chapter 22)*

⇨ *For more information about Shockwave movies,* **see** *"Making Shockwave Movies," p. 712 (Chapter 36)*

Figure 31.4
The browser window is broken
into two frames. The frame on the
left contains a page with a
Shockwave applet that controls
the frame on the right.

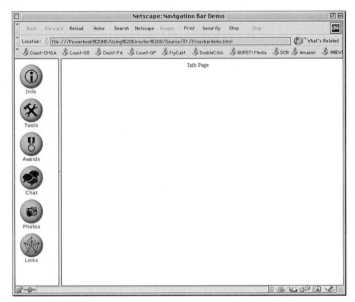

CREATING SHOCKWAVE ADS

Advertising is everywhere on the Web nowadays. At first, these were just static images. Now, Web advertisements are usually animated GIF images.

Sometimes, however, ads come in the form of Java applets, dynamic HTML, or Shockwave. Although Shockwave Flash movies as ads are more common than Shockwave for Director, it's not unheard of to have a movie as an ad. This is especially true because JavaScript can determine whether users have Shockwave, and simply display a less rich ad, such as an animated GIF, if they do not.

Making an ad in Director is another task that is relatively simple, but it doesn't have to be. Because Web ads are usually just animation, it is tempting to just do that in Director, too. But you can do so much more.

One idea is to use Lingo and behaviors to make animation that isn't possible to make with animated GIFs or Flash. For instance, take a look at the 3D cube script in Chapter 18, "Controlling Bitmaps." This script produced a 3D cube by manipulating six square bitmaps by their *quad* property. The cube rotated and changed angles depending on the mouse's location.

You can place that same script into a small advertising applet. Because it reacts to the mouse location, it can't be made in a simpler medium such as GIFs or Flash. The different possible angles also make it hard to do in other mediums, because the cube can be displayed in an almost infinite number of ways.

Figure 31.5 shows such a Web applet, which is set to 468 pixels by 60 pixels, a common Web advertisement size.

Figure 31.5
A small Shockwave applet can be used as an advertisement. This ad contains an interactive 3D cube on the right.

The only changes made to the 3D cube script were to make it a radius of 20 pixels, rather than 60, and to center it in a new position. The movie itself is several frames, rather than just one, so the three-color swipes can animate from left to right without any extra Lingo.

➯ *For more information using quad,* **see** *"Distorting Sprites," p. 374 (Chapter 18)*

PROCESSING AND DISPLAYING INFORMATION

An often-overlooked feature of Director is the power of the *getNetText* series of commands. With them, you can get any Web page from the Internet and process its raw HTML. You can also get a plain text file in the same way.

Because the Internet is full of information, there are plenty of uses for this. For instance, you can read in stock price information and display it in a ticker-like interface. You can even process the text of an HTML page to remove tags and find the information you want.

A good example of information retrieval is a Shockwave movie that reads reports from the National Weather Service, which provides simple conditions and forecasts on its Web site at `http://iwin.nws.noaa.gov`.

Checking out the site further, you can see that the forecasts are broken up by state. So, Colorado's forecast is at `http://iwin.nws.noaa.gov/iwin/co/state.html`, and California's forecast is at `http://iwin.nws.noaa.gov/iwin/ca/state.html`. The "co" and "ca" refer to the two-letter abbreviations for the states. Figure 31.6 shows a page with the forecast.

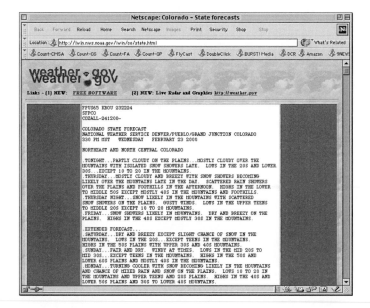

Figure 31.6
The browser window shows a forecast from the National Weather Service.

Figure 31.7 shows a small applet that presents weather forecasts in a "stock ticker" format. The buttons enable the users to specify which forecast the applet should retrieve.

Figure 31.7

This applet retrieves the text of a weather forecast and presents it like a stock ticker.

The following is the behavior for the buttons in Figure 31.7. Each button has two states, the down state representing that the button has been clicked, and an up state. The down state stays down until another button is clicked. So, a set of buttons such as these act like radio buttons.

```
property pStateCode, pUpMember, pDownMember, pNetID

on getPropertyDescriptionList me
  list = [:]
  addProp list, #pStateCode, [#comment: "State Code", #format: #string, \
#default: "XX"]
  return list
end

on beginSprite me
  pUpMember = sprite(me.spriteNum).member
  pDownMember = member(pUpMember.number + 1)
  gNetID = 0
end

on mouseDown me
  sendAllSprites(#reset)
  sprite(me.spriteNum).member = pDownMember
  pNetID = getNetText \
("http://iwin.nws.noaa.gov/iwin/"&pStateCode&"/state.html")
  sendSprite(sprite 12, #newData, "Loading a new forecast...")
end

on exitFrame me
  if pNetID > 0 then
    if netDone(pNetID) then
      text = netTextResult(pNetID)
      text = processReport(text)
```

```
      pNetID = 0
      sendSprite(sprite 12, #newData, text)
    end if
  end if
end

on reset me
  sprite(me.spriteNum).member = pUpMember
  pNetID = 0
end
```

This button behavior also starts a network operation with *getNetText* when the button is clicked. It checks every frame to see whether the information has been received. When that document has been received, the button behavior passes it along to the behavior attached to sprite 12, which is the stock ticker. The button behavior also gives that sprite a message immediately after the network operation begins.

There are many ways to make a stock ticker. This one simply makes the sprite move from right to left. The text member's width is set to the width of the text in it, assuming that each character is 7 pixels wide. When the entire text member has finished moving across the screen, it is reset to the right side of the screen and starts again.

```
property pText

on beginSprite me
  newData(me,"Click on a state button below to select a forecast.")
end

on newData me, text
  sprite(me.spriteNum).locH = (the stage).rect.width
  sprite(me.spriteNum).member.text = text
  sprite(me.spriteNum).member.width = text.length*7
end

on exitFrame me
  sprite(me.spriteNum).locH = sprite(me.spriteNum).locH - 3
  if sprite(me.spriteNum).rect.right < 0 then
    sprite(me.spriteNum).locH = (the stage).rect.width
  end if
end
```

This stock ticker behavior pads every piece of text it gets with 70 spaces. This forces the text to start off blank, and then the first character moves in from the right. It basically displays a different substring each frame. So, when the behavior starts, it displays characters 1 to 70, and then 2 to 71, and then 3 to 73, and so on.

When this behavior starts, it places some default text in the ticker. It also starts the ticker over again when the text runs out. You could handle this differently, by having it start with a forecast of a default state, or none at all. You could also have the behavior return to the default message to select a state when it is done.

Notice that the ticker calls a movie handler named "on processReport" to change the HTML text it receives before passing it along to the stock ticker. This handler is needed because the text at that Web location is certain to have some HTML tags and also some Return characters in it. To display it properly in the ticker, the tags and Returns should be removed. They are actually replaced with spaces to prevent pieces of information from appearing next to each other. The code also assumes that the real weather data appears between <TT> and </TT> tags. By focusing on the material inside these tags, a lot of the header and footer information is removed.

```
on processReport text
  text = betweenTT(text)
  text = removeTags(text)
  text = removeReturns(text)
  return text
end


on betweenTT text
  c1 = offset("<TT>",text)
  c2 = offset("</TT>",text)
  if c1 < 1 or c2 < 1 then return text
  return text.char[c1+4..c2-1]
end


on removeTags text
  inTag = FALSE
  newText = ""
  repeat with i = 1 to text.length
    if text.char[i] = "<" then
      inTag = TRUE
      put " " after newText
    else if text.char[i] = ">" then
      inTag = FALSE
    else if inTag = FALSE then
      put text.char[i] after newText
    end if
  end repeat
  return newText
end


on removeReturns text
```

```
repeat while TRUE
  c = offset(RETURN, text)
  if c < 1 then exit repeat
  put " " into text.char[c]
end repeat
return text
end
```

The actual function of the "on processReport" handlers depends on the content of the HTML page you are trying to read. Another page might present information in a table, and you might want to write a complex handler to extract it.

This program gives just an example of what can be done with the *getNetText* series of commands. You don't have to use a stock ticker to display information; you could just have it appear. Or, you could use graphics to show information, such as a line graph of stock prices. You could even have *getNetText* read in information from several pages and compile a report.

➡️ For more information about using getNetText, **see** "Getting Text over the Internet," **p. 450** (Chapter 22)

TROUBLESHOOTING SHOCKWAVE APPLETS

- To quickly test a movie in Shockwave, choose File, Preview in Browser. This tests the movie in your machine's default browser. You still need to test it in three other browsers. These should include both Netscape and Internet Explorer on both Windows and Mac. You might also want to check it in various versions of the browsers.

- Microsoft Internet Explorer 4.0 for the Mac had many problems that prevented Shockwave movies from working correctly. Therefore, developers should plan to support only version 4.01 and later on the Mac.

DID YOU KNOW?

- You don't necessarily need to embed a Shockwave applet inside an HTML page. You can point a browser directly to a Shockwave applet just as you can point it directly to a GIF or JPEG. The movie will fill the window, starting at the upper-left corner.

- Although *getNetText* can be used to retrieve data from a server stored in .html or .txt format, you can also use full CGI-like pathnames to access scripts. You can use *postNetText* to access scripts that respond only to posts.

- Use the Lingo function *netError* to determine whether something has gone wrong with a *getNetText* command, and what the problem is.

- You can use *getNetText*, *netDone*, and *netTextResult* without a network ID stored in a variable just as the examples in this book show. In that case, the program assumes that you mean the most recent network operation. It will work fine as long as you have only one network operation going on at a time.

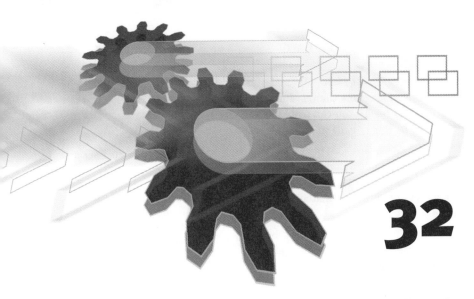

32

GAMES

Source movies for this chapter can be found on the CD-ROM in the "Book Movies" folder under folder 32.

Probably the most common use for Director is making games. Games can be used for many things. They can be used both to entertain and teach. You can even use them to demonstrate a point, or simply make information more fun.

Some games seem to be favorites among Director developers because they are fairly straightforward to make and can be used for a variety of purposes. Matching games are a good example.

Other games are more difficult to do in Director, but they are popular types of games, so Director developers have learned to make them anyway. Card games, such as blackjack, are examples of these types of games. This chapter shows you how to create various types of games.

> This chapter contains seven games. If you want even more information about creating games with Lingo, I've written an entire book on Lingo games called *Advanced Lingo for Games* published by another branch of the same publisher as this book, Hayden Books(ISBN: 0-7897-2331-X).

CREATING A MATCHING GAME

The basic object of a matching game is to correctly connect pairs of items on the screen. Each item is hidden, or face down, to use a card metaphor. You turn over one item, and then try to turn over its match. If you succeed, the two items are taken off the screen. If they do not match, both items are turned back over. This type of matching game is a memory game, in which you need to remember where items are located as you turn them over.

To make a game such as this, you first need a set of bitmaps to represent the items. Figure 32.1 shows a cast library with such a set. It includes 18 items. Because each is to be used in a pair of sprites, the Stage will include 36 sprites that form a six-by-six grid.

Figure 32.1
The Cast window shows a cast library with 18 items to be used in a matching game.

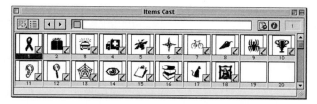

After you have the bitmaps for each item, you then need a bitmap to represent the items as they appear when they are laid face down. This should be a bitmap of the same size, in plain black. Name this member "Blank".

A movie script is used to control the whole game. You need two globals—one to contain a list of all the items according to the sprites in which they are placed and the other global needs to contain the sprite number of the one face-up sprite. The movie starts by randomizing the locations of the items in the sprites.

```
global gItemList, gSelected

on startMovie
  -- randomize items
  gItemList = createList()

  gSelected = 0
end
```

The items need to be placed in random sprites on the Stage, of course, or the game will be the same every time it is played. First, each item is added to the list twice, making a full set of pairs. Then, the list is shuffled into a new one.

```
on createList
  -- create ordered list
  templist = []
  repeat with i = 1 to 18
    add templist, i
    add templist, i
  end repeat

  -- shuffle list
  list = []
  repeat while templist.count > 0
    r = random(templist.count)
    add list, templist[r]
    deleteAt templist, r
  end repeat

  return list
end
```

All the sprites on the Stage should show the "Blank" member, so there is no need to set up the sprites in any way. The movie's Score has them as "Blank" members and they remain so until users click them.

When a user clicks one of the images, the "on clickItem" handler is called. The sprite number clicked is passed into this handler. The movie has the 36 items placed in sprites 11 to 46. So, to get the location of each item in the "gItemList" global, 10 needs to be subtracted from this number, giving you a number between 1 and 36.

When an item is clicked, the "Blank" member changes to the member corresponding to the item in the list. Then the handler checks to see whether this is the first item selected. If so, it sets the "gSelected" global to the sprite number. If not, it compares the items of the last sprite clicked with the current sprite. If they match, both are removed. If not, the previous sprite is turned back to "Blank" and the current sprite is stored in the "gSelected" global.

```
-- this handler is called by the item sprites when the user clicks
-- 10 is subtracted from the sprite number because the items
-- start with sprite 11
on clickItem sNum
  -- take control of sprite and turn over, use members from "items" cast
  puppetSprite sNum, TRUE
  sprite(sNum).member = member(gItemList[sNum-10],"Items")

  if gSelected = 0 then
    -- first item turned over
    gSelected = sNum

  else if gSelected = sNum then
    -- user clicked on selected item
    -- do nothing

  else if gItemList[sNum-10] = gItemList[gSelected-10] then
    -- user clicked on matching item
    -- make both go away
    sprite(sNum).memberNum = 0
    sprite(gSelected).memberNum = 0

    -- set items in list to 0
    gItemList[sNum-10] = 0
    gItemList[gSelected-10] = 0

    -- reset selection
    gSelected = 0

    -- check for end of game
    if checkForDone() then
      go to frame "done"
    end if

  else
    -- user clicked on wrong item
    -- turn last item back over
    sprite(gSelected).member = member("Blank")

    -- item clicked is now one selected
    gSelected = sNum
  end if
end
```

The "on clickItem" handler also calls the "on checkForDone" handler if a match is found. This handler looks at the member numbers of all the sprites where items should be. If all have been set to 0, it knows that the game is over. In that case, the movie jumps to another frame.

```
on checkForDone
  repeat with i in gItemList
    -- found an item still there
    if i <> 0 then return FALSE
  end repeat

  -- all were 0, so game is over
  return TRUE
end
```

Figure 32.2 shows this game in action. Often, an image is placed behind the game so that it is revealed as the users eliminate items. Because the item sprites start at 11, plenty of sprites in which to place this image are under the items.

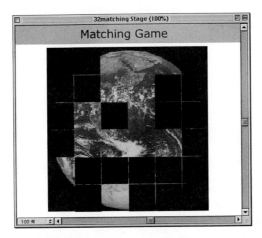

Figure 32.2
The matching game in progress. As the user finds pairs, a picture is revealed.

CREATING A SLIDING PUZZLE GAME

Another game that reveals an image as it is played is a sliding puzzle game. This is also played with squares on the screen. This time, all the items are shown, but they are all out of order. In addition, one piece is missing. Users can move any adjacent piece into the open spot. Users manipulate pieces in this way to try to put the image in order. Figure 32.3 shows this type of puzzle.

Figure 32.3
A partially solved sliding puzzle
with 15 pieces.

This puzzle was created with 15 different cast members, one for each piece. Because they will be randomized on the screen, the members need to know where they really belong. In order for the members to know where it belongs, each member needs a name that is also the correct horizontal and vertical position of the pieces in the puzzle. Look at Figure 32.4 to see an example.

Figure 32.4
A cast library with 16 puzzle
pieces. Each is named according
to its real position in the solved
puzzle. Only 15 are used in the
final puzzle.

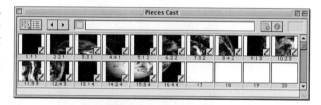

Like the matching game, this game consists mainly of a movie script. It needs to keep track of only one piece of information: the location of the blank spot in the puzzle. It stores this as two numbers, representing the horizontal and vertical location of the spot. The movie starts by setting this spot to position 1,1. It also uses the *puppetSprite* command to give Lingo control of the sprites with the pieces. This enables the movie script, as opposed to individual behaviors, to control the sprites.

```
global gOpenSpotX, gOpenSpotY

on startMovie
  gOpenSpotX = 1
  gOpenSpotY = 1
  repeat with i = 11 to 25
    puppetSprite i, TRUE
  end repeat
  scramble
end
```

The scramble can be done in a way similar to how the shuffle in the matching game was accomplished. The "on scramble" handler takes a more visual approach, however. It selects two sprites at random, and then switches them. It uses the *updateStage* command to make this switch visible to the users because it is an interesting effect.

```
on scramble
  repeat with i = 1 to 100
    -- pick two sprites at random and switch them
    s1 = random(15)+10 -- sprites between 11 and 25
    s2 = random(15)+10
    loc = sprite(s1).loc
    sprite(s1).loc = sprite(s2).loc
    sprite(s2).loc = loc
    updateStage
  end repeat
end
```

When a sprite with a piece is clicked, the "on clickOnPiece" handler is called. The sprite number is passed into it. The location of that piece in the puzzle is calculated by dividing the location of the sprite by 75. This is the number of pixels separating each piece from its neighbors. A 90 and 70 are subtracted horizontally and vertically because the puzzle's upper-left piece is located at 90,70.

After the piece's position is established, all four sides are checked to see whether any contains the empty spot. If the empty spot is found, the "on slide" handler is called.

```
on clickOnPiece sNum
  h = sprite(sNum).locH
  v = sprite(sNum).locV
  x =  (h-90)/75+1
  y = (v-70)/75+1

  -- check all surrounding spots
  if (gOpenSpotX = x-1) and (gOpenSpotY = y) then
    slide(sNum,-1,0)
  else if (gOpenSpotX = x+1) and (gOpenSpotY = y) then
    slide(sNum,1,0)
  else if (gOpenSpotX = x) and (gOpenSpotY = y-1) then
    slide(sNum,0,-1)
  else if (gOpenSpotX = x) and (gOpenSpotY = y+1) then
    slide(sNum,0,1)
  end if
end
```

The "on slide" handler moves the current piece up, down, left, or right, 75 pixels in 20 steps. You can add more steps to slow down the animation, or fewer steps to speed it up.

```
on slide sNum, dx, dy
  step = 20
  x1 = sprite(sNum).locH
  y1 = sprite(sNum).locV
  x2 = x1+(dx*75)
  y2 = y1+(dy*75)
  repeat with i = 0 to step
    p = float(i)/step
    sprite(sNum).locH = (p*x2)+((1.0-p)*x1)
    sprite(sNum).locV = (p*y2)+((1.0-p)*y1)
    updateStage
  end repeat
  gOpenSpotX = gOpenSpotX-dx
  gOpenSpotY = gOpenSpotY-dy
  if checkDone() then alert "You got it!"
end
```

At the end of each slide, the "on checkDone" handler compares all the sprite's positions with the location specified by the name of the member. If one does not match, it means that the puzzle is not complete. If they all match, the user has solved the puzzle.

```
on checkDone
  repeat with i = 11 to 25
    x = sprite(i).locH
    y = sprite(i).locV
    x = (x-90)/75+1
    y = (y-70)/75+1
    name = sprite(i).member.name
    if (value(name.word[1]) <> x) or (value(name.word[2]) <> y) then
      return FALSE
    end if
  end repeat
  return TRUE
end
```

The sliding puzzle game can be done with more or fewer pieces. You can also change the size of the pieces and their spacing. Just make sure that you adjust the numbers in the script accordingly. You can also standardize all the handlers so that they do not rely on hard-coded numbers such as 75, 90, and 70. Instead, they can use the member's width and the smallest horizontal and vertical positions in the puzzle.

CREATING A FALLING OBJECTS GAME

Another type of game that seems to be popular with Director developers is one that involves falling objects. The user controls something at the bottom of the Stage, such as a baseball glove or a cartoon character. Objects then fall from the top of the screen. Users must "catch" some of these objects and avoid others. Figure 32.5 shows a game such as this.

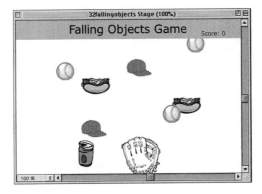

Figure 32.5
A falling objects game with baseball objects. The user moves the glove left and right and must catch balls while avoiding other objects.

The game is made up of several behaviors and a short movie script. The behavior that controls the glove movement is simple. It sets the horizontal location of the sprite to match the mouse.

```
on exitFrame me
  -- move glove with mouse
  sprite(me.spriteNum).locH = the mouseH
end
```

The falling object behavior is a little more complex. It uses a "pMode" property to determine whether the sprite is currently falling or awaiting instructions. It also enables itself to fall at different speeds, specified by the "pSpeed" property.

```
property pMode, pSpeed

on beginSprite me
  pMode = #none
  pSpeed = 10
end
```

In the *on exitFrame* handler, the "pMode" is checked. If it is set to #fall, the object's vertical position is changed. It then checks to see whether the sprite intersects the glove, which is in sprite 5.

If the two sprites intersect, another test is performed. This test makes sure that the center of the object is close to the center of the glove. Registration points are used to

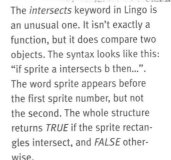

The *intersects* keyword in Lingo is an unusual one. It isn't exactly a function, but it does compare two objects. The syntax looks like this: "if sprite a intersects b then...". The word sprite appears before the first sprite number, but not the second. The whole structure returns *TRUE* if the sprite rectangles intersect, and *FALSE* otherwise.

determine the center—the registration point of the glove is set a little farther down than center, so it represents the "pocket" of the glove.

If this test proves true, the object is considered to be "caught." If it is the baseball, a point is added. If not, a point is subtracted. Either way, the sprite is reset.

```
on exitFrame me
  if pMode = #fall then
    -- move object down
    sprite(me.spriteNum).locV = sprite(me.spriteNum).locV + pSpeed

    -- see if it intersects the glove
    if sprite me.SpriteNum intersects 5 then

      -- see if it is close to the center of the glove
      if distance(me,sprite(me.spriteNum).loc,sprite(5).loc) < 20 then

        -- add points
        if sprite(me.spriteNum).member.name = "Baseball" then
          addPoint
        else
          subtractPoint
        end if

        -- reset object sprite
        pMode = #none
        sprite(me.spriteNum).locV = -100
      end if

    else if sprite(me.spriteNum).locV > 400 then
      -- went past bottom, reset
      pMode = #none
      sprite(me.spriteNum).locV = -100
    end if
  end if
end



-- utility handler
on distance me, p1, p2
  return sqrt(power(p1.locH-p2.locH,2)+power(p1.locV-p2.locV,2))
end
```

Because all the sprites start with the "pMode" of #none, something is needed to set it to #fall. The "on startFall" handler performs this task. It is called by the frame script. The handler specifies a speed and a member. If the sprite is already falling, the message is passed on to the next sprite.

```
on startFall me, speed, type
  if pMode <> #none then
    -- this sprite being used, go to next
    sendSprite(sprite(me.spriteNum+1), #startFall, speed, type)

  else
    -- set member, location, speed and mode
    sprite(me.spriteNum).member = member(type)
    sprite(me.spriteNum).loc = point(40+random(400),-20)
    pSpeed = speed
    pMode = #fall
  end if
end
```

In the "on startFall" handler, the horizontal location of the sprite is set randomly. Because the Stage in this example is 480 pixels across, a random number between 1 and 400 is chosen, and 40 is added. This gives a random number between 41 and 440, which keeps the object away from the edges.

The frame script is responsible for randomly telling sprites to drop. On a 1-in-10 chance, the script tells the first object sprite to drop. If that sprite is busy, it tells the next to drop, and so on.

The frame script also picks a random object, either a "baseball" member or one of three "object" members. It chooses a speed between 6 and 15, as follows:

```
on exitFrame

  -- drop object on 10% chance
  if random(10) = 1 then

    -- decide what type of object
    r = random(4)
    if r = 4 then type = "Baseball"
    else type = "Object"&&r

    -- send message to sprite(s)
    sendSprite(sprite 8, #startFall, 5+random(10), type)
  end if

  go to the frame
end
```

The movie script is present only to keep track of the score. It resets the score to 0 at the start of the movie, and then handles increasing or decreasing the score. It makes sure that the score does not go below 0, because a point is subtracted each time the user catches something that is not a baseball, but is one of the three other "object" types.

```
global gScore

on startMovie
  gScore = 0
  showScore
end

on addPoint
  gScore = gScore + 1
  showScore
end

on subtractPoint
  gScore = gScore - 1
  if gScore < 0 then gScore = 0
  showScore
end

on showScore
  member("Score").text = "Score:"&&gScore
end
```

The only thing that this sample game does not have is an ending. There are a lot of possibilities. You could have the game end when the user's score reaches a certain value. Or, you could count each object as it falls, and have the game end after a certain number of objects fall. You could also keep track of correct catches and incorrect catches, and stop the game after a certain number of incorrect catches. Another possibility is to set a timer and give the user a certain amount of time to collect as many points as possible.

EMULATING A SHOOTING GALLERY

Yet another common game that is easily done in Director is a shooting gallery. This is meant to emulate the shooting games at carnivals. Objects appear and move on the Stage, and the user tries to "shoot" them.

Figure 32.6 shows a typical setup. Some rectangles represent boxes or some other barrier. Ducks rise from them, and then descend back behind them. The cursor is changed to a crosshair and the user clicks to shoot. If the user clicks on a duck, the shot is recorded.

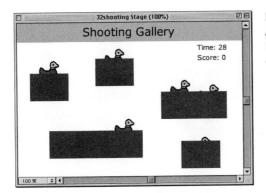

Figure 32.6
A shooting gallery game that challenges the user to shoot wooden ducks.

The movie consists mostly of a single behavior. This behavior controls the ducks. These ducks exist as sprites on the Stage, hidden behind rectangle sprites.

The behavior uses "pMode" to determine whether the duck is rising, falling, or not moving. If the duck is not moving, "pMode" is set to #down. Then, on a 1-in-30 chance, the duck begins to rise. A speed of 1 to 3 is chosen for this movement.

If the "pMode" is #rise, the duck moves up. If the pMode is #fall, the duck moves down. When the duck is rising, the behavior checks to see whether it has risen 30 pixels. If so, it changes the "pMode" to #fall.

A fourth mode is #hit, which means that the user has recently hit the duck. In that case, it resets to its original position and stops moving.

```
property pMode, pOrigLocV, pSpeed


on beginSprite me
  pMode = #down
  pOrigLocV = sprite(me.spriteNum).locV
end


on exitFrame me
  if pMode = #down then
    -- see if it is time to pop up
    if random(30) = 1 then
      pMode = #rise
      pSpeed = random(3) -- random speed
    end if

  else if pMode = #rise then
    -- move duck up
    sprite(me.spriteNum).locV = sprite(me.spriteNum).locV - pSpeed

    -- see if at highest point
    if sprite(me.spriteNum).locV < pOrigLocV-30 then
```

```
      pMode = #drop
    end if

  else if pMode = #drop then
    -- move duck down
    sprite(me.spriteNum).locV = sprite(me.spriteNum).locV + pSpeed

    -- see if at the lowest point
    if sprite(me.spriteNum).locV >= pOrigLocV then
      pMode = #down
    end if

  else if pMode = #hit then
    -- if recently hit, reset locV and member
    sprite(me.spriteNum).locV = pOrigLocV
    sprite(me.spriteNum).member = member("Duck")
    pMode = #down
  end if
end
```

The duck behavior also has an *on mouseDown* behavior. When the user clicks a duck, the duck is considered to be "hit." The following handler changes the member of the sprite to one that shows a duck being hit. In the example, the duck turns red. The movie handler "on addScore" is called, and the "pMode" is changed to #hit so that the *on exitFrame* handler can know that the duck has been hit.

```
on mouseDown me
  -- if already hit, then ignore
  if pMode = #hit then exit

  -- use other member
  sprite(me.spriteNum).member = member("Duck Hit")
  updateStage

  -- add point
  addScore
  pMode = #hit
end
```

This duck behavior comprises most of the game. All that is left is to position the duck sprites behind the rectangles on the Stage. These rectangles block mouse clicks, so the user cannot shoot "through" them. A simple behavior "eats" these mouse clicks.

```
-- block mouseDowns with boxes
on mouseDown
  nothing
end
```

The "on addScore" handler called by the duck behavior is in a movie script. In addition, some handlers are needed to take care of the game timer. This timer ticks down from 30 seconds. It actually works by noting the time, in ticks, when the movie starts. It adds 30 seconds to that time to determine the time when the game should end. It then subtracts the current time from that time to get the time remaining in the game.

The time remaining is displayed every frame, if needed. The handler also checks to see whether the game is over and then goes to another frame.

```
global gScore, gEndTime

on startMovie
  -- use sight cursor
  cursor([member "Sight",member "Sight"])

  -- reset score
  gScore = 0

  -- game ends 30 seconds from now
  gEndTime = the ticks + 30*60

  showScore
  showTime
end

on showScore
  member("Score").text = "Score:"&&gScore
end

on showTime
  -- convert ticks to seconds remaining
  timeLeft = (gEndTime - the ticks + 30)/60

  -- use this text
  text = "Time:"&&timeLeft

  -- if text is different than text displayed
  if member("Time").text <> text then
    member("Time").text = text
  end if

  -- time up?
  if timeLeft <= 0 then
    cursor(0)
    go to frame "Done"
  end if
end
```

```
on addScore
  gScore = gScore + 1
  showScore
end

on stopMovie
  cursor(0)
end
```

Another function that the movie handlers perform is the use of the *cursor* command to change the cursor to a crosshair. This cursor is stored as member "Sight". The program turns this cursor on during *on startMovie*, and turns it off when the game ends, or alternatively, when the game is interrupted through the *on stopMovie* handler.

The frame script completes the game. It just needs to call "on showTime" every frame to check the current time, display it if necessary, and end the game when the time comes.

```
on exitFrame
  showTime
  go to the frame
end
```

The game play is determined by the duck behavior. For instance, if you want to make a game where the ducks travel from side to side, you alter that behavior to make the ducks move that way, rather than rise and fall. You can even create several different behaviors that make targets move in different ways. You could combine these behaviors into one movie that has many different types of targets.

Another improvement would be to increase the speed of the sprites according to the time, or to the user's score. This makes the game more challenging for experienced players.

CREATING SPRITE INVADERS

The most classic of all games, Space Invaders, has given rise to hundreds, maybe thousands, of imitators. Some of these were done with Director. The following example is a simple version of a game of this genre. Figure 32.7 shows the game during play.

Making an invaders game is more involved than making any of the previous games in this section. It boils down to four behaviors: one for the invading sprites, one for the ship, one for bullets fired from the invaders, and one for bullets fired from the ship.

Creating the Invading Sprites

The game play is mostly dominated by the movement of the invaders. They move from side to side, all together. When they hit one side of the screen, they drop down, closer to the bottom.

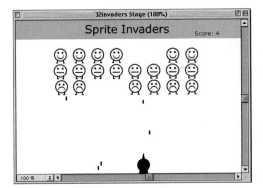

Figure 32.7
An "invaders" game that uses silly bitmaps as invaders.

A behavior for this kind of movement needs to worry about only one invader. The same behavior can be attached to all the invader sprites on the screen. However, two globals, "gHitWall" and "gHitBottom", are used so that when at least one sprite reaches a side of the screen or the bottom, the globals are set to *TRUE* and the frame script handles the situation.

The behavior begins by the direction and speed being set to 2, which means that the invader moves two pixels to the right every frame. It also records the member number of the sprite. The Cast is set up so that each invader has two members. They are essentially the same, but the feet reverse to give a "marching" feel. The invader behavior switches between these two members every frame.

```
global gHitWall, gHitBottom
property pDirection, pMemNum

on beginSprite me
  -- start moving 2 pixels to right
  pDirection = 2
  pMemNum = sprite(me.spriteNum).memberNum
end

on exitFrame me
  -- freeze if not on play frame
  if the frameLabel <> "Play" then exit

  if pDirection = 0 then
    -- no direction, must have been hit
    sprite(me.spriteNum).memberNum = 0 -- remove sprite

else
    -- move
    sprite(me.spriteNum).locH = sprite(me.spriteNum).locH + pDirection

    -- hit a wall?
```

```
  if pDirection > 0 and sprite(me.spriteNum).locH > 460 then
    gHitWall = TRUE
  else if pDirection < 0 and sprite(me.spriteNum).locH < 20 then
    gHitWall = TRUE
  end if

  -- toggle to other member to create animation
  if sprite(me.spriteNum).memberNum = pMemNum then
    sprite(me.spriteNum).memberNum = pMemNum + 1
  else
    sprite(me.spriteNum).memberNum = pMemNum
  end if

  -- fire 1 out of 200 times
  if random(200) = 1 then
    sendSprite(sprite 55, #fire, sprite(me.spriteNum).loc)
  end if
  end if
end
```

The *on exitFrame* handler also triggers an invader bullet to fire on a 1-in-200 chance. It sends a #fire message to sprite 55, which is where the invader bullets are located.

The *on exitFrame* handler sets the "gHitWall" global to *TRUE* if that sprite is too close to a side. The example shown previously in Figure 32.7 uses 24 invaders. It takes only one of the invaders being close to the wall to set this global. If it does become *TRUE*, the frame script handles it by sending a #changeDirection message to all sprites. Only the invader sprites use this message. The following handler is called. It moves the invaders down, and also reverses the direction of movement. The handler also checks to see whether any sprite has gone down too far and ends the game if one has.

```
on changeDirection me
  -- got change direction message

  -- move down
  sprite(me.spriteNum).locV = sprite(me.spriteNum).locV + abs(pDirection)

  -- hit bottom?
  if sprite(me.spriteNum).locV > sprite(5).rect.top then gHitBottom = TRUE

  -- reverse direction
  pDirection = -pDirection
end
```

Another message that can be sent to the invader is #hit. In this case, the member is changed to a bitmap that shows an explosion. The Stage is updated, so the explosion is shown right away. Then, the "pDirection" property is set to 0. This is used to let the *on exitFrame* handler know that the invader is dead, and it removes the sprite altogether in the next frame by setting its member number to 0.

```
on hit me
  -- got the message I was hit

  -- change to hit graphic
  sprite(me.spriteNum).member = member("Invader Hit")

  -- show me, since I will disappear next frame
  updateStage

  -- dead, so no direction
  pDirection = 0
end
```

Along with the invader behavior is the behavior for the invader bullets. These are assigned to a block of sprites from 55 to 75. You can assign more sprites if you want to enable the invaders to fire more shots at once, or assign fewer sprites if you want the invaders to be able to fire fewer shots at once.

The invader bullet behavior has a "pMode" property that tells it whether it is currently firing. The "on fire" handler causes the bullet to fire, or passes along the message to the next sprite if the bullet is already firing. The *on exitFrame* handler moves a firing bullet and also checks to see whether it hit anything or fell past the bottom.

```
property pMode

on beginSprite me
  pMode = #none
end

on fire me, loc
  if pMode = #fire then
    -- busy, send to next sprite
    sendSprite(sprite(me.spriteNum+1),#fire,loc)
  else
    -- set loc, mode
    sprite(me.spriteNum).loc = loc
    pMode = #fire
  end if
end

on exitFrame me
  -- freeze unless on play frame
  if the frameLabel <> "Play" then exit
```

```
if pMode = #fire then
  -- move down
  sprite(me.spriteNum).locV = sprite(me.spriteNum).locV + 8
  if sprite(me.spriteNum).locV > 330 then
    -- hit bottom
    pMode = #none
  else
    -- hit gun?
    didIHit(me)
  end if
end if
end
```

The *on exitFrame* handler calls "on didIHit" to determine whether the bullet ran into the ship. The ship, or gun, is in sprite 5.

```
on didIHit me
  -- hit gun?
  if sprite 5 intersects me.spriteNum then
    -- gun explodes
    sprite(5).member = member("Invader Hit")
    updateStage

    -- game over
    go to frame "Done"
  end if
end
```

Creating the Ship

Now that the invaders and the invader bullets are working, the next task is to get the ship to work. This is a fairly simple behavior that makes the ship move left and right with the left- and right-arrow keys. If the spacebar is pressed, a #fire message is sent to the block of sprites with the ship bullets.

```
property pFiredLastFrame

on exitFrame me
  if the frameLabel <> "Play" then exit

  if keyPressed(123) then
    -- left arrow
    sprite(me.spriteNum).locH = sprite(me.spriteNum).locH - 5
  end if
```

```
  if keyPressed(124) then
    -- right arrow
    sprite(me.spriteNum).locH = sprite(me.spriteNum).locH + 5
  end if

  -- check spacebar, plus check to make sure did not fire last frame
  if keyPressed(SPACE) and not pFiredLastFrame then
    -- space, fire
    sendSprite(sprite 6, #fire, sprite(me.spriteNum).loc)
    pFiredLastFrame = TRUE
  else
    pFiredLastFrame = FALSE
  end if
end
```

The ship behavior uses a property called "pFiredLastFrame", which prevents users from holding down the spacebar and creating a stream of bullets that would spell certain death for the invaders. Instead, bullets can be fired only every other frame. To space bullets even farther apart, you can use this property to count how many frames since the last bullet was fired, and allow a new bullet only every three, four, or more frames.

The ship's bullets have a behavior very similar to the invader bullets. The differences are that the bullet moves up, and it checks to see whether it hit any invader sprites.

Because a hit is scored every time a bullet hits an invader, the "gScore" global is referenced. The user's score is increased when a hit is determined.

```
global gScore
property pMode

on beginSprite me
  pMode = #none
end

on fire me, loc
  -- got signaled to fire
  if pMode = #fire then
    -- busy, send to next sprite
    sendSprite(sprite(me.spriteNum+1),#fire,loc)
  else
    -- fire
    sprite(me.spriteNum).loc = loc
    pMode = #fire
  end if
end

on exitFrame me
```

```
      -- freeze if not on play frame
    if the frameLabel <> "Play" then exit

    if pMode = #fire then
      -- move bullet up
      sprite(me.spriteNum).locV = sprite(me.spriteNum).locV - 16

      if sprite(me.spriteNum).locV < 0 then
        -- reached top of screen
        pMode = #none
      else
        -- check for hit
        didIHit(me)
      end if
    end if
end

on didIHit me
  -- loop through invader sprites
  repeat with i = 30 to 53
    -- see if it hit
    if sprite i intersects me.spriteNum then

      -- send hit message
      sendSprite(sprite i, #hit)

      -- get rid of bullet
      sprite(me.spriteNum).locV = -100
      pMode = #none

      -- add to score
      gScore = gScore + 1
      showScore
    end if
  end repeat
end
```

The movie script takes care of a few things, such as resetting the user's score and displaying a new score when needed:

```
global gScore

on startMovie
  gScore = 0
  showScore
```

```
      go to frame "Play"
end

on showScore
   member("Score").text = "Score:"&&gScore
end
```

Creating the Frame Script

Finally, the game needs a frame script. This script does more than your typical frame script. For one, it sends a #changeDirection to all sprites when a "gHitWall" flag is found. It also ends the game when a "gHitBottom" is found. These tasks are taken care of in the *on enterFrame* handler, which ensures that the tasks will execute before the *on exitFrame* handlers of all the behaviors attached to sprites.

```
global gHitWall, gHitBottom

on enterFrame me
   if gHitWall then
      -- an invader hit the wall
      sendAllSprites(#changeDirection)

   else if gHitBottom then
      -- an invader hit the bottom
      go to frame "Done"

   end if

   -- reset wall hit flag for this frame
   gHitWall = FALSE
end

on exitFrame
   go to the frame
end
```

This completes the scripts needed for the game. Many numbers, such as the speed of the ship, bullets, and invaders, can be changed. You can place as many or as few invaders as you want on the screen. You can also make them any bitmap image you want, but remember that every invader consists of two members that constantly switch to create animation.

Take this sample movie on the CD-ROM and try altering it. You can place the invaders in any formation you want. You can create a "shield" by adding some more sprites and writing a "shield" behavior script. You can go a lot of ways with this game to improve it.

CREATING TRIVIA GAMES

Trivia games can be found everywhere. They include popular board games, arcade machines, and even games you can play in bars. The hardest part of making a trivia game is coming up with the questions. The Director movie that asks the questions and keeps track of the score is fairly straightforward.

This example uses a movie script to do most of the work. The result is a game that looks like Figure 32.8. One question is asked at a time, and the user has to click one of four buttons to answer. A timer ticks down, so the longer the user takes to answer, the fewer points are rewarded. If the answer is incorrect, a full 100 points are removed from the timer.

Figure 32.8

A simple trivia game that asks one question at a time and provides four possible answers.

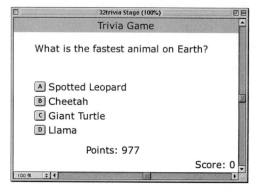

The movie script is needed to keep track of a few things in globals. It needs to know the question number that the user is on, the number of points possible if the answer is correct, the current score, and which answer is the correct one for the current question. The game starts by resetting these globals.

```
global gQuestionNum, gPossiblePoints, gScore, gCorrectAnswer

on startGame
  gQuestionNum = 1
  gScore = 0
  showScore
  askQuestion
  go to frame "Play"
end
```

The questions are stored in a field named "Data". This field holds one question per line. Each line contains three items, separated by a semicolon. The first item is the question; the second is the four possible answers, separated by commas; and the third is the number of the correct answer.

The "on askQuestion" handler takes care of retrieving all this information from the field and setting up the text on the screen.

```
on askQuestion
  text = member("Data").text.line[gQuestionNum]

  the itemDelimiter = ";"
  question = text.item[1]
  answers = text.item[2]
  gCorrectAnswer = value(text.item[3])

  member("Question").text = question
  the itemDelimiter = ","
  repeat with i = 1 to 4
    member("Answer"&&i).text = answers.item[i]
  end repeat

  gPossiblePoints = 1000
  showPossiblePoints
end
```

The "on gameTimer" handler is called every frame loop by the frame script. It subtracts one point from the number of points that the user can earn by answering the question correctly. The speed at which it does this depends on the frame rate. It calls "on showPossiblePoints" to change the text member on the Stage.

```
on gameTimer
  gPossiblePoints = gPossiblePoints - 1
  showPossiblePoints
end
```

```
on showPossiblePoints
  member("Possible Points").text = "Points:"&&gPossiblePoints
end
```

The "on showScore" handler changes the score text member on the Stage after the user answers a question.

```
on showScore
  member("Score").text = "Score:"&&gScore
end
```

To answer a question, the user must click one of four buttons on the Stage. They are all wired up with the complex button behavior discussed in Chapter 14, "Creating Behaviors." Each one is set to execute the Lingo handler "on clickAnswer" with the number 1, 2, 3, or 4 as the parameters, depending on the button.

This handler adds the potential points to the score if the user gets the question right, and then asks the next question. However, if the user answers wrong, it just subtracts 100 points from the potential points and does nothing. The user must try again.

```
on clickAnswer n
  if n = gCorrectAnswer then
    gScore = gScore + gPossiblePoints
    showScore
    nextQuestion
  else
    gPossiblePoints = gPossiblePoints - 100
    showPossiblePoints
  end if
end
```

The "on nextQuestion" handler advances the "gQuestionNum" global by one. If all the questions in the field have been asked, it jumps the movie to another frame.

```
on nextQuestion
  gQuestionNum = gQuestionNum + 1
  if gQuestionNum > member("Data").text.line.count then
    go to frame "done"
  else
    askQuestion
  end if
end
```

This movie can definitely benefit from sound. It should make a positive sound when the user clicks the correct answer, and a negative sound when the wrong answer is clicked. Maybe there should even be a ticking sound while the movie awaits the user's answer.

You can also try to take care of a lot of unusual situations that could arise in the game. For instance, what if the user continues to click wrong answers, or lets the clock run out? Should there be negative potential points? Or, should users just be advanced to the next question automatically?

Some popular trivia games use a lot of animation between the questions. Director can certainly do this easily enough. You might want to have a long movie with animated sequences between frames that ask a single question.

CREATING A BLACKJACK GAME

Implementing a card game, such as blackjack, is a far more difficult task than creating the games in the previous examples in the chapter. Even the following program, which does not take into account common blackjack rules such as splitting and doubling down, has a lot more Lingo code to it.

Figure 32.9 shows how this game can be complex. Two sets of cards are shown: the dealer's, at top, and the player's immediately below. Six decks are used, and any number of cards can be in each hand—up to 11 if the player or dealer draws all 2s. Below the cards, several text fields show the player's total cash, the player's bet, the player's hand value, the dealer's hand value, and an additional message. There are also three buttons (Deal, Hit, and Stay), as well as an editable text field that enables the player to enter a bet.

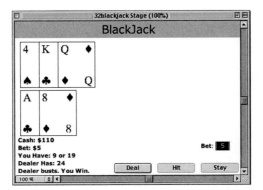

Figure 32.9
Even a simple blackjack program
has many parts to it.

This example uses a movie script to control the game. The globals include a list that contains the cards in the game, a list for the dealer's cards, a list for the player's cards, the total amount of cash the player has, and the current bet.

The movie uses two frames. The first has an active Deal button, and enables the user to enter a bet. A click on the Deal button takes the user to the second screen, which has active Hit and Stay buttons.

The movie starts by shuffling the cards with the "on shuffle" handler. This handler creates an ordered list of the six decks of cards and then randomizes it. Each card is represented by a short string, such as "5c" for the five of clubs or "Qh" for the queen of hearts.

Also notice that *the floatPrecision* is set to 2, which causes all dollar amounts in the game to display in a nicer format than with four digits after the decimal point.

```
global gDeck, gNextCardSprite, gDealer, gPlayer, gCash, gBet

-- Shuffles Deck, resets cash
on startMovie
  the floatPrecision = 2
  shuffle
  gCash = 100
  member("bet field").text = "5"
  clearScreen
  go to frame "Bet"
end

-- Set up deck list
on shuffle
  gDeck = []
  tempList = []
  suit = ["c","s","h","d"]
  number = ["2","3","4","5","6","7","8","9","10","J","Q","K","A"]
```

```
-- create an ordered deck
repeat with i = 1 to 6 -- six decks of cards
  repeat with s = 1 to 4
    repeat with n = 1 to 13
      card = getAt(number,n)&getAt(suit,s)
      add tempList, card
    end repeat
  end repeat
end repeat

-- pick cards out of tempList and place them in the deck
  repeat while tempList.count > 0
    r = random(tempList.count)
    add gDeck, getAt(tempList,r)
    deleteAt tempList,r
  end repeat
end
```

Another handler called from *on startMovie* sets up all the text members on the Stage. It also clears the members from sprites 10 through 40, which can be used for playing cards later in the game.

```
on clearScreen
  -- reset all text
  member("Cash").text = "Cash: $"&gCash
  member("Bet").text = ""
  member("Player Value").text = ""
  member("Dealer Value").text = ""
  member("Message").text = ""

  -- clear out sprites 10 to 40
  repeat with i = 10 to 40
    sprite(i).memberNum = 0
  end repeat
end
```

Every time a hand is dealt, several things happen. First, the text members are reset. Then, the "gDeck" list is checked to make sure that at least half of the deck remains in the list. If less than that amount remains, another shuffle is performed to create a new six-deck stack of cards.

Then, both the dealer's and the player's hands are reset to empty lists. Two cards are dealt to each, in the order that they are usually dealt in blackjack. The "on dealCard" handler is called to take care of selecting and placing a card on the Stage and in the dealer or player list. The first card dealt is dealt face down, signified by a second parameter to the "on dealCard" handler.

After the cards are dealt, the bet is deducted from the player's cash and several text members are updated to reflect this deduction.

In blackjack, if the player draws 21 to begin with, the player wins and the hand is over. So, the handler checks for this situation. An "on figureHand" handler is called to determine the value of any hand. It can return a list of either one or two values. A hand has two possible values if it contains an ace, because an ace is worth either 1 or 11.

Because it is undesirable for a hand to be worth more than 21, the program does not need to check for the case where there is more than one ace in a hand. Having both aces equal to 11 would mean a hand of at least 22, which is never desirable.

If the player initially draws blackjack, the player's score is increased by a total of 2.5 times the bet and the hand ends. The program shows the dealer's face-down card, and then returns to the "bet" screen.

```
-- Clears screen and deals initial hand
on dealHand
  clearScreen

  -- if less than half a deck left, shuffle before deal
  if gDeck.count <= 26 then
    shuffle
  end if

  -- start with sprite 10
  gNextCardSprite = 10

  gDealer = []
  gPlayer = []

  -- initial deal
  dealCard #dealer,TRUE -- deal face down
  dealcard #player
  dealcard #dealer
  dealCard #player

  -- deduct bet from cash
  gBet = value(member("bet field").text)
  gCash = gCash-gBet

  -- set screen text
  member("Cash").text = "Cash: $"&gCash
  member("Bet").text = "Bet: $"&gBet
  playerVal = figureHand(gPlayer)
  member("Player Value").text = "You Have:"&&displayVal(playerVal)
  go to frame "Play"
```

```
-- Check for initial Blackjack
if getLast(figureHand(gPlayer)) = 21 then
  member("Message").text = "BlackJack!"
  gCash = 2.5*gBet+gCash
  member("Cash").text = "Cash: $"&gCash
  sprite(10).member = member(gDealer[1])
  go to frame "bet"
end if
end
```

The "on dealCard" handler takes the first card in the "gDeck" list and uses it. It deletes this item from "gDeck". If the "toWho" parameter is #dealer, it adds the card to the "gDealer" list and sends a message to "on drawCard" to place it at vertical position 90. For #player, it adds it to the "gPlayer" list and places it at vertical position 190.

```
-- Pick the next card off the deck
on dealCard toWho, faceDown
  c = gDeck[1]
  deleteAt gDeck, 1
  if toWho = #dealer then
    add gDealer, c
    drawCard(90,gDealer.count,c,faceDown)
  else
    add gPlayer, c
    drawCard(190,gPlayer.count,c,faceDown)
  end if
  updateStage
end
```

The "on drawCard" handler takes care of creating the sprite that shows each card. It uses *puppetSprite* to take control of a sprite specified by "gNextCardSprite". It then sets the vertical position of that sprite according to the "y" parameter, and the horizontal position according to the "n" parameter. If the "faceDown" parameter is *TRUE*, it shows the member "back" as opposed to the card member.

For this handler to work, it needs 53 bitmap members: one for each card, and a card back for the card facing down. The cards can look like those shown earlier in Figure 32.9, or be of your own design.

```
-- Draw the card on the stage by assigning it to the next sprite
on drawCard y, n, card, faceDown
  -- control next sprite and set it to card location
  puppetSprite gNextCardSprite, TRUE
  sprite(gNextCardSprite).locV = y
  sprite(gNextCardSprite).locH = n*40+10
```

```
-- Card up or down
if not faceDown then
  sprite(gNextCardSprite).member = member(card)
else
  sprite(gNextCardSprite).member = member("back")
end if

gNextCardSprite = gNextCardSprite+1

-- Delay a bit
startTimer
repeat while the timer < 15
end repeat
end
```

The "on figureHand" handler takes a list of cards and computes its numerical value. It recognizes the cards with a 10, J, Q, or K as a value of 10. It also recognizes when the hand contains at least one ace, and then computes two values for it, one with the ace worth one, and one with it worth 11. It returns the value or values in a short list.

```
-- Calculate the value of a hand and return a list
on figureHand list
  total = 0

  -- Loop through hand, and add up cards
  repeat with i = 1 to list.count
    card = list[i]
    if "1JQK" contains card.char[1]  then
      total = total + 10
    else if card.char[1]  = "A" then
      total = total + 1
      haveAce = TRUE
    else
      total = total + value(card.char[1])
    end if
  end repeat

  -- If an ace is present, then there are two values
  if haveAce then
    if total+10 > 21 then return [total]
    else return [total,total+10]
  else
    return [total]
  end if
end
```

Although the "on figureHand" handler computes the value of a hand and returns a list, you will not want to display that list to users. Instead, it is a good idea to break the list apart and display the hand value as either a number or two numbers.

```
-- Take the returned value list and display it in English
on displayVal val
  if val.count = 1 then return string(val[1])
  else return val[1]&&"or"&&val[2]
end
```

The three buttons on the Stage use the complex button behavior described in Chapter 14. The Deal button calls "on dealHand". The Hit button, however, calls the following "on hitMe" handler, which deals a new card to the player. It checks to see whether the player busts. It also displays the new value of the hand.

```
-- Give the player another card
on hitMe
  dealCard #player
  playerVal = figureHand(gPlayer)
  if playerVal[1] > 21 then
    member("Player Value").text = "Bust."
    dealerWins
  else
    member("Player Value").text = "You Have:"&&displayVal(playerVal)
  end if
end
```

The Stay button calls the "on doDealer" handler. First, it turns over the face-down card. Then, this handler creates a loop and adds cards to the dealer's hand. It does this only as long as the dealer has a score of 16 or less. If the dealer has a score of 17 or more or busts, the dealer is finished. The "on decideWhoWins" handler is called for the next step.

```
-- Dealer hits until 17 or above
on doDealer
  -- Show face down card first
  sprite(10).member = member(gDealer[1])
  dealerVal = figureHand(gDealer)
  member("Dealer Value").text = "Dealer Has:"&&displayVal(dealerVal)
  updateStage

  -- Keep adding cards
  repeat while TRUE
    -- See if dealer is done
    if (dealerVal[1] > 16) or ((getLast(dealerVal) > 16) and \
      (getLast(dealerVal) < 22)) then
      decideWhoWins
      exit repeat
```

```
    else
      dealCard #dealer

      dealerVal = figureHand(gDealer)
      member("Dealer Value").text = "Dealer Has:"&&displayVal(dealerVal)
      updateStage

      -- wait a second
      startTimer
      repeat while the timer < 60
      end repeat
    end if

  end repeat
end
```

To decide who wins, first the dealer's hand is examined to see whether it is over 21. If it isn't, the two hand values are compared. In this program, if the player and dealer tie, the dealer wins.

```
-- Figure out who has highest valid hand
on decideWhoWins
  -- Get hand values
  dealerVal = figureHand(gDealer)
  playerVal = figureHand(gPlayer)

  -- Dealer busts
  if (dealerVal[1] > 21) then
    member("Message").text = "Dealer busts. You Win."
    playerWins

    -- Dealer and player have valid hands
  else
    -- Decide highest possible value of each hand, given aces present
    if (dealerVal[dealerVal.count] < 22) then dval = dealerVal[dealerVal.count]
    else dval = dealerVal[1]
    if (playerVal[playerVal.count] < 22) then pval = playerVal[playerVal.count]
    else pval = playerVal[1]

    -- Who wins
    if pval > dval then
      member("Message").text =  "You Win."
      playerWins
    else
      member("Message").text =  "You Lose."
```

```
        dealerWins
      end if
    end if
end
```

The "on decideWhoWins" calls two handlers to finish the hand. The first rewards the player with twice the bet, and the second returns to the bet screen.

```
-- Double money back
on playerWins
  gCash = 2*gBet+gCash
  member("Cash").text = "Cash: $"&gCash
  go to frame "bet"
end


-- No money back
on dealerWins
  go to frame "bet"
end
```

In addition to the movie script, a small script is attached to the bet amount field. This script prevents users from entering a number greater than the amount of cash they have. It also prevents them from typing anything other than number keys.

```
on keyDown
  if "0123456789" contains the key then
    pass
  end if
end


on keyUp
  global gCash
  if value(field "bet field") > gCash then
    put string(gCash) into field "bet field"
  end if
end
```

Check the sample movie on the CD-ROM to see how the whole thing fits together. Try adding some more features to it. You might want to add card shuffling and dealing sounds, and maybe even a "cheer" when the player gets a blackjack.

A much harder task is to enable users to split. With splitting, the user plays two separate hands. You can show both hands on the screen at the same time, or you can have them play each hand one at a time. Double-down is an easier rule, in which users double their bet and get one, and only one, extra card. You can deduct the same amount as the original bet from the user's cash and then deal them one card. To complete the game, you should consider situations in which users run out of cash.

TROUBLESHOOTING GAMES

- Many games combine behaviors and movie scripts. Remember to make sure that each type of script is set correctly, so that a behavior is not set to be a movie script and a movie script is not set to be a behavior.

- The function *keyPressed( )* has many game applications because it tells you exactly what is happening on the keyboard whereas *on keyDown* sends only a single message at a given time. However, watch out for the reality that users can have more than one key pressed at a time. Make sure your games can handle it when users press both the left- and right-arrow keys.

- Don't just worry about bugs and obvious errors when it comes to games. Also think about playability and fun. Games are supposed to be enjoyable entertainment. Consider it a bug if your game is not fun.

DID YOU KNOW?

- Many games use a shuffle to randomize playing pieces or cards. Shuffling uses the random function to pick cards out of the first list and place them in the second. If you want to keep the shuffle the same every time you play, which is good for testing, try setting the *randomSeed* property to a specific number, such as 1, 2, 3, and so on. This ensures that the same random numbers are generated each time and makes your shuffle the same for each game.

- Want more game examples? Remember that I've written an entire book on Lingo games called *Advanced Lingo for Games*, published by Que. You can find it in online stores and your local bookstores.

IX

FINISHING A PROJECT

IN THIS PART

33

DEBUGGING

Source movies for this chapter can be found on the CD-ROM in the "Book Movies" folder under folder 33.

If you create a Director movie that has more than a few lines of Lingo in it, chances are that you will have to do some debugging. This means, literally, getting rid of bugs. Bugs can be as obvious as error messages generated by a faulty Lingo line, or as vague as "something just not working right."

The reason program errors are called "bugs" is that the first bug was actually, well, a bug. An early computer produced an error when a moth flew in and short-circuited it. The name stuck.

WRITING GOOD CODE

An ounce of prevention goes a long way when programming. This means commenting your code, using descriptive handler and variable names, and dividing your code into sensible script members.

You can also use commenting to temporarily deactivate a line of code. This is called *commenting out*.

Well-written code has much less chance of containing an error. If it does contain bugs, well-commented code increases the chance that these bugs can be located and fixed.

Commenting Your Code

Knowing when to comment in your code is the trick. You can't add code comments for every line, because it clutters up your Script window and makes it even harder to read. At the same time, no commenting at all makes it very hard to debug or to alter your code in the future.

A comment is anything on a line that follows a double dash: (—). You can place comments in lines by themselves, or follow lines of actual code with a comment.

You can add three types of comments to your code. You can write blocks of comments before a handler or a section of code, write comment lines before a line or group of lines, or write a short comment at the end of a line of code.

Block Comments

Writing several lines of commentary before a handler is a common technique in Lingo and other programming languages. As shown in the following commentary, you can state what the handler does, talk about which parameters it needs and which type of value it returns, and specify when and how the handler is used.

Here is an example:

```
-- This handler will add a number to the gScore global
-- and place the global in the text member. It will
-- also check to make sure that the score is not less
-- than 0, and make it 0 if it is. The number passed in
-- should be an integer.
-- INPUT: integer
-- OUTPUT: none
-- EFFECTS: gScore, member "score"
```

```
on changeScore n
  gScore = gScore + n
  if gScore < 0 then gScore = 0
  member("score").text = string(gScore)
end
```

The main advantage of block comments is that they stay out of the way of actual code. Because Lingo code is written in English anyway, individual line comments are not always necessary.

Block comments are also good for situations in which other programmers will take your code and use it in their programs. They can read the block comment rather than the code itself. In these cases, the block comments should include information about the parameters, the return value, and perhaps a list of globals, members, and sprites that are affected by the handler.

Comment Lines

Placing a single line of commentary before important lines of code is another commonly used technique. The idea is to use the comments to clarify what the following line does and why it does it.

Here is an example:

```
on changeScore n

  -- add n to the score global
  gScore = gScore + n

  -- make sure score isn't less than 0
  if gScore < 0 then gScore = 0

  -- place score in text member on Stage
  member("score").text = string(gScore)
end
```

Although the preceding example used a comment line before each code line, a more typical example would use a comment line only before some of the lines. This way, the code doesn't get too cluttered with comments.

Comment lines are useful to remind you of what is going on inside the handler. This helps in debugging, and in altering the handler in the future.

Short Line Comments

Line comments appear on the same line as the code and explain what is going on in that line. Sometimes the comment points out a specific piece of information about a variable or function in that line.

Here are some examples:

```
on changeScore n
  gScore = gScore + n -- gScore is a global
  if gScore < 0 then gScore = 0 -- make sure it is less than 0
  member("score").text = string(gScore) -- show on screen
end
```

The first line of the handler demonstrates using a short line comment to point out something specific about a part of the line. The other comments serve the same purpose as the full comment lines.

Line comments are useful when you don't feel that full explanations are needed, and would rather just use short, helpful "hints" for the person reading the code. Like comment lines, they are useful when you need to go back and alter the code later.

The best strategy for commenting is often to combine all three types of comments. You might place a block comment at the start of a behavior, or before each handler in a movie script, and then use comment lines and line comments in tricky parts of the code.

For more information about writing code, *see* "Writing Lingo Code," *p. 213* (Chapter 12, "Learning Lingo")

Using Descriptive Names

Chapter 12, "Learning Lingo," contains some information about using descriptive handler and variable names. I cannot stress the importance of this enough. Several techniques that you can use to make your names more descriptive are described next.

Using Multiple Word Names

A convention among Lingo coders has been to use multiple words, all run together, as handler names. Each word, except the first, is capitalized.

Here is an example:

```
on addNumberToScore numberToAdd
  gTotalScore = gTotalScore + 1
end
```

The handler name and both variable names are descriptive little phrases all run together. You can see that this makes additional commenting almost unnecessary. It is obvious what the handler does and how it does it.

It might seem that using the long word has the disadvantage of taking up more space in your Script window and taking longer to type. However, if it eliminates the need for a comment on that line or before it, it more than pays for itself in keystrokes.

Using First-Letter Conventions

Throughout this book you might have noticed the letter "g" at the beginning of all global variables and a "p" in front of all property variables. This sort of convention makes it easier to remember where a variable originated and the range through which it is available.

You can use other conventions for the first letter of a variable. Sometimes the letter "l" is used in front of local variables. Most developers prefer to make local variables the only variable types without a letter prefix, however.

You might also see the letter "i" used in front of property variables in parent scripts. The "i" stands for instance.

You can also use a single-letter prefix in front of handler names. This used to be common in parent scripts, where "m" would be used to mean method, another term for a handler in a parent script. You can use "m" in front of handlers in behavior scripts as well.

If you are the only one to look at your code, or you have a small team that can agree on standards, you might want to implement your own prefixes. A "b" for behavior handlers, an "m" for movie handlers, and a "p" for parent script handlers might be a helpful combination. A custom set of prefixes such as this should be explained in your documentation somewhere, in case other programmers work on the code.

Using Descriptive Member Names

If you are being descriptive when it comes to variable names, you should apply the same techniques to member names. The only difference is that you can actually use separate words, not divided by spaces.

It's tempting to not use any name for a member. After all, a member placed on the Score and referenced by its sprite number doesn't need to be referenced by name in Lingo code. However, you can still benefit from naming that member. Just try cleaning up a Cast window that has dozens of unnamed members and you will learn why.

Member names should be descriptive and unique. It's useless to have a bunch of text members named "text". You can mention where and how these members are used in a name. For instance, if one text member shows the score during a game and another shows it in the "game over" frame, name the first "Score Text in Game" and the other "Score Text for Game Over".

Also, it is helpful to arrange your members in the Cast in a useful manner. You can arrange them by member type, or by how or when they are used in the Score.

For more information on Cast window preferences, **see** "Setting Preferences," **p. 157** (Chapter 9, "The Director Environment")

Using Variable Constants

Another way to make your code more usable and readable is to use variables to represent commonly used numbers and objects. For instance, if the number 2 is used several times in your code for similar reasons, you might want to set a variable to 2, and then use that variable. Look at this example:

```
on moveFromKeyPress charPressed, position
  case charPressed of
    "i": position.locV = position.locV - 2
    "m": position.locV = position.locV + 2
    "j": position.locH = position.locH - 2
    "l": position.locH = position.locH + 2
  end case
  return position
end
```

This handler is used in a program to change the position of a sprite on the Stage when a key is pressed. It makes the position change by 2 in any direction. However, if you want to change this code to make the position differ by three, you need to change it in four places. Instead, the following handler enables you to make the change in only one place:

```
on moveFromKeyPress charPressed, position
  diff = 2
  case charPressed of
    "i": position.locV = position.locV - diff
    "m": position.locV = position.locV + diff
    "j": position.locH = position.locH - diff
    "l": position.locH = position.locH + diff
  end case
  return position
end
```

As another example, consider the need to refer to a sprite several times. You can place a sprite object in a variable and use that instead. For instance, you can code:

```
thisSprite = sprite(34)
```

Then, anywhere in that handler, you can refer to "thisSprite" rather than "sprite(34)". If you ever need to change the code to refer to sprite 33, for example, you have to change it in just one place.

You can also use this technique with globals. You can set a global to a constant number, string, or object, and then refer to that global throughout your code. If you want to change that constant later, you need to change it in only one place. The disadvantage of using this method with globals, however, is that you must declare the global variable with the *global* command in every script in which it is used.

➪ For more information on writing code, **see** *"Writing Lingo Code," p. 213 (Chapter 12)*

Member Comments

A new feature of all members in Director 8 is the capability to add a comment to each member. You can do this for script members too, adding commentary about what the script does and what it is used for.

> You can even use member comments in Lingo. Just access the *comments* property of the member.

To add a comment, just use the Property Inspector. You will also see the created date, the modified date, and the modified by information. Although you can't change these fields, they do contribute to the information you have about scripts and other types of members.

Writing Error-Proof Code

Impossible, you say? Well, maybe. But you can get awfully close. Many Lingo handlers can be changed in such a way as to catch errors before users are affected by them.

Many times this involves writing code that recognizes that something is wrong, tells the users about it if they can do anything, and stops the code before it can do any harm. This sort of error-checking can and should be an integral part of your code.

Bug-Free FileIO Code

If you want to write some code to create a file and place some text in it, all that is required are a few short commands that use the FileIO Xtra. Here is an example:

```
on writeFile name, text
  fileObj = new(Xtra "FileIO")
  fileName = displaySave(fileObj, "Save"&&name, name&".txt")
  createFile(fileObj,fileName)
  openFile(fileObj,fileName,2)
  writeString(fileObj,text)
  closeFile(fileObj)
  fileObj = 0
end
```

This code works well most of the time. But what if there is a problem? For instance, what if the user clicks the Cancel button when the Save dialog box appears? In the preceding handler, the code marches directly to the *createFile* command with a bad filename. The result is that the file is never created and nothing happens. But the user doesn't know that.

It would be better to check to see whether the Cancel button has been clicked. If it has, the "filename" variable will contain an empty string. You can test for that, and report it to the user. You can then exit the handler before the other commands are used.

But what if the movie cannot create the file for some reason? Imagine that the user chooses a file that has the same name as one already present. You can check for this as well. If you don't check for this sort of thing, your program can be easily crashed by the user.

FileIO has two functions that enable you to test for errors. The first is the *status* function, which returns a number. If that number is 0, everything is fine; otherwise, there has been an error. You can then take the error number and feed it into the second function, the *error* function, to get a string that represents the error in plain English.

Here is the same handler as previously shown, but with comprehensive error checking. Every step of the file-creation process is checked to see whether there is a problem, and is handled accordingly.

```
on writeFile name, text
  fileObj = new(Xtra "FileIO")

  -- check to make sure object was created
  if not objectP(fileObj) then
    alert("FileIO failed to initialize")
    return FALSE
  end if

  fileName = displaySave(fileObj, "Save"&&name, name&".txt")

  -- check to see if a filename was returned
  if filename = "" then
    alert "File not created."
    return FALSE
  end if

  createFile(fileObj,fileName)

  -- check to see if file was created ok
  errorNum = status(fileObj)
  if errorNum <> 0 then
    alert "Error:"&&error(fileObj,errorNum)
    return FALSE
  end if

  openFile(fileObj,fileName,2)

  -- check to see if file was opened ok
  errorNum = status(fileObj)
  if errorNum <> 0 then
    alert "Error:"&&error(fileObj,errorNum)
    return FALSE
  end if

  writeString(fileObj,text)

  -- check to see if file was written to ok
  if errorNum <> 0 then
    alert "Error:"&&error(fileObj,errorNum)
    return FALSE
```

```
  end if

  closeFile(fileObj)

  -- check to see if file was closed ok
  if errorNum <> 0 then
    alert "Error:"&&error(fileObj,errorNum)
    return FALSE
  end if

  fileObj = 0
  return TRUE
end
```

Notice that every error found returns a *FALSE* from the handler. However, if the handler completes its task, it returns a *TRUE*. This doesn't need to be present, but it is a nice feature. Any handler that calls this "on writeFile" handler can then call it as a function and get an answer back as to whether the file was actually saved.

About 18 different error messages can be returned. Table 33.1 shows a complete list of errors that can be returned by the FileIO Xtra. If the error function is used, and the error number does not correspond to one of the numbers listed here, the text "Unknown Error" is returned.

Table 33.1   Error Codes Used by the FileIO Xtra

Code	Message
124	File is opened write-only
-123	File is opened read-only
-122	File already exists
-121	Instance has an open file
-120	Directory not found
-65	No disk in drive
-56	No such drive
-43	File not found
-42	Too many files open
-38	File not open
-37	Bad filename
-36	I/O error
-35	Volume not found
-34	Volume full
-33	File directory full
0	OK
1	Memory allocation failure

⇨ *For more information on reading and writing files, see "Text Files and the FileIO Xtra," p. 355 (Chapter 16, "Controlling Text")*

Bug-Free Shockwave Code

Although FileIO has the *status* and *error* functions, other categories of Lingo commands also have error-handling functions. Shockwave Lingo commands have the *netError* function. You can use this function to determine what has happened after the *netDone* function returns *TRUE*.

Here is an *on exitFrame* script that replaces the one from the section "Getting Text over the Internet" in Chapter 22, "Shockwave and Internet Access." It checks the *netDone*, as it did before, but then goes a step further and checks *netError*. This function returns an OK if the operation was successful. If not, it returns a number. That number corresponds to the numbers in Table 33.2.

```
on exitFrame
  global gNetID
  if netDone(gNetID) then
   err = netError(gNetID)
    if err = "OK" then
      text = netTextResult(gNetID)
      put text
      go to the frame + 1
      exit
    else
      if err = 4165 then
        alert "Could not find that URL."
      else
      -- handle error somehow
      end if
    end if
  end if
  go to the frame
end
```

This example looks for error code 4165, which usually happens when a file is not found. You might want to replace the comment line with some code that handles other errors too.

Table 33.2   Shockwave Lingo *netError* Codes

Number	Definition
0	Everything is okay.
4	Bad MOA class. The required network or non-network Xtras are improperly installed or not installed at all.
5	Bad MOA interface. See 4.

Table 33.2   Continued

Number	Definition
6	Bad URL or Bad MOA class. The required network or non-network Xtras are improperly installed or not installed at all.
20	Internal error. Returned by *netError()* in the Netscape browser if the browser detected a ne work or internal error.
4146	Connection could not be established with the remote host.
4149	Data supplied by the server was in an unexpected format.
4150	Unexpected early closing of connection.
4154	Operation could not be completed due to timeout.
4155	Not enough memory available to complete the transaction.
4156	Protocol reply to request indicates an error in the reply.
4157	Transaction failed to be authenticated.
4159	Invalid URL.
4164	Could not create a socket.
4165	Requested object could not be found (URL may be incorrect).
4166	Generic proxy failure.
4167	Transfer was intentionally interrupted by client.
4242	Download stopped by *netAbort(url)*.
4836	Download stopped for an unknown reason, possibly a network error, or the download was abandoned.

⇨ *For more information about getting text from the Internet,* ***see*** *"Getting Text Over the Internet," p. 450 (Chapter 22)*

Shockwave Audio Error Lingo

Error codes can also be returned by Shockwave Audio members. They return errors through use of the *getError()* function. The *on* parameter that it takes is the name of the SWA member.

Whereas *getError* produces a number, *getErrorString* returns a string that you can display to the users. Table 33.3 shows a list of these errors.

Table 33.3   Shockwave Audio Error Codes

GetError Code	getErrorString Message	Meaning
0	OK	No error
1	memory	Not enough memory available to load the sound
2	network	A network error occurred
3	playback device	Unable to play the sound
99	other	

⇨ *For more information about Shockwave audio,* **see** *"Using Shockwave Audio," p. 370 (Chapter 17, "Controlling Sound")*

Flash Error Lingo

You can also use *getError* with Shockwave Flash members that stream over the Internet. Rather than return a number, these return symbols. Table 33.4 shows them all.

Table 33.4 Flash Member Errors with *getError*

Symbol Returned	Meaning
FALSE or 0	No error
#memory	Not enough memory available to load the member
#fileNotFound	Could not locate the file
#network	A network error occurred
#fileFormat	File is not a Flash movie
#other	Some other return error occurred

⇨ *For more information about using Flash members,* **see** *"Using Flash Member Lingo," p. 406 (Chapter 20, "Controlling Vector Graphics")*

Other Error Lingo

In addition to those functions that relate to a specific type of media or Lingo category, some functions can be used to test variables to make sure they are a certain type. For instance, suppose you treat a number like a list. This generates an error message. However, you can check to see whether a variable is a list, before you try to use it.

Most of these functions end with the letter "P". This stands for predicate (to confirm). Here is a list of functions and what they test for:

- **listP()**—Is the variable a list?
- **integerP()**—Is the variable an integer?
- **floatP()**—Is the variable a floating-point number?
- **stringP()**—Is the variable a string?
- **symbolP()**—Is the variable a symbol?
- **objectP()**—Is the variable an object, such as a member, sprite, list, or Xtra instance?

Here are some examples in the Message window:

```
x = 1
put integerP(x)
-- 1
```

```
put floatP(x)
-- 0
put listP(x)
-- 0
put stringP(x)
-- 0
put objectP(x)
-- 0
x = [1,2,3]
put integerP(x)
-- 0
put listP(x)
-- 1
put objectP(x)
-- 1
x = "abc"
put integerP(x)
-- 0
put stringP(x)
-- 1
put objectP(x)
-- 0
x = member(1)
put listP(x)
-- 0
put objectP(x)
-- 1
```

The *listP* function is useful, but it doesn't tell the full story. Is the list a property list or a linear list? Another function, called *ilk*, tells you what type of list a variable is. Possible values are #list, #poplist, #integer, #float, #string, #rect, #point, #color, #date, #symbol, #void, #picture, #instance, #member, #xtra, #script, #castlib, #sprite, #sound, #window, #media, and #image.

Here are some examples in the Message window:

```
x = [1,2,3]
put ilk(x)
-- #list
put x.ilk
-- #list
x = [#a: 1, #b: 2, #c: 3]
put x.ilk
-- #propList
x = point(100,150)
put x.ilk
-- #point
```

```
x = rect(0,0,10,10)
put x.ilk
-- #rect
x = the systemDate
put x
-- date( 1999, 1, 5 )
put x.ilk
-- #date
x = rgb(0,0,0)
put x.ilk
-- #color
```

You can also use *ilk* to compare a variable and a type. The variable is the first parameter, and the type is the second. In this case, the function returns *TRUE* for more than one type per list, because some list types can be used in more than one way. A color, for instance, is a list, a linear list, and a color list. In addition to the symbols used by the one-parameter *ilk* function, you can also use #linearlist to test to see whether a variable is that specific type of list.

```
x = [1,2,3]
put ilk(x,#list)
-- 1
put ilk(x,#linearlist)
-- 1
put ilk(x,#proplist)
-- 0
x = [#a: 1, #b: 2, #c: 3]
put ilk(x,#list)
-- 1
put ilk(x,#linearlist)
-- 0
put ilk(x,#proplist)
-- 1
x = rgb(0,0,0)
put ilk(x,#list)
-- 0
put ilk(x,#linearlist)
-- 0
put ilk(x,#proplist)
-- 0
put ilk(x,#color)
-- 1
```

For more information about lists, see "Using List Variables," p. 248 (Chapter 13, "Essential Lingo Syntax")

Error-Handling Lingo

Even after implementing error checking along every step of the way, there is always a chance that a bug will persist and end up in your final product. There is one way you can minimize the effects of these nasty things, however. Director enables you to intercept errors when they happen.

You can use this power to send your own error message instead of the standard Director message. You can also use this power to display no error message at all. In many cases, the program can continue with little problem after a nonserious error.

The way it works is a little complicated. First, you set a system property called the *alertHook* to a parent script. A good place to set it is during the *on prepareMovie* or *on startMovie* handlers. In this case, *the alertHook* is set to a parent script that has the member name "Error Handling".

```
on prepareMovie
  the alertHook = script("Error Handling")
end
```

Then, you need to create the parent script itself. This script needs to contain an *on alertHook* handler. Here is an example:

```
on alertHook me, error, message
  alert "Error:"&&error&RETURN&message
  return 1
end
```

The *on alertHook* handler should have a first parameter of *me*, and then it can accept two more: the error and the message. They are actually both messages. They correspond to the two pieces of information displayed with every Director Lingo error. The first message is usually something like "Script runtime error" and is very general. The second message contains specific information about the error, such as "Handler not defined" or "Cannot divide by zero".

You can use these two strings to determine what to do next. For instance, if you want to handle an "Index out of range" error a specific way, you can look for that error and handle it one way, and then handle other errors another way.

The one last thing that the *on alertHook* handler needs to do is to return a value. If a value of 0 is returned, Director proceeds to display the error message that it wanted to show in the first place. A value of 1 suppresses the error message as long as it is not a fatal error.

If you plan to suppress error messages completely, it might be a good idea to at least check whether *the runMode* is "author" and handle that by returning 0. Otherwise, you could be getting errors while creating or altering the movie, and not know about it.

If you need to turn off *the alertHook* error handling, just set *the alertHook* to 0.

USING LINGO DEBUGGING TOOLS

The best thing to do when you find a bug, of course, is to fix it. Fixing bugs is actually a major part of coding. A Lingo program of any size is certain to need some debugging. It doesn't matter how experienced you are. Expert Lingo programmers tend to write more code, and this code is more complex. Thus, they have just as many bugs as beginning programmers, who are more conservative in their programming.

When a bug appears, it is usually in the form of an error message. Figure 33.1 shows a typical error message dialog box. The important items to notice are the Debug and Script buttons. These buttons take you to the two most powerful debugging tools: the Debugger and the Script windows.

Figure 33.1
A typical error message dialog box in Director shows the error type, the error message, and the Cancel, Script, and Debug buttons.

In addition to the Debugger and the Script windows, there is a Watcher window that displays the values of variables in your movies as they change. The Message window is also a valuable debugging tool.

Using the Debugger

The Debugger can be used on two occasions. The first is when you get an error message, and then click the Debug button in that message dialog box to bring up the Debugger. The result looks like Figure 33.2.

The Debugger window contains three panes and a set of buttons that enable you to examine the current state of the movie or walk through code step by step. You can see the code of a handler called "on forceError" in the Debugger window, in Figure 33.2. This is the code that was executed at the time the error occurred. The error message was the one shown earlier in Figure 33.1.

The upper-left pane in the Debugger window (called the History pane) shows a list of handler names. The last one in the list is the handler currently executing—in this case, "on forceError". The handlers listed above it are the handlers called that lead to the current situation. In this case, *on mouseUp* initiated the action, and that called "on forceError".

The upper-right pane (called the Variables pane) contains a list of local and global variables used in the current handler. Next to each is its value.

The largest pane in the Debugger window, appearing in the bottom half of the screen, is the Script pane. This pane displays the script that contains the current handler, along with a green arrow next to the line that was just executed.

Toggle   Script
Breakpoints   Window

Step   Watch
Into   Expression

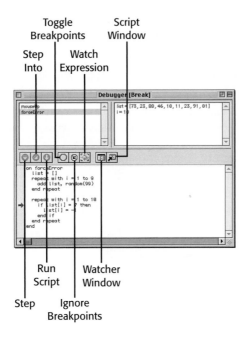

Figure 33.2
The Debugger window.

Run   Watcher
Script   Window

Step   Ignore
          Breakpoints

In this case, you can see that the Debugger has stopped on the line:

```
if list[i] = 7 then
```

The error was "Index out of range" (refer to Figure 33.1), so the first suspect would be that the "i" used to reference the "list" is a larger number than the number of items in "list". Sure enough, that is the case because "i" is 10, but "list" has only nine items.

Another way to use the Debugger is to set a breakpoint. You can see the Toggle Breakpoints button in Figure 33.2. The same button appears in the Script window. You can also set breakpoints in the Script window by clicking in the gray area to the left of any line of Lingo code.

Setting a breakpoint causes a movie to stop and open the Debugger window when the line containing the breakpoint is executed. This is different from using the Debugger when an error occurs, because you can start to step through the code, line by line.

The three arrow buttons shown in Figure 33.2, labeled Step, Step Into, and Run Script, enable you to continue. Step simply advances you to the next line. The Lingo code executes normally, changing variables and objects on the Stage. You can use this to slowly watch the progress of your code as it runs.

If, as you are stepping through code, you encounter a line that calls another handler, it executes that handler all as one step. However, if you use the Step Into button instead, it enables you to step, line by line, through that handler as well.

The last arrow button, Run Script, enables the program to run again at full speed. The Debugger does not track it anymore. However, if it encounters another breakpoint, it stops again.

This is why there is a Toggle Breakpoint button in the Debugger itself, so you can set a new breakpoint further down in the code, and click the Run button to have the program advance to that point.

USING THE WATCHER

In addition to the Debugger window, you can also use the Watcher to check on the values of expressions and variables. Figure 33.3 shows the Watcher window.

Figure 33.3
The Watcher window enables you to track changes in expressions as the movie runs.

The main area in the Watcher window lists the expressions you want to watch. Above that is an area for you to type new expressions and add them to the list. Below the main area, you can type a number, string, or other value, select a variable in the list, and set it to that value.

You can actually type in any Lingo code that evaluates to a value and see it change as your program runs. This means you can use operations, such as addition and subtraction, and movie properties, such as *the mouseLoc*.

The main use for the Watcher window is to enable you to track variables that you think might be causing a problem. You can watch them as the movie runs and see where they go wrong.

The Watcher window is so easy to use that it is sometimes more convenient to use it rather than to type *put* statements into the Message window to test values.

Using the Script Window

The importance of the Script window shouldn't be overlooked in any discussion on debugging. A lot of bugs can be squashed just by reading over your code.

In fact, it's my first stop when I find a new bug. When I see the error dialog box appear, as shown previously in Figure 33.1, I click the Script button and have a look. Most of the time I can see the bug right away and fix it without having to go to the Debugger window or using some other technique.

Usually, a question mark appears in the dialog box that tries to point out the exact location of the bug. However, because Director is not privy to what you were actually thinking when writing the script, it isn't always correct.

The Script window is also where you can set breakpoints for the Debugger, and, of course, place helpful comments to help you quickly and easily find and kill the trickier bugs.

Using the Message Window

The Message window can serve many purposes when it comes to writing error-free code and debugging code that is not so error-free.

First, you can use the Message window to test short bits of Lingo code that you are not quite sure about. The Message window is known as a command-line interpreter in other programming environments. So, for instance, rather than just assume that a text member's type is #text, you can test it.

```
put member("score").type
-- #text
```

Forget what the items in *the systemDate* are? Just try it out:

```
put the systemDate
-- date( 2000, 1, 5 )
```

Now you can program with confidence.

In addition, you can use the Message window to test individual movie handlers. Just type their names, add any parameters, and press Enter. If the handler is a function, you can place *put* before it to have the result placed in the next line of the Message window.

```
put addTwoNumbers(4,5)
-- 9
```

You can also test global variables in the Message window. So, if you want to see what the global "gScore" is currently set to, just try it:

```
put gScore
-- 405
```

You can even set globals in the Message window:

```
gScore = 10000000
```

Another way to use the Message window is to place the *put* command inside scripts. You can send variable contents to the Message window. This is similar to using the Watcher window, but you get to keep a record of values.

Using Trace

The Message window is also the primary tool for using a debugging method known as *tracing*. With tracing, Director sends a message to the Message window every time a line of Lingo executes, and every time a variable changes. Figure 33.4 shows a sample trace session.

> Make sure that you comment out or delete debugging *put* statements before finishing your movie. Sending lots of information to the Message window slows down your movie considerably.

Figure 33.4
Trace information is displayed in the Message window.

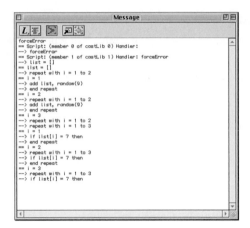

Note that the first line in the Message window is actually typed. After you press Enter, the trace begins. Director incorrectly states that the "forceError" message came from member 23128. However, this does not affect the rest of the trace, which starts on the next line.

To turn tracing on, simply click the Trace button at the top of the Message window. It is the middle button of the five shown in Figure 33.4.

In addition, you can set *the trace* to *TRUE* or *FALSE*, to turn tracing on or off. You can do this in the Message window, or you can insert it in your handlers. Doing either one enables you to start the trace before a sensitive piece of code, and stop it afterward.

Using Other Debugging Methods

Debugging works great in Director, but what if the bug only appears when the movie is running as a projector or in Shockwave?

There is no debugger for these situations, but you can still output messages at points in your code to let you know the settings for your variables, or at what point in the code your movie currently is.

In projectors, the *alert* command comes in handy for this. You can use *alert* at a sensitive part of your code to figure out what is going on. For instance, if your program isn't working correctly after a *getNetText* series of commands, you might want to check to see whether the text that your Shockwave movie is getting is actually the text you expect. Rather than just getting the text and moving on, you might want to try this:

```
text = netTextResult(gNetID)
alert text
```

Now, you can see the text and check to make sure it is what you expect. Of course, you should remove the *alert* command after the testing is done.

Shockwave also offers you the chance to use the *netStatus* command. This command places a message in the Netscape Navigator message space at the bottom of the browser window.

You can also use *netStatus* to display useful information to users, such as the potential destination or action of a button over which the user's cursor is hovering. This is similar to how it is used by plain HTML and JavaScript code.

TESTING YOUR CODE

It is a sad fact that most major pieces of software released today are released with bugs in them. Maybe it's not so much sad as unavoidable. After all, how do you thoroughly test software? Thousands of different computer configurations are available that vary by one item or another: processor type, processor speed, operating system type, operating system version, video card manufacturer, video card driver version, video settings, hard drive speed, CD-ROM speed, RAM size, system settings, system extensions, and so on.

It's impossible to test on every machine available. However, you can test on a variety of machines and find a majority of the problems. The key is to test on all target platforms and on as many configurations of hardware and operating systems as possible.

Test Early and Often

Any computer science professor or software project manager will tell you: Test early and test often. Take these words to heart.

Start your testing as soon as you have something that can be tested. If you are writing handlers, test each one individually if you can. For instance, if you write a handler that takes two points and finds the distance between them, why not use the Message window to try it out? Did you get an error? Did the result come out as expected?

Although this method of testing might seem tedious, consider the alternative. A large Lingo program might have a few dozen movie handlers, many behavior scripts, and a lot of named (or misnamed) members. If you try programming it all at once, never testing any piece individually, chances are very slim that it will work when you are initially finished. However, if you perform a minute of testing here and there, the program could work as soon as you write your last line of code.

Testing In-House

In-house testing is sometimes called *alpha testing*. It starts when the program is "done" and you give it a thorough test yourself. Run the program through its paces. Most of your bugs actually show up right away.

The next step is to let others in your company or organization test it. In a classroom situation, lab partners or classmates make good alpha testers. Maybe some of your friends, too.

This level of testing gives you a lot more control than the next stage. You can personally talk to people who use the software, and maybe even have them show you, firsthand, what went wrong.

You might even want to use the *alertHook* Lingo to give detailed reports when errors occur. This makes it easier for you to track down the problem, but it does not affect the final product because you can remove this code before the product is finished.

Beta Testing

After your program seems to work for you, and everyone in your company has tested it, you can start a *beta test*. This means that you can give out a copy of your program to people outside your company or organization. Many times these are people you don't even know.

Some developers do a private beta test, whereby only a few selected individuals get to test. These individuals can be found among the company's loyal customers, or among applications received from simply advertising.

Some companies do a public beta test, where anyone can download and test the software. This usually results in many people downloading, but few actually reporting errors. It does give you the widest range of testers, however.

Although I recommend that beta tests occur after the product is fully developed and somewhat tested, there are many companies that hold beta tests during development. This enables them to test out new features and get feedback from actual users while they develop.

Beta testing can be overkill if you have a small project, however. Also, if you are developing a Shockwave applet, consider how easy it is to update your movie after you make it live. The applet really exists only in one place: your Web site. If an error, even a big one, is found, you can correct it and upload a new version immediately.

DID YOU KNOW?

- Try using the Lingo command *nothing* as a place to put breakpoints. *nothing* does just that. You can place *nothing* inside a conditional statement and set a breakpoint on it to have the Debugger start at only a particular time. For instance:

```
if i = 8 then
  nothing
end if
```

- You can use the Lingo system property *the traceLogFile* to set a filename that will be used to write the contents of the Message window to the hard drive. This is useful for viewing Message window statements while playing back in a projector.

- You can also place *nothing* inside a conditional statement that looks for a keyboard function, such as *the shiftDown*. This way you can have the Debugger start when the code is at a certain spot, but only when you want it.

```
if the shiftDown then
  nothing
end if
```

- You can click in the handler history pane of the Debugger window to see the previous handlers and the point to which the program will return as soon as the more recent handler is done. This also changes the variables in the second pane to reflect the state of the handler selected.

34

PERFORMANCE ISSUES

Source movies for this chapter can be found on the CD-ROM in the "Book Movies" folder under folder 34.

Performance can be the difference between a good Director movie and a great one. Issues that you may not think about can sometimes spoil a multimedia experience for the users. For instance, issues such as a long download over the Internet, too long of a pause before a digital video starts, poor color quality in a picture, or a sound that isn't synchronized with the animation can spell disaster for your product.

Solving performance issues is usually about fine-tuning. Most of the time it is left for the last stage of development. However, at some point, performance issues must be examined and solved before a project can be considered done.

DESIGNING FOR A TARGET MACHINE

Every time you create a Director movie, you should think about the type of computer that will run it when it's done. You not only need to decide what a typical system will be, but what the minimum system requirements are.

Compromise

Kiosk builders have it easy. They know on exactly what computers the movie will run, and usually even get to test it on that machine during development.

If you are developing a project for yourself, a co-worker, or even a movie that will be seen by only a few co-workers and friends, it also makes the job easier. The best situation is when you are creating a presentation and plan to run the finished product only on your own computer, the same one on which you are developing it.

However, most developers are not that fortunate in a typical situation. If you are creating a CD-ROM, you will usually have to decide what the minimum specifications are for a computer that can use the CD-ROM. That information usually goes on the packaging.

The operative word is "minimum." You can expect most of your users to have fairly fast computers, but you always have to think of that one user who buys the product and has a machine with the bare minimum.

Shockwave developers have it even tougher. People use all sorts of computers to surf the Web. You have to think about your target audience and what they might have. Even if you specify minimum requirements, users with less powerful computers are still going to try to use your movie.

On one hand, you probably want to make the Shockwave experience available to as many people as possible. On the other hand, you don't want to build something that lacks quality, just so the movie works for a few more people with five-year-old computers. It is definitely a situation for compromise.

Sample Requirements

The computer industry is moving amazingly fast. A system that would have been typical two years ago is almost unacceptable today. Knowing that this book will be on shelves for many years makes it hard to talk about specifics.

In the beginning of 2001, computers are less expensive than ever. For less than $1,000, you can get a Windows machine running at 400MHz, with a video card and monitor capable of supporting millions of colors. Stereo speakers are almost always included.

However, that doesn't mean that everyone who bought a computer in 1997 ran out and upgraded. People hang on to old machines that work just fine for most things.

If you need to create for Windows 3.1 and Mac 68KB, have no fear. Director 6.5 is an excellent program that can be used to make projectors and Shockwave for these computers.

Worse yet, educational institutions often get hand-me-down computers. So, a 1997 machine will find its way into a school in 2002. A student might sit down and use that computer to try to run a movie made by you. You must decide whether it will work reasonably well on those machines.

Macromedia has made this a little easier for Director 8 developers. Director projectors can be made for only a 32-bit Windows system or a Macintosh PowerPC. Shockwave runs on only these two platforms as well. Windows 95, 98, and NT are the only 32-bit Windows systems.

So, this eliminates any worry about having to create movies for Windows 3.1 or Macintosh 68KB machines.

So, what should the minimum requirements be? If I were to make a mass-market CD-ROM right now, the minimum requirements for Windows would be as follows:

- Pentium 200MHz processor
- CD-ROM drive
- 640×480 monitor with 32-bit color
- 32MB of RAM
- 1GB hard drive
- Windows 95

On the Mac side, the requirements would be as follows:

- PowerPC processor
- CD-ROM drive
- 32MB RAM
- 640×480 monitor with 32-bit color
- 1GB hard drive
- System 8.0

These requirements are fairly conservative. But the idea is that the CD-ROM is supposed to be mass-market, possibly even educational. If I were creating something that contained a lot of digital video and other high-end effects, such as an adventure game, my Windows requirements would be

- 400MHz Pentium MMX processor

- 8x or better CD-ROM drive

- 32MB of RAM

- 800×600 monitor with 32-bit color

- 1GB hard drive

- Windows 98

On the Macintosh side, my requirements would be

- G3 processor

- 4x or better CD-ROM drive

- 32MB of RAM

- 800×600 monitor with 32-bit color

- 1GB hard drive

- System 8.0 or better

In early 2001, either a PC or an iMac that meets these requirements costs less than $1,000.

One important difference between my first set of requirements and my second is the monitor depth. If you have 640×480 as your minimum requirement, it forces you to use a Stage size of 640×480 or less. Even though 800×600 doesn't seem that much bigger, it will definitely give you the needed elbow room to create better interfaces.

Sometimes, a client or supervisor will specify the system requirements. Usually, they are fairly conservative: 8-bit color, 640×480 screen, and so on. It's important that you tell them about how much those specifications will degrade the movie for a majority of users. Sometimes, when a client or boss finds out that the colors will be poor and the screen will look tiny for most users, they decide to revise their minimum requirements.

3D Requirements

With the 3D capabilities of Director 8.5, a separate set of minimum system requirements is needed. Using 3D cast members requires that the computer have both advanced hardware and software.

On the hardware side, the computer must have a 3D video graphics card. There are many different manufacturers of these types of cards. Most inexpensive computers come with a video card made by the computer manufacturer. Some even come with a video card as part of the motherboard. Few of these low-power cards will work well with Shockwave 3D or any 3D application.

Most higher-end computers, especially those owned by graphic professionals or game players, will have a third-party video card. Here is a list of third-party cards that Macromedia has tested and found to work well with Shockwave 3D.

- 3Dfx Voodoo 3, 4, 5 and Banshee

- 3D Labs Permedia 2, 3

- ATI Radeon, Rage, All-in-Wonder, XPERT

- Intel i740

- Matrox Millennium G450, G400, G200

- Nvidia GeForce3, GeForce2, GeForce256, TNT2, Riva

- Rendition V2100, V2200

- S3 Virge, Savage

Each one of the cards listed has its own idiosyncrasies when playing back Shockwave 3D. 3D scenes rendered with each card will look slightly different. This is completely different than 3D graphics where you can be assured that things look the same from machine to machine. In the 3D world, the card is what handles screen display and each card handles it slightly differently.

For the Macintosh world, the hardware issue is much simpler. All modern Macs come with the ATI Rage card. This makes it very simple to test your Shockwave 3D content on Macs. However, other 3D cards are available for Macs. In fact, almost all cards will work in a Mac, as long as the company has written Mac drivers for the card. So you will run in to some people—particularly graphic professionals—who are using another type of card. Most older cards will not support 3D at all, while many newer ones do.

One factor you will see when buying a 3D card is a measurement of how much memory the card has. Anything less than 8MB of video RAM will not work very well. I recommend at least 16MB.

Even with the list above there are no guarantees. There are many variations of each type of card. The ATI Rage Mobility card, for example, has different configurations and drivers for each notebook it is on. This means that there are dozens of variations.

To the Director developer used to working in the 2D graphics world, this all must seem incredible. How can you create a product that will look different from machine to machine, and may not even work on some machines that would seem to fit the minimum requirements?

This is reality in the 3D graphics world, and many people with 3D-capable computer already know it. Gamers, for instance, are usually very familiar with what the card in their computer can and cannot do.

I would say that testing is an important part of 3D development. However, even a well-funded shop can't afford to get several rooms full of computers and graphics cards to test each possibility. But if you have a small range available, like one card from each manufacturer, then you will get a good idea if your program will work well on a majority of computers.

The second requirement of a 3D computer is software. You need an extension to your computer's operating system to handle 3D graphics. There are only two choices when it comes to Shockwave 3D: DirectX and OpenGL. The first is made by Microsoft and will run on any modern Windows computer. You can download the latest version from Microsoft's site. At the time of this writing, it is DirectX 8.0.

The other alternative is OpenGL. This is the only choice for Mac users, and Apple goes a long way to support OpenGL on the Mac. In fact, Mac users will be able to find OpenGL for Mac right on the Apple Web site. OpenGL will also work for many Windows cards.

DirectX or OpenGL will be the bridge between Shockwave 3D and the video card. Shockwave 3D knows how to talk to DirectX and OpenGL and these in turn talk to the video card.

If you are using a Windows machine, I encourage you to download the most recent versions of both DirectX and OpenGL from the Internet. You can easily switch which one Director is using in the Movie Properties dialog box. While playing content back in Shockwave, you can switch by right-clicking on the content.

Macromedia recommends using DirectX 7 or 8 for the best performance. They rate DirectX 5.2 as the second best, and OpenGL as third. In my tests, OpenGL and DirectX 8 were pretty close, while DirectX 5.2 performance was pretty poor. However, I was not able to test on a machine that only had DirectX 5.2 on it, and not a later version "dumbed-down" to act like DirectX 5.2. In fact it will be impossible for users to even get anything earlier than DirectX 8 from normal public channels.

Macromedia keeps updated lists of which video cards and drivers work and don't work, as well as issues with each card. Go to the Macromedia site and search for "Troubleshooting 3D Rendering" to find this information. At the time of this writing it is identified as "Tech Note 15297."

▷ *For more information about using Shockwave 3D, see Chapters 38 and 39.*

RECOGNIZING ISSUES AFFECTING PERFORMANCE

Many things affect performance on a computer. You should think about all these issues when developing your movie, and when writing the system requirements, if any.

To do this, it helps to understand each part of a computer system that could affect performance. You can break these into the categories of hardware, software, and network.

To really get into these issues, you need a knowledge of computer engineering. However, it helps to understand the basics. This way, you can know what to look for when testing, and have some idea of what might be happening in situations in which performance varies from machine to machine.

Hardware Considerations

The term "hardware" represents the computer itself. Just about everything except the case can affect performance.

Processor

All computer manufacturers love to talk about the processor speed of the latest machines in their ads. In early 2000, these speeds have topped 500MHz for both Mac and Windows computers. More importantly, low-priced consumer versions are usually above 400MHz.

Processor speed, of course, does affect the performance of your movies. Higher processor speeds enable you to attain higher frame rates and smoother transitions. Lingo computes faster.

Also, keep in mind that there are different types of processors. You can get a standard Pentium, a Pentium with MMX, a Pentium II, and a Pentium III, each one offering a little bit of a speed boost beyond just the MHz number. On the Mac side, *the 601 chip, the 603e, the 604, the G3 and G4 series* of chips offer increasing speeds as well. The new G4 processors include a wider path for data to enter and leave the processor, giving speed increases over a G3 processor of the same rating.

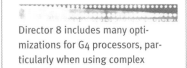

Director 8 includes many optimizations for G4 processors, particularly when using complex sprite inks.

Processor Cache

A cache is a memory chip that is super-fast, usually much faster than normal RAM. The cache is used to store things, such as code or data, which were recently accessed in memory. The idea is that something recently accessed in memory is likely to be accessed again soon. If it is, and it's still stored in the cache, it can be retrieved from the cache, rather than from the slower RAM memory.

The larger the cache and the faster it is, the faster the computer can process commands. It will appear as if the processor is even faster, and have a positive effect on the speed of your movie.

In early 2001, a good cache size is 1MB. Slower machines will have 512KB or 256KB caches, and many machines have none at all. The PowerMac G3 and G4 machines are specifically designed with large, fast caches called *backside caches*. They are located on the back side of the processor card, placing them that much closer to the processor and thereby increasing speed.

RAM

Random Access Memory (RAM) is usually just referred to as "memory." The more a computer has, the more programs it can run at one time. Also, for memory-intensive programs, such as movies with large cast members, RAM is very important.

Director stores all cast members in the file. However, as each one is used, it loads that cast member into memory. The more memory that is available to Director, the more cast members can be stored in memory. When no more memory is left, a cast member that has not been used recently is erased to make room for others. If the erased member is needed again, it has to be loaded again. This repeated loading slows things down.

Virtual Memory

Virtual memory is used by just about every home computer. The idea is for the computer to pretend that it has more RAM than it really does. It uses hard drive space to pull this off.

The hard drive stores a large file that is actually the total contents of the virtual memory that the computer thinks it has. The real RAM is used as a cache to store the most recently used parts of this virtual memory. Because recently used parts of memory are the most likely parts to be used again soon, a slowdown is caused only when new parts of memory need to be loaded into RAM.

Virtual memory therefore makes a computer slower, but it also increases the amount of memory, at least virtually. For many users, virtual memory is the only option, because their computers came with only 16MB or 32MB of RAM.

Disk Speed

All hard drives are not equal. Some hard drives read and write data faster than others. Although this is usually not an issue for consumer-based products, it can be for kiosks. If your kiosk includes media that needs to stream from the hard drive, such as full-screen video, you need to take this under consideration.

CD-ROM Speed

Although CD-ROM speed is not an issue for more recent machines, older ones came with single-speed (1x) or 2x CD-ROM drives. 1x CD-ROMs read data off the CD at the same rate as audio CD players.

At 1x, you can only hope to get to 150Mbps, which means an average of more like 90Mbps. This is too slow for decent digital video, and you will definitely see a performance hit in loading large cast members. 2x CD-ROMs double these numbers, but still make it hard to deliver high-quality video or fast-loading movies. At speeds above that, however, you can expect decent performance. In early 2000, even budget computers come with 32x CD-ROM drives, which perform very nicely for Director movies.

However, CD-ROM drives are still slower than regular hard drives. One way to compensate for this is to require users to install the projector onto their hard drives before running it.

Bus Speed

Although processor speed is the subject most frequently discussed when it comes to buying a new computer, bus speed is another concern. A bus is the vehicle through which the various parts of the computer, such as the processor, the cache, the keyboard, the video, the sound cards, and other pieces, communicate. It is usually set to match the speed of the processor.

Video Cards

Video cards also have different capabilities. Director does a lot of drawing to the screen. Drawing occurs as a result of communication between the software and the video card. If the video card is slow, drawing a frame takes longer and the frame rate suffers.

3D performance relies mostly on the video card. If the video card is not optimized for 3D, then you have little hope that 3D cast members will be displayed with any speed at all. The amount of memory on a 3D video card will also affect speed. You need at least 8MB video RAM, but 16MB or 32MB will be much better.

Sound Cards

Although a slow sound card may not slow down the frame rate, it could mean that sounds are delayed in starting. More commonly, a bad sound card just makes for poor-quality sound. Also, remember that on PCs, MIDI sounds are processed by the sound card. Cheap sound cards can make music sound as if it were being played on a child's toy keyboard. Some high-end sound cards, on the other hand, can make MIDI sound as if the music were being played on professional keyboards.

Speakers

Speakers are easy to overlook. If your movie has CD-quality sound in it, it will still sound only as good as the user's speakers. If the user has the cheap speakers that come with so many bargain computers, you can expect the worst.

Many developers have a great set of speakers, complete with subwoofers and a good range. They design sound for these speakers because that is what they have. Then, the end user's machine tries to play these sounds, which come out like mere noise. This usually occurs because the sound relies too much on the low- or high-end frequencies.

It is worth the $14.95 to buy a pair of cheap speakers to use for testing if you expect to make movies for users who have them.

Software Considerations

Hardware is only half the picture when it comes to an individual computer. The software is the other half. Your projector, or Shockwave, will be running your movie. It talks to the operating system, which in turn talks to the hardware. Every step of the way there is the potential for a performance problem.

Operating System

PCs will be using Windows 95, 98, NT, or 2000 to play back Director movies. There were two major releases of Windows 95, known as A and B. There are also many different versions of Windows NT. As of early 1999, PowerMacs were using everything from System 7.5 to System 9.0.

Windows NT, in particular, seems to be problematic for Director projectors and Shockwave. Sound problems and crashes seem to occur more frequently. Hopefully, users with the latest version of any operating system will not experience any problems, and Macromedia works closely with Apple and Microsoft to minimize problems.

Each upgrade of the operating systems incorporates better performance. Upgraded operating systems handle memory better, handle disk drive access better, and display your graphics better.

Extensions

Beyond the basic operating system, extensions add more functionality to a computer. Typically, the more extensions, the worse performance is. Extensions take up disk space, increase the amount of memory needed by the operating system, and slow down the machine with more information to process on a regular basis.

However, some extensions are designed specifically to increase the performance of the computer. QuickTime 4, for instance, makes QuickTime media available to the computer, and also gives Director movies a better way to mix sound on PCs. An extension such as DirectX enables a Windows machine to process graphics better and faster.

Drivers

Unlike extensions, drivers are a necessary part of the operating system. They tell it how to communicate with various pieces of hardware, such as video cards, sound cards, and printers.

What most users do not know is that drivers have updates. The driver that comes installed on their machines is usually the original driver for the hardware, such as a sound card. A few months later, the hardware company may release a newer version of the driver and make it available for download on the Web. The new version fixes bugs and increases performance.

Sometimes developers are savvy enough to know about driver upgrades and install them on their machines. But you cannot assume that about the end user. Testing with lowest-common-denominator drivers is a good idea for a mass-market product.

If you are using 3D cast members, then the user really should have DirectX or OpenGL drivers on their computer. Without them, Director cannot communicate with the 3D video card.

Display Settings

The two main display settings are screen resolution and color depth. One user may have the display set to 640×480 at 8-bit color, while another has the display set to 1,024×768 and 32-bit color.

The difference? Well, the first user can see only one palette of 256 colors at a time. Also, that user cannot fit a projector larger than 640×480, or a Shockwave movie larger than 640×480 minus the 200 pixels vertically and the 50 pixels horizontally that the browser uses.

However, the 640×480 8-bit setting is usually faster than the 1,024×768 32-bit setting, because there is less display information to process. Multiplying 640 by 480, and then by 8, you get 2.5 million bits of information. On the other hand, 1,024 times 768 times 32 gives you 25 million bits, or 10 times the first number.

On Macs, you can use *the colorDepth* property to change the user's color depth. A few Windows machines enable you to do this, too, but most do not. However, on both Mac and Windows, you can use the Buddy API Xtra to change the color depth and screen resolution. You might want to consider that for super-fast, arcade-style movies.

Network Activity

Although this is no longer much of a problem, it used to be that computers hooked up to a network were slowed down by the overhead of staying in touch with the network. Processors are so fast now that this is not a problem. However, if the hard drive on a computer is being accessed by the network, it does slow down a projector or Shockwave movie currently running.

Browsers

Browsers stand between your Shockwave movie and the rest of the computer. Although Shockwave draws most graphics and sounds directly to the portion of the browser window it owns—making it fairly fast—some activity does need to pass through the browser.

Internet text retrieval and media linking, for instance, rely on the browser for the connection. Browsers vary in their performance for this task. In some cases, such as in older Microsoft Internet Explorer versions on the Mac, they will not even allow you to use network Lingo.

Basically, the newer the browser version, the more compatible it is with the complex features of Shockwave. However, new versions can also introduce new bugs. As of this writing, Netscape 6 is expected to arrive soon, and this might mean new problems if it is not tightly integrated with Shockwave.

Network Considerations

Hardware and software describe what is inside a computer, but many factors outside a computer can also affect performance. This is especially true when the movie is a Shockwave movie that needs to be loaded from the Web. Keep in mind that projectors also sometimes call on the Internet for information or media.

Modems

In early 2001, a 28.8 modem is still the lowest common denominator. There are a lot of them out there. For these users, movies load at the top rate of about 2Kbps, which means that a 120KB movie takes a full minute to download.

Even people with digital subscriber line modems or cable modems still have limits. They can expect a normal rate of maybe 20Kbps. This means that a 1MB file still averages about a minute to download.

The Internet

In a perfect network situation, the user's computer and your server with the Shockwave movie on it would be directly connected. This is not true on the Internet. Chances are the data routes through all sorts of systems, and probably comes in and out of other servers. This is true even when the client and server are in the same town.

Data can even travel in different paths at different times. So, a user might experience a great connection to your server one time, and then a very slow one the next.

You can't do much about this as a Director developer. However, you can plan for it, and make sure that the movie-loading process works well at slow speeds.

➪ For more information about working with browsers, **see** "Making Shockwave Movies," p. 712 (Chapter 36, "Delivering the Goods")

Servers

If you or your company own your own servers, you should consider performance on those as well. Can your server handle 20 users? A hundred? A thousand? What happens when it goes down in the middle of the night? Although these are not issues that can be solved with Lingo, they are still important to the end user looking for your Shockwave game.

IMPROVING PERFORMANCE

Plenty of things can degrade the performance of your movie. But how can you improve performance? There are many ways.

Member Loading

In the section called "Member Loading" in Chapter 21, "Controlling the Director Environment," you learned how to use the different load settings for different members. You also learned how to use Lingo to preload members. Careful use of these techniques can improve performance.

For instance, suppose you have an animation that takes the movie through many frames. Somewhere in the middle of the animation, the background art changes. At first, it's a 640×480 8-bit graphic of one image, and then it changes to a whole different 640×480 8-bit graphic.

The movie is supposed to move smoothly through the frames, but instead it pauses for a time just before the frame in which the background is replaced. This happens because Director has to suddenly load that large graphic into memory.

But what if you use *preloadMember* to request that the member be in memory before the animation begins? Then, when that critical frame hits, the movie does not have to load the graphic into memory; it's already there.

Also, consider the Unload member settings in the member's Properties dialog box. Chapter 21 has more detail about it in the "Member Loading" section.

Shockwave File Size and Streaming

If the movie is playing from the Web in Shockwave, you should always take the download time of the movie into account. Does the value of the movie to the end user make the download time worth it?

Consider a Shockwave movie that introduces a Web site. You want it to look very cool, so it has all sorts of bitmap images and sounds. It is 300KB. But the movie is really nothing more than an animated introduction. There is very little information for the users; that is all further down in the site.

Well, if 28.8Kbps-modem users are coming into the site wondering what is there, they are going to be forced to wait for about three minutes to see the Shockwave movie. Then, they are going to be disappointed to learn that the movie does not tell them anything they want to know.

There is no way to tell the speed of a user's connection. Some developers have tried a method wherein they have the user load a small movie or external sound first, and the movie times how long it took to download. The results can easily be misleading, however.

The movie is clearly not worth the download time for the users. However, a 30KB movie might have been just fine.

On the other hand, if the Shockwave movie is a real program, such as a game, a business application, or a presentation of some information, it might be worth a 300KB download.

The first thing you should do with Shockwave movies that are too large is to use some trimming techniques to get the file size down to something more reasonable. See the section called "Trimming Media" later in this chapter.

After trimming, you should look at streaming techniques. The section "Shockwave Streaming" in Chapter 11, "Advanced Techniques," goes into detail about this.

Compensating with Alternatives

Another method of improving performance is to have alternatives to items that might not work well on some systems. A simple example is to create two Shockwave movies, one that uses some very small 1-bit graphics and plain-colored backgrounds, and one that is a much larger movie with sounds and all the images you want.

Then, just ask the users to choose to look at the "slim" movie, which you can recommend for 28.8 modem users, or the "full" version, which is recommended for people with faster connections. This also gives 28.8 users the option to select the full version if they really want. In that case, they will expect the long download time rather than be upset by it.

You can also offer alternatives at a smaller level. For instance, you can have a 32-bit image and an 8-bit image in your projector, and use the first if the user's monitor is set to 32-bit color depth, and the second otherwise. This maximizes performance for both users.

The same is true with sound and video. You can have alternative versions of these kinds of media in your movie, and play the appropriate one based on information you have about the user's system. You can check *the freeBlock* for instance, and see whether it is too small to fit a large, stereo sound, and instead play the smaller, mono sound. This way, both types of users can hear the sound at levels their machines support.

⇨ *For more information about member loading* **see "Memory Management," p. 440** *(Chapter 21)*

Trimming Media

Of course, you always want to trim your media as much as possible in a Shockwave movie to make the file size smaller. Even if you are delivering your product on a CD-ROM, you should pay attention to this. Smaller bitmaps and sounds load and display more quickly.

Bitmaps

With bitmaps, first make sure that you are using every part of every image. For instance, if you have a background image that is 700 pixels wide, but only 640 of those pixels are visible on the Stage, 60 pixels' worth of data in the image will never be seen by users. Cut the excess out.

Next, determine whether the color depth you are using for an image is as low as it can be. If you expect the end user to be at 32-bit color, you may be using 32-bit color images for your bitmaps. However, in most cases you can use 8-bit color with a custom palette. An image of a forest might have a palette that is mostly greens and browns, whereas an ocean view might use blues and grays. You can display as many graphics as you like on the screen in as many different palettes as you like if the user is in 32-bit color. These 8-bit images with custom palettes are smaller and draw more quickly.

Also, consider 1-bit images when the image contains only one or two colors. Remember that you can set the foreground and background colors of a 1-bit image after it is placed on the Stage. Just select the sprite and use the color chips in the Tool Palette.

⊏⟩ *For more information about bitmaps, **see** "Bitmap Member Properties," p. 86 (Chapter 3, "Bitmap Members")*

⊏⟩ *For more information on sprite colors, **see** "Setting Sprite Colors," p. 179 and "Using the Sprite Blend," p. 178 (Chapter 10, "Properties of Sprites and Frames")*

⊏⟩ *For more information about resizing sprites, **see** "Distorting Sprites," p. 374 (Chapter 18, "Controlling Bitmaps")*

Sounds

With sounds, consider whether the sound is too high-quality. Did you try it at a lower quality to see whether it was acceptable? If you are using Shockwave audio compression, which is recommended, try different settings. Try it at 16Kbps. This is acceptable for many uses.

Make sure that you are using compact, trim sounds. Many developers make the mistake of leaving a second or two of silence at the start or end of a sound. They probably do so because many sound effects collections store their sounds in this manner. Trim away this excess and your sounds will start when you want them to and use only as much file space as needed.

Figure 34.1 shows a sound in SoundEdit 16 on the Mac. You can see short periods of silence at the beginning and end of the sound. These add nothing to the movie, but they do take up extra space in the file that results in slower loading.

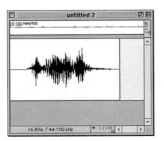

Figure 34.1
A SoundEdit 16 window shows a typical sound clip that contains useless and wasteful silence at the beginning and end of the sound. This can easily be trimmed out.

Video

The same is true for video and any other time-based media. Does a digital video sequence have excess seconds at the beginning or end? Also, is it stored at too high a quality setting for the use that you need? Consider these issues.

Cutting Out Dead Wood

One obvious thing to do to reduce the file size of your movie is to look for unused cast members. While developing, you may have created or imported members that didn't end up being used. You should cut away these useless members.

One way to make these cuts is to use the Find Cast Member window, shown in Figure 34.2. You can access this window by choosing Edit, Find, Cast Member, or by using ⌘+; (semicolon) on the Mac or Ctrl+; (semicolon) in Windows.

Figure 34.2
The Find Cast Member window enables you to search for members using all sorts of criteria.

If you use the Usage setting in this window, a list of all the members not used in the Score is shown. If you select one or more of these member names, you can use the Select All button to return to the Cast window and have all the unused members selected for you automatically.

But don't press Delete right away. The Find Cast Member window does not take into account any members that are referenced strictly in Lingo scripts. So, down states for buttons, for instance, may not be selected. You will have to look at each member on a case-by-case basis.

OPTIMIZING PROJECTOR PERFORMANCE

One of the biggest complaints that developers have when it comes to projector performance is that it takes a long time for the projector to start. This can be alleviated in a number of ways.

First, don't use embedded Xtras. Embedding Xtras just bundles the Xtras into your projector to make a single file, rather than requiring you to have an Xtras folder that comes along with the projector. However, when the projector runs, it extracts the Xtras from itself, and places them in an Xtras folder. It removes this folder when the projector quits.

You can eliminate the need for this whole process by choosing Modify, Movie, Xtras and making sure none of the Xtras are selected to be included in the projector. Then, you must make an Xtras folder that sits next to your projector and contains copies of all the Xtras that you need. You can copy these from the Director Xtras folder.

Of course, it will also speed things up a bit if you don't include Xtras that aren't necessary. You can very often look at projector's Xtras folders and see Xtras such as QuickTime and Flash, even when QuickTime and Flash are not used in the projector.

Projectors also typically run faster from the user's hard drive than from their CD-ROM drive. So, if performance is critical, you may want to make sure the user has a projector on their hard drive. You can use an installer to do this.

Another great way to speed up projector launching is to limit the size of the movie contained inside the projector. If you have a 40MB movie inside your projector, then the user is launching a 42MB projector. Instead, have very little in your projector and have the 40MB movie as a .DCR file outside the projector. Then, your projector is only 2MB and loads quickly. You can then use Lingo to call the large movie.

➭ *For more information about building "stub" projectors,* **see** *"Making Projectors," p. 710 (Chapter 36)*

➭ *For more information about installer-building programs,* **see** *"Making Installers," p. 716 (Chapter 36)*

OPTIMIZING LINGO PERFORMANCE

If your movie is Lingo-intensive, you might want to consider looking at the performance of your Lingo handlers. There is almost always more than one way to do tasks in Lingo, but that does not mean that different tasks are equal. Some methods take longer, and use more system resources, than others.

For instance, if you have a handler that runs many times in your movie, and refers to all the cast member names in a cast library, you might want to consider placing these names in a list when the movie starts, and referring to the list, rather than to the members themselves.

There are as many ideas for optimizing Lingo as there are tasks that can be accomplished with Lingo. The best way to learn how to optimize is to test.

Benchmark tests compare two methods of accomplishing the same task. Benchmarks are commonly used by expert Lingo programmers to determine the fastest method of doing something.

The idea is that you set up a fake handler that accomplishes a task. Chances are that it takes only a fraction of a tick to accomplish the task, so the task is repeated many times to get a better reading of how long it takes.

The following handler benchmarks a simple *if* statement. It runs the *if* statement 10,000 times, and marks the time before it began and then reports the total time to the Message window.

```
on testIf
  startTime = the milliseconds
  repeat with i = 1 to 10000
    r = random(3)
    if r = 1 then nothing
    else if r = 2 then nothing
    else if r = 3 then nothing
  end repeat
  totalTime = the milliseconds - startTime
  put totalTime
end
```

Of course, the *random* function takes up a large chunk of the time in this handler. However, the handler that you race this script against should also use the same *random* function, as well as the same *nothing* commands. The only difference between the two handlers is the Lingo syntax used to branch on the value of "r".

This next benchmark handler tests the *case* statement.

```
on testCase
  startTime = the milliseconds
  repeat with i = 1 to 10000
    r = random(3)
    case r of
      1: nothing
      2: nothing
      3: nothing
    end case
  end repeat
  totalTime = the milliseconds - startTime
  put totalTime
end
```

You can see that the two handlers are identical, except the first uses *if* and the second, *case*. This is important, because any other difference, other than the command you are testing, can skew the results.

When the first handler is run on my computer, it takes 64 ticks. I actually ran the handler several times from the Message window and averaged the results.

The second handler averaged about 68 ticks. This means that it is a little more than 5% slower to use a *case* statement rather than an *if* statement.

However, remember that the handlers were testing the commands 10,000 times apiece. So, don't stop using the *case* statement based on this. However, if a *case* statement is being executed in an *on exitFrame* script in a behavior that is attached to hundreds of sprites on the Stage, you might want to consider this sort of optimization.

The purpose of this example is not to show the speed difference between *if* and *case*, but to demonstrate how to do your own benchmark tests. If you are trying this on something that will have a larger effect, such as using different inks to draw animating sprites, chances are that you will see a much larger difference.

DID YOU KNOW?

- There are companies that specialize in taking your nearly finished product and testing it on different machines in a testing lab. They then report on bugs and performance issues.

- A cheap way to test your projector or Shockwave movies on other machines is to find public computers that you can use. For instance, you can find older machines in libraries. You can also use computers in Internet cafés.

- On Macs, you can use the Extensions Manager to set up an alternative set of system extensions to use for testing. Such a set might not include some of the performance-enhancing extensions that your development machine normally uses.

- Use the system property *the traceload* to have member loading and unloading information to the Message window. Set it to 1 to just see the members, and to 2 to see the members plus all sorts of other information.

- If you are a serious Shockwave developer, you might want to pay for a few $19.95-per-month dial-up Internet connections, even if you have a faster connection available. Then, every once in a while, try the applets on your site using these various services to see what your users are seeing.

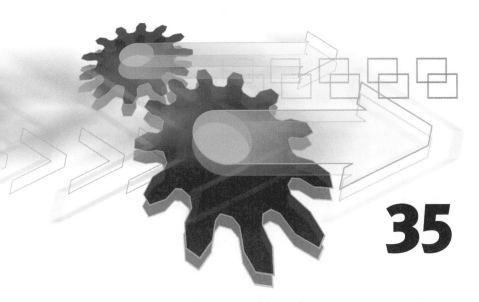

35

CROSS-PLATFORM ISSUES

IN THIS CHAPTER

Source movies for this chapter can be found on the CD-ROM in
the "Book Movies" folder under folder 35.

If you are developing for just the Mac or just Windows, you might not have to worry about cross-platform compatibility. However, this is usually not the case. Most of the time you need to consider both platforms.

The same is true for Shockwave and browsers. This time the competitors are Microsoft, again, with Internet Explorer, and Netscape Navigator. Your Shockwave movies can be run in both, so you must keep this in mind when developing your programs.

DEVELOPING FOR THE MAC AND WINDOWS

A typical Director movie is developed for both platforms. For Shockwave, you almost have no choice, unless you want to tell users from one platform or another that they can't look at your site.

Even with Projector-based products that are originally created for one platform only, you should take cross-platform issues into account. I have been in the situation many times in which a project that started as a single-platform delivery product suddenly expanded cross-platform when a demo CD-ROM was needed for a concern that used the other platform.

The issues that you need to consider for cross-platform compatibility are the differences in the two operating systems: fonts, system palettes, display brightness, non–cross-platform Lingo commands, and so on. Each of these issues is discussed in more detail in the following sections.

Fonts

Although the issue of Font compatibility across platforms was important in Director 6.5 and before, the capability to have font cast members makes this less of an issue.

If you import all the fonts that your movie needs, and then use only text members that use these font members as fonts, you won't run into a cross-platform font problem.

However, if you use any fields, you have to worry about fonts. Or, if you use text members that have fonts in them that are not imported fonts, you have to worry, too. After all, the same fonts don't appear across the two operating systems.

For instance, Arial is a popular font in Windows. However, there is no Arial on the Mac. The Mac uses a font named Helvetica instead. Many users still have Arial on their Macs, probably because they have installed a Microsoft program such as Word. However, you can't rely on this.

The Font Map

The Font Map is how Director decides which fonts on one operating system map to which fonts on the other. To access the Font Map, choose Modify, Movie, Properties. At the bottom of the Property Inspector are two buttons: Save Font Map and Load Font Map.

To make a change to the Font Map, you need to use the Save Font Map button to create a text file. Then you can edit it in a program such as SimpleText on the Mac or Notepad in Windows. Then, you must use the Load Font Map button to implement the change.

The Font Map file contains a lot of comment lines, all starting with a semicolon. It basically explains how to use the active part of the file, which consists of lines that map Mac fonts to Windows fonts, and vice versa. Here is the first set:

```
Mac:Chicago          => Win:System
Mac:Courier          => Win:"Courier New"
Mac:Geneva           => Win:"MS Sans Serif"
Mac:Helvetica        => Win:Arial
Mac:Monaco           => Win:Terminal
Mac:"New York"       => Win:"MS Serif"
Mac:Symbol           => Win:Symbol  Map None
Mac:Times            => Win:"Times New Roman" 14=>12 18=>14 24=>18 30=>24
Mac:Palatino         => Win:"Times New Roman"
```

Each line consists of a three-letter abbreviation for the name of the system, followed by a colon and the name of the font. The name of the font should be surrounded by quotes if it is more than one word. Then, any number of spaces separate the instructions for the first system from the three-letter abbreviation for the other system, and the name of the font to which it should map.

So, for instance, the font Helvetica on the Mac is mapped to Arial on Windows. If you make a movie on the Mac and you have a text field in your movie that contains text using Helvetica, and you run it on Windows, it is converted to Arial. If you want it, instead, to map to MS Sans Serif, you can just replace the "Helvetica" text with "MS Sans Serif" and then load the Font Map into your movie.

Also note the numbers listed after the Times to Times New Roman mapping. These numbers identify specific font sizes of text that use that font and changes them. So not only is text using Times converted to Times New Roman, but any of that text that is 14-point is converted to 12-point at the same time. You just need to specify the two sizes, with the => between them.

In addition to this mapping from Mac to Windows, the file also contains a mapping from Windows to Mac. Here it is:

```
Win:Arial             => Mac:Helvetica
Win:Courier           => Mac:Courier
Win:"Courier New"     => Mac:Courier
Win:"MS Serif"        => Mac:"New York"
Win:"MS Sans Serif"   => Mac:Geneva
Win:Symbol            => Mac:Symbol  Map None
Win:System            => Mac:Chicago
Win:Terminal          => Mac:Monaco
Win:"Times New Roman" => Mac:"Times" 12=>14 14=>18 18=>24 24=>30
```

You can see that this is just the opposite of the other mapping. It is important that you coordinate the two mappings. If not, you could end up in an odd situation. Suppose you map Times on the Mac to Times New Roman on Windows. Then, you take your movie and move it to a

Windows machine and open it to test. The conversion takes place. Then, if you take that movie back to the Mac, and have the conversion of Times New Roman to New York, you don't end up with the same fonts as before.

The Font Map file also includes character mappings, which are necessary because special characters, such as Yen signs and other symbols, are not in the same locations in Mac and Windows fonts. This mapping converts characters appropriately so that your symbols match up.

Some lines also deal with Japanese fonts. Comments around these lines explain their use if you need to alter them.

One way to make your Shockwave movies a little smaller is to edit the Font Map down to the bare minimum. You can get rid of font mappings that you don't use—such as the Japanese character translations and the other ASCII character translations—as long as you don't need them. You can trim 1KB or more from your files this way. Doesn't sound like much, but if you are expecting a million people to play your movie, it adds up.

Text Member Bitmaps

Another way to get text members to appear identical across platforms is to use the Save As Bitmap feature. This is an option you can set in the Property Inspector for text members, under the Text tab. First, choose either Copy Ink or Other Ink from the Pre-Render pop-up menu. Then, you can check the Save As Bitmap box.

The Copy Ink option should be used only when the member is displayed on the Stage only using Copy ink. If you are using any other ink at all, choose Other Ink. If you are using the member in multiple frames, sometimes with Copy ink and sometimes with something else, choose Other Ink and then place a white background behind the sprite when you want to simulate Copy ink.

Director then saves a copy of the text member as a graphic. When the movie is opened in a projector or in Shockwave, the graphic is used instead of the text. This means that the actual font is not needed.

The disadvantage is that the text cannot be edited and cannot be changed with Lingo. Another disadvantage is that the member increases the file size considerably. But the text member looks identical from platform to platform.

Continuing Font Problems

The text and font engines received a major overhaul between Director 7 and Director 8. The engines are now more accurate, stable, and much faster. However, many cross-platform font issues still persist.

The scope of the problems depend on your need for perfection. For most uses, text members will seem and act identical between Mac and Windows. However, there are some differences.

Another way to do this is to choose Modify, Convert to Bitmap, which permanently converts a text member to a bitmap member. The bitmap member cannot be edited, even in the authoring environment, ever again. This technique also works for fields.

Figure 35.1 shows two views of the same movie. The image on the left is from Director 8 for Mac and the one on the right is from Director 8 for Windows. The text uses a version of Geneva font imported in Director 8 for Mac. The point size is 18.

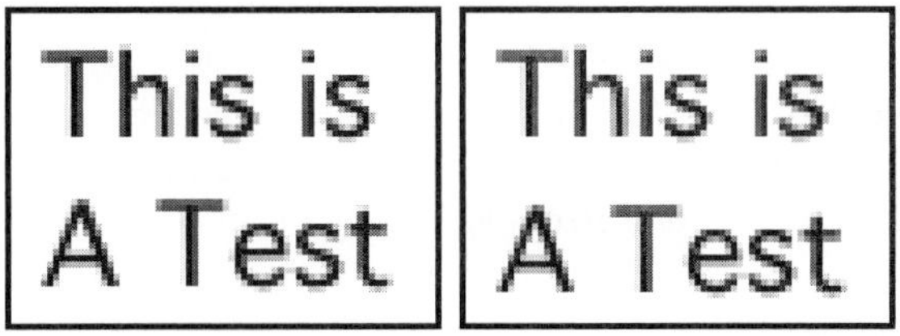

This is A Test | **This is A Test**

Figure 35.1
The left shows the text as it appears on the Mac, and the right shows it in Windows. They are nearly identical, except for line spacing.

The pixels making up the two views are almost identical. The width of each character, space, and line are perfect. However, the second line starts one pixel lower on Windows than it does on the Mac.

This small difference can make a huge impact on your final product. If the text member has a dozen lines in it, and it's set to Copy ink, the text will cover 12 pixels more vertically on Windows than on Mac. This could obscure an important button or other element.

One way to get around this is to set the text member frame style to "fixed". This will make sure that the text member does not grow to exceed its boundaries. However, it could mean that the last line of text extends beyond the visible portion of the member.

Another way to avoid this is to make the text sprite background transparent. This means that the text might still extend further than you planned, but at least other elements on the screen won't be completely covered.

Even with these solutions, other problems can occur. If you have a graphic of an arrow, for instance, that points out a line in the text, this arrow might be pointing in the wrong place.

These differences between platforms are minor, however, and can easily be avoided by simply checking your movie on both platforms before releasing it. As you become more familiar with cross-platform development, you will begin to recognize such potential problems ahead of time and compensate accordingly.

Color Palettes

The issue of cross-platform color palettes is another that is slowly going away. Because most computers are capable of displaying at greater than 8-bit color depth, you no longer have to worry about palettes as much.

However, if you are developing for 8-bit screens, you do need to know some things.

One way to get around this line spacing discrepancy is to specifically set the line spacing of the text in the text member. You can do this with the Text Inspector or in the toolbar of the text member editing window. If the default line spacing is used, in this case 24, it seems to then be altered in Windows to the default of 25 instead. However, if 23 is used, which is not the default, 23 is also used on Windows. However, if you really want to set the line spacing to 24 on both platforms, you are out of luck.

Both Mac and Windows use a default system palette when set to 8-bit color. These are the 256 colors that the screen uses when nothing but the operating system is running. They include the colors used by the different buttons, icons, menus, and other items seen on the desktop.

You can use your Director movie to change the screen's palette to the one being used by your movie. This happens automatically in a projector.

However, if the desktop is still visible around the edges of the projector, consider that the palette might not be providing the correct colors for the rest of the desktop—or any other running program—to display. As a result, your movie looks fine, but the rest of the screen does not.

There are some ways around this:

- You can set the projector to occupy the whole screen. This is the default setting when you make a projector. It hides everything else and makes it easy for you to use any palette you want.

- You might also want to consider using 16-bit or higher color depth. Users of computers capable of only 8-bit color depth will see a badly drawn Stage, but it is somewhat usable. You can use *the colorDepth* to detect this situation and add a message to users that strongly suggests they change their monitor settings if possible.

- You can also place all your bitmap cast members in an external Cast. Then, build a second version of this Cast with the same cast members in the same slots. One cast file uses bitmaps all set to the Mac system palette, and the other uses them set to the Windows system palette. Then, place the correct cast library on the correct partition of a cross-platform CD-ROM.

With this last technique, you must also use Lingo to tell the Stage to use a different color palette depending on the system. Use *puppetPalette* to set this.

You can also try playing with the *paletteMapping* property, which tries to map bitmap images that use a different palette than the Stage is currently using.

Display Brightness

One common cross-platform mistake is made by Mac developers. The Macintosh display is much brighter than a typical Windows display. Developers working in dark colors are surprised by how much darker they appear in Windows.

You can adjust for this by using your Mac's Monitors and Sound control panel and changing the Gamma setting. Then, compare a dark image on both Mac and Windows platforms before you get too far into your development. Many newer Macs are missing this functionality, however.

Digital Video

Although QuickTime 4 is available on both Mac and Windows platforms, you might want to consider the situation in which Windows users do not have QuickTime. You can certainly ask them to install it, or you can simply have a substitute Video for Windows movie waiting to be played instead.

Use the *quickTimeVersion* property to determine whether users have QuickTime installed.

File Pathnames

If you are using FileIO to read any text files, or you are using Lingo to set the *filename* property of a linked member, you need to think about pathnames. On the Mac, the character that goes between folder names in a path is a colon. On Windows, it's a backslash.

If you have an image in a folder that is at the same level as your projector, you might use a command like this one on the Mac:

```
member("linkedimage").filename = "images:newimage.jpg"
```

However, in Windows, you might use this command:

```
member("linkedimage").filename = "images\newimage.jpg"
```

If you try to use the wrong one on the wrong platform, the image cannot be found. Instead, first determine on which platform the movie is running and use the appropriate command, as follows:

```
if the platform contains "mac" then
  member("linkedimage").filename = "images:newimage.jpg"
else
  member("linkedimage").filename = "images\newimage.jpg"
end if
```

You can also use a variable to store an item delimiter character, and then refer to that character later. This works best if you need to set multiple pathnames.

```
if the platform contains "mac" then pathDel = ":"
else pathDel = "\"
member("linkedimage1").filename = "images"&pathDel&"newimage1.jpg"
member("linkedimage2").filename = "images"&pathDel&"newimage2.jpg"
member("linkedimage3").filename = "images"&pathDel&"newimage3.jpg"
```

Non–Cross-Platform Lingo

Many Lingo commands are just not available in both platforms or work differently in different platforms. The following list includes some of the most common ones:

- **shutdown**—Exits a projector on Windows, but exits the projector and shuts down the computer on Mac.

- **restart**—Exits a projector on Windows, but exits the projector and restarts the computer on Mac.

- **cursor**—The command and property works the same, but be aware that some cursors look different. For instance, the Watch cursor on Mac is the equivalent to the Hourglass in Windows.

- **optionDown**—Examines the state of the Option key on a Mac, but the Alt key on Windows.

- **commandDown**—Examines the state of the Command (Apple) key on the Mac, but the Ctrl key on Windows.

- **controlDown**—Examines the state of the Ctrl key on Windows, but only the Control key on Mac, not the Command key.

- **on rightMouseDown**—You can use *the emulateMultiButtonMouse* system property to accept Ctrl+Click on the Mac as a right-click.

- **on rightMouseUp**—See previous entry.

- **colorDepth**—Can be tested in both platforms, but set only on the Mac and some, but not all, Windows machines.

Also, all commands that depend on the operating system for execution behave differently on different platforms. So, the *alert* command brings up a different-looking alert box for each platform (and does not beep in Windows). The FileIO and MUI Dialog Xtra dialog boxes look slightly different to reflect the different systems.

➮ *For more information about changing the monitor's color depth, **see** "Learning About the Computer," p. 427 (Chapter 21, "Controlling the Director Environment")*

DEVELOPING FOR NETSCAPE NAVIGATOR AND MICROSOFT INTERNET EXPLORER

The biggest difference between Shockwave in the two browsers is the way that the Shockwave plug-in is installed. Netscape users have to download a Shockwave installer program and run it. This places a plug-in in their browser's plug-in folder that prompts them to download (and automatically install) all of Shockwave's components the next time they browse over to a Shockwave movie.

In Internet Explorer in Windows, the plug-in is wrapped inside an ActiveX control. ActiveX controls are files that extend the functionality of the operating system or of a program. In this case, the ActiveX control adds Shockwave to the browser. The way users get this control is better than the downloading scenario for Netscape users. It automatically looks for and loads the ActiveX control for Shockwave the first time the user browses over to a Shockwave movie.

In addition to installation differences, you need to prepare your HTML pages that contain Shockwave to send the correct signals to both Netscape and Internet Explorer. Netscape needs an <EMBED> tag, whereas Internet Explorer needs an <OBJECT> tag.

> ⇨ *For detailed information about these tags,* **see** *"Making Shockwave Movies," p. 712 (Chapter 36, "Delivering the Goods")*

If you want to talk to the browser through JavaScript, you also have to do it differently with each browser. In Internet Explorer, JavaScript cannot receive messages from Lingo. Instead, you have to route these messages through VBScript, Internet Explorer's alternative browser language.

> ⇨ *For examples of communication between browsers and Shockwave,* **see** *"Working with Browsers" p. 454 (Chapter 22, "Shockwave and Internet Access")*

One final consideration is screen size. As Netscape and Internet Explorer change, they have different elements at the top, bottom, and sides that take away screen space from the content. If you want your Shockwave movies to fit on the screen, you have to take into account a lot of different potential configurations by users.

Experiment with different Stage sizes and how they look inside both browsers on both platforms. Try the 640×480 monitor setting, the 800×600 monitor setting, and any others that you think your users might have. There is no ideal solution, because people with large monitors will think a 600×300 applet is too small, whereas people with small monitors will barely be able to fit it in their browsers.

> ⇨ *For more information about building Shockwave movies,* **see** *"Making Shockwave Movies," p. 712 (Chapter 36)*

THE CROSS-PLATFORM CHECKLIST

Developers need to have a checklist of potential problem areas for cross-platform development. Don't use this checklist only when the project is finished. Review it before you begin, and occasionally as the development continues.

- **Lingo**—Are you using any commands that might not work on another platform? Will commands that work differently on another platform still perform adequately?

- **Xtras**—Are you using Xtras that might not be available on another platform? Do all your Xtras behave the same on each platform?

- **Pathnames**—Are you using the colon or backslash (: or \) item delimiters to describe pathnames in your code? If so, does the code recognize when it is running on each platform and adjust as needed?

- **Color palettes**—If you are making an 8-bit color presentation, does it work cross-platform if it's set to 8-bit?

- **Fonts**—Are you using fields? If so, are the fonts that you are using properly mapped to fonts on the other platform?

- **Text**—Do you notice any difference between platforms for your text members? Do any extend too far? Do any need to be precisely lined up with other graphics on the Stage?

- **Screen size**—Does your Stage fit in the screen? How about with the Windows taskbar at the bottom? Do you want it to fit inside both browser windows without requiring the users to scroll? Does it?

- **Digital video**—Are you using digital video that might work on only one platform? How do you deal with situations in which users do not have the correct extensions, such as QuickTime?

- **Transitions**—Some transitions are slower on Windows than on the Mac. Be sure to test all your animations for speed.

DID YOU KNOW?

- If you are developing for the Mac, and you have a fast one, you can buy an emulator that runs Windows. Emulators are commonly used by Mac developers to test Windows projectors. The ones that emulate an actual Pentium chip, and then run Microsoft's version of Windows on top of that, are very reliable testing devices because they are usually more typical of a Windows configuration than a randomly selected Windows machine.

- When you create a new movie, the fontmap.txt file is read in from the Director folder and used as the Font Map. You can change that file so that the default font map settings for any new movie you create also change.

DELIVERING THE GOODS

Source movies for this chapter can be found on the CD-ROM in the "Book Movies" folder under folder 36.

After you are finished creating a movie, you always have to take those final steps to create a deliverable product. In some cases, these steps require you to create a projector. In others, they require you to make a compressed Shockwave movie. You might also want to export your Director movie as a Java applet. This chapter covers the steps you need to take to deliver the final product.

MAKING PROJECTORS

The section called "Creating a Standalone Projector" in Chapter 2, "Presentations with Director," goes into detail about creating a projector. In addition, there are many options to choose from when building a projector, and you should carefully examine each setting before you build one.

You also have some alternatives to the simple projector. You can build what is called a *stub projector*, which can run any external Director movie. Director also enables you to build Shockwave projectors, which rely on Shockwave components on the user's system.

Stub Projectors

The need for a stub projector is obvious after you think about it. Rather than creating a new projector each time you make a change to a movie, just create a simple projector that runs your movie as an external file.

The projector can have one movie that contains a *go to movie* command as the sole command of an on *exitFrame* script. This script is placed in the first frame of the movie:

```
on exitFrame
  go to movie "myrealmovie.dir"
end
```

Take this one-frame, one-member movie and create a projector from it. Then, when you run it, it jumps directly to the first frame of the external movie, which is the main (or first) movie of your presentation or program.

If you make a change to your movie later, you don't have to rebuild the projector. Just run it again and it will use the new, modified version of your movie.

You can even make more complicated stub projectors by having your Lingo code read in the name of the stub projector with *the movie* property, removing an .exe if there is one, and then appending a .dir to the end. This will then be the name of the movie it should run.

This way, a projector named present.exe looks for and runs present.dir. If you then create a movie called program.dir, you can copy the present.exe projector, change its name to pro-gram.exe, and it can run the new movie.

Here is a script that does this:

```
on exitFrame
  moviename = findMyMovie()
  go to movie moviename
end
```

```
on findMyMovie
  myname = the applicationName
  if myname contains ".exe " then
    myname = myname.char[1..offset(".",myname)-1]
  end if
  moviename = myname&".dir"
  return moviename
end
```

A more complex projector script can even check to make sure the file is there before running it. You use the *getNthFileNameInFolder* command to do this. Look for a .dcr file first, a .dxr file next, and then a .dir file if neither of the first two is there. This way, the projector works while you are testing and will also work when you decide to create a protected version of your movie.

Some projectors check to see what the user's machine is like, and then run a movie that is appropriate to the power of that machine. So, it might run myMovie640.dir if the user's monitor is 640×480, or myMovie800.dir if the monitor is larger. The same can be done for platform, memory, screen depth, and so on.

For more information on using getNthFileNameInFolder, **see** "Creating Slideshows," **p. 574** (Chapter 29, "Graphics Applications")

Compressed Projectors

Compressed projectors are really no different than normal projectors as far as development is concerned. The resulting projector is a compressed file, which decompresses and runs with a single click (or a double-click as the case might be).

Do not confuse this with using Shockwave compression on your movies. You can make normal projectors that call compressed movies or actually contain movies that are compressed. Compressed projectors, on the other hand, are also using a compressed version of the Director engine.

The amount of file size that you save with this option varies with the number of Xtras you use. However, it might be the key to fitting a small projector onto a floppy disk or making the download of such a projector faster.

Shockwave Projectors

Shockwave projectors are much smaller than full-sized projectors, but are not really standalone. They require users to have Shockwave 8 on their computers. A projector uses Shockwave 8 as the core engine to play the movie.

If the users do not have Shockwave, the Shockwave projector prompts them to download it first. You can include Xtras with your Shockwave projector, just like you can with your regular projectors. Your movies will then have access to both the Xtras in your Shockwave projector and the Xtras that the user's version of Shockwave contains.

⮕ *For more information about creating projectors,* see *"Creating a Standalone Projector," p. 64 (Chapter 2)*

MAKING SHOCKWAVE MOVIES

Making a Shockwave movie requires almost no effort. Actually, it can be said to require no effort at all because any Director movie, compressed or not, can be run in Shockwave.

However, most uses of Shockwave require that the movie be saved as a Shockwave movie so that it is compressed. "Showing Your Presentation" in Chapter 2 also goes into creating a basic Shockwave movie, which is simply a matter of choosing File, Publish.

Many times Shockwave projectors are much larger than they need to be because the developer has not chosen Modify, Movie, Xtras, and removed Xtras that are guaranteed to be present in Shockwave anyway. Typical ones to remove are the Text and Font Xtras, the network Xtras, and the audio Xtras. In fact, most Shockwave projectors will work if all Xtras are removed from the Modify, Movie, Xtras dialog box, as they are usually found in Shockwave anyway.

Chapter 9, "The Director Environment," takes a close look at all the options available to the Publish command. These are all set by choosing File, Publish Settings.

Publishing takes care of both the creation of a compressed Director movie and the creation of a sample HTML page. However, many developers don't want to use Director's built-in sample HTML pages, but rather use their own code in their own site's style.

Although you can use the Publish HTML output as sample code that can be cut and pasted into your own HTML code, you should also know the basics about how Shockwave is placed into HTML.

There are two main browsers: Netscape Navigator and Microsoft Internet Explorer. Shockwave has versions for both. For Navigator and IE on the Mac, Shockwave is a plug-in that handles Director movies inside a Web page. For Explorer on Windows, Shockwave is an ActiveX control, which is like an extension to the browser.

The result is the same: The Director movie appears in the browser directly on the Web page. However, the information needed to place the movie on the page differs for each browser.

Netscape Navigator <EMBED> Tag

With Navigator, a movie is placed in a page with the <EMBED> HTML tag. Here is an example:

```
<EMBED SRC="mymovie.dcr" WIDTH="400" HEIGHT="200">
```

This tag simply states that the movie file is named mymovie.dcr and the size of the movie is 400×200. You can use a more complex path for the file if the movie is not in the same directory as the HTML page.

In addition to the SRC, WIDTH, and HEIGHT parameters shown in the previous piece of code, you can also include several others. Here is a complete list:

- **SRC**—The relative or absolute location of the movie.

- **WIDTH, HEIGHT**—The screen size of the movie. The actual movie can be larger or smaller, but this parameter reserves a rectangle exactly this size on the page.

- **BGCOLOR**—Set to the hexagonal value for the color you want the rectangle to display while the movie downloads.

- **NAME**—This parameter is more for the HTML page and JavaScript than for use by the movie itself. It is how you refer to the movie object in HTML code.

- **SWREMOTE**—Contains a string that contains yet more parameters.

- **SWSTRETCHSTYLE**—Set to either "none" or "fill". The fill option stretches the Shockwave movie to fill the browser window.

- **TYPE**—Some versions of Netscape enable you to specify the MIME type of the object in the <EMBED> tag. You should set this to "application/x-director". This way, if your server is not set up for Shockwave movies, some users can still see the movie.

- **PLUGINSPAGE**—You can set the location of the download page for Shockwave here. Newer versions of Netscape use this to direct users to the place where they can get the plug-in. A good URL to use is `http://www.macromedia.com/shockwave/download/`.

If you use the <SWREMOTE> tag, you must include even more parameters inside it. These can be all set to TRUE or FALSE. Here is a list of what you can use:

- **swSaveEnabled**—Whether the movie can be saved and used in ShockMachine.

- **swVolume**—Whether the user can change the volume of the movie by right-clicking or using the Shockwave Remote.

- **swRestart**—Whether the user can restart the movie by right-clicking or using the Shockwave Remote. Set this to TRUE only when the movie is a plain animation.

- **swPausePlay**—Whether the user can pause the movie by right-clicking or using the Shockwave Remote. Set this to TRUE only when the movie is a plain animation or you are sure that pausing will not hurt your Lingo code.

- **swFastForward**—Whether the user can fast forward through a movie by right-clicking or using the Shockwave Remote. Set this to TRUE only when the movie is a plain animation.

- **swContextMenu**—Whether the user gets a context menu when right-clicking on Windows or Control+clicking on the Mac.

The following complex <EMBED> tag contains all the possible standard parameters:

```
<embed src="mymovie.dcr" name="myMovie" bgColor=#FFFFFF  width=70 height=50
swRemote="swSaveEnabled='true' swVolume='true' swRestart='true'
swPausePlay='true' swFastForward='true' swContextMenu='true' "
swStretchStyle=none type="application/x-director"
pluginspage="http://www.macromedia.com/shockwave/download/">
</embed>
```

Microsoft Internet Explorer <OBJECT> Tag

To achieve the same result as a Netscape <EMBED> tag, you need to write a different type of tag for Internet Explorer.

The <OBJECT> tag is used to embed an object for which an ActiveX control provides the engine. In this case, the ActiveX control is Shockwave.

The <OBJECT> tag specifies the identification code for the ActiveX control. Microsoft assigned this number to Shockwave. The browser uses the number to determine whether it already has this ActiveX control. If not, the browser use an Internet address, also specified in the tag, to download and install it.

The following is a sample <OBJECT> tag:

```
<OBJECT classid="clsid:166B1BCA-3F9C-11CF-8075-444553540000"
codebase="http://download.macromedia.com/pub/shockwave/cabs/director/
sw.cab#version=8,0,0,0"
ID=Credits WIDTH=400 HEIGHT=200>
<PARAM NAME=src VALUE="mymovie.dcr">
</OBJECT>
```

The first part of the <OBJECT> tag is the classid, which is the identification code mentioned earlier. The second part is the location on the Internet where the browser can get this ActiveX control if it is not already installed.

Notice that the last part of the location contains "version=8,0,0,0.", which tells Macromedia's Web site which version of the control is needed.

After those two pieces, the ID parameter is used in the same manner as the NAME parameter in the <EMBED> tag. It identifies the Shockwave movie object to any JavaScript or VBScript that needs to know about it.

The WIDTH and HEIGHT options are next, and they serve the same purpose as the equivalent parameters in the <EMBED> tag. This ends the first part of the <OBJECT> tag.

However, this is not the end of the <OBJECT> tag as a whole. It requires an </OBJECT> tag to end it. In between, there can and should be some <PARAM> tags. You can see one in the preceding example. Each <PARAM> tag specifies a parameter name and a value. In the example, the parameter is "src" and the value is "mymovie.dcr". This of course, denotes the location of the Shockwave movie itself.

You can also include other <PARAM> tag parameters such as "bgColor" and "swRemote" that do the same things as their <EMBED> counterparts. Here is a more complex <OBJECT> tag:

```
<object classid="clsid:166B1BCA-3F9C-11CF-8075-444553540000"
codebase="http://download.macromedia.com/pub/shockwave/cabs/director/sw.cab#ver
sion=8,0,0,0"
ID=mymovie width=70 height=50>
<param name=src value=" mymovie.dcr">
<param name=swRemote value="swSaveEnabled='true' swVolume='true'
swRestart='true' swPausePlay='true' swFastForward='true' swContextMenu='true' ">
```

```
<param name=swStretchStyle value=none>
<param name=bgColor value=#FFFFFF>
</object>
```

Using Both the <EMBED> and <OBJECT> Tags

Most of the time, you want to build an HTML page for both browsers. This requires you to use both the <EMBED> and <OBJECT> tags.

This works fine for Netscape Navigator, in which the <EMBED> tag is used and the <OBJECT> tag is ignored.

However, Internet Explorer recognizes both tags. The <OBJECT> tag is used to show the Shockwave movie as you expect. But Internet Explorer can also use the <EMBED> tag to use Netscape Navigator plug-ins. So, it attempts to display the Shockwave movie a second time with the <EMBED> tag. Chances are that the browser does not have the Shockwave plug-in available, but the rectangular area for the Shockwave movie is still reserved for its use and users might even be prompted for a download.

Fortunately, there is a simple solution for this problem. Just place the <EMBED> tag inside the <OBJECT> tag. Microsoft Internet Explorer is smart enough to ignore <EMBED> tags inside <OBJECT> tags, so the movie will not be displayed twice.

For example:

```
<object classid="clsid:166B1BCA-3F9C-11CF-8075-444553540000"
codebase="http://download.macromedia.com/pub/shockwave/cabs/director/sw.cab#ver
sion=8,0,0,0"
ID=mymovie width=70 height=50>
<param name=src value=" mymovie.dcr">
<param name=swRemote value="swSaveEnabled='true' swVolume='true'
swRestart='true' swPausePlay='true' swFastForward='true' swContextMenu='true'
">
<param name=swStretchStyle value=none>
<param name=bgColor value=#FFFFFF>
<embed src="mymovie.dcr" name="myMovie" bgColor=#FFFFFF  width=70 height=50
swRemote="swSaveEnabled='true' swVolume='true' swRestart='true'
swPausePlay='true' swFastForward='true' swContextMenu='true' "
swStretchStyle=none type="application/x-director"
pluginspage="http://www.macromedia.com/shockwave/download/">
</embed>
</object>
```

⇨ For more information about publishing, **see** "Publish Settings," **p. 162** (Chapter 9)

⇨ For more information about building HTML tags, **see** "Working with Browsers," **p. 454** (Chapter 22, "Shockwave and Internet Access")

BUILDING CD-ROMS

Next to the Internet, the most common way to deliver Director content is on CD-ROMs. The steps involved in making a CD-ROM depend on your CD-ROM burner, and your CD-ROM burning software. Usually, the software comes with documentation. Because software varies greatly, it is impossible to go into complete detail here.

If you are making a cross-platform CD-ROM, this usually involves building two descriptions of the CD-ROM contents. The popular CD-ROM burning software, Adaptec Toast, requires you to make the Mac description first by creating a temporary hard drive partition and copying all the files to it.

Next, you can describe the Windows side of the CD-ROM to it, pointing to files both on the Mac temporary partition and elsewhere. The program is then smart enough to place shared files on the CD-ROM once, in such a way that both platforms can read them.

This way, if you have a 650MB CD-ROM, you might have just a few megabytes of Mac-only data and a few megabytes of PC-only data. The Mac-only data and PC-only data can be the projector and all the Xtras. The rest can be nearly 650MB of shared data.

Optimization used to be an important topic for CD-ROM creators. Today's software is so advanced that it does a good job of optimizing the positions of the files on the CD-ROM even without more information from you. Check your software's documentation for more information.

MAKING INSTALLERS

If you are building a professional CD-ROM product, you might want to create an installer, rather than just having the projector play from the CD-ROM. Installers are created not with Director, but with third-party programs.

These programs do not care that you used Director to make your product. They will work with just about any type of standalone application, such as projectors.

Each third-party application works differently, so there is no use describing the steps needed to use one. The products all come with instructions and are relatively easy to use. Here is a list of some third-party applications:

- **InstallerMaker (Mac)**—http://www.aladdinsys.com/developers/installermaker/

- **InstallerVise (Mac and Windows)**—http://www.mindvision.com

- **InstallShield (Windows)**—http://www.installshield.com/

- **DragInstall (Mac)**—http://www.sauers.com/draginstall/

- **Wise and InstallBuilder (Windows)**—http://www.glbs.com

BUILDING SCREEN SAVERS

You can also turn your Director movies into screen savers. These are popular as promotional items.

Projectors, or any other executable, can be used as screen savers if the user knows how to manipulate the Windows screen saver resources. However, because the people in the target audience for screen savers probably don't know how to do that, a little help is needed.

If you are actually looking for the opposite functionality—disabling the screen saver while your Director movie runs—the Buddy API Xtra that comes on the Director 8 CD-ROM includes a *DisableScreenSaver* command.

A third-party program can be used to build an installer that creates a screen saver from a Director movie. Other third-party programs can be used to "bridge the gap" between projectors and screen savers. Some of these products are listed here:

- **CineMac (Mac and Windows)**—http://www.macsorcery.com/

- **AnySaver (Windows)**—http://dgolds.com/

- **AutoLaunch (Mac)**—http://www.stclairsoft.com

- **DirSaver (Windows)**—http://members.xoom.com/dirsaver/

- **EXE Screen Saver (Windows)**—http://www.ames.net/bsmith/exe_ss/

- **Buddy Saver (Windows)**—http://www.mods.com.au/

TROUBLESHOOTING DELIVERING THE GOODS

- Some computers, especially laptops, do not recognize CD-ROMs that have been created in one-off CD-ROM burners, such as the ones that you would typically have attached to your home or office computer. They still work well with CD-ROMs created in factories.

- If a Shockwave movie still does not appear on a page after you upload it to a server, it might be because the MIME type for Shockwave is not set on the server. MIME types enable the server to tell the browser what a media element is. Search the Macromedia Web site for MIME to find the latest information about setting MIME types for different servers.

- Check your browser cache settings before testing. Many browsers come with a default setting that has the movie check for new content only once per session. If you are uploading new versions constantly and then testing, you might actually be looking at the cached version of your old movie. Set the cache to check the server every time.

- More about caches: Even when you have the browser set to check the server each time for a new version, it still sometimes uses a cached version. Versions of both Internet Explorer and Navigator have exhibited this behavior for developers in the past. To make absolutely sure that you are using a new version of the Shockwave movie on your server, you must go to another page, clear the cache, and then return to the Shockwave page.

DID YOU KNOW?

- You can place an <IMG> tag inside an <OBJECT> tag for Internet Explorer users. If the browser is unable to display the Shockwave movie, the image appears instead.

- If you include a text file called LINGO.INI in the same folder as your projector, the projector will open this file and read it as Lingo. Any commands inside an *on startUp* handler will be executed. You can declare and set globals using this file.

- Director 8's Publish command uses sample HTML files from the Publish Templates folder inside your Director 8 folder. You can view these files with a text or HTML editor, and even make changes to them if you feel confident that it will not disturb the codes necessary for Director's Publish command to use the files.

X

ADVANCED TOPICS

IN THIS PART

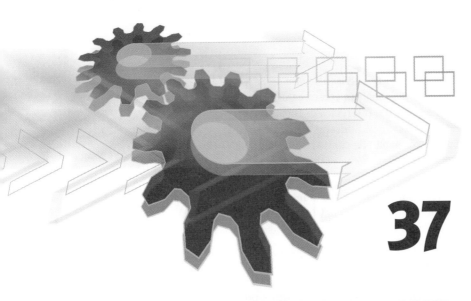

37

CREATING MULTIUSER APPLICATIONS

IN THIS CHAPTER

Source movies for this chapter can be found on the CD-ROM in the "Book Movies" folder under folder 37. Note that some of the files are in Director 8.0 format, while others need to be in Director 8.5 format.

Director 8.5 comes with the Shockwave Multiuser Server version 3.0, a program that enables you to connect your users to one another over the Internet. For Director, Shockwave, and Projectors, a Multiuser Xtra provides this connectivity. The server itself is a compact program that runs on a Mac or Windows machine with a dedicated Internet connection.

Shipping with Director 8.5 is version 3.0 of the Multiuser Server. An even newer version might be available by the time you read this. Check Macromedia's site to download an upgrade. You should always upgrade to the latest version.

The Multiuser Server can be used to send information to and from users, connect users with chat-room and whiteboard applications, and even make multiplayer games.

This chapter serves as an introduction to and an overview of the capabilities of the Multiuser Server and Xtra. There are also some examples of the server and Xtra at work. To write a complete reference would almost require another book. Macromedia's own documentation takes up quite a bit of space. With this chapter as a starting point and the official documentation as a reference guide, you should be able to use the Multiuser Server and Xtra to create a variety of applications.

SETTING UP THE MULTIUSER SERVER

The Multiuser Server is a program, just like Macromedia Director. When you install Director, Multiuser Server is installed in a folder inside the Director 8.5 folder called "Shockwave Multiuser Server 3.0." That folder contains a lot of files that support the server, as well as the application itself.

Running the Multiuser Server

To set up the server, all you need to do is run the program. First, make sure that the computer you are running it on is connected to the Internet. That computer should have a permanent static IP address, but a temporary IP address is fine for testing.

Figure 37.1 shows what the server program window looks like after you launch it. In addition, the figure includes the output obtained by choosing Status, Server from the menu.

Figure 37.1
The Multiuser Server window after it has been launched and server information has been requested.

The Multiuser Server application is simply a window that displays messages concerning the server. By choosing Status, Server, you can see the computer's IP address and the port that the server is using. You need this information to build multiuser movies.

Configuring the Server

There are many options that you can set to change the way your server works. These can all be found in the Multiuser.cfg file in the same folder as the application.

The Multiuser.cfg file is well commented and most settings are described in detail, along with how to change them. One of the first changes you can make in the file concerns ServerOwnerName and ServerSerialNumber. If you enter your Director serial number, you can go beyond the 50-connection limit of the server, all the way up to 2,000 connections. The actual number of connections can be set using the ConnectionLimit parameter, found further down in the file.

The next setting is the port number. A *port* is an addressing technique used by your computer to determine which incoming data goes where. The default port is 1626, which means that any information coming in to your computer on port 1626 is routed to the Multiuser Server.

Another useful setting is IdleTimeOut. This is set to the default of 600, which is 10 minutes. This means that if a Shockwave movie has not tried to contact the server in 10 minutes, the connection is dropped. This can be a problem if you plan on having long delays between communications, such as you might have in a chess game.

Most of the other settings pertain to user levels. These settings specify which commands a movie can or cannot use on the server. For instance, if a user has a level of 20, but a level of 40 is required to create a record in the database, messages sent to the server that ask it to create a new record are refused.

User levels are a great security feature, but they complicate things for developers who just want to build basic multiuser applications. I don't deal with user levels much in this chapter, but the server documentation contains all the details needed by advanced developers.

Just about every version of the Multiuser Server since 1.0 has brought about major changes to the Multiuser.cfg file. Use this chapter as a guideline to the file, but note that property names and options might change.

If your computer is properly configured, you can set up the server to run on multiple ports. This is called *multihoming*. See your computer's documentation for how to set it up.

You can also set many properties of the server on a movie level, rather than on the server level. This means that as different movies use the same server, they can have different settings. Check the Movie.cfg file for an example. You can duplicate this file and rename it to create unique settings for different movies.

USING THE MULTIUSER BEHAVIORS

After your server is up and running, creating a basic multiuser application takes very little effort. This is because Macromedia has included a set of multiuser behaviors in the behaviors library.

Taking these behaviors and building a simple chat room is easy. It took me less than 10 minutes, and I didn't have to use any Lingo at all.

The first screen simply needs a button and a text member. The text member should be editable and indicate to users that this is where they should enter the name they want to use in the chat room. Figure 37.2 shows what this screen might look like.

After the text member and the button are ready, choose Window, Library Palette, and select the Multiuser subcategory of the Internet category. Drag and drop the "Connect to Server" behavior onto the button. I used a simple Director pushbutton for the sample movie on the CD-ROM (see 37librarychat.dir), but you can use a nice bitmap instead.

It is a good idea to only do the bare minimum changes to the Multiuser.cfg file and use multiple movie.cfg files to customize the settings for each different movie that connects to the server. To do this, name each customized movie.cfg file the same as the movie that will be connecting to the server. Then, the correct .cfg file will be read and, in effect, a custom server will be set up for the movie.

After you drop the behavior onto the button, a Parameters dialog box appears (see Figure 37.3). It contains most of the information that your server needs to create and maintain the chat room.

Figure 37.2
The sign-in screen for a simple chat room.

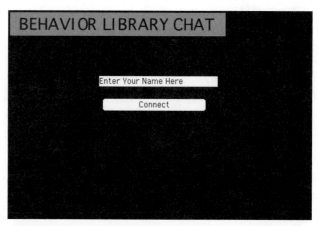

First, you must specify the name of the text member that is on the Stage. This is where the server gets the user's name. You can also create another text member and have the user type in a password.

Next, you should specify three frames: a wait frame, a frame that the movie goes to when the connection is in place, and a frame to go to if the connection fails. To keep this simple, I have the movie return to the sign-in frame when the connection fails.

To set these three frames, you might want to cancel the behavior Parameters dialog box and place "Sign In", "Connected", and "Waiting" frame labels in the Score. Then, drag and drop the "Connect to server" behavior onto the button again to set these parameters more easily.

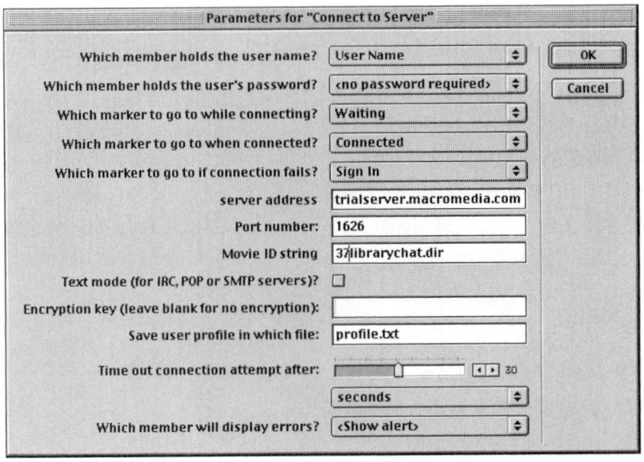

Figure 37.3
The "Connect to Server" behavior offers many customizable features in its Parameters dialog box.

The "server address" and "Port number" parameters should reflect the numbers that you see when you set up the server. Refer to Figure 37.1 to see where these are.

The "Movie ID string" is simply an identifier for the server. You can use a Multiuser Server to service more than one application. The server uses the movie ID to tell the applications apart. All the people using this chat movie will be connecting to the server with the same movie ID. If something else, like a game, is using the same server, it should have a different movie ID.

The rest of the parameters can be left as defaults.

The next step in creating the chat room is to place a "please wait" message on the "Waiting" frame. You need simple *go to the frame* handlers in each frame script for the "Sign In", "Waiting", and "Connected" frames. You can use the "Go Loop" standard behavior if you want to avoid Lingo entirely.

The main frame for the chat room is the chat frame. You can see this frame in Figure 37.4. It contains a title, a chat output text member, a chat input text member, a text member that displays the members in the chat room, a disconnect button, and a small whiteboard bitmap.

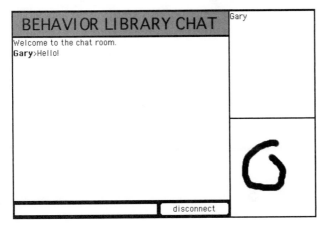

Figure 37.4
The "Connected" frame is where all the action takes place in the chat room movie.

Most of the elements in the chat room have an associated behavior that makes each element work. For instance, the chat input text member, at the bottom left, needs to have the "Chat Input" behavior dropped on it. There is also a "Chat Output" behavior, a "Display Group Members" behavior, and a "Disconnect from server" behavior. To make the whiteboard work, you need to first drop the "Canvas" behavior, found in the "Paintbox" behaviors category on to a bitmap sprite. Then, you can drop the "Whiteboard (Shared Canvas)" behavior on it.

Many of these behaviors have short Parameter dialog boxes that appear when you drop them on the sprites. In all cases, the default settings in those dialog boxes will work just fine to get your chat room up and running.

After the movie is complete, you can simply rewind and run your movie to see it in action. You need the server to be running on another computer for it to work, of course.

> **Caution**
>
> This is a bug in the "Chat Input" behavior that comes with Director 8.5 that you must fix to get this to work. In the handler "on init", the following two lines must be switched so that they are in this order:
>
> ```
> pCurrentGroupID = groupID
> me.setMessageSubjects(group
> ID)
> ```
>
> This bug is not present in the behavior that comes with Director 8.0.

The chat area functions as you might expect. You just type in the input area and press Return. The text appears in the output area.

For the whiteboard, just click and draw. If you want to create a more complex whiteboard, check out the other behaviors in the "Paintbox" category. These behaviors enable you to set brushes and colors as well as erase the canvas.

The only loose end is the "Disconnect" button. It successfully disconnects users from the server, but it does not jump to another frame. The users are left staring at a dead chat-room screen. You have to attach another button behavior to the button to make it go to another frame.

LEARNING BASIC MULTIUSER LINGO

Although the standard multiuser behaviors enable you to customize your chat room quite a bit, you have to use Lingo to build other types of multiuser applications.

You need to know about several main Lingo commands. They enable you to connect to the server, get messages, and send messages.

First, you need to create an instance of the Multiuser Xtra. All the commands you need are part of the Xtra. You can create an instance with the *new* command like this:

```
gMultiuser = new(xtra "Multiuser")
```

The variable "gMultiuser" should be global so that other handlers in other scripts can access it.

After you have an instance of the Xtra, you can establish the connection to the server. You need the *connectToNetServer* command to do this. It requires the IP address and port number for your server, as well as a movie ID. A common call looks like this:

```
err = gMultiuser.connectToNetServer(userName,"password", \
IPaddress,portNumber,"myMovie")
```

In this case, I use the password "password" to make it simple. You can provide a real password if you want. I use the name "myMovie" for the movie ID, but you can use something more relevant for yours.

You can check the error code that's returned by *connectToNetServer* to make sure that the connection was successful. If the error code is 0, it was successful. If it is some other number, you can feed that number to the *getNetErrorString* function to see a description of the problem.

After the connection has been established, you should call *setNetMessageHandler*. This call tells the Xtra which handler should be called every time a communication arrives from the server.

```
gMultiuser.setNetMessageHandler("myMessageHandler")
```

Now you are ready to send and receive messages from the server. To send a message, use the *sendNetMessage* command. This command takes three parameters. The first parameter is the name of the recipient, the second is the subject, and the third is the message content. Here is an example:

```
gMultiuser.sendNetMessage("@AllUsers","chat","Hello!")
```

Instead of specifying the name of a single user, I use the value "@AllUsers" for the recipient. This means that the message is broadcast to all the users on the server who are using the same movie ID.

The subject and content in this example are simple. In most cases, the subject is used to identify the type of message that is being sent, and the content is the message itself. The server doesn't really care. It will be your Lingo code that interprets the subject and content.

When a message is sent with *sendNetMessage*, you need to have a handler in the movies of all the connected users that retrieves this information. This is where the handler defined in *setNetMessageHandler* comes in. It is called whenever a message is sent to the user, whether it is sent specifically to a single user, or to "@AllUsers" as the *sendNetMessage* example does. Here is a simple handler:

```
on myMessageHandler
  message = gMultiuser.getNetMessage()
  subject = message.subject
  content = message.content
  senderID = message.senderID
end
```

The message handler uses the *getNetMessage* function to retrieve a property list that defines the message. This property list includes the properties #subject, #content,

"@AllUsers" defines a group on the server, as does any recipient that uses an @ before it. "@AllUsers" is set up automatically for you, but you can also define your own groups by using *sendNetMessage* with "system.group.join", "system.group.leave", and similar commands. See the user documentation for details.

and #senderID. In addition, the properties #errorCode, #recipients, and #timestamp are returned should you want to use them.

To disconnect from the server, all you need to do is throw away the Xtra instance. You can do it as simply as this:

```
gMultiuser = VOID
```

That's all the commands that you need to create many multiuser applications. Check the server documentation for more details and for other minor commands and updates. Here is a list of some of the other commands and functions you might use:

- **checkNetMessages**—Forces the Xtra to check for incoming messages.

- **getNetAddressCookie**—Returns the IP address of the computer. In Shockwave, this is encrypted as a weird string for security reasons. However, the encrypted string works like a regular IP address for all multiuser commands.

- **getNetOutgoingBytes**—Returns how many bytes are waiting to be sent.

- **getNumberWaitingMessages**—Returns how many messages have arrived that have not yet been processed.

- **setNetBufferLimits**—Sets the limit on how much information can be queued in memory.

Next, let's look at how you might use these commands to create a simple application.

CREATING YOUR OWN MULTIUSER APPLICATION

Using these Lingo commands, you can create a simple multiuser application. This simple example enables users to control a little smiley face in a shared space. It is simple so that the important Lingo syntax is the main feature.

You can do this all in one behavior. This behavior attaches to the frame script. In addition, sprites 1 through 8 will hold duplicates of little smiling face graphics.

The behavior starts off with property declarations. You can store the Xtra instance in a property, as well as the user ID. In this case, I use *getNetAddressCookie* to get a unique username for each person. The first word of every value returned by *getNetAddressCookie* is "MacromediaSecretIPAddressCookie:". You can discard that and use the second word, which is the encoded address. It is usually something like "be8759e422678e76c855f6fe521ff8".

This unique name guarantees that every user will have a unique ID and there will be no confusion about where messages are coming from.

You will also have a property that stores the list of user IDs and face locations on the screen. The "pLoc" property holds the location of the person using the movie.

```
property pMultiuser -- Xtra instance
property pUserID -- unique name
property pPeople -- list of people and positions
property pLoc -- your loc
```

The *on beginSprite* handler creates the Xtra instance, connects to the server, and places the user at a random location on the screen. It then broadcasts this location to the users already on the server.

```
on beginSprite me
  -- start Xtra
  pMultiuser = new(xtra "Multiuser")

  -- get a unique name
  pUserID = pMultiuser.getNetAddressCookie().word[2]

  -- connect and set up
  pMultiuser.connectToNetServer(pUserID,"",\
     "X.X.X.X",1626,"example")
  pMultiuser.setNetMessageHandler(#messageHandler,me)

  -- init people list and location
  pPeople = [:]
  pLoc = point(random(47)*10,random(31)*10)
  addProp pPeople, pUserID, pLoc

  -- send first message to all present
  pMultiuser.sendNetMessage("@AllUsers","move",pLoc)

  -- draw screen
  drawPeople(me)
end
```

The *setNetMessageHandler* specifies that the "on messageHandler" will take care of incoming messages. The second parameter in *setNetMessageHandler* tells the message to look for this handler in this behavior, not in a movie script.

When a message comes in, it is first broken into parts. Then, the subject is checked and different subjects trigger different events. In the following example, I handle the "move" event by setting a location in "pPeople" and updating the screen.

```
-- handle all incoming messages
on messageHandler me
  -- get message and break into parts
  message = pMultiuser.getNetMessage()
  subject = message.subject
  content = message.content
  sender = message.senderID

  -- handle move messages
  if subject = "move" then
    -- set or add person's location to list
```

```
      pPeople.setAProp(sender,content)
      -- update screen
      drawPeople(me)
    end if
  end
```

The "on drawPeople" handler takes care of positioning the faces on the screen. The handler is careful to position unused sprites off the screen so that when someone leaves the room the extra sprite doesn't hang around.

```
-- draw up to eight faces on the screen
on drawPeople me
  repeat with s = 1 to 8
    if s <= pPeople.count then
      -- person exists, place them
      sprite(s).loc = pPeople[s]
    else
      -- no one for this sprite, remove it
      sprite(s).loc = point(-1000,-1000)
    end if
  end repeat
end
```

When the sprite ends, either from the movie stopping or from a navigation button taking the movie off the frame, the Xtra instance is killed. This disconnects the user from the server.

```
-- kill Xtra instance
on endSprite me
  pMultiuser = VOID
end
```

The *on keyDown* handler accepts arrow keys, moves the person's face, and then broadcasts this move to the other users.

```
-- allow people to move
on keyDown me
  -- arrow keys
  case the keyCode of
    123: dx = -10
    124: dx = 10
    125: dy = 10
    126: dy = -10
  end case

  -- change location
  pLoc = pLoc + point(dx,dy)
```

```
-- broadcast location
pMultiuser.sendNetMessage("@AllUsers","move",pLoc)
end
```

Finally, as in so many other behaviors, you need a handler that holds the movie on the current frame.

```
-- loop on the frame
on exitFrame me
  go to the frame
end
```

The previous behavior is crude, in a way. All it does is allow nameless faces to float around in an empty space. However, it's important because these faces are controlled by different people, on different computers, possibly from entirely different places in the world.

The basic framework is here to turn this into something much bigger. The "on messageHandler" handler can easily handle more messages, such as "chat" to receive a chat message and append it to a text member. It can get "frown" messages to have faces frown. With a little more Lingo code, there is no reason why you can't have the faces interact: bumping into each other or shooting things at each other, for example.

USING PEER-TO-PEER CONNECTIONS

Not all multiuser programs need to use a server. You can also use the Multiuser Xtra to connect directly with another computer on the Internet. Even though this is a peer-to-peer connection without using an actual server, one computer is considered the "server" and the other the "client." The main difference is that the "server" starts up and waits for connections. The "client" will then try to contact the "server."

This has limited use since the client user must somehow know the IP address of the server user. If they are both Shockwave movies or Projectors running on someone's random computer on the Internet, then how is one to know the other exists?

There are two ways, then, to use peer-to-peer connections. The first is to use the Multiuser Server to allow two users to meet and decide that they want to connect directly, such as to play a game of chess. Then, the two players can exchange IP addresses and go off to play each other peer-to-peer. With a lot of complex programming, you can achieve this and the players will not even know the difference.

The other way to use peer-to-peer connections is to have two users that already know that they want to connect. This could work in a business setting. The users might decide in a meeting or via email who will be the server and where that server is located.

Caution

In my experience, setting up a game site using peer-to-peer connections does not work very well. This is because many business firewalls and some ISPs will prevent the type of connection needed. Using a central Shockwave Multiuser Server works much better if you plan on allowing the general public to use your application.

To create a peer-to-peer connection, you start off by issuing the *waitForNetConnection* command in the movie that is to be the server. This effectively turns the Shockwave movie or Projector into a mini Shockwave Multiuser Server.

```
gMultiuser = new(xtra "Multiuser")
gMultiuser.setNetMessageHandler(#messageHandler,script "MUS Scripts")
myUserID = "server movie"
gMultiuser.waitForNetConnection(myUserID,1627)
```

The client users can connect to the server user in the same way that they connect to a Shockwave Multiuser Server, using *connectToNetServer*. The trick is, of course, knowing the IP address of the server computer. The user who is running the server can get this by looking at the appropriate control panel for his operating system. You can also tell this user what his or her IP address is by using the *getNetAddressCookie()* function. While this function will return a real IP address if used in a Projector, it will return an encoded string of numbers and letters if used in Shockwave. Lingo can interpret either the real IP address or the encoded one, but the encoded one is much harder for client users to type.

When a client movie tries to connect to a server movie, the server movie will get a "waitForNetConnection" message. It is important that the message handler returns a *TRUE* with the *return* command. This will signal an acceptance of the connection. Otherwise, the connection will be refused by the Xtra.

One other specialized peer-to-peer function is the *getPeerConnectionList()* function. This works for the server movie only. It will return a list of all of the users connected to the movie.

One use for peer-to-peer connections has nothing to do with multiuser applications. You can actually establish a multiuser connection between two movies running on the same computer. In fact, you can do it with two movies running in the same Web page.

The way this works is that the movie loaded first uses *waitForNetConnection* to become a server and the second movie uses *connectToNetServer* to connect to it. They can then send messages back and forth.

Here is a single behavior that will demonstrate this. It is on the CD-ROM as "37moviecom.dir". The behavior starts by creating the Xtra. It then checked the "sw1" parameter on the Web page. There will be two of these movies in one page. The first instance will have an "sw1" tag that states "server". The second instance will not even have an "sw1" tag. Thus, the first movie will use *waitForNetConnection* and the second will use *connectToNetServer*.

The second movie will use the IP address from *getNetAddressCookie()* to call the server. This will return its own IP address, which is the same as the server's since they are both on the same machine. While the server started as user "server user", the client will start as "client user".

In order to complete the connection, the server must return a *TRUE* when it gets the initial message from the client user. Now that the connection is set, the two movies can communicate between each other with *sendNetMessage*. This simple example sends random numbers back and forth. The numbers are put into text members as proof that the communication is taking place.

```
property pMultiuser

on beginSprite me
  -- create server and get IP address
  pMultiuser = new(xtra "Multiuser")
  pMultiuser.setNetMessageHandler(#messageHandler,me)

  -- the server user waits for a connection while the client user connects
  if externalParamValue("sw1") = "server" then
    pMultiuser.waitForNetConnection("server user",1627)
  else
    pMultiuser.connectToNetServer("client
user","",pMultiuser.getNetAddressCookie(),1627,"37moviecom")
  end if
end


on messageHandler me
  message = pMultiuser.getNetMessage()

  if message.subject = "waitForNetConnection" then
    -- return TRUE to allow client to connect
    return TRUE
  else if message.subject = "number" then
    -- got a new number from other movie
    member("output").text = string(message.content)
  end if
end

on sendNumber me
  -- send random number to other movie
  if externalParamValue("sw1") = "server" then
    pMultiuser.sendNetMessage("client user","number",random(99))
  else
    pMultiuser.sendNetMessage("server user","number",random(99))
  end if
end

on exitFrame me
  go to the frame
end
```

On the CD-ROM there is a sample HTML page called "37moviecom.html". You will find two OBJECT/EMBED tags in the file, one with an "sw1" specifying "server" and the other without it. If you open this page with a browser, you'll see the cross-communication in action.

USING THE MULTIUSER SERVER DATABASE

A useful feature of the Multiuser Server is its ability to store data. This can be used to store information about the users that connect to the server, or it can contain pre-made information about a multiuser environment, such as an adventure game.

The Multiuser Server has four types of databases: user data, player data, application data, and read-only application data. The first two can be used to store information about users, the second two about environments.

User data, referred to as "DBUser" in commands, is a good place to store universal information that might cross over to multiple multiuser applications. These could be things such as the user's name and preferences. Player data, "DBPlayer", is similar, but is used to store information about a user only as it pertains to the current movie.

The first of the two types of application data, "DBApplication", can be used to store game states and environmental variables about your server that change. The second type, "DBApplicationData", is meant to be read-only by the users, but you can still set it with a movie that has high-level access.

To create a database entry, use the *sendNetMessage* command with a special recipient. For example, to create a user entry, use "system.DBAdmin.createUser". Here is an example:

```
gMultiuser.sendNetMessage("system.DBAdmin.createUser","",\
    [#userID: userID, #password: password, #userLevel: 20])
```

After there is a record of a user, you can store information about the user in that record. The first step toward doing this is to create the attribute. Then, you can store information with that attribute. Notice in the following example that the first line refers to "DBAdmin" to declare an attribute, but refers to "DBUser" to get the information.

```
gMultiuser.sendNetMessage("system.DBAdmin.declareAttribute","",\
    [#attribute: #userEmail])
gMultiuser.sendNetMessage("system.DBUser.setAttribute","",\
    [#userID: userID, [#userEmail: userEmail]])
```

After the user has a database entry and attributes, you can retrieve data with "system.DBUser.getAttribute". To get a list of available attributes, you can also send messages such as "system.DBUser.getAttributeName".

There are dozens of database commands to set and retrieve data from the four types of databases. To see the complete list, check the documentation, which is constantly updated on Macromedia's site to correspond to the latest version of the server.

The biggest problem I have had when creating database entries was that the *userlevel* of the user was not high enough to allow the creation of users and attributes. If you run into this problem, you can modify the Multiuser.cfg file to give new users a higher *userlevel*, or lower the *userlevel* required to perform database modifications.

USING UDP

The Multiuser Server and Xtra generally use TCP/IP connections, like most of the rest of the Internet. A connection like this consists of two steps. First, the message is sent to the destination. Then, the destination sends a message back confirming that the message arrived intact.

In fact, each message sent becomes two messages, one there and one back. This can create a long "lag" when sending messages. This lag can be a fraction of a second up to several seconds.

> Note that you are specifying a different port on your server for UDP addresses. This means that the server will be using two ports. This also means that every time someone connects to your server, they will be using two connections: one for TCP/IP and one for UDP. A server that is set to allow 50 connections will then only be able to handle 25 users.

However, there is a way to send a message without this second confirmation step. The Multiuser Server 3.0 supports UDP, User Data Protocol. With UDP, the message is sent one way and no checking is done to make sure it has arrived.

UDP is commonly used for games where lots of messages will be sent and mistakes will not matter so much. For instance, if UDP messages are sent every time a player moves a character in a game, then if one never arrives, it is no big deal. In fact, that character position will likely become obsolete in another second when another move is made.

On the other hand, using UDP for a chess game is not a good idea. If a move is missed, then the game is ruined. Plus, speed is not that important for chess, since it is a turn-based game.

Using UDP messages is not that different from using regular TCP/IP messages. First, you'll need to modify the "Multiuser.cfg" file to allow the server to use UDP. This is done by uncommenting the line that sets the "EnableUDP" property to 1.

```
EnableUDP = 1
```

Right above that line is another that will specify the IP address and port of the server. Uncomment it and set with your own server IP address and a port number other than the one you are using for TCP/IP messages.

```
UDPServerAddress = X.X.X.X:1627
```

When you want to use UDP, you need to connect to the server in a slightly different way. You need to add a #localUDPPort property when using *connectToNetServer*.

The following *connectToNetServer* command looks a lot different than *connectToNetServer* commands used previously in this chapter. The *connectToNetServer* command has changed a lot since the first version of the Xtra. However, it maintains backwards compatibility with earlier versions of the command. With version 3.0, you can use a single parameter to define all the properties of the connection. This format makes it very easy to figure out what is going on. For new functions, like UDP, you'll need to use this format.

```
gMultiuser.connectToNetServer([#remoteAddress:"X.X.X.X" #logonInfo: [#userID:
myUserID, #password: "", #movieID: "myMovie"], #localUDPPort: 1627])
```

The #localUDPPort setting needs to match the setting on the server. Just by using this property, you have set up the movie to allow UDP messages. The next step is figuring out how to send a UDP message. It turns out that this is the same *sendNetMessage* command, but with one more parameter, #udp. Set this parameter to *TRUE* and the message will be sent via UDP instead of TCP/IP.

```
gMultiuser.sendNetMessage([#recipients:  "@AllUsers", #subject: "mySubject",
#content: "myMessage", #udp: TRUE])
```

If you set the #udp parameter to FALSE, or just leave it out, then the message will be sent via TCP/IP.

Note that the speed improvement that UDP messages will give you is very hard to demonstrate. If you are connected over a local network, then the difference will be almost undetectable. It is over a long distance, like half way around the world, where UDP speed is more apparent.

USING SERVER-SIDE LINGO

The most powerful addition to Director 8.5, apart from 3D, is server-side scripting for the Multiuser Server. For the first time, the Lingo programming language has been extended to operate outside of Macromedia Director. The Multiuser Server, a completely different application, can now be programmed with Lingo.

Creating scripts for the server can range in difficulty from relatively easy, to very difficult. It all depends on how deep you want to go. For instance, the server can be programmed to use "threads." Threads are like parent scripts or behaviors, except that they are running virtually at the same time as other scripts. Plus, "threads" are not, in themselves, scripts. They created, and then told what handlers to run. The handlers themselves come from outside the threads.

While threads are an advanced topic for anyone who is not an expert programmer, you can also create a server-side script that uses the same basic Lingo that you would use to control a sprite. Before we look at an example, let's examine what server-side scripting can and cannot do.

Lingo Outside of Director

So where do these Lingo scripts go? The Multiuser Server does not have a Script window. Instead, scripts are contained in ordinary text files. One of the server's subfolders is named "Scripts" and there are already several scripts present.

If you open up the "dispatcher.ls" script or the "scriptmap.ls" files, you will see a lot of complex Lingo code. In fact, these two files are well-commented, but the code is expert-level stuff. You'll be relieved to learn that you don't have to know much about these two scripts.

You might have trouble editing these files at first. For instance, on the Mac, these .ls files are recognized as Director files, and so Director is used to open them if you double-click them. However, Director won't do anything with the files. You can also open them from a text editor like SimpleText, BBEdit, or WordPad. If you know how to modify your operating system so that it handles .ls files by opening them with a text editor, I recommend doing that.

The dispatcher.ls and scriptmap.ls are always present with the Multiuser Server. The dispatcher is what actually handles most server-side scripting. When you create new scripts, it is in charge of passing control of incoming messages on to these scripts. The scriptmap.ls is what tells the dispatcher which movies send messages to which scripts.

To create your own server-side script, start a new text file. Name it with the .ls extension and place it in the "Scripts" folder.

In order for the server to recognize the new script, the scriptmap will need to be changed. Open that up with a text editor and take a look. You will see two commented-out examples of scripts being mapped to movies. You can modify one of these or create your own line. Here is a line that will map all messages from the movie "serverside" to the script "serverside.ls".

```
theMap.append([#movieID: "serverside", #scriptFileName: "serverside.ls"])
```

Now all that is left is to populate "serverside.ls" with a script. You'll need to know more about what events the server responds to first.

New Lingo Syntax

When you are creating a sprite behavior, you know that there are certain messages that the behavior will respond to, like "mouseUp" or "exitFrame". You would write handlers to handle these messages.

Server-side scripts are the same. They also have a set of possible messages that need handlers if you choose to handle them. Here is a complete list of these handlers.

- **on groupCreate**   This handler gets called when the first user joins a new group
- **on groupDelete**   This handler gets called when the last user leaves group
- **on groupJoin**   This handler gets called when a new user joins a group
- **on groupLeave**   This handler gets called when a user leaves a group
- **on incomingMessage**   This handler gets called every time a user sends a message to "system.script"
- **on movieCreate**   This handler gets called when the first user logs on to the server
- **on movieDelete**   This handler gets called when the last user leaves the server
- **on new**   This handler gets called when the first user logs on to the movie. Use *return(me)* to complete the creation on the script object.
- **on serverShutDown**   This handler gets called just before the server is shut down
- **on userLogOff**   This handler gets called whenever a user leaves
- **on userLogOn**   This handler gets called when a new user arrives

The three most useful of these handlers are the *on incomingMessage* handler, the *on userLogOn*, and *on userLogOff* handlers. With them, most simple tasks can be accomplished.

Server-side scripts look a lot like behaviors. Instead of *on beginSprite*, use *on new* to start it off. You can define properties with the *property* statement that will persist between handlers.

The *on incomingMessage* is the main way to get messages to the script. The Director movie would send a message to "system.script" in order for the message to reach the *on incomingMessage* handler.

The *on incomingMessage* handler will take four parameters after the *me*. They are: movie, group, user, and message. The movie, group and user are three objects that can be used as references to send messages to. The message is a property list of items from the original message sent by the Director movie.

To send a message back to the user, the server-side script would use the *sendMessage* command. This is called using the object that defines where the message should be sent. You can use the movie, group or user as the object for the *sendMessage* command. Here is an example:

```
on incomingMessage me, movie, group, user, message
    if message.subject = "test" then
          user.sendMessage("system.script.subject","content")
    end if
end
```

When you are using the user as the object, you can just pass two parameters in to *sendMessage*: the subject and the content. However, if you use the group or movie object, then your first parameter should be the recipients, such as the user id, a list of ids, the group name, and so on.

The subject of any message that comes from the server should start with "system.script" and then a short subject name. The content can be anything you like.

Server-Side Script Limits

Remember that the server is not Director. Things like sprites, members, and the Stage do not exist. All Lingo that pertains to them doesn't exist either.

What you can use is standard programming syntax like *if*, *repeat*, variables and lists, strings, math function, and custom handlers. If you like parent/child script, there is even a way to do that.

Server-side scripting also has a whole set of new commands that deal with threads and file management. The *exists*, *read*, and *write* commands do what you would expect. For instance, to read a text file into a variable, you can do this:

```
myText = file("myFile").read()
```

You can also use *readValue* and *writeValue* to read and write binary data, like lists. The file functions are quite powerful and will let your server-side script access or create small database-like files which can contain valuable data pertaining to your multiuser application.

A Server-Side Script Example

Earlier in this chapter we looked at a multiuser application where people could log in to the server and move little faces around on the screen. Without server-side scripting, the faces just appeared at random on the screen and were able to move on top of and underneath each other. With central server control, we can have the server be in charge of making sure that the faces never overlap.

We'll start with a script that looks a lot like the one earlier in the chapter. However, it will be a little simpler. First of all, it will not keep track of its own location, so no "pLoc" property is needed. In fact, it will connect to the server and not even establish its location or add itself to the "pPeople" list.

```
property pMultiuser -- Xtra instance
property pUserID -- unique name
property pPeople -- list of people and positions

on beginSprite me
  -- start xtra
  pMultiuser = new(xtra "Multiuser")

  -- get a unique name
  pUserID = pMultiuser.getNetAddressCookie().word[2]

  -- connect and setup
  pMultiuser.connectToNetServer(pUserID,"","X.X.X.X",1626,"serverside")
  pMultiuser.setNetMessageHandler(#messageHandler,me)

  -- init people list
  pPeople = [:]
end
```

The "*on messageHandler*" looks different too. It will accept only two messages: "system.script.move" and "system.script.remove". The first will add or replace the location of a user in the "pPeople" list and the second will remove a user from that list. In both cases the "*on drawPeople*" handler is called.

Notice that there is a complete absence of any mention of the real location of the faces. The server will be handling that, not the individual movies.

```
-- handle all incoming messages
on messageHandler me
  -- get message and break into parts
  message = pMultiuser.getNetMessage()
  subject = message.subject
  content = message.content
  sender = message.senderID
```

```
  -- handle messages
  if subject = "system.script.move" then
    -- set or add person's location to list
    pPeople.setAProp(content.id,content.loc)
    -- update screen
    drawPeople(me)

  else if subject = "system.script.remove" then
    -- delete user from list
    pPeople.deleteProp(content.id)
    -- update screen
    drawPeople(me)
  end if
end
```

The "*on drawPeople*" handler is exactly the same as the previous script version. So is the "*on endSprite*".

```
-- draw up to 8 faces on the screen
on drawPeople me
  repeat with s = 1 to 8
    if s <= pPeople.count then
      -- person exists, place them
      sprite(s).loc = pPeople[s]
    else
      -- no one for this sprite, remove it
      sprite(s).loc = point(-1000,-1000)
    end if
  end repeat
end
```

```
-- kill xtra instance
on endSprite me
  pMultiuser = VOID
end
```

The "*on keyDown*" handler will define a variable "d" according to how much the face should move. It is not actually changing the location of anything. It simply gets the amount that the face should move and sends that amount on to the server-side script.

```
-- allow people to move
on keyDown me
  -- arrow keys
  case the keyCode of
    123: d = point(-10,0)
    124: d = point(10,0)
```

```
   125: d = point(0,10)
   126: d = point(0,-10)
  end case

  -- send new potential location to server-side script
  pMultiuser.sendNetMessage("system.script","move",d)
end

-- loop on the frame
on exitFrame me
  go to the frame
end
```

There seems to be a lot missing from this script. For instance, how is the starting location of the face determined? How is the location of the face changed each time an arrow key is pressed? And how are the faces prevented from colliding? This will all be handled by the server-side script "serverside.ls".

This script starts off by creating an empty property list "pPeople" just like the Director movie. It will also put a nice message to the server text window when the script starts.

```
property pPeople

on new me
    put "Server-side example program loaded and ready!"
    pPeople = [:]
    return(me)
end
```

When a new user logs on, a message is put out to the server window. Then an entry is added to the "pPeople" list. The property name is the user's ID, taken from the "user" object as the "user.name". The value added to the list contains both the id and the location of the user. This will make it easy to send along in a message.

The "*on userLogOn*" handler finishes by sending a message to all of the users in the movie. This message will contain the location of the new face. This location comes from "*on getOpenLocation*" which we will look at later.

```
on userLogOn me, movie, group, user
    put "User"&&user.name&&"has entered."

    -- put new person into list and give them a unique location
    pPeople.addProp(user.name, [#id: user.name, #loc: getOpenLocation(me)])
    movie.sendMessage("@AllUsers","system.script.move",pPeople[user.name])
end
```

When a user leaves the server, the "system.script.remove" message is sent to everyone. Also, the user is removed from the "pPeople" list.

```
on userLogOff me, movie, group, user
    put "User"&&user.name&&"has left the arena."
    movie.sendMessage("@AllUsers","system.script.remove",pPeople[user.name])
    pPeople.deleteProp(user.name)
end
```

The only custom message that is sent to the server script is the "move" message. The content of this message is a point representing the direction of movement. This is used to calculate the "newloc" variable. Then the handler "*tooClose*" is used to determine if this new location is too close to another face. Only if it is not is the new location placed into "pPeople" and a "system.script.move" message sent to all of the users.

```
on incomingMessage me, movie, group, user, message
    if message.subject = "move" then
            newloc = pPeople[user.name].loc + message.content
            if not tooClose(me,user.name,newloc) then
                    pPeople[user.name].loc = newloc

movie.sendMessage("@AllUsers","system.script.move",pPeople[user.name])
            end if
    end if
end
```

The handler "*on getOpenLocation*" will create a random point and then call "*tooClose*" to see if that overlaps with another face.

```
on getOpenLocation me
    repeat while TRUE
            loc = point(random(350)+25,random(250+25))
            if not tooClose(me,VOID,loc) then return(loc)
    end repeat
end
```

The "*on tooClose*" handler will loop through the existing faces and see if any is closer than 25 pixels from a point. The "username" variable is passed in so that the handler can avoid comparing a new location to the present location of the same face.

```
on tooClose me, username, loc
    repeat with i = 1 to pPeople.count
            if username = getPropAt(pPeople,i) then next repeat
            if distance(me,pPeople[i].loc,loc) < 25 then return(TRUE)
    end repeat
    return(FALSE)
end
```

The "*on distance*" handler is a utility function that returns the distance between two points.

```
on distance me, loc1, loc2
    return sqrt(power(loc1.locH-loc2.locH,2)+power(loc1.locV-loc2.locV,2))
end
```

The outcome of the "serverside.ls" script is that it will handle the initial placement and all forthcoming movements of the users. The user simply requests a movement and the server determines if it is valid. The server keeps the master list of user and locations, and passes that information on to the clients when a change is made.

This is just a simple example of a server-side script. Developers have only begun to tap the power of master control scripts like this. They allow Director developers to basically create a custom server to do specifically what an application requires.

TROUBLESHOOTING MULTIUSER APPLICATIONS

- Do you have trouble using the demo movies on the CD-ROM or the text example in this book? Note that the IP addresses of the server in many cases is set to "X.X.X.X". You need to run your own server and set this IP address to match that server for any of this to work.

- If you are behind a firewall, you might not be able to connect to a Multiuser Server, or run one. Talk to the administrator of that firewall and let them know the port number of your server. They might be able to allow access to it.

DID YOU KNOW?

- You can also use the Multiuser Xtra to communicate with text-based servers. For example, you can communicate with a text-based mail server to send email. Search the technotes on Macromedia's site for examples of this.

- If you don't have a computer that you can use as a server to test your Multiuser applications, Macromedia can come to your rescue! Check out http://www.macromedia.com/support/director/multiuser/ for a link to a page that tells you how to sign up to use Macromedia's test server.

- You can run the Multiuser Server on the same computer that you are using to run Director, a projector, or a Shockwave movie that accesses the server. That way, with two computers, you can run the server and one movie on one computer, and the other movie on the other computer and check out how your application works with two users connected to the server.

USING 3D MEDIA

IN THIS CHAPTER

Source movies for this chapter can be found on the CD-ROM in the "Book Movies" folder under folder 38.

Director 8.5's biggest addition, without a doubt, is its 3D capability. In fact this may be the biggest addition to Director since the introduction of Lingo.

In this chapter we'll look at 3D basics, how to use the 3D cast member, and how to import and use 3D models. We'll also add some interactivity by using the 3D behaviors that come with Director 8.5.

3D BASICS

Using 3D worlds and models is almost completely different than the 2D graphics space that Director developers are used to. To really be able to use the new Director 8.5 3D capabilities, it will help to understand the basics of 3D computer graphics.

The Third Dimension

The three dimensions of 3D are horizontal distance, vertical distance and depth. These are also referred to with the letters x, y and z. Locations of objects in a 3D world can be specified by x, y and z coordinates just as locations in a 2D space can be defined by horizontal and vertical, or x and y, coordinates. Figure 38.1 shows you how to think of this three-coordinate system.

Figure 38.1
The z coordinate usually represents depth.

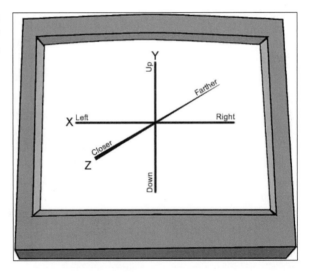

The world we live in is 3D, so you would think that it would be easy to build and manipulate 3D computer models. But it isn't easy at all. This is because computers really don't display anything in 3D at all. The computer monitor is hopelessly a flat 2D surface. 3D computer graphics are not really about 3D spaces, but about representing 3D spaces on a 2D screen. This complicates things quite a bit. You can't reach your hand into a computer monitor and move something around in three dimensions. Instead, we have all sorts of expensive complex tools to help us create 3D illusions on a 2D screen.

Two of the three dimensions, x and y, are easy to talk about. They correspond to the horizontal and vertical position on a computer screen. The z dimension, depth, is supposed to represent locations *into* the computer screen. But there is really no such thing. It is all an optical illusion.

So when you are dealing with 3D graphics, you are always dealing with five numbers. There are the x, y and z coordinates of the 3D object in 3D space. There are also the x and y coordinates that indicate where the 3D object appears on the 2D computer screen. Fortunately, the 3D engine built in to Director will take care of determining where things appear on the screen. All you need to worry about is where objects are in the x, y, and z coordinate system of the imaginary 3D world.

The Imaginary 3D World

With 2D graphics, usually what you see is what you get. As you create a 2D picture, you know exactly what it will look like on the screen in the final product. You may stretch or shrink the image, but the basic image will look exactly as you created it.

3D graphics are totally different. Instead of a flat painting, 3D graphics are made of models. A model is a mathematical representation of a 3D object. For instance, you may have a model of a tea cup or an airplane.

So what does this model look like? Well, it doesn't look like anything. In order to get a visual representation of the model, you have to create a rendering of it. A rendering is a snapshot of the model taken from a particular angle and distance. There are other factors involved in determining what the rendering looks like. For instance, you could use different lighting, a different type of camera lens, or even a different mathematical method of creating the rendering. Figure 38.2 shows several renderings of the same 3D model.

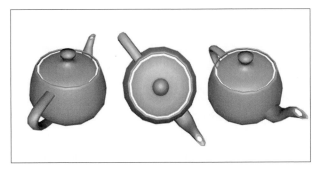

Figure 38.2
All of these images use the exact same model; only the viewpoint has changed.

When you create a 3D graphic in a 3D modeling program, you usually see the model as you create it. This is a preview rendering of the model that is created on the fly as the model is being built. This is usually a low-quality rendering since the image needs to be updated constantly as the artist changes the 3D model. If you are a 3D artist, you may request from the 3D program a high-quality rendering of the model. This would usually take a few seconds or minutes to create.

When a 3D engine like the one in Director 8.5 is used, the purpose is usually to have a live rendering which is updated as the model changes position, or the viewpoint changes. So instead of creating a model and making a single 2D rendering of it, we will be creating a model to place in a live environment.

Shockwave 3D Terminology

There are certain terms that you should master before beginning to work with 3D graphics. Note that we'll be talking about what these terms mean for Shockwave 3D. This may differ slightly than what you may have learned when using other 3D tools. Unfortunately, terms can sometimes mean slightly different things as you use tools created by different companies.

Models

We have already talked about *models*. A model is a mathematical representation of an object, like a goldfish or an automobile. A model can also define a smaller sub-object, like the goldfish's eye or the automobile's front left tire. Or, you can go the other way and have a model that contains lots of other models, like the model of a goldfish bowl or a city street.

Cameras

Next to models, the most important thing in a 3D environment is the *camera*. A camera is a viewpoint though which the world is seen. You can have one or more cameras in a 3D world and switch between them. A camera, like a model, can be positioned and rotated in the world. The result would be that the view of the world through that camera will change to reflect the position and rotation of the camera. In addition, cameras have some other minor properties, like the field of view of the lens.

Lights

Another very important part of 3D worlds are *lights*. In the real world, we can see things because light comes from a source, like the sun or a light bulb, reflects off a surface, and bounces into our eyes. The same is true for 3D worlds. There needs to be one or more light sources or the world is just completely dark.

A light source can be a point of light that radiates in all directions, or a spotlight that shines in a particular direction. A light can have a particular color and intensity.

A light that shines universally throughout a 3D world is called an *ambient* light. The location of such a light doesn't matter, as the light is treated like it is coming from all directions and hitting everything evenly.

One model, one light and one camera make up the bare minimum you need to have a 3D world. Most 3D creation programs start off with a default camera and light, so all you need to do is add a model.

Parts of a Model

Models are made up of *faces*. For instance, a cube would have six faces. Each face is made up of *polygons*. These are three-sided planes that fit together to make up a face and thus make up the whole model. Each polygon is defined by its three corner points. These points are called *vertices*. Figure 38.3 shows all of these elements as they relate to a cube.

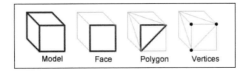

Figure 38.3
A cube model can be broken into faces, then polygons, then vertices.

Shaders

What the surface of a model looks like is determined by a *shader*. A shader can be defined as a color and how the surface reflects light. Or, a shader can use a *texture* for a more complex surface. A texture is usually a 2D bitmap graphic that represents what the surface looks like if viewed under simple straight-on conditions.

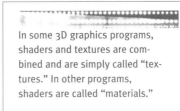

In some 3D graphics programs, shaders and textures are combined and are simply called "textures." In other programs, shaders are called "materials."

Shaders are one of the most complex aspects of 3D worlds. Shaders are also what give the world character. Without shaders, the world would be made up of flat-colored polygons.

For instance, if you have a model of a brick, you will probably want to apply a shader to the brick to make it red. Or, you could have a shader that uses a texture to make the surface of the brick look red and resemble rough stone. A brick wall model might be a simple wide and tall box that uses a bitmap texture to represent a whole wall of bricks.

Some models will use one shader to color in the entire model. More complex models will use several shaders to represent different parts of the model.

Now that you know some 3D terminology, let's import a model into Director and play with it a bit.

IMPORTING MODELS

While Director 8.5 can manipulate 3D models, there is no tool in Director that can be used to create them. Instead, you would normally use a 3D graphics tool to create the models, then a special exporter to create a Shockwave 3D file that can be imported into Director.

Where to Get 3D Models

While having a 3D engine in Director is great, it is useless unless you have some 3D media to display. There are three ways to make or obtain models to be used in Director.

Make Them Yourself

If you want to make your own 3D models, then you are going to need a 3D graphics program. There are dozens of such programs out there, and they range in price from a few hundred dollars to several thousand dollars. Whichever one you choose, make sure it has a Shockwave 3D export function. Here is a list of 3D graphics programs that have, or are planning to have, Shockwave 3D exporters at the time of this writing:

Alias|Wavefront: Maya

Caligari: TrueSpace

Curious Labs: Daz3D

Discreet: 3DS Max

Maxon Computer: Cinema 4D

NewTek: Lightwave

RealViz: ImageModeller

SoftImage: XIS

Tabuleiro: ShapeShifter 3D

TGS: AMAPI 3D

ShapeShifter stands out as the only tool created specifically for Shockwave 3D model creation. It also is different in that it works as a window inside of Director. It is a very simple tool, however, whereas tools like Maya, 3DS Max and Lightwave are used to create high-end 3D graphics you might see on television or in the movies.

Making 3D models is a skill all to itself. Do not expect to be able to buy one of these tools and be able to instantly create jet fighters and jellyfish. 3D modeling is a skill usually developed over years of work or education.

As the explanation of how to use a 3D program is a topic for a book all by itself, I won't spend any more time with it here. If you want to make your own models, pick your 3D program of choice and then look for a way to learn it: for instance a good book or a training course. Otherwise, you may want to consider other ways of getting 3D models.

Shockwave 3D Model Libraries

Just like there are 2D image clipart collections, there are also 3D model collections. You can purchase them on a CD-ROM or subscribe to a Web site that allows you to purchase models a la carte.

The Director 8.5 CD-ROM comes with a folder full of example Shockwave 3D files. These files are examples from 3D model collections that can be purchased. Even though Shockwave 3D is relatively new, several 3D model companies are already offering models in ready-to-use Shockwave 3D format. By the time you read this, many more collections may also be available.

Convert Other 3D Models

A third way to get 3D models is to obtain models in universal 3D formats. Then, import these models into a 3D program that has a Shockwave 3D exporter and export them as Shockwave 3D.

While this method seems simple, there are some complications. Often, the 3D models you get in collections will be too simple or too complex for what you need. For instance, a detailed model of an airplane may contain tens of thousands of polygons. While this is required for a film or television rendering of the airplane, it will be too complex for the fast on-the-fly rendering of a Shockwave 3D application. Plus, it may be so huge that the download time for a movie with this model in it may be too long.

Textures are often a problem as well. Often textures from standard 3D formats will not import correctly into a 3D program. Even if they do, these textures may not export correctly to Shockwave 3D.

Converting non-Shockwave 3D models into Shockwave 3D models will sometimes work and sometimes not. It all depends on what you start with and what your expectations are.

Importing Into Director

No matter how you create your Shockwave 3D model, you should end up with a Shockwave 3D file, also called a ".w3d" file after its dot-three filename extension. To bring this .w3d file into Director is simple. It is the same process that you use to bring in any other piece of media, like a picture or a sound.

By choosing File, Import, you can find and select one or more .w3d files. The only options you have at this point are whether to import the 3D models completely into Director, or whether to create a cast member that links to an external file. You can do this by using the pop-up menu at the bottom of the Import dialog box.

Now the 3D model is a Shockwave 3D cast member. The fun is just beginning. Next, we'll use Director's 3D member window to inspect the model.

THE SHOCKWAVE 3D WINDOW

To open the Shockwave 3D Window, just double-click on the 3D member in the Cast window. You'll get a window like the one in Figure 38.4, except that your model will be shown in the middle area. This middle area is the 3D preview area.

The Shockwave 3D window is not like Director's Paint window. You can't actually create or modify models. What you can do is preview your 3D member and make changes to the initial camera position.

All of the buttons on the left side of the window control the camera. The first three buttons allow you to dolly, rotate and pan the camera. Click the button of the function you want to use, and then click and drag in the preview area to move the camera. A dolly move will zoom the camera in and out. A pan will move the camera horizontally and vertically.

Figure 38.4
The Shockwave 3D window allows you to view your 3D member and make some changes to the position of the camera.

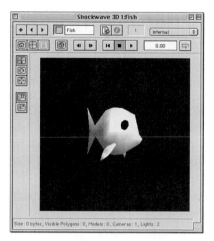

A rotation movement depends on which of the two buttons on the left is depressed, the "y-axis" button or the "z-axis" button. If you rotate using the z-axis, then the camera can move above and below the model, and the camera can lean left and right. If you use the y-axis then the camera can move to the left and right around the model as well as above and below it. Give these tools a try. It takes a while to get used to them if you have never used a 3D tool before.

The button with a picture of a house on it will reset the camera to its default position. The button next to it will set the default to match the view you have at the moment. Any changes you make to the camera view will disappear the moment you close the Shockwave 3D window if you do not use this Set Camera Transform button.

The Reset World button, with the little picture of the Earth on it, will reset the camera and everything else in the 3D member. This is handy if you have been using Lingo to manipulate models in the 3D member.

The rest of the controls have to do with 3D members that have been created with a 3D animation tool. Once imported into Director, these 3D animations can be played just like Flash members. You can use these video tape recorder-like buttons to play the animation and view each frame if you like.

At the bottom of the Shockwave 3D window, you will see some information about the 3D member. The total size, number of polygons, number of cameras and number of lights is shown. This will help you judge how complex a 3D member is and how much space it will occupy in the final Shockwave movie.

DISPLAYING A 3D MODEL ON THE STAGE

You can place a 3D member on the Stage just like a bitmap or Flash member. Once there, you can use the Property Inspector to make some adjustments to it. You can also select the member in the Cast and use the Property Inspector to make adjustments before you ever place it on the Stage.

Figure 38.5 shows the Property Inspector's 3D Model pane. It actually looks a lot like the 3D Text pane from Chapter 4, "Text and Field Members."

Once a Shockwave 3D member is on the Stage, you can stretch it or shrink it like a bitmap member. However, while bitmaps will not look very nice when stretched, Shockwave 3D was built so it can be stretched without losing any quality. In fact, you should feel free to stretch the sprite to fit any size you want. This should not affect quality or performance.

Figure 38.5
The 3D Model pane of the Property Inspector allows you to change the camera position and lighting of a 3D member.

The six number fields at the top of the pane allow you to change the camera position and angle. This will have the same effect as moving the camera around in the Shockwave 3D window, but it is more precise.

Probably the most important setting for any 3D member is whether it is "Direct to Stage" or not. If it is "Direct to Stage" then no other sprites can be placed on top of the 3D member. The benefit is speed. A "Direct to Stage" 3D member will display much faster than one that is not. Unless you know your users will have very fast 3D computers, it is best to always have 3D members set to "Direct to Stage."

The "Play Animation" and "Loop" options only apply if the 3D member contains a 3D animation. The "Preload" option will make sure that the entire member has been loaded into memory before it is displayed on the screen.

The "Revert to World Defaults" button will come in handy when you begin to use behaviors or Lingo to change a 3D member on the fly. The 3D member will always start off with models in their default position when you first run a movie. However, when you are working in Director, changes to a 3D member may persist as you build the movie. It is often useful to hit this

"Revert to World Defaults" button to manually reset the member so it looks like it will when a user first runs the final movie.

The next part of the Shockwave 3D panel deals with the default directional light present in the 3D member. The little pop-up menu reads "Top Center" in Figure 38.5, but you can change it to one of nine positions. You can also select "None" to have no default directional light at all. Once you have selected the position of the directional light, you can set its color. The color will also determine

When I import a 3D file that was made in an external graphics program, the first thing I do is check the directional and ambient lights. Sometimes these are black or turned off and I need to turn them on to brighten the scene.

the intensity. For instance, to have a weak white light, choose a gray color instead of white. A directional light appears to originate from a point in the 3D world. That's why changing its position will affect how much light is on certain parts of your model.

There is also an ambient light present in every 3D member. You can select its color here as well. If you don't want any ambient light, just set it to black. The ambient light doesn't have a location, it just comes from everywhere and reflects off of all surfaces equally.

The "Background" color chip will determine what color is seen in the background of the 3D member. Black is the default and creates the illusion of empty space around the model. However, white can work just as well in many cases.

The final set of controls in the Shockwave 3D pane are the default shader controls. These come in to play if a model is imported that has no shader applied to its surface, or if Lingo is used to create new objects in the 3D member.

You can pick a bitmap cast member as the default texture, or use the red and white checkerboard default bitmap. You can also adjust how diffuse and specular light is reflected on the shader surface. These basically tint the shader to a certain color. The specular color defines what color is used to show highlights, while the diffuse color is used to tint the rest of the surface. The reflectivity setting determines how shiny the surface is.

The controls in the Shockwave 3D window and the Shockwave 3D Property Inspector panel are the sum total of what you can do to change the appearance of a 3D member without using behaviors or Lingo. The only benefit of Shockwave 3D so far is the ability to display 3D media on the Stage. Next, we'll look at how to use behaviors to manipulate 3D models.

USING 3D BEHAVIORS

Director 8.5 comes with a good set of behaviors that allow you to add interactivity to your 3D movies without needing to know Lingo. You can find these behaviors by choosing Window, Library Palette, and then selecting the "3D" behavior set.

There are two subsets under "3D." The first subset, "Actions," contains all of the behaviors that actually manipulate 3D members. Figure 38.6 shows the entire set. We'll look at the second set, "Triggers," later.

Figure 38.6
The Actions behaviors allow you
to control a 3D member.

Rotating a Model

The simplest behavior is the "Automatic Model Rotation" behavior. To use it, you'll first need a Shockwave 3D member. The sample movie "38autorotate.dir" has a simple model of a goldfish. You can use this example movie, or you can use one of the models that comes as a sample on the Director 8.5 CD.

After importing this model, drag and drop the cast member on to the Stage. Then, drag and drop the "Automatic Model Rotation" behavior from the Library Palette on to this sprite. This will copy the behavior in to your Director movie. It will also prompt you for some parameters with a dialog box seen in Figure 38.7.

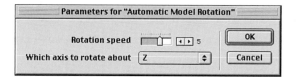

Figure 38.7
The Parameters dialog box for the
"Automatic Model Rotation"
behavior.

The first parameter, "Rotation Speed," determines how fast the model rotates. Leave it at the default of 5 for now. The second parameter, "Which axis to rotate about," should be set to "Z." You can try other values as well to make the fish rotate faster and along other axes.

Actually, the axis you use for a rotation depends on the camera settings. If you have a model where the default camera is set to look at the model from above, or if the camera is facing the other way, then you will need to use another axis of rotation to get the right effect. Default cameras can be set in the 3D graphics program used to create the model, so it is hard to tell what you are going to get. This is especially true if the model is from a third-party collection.

When you run the movie, the fish will rotate. This simple effect is extremely useful. For instance, if you want to make a product viewer, you could have a 3D model of a product and have it spin around. Or, you could have a graphic like a planet or logo element spinning. What used to take dozens or hundreds of pre-rendered bitmaps of a spinning product can now be done with a single model and a single behavior. This not only cuts down on development time, but also will shrink the file size to almost nothing.

Controlled Rotation

The next step is to give the user control over the rotation of the model. This can be done with the "Drag Model to Rotate" behavior.

Start again with a movie that just contains a single 3D member on the Stage. The completed example movie on the CD-ROM is "38controlledrotate.dir". I've used the same goldfish model again.

Drag and drop the "Drag Model to Rotate" behavior on to the sprite. You will be prompted with the Parameters dialog seen in Figure 38.8.

Figure 38.8
The "Drag Model to Rotate"
behavior parameters.

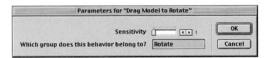

The first parameter, "Sensitivity," will determine how fast the model rotates as the user drags the mouse. The default setting of 1 is fast enough for most uses, so we'll leave it there. The second parameter, labeled "Which group does this behavior belong to?" allows you to organize several behaviors on a single sprite. We don't really need it here, but the default "Unassigned!" is pretty ugly, so change it to "Rotate."

If you run the movie now, you'd expect to be able to click and drag the sprite and see the goldfish rotate. However, nothing happens. This is because the 3D behaviors use an actions/triggers system. We've attached an action, but there is nothing to trigger it to happen. A trigger is an event like a mouse click, drag, or key press.

The trigger behaviors can be found in the second subset of 3D behaviors. Figure 38.9 shows the complete set of trigger behaviors.

Figure 38.9
The trigger behaviors allow you to
link a user action to a 3D behavior.

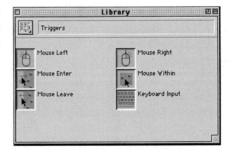

Drag and drop the "Mouse Left" behavior on to the sprite. You'll be presented with another behavior parameters dialog box. You can see it in Figure 38.10. We'll leave all of the parameters at the default settings.

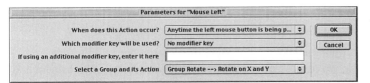

Figure 38.10
The "Mouse Left" trigger can be linked to most "actions" behaviors.

Trigger actions are pretty smart. They will look for 3D action behaviors already attached. If you use the pop-up labeled "Select Group and its Action," you will see that there is a whole list of possibilities set up by the "Drag Model to Rotate" behavior. You can allow the user to rotate around any single axis or pair of axes.

You can also set how the left mouse button is used to trigger the action. In this case, only "Anytime the left mouse button is being pressed" is the only choice that makes sense. The next option lets you add a modifier key. You would use this if you wanted the action to only occur if the user was holding down the Shift and/or Control key.

If you run the movie now, you can click and drag the model and it will rotate. Try playing with the parameters so that it rotates around different axes.

For a product demonstration movie, this example is even more useful than the previous one. Now you can have a product demonstration that the user can manipulate and move around to view from different angles.

Combining Rotation Behaviors

Suppose you wanted to give the user the ability to rotate the model in any direction. The "Drag Model to Rotate" behavior only lets you drag in one or two axes at a time. This makes sense since you can only move the mouse in two dimensions.

But you can use multiple applications of a trigger behavior on a single sprite to trigger different actions. The example movie "38combinedrotate.dir" is an example of this.

The behavior "Drag Model to Rotate" is applied first, just like in the previous example. Then, the "Mouse Left" action is applied. No modifier key is used, but the action selected is "Rotate on X axis." So clicking and dragging on the sprite will now allow the user to rotate around the x axis.

To apply the "Mouse Left" trigger a second time, drag and drop it on to the sprite again. Make sure you drag it from your Cast rather than from the Library Palette. If you drag it from the Library Palette, you will get a second copy of the behavior in your Cast.

In this application of the "Mouse Left" trigger, select the modifier "Shift Key" and the action "Rotate on Y axis." Add a third application of the "Mouse Left" trigger with the "Control Key" modifier and the "Rotate on Z axis" action.

When you run the movie now, you can click on the sprite and rotate it around the x axis, Shift+Click and rotate around the y axis and Control+Click to rotate around the z axis. You can even press and release the Shift and Control keys while dragging to change the axis of rotation.

Moving Models

Movement in 3D can mean one of two things. Usually, movement means camera movement. After all, the camera acts as your viewpoint, so moving the camera simulates what it would look like if you moved. So far, we have seen what happens when you rotate the camera and when you rotate a model. Next, we'll look at moving the camera and moving a model.

Since a 3D world can involve more than one model, moving a model is very different than moving the camera. The latter will appear to change everything, while moving a model will only change that one model.

In the example "38movemodel.dir," I've used the "Drag Model" behavior with the "Left Mouse" trigger. When you drop the "Drag Model" behavior onto a 3D sprite with only one model in it, it is assumed that you will want to drag that one model. However, if there is more than one model in the member, then you will be prompted as to which model you want to drag.

You can assign the same behavior multiple times to the same sprite so the user can drag several models. In the example, there are two fish and a ground plane. That's three models. You can see what they look like when the movie starts in Figure 38.11.

Figure 38.11
In this 3D member there are three
objects: two fish and a plane.

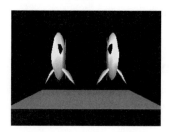

The "Drag Model" behavior is applied once with "Any Model" selected as the model to rotate. The "Mouse Left" trigger is applied once and linked to the "Drag Model" behavior.

When the user clicks and drags on the sprite, the behavior determines which, if any, model has been clicked on. That model then becomes draggable. Another option for the "Drag Model" behavior is to specify a specific model that is draggable. In that case, only that one model will react to the mouse.

You could also apply the "Drag Model to Rotate" behavior in the same way. You can make one of the models rotate when you drag it, and the other move. Or, you could make both models move when you left-mouse click and drag them, and have then rotate when you do the same but with the Shift key down.

Simple Camera Movement

So far, I have shown you how to move models. The camera has remained in one stationary spot. Leaving the models stationary and moving the camera around is a very common way to manipulate the view of a 3D world. There are several behaviors for doing this.

The first camera behavior is the "Dolly Camera" behavior. This will move the camera closer or farther from the center of the 3D world.

The example movie "38dollycamera.dir" uses this behavior. I started with the same 3D world used in the previous example, the one with the two fish and the plane. Then, I dropped the "Dolly Camera" behavior on to it. I used the default settings, but changed the group from "Unassigned!" to "Camera."

Next, I used the "Keyboard Input" trigger behavior. This presents a dialog box seen in Figure 38.12. You can assign an arrow key, or any alphanumeric key, to the trigger. You can also pick a modifier key like Shift or Control. Then, you can assign a group and action. In this case, you can use the action "Camera In" or "Camera Out."

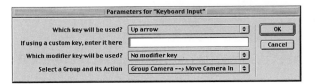

Figure 38.12
The "Keyboard Input" trigger allows you to link a key to an action.

In the example movie, I have applied the "Keyboard Input" trigger twice. The first time I mapped the "Up Arrow" to "Camera In" and the second time I mapped the "Down Arrow" to "Camera Out."

When you run this movie, you can use the up and down arrow keys to move the camera forward and backward. You could have also mapped other keys, like the "A" and "Z" keys to these two functions.

Complete Camera Movement

The previous example allowed you to move the camera in and out. This next example, "38movecamera.dir," will allow you to move the camera as well as rotate it.

First, start off with a movie just like in the previous example. The "Dolly Camera" behavior has been applied with the up and down arrow keys hooked up. Now, add the behavior "Pan Camera Horizontal." Then, add the "Keyboard Input" trigger to the sprite two more times. The first time, map the left arrow key to the "Pan Camera Left" action. The second time, map the right arrow key to the "Pan Camera Right" action.

Next, add the "Pan Camera Vertical" behavior to the sprite. Then, add the "Keyboard Input" trigger two more times. Since we have used all four arrow keys, map the "a" key to the "Pan Camera Up" action and the "z" key to the "Pan Camera Down" action.

You should now have a total of three action behaviors attached to the sprite and six "Keyboard Input" trigger behaviors. This makes a total of six keys that can be pressed to change the camera's position and angle.

When you run this movie, you can play with the arrow keys and the "a" and "z" keys to get any position and angle you want. Note that the up and down arrow keys are actually moving the camera, while the left and right arrow keys and the "a" and "z" key just rotate the camera.

Creating New Models with Behaviors

The behavior library that comes with Director 8.5 also has some unusual behaviors that don't serve much of a purpose, but are fun to play with. The "Create Box" behavior, when mixed with the "Mouse Left" trigger, will create a new 3D box wherever you click the sprite. Figure 38.13 shows a 3D sprite that has been clicked on a few times.

Figure 38.13
This 3D sprite has been clicked on many times to create little boxes with the "Create Box" behavior.

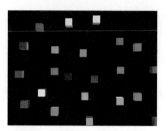

Take a look at the example movie "38createbox.dir." When I applied the "Create Box" behavior, I used all of the defaults, but I made it part of the group "Box." I then applied the "Mouse Left" trigger behavior, but with the "Only when the left mouse button is first pressed" option. This means that a click will create a box, but continuing to hold down the mouse button will do nothing.

Other options for the "Create Box" behavior allow you to specify the size of the box, or to make the boxes random sizes. The color can be random, or set to a specific color.

You can also use the "Create Sphere" behavior instead of "Create Box" to make random spheres instead of boxes.

Creating Particle Systems

Particle systems sound like something nuclear scientists should be dealing with. In fact, they are one of the most complex elements of 3D graphics. But the "Create Particle System" behavior makes them easy to use.

A particle system is a single model, but it does not look like a typical model. Instead, it is a collection of small shapes, usually single-pixel dots, that originate from a single point, line or area, move away, and fade out over a period of time.

Figure 38.14 is a snapshot of a simple particle system in progress. It is hard to capture the idea of a particle system in a still image because a particle system is always changing as new particles are born and old ones fade away.

Particle systems are important to 3D modeling because they can show some real-life objects that would not be easy to re-create otherwise. Typical examples of what particle systems can represent are: fireworks, smoke, running water, kicked-up dirt or dust, confetti, rain, and explosions.

Figure 38.14
This snapshot of a simple particle system shows the particles originating at a point in the center and fading away as they move away from the origination point.

By using the "Create Particle System" default settings with the "Mouse Left" trigger, you can create a sort of sparkler effect. If you run the example movie "38createpartsys.dir," you can click once to create a little explosion of particles at the mouse location. If you click and hold down the mouse, you can create a stream of particles that follow the cursor like sparks.

The "Create Particle System" can actually be used for a lot more than just this simple example. If you look at the parameters dialog for the behavior, shown in Figure 38.15, you'll see that there are many ways to customize the behavior.

Parameters for "Create Particle System"	
How many particles?	50
What is the lifetime a particle?	1.0000
What is the starting size of a particle?	1.0000
What is the final size of a particle?	1.0000
What is the angle of the emission?	180
What is maximum speed of a particle?	250.0000
What is minimum speed of a particle?	50.0000
What is distribution method?	Linear
Strength of GRAVITY along axis X?	0
Strength of GRAVITY along axis Y?	0
Strength of GRAVITY along axis Z?	0
Strength of WIND along axis X?	0
Strength of WIND along axis Y?	0
Strength of WIND along axis Z?	0
How should the colors be selected?	Randomly
What is the starting color of a particle?	rgb(255, 255, 255)
What is the final color of a particle?	rgb(255, 0, 0)
What is the starting BLEND of a particle?	100
What is the final BLEND of a particle?	10
Repeat the emissions?	☐
How will the emissions be released?	All at once
Which group does this behavior belong to?	Unassigned!

OK
Cancel

Figure 38.15
The "Create Particle System" behavior parameters dialog has many customizable settings.

The example movie "38createrunningwater.dir" uses the same behaviors as the previous example. However, the parameters are set differently.

To create the illusion of running water, I first set the number of particles to 2,000 and the "Repeat Emissions" to true. I also changed the "How will the emissions be released" setting to "Streaming." This will provide a constant stream of a lot of particles rather than a single burst.

Next, I kept the final size of the particles at 1, but changed the starting size to 5. So the particles will start as 5-by-5 boxes and get smaller as they move.

I changed the maximum speed of a particle to 50 and the minimum speed to 10. The larger these speeds, the faster the particles will move away from the origin.

> **Caution**
>
> If you try to set the "Wind" in the "Create Particle System" behavior, you will find it has no effect. This is because the critical *drag* property was left out of the behavior. You'll learn more about particle effects and the proper way to use wind in the next chapter.

Water falls. To make the water fall, I changed the y-axis gravity to -10. A value of 10 would make the particles fly upward, while this negative number pulls them down.

I also set the colors of the particles to start with a plain blue and change to a lighter blue over time. The starting blend I set to 100, and the final blend to 0. This will make the particles fade away.

When you run this movie, click once on the sprite to start a waterfall. The particles start off big and blue and spread outward from the origin. They are also falling downward. As they fall, they are changing color and fading away. Figure 38.16 shows this waterfall effect.

Figure 38.16
This simple waterfall was created with the "Create Particle System" behavior.

If you click on the sprite again, a second waterfall will start. You can create even more, but you'll quickly see that performance is affected. Particle systems take up a lot of processor power. You can alleviate this slowdown by reducing the number of particles used.

Playing 3D Animation

Some, but not all, 3D graphic programs will allow you to export 3D animations into Shockwave 3D files. You can then use behaviors to control the playback of these animations.

After you import an animated Shockwave 3D file, first test it out in the Shockwave 3D window. You can use the playback controls at the top of the window for this.

The example movie "38animation.dir" contains a simple animated scene that features a ball that bounces through some boxes. I've also attached the behavior "Play Animation" to it. Figure 38.17 shows the options for this behavior.

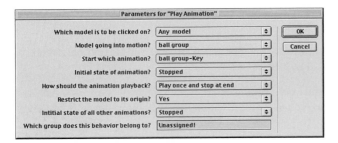

Figure 38.17
The "Play Animation" behavior allows you to select the model and motion to be played.

In Figure 38.17, you can see that the model is called "ball group" and the animation is called "ball group-Key." These names were assigned in the 3D graphics program. The behavior simply reads these names and uses them in the Parameters dialog box.

One change that we need to make in the behavior parameters is to change the "Restrict the model to its origin" property to "No." Otherwise, the model will not be allowed to move. It will only go through its motions, in this case spinning, while standing still.

Next, I dropped the "Mouse Left" trigger on to the sprite and set it to "Only when the left mouse button is first clicked." Now when you run the movie the sprite will start off stopped, with the ball in place, and then the animation will play when you click on the sprite.

The "Play Animation" behavior will also let you set the animation to loop. This comes in handy when the animation is something that is meant to loop. In fact, you can have a looping animation and still use other behaviors like the camera movement behaviors. The user can then navigate through an animated 3D world.

TROUBLESHOOTING USING 3D MEDIA

- Almost every 3D graphics program will export Shockwave 3D files in a slightly different way. Be prepared to spend some time getting used to how your 3D program does it.

- When exporting from 3DS Max, the camera view is completely dependent on which window is selected when you choose to export. Usually, you want the perspecive view window, not the front, back or side windows.

- Not all triggers work on all behaviors. If you cannot drag and drop a trigger onto a sprite, this is because the action behavior on the sprite does not support that trigger.

- When you create a model in a 3D graphics program, you may be creating it from several different shapes. You must tell the 3D program that you want these shapes grouped together into a single model or they will all appear as separate models when you get the file into Director.

- You can change the 3D software drivers that Director is using by choosing Modify, Movie, Properties. Test your movies out with each available driver to make sure it looks good and is fast enough. You never know what the end-user will have.

DID YOU KNOW?

- You can stretch the 3D sprite to any size you want without hurting performance. You don't need to stick to 320 by 240.

- You can still assign normal behaviors to a 3D sprite. For instance, if you have a small 3D sprite that shows a logo, you can assign an *on mouseUp* behavior to it so that it acts like a button.

- All behavior-based changes to a 3D member will be erased when you close and then open the movie again. You can force this change with the Reset World button in the Shockwave 3D window.

- If you are making a Shockwave movie that will stretch with the size of the browser window, the 3D sprites in your movie will stretch very nicely with the Stage size.

3D LINGO

Source movies for this chapter can be found on the CD-ROM in the "Book Movies" folder under folder 39.

Importing 3D models into Director and using the behavior library to move them around is nice, but the real power of the Director 3D engine is in the extensive addition of Lingo commands to Director 8.5

Hundreds of new commands, functions and properties allow you to control and even create 3D worlds. The power in these commands rivals the control in expensive 3D game engines.

MOVING 3D MODELS

The first aspect of 3D Lingo that we will examine is simply to move 3D models around in the 3D world. This will give you a basic understanding of how to manipulate 3D members.

Changing the Position of a Model

Let's start off simple by using the Message window to examine and then alter a 3D member. Load up the file "39movemodels.dir." You can see this movie in Figure 39.1.

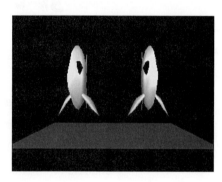

Figure 39.1
We will be playing with the properties of this simple example movie.

Leaving the Stage visible, open and position the Message window. Now try this:

```
put sprite(1).member.model.count
-- 3
```

Sprite 1 contains the member "goldfishpair" which is a 3D member. We could refer to this member by name, but instead, I referred to it as the member of sprite 1. The *put* statement gives us the *count* of the member property *model*. This *model* property gives us access to all of the models in the member. The output from this *put* statement shows us that there are three models in the member.

Next, let's get the names of these models. We can do this by treating the *model* property like a list. We can then get the *name* of each item in this list.

```
put sprite(1).member.model[1].name
-- "right goldfish"
put sprite(1).member.model[2].name
-- "left goldfish"
put sprite(1).member.model[3].name
-- "plane"
```

Where did these names come from? They were assigned when the 3D world was created. In this case, I used 3DS Max to create the world. While building the world, I took the time to name the three objects "right goldfish", "left goldfish", and "plane".

Next, let's find out something about one of these models. We can get the location of a model by looking at the *position* property of the *transform* property.

```
put sprite(1).member.model[1].transform.position
-- vector( 70.8987, 118.1114, 30.6382 )
```

The *transform* of a model is a long, complex list of numbers that contains information about a model's location, scaling and orientation. To access just the location information, the *position* property is used.

The result of *transform.position* is a *vector*. A vector is a three-part list of numbers that gives the location of an object in 3D space. The numbers represent the horizontal position, vertical position and depth. You can get the components of a vector by using the *x*, *y*, and *z* properties.

```
myModelPos =
sprite(1).member.model[1].transform.position
put myModelPos.x
-- 70.8987
put myModelPos.y
-- 118.1114
put myModelPos.z
-- 30.6382
```

To change the position of a model, you can use the same properties. For instance, to move the right fish slightly to the right, try this:

```
sprite(1).member.model[1].transform.position.x =
100
updateStage
```

The *updateStage* is necessary only because the movie is not running. It forces an update of the Stage, as well as any 3D sprites on it.

You can also refer to the model by name. Use parentheses instead of brackets, and then the model name.

```
sprite(1).member.model("right goldfish").transform.position.x = 100
updateStage
```

If you look at the *transform* property of a model or other object, you will get a list of 16 numbers. This corresponds to a 4-by-4 matrix that describes the location, orientation, and scale of the object. However, you will need to use sub-properties like *position* to effectively alter the *transform* of an object.

Caution

Remember that positions in a 3D member depend completely on the orientation of the camera. If you try these commands with a different 3D world, you might get different specific results if the camera is not the same as in the example. However, the basic principles of position and orientation are the same.

Instead of using *updateStage*, I find that I can update the screen by simply clicking on the 3D sprite. However, I'm not positive that this will work with all computer hardware and software configurations. Give it a try.

To get the fish back to its original location, you can use the *resetWorld* command. For some reason, this does not need an *updateStage* to be called after it.

```
sprite(1).member.resetWorld()
```

The *resetWorld* command comes in handy because a 3D member will remember any changes that you force upon it until you quit Director or reload the movie. If it is important to start off fresh each time your play the movie, then you will want to use the *resetWorld* command at the start of your movie.

That's right, a vector can sometimes contain positional units, and sometimes contain angular units. So if you are used to the physics definition of a vector as speed and direction, remember that sometimes it is used by Director as just a collection of three numbers.

Changing the Orientation of a Model

You can also examine and change the orientation of a model in the Message window. The *transform* property is used again, but this time the *rotation* sub-property is what we want.

```
put sprite(1).member.model("right goldfish").transform.rotation
-- vector( 0.0000, 0.0000, 0.0000 )
```

As you can see, a vector is returned. Each of the three parts of the vector represents an angle, in degrees.

To change the orientation of a model, you can set the entire vector. For instance, to turn the fish completely on its side, try this:

```
sprite(1).member.model("right goldfish").transform.rotation = vector(0,0,-90)
updateStage
```

Moving a Model

So far we have seen how we can set the position and orientation of a model, but how about movement?

What's the difference between setting the position of a model and moving it? Moving a model means that you are taking the current position and orientation of a model and moving it from that spot by a certain distance. So the starting point is important and so is its orientation.

To move a model, we use the *translate* command. This takes a vector and will move the model from its current spot by the distance of the vector. The following lines will move one of the fish closer by 10 units. Remember to use *resetWorld* first if you have just completed the code in the previous section.

```
sprite(1).member.model("right goldfish").translate(0,-10,0)
updateStage
```

Now, try the same two lines of code again. The model will move closer by another 10 units. You can keep issuing these same commands and the model will continue to move closer.

The *translate* command is not just using the current location of the model, but it is also using the orientation of the model. Try rotating the model and then moving it.

```
sprite(1).member.model("right goldfish").transform.rotation = vector(0,0,-90)
updateStage
sprite(1).member.model("right goldfish").translate(0,-10,0)
updateStage
```

The model is first rotated to the left, and then moved. The result is that the model moves to the left. This is the same exact *translate* command that moved the model toward you before. So the translate command is not just moving the model relative to the rest of the world, it is moving the model relative to the orientation of the model.

This is the way to get models to move at a constant rate and a consistent direction. First, you orient the model in the directoion you want it to go, then you use *translate* to move the model in that direction.

Rotating a Model

While the *translate* command will move a model relative to its current location, the *rotate* command will rotate it relative to its orientation.

To rotate one of the models in the example movie, try these lines in the Message window. They will rotate one of the fish by 5 degrees.

```
sprite(1).member.model("right goldfish").rotate(0,0,-5)
updateStage
```

You can keep issuing these lines to make the fish rotate even more. Here is a simple behavior that will rotate the model at a constant rate:

```
on beginSprite me
  sprite(me.spriteNum).member.resetWorld()
end

on exitFrame me
  sprite(me.spriteNum).member.model("right goldfish").rotate(0,0,-5)
end
```

You can find this simple behavior in the movie "39constantrotate.dir". You can make the fish rotate in the other direction by changing the -5 to 5.

Making the Fish Swim

So to make the fish swim, all you would need to do is write behavior that moves the fish a little bit every frame. This would be just like the rotation behavior above, except using the *translate* command instead of the *rotate* command.

However, this would create a problem. The fish would swim right off of the screen! That's not much fun. Fish usually swim around in circles, so let's try to make our fish behave that way.

To make a fish swim in a circle, all we need to do is both rotate the fish and move the fish a little each frame. Here is a script that does just that.

```
on beginSprite me
  sprite(me.spriteNum).member.resetWorld()
end

on exitFrame me
  sprite(me.spriteNum).member.model("right goldfish").rotate(0,0,-5)
  sprite(me.spriteNum).member.model("right goldfish").translate(0,-10,0)
end
```

Now the goldfish on the right swims in circles around the goldfish on the left. Changing the numbers in this script will make the goldfish swim in a wider or smaller circle. Check the movie "39fishorbit.dir" to see it in action.

MOVING THE CAMERA

Most of the time that a 3D world is used, the camera represents the viewpoint of the user. It is the user's eye into the world.

Moving the camera, then, is like moving the user. While objects like goldfish tend to move around themselves, most objects in 3D worlds are stationary. It is the users' perspective that changes as they walk or fly through the world.

Camera Position

To get the position and orientation of the camera, use the *position* and *rotation* properties just like you would if the camera was a model.

```
put sprite(1).member.camera[1].transform.position
-- vector( 0.0000, -400.0000, 0.0000 )
put sprite(1).member.camera[1].transform.rotation
-- vector( 90.0000, 0.0000, 0.0000 )
```

You can also address the camera by its name. In this case, the name of the camera was assigned when it was created in the 3D modeling program.

```
put sprite(1).member.camera[1].name
-- "DefaultView"
put sprite(1).member.camera("DefaultView").transform.position
-- vector( 0.0000, -400.0000, 0.0000 )
```

Another way to refer to a camera is directly through the sprite reference. A 3D member can have one or many cameras. The camera that is currently being used to view the 3D world can be accessed with the *camera* property of the sprite.

```
put sprite(1).camera.transform.position
-- vector( 0.0000, -400.0000, 0.0000 )
```

To move the camera, we could assign a new *position* or *rotation* to it. However, a better way is to use the *translate* command to move the camera a certain distance from its current location. This is the same process that we used to move models. These commands will move the camera closer to the goldfish.

```
sprite(1).camera.translate(0,0,-1)
updateStage
```

Using different *translate* commands, we can assign a direction to each of the four arrow keys. Here is a simple behavior that will allow the user to move the camera in four directions. You can test it out yourself in the example movie "39repositioncamera.dir".

```
on beginSprite me
  sprite(me.spriteNum).member.resetWorld()
end


on exitFrame me
  if keyPressed(123) then -- left arrow
    sprite(me.spriteNum).camera.translate(-1,0,0)
  else if keyPressed(124) then -- right arrow
    sprite(me.spriteNum).camera.translate(1,0,0)
  else if keyPressed(125) then -- down arrow
    sprite(me.spriteNum).camera.translate(0,0,1)
  else if keyPressed(126) then -- up arrow
    sprite(me.spriteNum).camera.translate(0,0,-1)
  end if
end
```

If you try this example movie, you will see that it works to reposition the camera just fine, but the movement is not natural. That is because the camera is always oriented in the same exact direction. A better way to move the camera would be to allow the user to spin the camera around left and right, and move forward and backward. This will better simulate how we walk.

Natural Camera Movement

To get the camera to change orientation, you can use the *rotation* property. In the goldfish example we have been using, the camera starts off at 90,0,0. This was set when the models were made in a 3D modeling program. We can change the *rotation* of the camera to point in another direction.

```
put sprite(1).member.camera[1].transform.rotation
-- vector( 90.0000, 0.0000, 0.0000 )
sprite(1).camera.transform.rotation = vector(90,0,5)
updateStage
```

The result is that the camera turns slightly to the left. You could use a -5 to turn the camera slightly to the right.

Instead of setting the *rotation* of the camera, we can use the *rotate* command to turn the camera relative to the current orientation.

```
sprite(1).camera.rotate(0,5,0)
updateStage
```

I know it seems a little odd that at first we changed 90,0,0 to 90,0,5 to make the camera re-orient itself, and then used 0,5,0 with the *rotate* command to achieve the same effect. The result is that the camera is oriented to 90,0,5 either way. It is always good to experiment with the *rotate* command in the Message window as its effect depends on how your 3D world was originally built.

Here is a behavior that will allow the user to rotate the camera with the left and right arrow keys, and move the camera forward and back with the up and down arrow keys. See the example movie "39movecamera.dir" to see it in action.

```
on beginSprite me
  sprite(me.spriteNum).member.resetWorld()
end


on exitFrame me
  if keyPressed(123) then -- left arrow
    sprite(me.spriteNum).camera.rotate(0,1,0)
  else if keyPressed(124) then -- right arrow
    sprite(me.spriteNum).camera.rotate(0,-1,0)
  else if keyPressed(125) then -- down arrow
    sprite(me.spriteNum).camera.translate(0,0,5)
  else if keyPressed(126) then -- up arrow
    sprite(me.spriteNum).camera.translate(0,0,-5)
  end if
end
```

Complete Camera Movement

There are actually twelve ways in which a camera can be moved. It can be moved up, down, left, right, forward and backward. It can also be rotated in any one of these directions.

Most 3D applications will restrict the camera movement. For instance, if the user is supposed to be walking through a 3D world, then the movement will be restricted so that they can't fly up off the ground or go down into the ground.

However, it is useful to have a behavior that allows all 12 movements. Here is such a behavior. It uses the arrow keys and the "a" and "z" keys to get movement in all directions. Then, if the Shift key is held, you get rotation in all directions with the same keys.

```
on beginSprite me
  sprite(me.spriteNum).member.resetWorld()
end

on exitFrame me
  if the shiftDown then
    -- rotation
    if keyPressed(123) then -- left arrow
      sprite(me.spriteNum).camera.rotate(0,1,0)
    else if keyPressed(124) then -- right arrow
      sprite(me.spriteNum).camera.rotate(0,-1,0)
    else if keyPressed(125) then -- down arrow
      sprite(me.spriteNum).camera.rotate(-1,0,0)
    else if keyPressed(126) then -- up arrow
      sprite(me.spriteNum).camera.rotate(1,0,0)
    else if keyPressed("a") then -- A
      sprite(me.spriteNum).camera.rotate(0,0,-1)
    else if keyPressed("z") then -- Z
      sprite(me.spriteNum).camera.rotate(0,0,1)
    end if

  else
    -- movement
    if keyPressed(123) then -- left arrow
      sprite(me.spriteNum).camera.translate(-5,0,0)
    else if keyPressed(124) then -- right arrow
      sprite(me.spriteNum).camera.translate(5,0,0)
    else if keyPressed(125) then -- down arrow
      sprite(me.spriteNum).camera.translate(0,0,5)
    else if keyPressed(126) then -- up arrow
      sprite(me.spriteNum).camera.translate(0,0,-5)
    else if keyPressed("a") then -- A
      sprite(me.spriteNum).camera.translate(0,5,0)
    else if keyPressed("z") then -- Z
      sprite(me.spriteNum).camera.translate(0,-5,0)
    end if
  end if
end
```

Take a look at the example movie "39movecameraall.dir" to see this behavior in action.

Constant Camera Movement

Moving the camera around as a reaction to a key press makes sense if the user is supposed to be standing or walking. But what if the user is driving a car or flying a plane? In that case, the forward movement doesn't stop immediately when the user lifts up the key on the keyboard.

To get this type of movement, we need to remember the speed and direction in which that camera is moving, and then allow the user to accelerate or decelerate (brake) to change that speed. The movement continues each frame even if the user is not issuing a new command.

The example movie "39smoothmove.dir" contains a behavior that will do just this. It stores the current speed of the camera movement in the property "pSpeed". If the user hits the left or right arrow keys, the orientation of the camera turns just like in the last few examples. However, pressing the up or down arrow keys simply changes "pSpeed". Then, as each frame passes, the camera is moved by "pSpeed".

```
property pSpeed

on beginSprite me
  sprite(me.spriteNum).member.resetWorld()

  -- user starts standing still
  pSpeed = 0.0
end

on exitFrame me
  if keyPressed(123) then -- left arrow
    sprite(me.spriteNum).camera.rotate(0,1,0)
  else if keyPressed(124) then -- right arrow
    sprite(me.spriteNum).camera.rotate(0,-1,0)
  end if

  if keyPressed(125) then -- down arrow
    pSpeed = pSpeed + .1 -- speed up
  else if keyPressed(126) then -- up arrow
    pSpeed = pSpeed - .1 -- slow down
  end if

  -- move every frame according to speed
  sprite(me.spriteNum).camera.translate(0,0,pSpeed)
end
```

One simple improvement to this behavior is to add the following lines to the middle of the *on exitFrame* handler. They will check to see if the speed is positive or negative, and decrease or increase the speed slightly so that it tends toward being 0. This will act like friction to slow the camera down when the user is not pressing the up or down arrow key.

```
-- move the speed closer to 0 to simulate friction
  if pSpeed >= 0.1 then
    pSpeed = pSpeed - .01
```

```
else if pSpeed <= -0.1 then
  pSpeed = pSpeed + .01
else
  pSpeed = 0 -- close to 0, so stop completely
end if
```

Take a look at the example movie, "39smoothmove.dir". If you press the up arrow for a few seconds, you will see the speed increase. When you release, the speed will slowly decrease until you stop.

Following an Object

So far we have treated the camera like the eye of the user. It is the portal through which the user sees the 3D world. However, in many 3D applications, the user sees the world from just behind the object that represents the user. For instance, in a racing game, the camera might be just behind and above the player's car. In a first-person shooter, the player's character might be right in front of the camera, so that the player sees the back of his or her head.

To get this type of view, you must lock the camera to the player's character. This means that as the character moves, so does the camera. It stays right in synch with the character, always the same distance from it and always the same viewpoint relative to the character.

In the example movie "39followobject.dir" there are three fish. The left and right fish are still there, but there is also a fish right in front of the camera, facing the same direction as the camera. The camera is right on top of this fish so you are looking right over it. Figure 39.2 shows this view.

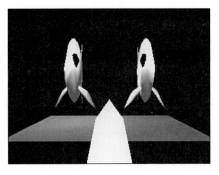

Figure 39.2
The camera is poised right above a fish that is facing two other fish.

Locking the camera so it stays in the same position relative to the new fish is easy. The *addChild* command will make the camera a child of the fish.

Parents and children are terms used to describe grouping in 3D members. When we say that a model is a child of another model, we mean that the models are locked to each other. Any change in the parent, like movement or rotation, will also happen for the child. The two models are locked together as if they were one larger model. Note that any movement of the child will not affect the parent.

Suppose model B is a child of parent A. When model A moves, model B moves with it. When model B moves, model A is not affected. We'll look at more examples of grouping in the section called "Grouping" later in this chapter.

The new fish model is called "character goldfish" since it is the representation of the player's character in the environment. The behavior starts just like the previous example, except for the *addChild* command.

```
property pSpeed

on beginSprite me
  sprite(me.spriteNum).member.resetWorld()

  -- lock camera to fish
  sprite(1).member.model("character goldfish").addChild(sprite(1).member.cam-
era[1])

  -- user starts standing still
  pSpeed = 0.0
end
```

The rest of the behavior also looks like the previous example. However, instead of the camera moving, the fish is moved. The camera is never even referred to. It doesn't have to be. It is locked to the fish, so as the fish moves, so does the camera.

```
on exitFrame me
  if keyPressed(123) then -- left arrow
    sprite(me.spriteNum).member.model("character goldfish").rotate(0,0,1)
  else if keyPressed(124) then -- right arrow
    sprite(me.spriteNum).member.model("character goldfish").rotate(0,0,-1)
  end if

  if keyPressed(125) then -- down arrow
    pSpeed = pSpeed + .1 -- speed up
  else if keyPressed(126) then -- up arrow
    pSpeed = pSpeed - .1 -- slow down
  end if

  -- move the speed closer to 0 to simulate friction
  if pSpeed >= 0.1 then
    pSpeed = pSpeed - .02
  else if pSpeed <= -0.1 then
    pSpeed = pSpeed + .02
  else
    pSpeed = 0 -- close to 0, so stop completely
  end if
```

```
-- move every frame according to speed
sprite(me.spriteNum).member.model("character goldfish").translate(0,pSpeed,0)
end
```

Switching Cameras

You don't have to settle for just one camera view. You can create several cameras and allow the user to switch back and forth between them.

To create a new camera, use the *newCamera* command.

```
sprite(1).member.newCamera("my other camera")
```

Notice that this new camera is created as a property of the member. You can use the *camera* property as a property of the member or a property of the sprite. When used as a property of the sprite, it refers to the actual camera being used. When used as a property of a member, you need to include the number of the camera in brackets or the name of the camera in quotes, even if there is only one camera.

In order to set the view to a certain camera, just set the sprite's *camera* property to a member *camera* property.

```
sprite(1).camera = sprite(1).member.camera("my other camera")
```

This way, you can have the user switch between cameras. For instance, they can press one key to get the cockpit view, another key to get a behind-the-car view and another key to get an overhead view of the race track.

PLAYING WITH LIGHTS

Lights are a critical part of a 3D world. Without any lights, there would be nothing to see. The brightness and color of surfaces depends on having lights in the 3D world to reflect off of the surfaces.

We can deal with lights in Lingo in the same way that we deal with models. They have a position and orientation. They also have a few properties that are unique to lights.

Examining Lights in the Message Window

First, let's examine lights by using the Message window. Open the file "39basiclights.dir". In this simple 3D world, there is a single goldfish. Let's find out how many lights are present.

```
put sprite(1).member.light.count
-- 2
```

Now, let's find out what these lights are named.

```
put sprite(1).member.light[1].name
-- "UIAmbient"
put sprite(1).member.light[2].name
-- "Default MAX Light"
```

Both of these lights come from the 3D program that created the model. The default names were left there, although they could have been changed in the 3D program to something more relevant.

Lights have a color and intensity. Both of these properties are represented by their *color*. For instance, the *color* "FFFFFF" would be a pure white, while "999999" would be a medium gray. "000000" would be black, or the complete absence of any intensity. If you wanted a bright red light, you could use "FF0000", while "990000" would be a darker red light.

Let's find out the colors of the two lights in the model.

```
put sprite(1).member.light("UIAmbient").color
-- rgb( 0, 0, 0 )
put sprite(1).member.light("Default MAX Light").color
-- rgb( 191, 191, 191 )
```

The color of the first light is set to 0,0,0 or "000000" which is black. This means that the light is turned off. The second light is 191,191,191 with is "CCCCCC" or a light gray. Figure 39.3 shows the effect of these lights on the model in the example movie. The fish is lit only by the "Default MAX Light" since the ambient light is black.

Figure 39.3
The goldfish model is lit from a single light gray light.

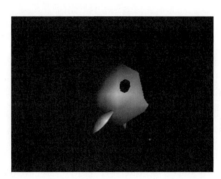

The color of a light doesn't tell the full story. The *type* of light determines where the light originates and how it shines.

```
put sprite(1).member.light("UIAmbient").type
-- #ambient
put sprite(1).member.light("Default MAX Light").type
-- #point
```

The first light is an #ambient light. This means that the position of the light is irrelevant. The light shines as it if it is coming from all directions at an even brightness. This is usually used to simulate outdoor lighting, strong lighting like the sunlight coming in from a window, or when you just want to ignore lighting and have all surfaces equally visible.

The #point type of light is similar to a light bulb. It comes from a point in space and shines in all directions from that point.

There are also #directional and #spot lights. Directional lights are at a point in space, like #point lights, but they only shine in one direction. Therefore, the orientation (*rotation* property) of the light is important. Spot lights are the same as directional lights, but the light fades as it gets further from the source.

To see how these lights work, let's play with them a bit more in the Message window. First, let's turn off the directional light and create a medium gray ambient light.

```
sprite(1).member.light("Default MAX Light").color = rgb("000000")
updateStage
sprite(1).member.light("UIAmbient").color = rgb("999999")
updateStage
```

In Figure 39.3, the light was of type #point, so it affects different surfaces in different ways, depending on the angle of the surface in relation to the location of the light. In Figure 39.4, however, you can see that the ambient light affects the surfaces evenly.

Figure 39.4
A single ambient light illuminates the goldfish.

As one last experiment in the Message window, let's change the color of the default light to red. This will show how the color of the light can change the color of the surface.

```
sprite(1).member.light("UIAmbient").color =
rgb("000000")
updateStage
sprite(1).member.light("Default MAX Light").color
= rgb("FF0000")
updateStage
```

The color "FF0000" is a bright red and will change the yellow surface of the goldfish almost completely to red. You could use a more subtle red light with a color like "FFCCCC".

> Director's 3D engine doesn't do shadows. Most 3D engines don't. Shadows are very time-consuming for a render-in-real-time engine to show. This means that light will affect objects regardless of what other objects are between it and the light. Many 3D games don't use shadows either, but instead create dark fuzzy-shaped models that follow characters around acting as their shadows.

Moving Lights

Let's continue to play with the same model. Using the Message window, we can find out where the light is located. The *worldPosition* property will tell us this.

```
put sprite(1).member.light("Default MAX Light").worldPosition
-- vector( 0.0000, -400.0000, 0.0000 )
```

So the light is 400 units away from the center of the world. This happens to be exactly where the default camera is located, which is a good location for a default light.

Here is a simple behavior that will start the light out further to the left of the camera, and then gradually move it to the right. This will show how the surfaces appear to change as the light moves. The example movie "39movinglight.dir" will let you try this out.

```
property pLightLoc

on beginSprite me
  sprite(me.spriteNum).member.resetWorld()

  -- set the starting position of the light
  pLightLoc = vector(-1000,-400,0)

  -- set the light the first time
  moveLight(me)
end

on moveLight me
  -- move the light to the right
  pLightLoc = pLightLoc + vector(10,0,0)

  -- set the positon of the light
  sprite(me.spriteNum).member.light("Default MAX Light").worldPosition =
pLightLoc
end

on exitFrame me
  -- move the light a little each frame
  moveLight(me)
end
```

Rotating Light

We can use the *rotate* command to rotate a light just as we used it to rotate a model. First, we'll want to change the light from a #point light to a #directional one. Otherwise, the orientation of the light doesn't matter.

The example movie "39rotatinglight.dir" contains a simple behavior that rotates the light. Try it as-is first, and then try it after changing the code so it presents a #spot light rather than a #directional one.

```
on beginSprite me
  sprite(me.spriteNum).member.resetWorld()

  -- change the light to a directional light
  sprite(me.spriteNum).member.light("Default MAX Light").type = #directional
end

on exitFrame me
  -- rotate the light
  sprite(me.spriteNum).member.light("Default MAX Light").rotate(0,1,0)
end
```

SHADERS AND TEXTURES

You can use Lingo to change the appearance of a surface in a 3D world. You do this by creating or changing *shaders*. A shader is what defines what a surface looks like. It can be a simple definition, like a color, or a complex one like a bitmap image.

Figure 39.5 shows a 3D world created in a 3D graphics program. The walls use a bitmap texture and there is a bitmap displayed on the television set and as a window. The floor has a repeating bitmap as well. The chair and table, however, have a simple color as a shader.

Figure 39.5
This simple 3D room contains many different shaders.

Using the Message window, we can find out about the shaders in this room. First, let's get a list of the models in the room. If you want to try this yourself, you can use the example movie "39shaderroom.dir".

```
put sprite(1).member.model.count
-- 6
put sprite(1).member.model[1].name
-- "Room"
put sprite(1).member.model[2].name
-- "TV"
put sprite(1).member.model[3].name
-- "Table"
put sprite(1).member.model[4].name
-- "Chair"
```

```
put sprite(1).member.model[5].name
-- "Lamp"
put sprite(1).member.model[6].name
-- "Remote Control"
```

The names of the six models in this 3D member were assigned when they were created in the 3D graphic program. Using good names like these makes it easy for us to identify the models in the member.

Each model contains a list of shaders. We can see this list by using the *shaderList* property of the model.

```
put sprite(1).member.model("Room").shaderList
-- [shader("ceiling"), shader("floors"), shader("picture map"),
shader("walls")]
```

There are four shaders used by this model. The ceiling and floor have their own shaders, while the walls all share a common shader. There is also a "picture map" shader that represents the image in the window.

Let's look at the shaders used by the chair. This shader is actually used by both the chair and the table. The shader name tips us off of that fact.

```
put sprite(1).member.model("Chair").shaderList
-- [shader("chair and table texture")]
```

This shader is just a solid color. You can change the color of a shader like this by altering several properties. The *ambient*, *diffuse* and *specular* properties determine how light is reflected off of the surface. For instance, if we examine the *ambient* property of the shader, we can see that it is a light brown.

```
put sprite(1).member.shader("chair and table texture").ambient
-- rgb( 112, 99, 74 )
```

To change this to a red, just set the *ambient* property of the shader. To make sure that the change happens no matter what types of lights are present, let's change all of the color properties.

```
sprite(1).member.shader("chair and table texture").ambient = rgb("FF0000")
sprite(1).member.shader("chair and table texture").diffuse = rgb("FF0000")
sprite(1).member.shader("chair and table texture").specular = rgb("FF0000")
updateStage
```

Now the chair and table should be red. Changing the color of a solid shader is easy. However, it gets a little more complex when you want to change a shader that uses a bitmap image.

First, let's look at the shaders used by the television model.

```
put sprite(1).member.model("TV").shaderList
-- [shader("tv outside texture"), shader("tv picture texture")]
```

Next, let's look at the *texture* property of "tv picture texture" shader. The *texture* defines which bitmap image is used in the shader.

```
put sprite(1).member.shader("tv picture texture").texture
-- texture("tv earth")
```

The image "tv earth" is embedded inside the 3D member. It was added to the shader while the models were created in the 3D graphic program.

To change this image, we need to create a new texture and add it to the member. The *newTexture* command let's you do this.

```
myTexture = sprite(1).member.newTexture("My Texture", #fromCastMember,
member("Natasha"))
```

The *newTexture* command can either take a bitmap member, like above, or a Lingo image object. All you need to do is swap out the #fromCastMember symbol with a #fromImageObject symbol.

The 3D member now has a "My Texture" texture stored in it. You can force the "tv picture texture" to use your new texture by changing its *texture* property.

```
sprite(1).member.shader("tv picture texture").texture = myTexture
```

After using an *updateStage* to force the screen to redraw, you should see the picture on the television change to show the picture of Natasha. Figure 39.6 is what the screen should look like now.

Figure 39.6
The picture of the Earth has been replaced by a picture of my dog.

Another way that we could have replaced the image on the television would be to create a completely new shader. This is done with a series of steps.

First, you want to use the *newShader* command to create a new shader object in the member. Next, you want to create a new texture to be placed in the shader. Then, you want to assign the texture to the shader. Finally, you would replace the existing shader in the model's *shaderList* with your new shader. Here is the complete process:

```
myShader = sprite(1).member.newShader("My Shader", #standard)
myTexture = sprite(1).member.newTexture("My Texture", #fromCastMember, mem-
ber("Natasha"))
myShader.texture = myTexture
sprite(1).member.model("TV").shaderList[2] = myShader
```

The technique of completely replacing the shader is what you would normally use, since it allows you to start off with a fresh shader. By just changing the *texture* property of an existing shader, you could have problems if the shader has other custom settings for lights, blend, and so on.

CREATING PRIMITIVES

So far we have been using Lingo to modify models in a 3D world created by an external 3D program. You can also use Lingo to start with a completely blank 3D world and create objects in it.

These simple objects are called primitives. There are four types of primitives: the box, the sphere, the cylinder, and the plane. Figure 39.7 shows them all.

Figure 39.7
These are all four basic primitives.

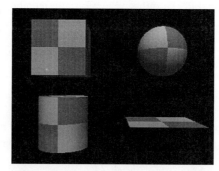

Starting From Scratch

Let's start by creating a completely blank 3D cast member. This is not as easy as it sounds. If you choose Insert, Media Element, Shockwave 3D, a new 3D member is created. However, it will disappear as soon as you close the Shockwave 3D window.

The way to keep a blank member around is to name it. So choose Insert, Media Element, Shockwave 3D. Then name the member in the Shockwave 3D window. When you close the window, the 3D member will remain in the Cast.

You could also use Lingo in the Message window to create a new 3D member. The *new* command works with the #Shockwave3D symbol to do this. However, you'll have to name the member right away or risk losing it again.

```
my3Dmember = new(#Shockwave3D)
my3Dmember.name = "My 3D Member"
```

Either way you create a 3D member, you'll want to drag it on to the Stage next. If you drag it right into the Score, then the member will be centered on the Stage. Or, you could drag it on to the Stage and position it as you like.

Creating a Box

To create a primitive, you need to do two things. First, you need to create a model resource. This is like a template for creating models. Then, you need to use the model resource to create the actual model.

The *newModelResource* command creates one of these templates. You just need to tell it what you want to name the template and what type of primitive it will represent. Here is a line of code that will create a box model resource.

```
myModelResource = sprite(1).member.newModelResource("My Box Resource",#box)
```

The model resource can be referred to by its name, or it can be referenced with the variable "myModelResource" that we used in the previous line. Using variable references can greatly reduce the length of your Lingo statements.

To create a model from this resource, use the *newModel* command. The new model will appear in the center of the 3D world.

```
myModel = sprite(1).member.newModel("My Box",myModelResource)
```

Since you are looking straight-on at the box, you can't see any of the sides or the back. Figure 39.8 shows the one face you can see.

Figure 39.8
A single box primitive placed in the middle of the 3D world.

You can now reposition the box and re-orient it. For instance, to spin the box around 45 degrees and tilt it 45 degrees, try this in the Message window:

```
sprite(1).member.model("My
Box").rotate(45,45,0)
```

When you create primitives with Lingo, these primitive models only exist until the member is reset. If you quit Director and return to the movie later, they will be gone.

All primitives have unique properties. Boxes, for instance, have the *height, length* and *width* properties. These are not properties of the individual models, but properties of the model resource.

By default, a box is 50 units high by 50 units wide by 50 units long. But you could make a box that has different dimensions. For instance, if you wanted to make a box that is 10 high by 20 wide by 100 long, you could do this:

```
sprite(me.spriteNum).member.resetWorld()

-- create the model resource
myModelResource = sprite(me.spriteNum).member.newModelResource("My Box
Resource",#box)
myModelResource.height = 10
myModelResource.width = 20
myModelResource.length = 100

-- create the model
myModel = sprite(me.spriteNum).member.newModel("My Box",myModelResource)

-- rotate to see it better
sprite(me.spriteNum).member.model("My Box").rotate(45,45,0)
```

The example movie "39createbox.dir" contains this code if you want to play with the numbers more. Figure 38.9 shows this odd-sized box.

Figure 39.9
This odd-sized box was created by setting the properties of the box resource.

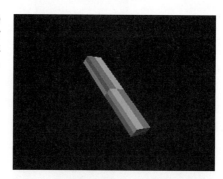

Besides the *height, width* and *length*, there are a few other properties of box resources. Here is a complete list:

- **height**, **width**, **length**: This affects the dimensions of the box. The default for each is 50.

- **top**, **bottom**, **front**, **back**, **left**, **right**: These *true* or *false* values determine if a face of the box is present or not. The default for all is *true*.

- **lengthVertices**, **widthVertices**, **heightVertices**: This refers to the number of polygons used to draw each side of the box. The default is 4. Increasing this number will result in more detailed light reflection.

Note that you can change the properties of a box resource after you have created a model from it. The model will then change to reflect this change. So you could create a model resource, create 100 models from that resource, then change the model resource. The result would be that all 100 models would change.

Creating a Sphere

Spheres can be created in the same way as boxes. The only difference is that you need to use a #sphere symbol rather than a #box symbol.

```
myModelResource = sprite(1).member.newModelResource("My Sphere
Resource",#sphere)
myModel = sprite(1).member.newModel("My Sphere",myModelResource)
```

The default sphere looks like the one in Figure 39.10. Spheres don't use the *width*, *height* and *length* properties that boxes do. Instead, they use the *radius* property. The default *radius* is 25.

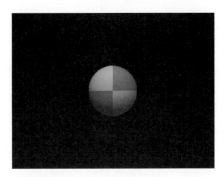

Figure 39.10
The default sphere is 25 units in radius.

In addition to the *radius* property, there are also *startAngle* and *endAngle* properties. Normally, these are set to 0 and 360 respectively. This will create a complete sphere. However, you could set them to other amounts to make an incomplete sphere. Figure 39.11 shows such a sphere.

Figure 39.11
This sphere has a *startAngle* of 0, but an *endAngle* of 330. So 30 degrees have been cut out of this sphere.

You can see the behavior that created this sphere in the example movie "39createsphere.dir". Here is a complete list of sphere resource properties:

- **radius**: The size of the sphere. The default is 25.

- **resolution**: The number of polygons used to make the sphere. The default is 20.

- **startAngle, endAngle**: Where the sweep of the sphere starts and ends.

Another thing you can see in Figure 39.11 is that the inside of the sphere is dark. In fact, it is transparent, showing the background color. This is because the surface of the sphere only reflects light on the outside of the sphere. The inner surface is invisible, kind of like a two-way mirror.

You can make both sides of the surface reflect light by altering the *newModelResource* command to include a third parameter. This third parameter tells the 3D engine which side of the surface to make reflective. The default value is #front, but you can also use #back or #both. Using #both will make the inside of the sphere reflect light.

Creating a Cylinder

Cylinders are the most complex of the four basic primitives. To create a default cylinder, just use the symbol #cylinder in the *newModelResource* command.

```
myModelResource = sprite(me.spriteNum).member.newModelResource("My Cylinder
Resource",#cylinder)
myModel = sprite(me.spriteNum).member.newModel("My Cylinder",myModelResource)
```

Figure 39.12 shows the default cylinder created. A cylinder is made up of a circular top, a circular bottom, and a surface wrapped around between the top and the bottom.

Figure 39.12
A default cylinder is 50 units tall with a uniform radius of 25.

You can adjust the cylinder to make it thinner by changing both the *topRadius* and the *bottomRadius* properties of the model resource. You can also make the cylinder shorter by adjusting the *height* of the model resource. Here is a complete list of model resource properties:

- **topRadius, bottomRadius**: The radius of the top and bottom circle. The default is 25.

- **height**: The height of the cylinder. The default is 50.

- **numSegments, resolution**: The first is the number of polygons from top to bottom and the second is the number of polygons around the circumference of the cylinder.

- **topCap, bottomCap**: Whether the top or bottom of the cylinder is present.

- **startAngle, endAngle**: These two properties allow you to define how much of the main part of the cylinder to draw. For instance, to draw only half of the cylinder, use 0 and 180.

Since the top and bottom radii of a cylinder are independent properties, it is easy to set them to different values. This would create a cone, or at least a portion of a cone. Here is how it can be done. Figure 39.13 shows the result.

```
myModelResource = sprite(me.spriteNum).member.newModelResource("My Cone
Resource",#cylinder)
myModelResource.topRadius = 0
myModelResource.bottomRadius = 40
myModelResource.height = 50
myModel = sprite(me.spriteNum).member.newModel("My Cone",myModelResource)
```

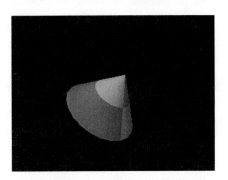

Figure 39.13
A cone was created by using a cylinder with a top radius of 0.

The example movie "39createcylinder.dir" has two behaviors. The first creates a default cylinder. The second creates the cone in Figure 39.13. You can play with this behavior to create different cones, even ones that have somewhat flat tops.

Creating a Plane

Planes are the simplest of the primitives. A plane is just a flat surface. A default plane is a 1-by-1 flat square that is facing the camera. This is too small to be easily seen, so here is the code to create a 10-by-10 plane.

```
myModelResource = sprite(me.spriteNum).member.newModelResource("My Plane
Resource",#plane)
myModelResource.width = 100
myModelResource.length = 100
myModel = sprite(me.spriteNum).member.newModel("My Plane",myModelResource)
```

Since this plane faces you, it just looks like a large square. For all the viewer knows, it may even be hiding a whole cube behind it. To prove that it is just a plane, we can rotate it a bit with this code to produce Figure 39.14.

```
sprite(me.spriteNum).member.model("My Plane").rotate(-60,0,0)
```

Figure 39.14
This 100-by-100 plane has been rotated from its default position so you can see it better.

The movie "39createplane.dir" contains all of this code if you want to play with these settings. Here is a complete list of the properties of a plane model resource:

- **width**, **length**: The size of the plane. The default is 1, which makes a very small plane.
- **lengthVertices**, **widthVertices**: The number of points in the plane used to determine the number of polygons in it.

Planes, like spheres and all of the other primitives, can use a third parameter during the *newModelResource* command. In the case of all of the other primitives, the default third parameter is #front, which means that only the outside surfaces of the primitives reflect light. However, in the case of the plane, #both is the default property, which means that both the top and bottom of the plane reflect light. You can set it to #front or #back if you don't want to use the default.

Assigning Shaders to Primitives

So far, the primitive shapes we have created have a strange red-and-white checkerboard pattern. This is the default default texture. A 3D member has a default texture that is used on every new item created. The red-and-white texture is the default for the default texture.

You can change this default texture by bringing up the property inspector, selecting the 3D member, and changing the "Shader Texture" to something else. Then, when you create new primitives, they will use this default texture.

However, it is more likely that you want to create primitives that use varied colors and textures. To do this, you will need to create shaders and textures, and assign them to the faces of the primitives you create.

First, let's create a primitive box.

```
myResource = sprite(1).member.newModelResource("My Box Resource",#box)
sprite(1).member.newModel("My Box",myResource)
```

Now, let's look at the *shaderList* for this box.

```
put sprite(1).member.model("My Box").shaderList
-- [shader("DefaultShader"), shader("DefaultShader"), shader("DefaultShader"),
shader("DefaultShader"), shader("DefaultShader"), shader("DefaultShader")]
```

You can see that each of the six sides of the box has been assigned the shader "DefaultShader". That's the red-and-white checkerboard.

Now, let's create a new shader and assign that shader to the first side of the box.

```
thisShader = sprite(1).member.newShader("Shader 1",#standard)
thisTexture = sprite(1).member.newTexture("Texture
1",#fromCastMember,member("texture 1"))
thisShader.texture = thisTexture
sprite(me.spriteNum).member.model[1].shaderList[1] = thisShader
```

The example movie "39primitiveshaders.dir" contains a little behavior that will create six shaders with six textures, assign one shader to each side of the box, and then rotate the box around so you can see all of the sides. Figure 39.15 shows the resulting box.

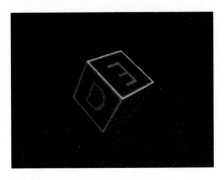

Figure 39.15
This box was created from a primitive model resource and then new shaders were created for each side.

Here is the behavior from that example movie.

```
on beginSprite me
  sprite(me.spriteNum).member.resetWorld()

  -- create a box
  myResource = sprite(me.spriteNum).member.newModelResource("My Box
Resource",#box)
  sprite(me.spriteNum).member.newModel("My Box",myResource)

  -- create 6 shaders, each with a texture, and assign
  repeat with i = 1 to 6
    thisShader = sprite(me.spriteNum).member.newShader("Shader"&&i,#standard)
    thisTexture =
sprite(me.spriteNum).member.newTexture("Texture"&&i,#fromCastMember,member("tex
ture"&&i))
    thisShader.texture = thisTexture
    sprite(me.spriteNum).member.model[1].shaderList[i] = thisShader
  end repeat
end
```

```
on exitFrame me
  -- tumble the box so you can see all sides
  sprite(me.spriteNum).member.model("My Box").rotate(5,5,0)
end
```

If you want to simply color in a side of a box instead of using a bitmap, then you can create shaders that don't use any texture at all. Instead, just set the *ambient* and/or *diffuse* colors of the shaders.

The example movie "39primitiveshaders2.dir" contains a behavior that will assign a different color to each face of the box. Here is that behavior.

```
on beginSprite me
  sprite(me.spriteNum).member.resetWorld()

  -- create a box
  myResource = sprite(me.spriteNum).member.newModelResource("My Box
Resource",#box)
  sprite(me.spriteNum).member.newModel("My Box",myResource)

  -- create shaders for each color
  redShader = sprite(me.spriteNum).member.newShader("Red Shader",#standard)
  redShader.ambient = rgb("FF0000")
  redShader.texture = VOID

  greenShader = sprite(me.spriteNum).member.newShader("Green Shader",#standard)
  greenShader.ambient = rgb("00FF00")
  greenShader.texture = VOID

  blueShader = sprite(me.spriteNum).member.newShader("Blue Shader",#standard)
  blueShader.ambient = rgb("0000FF")
  blueShader.texture = VOID

  cyanShader = sprite(me.spriteNum).member.newShader("Cyan Shader",#standard)
  cyanShader.ambient = rgb("00FFFF")
  cyanShader.texture = VOID

  magentaShader = sprite(me.spriteNum).member.newShader("Magenta Shader",#stan-
dard)
  magentaShader.ambient = rgb("FF00FF")
  magentaShader.texture = VOID

  yellowShader = sprite(me.spriteNum).member.newShader("Yellow Shader",#stan-
dard)
  yellowShader.ambient = rgb("FFFF00")
  yellowShader.texture = VOID
```

```
-- assign shaders to each face
sprite(me.spriteNum).member.model[1].shaderList[1] = redShader
sprite(me.spriteNum).member.model[1].shaderList[2] = greenShader
sprite(me.spriteNum).member.model[1].shaderList[3] = blueShader
sprite(me.spriteNum).member.model[1].shaderList[4] = cyanShader
sprite(me.spriteNum).member.model[1].shaderList[5] = magentaShader
sprite(me.spriteNum).member.model[1].shaderList[6] = yellowShader
end


on exitFrame me
  -- tumble the box so you can see all sides
  sprite(me.spriteNum).member.model("My Box").rotate(5,5,0)
end
```

PARTICLE SYSTEMS

I described what particle systems were in the previous chapter. The behavior that comes with Director 8.5 allows you to create all sorts of interesting particle systems, but it only scratches the surface of what you can do with Lingo.

Particle System Basics

The default particle system can be created with only two lines of code. The first line will create a new model resource, just like we did with the primitives. The second line will add the particle system to the world.

```
myPartRes = sprite(1).member.newModelResource("My Particle Resource",#particle)
myPartSys = sprite(1).member.newModel("My Particle System",myPartRes)
```

To get this working using the Message window, you must first place a 3D member in sprite 1 and then set the movie playing.

What the default particle system looks like is a small blob of particles in the center of the screen. We can make it more interesting by adjusting a few parameters of the particle resource. This next line will get the particles moving faster, and thus get them to move further away from the center of the particle system before they dissolve.

```
myPartRes.emitter.minSpeed = 10
```

Now we have a particle system that I can show you an image of. Figure 39.16 shows the default particle system with a *minSpeed* of 10.

Figure 39.16
This particle system uses all the
default settings, except for a
minimum speed of 10.

For good measure, let's set the maximum speed of the particles to 15. This means that the particles will travel at random speeds between 10 and 15.

```
myPartRes.emitter.maxSpeed = 15
```

Now, let's change the number of particles being generated.

```
myPartRes.emitter.numParticles = 100
```

As soon as you change the number of particles, the particle system resets itself. But pretty soon it is back to full speed. Notice that with 100 particles, there are far less particles on the screen at any one time. Try different numbers like 1000 or 5000 to see what you get.

You can also play with the color of the particles. Try this:

```
myPartRes.colorRange.start = rgb("FF0000")
```

The particles will now start off red, but change to white as they get older. You can adjust the destination color too.

```
myPartRes.colorRange.end = rgb("0000FF")
```

Notice that the *colorRange* properties don't require the *emitter* property to be placed before it. Some particle system properties need the word *emitter* before them and some don't.

Another fun property to play with is the *lifetime* of the particles. Try changing it to one second.

```
myPartRes.lifetime = 1000
```

So far we have only played with particle systems that emit particles at a constant rate. The particles keep coming. However, you can turn this off by setting the *loop* property to false. So, instead of a constant stream of particles, you get a finite number of particles.

```
myPartRes.emitter.loop = FALSE
```

Particle systems have a ton of properties. Here is a complete list of properties and what they are good for:

- **lifetime**: How long the particles last, in milliseconds.

- **colorRange.start**, **colorRange.end**: A particle will start with one color and change to the other color over its lifetime.

- **tweenMode**: If set to #velocity, the color will change according to its speed. Otherwise, the default #age setting will have it change over the course of its lifetime.

- **sizeRange.start**, **sizeRange.end**: The particles will start at one size and gradually change to the other. The default for both is 1.

- **blendRange.start**. **blendRange.end**: The particles will go from one blend setting to the other. For instance, to make the particles fade away, set *blendRange.start* to 100, but *blendRange.end* to 0.

- **texture**: This texture will be applied to each particle. The default, *VOID*, means no texture at all.

- **emitter.numParticles**: The number of particles that can exist at one time in a stream, or the number of particles that are created at once if the system is a burst.

- **emitter.minSpeed**, **emitter.maxSpeed**: The slowest and fastest possible speed for a particle.

- **emitter.mode**: If set to #burst, then all of the particles will be emitted immediately. If set to #stream, then the particles will be emitted gradually.

- **emitter.loop**: Whether the particles are recycled or not. If the system is a stream, then setting this to *TRUE* will ensure a constant stream of particles. If set to *TRUE* when the system is a burst, then the burst will repeat over and over again.

- **emitter.angle**: The distribution of directions in which the particles are emitted. A value of 180 degrees means that the particles are emitted from any direction. A value of 90 means that they are distributed from only one hemisphere. A value of 0 means that they all go in exactly the same direction.

- **emitter.direction**: The direction of the particles. If the *emitter.angle* is set to 180, then this will have no effect.

- **emitter.region**: Usually, particles are emitted from a single point. You could set this point using the *emitter.region*. Instead, if you want the particles to come from a line, then give this property a list of two vector points. If you want the particles to come from a larger area, give this property four vector points.

- **emitter.distribution**: Determines the distribution of the particles, either #linear or #gaussian.

> **Caution**
>
> Note that the "What's New In Director Shockwave Studio" book that comes with Director 8.5 and the online documentation is wrong in a number of places. The entries on pages 95-97 have incorrect information about *emitter.distribution*, *drag*, *gravity*, *wind*, and the *emitter.angle* property is completely missing.

- **emitter.path**: A list of vector points that define a path for the particles to follow.

- **emitter.pathStrength**: A value from 0 to 100 of how strictly the particles should follow the path.

- **gravity**: The force and direction of gravity that affect the particles.

- **wind**: The force and direction of wind that affects the particles. This requires that the *drag* property be set.

- **drag**: How much a particle is affected by wind, from 0 to 100.

Now let's look at how some of these properties can be used to create various interesting effects.

Fountain

Particle systems can be used to simulate running water. You could use them to show water falling from a faucet or a waterfall. You could also use them to simulate fountains.

Figure 39.17 shows a simple fountain. The particles are streaming out of a point and going straight up.

Figure 39.17
A fountain made with particles.

To achieve this effect, I created a particle system that used a very narrow *angle* and *direction* vector to point the particles up. I also set the *gravity* so that the particles fell back down. To complete the effect, I had the blend range from 100 to 0, so the particles faded away as they aged.

Here is the complete behavior, which can be found in the movie "39particlesystems.dir". The speed and gravity numbers were obtained through trial and error until I had a combination that looked good.

```
on beginSprite me
  sprite(me.spriteNum).member.resetWorld()

  -- create particle system
  myPartRes = sprite(me.spriteNum).member.newModelResource("My Particle
Resource",#particle)

  -- range of speeds
  myPartRes.emitter.minSpeed = 20
  myPartRes.emitter.maxSpeed = 30
```

```
-- just enough particles to make it look like water
myPartRes.emitter.numParticles = 1000

-- narrow stream, straight up
myPartRes.emitter.angle = 5
myPartRes.emitter.direction = vector(0,1,0)

-- gravity to pull back down
myPartRes.gravity = vector(0,-0.2,0)

-- live about long enough to get back down
myPartRes.lifetime = 7000

-- start full blend, then fade
myPartRes.blendRange.start = 100
myPartRes.blendRange.end = 0

-- place particle system
myPartSys = sprite(me.spriteNum).member.newModel("My Particle
System",myPartRes)
end
```

Smoke

Imagine the smoke coming from a factory smokestack or a locomotive. To create a particle system like this, we can use wind and drag. Figure 39.18 shows the result.

Figure 39.18
Smoke created with a particle system.

I've taken a similar approach to making smoke as I did to making the fountain. There will be a narrow stream pointed up. But I have turned off gravity, since smoke rises, and turned on wind. I played with the *drag* property until I found that a value of 5 worked well to make this effect.

```
on beginSprite me
  sprite(me.spriteNum).member.resetWorld()

  -- create particle system
  myPartRes = sprite(me.spriteNum).member.newModelResource("My Particle
Resource",#particle)
```

```
-- range of speeds
myPartRes.emitter.minSpeed = 20
myPartRes.emitter.maxSpeed = 80

-- just enough particles to make it look like smoke
myPartRes.emitter.numParticles = 5000

-- narrow stream, straight up
myPartRes.emitter.angle = 15
myPartRes.emitter.direction = vector(0,1,0)

-- live about long enough to get off the screen
myPartRes.lifetime = 10000

-- start full blend, then fade
myPartRes.blendRange.start = 100
myPartRes.blendRange.end = 0

-- wind to blow the smoke away
myPartRes.wind = vector(15,0,0)
myPartRes.drag = 5

-- place particle system
myPartSys = sprite(me.spriteNum).member.newModel("My Particle
System",myPartRes)
end
```

To use this behavior, you'll need to remove the current behavior in the "39particlesystems.dir" movie and drag and drop the "smoke" behavior on to the 3D sprite.

Tornado

You can force particles to follow a path. This gives you the artistic license to create all sorts of things. However, finding something that looks good can be tough.

By using just two points in a path, and playing with the number of particles and their speed, I was able to come up with something that looks a little like a tornado. Figure 39.19 is a still image of it, but it looks a lot better when animating.

Here is the behavior, which can be found in "39particlesystems.dir". Try playing with the number of particles and the speeds to see what else you can make it look like. Also, try inserting other points in the *path*.

```
on beginSprite me
sprite(me.spriteNum).member.resetWorld()

-- create particle system
```

```
myPartRes = sprite(me.spriteNum).member.newModelResource("My Particle
Resource",#particle)

  -- range of speeds
  myPartRes.emitter.minSpeed = 20
  myPartRes.emitter.maxSpeed = 10

  -- just enough particles to make it look like smoke
  myPartRes.emitter.numParticles = 1000

  -- start with narrow stream, straight up
  --myPartRes.emitter.angle = 0
  --myPartRes.emitter.direction = vector(0,1,0)

  -- live about long enough to get off the screen
  myPartRes.lifetime = 5000

  -- define a path to follow
  myPartRes.emitter.path = [vector(0,-30,0),vector(0,30,0)]

  -- place particle system
  myPartSys = sprite(me.spriteNum).member.newModel("My Particle
System",myPartRes)
end
```

Figure 39.19
This tornado effect looks better when animating in Director.

Explosions

One of the main properties of particle systems is the *mode*, which can be set to #stream or #burst. Changing it to #burst allows us to create quick bursts of particles which look like explosions.

Figure 39.20 shows such an explosion in progress. All of the particles are generated at once and expand outward. I also set them to fade away with the *blendStart* and *blendEnd* properties.

Figure 39.20
An explosion in progress.

Here is the behavior for this. Note that you can change the *loop* property to *FALSE* if you don't want the explosion to repeat again and again.

```
on beginSprite me
  sprite(me.spriteNum).member.resetWorld()

  -- create particle system
  myPartRes = sprite(me.spriteNum).member.newModelResource("My Particle
Resource",#particle)

  -- burst, not stream
  myPartRes.emitter.mode = #burst

  -- change loop to FALSE if you don't want it to repeat
  myPartRes.emitter.loop = TRUE

  -- range of speeds
  myPartRes.emitter.minSpeed = 20
  myPartRes.emitter.maxSpeed = 10

  -- just enough particles
  myPartRes.emitter.numParticles = 1000

  -- live about long enough to see real
  myPartRes.lifetime = 5000

  -- start full blend, then fade
  myPartRes.blendRange.start = 100
  myPartRes.blendRange.end = 0

  -- place particle system
  myPartSys = sprite(me.spriteNum).member.newModel("My Particle
System",myPartRes)
end
```

If you set up an explosion like this, you can always force it to start over again by setting the *numParticles* again, even if it is to the exact same amount.

Fireworks

Modifying the explosion to make it look like fireworks is pretty simple. All that is needed is to add gravity. I've also slowed down the particles quite a bit since fireworks cover a large area and take a long time to expand and fall.

```
on beginSprite me
  sprite(me.spriteNum).member.resetWorld()

  -- create particle system
  myPartRes = sprite(me.spriteNum).member.newModelResource("My Particle
Resource",#particle)

  -- burst, not stream
  myPartRes.emitter.mode = #burst

  -- change loop to FALSE if you don't want it to repeat
  myPartRes.emitter.loop = TRUE

  -- range of speeds
  myPartRes.emitter.minSpeed = 12
  myPartRes.emitter.maxSpeed = 8

  -- just enough particles
  myPartRes.emitter.numParticles = 500

  -- live about long enough to see real
  myPartRes.lifetime = 10000

  -- start full blend, then fade
  myPartRes.blendRange.start = 100
  myPartRes.blendRange.end = 0


  -- add gravity
  myPartRes.gravity = vector(0,-.2,0)

  -- place particle system
  myPartSys = sprite(me.spriteNum).member.newModel("My Particle
System",myPartRes)
end
```

These were just a few examples of what you can do with particle effects. I have used them in many different ways. For instance, I have a few particles fly out of a point where two objects collide, so they look like sparks. I have also used them to draw attention to a model, like a magic item in a game.

If you plan on creating a lot of products with Director's 3D engine, I definitely recommend investing some time playing around with particle systems first. This will give you some good ideas that you can use later on.

MODIFIERS

There are many procedures and special effects that you can perform on models once they are a part of a 3D member. Some of these affect the appearance of models, while others have to do with the balance of quality versus performance.

Level of Detail

Level of detail, or "lod," is a way to get Director's 3D engine to remove polygons from a model so that it renders faster. It only works on models imported from a 3D graphics program, not primitives.

Normally, the level of detail is handled automatically. Director will remove polygons from a model when it is far away from the camera and such extra polygons make little difference. When the object is close to the camera, then all of the polygons will be used.

To take control over the level of detail in a model, you must first add the #lod modifier to the model. Adding a modifier is just a matter of using the *addModifier* command. Open up "39lod.dir" and try this:

```
sprite(1).member.model("left teapot").addModifier(#lod)
```

Now that the model has a lod modifier, you can access several new properties of the model. The first is the *lod.auto* property. When set to *TRUE*, Director handles changes in the level of detail. Set this to *FALSE* to take control of the level of detail yourself.

```
sprite(1).member.model("left teapot").lod.auto = FALSE
```

Now that you have control, you can use the *lod.level* property to set the level of detail. A value of 100 means that all of the polygons should be used to render the model. Let's set this to 20, so that only 20 percent of the polygons will be used.

```
sprite(1).member.model("left teapot").lod.level = 20
```

The result can be seen in Figure 39.21. The two teapots are identical, but the one on the left has been given a lod modifier and the *lod.level* has been set to 20.

Another way to use the lod modifier is to keep the *lod.auto* setting at *TRUE*, but set the *lod.bias* setting to something between 0 and 100. This will change how aggressive Director is in adding or removing polygons as the model gets closer or further from the camera.

Subdivision Surfaces

The subdivision surfaces, or "sds," modifier is sort of the opposite of level of detail. Sds will add geometry to a model, rather than take it away. This added detail comes from information provided by the 3D graphics program.

Figure 39.21
The teapot on the left has a lower level of detail setting.

After adding the #sds modifier to a model, set the *sds.depth* property to a value from 1 to 5. A value of 0 is the same as not using sds at all. Use the example movie "39sds.dir" to test out these changes.

```
sprite(1).member.model("left box").addModifier(#sds)
sprite(1).member.model("left box").sds.depth = 3
```

Figure 39.22 shows the result. The box on the left has been given very smooth, rounded corners rather than the sharp ones of the original box.

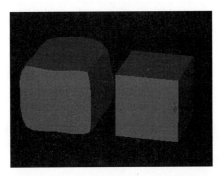

Figure 39.22
The box on the left has been altered using the subdivision surfaces modifier.

In addition to the *sds.depth* property, you can also set the *sds.tension* to a percentage that indicates how much the new surfaces match the old ones. The *sds.subdivision* property can be set to either #uniform or #adaptive. Using #adaptive means that the changes will only take place when there is a major vertex and when that vertex is visible. If you use #adaptive, you can use the *sds.error* to set the tolerance level for these changes.

Inker

The inker modifier allows you to accentuate the lines between faces in a model. The effect looks like someone traced the wireframe of a model to make it stand out.

Figure 39.23 shows a simple box model that has been given the inker modifier.

Figure 39.23
The box on the left has been given the inker modifer and the *lineColor* has been set to white to make the lines more visible.

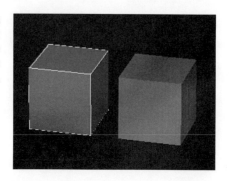

To turn on the inker modifier, use the *addModifier* command. The effect will be rather pronounced right away, but you can alter it in a few different ways.

The *lineColor* property allows you to set the color of the lines drawn. To obtain Figure 39.23 I set the line color to white, since the default black lines were a little hard to see in the figure. You can see this code in movie "39inker.dir".

```
sprite(1).member.model("left box").addModifier(#inker)
sprite(1).member.model("left box").inker.lineColor = rgb("FFFFFF")
```

The lines are drawn along creases in the model. This is typically where one face begins and another ends. However, if the angle between these two faces is shallow, then no line will be drawn. Only sharp angles, like the ones at the edges of the box in Figure 39.24, are used for lines.

You can adjust the sensitivity for which creases get lines and which don't using the *inker.creaseAngle* property. If you set this all the way up to 1.0, then lines are drawn at every crease. The default value is .01.

There are actually three different types of lines that are drawn: creases, boundary lines, and silhouette lines. You can turn on and off these lines with the *inker.creases*, *inker.boundary*, and *inker.silhouettes* properties. By default they are all on.

Toon

The toon modifier will take a 3D model and flatten it so that it looks similar to a 2D cartoon. Figure 39.24 shows a teapot that has been given the default toon modifier.

Figure 39.24
The teapot on the left has been flattened with the toon modifier.

To get this effect, all you need to do is apply the toon modifier like this:

```
sprite(1).member.model("left teapot").addModifier(#toon)
```

There are also a lot of ways in which you can customize the toon modifier. Here is a complete list of properties:

- **toon**: This can either be #toon, #gradient or #blackandwhite. The difference between #toon and #gradient is that #gradient provides smoother transitions between colors.

- **colorSteps**: This is the number of colors that can be used. Figure 39.25 shows the default 2 colors. You can increase the number of colors to 4, 8 or 16.

- **shadowPercentage**: This is the percentage of the *colorSteps* to be used for shadows. A default value of 50 means that half the colors will be used for shadows.

- **highlightPercentage**: This is the percentage of *colorSteps* to be used for highlights. This number is linked to the *shadowPercentage*, so changing one will change the other.

- **shadowStrength**, **highlightStrength**: The darkness of the shadow colors and the brightness of the highlight colors.

In addition to the properties listed above, the toon modifier can also use all of the properties of the inker modifier. So you can set *lineColor*, *creases*, *silhouettes*, *boundary*, and *creaseAngle*.

MESH DEFORM

We have already seen that you can create primitives of various shapes and sizes and even apply your own textures to them. You can also modify the points that make up a primitive model.

To do this, you must attach the mesh deform modifier to the model. Once you do that, you can modify every vertex in the model.

For a simple example, let's take a plane. To create a plane, just use a few simple lines in the Message window. The following code assumes that you have placed a blank 3D member in sprite 1.

```
myModelResource = sprite(1).member.newModelResource("My Plane Resource",#plane)
myModelResource.width = 200
myModelResource.length = 200
myModel = sprite(1).member.newModel("My Plane",myModelResource)
```

This creates a huge plane that just about fills the 3D sprite. Use *updateStage* to update the image on the screen.

To make the plane easier to see, let's rotate it and move it down, so it becomes a ground plane in our 3D world.

```
sprite(1).member.model("My Plane").rotate(90,0,0)
sprite(1).member.model("My Plane").transform.position = vector(0,-50,-50)
```

Figure 39.25 shows this simple plane. Our goal is to alter the plane so that it is not flat, but shows some irregularities.

Figure 39.25
This is a normal flat plane primitive.

The plane is made up of vertices. In this case, there is one vertex on each corner of the plane. However, we can define the plane to be made up of a whole matrix of vertices instead. To make the plane a grid of 5-by-5 vertices, just change the *widthVertices* and *lengthVertices* properties of the model resource. But you must do this before you create the model. So it is important to start over again.

```
sprite(1).member.resetWorld()
myModelResource = sprite(1).member.newModelResource("My Plane Resource",#plane)
myModelResource.width = 200
myModelResource.length = 200
myModelResource.widthVertices = 5
myModelResource.lengthVertices = 5
myModel = sprite(1).member.newModel("My Plane",myModelResource)
sprite(1).member.model("My Plane").rotate(90,0,0)
sprite(1).member.model("My Plane").transform.position = vector(0,-50,-50)
```

Now it is time to add the mesh deform modifier. Once this is done, the plane becomes a matrix of vertices that you can access and alter.

```
myModel.addModifier(#meshDeform)
```

To see that the model is now made up of a grid of 5 vertices by 5 vertices, look at the *count* of the *vertexList* property.

```
put myModel.meshDeform.mesh[1].vertexList.count
-- 25
```

There are 25 vertices in the model. It follows that the thirteenth vertex is the one in the middle of the grid. Let's get the position of that vertex.

```
put myModel.meshDeform.mesh[1].vertexList[13]
-- vector( 0.0000, 0.0000, 0.0000 )
```

That makes sense. The model is at 0,0,0, so the vertex right in the middle of the model should be at 0,0,0. Now, let's try moving that vertex up to create a bump in the plane.

```
myModel.meshDeform.mesh[1].vertexList[13] = vector(0,0,-30)
updateStage
```

You should now see something like Figure 39.26. The middle vertex has been moved up by 30 units. This creates a bump in the middle of the plane.

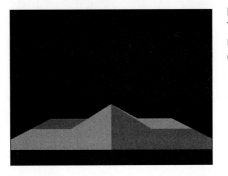

Figure 39.26
The plane has been altered by moving the middle vertex up to create a bump.

Notice that we are altering the first *mesh* in the *meshDeform* property. A plane actually has two meshes: the top and the bottom. Other primitives have even more meshes when they are given the mesh deform modifier.

The example movie "39meshdeform.dir" will actually perform a similar set of commands to what we just learned. However, it will randomly assign vertical positions to all of the vertices in the mesh, rather than just the middle one. It will then assign a whole new set of vertices in the next frame, and so on. This creates a little earthquake, or water ripple animation.

COLLISION DETECTION

Objects in 3D worlds tend to be like ghosts: they can move through other objects and even exist inside other objects. This is not typically how things work in the real world. In most cases, you will want to limit the movement of 3D objects so that they do not pass through other objects.

To do this, you need collision detection. There are four ways to do collision detection in 3D Director members. The first way is to use the collision modifier and the second way is to use *modelsUnderRay*. We'll examine both of these next. You could also use pure math to determine when two objects are too close to each other. A fourth way is to use the Havok physics engine, which we'll get to later on in this chapter.

The Collision Modifier

You can apply the collision modifier to a model in the same way that you apply the inker or toon modifier. Once the collision modifier is there, you can get and set properties of the model related to collisions.

Let's start by creating a playground of 3D objects. Figure 39.27 shows a 3D world created in a 3D graphics program. There are four models and a ground plane.

Figure 39.27
This 3D playground is a good
place to experiment with collision
detection.

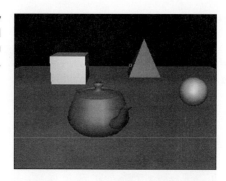

To test collisions, we'll need to be able to move around one of the objects in the world. Here's a behavior that will allow us to move the teapot around. You can find this behavior and the other versions of it to come in the file "39collision.dir".

```
property myModel

on beginSprite me
  sprite(me.spriteNum).member.resetWorld()

  -- store reference to the teapot
  myModel = sprite(me.spriteNum).member.model("teapot")
end

on exitFrame me
  -- rotate with left and right arrows
  if keyPressed(123) then myModel.rotate(0,0,5)
  if keyPressed(124) then myModel.rotate(0,0,-5)

  -- move with up and down arrows
  if keyPressed(126) then myModel.translate(5,0,0)
  if keyPressed(125) then myModel.translate(-5,0,0)
end
```

Open the example movie and make sure that only the "Quick Movement Behavior" is attached to the sprite. If you run the movie, you will be able to use the arrow keys to move the teapot around. You can easily drive the teapot through other objects.

To add collision detection, first add the collision modifier to the teapot. The behavior has stored a reference to the model in "myModel". Add this code to the *on beginSprite* handler:

```
myModel.addModifier(#collision)
```

Just adding the modifier to the teapot is not enough. Models with the collision modifier attached can only detect collisions with other models that also have the collision modifier attached. So, here is the code to attach the collision modifier to all of the other models.

```
sprite(me.spriteNum).member.model("sphere").addModifier(#collision)
sprite(me.spriteNum).member.model("box").addModifier(#collision)
sprite(me.spriteNum).member.model("pyramid").addModifier(#collision)
```

If you run the movie now, you can still move the teapot around, but it will not be able to pass through the other three objects.

This isn't really "collision detection" so much as "collision prevention." However, you can add another line to have the collision event reported back to your Lingo code. The following line uses the *registerForEvent* command to tell Director that any collisions should be reported to a handler named "on handleCollision" in the current script object.

```
sprite(me.spriteNum).member.registerForEvent(#collideAny,#handleCollision,me)
```

Now all we need is an "on handlerCollision" handler. Here is a simple one:

```
on handleCollision me, collisionData
  put collisionData.modelA.name&&"collided with"&&collisionData.modelB.name
end
```

The handler you define as the collision handler will get back a parameter, called "collisionData" in the example above. The Director documentation refers to this parameter as "collisionData" as well, although you could name it whatever you want.

The collisionData parameter is actually an object that has a few properties. The *modelA* and *modelB* properties tell you which models were involved in the collision. The previous handler will simply display the model names in the Message window.

Right now, the code looks just like the behavior "Basic Collision Detection" in the "39collision.dir" movie. Swap out the previous behavior for this one to see it in action.

One of the things you will notice about the collisions is that they seem to happen when the teapot is still quite a distance from the objects. For instance, Figure 39.28 shows the teapot and the box at the point of collision, but they are not very near each other. In addition, the *debug* property of both models has been turned on so that you can see the bounding spheres of these models. It is easy to see, then, that it is the spheres around these models that have collided, not the models themselves.

There are actually three different modes for collision detection. The first, #sphere, will use the bounding spheres of the objects. This is the default. It is the quickest method, since the only calculation that needs to be done is to determine how far the center of one object is from the other.

Another fast method is the #box mode. This will use the bounding box of the models instead of the sphere. This comes in handy when you have walls or roads that may be very long or tall, thus making their bounding spheres huge.

The ultimate mode for collision detection is #mesh. This gives accurate collision detection right down to the polygon. It is also very slow. Here's how to modify the current behavior to use #mesh mode collision detection. You can find a new behavior in the file as "Mesh Collision Detection."

```
myModel.collision.mode = #mesh
sprite(me.spriteNum).member.model("sphere").collision.mode = #mesh
sprite(me.spriteNum).member.model("box").collision.mode = #mesh
sprite(me.spriteNum).member.model("pyramid").collision.mode = #mesh
```

Figure 39.28
The teapot and box collide when their bounding spheres touch.

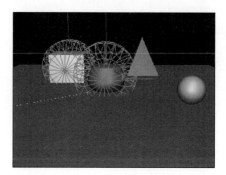

It is important to set all of the objects to #mesh as if you set only one object to #mesh and leave the others at #sphere mode. Then #sphere mode will be used to determine any collisions.

When you run the movie with this new behavior applied, you can see that the teapot can get right up to the other objects. As a matter of fact, you can see that collision detection works when you rotate objects as well. Just bring the teapot up alongside another object, and try rotating it so that the spout or handle hit the other object. The collision detection works in this case too.

The *collisionData* object you get back when a collision occurs contains more than just the two models that collided. A *pointOfContact* property will tell you exactly where the collision occurred and a *collisionNormal* property will tell you the direction of the collision.

Casting Rays

The collision modifier is a great function that is easy to use and has a lot of versatility. However, this versatility comes with a price: It is slow.

Our example with the teapot and other shapes is a pretty simple 3D world. If you try to make a game that has hundreds of models, some of which are quite large, then the collision modifier is just not fast enough.

One way that I have found to detect and avoid collisions is to use the *modelsUnderRay* function. What this does is to cast a ray from one point in the 3D world in a certain direction. In other words, it draws an invisible line. It then reports back what models this line came in contact with.

So, if we start at the location of the moving object, then cast a ray in the direction that the object is supposed to move, we can get a list of what objects are in the way. Better yet, we also find out how far away these objects are.

So, for instance, if the teapot is supposed to move 5 units in a certain direction, we can cast a ray before the teapot moves, find out if anything is in front of the teapot, then find out how far it is in front of the teapot. If the object in the way is too close, we can simply not allow the teapot to move in that direction.

The first step in setting something like this up is to determine how close the moving model can get to something else. If the object is roughly circular, like the teapot, then we can get the radius of the object and use that as the minimum distance that the teapot can get to another object. Any closer and the other object and the teapot will overlap, since the distance is measured from the middle of the teapot.

To get the radius of a model, we can use the *boundingSphere* function. This will return a list where the first item is the center of the object and the second item is the radius of the object.

```
modelRadius = myModel.boundingSphere[2]
```

The next step is to monitor the keyboard for up and down arrow keys so that the requested movement is recorded in a variable. This is different than in the previous example where we just tried the movement immediately. This time, we will record the requested movement and perform calculations on it before doing the movement.

```
if keyPressed(126) then move = vector(5,0,0)
else if keyPressed(125) then move = vector(-5,0,0)
else move = vector(0,0,0)
```

If there is a movement, then we want to use *modelsUnderRay* to determine if there is an object in the way. This function requires two parameters. The first is the location of the starting point of the ray. The second is a vector that represents the direction of the ray.

To get the direction, you would think that we could just use the *transform.rotation* of the model. Not so. This will return a vector with angles, like vector(0,90,0) for a 90 degree angle. What we need is a real vector, like vector(0,0,1) that shows the movement, sort of like a short arrow pointing in the right direction.

Getting this vector becomes a little complex. First, we create a blank transform variable. Everything is set to 0 in this variable. Then we rotate this transform by the same amount that the model is rotated. Next we move the transform by the amount that the model is to be moved. We can't use *translate* for this, however, since that will not take into account the rotation of the transform. However, *preTranslate* will rotate the transform first, then move it.

The result is that the position of the transform is now a certain distance from the origin. This makes a little arrow for us to use, drawn from the center of the world to the position of our "t" transform. Here is the code:

```
t = transform()
t.rotate(myModel.transform.rotation)
t.preTranslate(move)
rayMove = t.position
```

I realize that the concepts here are getting a little deep into 3D mathematical concepts.

Unfortunately, this is necessary in order to use this technique.

The first parameter of the *modelsUnderRay* function is the location of the starting point of the ray. However, we cannot just use the location of the teapot for this. Why? Well the teapot rests on the ground plane, at y location 0. If we cast a ray from here, then the ray is drawn along the ground. This will miss an object like the sphere, since the sphere barely touches the ground at its bottom point. However, if we simply raise the location of the ray's starting point a little off of the ground, then it will find the sphere and any other objects that are off the ground.

```
rayLoc = myModel.transform.position
rayLoc.z = 5
```

The *modelsUnderRay* function returns a list of models. You can set a third parameter to the number of models to return. We'll use 1 so that it returns the closest model. If we used, say, 4, then the closest 4 models would be returned. We'll also use the optional #detailed parameter so that we get a list back that includes the distance to the closest model, rather than just a reference to the model.

```
list = sprite(me.spriteNum).member.modelsUnderRay(rayLoc, rayMove,1,#detailed)
```

If the "list" contains any items, then it means that there is an object in the way. If this object is closer than our "modelRadius" then we will not allow the user to move in that direction.

```
if list.count > 0 then
   d = list[1].distance
   if d < modelRadius then move = vector(0,0,0)
end if
```

You can see this code in action in the movie "39raycast.dir". Play with moving the teapot around to see how it collides with other objects.

There are many flaws in this method of collision detection. For one thing, the moving object can easily sideswipe another object and the two objects will overlap. This is because only one ray is being cast from the middle of the moving object. If this ray comes from the center of the object and misses an object that is off to one side, no collision will occur.

The way I get around this is to use two rays, one from each side of the object. For instance, if the object were an airplane, then I would cast a ray from the tip of each wing.

You could also use the *modelsUnderRay* function to determine how far an object is from the ground, or the altitude of the ground at a certain point. Just cast a ray down from above and measure the distance to the "ground" model. This is great for making hover cars that try to maintain a constant distance from the ground, or for having normal cars or characters follow the contours of the ground as they move.

WORLD TO MOVIE COMMUNICATION

Your 3D world exists inside a sprite which is inside a member. This sprite can either be displayed as a normal sprite, or drawn directly to the screen. The latter option, which is the default, is much faster. You can change this setting using the *directToStage* property of the member.

If you decide to turn off *directToStage*, then you gain only one advantage: other sprites can appear on top of the 3D sprite. However, the speed decrease is so profound that the 3D world needs to be pretty simple in order to get any performance at all.

Once a 3D scene is on the screen, you may want to have it react to user clicks. There are several ways to determine which 3D object the user clicked on. The simplest is to use *modelUnderLoc*.

Here is a behavior that uses *modelUnderLoc* to determine which model has been clicked on. First, you need to calculate the upper-left corner of the sprite. Then, you need to subtract that from the screen click location. This will get you the location of the click relative to the upper-left corner of the sprite.

```
on mouseUp me
  -- get upper left corner
  upperLeft = point(sprite(me.spriteNum).left, sprite(me.spriteNum).top)

  -- calculate the click location
  clickLocation = the mouseLoc - upperLeft

  -- get the model there
  model = sprite(me.spriteNum).camera.modelUnderLoc(clickLocation)

  -- send to message window
  put model
end
```

The example movie "39selection.dir" contains this simple behavior wired up to the same 3D member as seen back in Figure 39.5. If you click on the television, chair, table or remote control, you will see the model references send to the Message window. However, if you click anywhere else, you will see a reference to "Room" instead. This is the model that represents the walls, floor and ceiling. If you click on the window, you will also get a reference to "Room", since the window is just part of the "Room" model and not its own model.

The *modelsUnderLoc* function will only return a reference to the closest model that is in the click location. You can use *modelsUnderLoc* to get a complete list of models under the click location, ordered by distance from the camera.

There are also two other commands: *spriteSpaceToWorldSpace* and *worldSpaceToSpriteSpace* that can be used to convert 2D screen coordinates to or from 3D world coordinates.

GROUPING

Earlier in this chapter, in the "Moving the Camera" section, I showed you a command called *addChild* that grouped the camera with another model. Grouping is an important part of controlling a 3D world.

When you create a world in a 3D graphics program, grouping is used to create models. For instance, you might create a car out of a few boxes for the body and four cylinders for the tires. Then, you would group them together to create a car model. Once this world was brought into Director, this would just be seen as a model, not as a group. So grouping doesn't necessarily mean the same thing between graphics programs and Director's 3D engine.

Grouping does come in handy when you want to bring together different primitives that you created with Lingo. They can then act as one model rather than individual models.

The main command for grouping is *addChild*. However, this will only link one model to another. Much of the time it is easier to create a group and to link models to that group.

A group is like an empty model. It has no geometry or shader. However, it can be moved, rotated and scaled. It can have children and even a parent. To create a group, use the *newGroup* command.

```
myGroup = sprite(1).member.newGroup("my group")
```

Now that you have a group, you can set its *position, rotation,* and *scale*. You can also *translate* or *rotate* it. None of this does anything that is visible until you assign some children to it. To add a child, just use this *addChild* command. This line will add a model to the group.

```
myGroup.addChild(sprite(1).member.model("my model"))
```

You can then add other models to the same group as well. It is a good idea to position the models in the right spot, relative to the group or other models in the group, before grouping them.

If you want to remove a model from a group, simply assign its *parent* property to the *group("World")*.

```
sprite(1).member.model("my  model").parent =
sprite(1).member.group("world")
```

CONTROLLING ANIMATION

Director 8.5 3D members can contain animated sequences. There are actually two types of animation in 3D members: keyframe player animations and bones player animations.

The bones player animations involve skeletons that map out how the pieces of a model are connected. For instance, if you have a model of a person, then the arms, legs and joints may all form a skeleton map inside the model. The bones player animations can be things like walking, picking something up, looking around, etc.

As of the time of this writing the only way to create bones and bones player animations is by using an old version (3.1) of the 3D graphics program 3D Studio Max. No other package supports the exporting of bones or bones player animations. Even if you have an old copy of this program, you will also need another software package called "Character Studio" to be able to easily create bones, though it is theoretically possible to create bones without Character Studio. Since bones player animation is, for practical purposes, not available, I will not discuss it any more. Hopefully, we will see more support for this in the future.

The other type of animation is more what you would be used to with Flash or digital video. Keyframe player animation can be created with a variety of 3D graphics tools. Only a few support exporting to Shockwave 3D, but more will probably do so by the time this book is published.

Once an animation has been included in the Shockwave 3D file, you can control it with Lingo. Open the file "39animation.dir" to see a simple animated scene. Figure 39.29 shows this scene.

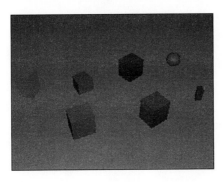

Figure 39.29
In this animated scene, the ball will bounce through the boxes.

To access the properties of such an animation, you must use the *keyframePlayer* modifier. However, you don't have to add the modifier with the *addModifier* command. Since the member includes an animation, the modifier is automatically attached.

You can use the Message window to find out about this animation. The model has a *playList* that lists the different animations queued up and ready to play. If you have used Director 8.X's sound Lingo, you will recognize this sort of list.

```
put sprite(1).member.model("ball group").keyframePlayer.playlist.count
-- 1
put sprite(1).member.model("ball group").keyframePlayer.playlist[1]
-- [#name: "ball group-Key", #loop: 0, #startTime: 0, #endTime: 5000, #scale:
1.0000]
```

The name of the animation is "ball group-Key". This name was assigned when the animation was created in the 3D program. You can see all of the animations by using the *motion* property of the member. In this case, there is a blank "DefaultMotion" and the motion above. You can also get the *duration* of a motion.

```
put sprite(1).member.motion.count
-- 2
put sprite(1).member.motion[1]
-- motion("DefaultMotion")
put sprite(1).member.motion[2]
-- motion("ball group-Key")
put sprite(1).member.motion[2].duration
-- 5000
```

When you start playing the movie, the animation will begin automatically. To stop that, we'll place a behavior on the sprite that will issue a *pause* command to the model's keyframe player modifier.

```
property myModel

on beginSprite me
   -- reset the model
   sprite(me.spriteNum).member.resetWorld()

   -- get easy reference to the ball
   myModel = sprite(me.spriteNum).member.model("ball group")

   -- don't let it play the first time
   myModel.keyframePlayer.pause()
end
```

Now that we have stopped the animation, we can play the movie and the ball will not bounce. To start the ball bouncing, we can just issue the *play* command. Here is a behavior that will do this when the user clicks on the sprite.

```
on mouseUp me
   myModel.keyframePlayer.play()
end
```

When the user clicks, the animation will play out. If you check the *playList* when it is done, you will find it empty. This is because the motion has been used and is now over.

The *playList* can contain a whole series of motions. Each will be performed one after the other. You can also add motions with the *queue* command that will be added to the *playList* while the current animation is playing.

The following *on mouseUp* handler will check the *playing* state of the animation. It will also check to see if there is an animation currently in the *queue*. If there is an animation there, it will use *playNext* to skip the rest of that animation just after it adds one to the end of the *queue*. This will cause the animation to play again when the user clicks the sprite. If no animation was playing, it will simply start a new one. If the animation has never started playing, then the *play* command is used to start it.

```
on mouseUp me

   if myModel.keyframePlayer.playing and myModel.keyframePlayer.playList.count >
0 then
      -- if one already playing, then que another and skip to it
      myModel.keyframePlayer.queue("ball group-Key")
      myModel.keyframePlayer.playNext()

   else if myModel.keyframePlayer.playList.count = 0 then
      -- if none queued or playing, start a new one
      myModel.keyframePlayer.queue("ball group-Key")
      myModel.keyframePlayer.play()

   else
```

```
    -- not playing yet, so start it
    myModel.keyframePlayer.play()
  end if
end
```

If you run the movie "39animation.dir" and click on the sprite several times, you will notice something very interesting. The ball will not just pop back into its original position and start again; it will actually fly back to its original position.

This is because animation in 3D members uses tweening to make smooth transitions between motions. So the ball will actually travel back to its starting position rather than just teleport there.

> The Havok physics engine is really an Xtra. It comes with Director 8.5 and can easily be added to your Projectors. The default download for Shockwave 8.5 does not include Havok, but it is automatically added when the user runs into the first movie that needs it. Since this is a Macromedia "blessed" Xtra, the user doesn't even see a confirmation dialog box as Havok is installed. It just happens automatically.

You can change this tweening behavior by using the *autoBlend*, *blendFactor*, and *blendTime* properties of the keyframe player modifier. If the *autoBlend* property is set to *TRUE*, then blending between animations is automatic. Otherwise, you can control the amount of blending with the *blendFactor* setting of 0 to 100. The *blendTime* is the time it will take to transition.

HAVOK PHYSICS ENGINE

In addition to the 3D engine that comes with Director 8.5, there is an additional physics engine provided by Havok. Havok makes 3D physics engines for many popular computer games, so having part of this engine included in Director 8.5 is quite a treat.

The Havok physics engine makes it easy to have 3D objects that behave like normal real-world objects. You can assign a mass to a model and apply forces to it. Using Havok is relatively simple.

The first thing you need to do is add a "Havok Physics Scene" to the movie. Choose Insert, Media Element, Havok Physics Scene to do this.

This Havok member is referenced by Lingo. You don't have to do anything else with it like place it in the score or set its properties. This is just a placeholder for Havok to be able to store information about the physics going on in your 3D world.

The Director 8.5 CD-ROM comes with a folder of Havok behaviors. You can use these to quickly create worlds with accurate physics. If you want to write your own Lingo scripts, here is a simple introduction to Havok physics Lingo.

The example movie "39havok.dir" contains a simple scene with a car and some boxes. You can see it in Figure 39.30. If you run the movie, you'll find that you can drive the car around with the arrow keys. You can also smash into the boxes and push them around. This was all done with Havok.

Figure 39.30
This scene includes a car that you can drive and boxes that can be pushed around.

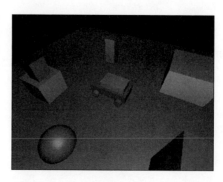

The behavior that controls the car starts off by defining the entire world. It gets a reference to the Havok cast member and then uses *initialize* to start the physics simulation. Next, all of the objects in the world are assigned masses. Some objects are fixed in place, while others are free to move. Before this is done, the mesh deform modifier needs to be added to all of these models.

```
property pHavok, pMember, pCar

on beginSprite me
  -- get the member for easy reference
  pMember = sprite(me.spriteNum).member

  -- reset the world
  pMember.resetWorld()

  -- get reference to havok member
  pHavok = member("carscene physics")

  -- start havok at scale of 1
  pHavok.initialize(pMember,1,1)

  -- add mesh deform to all models
  pMember.model("Ground").addModifier(#meshdeform)
  pMember.model("Car").addModifier(#meshdeform)
  pMember.model("Green Box").addModifier(#meshdeform)
  pMember.model("Blue Box").addModifier(#meshdeform)
  pMember.model("Pink Box").addModifier(#meshdeform)
  pMember.model("Top Box").addModifier(#meshdeform)
  pMember.model("Purple Box").addModifier(#meshdeform)
  pMember.model("Sphere").addModifier(#meshdeform)

  -- fix ground, one box and the sphere
  pHavok.makeFixedRigidBody("Ground",TRUE,#box)
  pHavok.makeFixedRigidBody("Blue Box",TRUE,#box)
  pHavok.makeFixedRigidBody("Sphere",TRUE,#sphere)
```

```
-- assign mass to other boxes
pHavok.makeMovableRigidBody("Green Box",20,TRUE,#box)
pHavok.makeMovableRigidBody("Pink Box",20,TRUE,#box)
pHavok.makeMovableRigidBody("Top Box",20,TRUE,#box)
pHavok.makeMovableRigidBody("Purple Box",40,TRUE,#box)

-- assign mass to car
pCar = pHavok.makeMovableRigidBody("Car",100,TRUE,#box)
end
```

Now that the world is set, we need to look for key presses and move the car when needed. We'll use the *applyImpulse* command to move the car, and the *applyAngularImpulse* to turn the car.

```
on exitFrame me
  -- if up arrow pressed, move forward
  if keyPressed(126) then
    -- calculate forward vector
    t = pMember.model("Car").transform.duplicate()
    t.position = vector(0,0,0)
    v = t*vector(0,1,0)

    -- move forward
    pCar.applyImpulse(v*100)
  end if

  -- if down arrow pressed, move backward
  if keyPressed(125) then
    -- calculate forward vector
    t = pMember.model("Car").transform.duplicate()
    t.position = vector(0,0,0)
    v = t*vector(0,1,0)

    -- move backward
    pCar.applyImpulse(v*-50)
  end if

  -- if arrows pressed, apply angular impulse to turn
  if keyPressed(123) then
    pCar.applyAngularImpulse(vector(0,0,300))
  end if
  if keyPressed(124) then
    pCar.applyAngularImpulse(vector(0,0,-300))
  end if
```

```
-- set the physics simulation
  pHavok.step()
end
```

The last line of the behavior issues the *step* command. In the physics simulation, time does not move forward until you tell it. The *step* command will push time forward and move all of the objects according to the forces applied to them.

If you play with the movie, you'll see that the car can bump into the boxes and push them away. There is even a box stacked on top of another box that you can knock off.

The sphere that is embedded in the ground will act as an immovable obstacle for the car. If you hit it hard enough, you can get the car to flip over.

Since the ground plane, really a box in this case, is finite, you can easily run the car off of it. In that case, the car will fall into the void.

If you want to have the camera follow around behind the car, just add the following code to the end of the *on beginSprite* handler. I've left it in the example movie too, but commented out.

```
-- camera follows the car
pMember.camera[1].transform.position = pMember.model("Car").transform.position
+ vector(0,-80,30)
pMember.camera[1].transform.rotation = pMember.model("Car").transform.rotation
+ vector(90,0,0)
pMember.model("Car").addChild(pMember.camera[1])
```

This example only scratches the surface of the Havok physics engine. The documentation from Havok is excellent, and I encourage you to read it to see what else you might find useful.

SPECIAL EFFECTS

There are a variety of special effects that you can apply to a 3D member. Let's take a look at some of them.

Fog

Fog is a camera effect that will obscure models the further they are from the camera. You can set up fog with a variety of properties.

Figure 39.31 shows the same member as seen in Figure 39.27, but the fog is obscuring the pyramid in the distance. The other models are faded from the fog as well.

To turn fog on, you must first set the *fog.enabled* property of the camera to *TRUE*. There are also a variety of other settings. Here is a complete list:

- **enabled**: This turns fog on and off.
- **decayMode**: The *decayMode* can either be #linear, #exponential or #exponential2. The default is #exponential, which means the fog starts immediately and grows exponentially

until the *far* distance. #exponential2 is the same, but the fog grows until the *near* distance. The #linear setting means that the fog grows steadily between the *near* and *far* distances.

- **color**: The color of the fog.

- **far**: The distance where the fog reaches its maximum.

- **near**: The distance where the fog begins.

Figure 39.31
This member is the same as Figure 39.27, but fog obscures some of the models.

The code to get the fog to look like Figure 39.31 is in the example file "39fog.dir". I had to set the *near* and *far* properties very carefully to get the pyramid to be totally hidden while the teapot was still pretty bright.

```
on beginSprite me
  -- reset the member
  sprite(me.spriteNum).member.resetWorld()

  -- get a reference to the camera
  pCamera = sprite(me.spriteNum).camera

  -- turn fog on
  pCamera.fog.enabled = TRUE

  -- recognize but near and far
  pCamera.fog.decayMode = #linear

  -- set near and far just right
  pCamera.fog.near = 200
  pCamera.fog.far = 300
end
```

Engraver and Newsprint Shaders

So far, we have only used the standard shaders. There are actually a few specialty shaders that you can use as well.

The engraver and newsprint shaders will render the model so that they appear as if they have been either carved or printed in a black and white newspaper. To me, they appear to be using a printing style called "halftoning" that is used in newspaper printing.

Figure 39.32 shows the teapot with these effects applied. The one on the left is using the default engraver shader and the one on the right is using the default newsprint shader.

Figure 39.32
The left teapot uses the engraver shader while the right teapot uses the newsprint shader.

Since these are the default shaders, I haven't done anything except create new shaders and apply them to the models.

```
on beginSprite me
  -- reset the member
  sprite(me.spriteNum).member.resetWorld()

  -- Create an engraver shader and apply it
  engraverShader = sprite(me.spriteNum).member.newShader("Engraver
Shader",#engraver)
  sprite(me.spriteNum).member.model[1].shaderList[1] = engraverShader

  -- Create a newsprint shader and apply it
  newsprintShader = sprite(me.spriteNum).member.newShader("Newsprint
Shader",#newsprint)
  sprite(me.spriteNum).member.model[2].shaderList[1] = newsprintShader
end
```

In addition to all of the normal shader properties, these shaders also have additional properties. Engraver shaders have *brightness*, *density*, and *rotation* properties. Newsprint shaders have *brightness* and *density*.

There is also one other type of shader: the painter shader. This is very much like the toon modifier. In fact, the toon modifier is really just a combination of the inker modifier and the painter shader. If you want the surface to have flat colors, then use the painter shader.

Backdrops and Overlays

Until now, all of our 3D worlds have had solid-colored backgrounds. You can change this by making a bitmap graphic the background for the world. This is called a backdrop.

A backdrop is not really a part of the 3D world. It does not rotate around as the camera moves, for instance. It remains as a steady image behind the 3D models.

To add a backdrop, just use the *addBackdrop* command on the current camera. You must first create a texture object, however. You do this in the same way that you would create a texture object to use in a shader. Here are two lines that will add a backdrop:

```
backdropTexture = sprite(me.spriteNum).member.newTexture("my backdrop",
#fromCastMember, member("backdrop"))
sprite(1).camera.addBackdrop(backdropTexture,point(0,0),0)
```

The *addBackdrop* command also wants to have a position and a rotation value. The position is measured from the upper-left corner.

An overlay is just like a backdrop, except that it appears in front of the 3D models in the member. You can have an overlay that is a small graphic floating in front of the 3D world. Or, you could have an overlay that covers the entire member, but uses alpha-channels to reveal a part of the world.

In Figure 39.33, I used an overlay bitmap that I made in Fireworks. Only the border is opaque, I simply left the middle part transparent. You can do the same thing in Photoshop, but not in the Director Paint window.

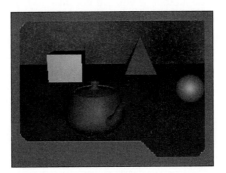

Figure 39.33
This world has been given one backdrop and one overlay.

Here is the behavior used to apply the backdrop and the overlay in Figure 39.33. You can see the movie itself as example "39backdrop.dir".

```
on beginSprite me
   sprite(me.spriteNum).member.resetWorld()

   -- create backdrop texture from bitmap
   backdropTexture = sprite(me.spriteNum).member.newTexture("my backdrop",
#fromCastMember, member("backdrop"))

   -- add backdrop to world
   sprite(1).camera.addBackdrop(backdropTexture,point(0,0),0)

   -- create overlay texture from bitmap
```

```
  overlayTexture = sprite(me.spriteNum).member.newTexture("my overlay",
#fromCastMember, member("overlay"))

  -- add overlay to world
  sprite(1).camera.addOverlay(overlayTexture,point(0,0),0)
end
```

Note that commands are prefixed with the word "add". This is because you are not setting the backdrop and overlay, but adding one. You can add more than one backdrop or overlay. For instance, you may want to use the starfield bitmap as the first backdrop, and then have a smaller graphic of a planet as a second backdrop. You may want to add a title graphic as a second overlay to appear in the enlarged area of the border to the lower left.

Movement Effects

There are several ways you can easily move and orient objects around in 3D worlds. One way is to use the *pointAt* function to orient an object so it is pointed directly at another object.

The first step in using *pointAt* is to use *pointAtOrientation* to tell Director what the "up" direction is, according to the object, and what the forward direction is. If you are into 3D math, you can easily calculate these vectors. If you are not into 3D math, you can use trial and error to get these vectors soon enough.

Once you set the *pointAtOrientation*, you can use *pointAt* to spin the object around to point at a vector location, such as the location of another object.

The movie "39pointat.dir" does just this. If you run the movie and click on one of the three shapes, the teapot will re-orient itself to point at it. Here is the behavior from that movie.

```
property pTeapot
on beginSprite me
  sprite(1).member.resetWorld()

  -- get model references
  pTeapot = sprite(me.spriteNum).member.model("teapot")

  -- set forward direction of teapot
  pTeapot.pointAtOrientation = [vector(1,0,0), vector(0,0,-1)]
end

on mouseUp me
  -- get the click location
  loc = the mouseLoc -
point(sprite(me.spriteNum).rect.left,sprite(me.spriteNum).rect.top)

  -- determine which model is there
  model = sprite(1).camera.modelUnderLoc(loc)
```

```
     -- if a model was there
   if not voidP(model) then

      -- if it is one of these three models
      if getOne(["Box","Sphere","Pyramid"],model.name) then

         -- point teapot at it
         pTeapot.pointAt(model.transform.position,vector(0,0,-1))

      end if
   end if
end
```

The *pointAtOrientation* is set so the forward vector is directly along the x-axis and the up vector is back along the z-axis. This will be different depending on how you created your world. In the case of this example, 3DS Max likes to use the z-axis for up and down, and the teapot happened to have a spout pointed along the x-axis.

I needed to restate the up vector as the second parameter to the *pointAt* command. If the teapot was not oriented so that its "up" was the same as the world's "up" then I may have had to use different up vectors for the *pointAtOrientation* property and the *pointAt* command.

You can also use the *pointAt* command and *pointAtOrientation* for lights and cameras. Using them with cameras is particularly useful as you can have a camera point directly at an object of interest.

Camera Projection

One of the major things that 3D scenes do differently from 2D scenes is to bring depth into the picture. Objects that are farther away are behind other objects that are closer. Also, objects that are farther away appear smaller.

However, sometimes it is useful to not have objects that are farther away look smaller. Many games use a technique called orthographic projection. This means that the screen dimensions of objects do not change as they get further from the camera. This allows artwork to be kept the same size through the world. You see this in strategy games like Age of Empires and SimCity.

To switch Director's 3D engine to use orthographic projection, just change the *projection* property of the current camera.

```
sprite(1).camera.projection = #orthographic
```

If you want to switch back to use the normal perspective mode, set this property to *#perspective*.

Figure 39.34 shows the same world that was in Figure 39.5, but this time the camera is switched to orthographic projection.

Figure 39.34
The room is rendered using orthographic camera projection.

Figure 39.34
The room is rendered using orthographic camera projection.

If you use perspective projection with your camera, you can adjust the *projectionAngle* of the camera to fit more into the screen rectangle. The default value is 30 degrees. If you want to see more of the scene, increase the number. However, the further you get from 30 degrees, the more distorted the models will look.

Figure 39.35 shows the same scene but with perspective projection with a *projectionAngle* set to 60 degrees.

Figure 39.35
The room is rendered using perspective camera projection with a
projection angle of 60 degrees.

If you are using orthographic projection, then the equivalent to *projectionAngle* is *orthoHeight*. This is the number of world units that fit the vertical length of the 3D sprite.

CREATING COMPLEX SCENES

All of Chapter 38, "Using 3D Media," and the start of this chapter assumed that you had some way to build 3D worlds using external 3D graphics programs. However, these programs are expensive and tend to have steep learning curves, especially if you have never used one before.

Fortunately, you don't need to have a 3D graphics tool to use Director's 3D engine. We have already seen how you can create primitives and particle effects with Lingo. Now, let's try to use those commands to create an entire scene from scratch.

With Lingo and a blank 3D member, you can do a lot. Figure 39.36 shows the complete scene that we will create. There is an uneven ground, a volcano complete with spewing ash, a distant planet and a fireball trailing dust. The fireball is moving and when it hits the ground, it even causes an explosion.

Figure 39.36
This scene can be created with Lingo.

Each object in this world will be created in its own handler. The *on beginSprite* handler will call each of these custom handlers to create the entire world.

To make the lines of code a bit shorter, I've stored a reference to the sprite in "pSprite" and a reference to the member in "pMember". I've also create properties to store the references to each object, like "pFireball".

```
property pSprite, pMember
property pPlanet, pGround, pVolcano, pFireball
property pViewType

on beginSprite me

  -- choose view type
  pViewType = #normal -- still camera
  --pViewType = #fireball -- follow fireball down
  --pViewType = #orbit -- swing camera around

  -- get easy reference variables
  pSprite = sprite(me.spriteNum)
  pMember = pSprite.member

  -- reset world
  pMember.resetWorld()

  -- make the elements of the world
  makeGround(me)
  makeVolcano(me)
  makeSmoke(me)
  makePlanet(me)
  makeFireball(me)
  makeBackdrop(me)
  makeFireballCamera(me)
```

```
-- register for fireball impact
  pMember.registerForEvent(#collideAny,#collisionHandler,me)
end
```

The last line of the *on beginSprite* handler will make sure that collisions get passed to the "on collisionHandler" handler that we'll define later on. We'll be adding the collision modifier to the ground and the fireball so that we know when these two items collide.

The first custom handler will make the ground plane. It starts with a plane resource, but then uses the mesh deform modifier to break it into adjustable polygons. The plane is then rotated to be oriented like a ground plane. The position is set back a bit, and further down.

To make the ground uneven, all of the points in the ground's mesh are given random z values. This makes some ground points higher than others.

The handler then creates a texture from the bitmap member "ground". This texture is applied to a new shader. This shader is then applied to the ground model.

The collision modifier is then added. The *mode* is set to #mesh to make it the most accurate.

```
on makeGround me
  -- create the model resource
  groundResource = pMember.newModelResource("My Plane Resource",#plane)

  -- make it big enough to be seen
  groundResource.width = 1000
  groundResource.length = 1000

  -- make the mesh out of 10 by 10 vertices
  groundResource.widthVertices = 15
  groundResource.lengthVertices = 15

  -- create the model
  pGround = pMember.newModel("My Plane",groundResource)

  -- rotate it and reposition it to see it better
  pGround.rotate(90,0,0)
  pGround.transform.position = vector(0,-50,-250)

  -- add the mesh deform modifier
  pGround.addModifier(#meshDeform)

  -- loop through all of the vertices
  repeat with i = 1 to pMember.model("My
Plane").meshDeform.mesh[1].vertexList.count
    -- lower vertice by a random amount
    v = pGround.meshDeform.mesh[1].vertexList[i]
    v.z = random(30)
```

```
    pGround.meshDeform.mesh[1].vertexList[i] = v
  end repeat

  -- create ground texture and shader
  groundtexture = pMember.newTexture("Ground
Texture",#fromCastmember,member("Ground"))
  groundShader = pMember.newShader("Ground Shader",#standard)
  groundShader.texture = groundtexture
  pGround.shaderList[1] = groundShader

  -- add collision modifier
  pGround.addModifier(#collision)
  pGround.collision.mode = #mesh
end
```

The volcano is actually a cylinder with a narrower top than bottom. Once it is created and placed, the same shader used for the ground is applied to this model as well.

```
on makeVolcano me
  -- create the model resource
  volcanoResource = pMember.newModelResource("Volcano Resource",#cylinder)
  volcanoResource.topRadius = 5

  -- create the model
  pVolcano = pMember.newModel("Volcano",volcanoResource)

  -- place the model
  pVolcano.transform.position = vector(-70,-50,0)

  -- set the ground shader
  pVolcano.shaderList[1] = pMember.shader("Ground Shader")
end
```

The ash coming from the top of the volcano is a particle system. The settings were achieved by trial and error to get the system to look just right. Some wind will blow the particles away. The particle system originates from the inside of the volcano.

```
on makeSmoke me
  -- create the resource
  smokeResource = pMember.newModelResource("Smoke Resource",#particle)
  smokeResource.emitter.angle = 10
  smokeResource.emitter.direction = vector(0,1,0)
  smokeResource.emitter.maxSpeed = 150
  smokeResource.emitter.minSpeed = 75
  smokeResource.drag = 5
  smokeResource.wind = vector(5,0,0)
```

```
  smokeResource.lifetime = 10000
  smokeResource.blendRange.start = 100
  smokeResource.blendRange.end = 0

  -- make the model
  pSmoke = pMember.newModel("Smoke",smokeResource)

  -- place the model
  pSmoke.transform.position = vector(-70,-50,0)
end
```

The planet appears to be a small sphere, but it is actually quite huge. It has been placed very far away. This will make the scene more realistic when we move the camera around.

The planet uses a new texture and shader that comes from a bitmap that is a flattened picture of Jupiter.

```
on makePlanet me
  -- make the resource
  planetResource = pMember.newModelResource("Planet Resource",#sphere)

  -- a very large sphere
  planetResource.radius = 30000

  -- make the model
  pPlanet = pMember.newModel("Planet",planetResource)

  -- place it a long way away
  pPlanet.transform.position = vector(0,100000,-500000)

  -- create the planet texture and shader
  planetShader = pMember.newShader("Planet Shader",#standard)
  planetTexture = pMember.newTexture("Planet
Texture",#fromCastmember,member("Jupiter"))
  planetShader.texture = planetTexture
  pPlanet.shaderList[1] = planetShader
end
```

The fireball is actually two models. The first is a small sphere. This sphere is oriented so that moving it forward along its z axis will move the sphere diagonally down toward the ground. It is positioned off the screen so that it comes into the scene later on.

The other part of the fireball is a particle system that is oriented so that the particles shoot out away from the fireball as it descends. The particle system model is made a child of the sphere so that it moves with the sphere.

The fireball model gets a collision modifier too. Since the tail is a part of the fireball, we want to use the #mesh *mode* for accuracy as the default #sphere *mode* will mean too big of a collision area when the particles are included.

```
on makeFireball me
  -- create a small sphere
  fireballResource = pMember.newModelResource("Fireball Resource",#sphere)
  fireballResource.radius = 3
  pFireball = pMember.newModel("Fireball",fireballResource)

  -- place it and rotate it pointed to where it is going
  pFireball.transform.position = vector(150,150,0)
  pFireball.transform.rotation = vector(0,90,45)

  -- use the ground shader
  pFireball.shaderList[1] = pMember.shader("Ground Shader")


  -- create a particle system for the tail
  fireballParticleResource = pMember.newModelResource("Fireball Particle
Resource",#particle)
  fireballParticleResource.emitter.angle = 20
  fireballParticleResource.emitter.direction = vector(1,0,0)
  fireballParticleResource.emitter.maxSpeed = 150
  fireballParticleResource.emitter.minSpeed = 75
  fireballParticleResource.lifetime = 1000
  fireballParticleResource.blendRange.start = 100
  fireballParticleResource.blendRange.end = 0
  fireballParticles = pMember.newModel("Fireball
Particles",fireballParticleResource)

  -- place the particle system with the fireball and aim it pointing out the
back
  fireballParticles.transform.position = pFireball.transform.position
  fireballParticles.transform.rotation = vector(0,0,45)

  -- add collision modifier
  pFireball.addModifier(#collision)
  pFireball.collision.mode = #mesh

  -- group the tail with the fireball
  pFireball.addChild(fireballParticles)
end
```

The backdrop is simply a bitmap of stars that adds some realism to the scene. It is added to the main camera for the scene.

```
on makeBackdrop me
  -- create the backdrop texture
  backdroptexture =
pMember.newTexture("Backdrop",#fromCastmember,member("Backdrop"))

  -- add the backdrop
  pSprite.camera.addBackdrop(backdropTexture,point(0,0),0)
end
```

When the fireball collides with the ground, we'll want to have an explosion. This next handler will create a particle system with a *type* #burst and place it at the location passed into the handler.

```
on makeExplosion me, loc
  -- create a burst particle resource
  explosionResource = pMember.newModelResource("Explosion Particle
Resource",#particle)
  explosionResource.emitter.maxSpeed = 150
  explosionResource.emitter.minSpeed = 75
  explosionResource.emitter.mode = #burst
  explosionResource.emitter.loop = FALSE
  explosionResource.emitter.numParticles = 5000
  explosionResource.lifetime = 1000
  explosionResource.blendRange.start = 100
  explosionResource.blendRange.end = 0

  -- make the model and place it
  explosion = pMember.newModel("Explosion Particles",explosionResource)
  explosion.transform.position = loc
end
```

If you change the "pViewType" to #fireball, then a new camera is created. This camera is set to a point just above and behind the fireball. It is also grouped with the fireball. Then, the sprite's main camera is changed to this new camera. This way, the view will be from this "fireball cam" as the fireball descends.

```
on makeFireballCamera me
  if pViewType = #fireball then
    -- create a new camera
    pMember.newCamera("Fireball Cam")

    -- place the new camera on top of the fireball
    pMember.camera("Fireball Cam").transform.position =
pFireball.transform.position + vector(20,30,0)
```

```
pMember.camera("Fireball Cam").transform.rotation =
pFireball.transform.rotation

    -- group the camera with the fireball
    pMember.model("FireBall").addChild(pMember.camera("Fireball Cam"))

    -- change the sprite's camera to this one
    sprite(me.spriteNum).camera = sprite(me.spriteNum).member.camera("Fireball
Cam")
  end if
end
```

As the movie plays, the fireball will need to descend a little bit every frame.

```
on moveFireball me
  -- move the fireball one step
  if not voidP(pFireball) then
    pFireball.translate(0,0,-1)
  end if
end
```

If the "pViewType" is set to #orbit, then the camera will orbit around the center of the scene. To do this, use the *transform.rotate* function. If you were to simply use the *rotate* function, then the camera would spin around its own axis. However, by using *transform.rotate*, the camera spins around the center of the world, always pointing as the same location. This creates a nice visual fly-around effect as the scene unfolds. It also brings out the fact that this is a 3D scene, not a 2D scene that is just faking it.

```
on orbitCamera me
  -- move the camera one degree
  if pViewType = #orbit then
    sprite(1).camera.transform.rotate(0,1,0)
  end if
end
```

The *on exitFrame* handler will call "on moveFireball" and "on orbitCamera" every frame.

```
on exitFrame me
  -- move fireball
  moveFireball(me)

  -- move camera
  orbitCamera(me)
end
```

When the fireball hits the ground, the "on collisionHandler" will be called. Since this is the only collision that will take place in this scene, we don't need to examine *modelA* and *modelB* of the "data" parameter to find out which two objects collided. Instead, we can just handle the collision.

The first thing that happens, is the camera is restored to the default view if "pViewType" is set to #fireball. This is needed because if the camera is riding the fireball down, then the camera will cease to exist when we get rid of the fireball. Also, the viewpoint just above the fireball is a lousy place to witness the collision.

The fireball is then removed from the world. This also gets rid of its children, in this case the fireball's particle system tail. The "pFireball" property is set to *VOID* so that the "on moveFireball" handler ceases to worry about the fireball.

Then, the "on makeExplosion" handler is called to display the explosion particle system.

```
on collisionHandler me, data

  if pViewType = #fireball then
    -- return to default camera view
    sprite(me.spriteNum).camera = sprite(1).member.camera("DefaultView")
  end if

  -- remove fireball
  pFireball.removeFromWorld()

  -- don't need fireball again
  pFireball = VOID

  -- particle system explosion
  makeExplosion(me,data.pointOfContact)
end
```

Try the example movie "39scene.dir" to see this behavior in action. Try changing the beginning of the behavior to use one of the different "pViewType" values.

I strongly encourage you to tinker with this scene even further. Try different textures. Try having ground that is more or less uneven. Try a volcano that spews more or less, or maybe several volcanoes that spew different colors. Perhaps the collision of the fireball should form a new volcano? The best way to get good at creating 3D scenes with Lingo is to practice.

TROUBLESHOOTING 3D LINGO

- Remember that when you use the Message window to change a 3D world, you often need to use *updateStage* to see the change take effect on the screen.

- The result of the *translate* and *rotate* commands depends on whether you are applying these commands directly on the model, or if it is on the model's *transform* property.

- Different 3D graphics programs produce different default settings in the Shockwave 3D file. For instance, sometimes the z-axis is vertical and other times the y-axis is vertical.

- When using the Havok physics engine, always remember to use realistic values. If you have a huge object that has a mass of 1 and a small object that has a mass of 1,000, then you can only expect unusual results.

- Either the Director 8.5 documentation is wrong, or there is a bug: You must use the *drag* property of a particle system to make *wind* have any effect at all.

- Particle systems are cool, but they are also expensive. If you add a few particle systems to your world, you will find that your movie runs very slowly on slower machines. Try particle systems that have very few particles and a short *lifetime* to speed things up.

- Always remember to use a *resetWorld* command at the start of your movie or behavior. Otherwise, conditions in the world will persist from play to play and you may end up with different results for that if you started the movie fresh. Also, you will get errors when you try to create models and model resources that are already in place from the previous play.

- Sometimes rendering with software mode can produce significantly different results from using DirectX or OpenGL. If you are forced to author in software mode, make sure you test often on a machine with DirectX or OpenGL. Alternatively, if you are using a machine with DirectX or OpenGL, switch to software mode every once and a while to test.

- In my tests, the wireframe and point shaders do not work in software mode.

- Bones player animations are extremely difficult to get working. At the time of this writing, only 3D Studio Max version 3.2 can be used to create them, and Character Studio is needed to make the work tolerable. I have seen a few examples of bones player animation working, but have yet to get it working myself.

- Remember that speed is always an issue. When you use 3D Lingo, be sure to test often on a basic computer that has your minimum requirements for playing the finished product.

DID YOU KNOW?

- You can apply a texture to the particles in a particle system resource.

- You can create a primitive model called a #mesh that will allow you to define each and every polygon in the model. This is the most versatile part of 3D Lingo, but it is also steeped in advanced 3D math concepts.

- The *extrude3d* function can be used to take a font member and some text and convert it to a model resource of that text. This is the basic function used by 3D text members. However, by using *extrude3D*, you can also insert 3D text into your 3D world.

- You can also use *extrude3D* to convert a vector shape into a 3D model resource. Just replace the *vertexList* of the model resource created by *extrude3D* with the *vertexList* of your vector shape member. This is an undocumented feature, but you can get it to work with some experimentation.

- The undocumented *fileSaveMode* property of a 3D member let's you save the changes made in a 3D member by Lingo. Look it up in the Lingo Reference appendix.

- You can get the *boundingSphere* property of a model or a group. This returns a list with the location of the center of the model or group and the radius of the sphere. You can roll your own collision detection this way, or use this information for other purposes.

- Set the *debug* property of a model to *TRUE* to get a wireframe bounding sphere drawn around a model, plus three colored lines to show the axes of the model. This really helps to understand what a model is doing while you are tinkering with it with Lingo.

APPENDIXES

XI

A

WHAT'S ON THE CD-ROM

This CD-ROM is packed with material to increase your productivity when using Macromedia Director 8.

USING THE CD-ROM GRAPHICAL INTERFACE

The enclosed CD-ROM has been designed to work on both Macintosh and PC computers. Once running, the interface is straightforward in guiding you to the content that you are seeking. Click the options on the left side of the window to navigate the various content contained on the CD-ROM.

To Install on a Windows-Based PC

With Auto-Run enabled, you can simply insert the CD-ROM and the interface will start up automatically.

If you do not have Autorun enabled, you will need to execute the START.EXE file from the root directory of your CD-ROM drive.

To Install on a Macintosh Computer

On a Macintosh computer, you should see the CD-ROM icon on your desktop upon inserting it into your machine. Double-click that icon to view the contents of the root directory. Within this directory is an executable called START. Double-click this program to run the interface.

AUTHOR FILES

Included on this CD-ROM are all the author files used throughout the book. All together there are more than 160 development files included in the \SOURCE directory on this disc. The files are all separated by chapter to help you quickly find what you are looking for. (*NOTE: If you do not already have Macromedia Director 8 on your system, you can view all the author material by using the Trial edition provided on the CD-ROM.*)

Also included are two full projects completely unprotected which you can open and examine closely. These project files can be found in the \BONUS directory on the CD-ROM. The first bonus project is The Lingo Infinite Possibility Machine. This program will demonstrate many Lingo techniques that you can learn from and apply to your own projects. The second bonus project is The Planetary Detective. This is another program that you can open up and view how it was created.

DIRECTOR XTRAS

One of the important capabilities that Director 8 has as an authoring environment is the capability to be modified to adapt to the developer's needs. This capability is utilized by installing Xtras. The author has provided four free Xtras located in the \Xtras directory on the CD-ROM.

Included on the CD-ROM is a huge collection of Xtras from various third-party developers including DirectXtras, MagicModules, Penworks, updateStage, RavWare, Tabuleiro, Ballard, CatEffects, DirectMedia Lab, Penworks, and more! By installing these various Xtras, you can extend the functionality of Director, giving you the ability to enhance your projects.

For updated versions of these Xtras you can check the author's Web site at `http://www.clevermedia.com/resources/`.

THIRD-PARTY SOFTWARE

Once again, our media development team has worked with the author to determine what third-party software would provide you with the most significant value as a Director developer.

- *Macromedia's Director 8.5 30-Day Trial edition.* Director is the industry standard in creating dynamic multimedia presentations and applications. In its latest version, Macromedia has combined synergy with the Internet to its already powerful software to create the ultimate development tool!

- *Viscosity 1.5 Trial Edition by Sonic Foundry.* Viscosity is an affordable Windows-based software package that creates and edits bitmap-based graphics, animations, and digitized video frames. This complete set of image-editing tools is essential for perfecting animation and video sequences for the Web, multimedia CD-ROMs, and video games.

- *Adobe's PhotoShop 6 Tryout Version.* Adobe's latest version of its excellent image editor. Use advanced design features such as layers and various effects to create high-quality graphics for use in projects and applications.

- *Aladdin FlashBack 1.130 Trial Edition.* Aladdin Flashback provides unlimited Undos for any application with instant access to all previous versions of a document. With FlashBack, users can create, compose, edit, and save documents in any application without fear of losing their work.

- *FastSplash 1.0.6.3 by Britton Smith.* What FastSplash does is display a bitmap splash screen and launches your application. You can have FastSplash check the Registry to see whether your application has been installed and run your installer program, if needed. Either way, FlashSplash will automatically quit.

- *Moho 2.7 Limited Demonstration.* Lost Marble's Moho is a 2D vector-based cartoon animation application. Moho provides the complete set of tools you need to create an animation, from drawing and painting to keyframe animation, and multilayer compositing and final output of QuickTime, AVI, and Flash movie files.

There are MANY additional programs included in the "/Software Library" directory on the CD-ROM. *(NOTE: Where available, Macintosh versions have been supplied. However, some of the software might be available only for the Windows platform).*

GRAPHIC ACCESSORIES

We have also included Ari Feldman's SpriteLib v1.01. SpriteLib is a free collection of more than 700 professional-quality, animated images that are ready to be plugged into your game and multimedia creations. Supporting more than a dozen different themes and styles, you'll find SpriteLib an indispensable resource for your game projects.

NOTE: To utilize the included SpriteLib, you'll need to register at `www.arifeldman.com/free/register.html`. *This is a free process.*

DIRECTOR GLOSSARY

Action: A script in Macromedia Flash.

ActionScript: The programming language of Macromedia Flash.

ActiveX: ActiveX controls are files that extend the operating system or a program, such as Internet Explorer. Shockwave is available as an ActiveX control for Microsoft Internet Explorer for Windows. The ActiveX Xtra enables Projectors to use other controls.

AIFF: Audio Interchange File Format. The most common sound format used on Macintosh computers. It is also used in the digital music recording industry. You will see these files on both Mac and Windows machines, usually represented with an .aif extension.

Alpha Channel: An extra channel of information in an image file. (The other channels are usually red, green, and blue color amounts.) This channel determines how transparent each pixel is.

Ambient Light: A light in a 3D world that doesn't come from a specific spot, but instead illuminates all objects in the world equally from all sides. *See also* Light.

Anchor: A tag in an HTML page that can be used to allow a link to go directly to that line on the HTML page, rather than starting at the top and requiring that users search for it.

Animated GIF: A file using Graphic Image Format that contains more than one frame of animation.

Anti-Aliasing: A technique that takes the edges of a text graphic and blends them with the background colors to make a smooth edge.

ASCII: American Standard Code for Information Interchange. The number system that corresponds to the 255 characters. In Director, it is used in the *charToNum* and *numToChar* functions.

Author: *See* Multimedia Author.

AVI: *See* Video For Windows.

Axis: An imaginary line through the center of a 3D world. You can rotate a model or the world around an axis, or move it along an axis. The X-axis is a line usually going from left to right, representing the horizontal; the Y-axis is a line usually going up and down, representing vertical; and the Z-axis is a line going straight into the screen, representing depth.

Backdrop: A 2D image that appears as a static background in a 3D scene.

BASIC: Beginners All-Purpose Symbolic Instruction Code. A simple programming language popular in the '70s and '80s that was a good first language for new programmers.

Behavior: A script member that controls a sprite or a frame. You can have only one behavior attached to a frame, but multiple behaviors can be attached to a sprite. You can create one with the Behavior Inspector or by writing raw Lingo, or use one from the Library palette.

Bézier: A curved line that is generated with a mathematical formula based on a series of points.

Bevel: When a 3D shape or text is extruded with a round or angled edge.

Bit Depth: The number of bits used to represent a single unit in a file. In an 8-bit image, for instance, each pixel is represented by 8 bits of information. In a 16-bit sound, each sound sample is represented by 16 bits of information. Higher bit depth usually means higher quality, but may be slower to view and download because of a larger file size.

Bitmap: An image cast member. You can edit most bitmaps in Director by using the Paint window.

Blend: A sprite property also used in image Lingo. It determines the amount that each pixel should blend with the pixels behind it. A blend of 100 makes the pixels in a bitmap opaque, whereas a blend of 0 makes it invisible. A blend of 50, for instance, would mean that the screen would show the user 50% of the color in the bitmap and 50% of the color behind the bitmap.

BlendLevel: The same as blend, except that the scale goes from 0 to 255 rather than 0 to 100.

BMP: Windows format for plain bitmap files.

Boolean: Math involving only two states: true and false. Used in programming to determine branching, as in *if* statements.

Bones: Lines running throughout a 3D model that define which parts of the model link to which other parts. With bones, parts of a model can be manipulated without it breaking apart. You can use bones to animate movements such as walking.

Braces: The term sometimes used to define { } characters, also called "curly brackets."

Buttons: This can refer to the quick, simple buttons made in Director with the Tool palette. It is also a term used to describe any bitmap or other member that is assigned a script that reacts to a mouse click.

C/C++: A general programming language used to create operating systems, applications, and even Macromedia Director. C++ is the object-oriented version of the language and is used most often today.

Cache: When a browser loads a document or a media element, it places it in a folder called the cache. When users want that document again sometime very soon, they can get it from the cache rather than load it again from the Internet. This is much faster. The same principle is applied to computer memory contents when you are using virtual memory on your machine.

Callback: When an Xtra or other process is called and left running, it will sometimes communicate back with the movie by calling a handler, called a callback handler.

Camera: A point through which a 3D world is viewed. A camera has a location and a direction, as well as some other properties. A 3D world can have one or more cameras and the view of that 3D world can switch between them.

Cast: The list of cast members used in a movie. All movies have at least one internal Cast, but movies can have many other internal Casts and external Casts. An external Cast is its own file, usually with a .cst extension.

cct: The file extension for a Director external cast library that has been compressed for use on the Internet. These cannot be reopened in Director.

Cell: Sometimes used to refer to the intersection of a frame and a sprite channel.

CGI: Common Gateway Interface. Scripts that run on servers to handle communication between the users and the server. CGI scripts are used to receive information in HTML forms, such as requests for more information or online transactions. CGI also stands for Computer Generated Image, as in the special effects used in modern films.

Channel: A numbered position in the Score. The Score has channels 1 through 1,000, as well as a few special channels at the top of the Score. Which channel a sprite is in determines whether it gets drawn on top of or under another sprite.

Check Box: A button that has an on or off state. The state of the button is usually reflected by a check mark or X that is visible only when the button state is on.

Child: An instance of a parent script, stored in a variable or list. Created with the *new* command.

Chunk: A piece of a string, such as a character or series of characters; a word or series of words; or a line or series of lines.

Client: In the realm of multiuser communication, a client is a computer that communicates only with the server and not directly with other computers. *See also* Server.

Clip Art: A set of graphics, usually created by a third-party company, which are used in print and multimedia.

Codec: A piece of hardware or a software algorithm that converts sound or video to digital code and then back again. You compress audio and video files with codecs.

Color Cycling: This describes when the Stage is using an 8-bit palette to define its colors, and then the palette is shifted to redefine those colors. The color in each pixel then adjusts to fit the new palette, thus shifting all the colors on the screen. The term also describes the simpler process of taking a graphic and shifting its colors through a rainbow.

Color Depth: The amount of information stored per pixel in an image or on the screen. With 8-bit color depth, for example, 8 bits (256 possible values) are stored per pixel.

Compression: When a file is changed in such a way that the information can be stored in less space. Compressed files may have to be decompressed before they can be used. Director compresses bitmaps, text, and sounds when a movie is made into a Shockwave movie.

CSS: Cascading Style Sheets. *See also* Style Sheets.

cst: The file extension for a Director external cast library. These external cast libraries can also be used as files in the Lib director to add more elements to your Director Library palette.

Cue Point: A marker in a sound or digital video file. These markers can be read and reacted to with Lingo.

cxt: The file extension for a Director external cast library that has not been compressed but has been protected from being re-opened in Director.

Dancing Baloney: A slang term used to describe a purely cosmetic element in a multimedia presentation or Web page.

Database: A collection of organized information that can be accessed and altered. Examples are a collection of names and addresses, or a description of levels in a game.

dcr: The file extension for a Director movie that has been compressed for use on the Internet. These files can be used on Web pages, by Projectors, or even as Xtras, but cannot be reopened in Director.

Depth: The third dimension in computer graphics. The horizontal and vertical dimensions correspond to the horizontal and vertical of your screen, but depth is the illusion of graphics being closer or farther from the camera.

DHTML: Dynamic Hypertext Markup Language. Using JavaScript and Style Sheets to create complex Web pages, often with interactivity. *See also* Style Sheets.

Diffuse: Light that is spread evenly over an area.

Digital Video: An external file that is linked to the Director movie. It can display video or a time-based animation, such as a 3D rendering. Video members can come in a variety of formats but are usually in Apple QuickTime format or Windows AVI format. The definition can be extended to hold a variety of QuickTime formats, such as QuickTime VR and MIDI files. *See also* DV.

dir: The file extension for a Director movie.

DirectX: A set of extensions to the Microsoft Windows operating system that improves the graphics and sound capabilities of PCs. Parts are called DirectSound, Direct3D, and DirectDraw.

Dithering: The process whereby pixels in an image are colored with available colors to simulate a color that is not available. For instance, two pixels next to each other might be colored two shades of red to produce the visual effect of the shade of red exactly between the two colors.

Dolly: A camera movement that takes the camera closer or farther from its original position.

DOS: Short for Disk Operating System. The underlying code that enables PCs to access files.

Down State: A graphic used to portray a screen button when it is in the process of being pushed by users.

Dreamweaver: A popular HTML authoring package from Macromedia that specializes in adding interactivity to Web pages.

DV: Digital Video. Also used to describe the standard digital video format used by camcorders and FireWire devices.

dxr: The file extension for a protected Director movie. These are not compressed, but are still protected against being reopened in Director.

Easter Egg: A hidden function in a piece of software. A common example would be a hidden button that reveals the names of the software engineers that built the product.

Engraver: A 3D shader that gives the model the appearance of an engraved metal surface.

Event: Something that affects the computer or Director environment. Examples are a mouse click, a frame advance, a key press, or a window movement. Messages are sent to parts of the Director environment when an event occurs. Handlers can be written to respond to these messages.

Extrude: To take a 2D shape, like a circle, square, or even text, and expand it into a 3D model.

Fields: The original text member from before Director 5. It still has a few properties that text members do not, such as borders and drop shadows.

Film Loop: A cast member that contains a complete animation. Any Score selection can be copied and pasted into the Cast as a film loop and used as a single cast member.

Filters: Defines plug-ins to imaging programs, such as PhotoShop. Some PhotoShop-compatible filters can be used as Xtras in Director to extend the functionality of the Paint window.

FireWire: A high-speed connection method for digital video and high-speed hard drives. Common on newer Macintosh computers. Also available on PCs, but it is called IEEE 1394.

Fireworks: A popular image-editing tool from Macromedia that specializes in creating graphics for the Web. It's also an excellent tool to use to create graphics for Director.

fla: The file extension for a Flash movie file. *See also* swf.

Flash: A program and the files it creates. Flash is another Macromedia tool that enables you to create mostly vector-based animation for the Web. Flash files can be imported and used as Director members.

Float: A floating point number. This is a number that contains a fractional component. For instance, 4 is an integer, but 4.5 is a float. Also, 4.0 is a float because it has a defined fractional component, even though that component is 0.

Fog: A 3D effect that obscures models farther away from the camera just like natural fog would.

Font: The description of how a set of characters appears on the screen. In Director, fonts can be imported so that they can be used in the movie even if the font does not exist on the user's computer.

FPS: Frames Per Second, such as in the tempo of movement through a Director movie.

Frame: An instant of time in Director. Also, a column in the Score. While you are working on a movie, the Stage shows a single frame. While the movie is animating, the Stage moves through frames to create the visual effect of animation.

Frame Script: A script that controls a frame. It appears in the script channel. Only one script can be attached to a frame. In the Cast, frame scripts are shown as behaviors.

FTP: File Transfer Protocol. This is the technology used to send raw files over the Internet. It is commonly used by developers to send files back and forth when they are too large to comfortably send via email.

GIF: Graphics Interchange Format. This is an image format that stores 8-bit images with a custom palette.

Global Variable: A variable that can be accessed by any script in Director, as long as it is declared in a global command in that script.

GUI: Graphical User Interface. Pronounced "Goo-ee."

Handle: One or two points applied to a vertex point used to define the curvature of the lines in a vector shape.

Handler: A Lingo function or procedure. Sometimes incorrectly referred to as a "script," which is actually a collection of handlers.

Home Page: The main index page of a Web site. Also used to describe a personal Web site created by an individual.

Hot Spot: An active part of a user interface. An area of the screen on which users can click is a hot spot.

HTML: Hypertext Markup Language. The language used to compose Web pages. It consists of plain text with special tags that are interpreted by Web browsers and other programs. The tags style and position the text, and add elements such as links, images, and other media.

HTTP: Hypertext Transport Protocol. This is the technology used to access Web pages over the Internet.

Hyperlink: A piece of text that, when clicked, takes users to another page, frame, or piece of information.

Icon: A small graphical element that helps define a file, action, tool, or other part of a computer's interface.

IDE: Integrated Drive Electronics. A common method for connecting hard disk drives inside computers. Also known as ATA.

IEEE 1394: *See* FireWire.

IMAP: Internet Messaging Access Protocol. An up-and-coming method for receiving email over the Internet. It's a little more sophisticated than POP3. *See also* POP *and* SMTP.

Ink: The rules by which a sprite is drawn on the Stage. Copy ink places the sprite on the Stage as an opaque rectangle. Background Transparent ink treats white pixels as transparent. You can also choose from dozens of other inks.

Inspectors: Small, palette-like Windows in Director that enable you to see and change information about selected items. An example is the Property Inspector. (Others include the Text and Behavior.)

Integer: A number that has no fractional component. A 4 is an integer, but a 4.5 or a 4.0 are floats. *See also* Float.

Java Applets: Small programs created in Java that are usually presented on Web pages. Director has the capability to save movies as Java applets through the Save As Java command in the File menu.

JavaScript: The scripting language built in to the Netscape Navigator browser that enables Web authors to create interactive content. *See also* JScript *and* DHTML.

JPEG: The Joint Photographic Experts Group format for images. It takes 32-bit images and compresses them a variable amount, depending on the decisions you make concerning file size versus quality.

JScript: The version of JavaScript included in the Microsoft Internet Explorer browser. Very similar to JavaScript, but not completely compatible. *See also* JavaScript and DHTML.

Kerning: Modifications made to the spacing of characters in a text member.

Keyframe: A frame in a sprite that denotes a specific position and other properties of the frame that the Stage must show exactly when that frame is reached. Between keyframes, the position and state of a sprite is tweened. *See also* Tweening.

Kiosk: A single computer set up in a public place running a multimedia program.

Label: A label is a name given to a frame in the Score. Frames in the Score can be labeled and referred to by that label. Also called *markers*. *See also* Marker.

LAN: Local Area Network. What you would call the network in your office.

Level of Detail: Refers to the number of polygons used to render a model. The more polygons used, the higher the level of detail.

Light: An object in a 3D world that creates light. The light will bounce off of objects to make them viewable. 3D worlds can have one or many lights. *See also* Ambient Light.

Lingo: The programming language of Director.

Link: *See* Hyperlink.

Loading Movie: The term used to describe a small movie that loads before a Shockwave movie. A loading movie loads quickly, and then entertains or distracts users while the larger movie downloads in the background. When the larger movie is done downloading, it replaces the loading movie.

Local Variable: A variable available only inside the handler. When the handler is done, the variable ceases to exist, although variables with exactly the same name can be used in other handlers.

Mac OS: The operating system used by Macintosh computers. The most recent version is 9.0, as of this writing, but 10.0, otherwise known as Mac OSX, is due out soon.

Marker: A name given to a frame in the Score. Frames in the Score can be labeled and referred to by that marker. Also called *labels*. *See also* Label.

Mask: An image used to define the opaqueness of another image. The black pixels in a mask image would map onto the other image and define which pixels are seen.

Matte: Taking an image and making the white (or background color) pixels transparent, while all other pixels are opaque.

Member: A single element such as a bitmap, a bit of text, a sound, a shape, a vector drawing, or a piece of digital video, stored in the Cast.

Mesh: An interconnected network of points that creates a 3D model surface.

MIAW: Movie in a Window. A Director movie that exists in a window other than the Stage. Sometimes pronounced "meow."

MIDI: Musical Instrument Digital Interface. The means by which computers communicate with keyboards and other instruments. MIDI files contain musical compositions that can be played back with a MIDI device, such as a Windows sound card or QuickTime.

MIP Mapping: The use of both large and small textures that map to a 3D surface, where the smaller texture is used for speed and the larger is only used when needed.

Model: A 3D object, such as a simple shape, a complex object like a car, an airplane, or a character. Models are usually created in third-party 3D programs and imported into Director inside a Shockwave 3D member.

Movie: The primary Director file; contains one or more cast libraries and a Score. It is the only Director file you need for most productions.

Movie Script: A script that controls the entire movie. You can have as many movie scripts as you want. They do not appear in the Score.

MP3: A popular audio compression format. Actually means MPEG 1, Level 3. This is similar to Shockwave Audio. MP3 can be used in Director just as Shockwave Audio can.

MPEG: Motion Picture Experts Group. A digital video format that uses a lot of compression, but still retains high quality.

Multimedia Author: A term used to describe someone who uses Director, or a similar tool, to create animation and presentations. They may use Lingo scripts created by others, but do not do much programming themselves.

Multithreading: When an application runs several programs at once. Because there is only one processor, the programs are not actually all running at once, but they are taking turns using the processor. Lingo running as server-side scripts on the Shockwave Multiuser Server can use multithreading.

Node: A model, group, light, or camera in a 3D scene.

Normal: A vertex that indicates which direction a vector is facing.

Object Movie: A term used to describe a QuickTime VR movie that contains a three-dimensional object. *See also* QuickTime VR.

Onion Skinning: The technique used by animators to create animation by seeing a shaded copy of the previous or next step in the animation underneath the image that they are currently working on.

OOP: Object-Oriented Programming. A method of programming that assigns code to objects, such as sprites or data.

Overlay: A 2D graphic that is shown in front of the 3D scene.

Palette: A list of colors that can be used by an image or by the whole screen to display graphics using only those colors.

Palette Window: A small window in a user interface, such as Director, which floats above other windows. Examples are the Property Inspector, the Control Strip, and the Library palette.

Pan: To move the camera across a 3D scene, usually horizontally.

Panoramic Image: An image that shows the scene in a 360-degree view around the camera. Typically, users interact with the image to change the view angle because only a portion of the image can be shown at a time.

Parent Script: A script member that is not used directly, but is instead used to create a script instance or instances. It is used for object-oriented programming.

Particle System: A 3D object that is actually a large number of small moving objects. Particle systems can be used to simulate things like fireworks, running water, smoke, and dust.

Pascal: A basic object-oriented programming language used mostly in colleges.

PDA: Personal Digital Assistant. Refers to handheld devices, such as the Palm Pilot.

Peer-To-Peer: A system where users are connected directly to each other through a network, as opposed to both users connecting through a third-party computer server.

Perl: A simple text-handling programming language used on many Web servers to create CGI scripts. *See also* CGI.

PICS: A single file that contains multiple images. It can be imported into a variety of programs. It can also be imported into Director as a film loop and series of members. Available on the Mac only.

PICT: The standard image file for Macintosh computers.

Pixel: The smallest possible dot on a computer screen. The screen is actually made up of rows and columns of pixels.

Plug-In: An extension to Netscape Navigator that is used to add new media types to the browser. Shockwave for Director is a plug-in that adds to browsers the capability to display Director movies.

PNG: Portable Network Graphics. This is an up-and-coming format that newer browsers support. It's the native format of Macromedia Fireworks.

POP: Post Office Protocol. Also called POP3. The most used way to receive email over the Internet. The messages are stored on the server until users request that they be transferred to their computer. *See also* SMTP and IMAP.

Pop-Up Menu: Describes a button that, when clicked, changes to a list of items that can be selected.

Port: While computers usually have a single IP address to identify them on the Internet, a computer will have many ports used for communication. Port 80, for instance, is used for http (HTML pages). The Shockwave Multiuser Server defaults to using port 1626.

Primitive: A simple 3D shape, like a cube, sphere, cylinder or plane. Primitives can be created by Lingo and inserted into a 3D member.

Progress Bar: A graphic element that shows the progress of a download or other long computer action. A rectangular-shaped element grows to fill a space on the screen as the process nears completion.

Projector: A standalone application program created from a Director movie.

Property Inspector: A palette window that contains information about the element currently selected. The Property Inspector, sometimes abbreviated PI, can contain information about sprites, members, the Stage, the movie, and a number of other things.

Pull-Down Menu: Describes a menu at the top of the screen or window that expands to a list of items that the users can select.

QuickTime: The standard video format for Macintosh computers and also used by about half of all Windows machines. Currently version 4.02.

QuickTime VR (QTVR): A QuickTime movie that contains a panoramic image or a three-dimensional object. Instead of simply playing the movie, users interact with the image to see a different view of the panoramic image or object.

Radians: A definition of an angle, like degrees. Whereas 360 degrees make a complete circle, 6.28 (two times pi) radians make a complete circle.

Radio Button: A button that is part of a set of buttons that displays an on or off state. Only one button out of a set can be on at one time. When another is chosen, the previous choice is turned off.

RAM: Random Access Memory. This is usually just referred to as "memory" in the computer.

Registration Point: The location in a bitmap image or other member that is used to position the sprite on the Stage. When the sprite is set to an X,Y location, it is the registration point of the image that appears at that exact location.

Rollover: An element on the screen that performs an action when the cursor is over it. The element itself can change, or another element on the screen can change as a reaction to the rollover.

RTF: Rich Text Format. An old standard format for transferring styled text between word-processing programs. It consists of plain text, with special tags that are interpreted as styles and media elements.

Sample Frequency: In a sound file, the measurement describes how often a sound sample was taken of the original file to build the data that exists in the current file. The higher the sample frequency, the better the quality.

Score: A chart showing which members appear on the Stage at what times.

Script: Used to describe a Lingo cast member. Sometimes used to describe a single handler.

SCSI: Small Computer System Interface. Pronounced "scuzzy." A method for hooking up external devices, such as CD-ROM drives and scanners, to your computer. This used to be the main external hookup for Macintosh computers but has now been replaced with FireWire and USB.

Server: In the realm of multiuser communication, a server is a computer that enables many other computers to communicate with one another. Of course, a server is also any computer that answers requests for information, such as a Web server or a file server. *See also* Client.

Shader: Something that describes the surface of a 3D object. A shader can be a bitmap texture or a simple color.

Shapes: Director has a few special cast member types called shapes. You can draw lines, ovals, rectangles, and rounded rectangles. All but lines can appear either filled or as outlines. You can use these shapes to add quick graphic elements to your movies without having to create bitmaps for them.

Shockwave: Technology that enables Director movies to play back inside Web browsers. "Shockwave" usually means "Shockwave for Director," whereas "Flash" usually means "Shockwave Flash."

Shockwave Audio: A sound file format that can be used by Director to stream sound over the Internet. Similar to the MP3 format. Also called SWA.

Slider: A graphical interface element that enables users to slide an element across a line to define a number among a range of numbers. A typical example is a slider that enables users to control volume.

SMTP:Simple Mail Transfer Protocol. This is the technology that enables you to send mail over the Internet. *See also* POP and IMAP.

Sorenson: A video compression algorithm available in QuickTime that compresses digital video to very small files.

Sounds: Director can import many different types of sound formats, but does not really have the capability to create or edit sounds. Sounds can be quick, simple buzzes and beeps, or long music pieces.

Sprite: The description of what member is shown, where it is in the Score, where it appears on the Stage, and many other properties.

Stage: The main Director screen where all the action takes place.

Streaming: The process by which a movie or other media is played for users while the file is gradually loaded in from a network or the Internet.

String: A variable that contains alphanumeric characters.

Style Sheets: Information contained in an HTML document, or linked from the HTML document, that describes how text should be displayed under various circumstances in Web browsers.

swf: The file extension for a Shockwave Flash movie. These can be imported into Director or used on a Web page. However, they cannot be reopened in Flash.

Targa: A bitmap graphics format used by some 3D programs.

TCP/IP:Transmission Control Protocol/Internet Protocol. The technology used to send information over the Internet.

Tempo: The speed at which the movie plays. Usually measured in frames per second.

Text Member: A text member contains formatted characters. You can create them in Director with the text-editing window, or you can import files created in word-processing programs. Director has the capability to display graphically pleasing anti-aliased text. In anti-aliased text, the edges of characters are smooth rather than jagged. Also in Director, you can create text members that use fonts that don't need to be on the user's machine to display properly.

Texture: A bitmap image that is used as the surface of a 3D object. In Director, a texture is usually the property of a shader, which in turn is applied to a surface. *See also Shader.*

Thread: A single program running in a multithreaded environment. *See also* Multithreading.

Thumbnail: A small image that represents the cast member in the cast window.

TIFF: Tagged Image File Format. An older image file format.

Toolbar: The strip of buttons that appears at the top of the Director screen.

Transform: An object that defines the position, rotation, and scale of a model in a 3D world.

Transition: A method of changing the screen, such as a dissolve or wipe.

Tweening: The process whereby you tell Director to place a sprite in a certain location and with certain properties in one frame, and then in a new location and new properties in another (keyframes). Then, Director animates the sprite between the two positions and the property sets in the frames in between. *See also* Keyframe.

URL: Uniform Resource Locator. This is the address of an item on the Internet.

USB: Universal Serial Bus. The modern method for hooking up low-bandwidth devices to Macintosh computers and PCs. It replaces standard serial connections used for digital cameras, MIDI devices, and small removable drives. On Macintosh computers, it can also be used for keyboards and mice.

Variables: Storage areas for values. *See also* Global Variable, Local Variable.

Vector Shapes: Vector shape members are similar to the media created with programs such as Macromedia Freehand and Adobe Illustrator. A vector member is one long line that can be bent and curved. A closed loop in a vector member can be filled. Vector members can be scaled to any size and still maintain their shape and clarity.

Vertex: A single point in a vector shape.

Video For Windows: The video format built in to Windows. Sometimes called AVI files. Available in Windows only.

Watermark: A small mark in photographs and other media that identifies the origin of the content. Used primarily to prevent people from using the content without permission.

WAV: A Windows sound format.

Windows: The name of the operating system used on most PCs. Developed by Microsoft, Windows comes in many flavors: the obsolete Windows 3.1, the old Windows 95, the modern Windows 98, the high-tech Windows NT, and the new Windows 2000.

Wizard: A feature of a piece of software that enables you to use a function of the software while being walked, step-by-step, through the process.

World: A complete 3D environment. A world can be completely empty, or could contain many models and primitives. Worlds include models, lights, cameras, and other elements. A 3D world corresponds to a Shockwave 3D cast member.

WYSIWYG: What You See Is What You Get. Pronounced "wiz-ee-wig." Used to describe an authoring environment that lets users work with information in the same way the information will later be displayed. For instance, an HTML editor is WYSIWYG if you can edit the HTML and see exactly what the page will look like in the browser while you are editing.

XML: Extensible Markup Language. Similar to HTML, but rather than using predefined tags, such as <P>, it enables you to define your own tags and what they mean. An Xtra that comes with Director enables you to parse such documents.

Xtras: Extensions to Director, developed by Macromedia and by third parties, that add or enhance functionality. Some Xtras enable you to have new types of cast members, such as cursor cast members or 3D graphics.

C

ONLINE RESOURCES

The Director world is constantly changing. New Xtras are released constantly. Developers discover new techniques and share them with the rest of the community. New updates of Director and Shockwave produce new features.

To keep up-to-date, developers should be checking Internet sources of Director information frequently.

TOP RESOURCES

The following lists the 10 best places to find and share information about Director. There are actually more than 100 sites, but because most of these sites have links to others, you are only a few clicks away from all of them.

Director Online Users Group (DOUG)

http://www.director-online.com/

This site has quickly become the leading independent resource site for Director developers. You can find the latest news about Director and Director-related products. There are how-to columns, message boards, and job listings. It also has a lot of interviews and articles written by developers.

Director Web

`http://www.mcli.dist.maricopa.edu/director/`

This is an intense, yet well-organized and often-updated site put together by Alan Levine at Maricopa Center for Learning and Instruction. It is sometimes referred to as the *Maricopa site*. This resource is completely independent of Macromedia and has different information and technical notes than Macromedia's site. It includes tips and tricks, lists of known bugs, links to other resources on the Web, and a huge list of Shockwave sites.

Macromedia

`http://www.macromedia.com/software/director/`

This is the official Macromedia site. You'll find technical notes, the latest updates, and an excellent list of Xtras.

The most important part of the site for developers is the TechNotes. They are currently located in the support section of the Director product pages. They include some valuable information on how to perform difficult tasks in Director. Just make sure the TechNote you read is for Director 8, not an earlier version. This is also where to go to get upgrades, the latest Shockwave plug-ins, and some cool free Xtras.

Developer Dispatch

`http://www.developerdispatch.com/`

Okay. So, I am a little biased with this one. At least I restrained myself from placing it first. My site includes all sorts of Director, Lingo, and Shockwave information. The main feature is an email newsletter I send out as often as I can. It also includes message boards for both Director and Flash. You can also find a huge collection of Shockwave games at `http://clevermedia.com/`.

Shockwavemovies.com

`http://www.shockwavemovies.com`

This up-and-coming site has already gotten a lot of attention by posting Director 8.5 undocumented features and oddities. There are also some sample behaviors and demos.

Direct-L

`DIRECT-L@UAFSYSB.UARK.EDU`

This is a mailing list with more than 2,000 subscribers. To subscribe, send email to the above address with "SUBSCRIBE DIRECT-L *YOUR_NAME*" in the body of the message. Check out its Web site at `http://www.mcli.dist.maricopa.edu/director/direct-l/manners.html` first. Mailing lists are a great way to stay in touch with the Director community around the world.

However, it can be a bit overwhelming, because 2,000 people can generate a lot of email over the course of a day.

To search the archives of this mail list, go to `http://www.mcli.dist.maricopa.edu/director/digest/`. If you are an advanced user, you might want to remember that this list is full of novices, and you might find yourself answering questions, not asking them (which is not all bad—it's a great way to land consulting gigs).

DirectorU.com

`http://www.directoru.com/`

Terry Schussler, of *gmatter* fame, maintains this site, which is a repository for behaviors, tips, and some Xtras. There is also information about Terry's popular training seminars.

DirectOregon

`http://www.moshplant.com/direct-or/`

Darrel Plant, author of a few books on Director and Flash, runs this site. He is also the technical editor of the Macromedia User Journal. He likes to play around a lot with new features in Director, and has posted many features, such as his EPS-to-vector-shape converter tool. You can also search the Direct-OR list, an Oregon-based developer mailing list.

MediaMacros

`http://www.mediamacros.com`

This site contains a huge list of open source behaviors and a large list of Xtras. It also has frequent news updates.

MultiMedia Help

`http://www.multimediahelp.8m.com/`

Lots of demo files to download, a forum, free audio links and free 3D models.

GENERAL DIRECTOR RESOURCES

Lots of Xtras, other products and Director quirks: `http://www.updatestage.com`

Message board and chat: `http://clubs.yahoo.com/clubs/macromediadirector`

Free resources, links, and info: `http://www.director8.com`

Lingo examples at The SuperLingo Pages: `http://superlingo.level.nl/`

Library of game source: `http://www.bowy.com/`

Artificial life with Lingo: `http://www.geocities.com/ResearchTriangle/Lab/1394/index0.html`

Lingo-based Director tools: `http://brennan.young.net/Comp/tools.html`

Code examples: `http://www.the-castle.com/examples.htm`

Chicago Area Users Group: `http://www.mmugchicago.org/`

Source code examples: `http://perso.planetb.fr/newton/`

Lingo tips: `http://www.xtramedia.com/lingoTips.shtml`

Changing projector icons: `http://etosoftware.hypermart.net/Minirun.htm`

Director examples: `http://users.aol.com/jrbuell/index.html`

The home page of John Thompson, the "Father of Lingo": `http://www.lingoworks.com/`

Director tutorials: `http://www.kkti.com`

A tutorial on how to write Director ActiveX controls: `http://www.mods.com.au/ActiveX/`

Experiments using Lingo threads: `http://ds.dial.pipex.com/andy.white/`

Expert Lingo programming technotes: `http://venuemedia.com/mediaband/collins/technotes.html`

Shockwave Multiuser Server information: `http://poppy.macromedia.com/multiuser/`

NON-ENGLISH DIRECTOR RESOURCES

A Spanish Director developer site: `http://www.directorzone.com/`

Macromedia User Group Argentina: `http://www.mmug-ar.com.ar/`

A German Director site: `http://www.lingopark.com/`

A German Director site: `http://www.director-workshop.de/`

A German Director site: `http://www.lingo.de/`

A French Director site: `http://www.yazo.net/`

A French Director site: `http://www.director-fr.com/`

A French Director site: `http://perso.wanadoo.fr/g.hocquet/`

DIRECTOR-RELATED MAILING LISTS

Direct-L, the largest list: `http://www.mcli.dist.maricopa.edu/director/`

3D, Multiuser and Xtra development mailing lists: `http://www.trevimedia.com/mailinglists/`

Director game development mailing list:
`http://nuttybar.drama.uga.edu/mailman/listinfo/dirgames-l/`

Lingo Programmers mailing list: `http://www.penworks.com/LUJ/lingo-l.cgi`

Yahoo club: `http://clubs.yahoo.com/clubs/lingo`

3D-RELATED RESOURCES

Lots of information, links and free textures and models:
http://www.3dcafe.com/asp/default.asp

Models, textures and other things, with some available in Shockwave 3D format:
http://www.turbosquid.com

Home of the Maya Shockwave 3D exporter : http://www.aliaswavefront.com/sw3d

Home of TrueSpace, another 3D tool with a Shockwave 3D exporter:
http://www.caligari.com/

Home of a 3D exporter of Poser: http://www.daz3d.com/

3D Studio Max exporter: http://www2.discreet.com/web/

3D exporter for SoftImage: http://www.softimage.com/download/xsi/converters/

A 3D modeling tool made specifically for Shockwave 3D: http://www.shapeshifter3D.com/

Developers page for the Havok Xtra: http://www.havok.com/xtra/

TABLES AND CHARTS

ASCII CHARACTER CHART

These are the numbers used by *charToNum* and *numToChar* functions. Some characters, especially those above 127, vary from font to font and platform to platform.

3	Enter		37	%		52	4
8	Delete		38	&		53	5
9	Tab		39	'		54	6
10	Line Feed		40	(		55	7
13	Return		41	)		56	8
27	Clear		42	*		57	9
28	Left Arrow		43	+		58	:
29	Right Arrow		44	,		59	;
30	Up Arrow		45	-		60	<
31	Down Arrow		46	.		61	=
32	[space]		47	/		62	>
33	!		48	0		63	?
34	"		49	1		64	@
35	#		50	2		65	A
36	$		51	3		66	B

67	C	100	d	133	...		
68	D	101	e	134	†		
69	E	102	f	135	‡		
70	F	103	g	136	ˆ		
71	G	104	h	137	‰		
72	H	105	i	138	ˇ		
73	I	106	j	139	‹		
74	J	107	k	140	Œ		
75	K	108	l	141	≤		
76	L	109	m	142	≥		
77	M	110	n	143	$\sum$		
78	N	111	o	144	$\prod$		
79	O	112	p	145	`		
80	P	113	q	146	'		
81	Q	114	r	147	"		
82	R	115	s	148	"		
83	S	116	t	149	•		
84	T	117	u	150	–		
85	U	118	v	151	—		
86	V	119	w	152	~		
87	W	120	x	153	™		
88	X	121	y	154	π		
89	Y	122	z	155	›		
90	Z	123	{	156	œ		
91	[	124	|	157	∫		
92	\	125	}	158	Ω		
93	]	126	~	159	Ÿ		
94	^	127	DEL	160	á		
95	_	128	≠	161	¡		
96	`	129	∞	162	¢		
97	a	130	‚	163	£		
98	b	131	f	164	¤		
99	c	132	„	165	¥		

166	¦	197	Å	228	ä		
167	§	198	Æ	229	å		
168	¨	199	Ç	230	æ		
169	©	200	È	231	ç		
170	ª	201	É	232	è		
171	«	202	Ê	233	é		
172	¬	203	Ë	234	ê		
173	–	204	Ì	235	ë		
174	®	205	Í	236	ì		
175	¯	206	Î	237	í		
176	°	207	Ï	238	î		
177	±	208	q	239	ï		
178	²	209	Ñ	240	u		
179	³	210	Ò	241	ñ		
180	´	211	Ó	242	ò		
181	µ	212	Ô	243	ó		
182	¶	213	Õ	244	ô		
183	·	214	Ö	245	õ		
184	¸	215	r	246	ö		
185	¹	216	Ø	247	÷		
186	º	217	Ù	248	ø		
187	»	218	Ú	249	ù		
188	¨	219	Û	250	ú		
189	´	220	Ü	251	û		
190	p	221	s	252	ü		
191	¿	222	t	253	v		
192	À	223	ß	254	w		
193	Á	224	à	255	ÿ		
194	Â	225	á				
195	Ã	226	â				
196	Ä	227	ã				

MEMBER TYPES

These are the possible values returned by the *type* property of a member.

#animgif	#flash	#shape
#bitmap	#font	#sound
#button	#movie	#swa
#cursor	#ole	#text
#digitalVideo	#palette	#transition
#empty	#picture	#vectorShape
#field	#QuickTimeMedia	
#filmLoop	#script	

TRANSITIONS

The following list shows each transition with its Lingo number, which can be used in *puppetTransition* commands.

Lingo Number	Transition	Lingo Number	Transition
1	Wipe right	27	Random rows
2	Wipe left	28	Random columns
3	Wipe down	29	Cover down
4	Wipe up	30	Cover down, left
5	Center out, horizontal	31	Cover down, right
6	Edges in, horizontal	32	Cover left
7	Center out, vertical	33	Cover right
8	Edges in, vertical	34	Cover up
9	Center out, square	35	Cover up, left
10	Edges in, square	36	Cover up, right
11	Push left	37	Venetian blinds
12	Push right	38	Checkerboard
13	Push down	39	Strips on bottom, build left
14	Push up	40	Strips on bottom, build right
15	Reveal up	41	Strips on left, build down
16	Reveal up, right	42	Strips on left, build up
17	Reveal right	43	Strips on right, build down
18	Reveal down, right	44	Strips on right, build up
19	Reveal down	45	Strips on top, build left
20	Reveal down, left	46	Strips on top, build right

Lingo Number	Transition	Lingo Number	Transition
21	Reveal left	47	Zoom open
22	Reveal up, left	48	Zoom close
23	Dissolve, pixels fast*	49	Vertical blinds
24	Dissolve, boxy rectangles	50	Dissolve, bits fast*
25	Dissolve, boxy squares	51	Dissolve, pixels*
26	Dissolve, patterns	52	Dissolve, bits*

TRANSITIONS MARKED WITH AN ASTERISK (*) DO NOT WORK ON MONITORS SET TO 32 BITS.

INKS

The following table includes the Lingo number for each ink, which you can use to set a sprite's ink property.

Lingo Ink Number	Ink Name	Description
0	Copy	Each pixel, including all white pixels, completely overrides the pixels under the sprite.
1	Transparent	A pixel's red, green, and blue values are compared to the pixel behind it. The darkest value of each color is used. So, a light red on a dark red shows up as dark red.
2	Reverse	Performs a logical "exclusive or" between each red, green, and blue color value of the pixel and the one under it. The resulting value is then reversed. This transforms colors in all sorts of odd ways that are hard to predict.
3	Ghost	Like Reverse, this performs a complex mathematical transformation of the color values. In this case, a logical "or" is performed between the color under the pixel and the opposite of the pixel's color.
4	Not Copy	A reverse effect is applied to all colors in the sprite, and then the Copy ink is applied.
5	Not Transparent	A reverse effect is applied to all colors in the sprite, and then the Transparent ink is applied.
6	Not Reverse	A reverse effect is applied to all colors in the sprite, and then the Reverse ink is applied.
7	Not Ghost	A reverse effect is applied to all colors in the sprite, and then the Ghost ink is applied.
8	Matte	A mask is created for the sprite that makes white pixels on the outside of the image transparent. All other pixels, including white ones completely enclosed in the image, are shown as in Copy ink.
9	Mask	Uses the next cast member in the Cast window to block or unblock background colors. Rules for a Mask are as follows: must be the same size as the masked cast member, must be the next cast member position in the Cast window, and must be 1 bit. If there is a black pixel in the mask, the same pixel position of the sprite is the color of the sprite. Otherwise, it is completely transparent.

Lingo Ink Number	Ink Name	Description
32	Blend	Applies a blend to the sprite. The amount used in the blend is set in Sprite Properties from the Modify menu or in the Score or Property Inspector. The amount of each color used from the sprite and the pixels under it is determined by the blend percentage.
33	Add Pin	The same as Add with the exception that if the color value exceeds 255, 255 is used.
34	Add	Takes the red, green, and blue color values of the pixel and the pixel under it and adds them. If this is greater than 255, the number wraps back around starting at 0.
35	Subtract Pin	The same as Subtract with the exception that if the color value is less than the minimum visible color, the minimum color is used.
36	Background Transparent	Sets all the white pixels within an image to transparent.
37	Lightest	Takes the lightest color values from the pixel and the pixel behind it.
38	Subtract	Takes the red, green, and blue color values of the pixel and subtracts them from the pixel under it. If this is less than 0, the number wraps back around from 255.
39	Darkest	Takes the darkest color values from the pixel and the pixel behind it.
40	Lighten	This ink uses the foreground and background colors of the sprite. It does not use color information from the pixels under the sprite. In addition to the color translation, it behaves like the Matte ink by making exterior white pixels transparent. It takes the red, green, and blue values of each pixel and multiplies them by the red, green, and blue values of the sprite's background color. Then it adds the color values from the foreground color.
41	Darken	The same as Lighten, but in addition, the red, green, and blue values of the background color are reversed and then added to the color for each pixel.

COMMON COLORS

Director enables you to set colors using the *rgb* object and a string with a hexadecimal value. Because it's not easy to remember the code for "maroon" (800000), it's handy to have a name-to-color chart. The names used here are the official color names for Netscape Navigator colors.

Color	RGB Hexadecimal Code	Color	RGB Hexadecimal Code
aliceblue	F0F8FF	darkorange	FF8C00
antiquewhite	FAEBD7	darkorchid	9932CC
aqua	00FFFF	darkred	8B0000
aquamarine	7FFFD4	darksalmon	E9967A
azure	F0FFFF	darkseagreen	8FBC8F
beige	F5F5DC	darkslateblue	483D8B
bisque	FFE4C4	darkslategray	2F4F4F
black	000000	darkturquoise	00CED1
blanchedalmond	FFEBCD	darkviolet	9400D3
blue	0000FF	deeppink	FF1493
blueviolet	8A2BE2	deepskyblue	00BFFF
brown	A52A2A	dimgray	696969
burlywood	DEB887	dodgerblue	1E90FF
cadetblue	5F9EA0	firebrick	B22222
chartreuse	7FFF00	floralwhite	FFFAF0
chocolate	D2691E	forestgreen	228B22
coral	FF7F50	fuchsia	FF00FF
cornflowerblue	6495ED	gainsboro	DCDCDC
cornsilk	FFF8DC	ghostwhite	F8F8FF
crimson	DC143C	gold	FFD700
cyan	00FFFF	goldenrod	DAA520
darkblue	00008B	gray	808080
darkcyan	008B8B	green	008000
darkgoldenrod	B8860B	greenyellow	ADFF2F
darkgray	A9A9A9	honeydew	F0FFF0
darkgreen	006400	hotpink	FF69B4
darkkhaki	BDB76B	indianred	CD5C5C
darkmagenta	8B008B	indigo	4B0082
darkolivegreen	556B2F	ivory	FFFFF0

Color	RGB Hexadecimal Code
khaki	F0E68C
lavender	E6E6FA
lavenderblush	FFF0F5
lawngreen	7CFC00
lemonchiffon	FFFACD
lightblue	ADD8E6
lightcoral	F08080
lightcyan	E0FFFF
lightgoldenrodyellow	FAFAD2
lightgreen	90EE90
lightgray	D3D3D3
lightpink	FFB6C1
lightsalmon	FFA07A
lightseagreen	20B2AA
lightskyblue	87CEFA
lightslategray	778899
lightsteelblue	B0C4DE
lightyellow	FFFFE0
lime	00FF00
limegreen	32CD32
linen	FAF0E6
magenta	FF00FF
maroon	800000
mediumaquamarine	66CDAA
mediumblue	0000CD
mediumorchid	BA55D3
mediumpurple	9370DB
mediumseagreen	3CB371
mediumslateblue	7B68EE
mediumspringgreen	00FA9A
mediumturquoise	48D1CC
mediumvioletred	C71585
midnightblue	191970
mintcream	F5FFFA

Color	RGB Hexadecimal Code
mistyrose	FFE4E1
moccasin	FFE4B5
navajowhite	FFDEAD
navy	000080
oldlace	FDF5E6
olive	808000
olivedrab	6B8E23
orange	FFA500
orangered	FF4500
orchid	DA70D6
palegoldenrod	EEE8AA
palegreen	98FB98
paleturquoise	AFEEEE
palevioletred	DB7093
papayawhip	FFEFD5
peachpuff	FFDAB9
peru	CD853F
pink	FFC0CB
plum	DDA0DD
powderblue	B0E0E6
purple	800080
red	FF0000
rosybrown	BC8F8F
royalblue	4169E1
saddlebrown	8B4513
salmon	FA8072
sandybrown	F4A460
seagreen	2E8B57
seashell	FFF5EE
sienna	A0522D
silver	C0C0C0
skyblue	87CEEB
slateblue	6A5ACD
slategray	708090

Color	RGB Hexadecimal Code		Color	RGB Hexadecimal Code
snow	FFFAFA		turquoise	40E0D0
springgreen	00FF7F		violet	EE82EE
steelblue	4682B4		wheat	F5DEB3
tan	D2B48C		white	FFFFFF
teal	008080		whitesmoke	F5F5F5
thistle	D8BFD8		yellow	FFFF00
tomato	FF6347		yellowgreen	9ACD32

SHOCKWAVE AUDIO STATES

These numbers are returned from the *state* property of a Shockwave audio member:

Lingo Number	Description
0	Cast streaming has stopped.
1	The cast member is reloading.
2	Preloading ended successfully.
3	The cast member is playing.
4	The cast member is paused.
5	The cast member has finished streaming.
9	An error occurred.
10	There is insufficient CPU space.

FLASH MEMBER STATES

These values are returned by Flash members while the movie is running:

Lingo Number	Description
0	The cast member is not in memory.
1	The header is currently loading.
2	The header has finished loading.
3	The cast member's media is currently loading.
4	The cast member's media has finished loading.
-1	An error occurred.

MOVIE IN A WINDOW (MIAW) TYPES

Table D.1 and D.2 describe the MIAW types for both Windows and Mac.

Table D.1 MIAW Types for Windows

Type Number	Description	Movable	Close Box	Maximize	Minimize
-1	Default	Yes	Yes	No	No
0	Standard	Yes	Yes	No	No
1	Alert Box	No	No	No	No
2	Rectangle	No	No	No	No
3	Rectangle	No	No	No	No
4	Document	Yes	Yes	No	No
5	Document	Yes	Yes	No	No
8	Document	Yes	Yes	Yes	No
12	Document	Yes	Yes	Yes	No
16	Document	Yes	Yes	No	No
49	Palette (Not in Projectors)	Yes	Yes	No	No

Table D.2 MIAW Types for Mac

Type Number	Description	Resize Box	Movable	Close Box	Stretch Box
-1	Default	Yes	Yes	Yes	No
0	Standard	Yes	Yes	Yes	No
1	Alert Box	No	No	No	No
2	Rectangle	No	No	No	No
3	Rectangle with Drop Shadow	No	No	No	No
4	Document	Yes	Yes	No	No
5	Document	Yes	No	No	No
8	Document	Yes	Yes	Yes	Yes
12	Document	Yes	Yes	No	Yes
16	Curved Border Box	Yes	Yes	No	No
49	Palette (Not in Projectors)	Yes	Yes	No	No

LINGO CURSOR NUMBERS

The following numbers can be used with the *cursor* command and the *cursor* sprite property.

Lingo Number	Description	Lingo Number	Description
-1	(Reset Cursor)	292	Copy Closed Hand
0	Arrow	256	Pencil
1	I-Beam	257	Eraser
2	Crosshair	258	Select
3	Crossbar	259	Bucket
4	Watch/Hourglass	272	Lasso
200	Blank	281	Dropper
254	Help	301	Air Brush
280	Finger	302	Zoom In
260	Hand	303	Zoom Out
290	Closed Hand	284	Vertical Size
291	No Drop Hand	285	Horizontal Size
286	Diagonal Size		

LINGO BY SUBJECT

In addition to having an alphabetical listing of all Lingo keywords, it's useful to have a list of keywords arranged by subject. This comes in handy when you can't remember the name of a certain command or property. It can also be a good way to familiarize yourself with a set of keywords for a part of Lingo that you might not have used before. This appendix provides just that list.

3D, Animation

animationEnabled
autoblend
blendFactor
blendTime
cloneMotionFromCastmember
currentLoopState
currentTime
deleteMotion
keyframePlayer
lockTranslation
motion
newMotion
pause
play
playing
playlist
playNext
playRate
positionReset
queue
removeLast
rootLock
rotationReset
type
update

3D, Backdrops and Overlays

addBackdrop
addOverlay
blend
insertBackdrop
insertOverlay

loc
regPoint
removeBackdrop
removeOverlay
rotation
scale
source

3D, Bones Player

autoblend
blendTime
bonesPlayer
currentLoopState
currentTime
getBoneID
getWorldTransform
lockTranslation
pause
play
playing
playlist
playNext
playRate
positionReset
queue
removeLast
rootLock
rotationReset
transform

3D, Box Primitives

back
bottom
front
height

heightVertices
left
length
lengthVertices
right
top
width
widthVertices
isInWorld
newCamera
orthoHeight
pointAt
pointAtOrientation
position
projection
projectionAngle
rect
removeFromWorld
rootNode
rotate
scale
transform
translate
userData
worldPosition
yon

3D, Collision Detection

collision
collisionData
collisionNormal
enabled
immovable
mode

modelA

modelB

modelsUnderRay

pointOfContact

registerForEvent

registerScript

resolve

resolveA

resolveB

setCollisionCallback

unregisterAllEvents

3D, Cylinder Primitives

bottomCap

bottomRadius

endAngle

height

numSegments

resolution

startAngle

topCap

topRadius

3D, Fog

color

decayMode

enabled

far

fog

near

3D, Groups, Parents and Children

addChild

addToWorld

boundingSphere

child

clone

cloneDeep

deleteGroup

group

isInWorld

newGroup

parent

pointAt

pointAtOrientation

position

removeFromWorld

rotate

scale

transform

translate

userData

worldPosition

3D, Inker

boundary

creaseAngle

creases

inker

lineColor

lineOffset

silhouettes

useLineOffset

3D, Level of Detail

auto

bias

Level of Detail

lod

3D, Lights

addToWorld

ambientColor

attenuation

boundingSphere

clone

cloneDeep

color

deleteLight

directionalColor

directionalPreset

isInWorld

light

newLight

pointAt

pointAtOrientation

position

removeFromWorld

rotate

scale

specular

spotAngle

spotDecay

transform

translate

type

userData

worldPosition

3D, Mesh Deform

add
face
mesh
meshDeform
neighbor
normalList
textureCoordinateList
textureLayer
vertexList

3D, Mesh Primitives

build
colorList
count
face
generateNormals
newMesh
normalList
shader
textureCoordinateList
textureCoordinates
vertexList

3D, Miscellaneous and Universal Syntax

active3dRenderer
clearAtRender
clearValue
colorBufferDepth
count
depthBufferDepth
directToStage

getHardwareInfo
getRendererServices
loadFile
name
preferred3DRenderer
primitives
registerForEvent
registerScript
renderer
rendererDeviceList
resetWorld
revertToWorldDefaults
sendEvent
setCollisionCallback
unregisterAllEvents

3D, Model Resources

deleteModelResource
modelResource
newModelResource
resolution
resource
type

3D, Models and Nodes

addToWorld
boundingSphere
clone
cloneDeep
cloneModelFromCastmember
deleteModel
isInWorld
model

modifier
newModel
pointAt
pointAtOrientation
position
removeFromWorld
renderStyle
resource
rotate
scale
shader
shaderList
transform
translate
userData
visibility
worldPosition

3D, Modifiers

addModifier
modifier
modifiers
removeModifier

3D, Particle System Primitives

angle
blendRange
colorRange
direction
distribution
drag
gravity
lifetime
loop

maxSpeed

minSpeed

mode

numParticles

path

pathStrength

region

sizeRange

texture

tweenMode

wind

3D, Plane Primitives

length

lengthVertices

width

widthVertices

3D, Selecting Models

modelsUnderLoc

modelsUnderRay

modelUnderLoc

spriteSpaceToWorldSpace

worldSpaceToSpriteSpace

3D, Shaders

ambient

blend

blendConstant

blendConstantList

blendFunction

blendFunctionList

blendSource

blendSourceList

brightness

colorSteps

deleteShader

density

diffuse

diffuseColor

diffuseLightMap

emissive

flat

glossMap

highlightPercentage

highlightStrength

newShader

reflectionMap

reflectivity

renderStyle

renderStyle

rotation

shader

shaderList

shadowPercentage

shadowStrength

shininess

specular

specularColor

specularLightMap

style

textureMode

textureModeList

textureRepeat

textureRepeatList

textureTransform

textureTransformList

transparent

type

useDiffuseWithTexture

wrapTransformList

3D, Sphere Primitives

endAngle

radius

resolution

startAngle

3D, Streaming

bytesStreamed

preLoad

state

streamSize

3D, Subdivision Surfaces

depth

enabled

error

sds

subdivision

tension

3D, Text

bevelDepth

bevelType

displayFace

displayMode

extrude3D

smoothness

tunnelDepth

3D, Textures

compressed

deleteTexture

height

member

nearFiltering

newTexture

quality

renderFormat

texture

textureRenderFormat

textureType

type

3D, Toon Modifier

boundary

colorSteps

creaseAngle

creases

highlightPercentage

highlightStrength

lineColor

lineOffset

shadowPercentage

shadowStrength

silhouettes

style

toon

useLineOffset

3D, Transforms

duplicate

getWorldTransform

identity

interpolate

interpolateTo

inverse

invert

multiply

pointAt

pointAtOrientation

position

preMultiply

preRotate

preScale

preTranslate

rotate

rotation

scale

transform

translate

worldPosition

xAxis

yAxis

zAxis

3D, Vector Math

angleBetween

axisAngle

cross

crossProduct

distanceTo

dot

dotProduct

duplicate

getNormalized

magnitude

normalize

randomVector

vector

x

y

z

Animated GIF

directToStage

fixedRate

linked

pause

playBackMode

resume

rewind

Behaviors

beginSprite

currentSpriteNum

endSprite

enterFrame

exitFrame

getBehaviorDescription

getBehaviorTooltip

getPropertyDescriptionList

idle

isOKToAttach

me

mouseDown

mouseEnter

mouseLeave

mouseUp

mouseUpOutSide

mouseWithin

prepareFrame

property

rightMouseDown

rightMouseUp

runPropertyDialog

scriptInstanceList

scriptList

sendAllSprites

sendSprite

spriteNum

stopEvent

Bitmap

alphaThreshold

antiAlias

blend

centerRegPoint

crop

depth

dither

imageCompression

imageQuality

mapMemberToStage

mapStageToMember

palette

paletteRef

picture

regPoint

useAlpha

Button

buttonStyle

buttonType

checkBoxAccess

checkBoxType

font

fontSize

fontStyle

hilite

text

Casts

activeCastLib

castLib

castLibs

erase

fileName

findEmpty

name

new

number

preloadMode

save castLib

selection

Color

bgColor

blue

color

colorType

green

paletteIndex

red

rgb

Cursor

autoMask

castMemberList

cursor

cursorSize

hotSpot

interval

Date and Time

abbr, abbrev, abbreviated

date

day

long

milliSeconds

month

seconds

short

startTimer

systemDate

ticks

time

timer

year

Debug

alert

alertHook

showGlobals

showXLib

trace

traceLoad

traceLogFile

Digital Video

center

controller

crop

cuePassed

cuePointNames

cuePointTimes

currentTime

digitalVideoTimeScale

digitalVideoType

directToStage

duration

frameRate

invertMask

isVRMovie

loop

loopBounds

mask

mostRecentCuePoint

movieRate

movieTime

pausedAtStart

preLoad

preloadRam

qtRegisterAccessKey

qtUnRegisterAccessKey

quickTimeVersion

scale

setTrackEnabled

sound

startTime

stopTime

timeScale

trackCount

trackEnabled

trackNextKeyTime,
trackPreviousKeyTime

trackNextSampleTime,
trackPreviousSampleTime

trackStartTime,
trackStopTime

trackText

trackType

translation

video

videoForWindowsPresent

volume

Field

alignment

autoTab

backColor

bgColor

border

boxDropShadow

boxType

charPosToLoc

color

dropShadow

editable

field

font

fontSize

fontStyle

foreColor

hilite

lineCount

lineHeight

linePosToLocV

locToCharPos

locVToLinePos

margin

mouseChar

mouseItem

mouseLine

mouseWord

pageHeight

scrollByLine

scrollByPage

scrollTop

selection

selEnd

selStart

text

wordWrap

Flash

actionsEnabled

antiAlias

broadcastProps

bufferSize

buttonsEnabled

callFrame

centerRegPoint

clearError

clickMode

defaultRect

defaultRectMode

directToStage

endTellTarget

eventPassMode

findLabel

fixedRate

flashRect

flashToStage

frame

frameCount

frameRate

frameReady

getError

getFlashProperty

getFrameLabel

getVariable

goToFrame

hitTest

hold

imageEnabled

linked

loop

mouseOverButton

obeyScoreRotation

originH

originMode

originPoint

originV

pathName

pausedAtStart

percentStreamed

playBackMode

playing

posterFrame

preLoad

print

printAsBitmap

quality

regPoint

rewind

scale

scaleMode

sendXML

setFlashProperty

setVariable

showProps

sound

soundMixMedia

stageToFlash

state

static

stop

stream

streamMode

streamSize

tellTarget

viewH

viewPoint

viewScale

viewV

Font

bitmapSizes

characterSet

font

fontList

fontStyle

generateOutline

originalFont

outlineFontList

recordFont

Image

copyPixels

createMask

createMatte

crop

draw

duplicate

extractAlpha

fill

floodFill

getPixel

image

picture

pictureP

setAlpha

setPixel

trimWhiteSpace

useAlpha

Keyboard

commandDown

controlDown

editShortCutsEnabled

exitLock

inlineImeEnabled

key

keyboardFocusSprite

keyCode

keyDown

keyDownScript

keyPressed

keyUp

keyUpScript

lastKey

optionDown

shiftDown

List

[ ]

add

addAt

addProp

append

count

deleteAll

deleteAt

deleteOne

deleteProp

duplicate

findPos

findPosNear

getaProp

getAt

getLast

getOne

getPos

getProp

getPropAt

list

listP

setaProp

setAt

setProp

sort

Logic

( )

<

<=

<>

=

>

>=

and

FALSE

not

objectP

or

TRUE

Math

-

*

/

+

abs

atan

bitAnd

bitNot

bitOr

bitXor

cos

exp

float

floatP

floatPrecision

inflate

inside

integer

integerP

intersect

log

map

mapMemberToStage

mapStageToMember

max

maxInteger

min

mod

offset

PI

power

random

randomSeed

sin

sqrt

tan

union

Member

castLibNum

comments

copyToClipBoard

creationDate

duplicate

fileName

height

importFileInto

media

member

members

modified

modifiedBy

modifiedDate

move

name

new

number

pasteClipBoardInto

purgePriority

rect

size

thumbnail

type

width

Memory

cancelIdleLoad

finishIdleLoad

frameReady

freeBlock

freeBytes

idleLoadDone

idleLoadMode

idleLoadPeriod

idleLoadTag

idleReadChunkSize

loaded

mediaReady

memorySize

movieFileFreeSize

movieFileSize

preLoadRAM

purgePriority

preLoad

preLoadEventAbort

preLoadMember

preLoadMode

preLoadMovie

ramNeeded

unLoad

unloadMember

unloadMovie

Menu

checkMark

enabled

installMenu

menuItem

name

script

MIAW

activateApplication

activateWindow

activeWindow

close

closeWindow

deactivateApplication

deactivateWindow

drawRect

fileName

forget

frontWindow

modal

moveToBack

moveToFront

moveWindow

name

open

openWindow

rect

resizeWindow

sourceRect

tell

title

titleVisible

visible

window

windowList

windowPresent

windowType

Misc

alert

beep

beepOn

bottom

color

colorType

count

framesToHMS

getNthFileNameInFolder

HMStoFrames

left

mci

number

open

point

printFrom

put

rect

right

scriptsEnabled

sound

top

value

zoomBox

Mouse

clickLoc

clickOn

doubleClick

emulateMultiButtonMouse

flushInputEvents

lastClick

lastEvent

lastRoll

mouseCast

mouseChar

mouseDown

mouseDownScript

mouseEnter

mouseH

mouseItem

mouseLeave

mouseLevel

mouseLine

mouseLoc

mouseMember

mouseOverButton

mouseUp

mouseUpOutSide

mouseUpScript

mouseV

mouseWithin

mouseWord

rightMouseDown

rightMouseUp

rollOver

stillDown

Movie

activateApplication

bgColor

centerStage

deactivateApplication

fixStageSize

frame

frameLabel

framePalette

frameScript

frameSound1

frameSound2

frameTempo

frameTransition

label

labelList

lastChannel

lastFrame

marker

markerList

mouseDownScript

mouseUpScript

movie

movieAboutInfo

movieCopyrightInfo

movieFileFreeSize

movieFileSize

movieFileVersion

movieImageCompression

movieImageQuality

movieName

moviePath

paletteMapping

prepareMovie

puppetPalette

puppetTempo

puppetTransition

savedLocal

saveMovie

score

showGlobals

showLocals

stage

stageBottom

stageColor

stageLeft

stageRight

stageTop

startMovie

stopMovie

updateMovieEnabled

updateStage

Multiuser Server-Side Scripting

abort

addUser

appendRecord

awaitValue

breakConnection

breakPointList

call

checkNetMessages

close

connectToNetServer

copyTo

count (thread)

createApplication

createApplicationData

createFolder

createScript

createUniqueName

createUser

creator

declareAttribute

delete

delete (file)

deleteApplication

deleteApplicationData

deleteAttribute

deleteFolder

deleteMovie

deleteRecord

deleteUser

disable

disableMovie

disconnectUser

enable

enableMovie

exchange

exists

flush

folderChar

forget (thread)

frame (thread)

frameCount (thread)

getAddress

getApplicationData

getAt

getAttribute

getAttributeNames

getFields

getGroupCount

getGroupList

getGroupMembers

getGroups

getListOfAllMovies

getMovieCount

getMovies

getNetAddressCookie

getNetErrorString

getNetMessage

getNetOutgoingBytes

getNewGroupName

getNumberOfMembers

getNumberWaitingNetMessages

getPeerConnectionList

getReadableFieldList

getRecordCount

getRecords

getServerTime

getServerVersion

getTempPath

getTime

getUserCount

getUserGroups

getUserIPAddress

getUserNames

getUsers

getVersion

getWriteableFieldList

goToRecord

handler

isRecordDeleted

join

joinGroup

language

leave

leaveGroup

line

list

lock

locked

lockRecord

name (script)

name (thread)

name (variable)

new (thread)

notify

notifyAll

open

pack

position

produceValue

read

readValue

recallRecord

reIndex

removeUser

rename

resume

script (thread)

seek

selectDatabase

selectTag

sendMessage

sendNetMessage

setAttribute

setBreakPoint

setFields

setNetBufferLimits

setNetMessageHandler

size

skip

sleep

stackLevel

stackSize

status

stepInto

stepOver

sweep

thread

type (variable)

type (file)

unlock

unlockRecord

value (variable)

variable

variableCount

volumeInfo

wait

waitForNetConnection

write

writeValue

Navigation

delay

exitLock

go

go loop

go next

go previous

halt

loop

marker

next

pauseState

play

play done

previous

Network

browserName

cacheDocVerify

cacheSize

clearCache

downloadNetThing

getLatestNetID

getNetErrorString

getNetText

getStreamStatus

gotoNetMovie

gotoNetPage

mediaReady

netAbort

netDone

netError

netLastModDate

netMIME

netPresent

netStatus

netTextResult

netThrottleTicks

postNetText

preloadNetThing

proxyServer

streamStatus

tellStreamStatus

URLEncode

OOP

actor

actorList

ancestor

birth

call

callAncestor

me

new

property

rawNew

stepFrame

Programming

abort

case

clearGlobals

do

dontPassEvent

else

end

exit

exit repeat

global

handler

handlers

if

ilk

in

into

next repeat

nothing

on

otherwise

param

paramCount

pass

repeat

result

return

set

the

then

to

VOID

voidP

while

with

QTVR

enableHotSpot

fieldOfView

getHotSpotRect

hotSpotEnterCallback

hotSpotExitCallback

motionQuality

mouseLevel

node

nodeEnterCallback

nodeExitCallback

nodeType

nudge

pan

ptToHotSpot

staticQuality

swing

tilt

triggerCallback

warpMode

Score Recording

activeCastLib

beginRecording

clearFrame

deleteFrame

duplicateFrame

endRecording

frameLabel

framePalette

frameScript

frameSound1

frameSound2

frameTempo

frameTransition

insertFrame

scoreColor

scoreSelection

scriptNum

setScriptList

tweened

type

updateFrame

updateLock

Script

linkAs

linked

scriptText

scriptType

Shape

filled

lineDirection

lineSize

pattern

shapeType

Shockwave

EvalScript

externalEvent

externalParamCount

externalParamName

externalParamValue

frameReady

getPref

gotoNetMovie

gotoNetPage

netStatus

preLoadNetThing

safePlayer

setPref

Shockwave Audio

bitRate

bitsPerSample

copyrightInfo

duration

getError

getErrorString

numChannels

pause member

percentPlayed

percentStreamed

play member

preLoadBuffer

preLoadTime

sampleRate

soundChannel

state

stop member

streamName

url

volume

Sound

beep

beepOn

breakLoop

channelCount

cuePassed

cuePointNames

cuePointTimes

currentTime

elapsedTime

endTime

fadeIn

fadeOut

fadeTo

getPlaylist

isBusy

isPastCuePoint

loop

loopCount

loopEndTime

loopsRemaining

loopStartTime

member

mostRecentCuePoint

pan

pause

play
playNext
puppetSound
queue
rewind
sampleCount
sampleRate
sampleSize
setPlayList
showProps
sound
sound fadeIn
sound fadeOut
sound playFile
sound stop
soundBusy
soundDevice
soundDeviceList
soundEnabled
soundKeepDevice
soundLevel
startTime
status
stop
volume

Sprite

backColor
bgColor
blend
blendLevel
bottom
castLibNum
color
constrainH

constraint
constrainV
cursor
editable
endFrame
flipH
flipV
foreColor
height
ink
intersects
left
loc
locH
locV
locZ
mapMemberToStage
mapStageToMember
member
memberNum
moveableSprite
puppet
puppetSprite
quad
rect
right
rotation
scriptList
setScriptList
skew
sprite
startFrame
top
trails
tweened

type
useFastQuads
visible
width
within

Strings

&
&&
..
after
BACKSPACE
before
char
chars
charToNum
contains
count
delete
EMPTY
ENTER
item
itemDelimiter
last
length
line
number
numToChar
offset
paragraph
QUOTE
ref
RETURN
SPACE
starts

string
stringP
TAB
value
word

Symbols

\#
symbol
symbolP

System

applicationPath
appMinimize
buttonStyle
clearGlobals
colorDepth
cpuHogTicks
date
deskTopRectList
environment
flushInputEvents
freeBlock
freeBytes
globals
idle
idleHandlerPeriod
machineType
memorySize
mouseH
mouseLoc
mouseMember
multiSound
organizationName
platform

productName
productVersion
quit
restart
romanLingo
runMode
searchCurrentFolder
searchPaths
serialNumber
shutDown
switchColorDepth
time
userName
version

Text

alignment
antiAlias
autoTab
backColor
bgColor
bottomSpacing
boxType
charPosToLoc
charSpacing
color
editable
editShortCutsEnabled
firstIndent
fixedLineSpace
font
fontSize
fontStyle
foreColor
html
hyperlink

hyperlinkClicked
hyperlinkRange
hyperlinks
hyperlinkState
inlineImeEnabled
kerning
kerningThreshold
leftIndent
linePosToLocV
locToCharPos
locVToLinePos
missingFonts
pageHeight
pointInHyperLink
pointToChar
pointToItem
pointToLine
pointToParagraph
pointToWord
rightIndent
rtf
scrollByLine
scrollByPage
scrollTop
selectedText
selection
setContents
setContentsAfter
setContentsBefore
substituteFont
tabCount
tabs
text
useHyperTextStyles
wordWrap

Timeout

forget

lastClick

lastEvent

lastKey

lastRoll

new

period

persistent

target

time

timeout

timeoutHandler

timeoutKeydown

timeoutLapsed

timeoutLength

timeoutList

timeoutMouse

timeoutPlay

timeoutScript

Transition

changeArea

chunkSize

duration

puppetTransition

transitionType

zoomBox

Vector

addVertex

antiAlias

bgColor

broadcastProps

centerRegPoint

closed

color

curve

defaultRect

defaultRectMode

deleteVertex

directToStage

endColor

fillColor

fillCycles

fillDirection

fillMode

fillOffset

fillScale

flashRect

gradientType

hitTest

imageEnabled

moveVertex

moveVertexHandle

newCurve

originH

originMode

originPoint

originV

regPoint

regPointVertex

scale

scaleMode

showProps

stageToFlash

strokeColor

strokeWidth

vertex

vertexList

viewH

viewPoint

viewScale

viewV

Xtras

closeXLib

interface

movieXtraList

name

new

number

openXLib

showResFile

showXLib

xtra

xtraList

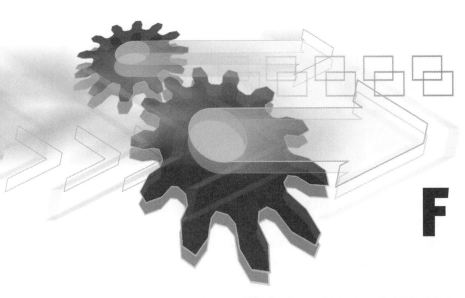

BEHAVIOR LIBRARY QUICK REFERENCE

Director 8.5 comes with a large collection of behaviors available through the Library palette. Although you can browse these in Director and view ToolTip information on each one, you might find this printed quick reference guide handier to use.

The main differences between the Director 8.0 behavior library and the 8.5 library is the addition of 3D and RealMedia behaviors. The 3D behaviors use a new behavior technique defined by "actions" and "triggers." The first set of 3D behaviors are "actions," which change the 3D sprite somehow. The second set are "triggers," which define the user interaction that triggers the actions. An "action" and a "trigger" are used together to allow the user to interact with the 3D sprite.

3D, ACTIONS

Dolly Camera—This behavior will move the camera closer in and farther out, depending on how the user uses the trigger.

Drag Camera—Allows the user to pan, dolly, or zoom the camera with a trigger event.

Fly Through—Allows the user to use the mouse and other triggers to move the camera through the 3D scene.

Pan Camera Horizontal—Allows triggers to cause the camera to pan left and right.

Pan Camera Vertical—Allows triggers to cause the camera to pan up and down.

Orbit Camera—Allows the user to rotate the camera around a specific model.

Reset Camera—Takes the camera back to its starting values.

Rotate Camera—Keeps the camera in the same place, but rotates it around in various directions.

Automatic Model Rotation—This will make a single model in the 3D world rotate about either the x, y, or z axis. It does not need a trigger, but instead rotates at a constant rate.

Click Model To Go To Marker—When the indicated model is clicked, the movie will jump to another frame.

Drag Model—When used with a trigger, will allow the user to drag a single model or any model in one or two dimensions.

Drag Model To Rotate—When used with a trigger, will allow the user to rotate the model around an axis.

Model Rollover Cursor—The user's cursor will change when the user moves it over a specific model.

Play Animation—If the 3D sprite includes an animation, this behavior can be used to start it playing.

Create Box—When triggered, a new box primitive will appear in the 3D world at the cursor location.

Create Particle System—When triggered, a new particle system will appear in the 3D world at the cursor location. The default particle system looks like fireworks.

Create Sphere—When triggered, a new sphere primitive will appear in the 3D world at the cursor location.

Level of Detail—Allows you to set the level of detail used to display the models. You can also have the level change in cycles or randomly.

Sub Division Surface—Allows you to set the number of surfaces used to display a model.

Generic Do—This behavior will call a custom script that you write. It is basically an empty behavior that has all the code to use the triggers, but performs no action until you define one for it.

Toggle Redraw—This behavior allows you to turn on and off redraw for the 3D sprite.

Toon—This behavior will render the entire 3D sprite using the toon renderer, making it look like a 2D drawing or cartoon.

Show Axis—This will draw lines and other marks so you can see clearly where each model is and how it is oriented in the 3D world.

3D, TRIGGERS

Mouse Left—This triggers a 3D action when the user clicks on the 3D sprite with the left mouse button.

Mouse Right—This triggers a 3D action when the user clicks on the 3D sprite with the right mouse button.

Mouse Enter—This triggers a 3D action when the user moves the mouse over the 3D sprite.

Mouse Within—This triggers a 3D action when the user moves the mouse over the 3D sprite. Many actions then track the mouse position and use it to define movement or placement.

Mouse Leave—This triggers a 3D action when the user moves the mouse away from the 3D sprite.

Keyboard Input—This triggers some 3D actions. You can define which key controls which type of action.

ANIMATION, AUTOMATIC

Color Cycling—Changes the foreground color of a sprite from one value to another once, many times, or forever.

Cycle Graphics—Cycles through a series of consecutive cast members.

Fade In/Out—Uses a blend to fade a sprite in or out once, many times, or forever.

Random Movement and Rotation—Moves and spins a sprite in a defined area.

Rotate Continuously (frame-based)—Rotates a sprite through a certain number of degrees per frame.

Rotate Continuously (time-based)—Rotates a sprite at a constant rate, regardless of the tempo.

Rotate to Follow Path—The sprite always faces a certain angle relative to its initial location on the Stage.

Rotation (frame-based)—Rotates a sprite a specific number of degrees with speed determined by the tempo.

Rotation (time-based)—Rotates a sprite a specific number of degrees over a period of time.

Scale and Clip—Scales a Flash or vector shape sprite from one size to another. Clipping occurs if one of the sizes is greater than 100%.

Slide In/Out—Moves a sprite from one position on the screen to another.

Sway—Rotates a sprite between two angles.

Waft—Uses a random movement to make a sprite zigzag and rise from the bottom of the screen.

Zoom In/Out—Scales the sprite up to the Score size, or down to nothing.

ANIMATION, INTERACTIVE

Avoid Mouse—The sprite moves away from the cursor.

Avoid Sprite—The sprite moves away from another sprite.

Constrain to Line—Enables users to drag the sprite along a line. Useful for sliders.

Constrain to Sprite—Enables users to drag a sprite around the Stage, but the sprite is still constrained to the rectangle of another sprite.

Drag and Toss—Enables users to move the sprite around the Stage; the sprite maintains some momentum when the mouse button is released.

Drag Quad Points—Enables users to grab a corner of a sprite and drag it.

Drag to Rotate—Enables users to rotate a sprite around its registration point.

Drag to Scale—Enables users to grab the sprite and drag it to scale it.

Drag to Stretch and Flip—Enables users to stretch and flip a sprite by clicking and dragging.

Draggable—Enables users to reposition the sprite by clicking and dragging.

Follow Sprite—Makes a sprite follow another one. Can be used to have another sprite movie along with one that has another behavior attached to it.

Move, Rotate, and Scale—Enables users to click and drag the sprite. If a modifier key is pressed, the sprite scales. Another modifier key enables users to rotate the sprite.

Multiple Sprite Drag—Enables users to grab a sprite and drag it, and other sprites will follow.

Rollover Cursor Change—The cursor changes when the mouse is over the sprite.

Rollover Member Change—Changes the sprite's member when the mouse is over the sprite.

Snap to Grid—Enables you to define an invisible grid for the sprite that makes it align itself with the nearest grid point when the grid is active.

Sprite Track Mouse—Moves a sprite so that it is under the cursor.

Turn to Fixed Point—The sprite turns to face a point on the Stage.

Turn Towards Mouse—The sprite turns so that it always faces the cursor location.

Turn Towards Sprite—The sprite turns so that it always faces the location of another sprite, even while that sprite is moving.

Vector Motion—The sprite moves in a straight line.

ANIMATION, SPRITE TRANSITIONS

Barn Door—New graphic comes in like opening or closing doors.

Pixelate—New graphic resolves in from large blocky pixels.

Slide—New graphic slides in.

Soft Edge Wipe—A wipe, but with a blended edge.

Stretch—New sprite stretches into position.

Wipe—New sprite appears with a basic wipe.

CONTROLS

Analog Clock—Turns a vector shape into a clock hand.

Display Text—Used by the "ToolTip" or "hypertext—Display Status" behaviors to show a text field.

Draw Connector—Takes a line member and enables users to draw with it.

Dropdown List—Creates a pop-up menu from a field member.

Jump Back Button—Takes users back through frames, reversing the "Jump to Marker Button," "Jump to Movie Button," or "Jump Forward Button" behaviors.

Jump Forward Button—Enables users to go "forward" frames after using "Jump Back Button" to go back.

Jump to Marker Button—Takes users to another frame. "Jump Back Button" enables users to go back.

Jump to Movie Button—Takes users to another movie. "Jump Back Button" enables users to go back.

Multi-State Button—Creates a graphic check box button.

Push Button—Standard button behavior.

Radio Button Group—Enables you to group graphic radio buttons.

ToolTip—Displays a ToolTip when users roll over the sprite.

INTERNET, FORMS

Form Post—Dropdown List—Used to create a pop-up menu to create data to be sent using *postNetText*.

Form Post—Field—Enables users to type data to be sent using *postNetText*.

Form Post—Hidden Field—Acts as a hidden text field that is to be sent using postNetText.

Form Post—Submit Button—The submit button that works with the posting interface behaviors described previously.

INTERNET, MULTIUSER

Connect To Server—Begins a client/server multiuser session.

Disconnect From Server—Ends a client/server multiuser session.

Display Group List—Displays the names of groups on the server.

Display Group Member Names—Displays the names of users in a group.

Chat Input—Used on a field to type chat messages. See the "Caution" note in Chapter 37 about this behavior.

Chat Output—Used on a field to display the chat text.

Send Chat Button—Sends the chat input.

Whiteboard (Shared Canvas)—Enables users in the group to draw on a bitmap image and other users to see the result.

 Join Group—When used with the Connect to Server and Chat Input behaviors, it will allow you to create a chat room that has multiple groups that people can join and leave.

INTERNET, STREAMING

Loop Until Next Frame Is Available—Waits on a frame until the media for the next frame is ready.

Loop Until Member Is Available—Waits on the frame until a specific member is ready.

Loop Until Media in Frame Is Available—Waits on the frame until the specified frame is ready.

Loop Until Media in Marker Is Available—Waits on the frame for a range of frames to be ready.

Jump When Member Is Available—Jumps to a point in the Score when a specific member is ready.

Jump When Media in Frame Is Available—Jumps to a specific frame when the media in a frame is ready.

Jump When Media in Marker Is Available—Jumps to a specific frame when the media in a range of frames is ready.

Progress Bar for Streaming Movies—Uses the sprite as a progress bar that shows the streaming percentage.

Progress Bar for URL Linked Assets—Uses the sprite as a progress bar that shows the streaming percentage.

Show Placeholder—Places a vector in place of a member until the media is available.

MEDIA, FLASH

Set Click Modes—Sets how the Flash sprite responds to clicks.

Set Playback Quality—Enables you to set the quality at which Flash sprites are displayed.

Set Scale, Origin and View—Enables you to set these properties before the sprite appears.

MEDIA, QUICKTIME

QuickTime Control Button—Can turn a sprite into a play, pause, rewind, fast forward, fast rewind, or jump button.

QuickTime Control Slider—Enables the sprite with the "Constrain To Line" behavior to control the position of the QuickTime video.

MEDIA, REALMEDIA

RealMedia Target—For the rest of the RealMedia behaviors to work, drop this behavior on to a RealMedia sprite. The other behaviors are controls that go on to other sprites.

RealMedia Control Button—Drop this behavior on a button sprite to create a Play, Pause, Stop, Forward Fast, Rewind, or other type of control.

RealMedia Slider Bar—To create a slider to control RealMedia playback, first drop this on to a graphic that represents the slider.

RealMedia Slider Knob—To add a knob to the slider, create a knob graphic and attach this behavior to it.

RealMedia Buffering Indicator—This turns a graphic into an indicator that shows how much of the RealMedia stream has been placed in the buffer.

RealMedia Stream Information—This turns a text member into a readout for various information about the RealMedia stream.

MEDIA, SOUND

Play Sound—Starts a sound.

Pause Sound—Pauses a sound. The sound can then be unpaused with the previous behavior.

Stop Sound—Stops the sound.

Sound Beep—A mouse click produces a system beep.

Channel Volume Slider—Enables you to make a slider that controls the volume of a sound.

Channel Pan Slider—Enables you to create a balance control.

NAVIGATION

Go Loop—Loops the movie from the current frame to the most recent marker.

Go Next Button—Jumps to the next marker.

Go Previous Button—Jumps the movie to the marker before the current one.

Go to Frame X Button—Jumps to a specific frame.

Go to URL—Uses *gotoNetPage* to jump to a new location in a Web browser.

Hold on Current Frame—Simple looping frame script.

Loop for X Seconds—Loops on a frame for a specific amount of time.

Play Done—Issues a play done command.

Play Frame X—Issues a simple play command.

Play Movie X—Issues a play movie command.

Wait for Mouse Click or Keypress—Holds the movie on the current frame until users respond.

PAINTBOX

Canvas—Turns a bitmap sprite into a user paint area.

Color Selector—Enables you to set the color of the user's brush.

Erase All Button—Clears the paint area.

Tool Selector—Brush—Sets the bitmap to be used as the user's brush.

Tool Selector—Eraser—Sets the user's paint tool to be an eraser instead of a brush.

Undo Paint—Undoes the last action by the user in the paint area.

TEXT

Add Commas to Numbers—Automatically inserts commas into large numbers.

Calendar—Creates a calendar in a Text member.

Countdown Timer—Displays numbers, counting backward.

Custom Scrollbar—Can be used on four graphic members to build a custom text scrollbar.

Filter Input Characters—Enables you to limit the characters that users can input in an editable text or field member.

Force Case—Forces the text typed into editable field and text members to upper- or lowercase.

Format Numbers—Enables you to display the numbers in a field or text member in a variety of formats.

Get Net Text—Retrieves text from a location on the Internet.

Hypertext—Display Status—Displays the link in a text member when users roll over a hyperlink.

Hypertext—General—Enables you to perform a variety of tasks when users click a hyperlink.

Hypertext—Go to Marker—Jumps to a marker according to the hyperlink data.

Password Entry—Enables users to type in a field, but the field displays only bullet characters.

Tickertape Text—Scrolls text in a field or text member horizontally.

Typewriter Effect—Slowly types text in a field or text member.

G

KEYBOARD SHORTCUTS

Director has a very intuitive interface. If you have never used a function before, and are not sure where to find it, just look at the menu names and think about their meanings. You can make an educated guess.

However, if you use Director eight hours a day, you want to learn all the tricks. The following lists will help you find the items you are likely to need to perform.

MACINTOSH SHORTCUTS

File Menu

Command	Shortcut
New Movie	⌘+N
New Cast	⌘+Option+N
Open	⌘+O
Close	⌘+W
Save	⌘+S
Import	⌘+R
Export	⌘+Shift+R
Publish	⌘+Shift+S
Page Setup	⌘+Shift+P
Print	⌘+P
General Preferences	⌘+U
Quit	⌘+Q

Edit Menu

Command	Shortcut
Undo	⌘+Z
Repeat	⌘+Y
Cut	⌘+X
Copy	⌘+C
Paste	⌘+V
Clear	Delete
Duplicate	⌘+D
Select All	⌘+A
Find Text	⌘+F
Find Handler	⌘+Shift+; (semicolon)
Find Cast Member	⌘+; (semicolon)
Find Selection	⌘+H
Find Again	⌘+Option+F
Replace Again	⌘+Option+E
Edit Sprite Frames	⌘+Option+]
Edit Entire Sprite	⌘+Option+[
Exchange Cast Members	⌘+E
Launch External Editor	⌘+, (comma)

View Menu

Command	Shortcut
Next Marker	⌘+→
Previous Marker	⌘+←
Zoom In	⌘+ + (plus)
Zoom Out	⌘+ – (minus)
Show Guides	⌘+Shift+Option+D
Snap to Guides	Shift+Option+G
Show Grid	⌘+Shift+Option+G
Snap to Grid	⌘+Option+G
Temporarily Turn on Snap to Grid	G+drag sprite
Rulers	⌘+Shift+Option+R
Show Info	⌘+Shift+Option+O
Show Paths	⌘+Shift+Option+H
Toolbar for Current Window	⌘+Shift+H
Keyframes	⌘+Shift+Option+K

Modify Menu

Command	Shortcut
Cast Member Properties	⌘+I
Cast Member Script	⌘+' (apostrophe)
Sprite Properties	⌘+Shift+I
Sprite Script	⌘+Shift+' (apostrophe)
Sprite Tweening	⌘+Shift+B
Movie Properties	⌘+Shift+D
Movie Casts	⌘+Shift+C
Font	⌘+Shift+T
Paragraph	⌘+Shift+Option+T
Join Sprites	⌘+J
Split Sprite	⌘+Shift+J
Extend Sprite	⌘+B
Bring to Front	⌘+Shift+↑
Move Forward	⌘+↑
Move Backward	⌘+↓
Send to Back	⌘+Shift+↓
Align	⌘+K
Tweak	⌘+Shift+K

Control Menu

Command	Shortcut
Play	⌘+Option+P
Stop	⌘+. (period)
Rewind	⌘+Option+R
Step Backward	⌘+Option+←
Step Forward	⌘+Option+→
Loop Playback	⌘+Option+L
Volume: Mute	⌘+Option+M
Toggle Breakpoint	F9
Watch Expression	⌘+Shift+Option+W
Ignore Breakpoints	⌘+Shift+Option+I
Step Script	⌘+Shift+Option+↓
Step Into Script	⌘+Shift+Option+→
Run Script	⌘+Shift+Option+↑
Recompile All Scripts	⌘+Shift+Option+C

Insert Menu

Command	Shortcut
Keyframe	⌘+Option+K
Frames	⌘+Shift+]
Insert One Frame	⌘+]
Remove Frame	⌘+[

Window Menu

Command	Shortcut
Toolbar	Control+Shift+Option+B
Tool Palette	Control+7
Property Inspector	⌘+Option+S
Behavior Inspector	Control+Option+;(semicolon)
Text Inspector	⌘+T
Stage	⌘+1
Control Panel	⌘+2
Markers	⌘+Shift+M
Score	⌘+4

Window Menu

Command	Shortcut
Cast	⌘+3
Paint	⌘+5
Vector Shape	⌘+Shift+V
Text	⌘+6
Field	⌘+8
Color Palettes	⌘+Option+7
Video	⌘+9
Script	⌘+0
Message	⌘+M
Debugger	⌘+` (single open quote)
Watcher	⌘+Shift+` (single open quote)

The Stage

Action	Shortcut
Resize the Stage to 100 percent	⌘+Option+0 (zero)
Full Screen Stage	⌘+Option+1
Full Screen playback	⌘+Shift+Option+P
Black Stage	– (minus) on numeric keypad
White Stage	Shift+– (minus) on numeric keypad
Invert Stage colors	Option+– (minus) on numeric keypad
Select Only the Current Frame of the Sprite	Option+click the sprite
Show/hide Sprite paths	⌘+Shift+Option+H
Create a keyframe within a Sprite path	Option-click a tick mark in the sprite path
Show/hide Sprite Overlay	⌘+Shift+Option+O
Change the opacity of Sprite Overlay	Drag the horizontal line on the right side of the overlay
Open Cast Member Editor	Double-click sprite
Open Paint window	⌘+5
Ink pop-up	⌘-click
Real-Time Record	⌘+Spacebar+drag a sprite on the Stage
Display Shortcut Menu for Selection	Control-click
Hide Selection Indicators	+ (plus) on the numeric keypad
Select a Locked Sprite	L+click locked sprite
Move Sprite by 1 pixel	Arrow keys
Move Sprite by 10 pixels	Shift+arrow keys

The Score

Action	Shortcut
Open shortcut menu for Score display options and preferences	Control-click in the channel number area of the Score
Duplicate selection (sprite or keyframe)	Drag with Option held down
Select a frame within a sprite	Option-click a frame within sprite
Turn on or off Edit Sprite Frames	Option+double-click a frame within sprite
Select empty frames and sprite frames	Option+drag, beginning in an empty frame
Select all the frames in a channel	Double-click channel number, drag to select multiple frames
Select all sprites in a channel	Click the channel number, drag to select multiple sprites
Previous keyframe	Shift+1 on numeric keypad
Next keyframe	Shift+2 on numeric keypad
Scroll the Score to view selected sprites	Shift+5 on numeric keypad
Switch sprites in the Score	⌘+E
Shuffle backward	⌘+↑
Shuffle forward	⌘+↓
Overwrite sprite frames while dragging a selection to a new location	⌘+drag
Move sprite on the Stage by 1 pixel	Select in the Score and use arrow keys
Move sprite on the Stage by 10 pixels	Select in the Score and use Shift+arrow keys
Move entire sprite (instead of keyframe)	Spacebar+drag
Stretch a sprite without proportionally relocating keyframes	⌘+drag the end frame
Stretch a sprite without proportionally relocating keyframes	⌘+drag the end frame
Lock Sprite	⌘+L
Unlock Sprite	⌘+Shift+L
Join Sprites	⌘+J
Split Sprite	⌘+Shift+J
Extend Sprite	⌘+B
Sprite Tweening	⌘+Shift+B
Select a single frame within a sprite	Option-click the sprite on the Stage, or a frame within the sprite in the Score
Move entire sprite between frames (instead of keyframes)	Spacebar+drag
Select all the sprites in a channel	Click the channel number, drag to select multiple sprites
Select all the frames in a channel	Double-click channel number, drag to select multiple sprites
Turn on or off Edit Sprite Frames	Option+double-click a frame within sprite

Select empty frames and sprite frames	Option+drag, beginning in an empty frame
Overwrite sprite frames while dragging a selection to a new location	⌘+drag
Move sprite on the Stage by 1 pixel	Select on the Stage or in the Score and use arrow keys
Move sprite on the Stage by 10 pixels	Select on the Stage or in the Score and use Shift+arrow keys
Show/hide sprite paths	⌘+Shift+Option+H
Create a keyframe within a sprite path	Option-click a tick mark in the sprite path on the Stage

Playback

Action	Shortcut
Move playback head to end of movie	Tab
Move playback head to beginning of movie	Shift+Tab
Move playback head to beginning	⌘+Shift+←
Move playback head to end	⌘+Shift+→
Go to next marker (or jump 10 frames)	⌘+→
Go to previous marker (or back 10 frames)	⌘+←
Hide cursor during playback	Shift+Enter on numeric keypad
Mute sound	⌘+Option+M

Paint Window

Action	Shortcut
Next/Previous Cast Member	Arrow keys
Open Transform Bitmap dialog box	Double-click color resolution indicator
Toggle Zoom In/Zoom Out	Control-click in window or double-click Pencil tool
Nudge selection rect or lasso selection	Arrow keys with selection rectangle or lasso
Change airbrush size (while painting)	↑/↓ with airbrush selected
Change airbrush flow (while painting)	←/→ with airbrush selected
Change foreground color (not painting)	↑/↓, all tools
Change background color (not painting)	Shift+↑/↓, all tools
Change destination color (not painting)	Option+↑/↓, all tools
Draw border with current pattern	Option+Shape or Line tools
Select background color	Shift+Eyedropper tool
Select destination color	Option+Eyedropper tool
Toggle between custom and grayscale patterns	Option-click pattern
Polygon lasso	Option+drag Lasso tool
Duplicate selection	Option+drag

Paint Window

Action	Shortcut
Stretch	⌘+drag
Draw with background color	Option+Pencil tool
Clear visible part of window	Double-click Eraser tool
Open Color Palettes window	Double-click foreground, background, or destination color chip
Airbrush	A
Brush	B
Arc	C
Pick up color under cursor	Option
Eraser	E
Bucket	F, K
Registration Point	G
Hand	H
Eyedropper	I
Lasso	L
Marquee	M. S
Line	N, /, \, |
Circle	O
Filled circle	Shift+O
Polygon	P
Filled polygon	Shift+P
Rectangle	R
Filled Rectangle	Shift+R
Text	T
Switch to black and white foreground color and background color	W
Switch foreground color and background color	X
Pencil	Y
Magnifying Glass	Z
Zoom in	+ (Plus sign)
Zoom out	– and 1 (minus sign and 1)
Zoom out 200%	– and 2 (minus sign and 2)
Zoom out 400%	– and 4 (minus sign and 4)
Zoom out 800%	– and 8 (minus sign and 8)
Move selection by 10 pixels	Shift+arrow keys

Paint Window

Action	Shortcut
Open Gradient Settings dialog box and set ink to gradient	Double-click Brush, Rectangle, Bucket, or Polygon tool
Open Airbrush Settings dialog box	Double-click Airbrush tool
Open Pattern Settings dialog box	Double-click pattern chip
Open Brush Settings dialog box	Double-click Brush tool
Open Paint Window Preferences	Double-click line width selector
Turn selected tool into foreground eyedropper	D
Turn selected tool into background eyedropper	Shift+D
Turn selected tool into Hand tool	Spacebar
Turn selected tool into destination eyedropper	Option+D

Cast Window and Editing

Action	Shortcut
Open cast member editor	Double-click a paint, text, palette, or script cast member or select the cast member and press Return
Cast member script	⌘+' (apostrophe)
Display cast member info	Control-click cast thumbnail
Rename cast member	⌘+Shift+N
Open script in new window	Option-click Script button
Cast to Time (Option+Place button)	⌘+Shift+Option+L
Create a new cast member	⌘+Shift+A
Previous cast member	⌘+←
Next cast member	⌘+→
Scroll up/down one window	Page Up, Page Down
Scroll to top left of Cast window	Home
Scroll to show last occupied cast member	End
Type-select by cast member	Type number

Text

Command	Shortcut
Bold	⌘+Option+B
Italic	⌘+Option+I
Underline	⌘+Option+U

Script

Command	Shortcut
New Movie Script	⌘+Shift+U
Comment	⌘+Shift+. (period)
Uncomment	⌘+Shift+, (comma)

WINDOWS SHORTCUTS

File Menu

Command	Shortcut
New Movie	Ctrl+N
New Cast	Ctrl+Alt+N
Open	Ctrl+O
Close	Ctrl+F4
Save	Ctrl+S
Import	Ctrl+R
Export	Ctrl+Shift+R
Publish	Ctrl+Shift+S
Page Setup	Ctrl+Shift+P
Print	Ctrl+P
General Preferences	Ctrl+U
Exit	Alt+F4

Edit Menu

Command	Shortcut
Undo	Ctrl+Z
Repeat	Ctrl+Y
Cut	Ctrl+X
Copy	Ctrl+C
Paste	Ctrl+V
Clear	Delete
Duplicate	Ctrl+D
Select All	Ctrl+A
Find Text	Ctrl+F
Find Handler	Ctrl+Shift+; (semicolon)

Edit Menu

Command	Shortcut
Find Cast Member	Ctrl+; (semicolon)
Find Selection	Ctrl+H
Find Again	Ctrl+Alt+F
Replace Again	Ctrl+Alt+E
Edit Sprite Frames	Ctrl+Alt+]
Edit Entire Sprite	Ctrl+Alt+[
Exchange Cast Members	Ctrl+E
Launch External Editor	Ctrl+, (comma)

View Menu

Command	Shortcut
Next Marker	Ctrl+→
Previous Marker	Ctrl+←
Zoom In	Ctrl+ + (plus)
Zoom Out	Ctrl+ − (minus)
Show Guides	Ctrl+Shift+Alt+D
Snap to Guides	Ctrl+Shift+G
Show Grid	Ctrl+Shift+Alt+G
Snap to Grid	Ctrl+Alt+G
Temporarily Turn On Snap to Grid	G+drag sprite
Rulers	Ctrl+Shift+Alt+R
Show Info	Ctrl+Shift+Alt+O
Show Paths	Ctrl+Shift+Alt+H
Toolbar for Current Window	Ctrl+Shift+H
Keyframes	Ctrl+Shift+Alt+K

Modify Menu

Command	Shortcut
Cast Member Properties	Ctrl+I
Cast Member Script	Ctrl+' (apostrophe)
Sprite Properties	Ctrl+Shift+I
Sprite Script	Ctrl+Shift+' (apostrophe)
Sprite Tweening	Ctrl+Shift+B
Movie Properties	Ctrl+Shift+D

Modify Menu

Command	Shortcut
Movie Casts	Ctrl+Shift+C
Font	Ctrl+Shift+T
Paragraph	Ctrl+Shift+Alt+T
Join Sprites	Ctrl+J
Split Sprite	Ctrl+Shift+J
Extend Sprite	Ctrl+B
Bring to Front	Ctrl+Shift+↑
Move Forward	Ctrl+↑
Move Backward	Ctrl+↓
Send to Back	Ctrl+Shift+↓
Align	Ctrl+K
Tweak	Ctrl+Shift+K

Control Menu

Command	Shortcut
Play	Ctrl+Alt+P
Stop	Ctrl+Alt+. (period)
Rewind	Ctrl+Alt+R
Step Backward	Ctrl+Alt+←
Step Forward	Ctrl+Alt+→
Loop Playback	Ctrl+Alt+L
Volume: Mute	Ctrl+Alt+M
Toggle Breakpoint	F9
Watch Expression	Shift+F9
Ignore Breakpoints	Alt+F9
Step Script	F10
Step Into Script	F8
Run Script	F5
Recompile All Scripts	Ctrl+Shift+Alt+C

Insert Menu

Command	Shortcut
Keyframe	Ctrl+Alt+K
Frames	Ctrl+Shift+]
Insert 1 Frame	Ctrl+]
Remove Frame	Ctrl+[

Window Menu

Command	Shortcut
Toolbar	Ctrl+Shift+Alt+B
Tool Palette	Ctrl+7
Property Inspector	Ctrl+Alt+S
Behavior Inspector	Ctrl+Alt+; (semicolon)
Text Inspector	Ctrl+T
Stage	Ctrl+1
Control Panel	Ctrl+2
Markers	Ctrl+Shift+M
Score	Ctrl+4
Cast	Ctrl+3
Paint	Ctrl+5
Vector Shape	Ctrl+Shift+V
Text	Ctrl+6
Field	Ctrl+8
Color Palettes	Ctrl+Alt+7
Video	Ctrl+9
Script	Ctrl+0
Message	Ctrl+M
Debugger	Ctrl+` (open single quote)
Watcher	Ctrl+Shift+` (open single quote)

The Stage

Action	Shortcut
Resize the Stage to 100 percent	Ctrl+Alt+0 (zero)
Full screen Stage	Ctrl+Alt+1
Full screen playback	Ctrl+Shift+Alt+P
Black Stage	– (minus) on numeric keypad

The Stage

Action	Shortcut
White Stage	Shift+ –(minus) on numeric keypad
Invert Stage colors	Alt+ – (minus) on numeric keypad
Show/hide sprite paths	Ctrl+Shift+Alt+H
Select only the current frame of the sprite	Alt-click the sprite
Create a keyframe within a sprite path	Alt-click a tick mark in the sprite path
Show/hide Sprite Overlay	Ctrl+Shift+Alt+O
Change the opacity of Sprite Overlay	Drag the horizontal line on the right side of the overlay
Open cast member editor	Double-click sprite
Open Paint window	Ctrl+5
Ink pop-up	Ctrl-click
Real-time record	Ctrl+Spacebar+drag a sprite on the Stage
Display shortcut menu for selection	Right-click
Hide selection indicators	+ (plus) on the numeric keypad
Move sprite by 1 pixel	Arrow keys
Move sprite by 10 pixels	Shift+arrow keys
Select a locked sprite	L+click locked sprite

Score

Action	Shortcut
Duplicate selection (sprite or keyframe)	Alt
Select a frame within a sprite	Alt+click a frame within sprite
Turn on or off Edit Sprite Frames	Alt+double-click a frame within sprite
Select empty frames and sprite frames	Alt+drag, beginning in an empty frame
Select all the frames in a channel	Double-click channel number, drag to select multiple
Select all sprites in a channel	Click the channel number, drag to select multiple sprites
Previous keyframe	Shift+1 on numeric keypad
Next keyframe	Shift+2 on numeric keypad
Scroll the Score to view selected sprites	Shift+5 on numeric keypad
Open shortcut menu for Score display options and preferences	Right-click in the channel number area of the Score
Switch sprites in the Score	Ctrl+E
Shuffle backward	Ctrl+↑
Shuffle forward	Ctrl+↓
Overwrite sprite frames while dragging a selection to a new location	Press Control while dragging

Score

Action	Shortcut
Move sprite on the Stage by 1 pixel	Select in the Score and use arrow keys
Move sprite on the Stage by 10 pixels	Select in the Score and use Shift+arrow keys
Move entire sprite (instead of keyframe)	Spacebar+drag
Stretch a sprite without proportionally relocating keyframes	Ctrl+drag the end frame
Open cast editor for selected sprite	Double-click a sprite frame or the cast thumbnail
Open Frame Settings dialog box	Double-click Tempo, Palette, or Transition channel
Stretch a sprite without proportionally relocating keyframes	Ctrl+drag the end frame Lock Sprite Ctrl+L
Unlock Sprite	Ctrl+Shift+L
Join Sprites	Ctrl+J
Split Sprite	Ctrl+Shift+J
Extend Sprite	Ctrl+B
Sprite Tweening	Ctrl+Shift+B
Select a single frame within a sprite sprite in the Score	Alt+click the sprite on the Stage, or a frame within the
Move entire sprite between frames (instead of keyframes)	Spacebar+drag
Select all the sprites in a channel	Click the channel number, drag to select multiple
Select all the frames in a channel sprites	Double-click channel number, drag to select multiple
Turn on or off Edit Sprite Frames	Alt+double-click a frame within a sprite
Select empty frames and sprite frames	Alt+drag, beginning in an empty frame
Overwrite sprite frames while dragging a selection to a new location	Ctrl+drag
Move sprite on the Stage by 1 pixel	Select on the Stage or in the Score and use arrow keys
Move sprite on the Stage by 10 pixels keys	Select on the Stage or in the Score and use Shift+arrow
Show/hide sprite paths	Ctrl+Shift+Alt+H
Create a keyframe within a sprite path	Alt+click a tick mark in the sprite path on the Stage

Playback

Action	Shortcut
Move playback head to end of movie	Tab
Move playback head to beginning of movie	Shift+Tab
Move playback head to begginning/end	Ctrl+Shift+←/→
Go to next marker (or jump 10 frames)	Ctrl+→
Go to previous marker (or back 10 frames)	Ctrl+←
Hide cursor during playback	Shift+Enter on numeric keypad

Paint Window

Action	Shortcut
Next/previous cast member	←/→ keys
Open Transform Bitmap dialog box	Double-click color resolution indicator
Toggle Zoom In/Zoom Out	Ctrl+click in window or double-click Pencil tool
Xtra properties	Ctrl+Shift+O
Nudge selection rect. or lasso selection	Arrow keys with selection rectangle or lasso
Change airbrush size (while painting)	↑/↓ with airbrush selected
Change airbrush flow (while painting)	←/→ with airbrush selected
Change foreground color (not painting)	↑/↓, all tools
Change background color (not painting)	Shift+↑/↓, all tools
Change destination color (not painting)	Alt+↑/↓, all tools
Draw border with current pattern	Alt+Shape or Line tools
Select background color	Shift+Eyedropper tool
Select destination color	Alt+Eyedropper tool
Toggle between custom and grayscale patterns	Alt+click pattern
Polygon lasso	Alt+drag Lasso tool
Duplicate selection	Alt+drag
Stretch	Ctrl+drag
Draw with background color	Alt+Pencil tool
Clear visible part of window	Double-click Eraser tool
Open Color Palettes window	Double-click foreground, background, or destination color chip
Airbrush	A
Brush	B
Arc	C
Pick up color under cursor	Alt
Eraser	E
Bucket	F, K
Registration point	G
Hand	H
Eyedropper	I
Lasso	L
Marquee	M. S
Line	N, /, \,	
Circle	O
Filled Circle	Shift+O

Paint Window

Action	Shortcut
Polygon	P
Filled Polygon	Shift+P
Rectangle	R
Filled Rectangle	Shift+R
Text	T
Switch to black and white foreground color and background color	W
Switch foreground color and background color	X
Pencil	Y
Magnifying Glass	Z
Zoom in	+ (Plus sign)
Zoom out	– and 1 (minus sign and 1)
Zoom out 200%	– and 2 (minus sign and 2)
Zoom out 400%	– and 4 (minus sign and 4)
Zoom out 800%	– and 8 (minus sign and 8)
Move selection by 10 pixels	Shift+arrow keys
Open Gradient Settings dialog box and set ink to gradient	Double-click Brush, Rectangle, Bucket, or Polygon tool
Open Airbrush Settings dialog box	Double-click Airbrush tool
Open Pattern Settings dialog box	Double-click pattern chip
Open Brush Settings dialog box	Double-click Brush tool
Open Paint Window Preferences	Double-click line width selector
Turn selected tool into foreground eyedropper	D
Turn selected tool into background eyedropper	Shift+D
Turn selected tool into Hand tool	Spacebar
Turn selected tool into destination eyedropper	Alt+D

Cast Window

Action	Shortcut
Open cast member editor	Double-click a paint, text, palette, or script cast member or select the cast member and press Return
Cast member script	Ctrl+' (apostrophe)
Switch selected cast member with score selection	Alt+double-click thumbnail
Display cast member info	Ctrl-click cast thumbnail
Rename cast member	Ctrl+Shift+N
Open script in new window	Alt+Script button
Cast to Time (Option+Place button)	Ctrl+Shift+Alt+L
Create a new cast member	Ctrl+Shift+A
Previous cast member	Ctrl+←
Next cast member	Ctrl+→
Scroll up/down one window	Page up, Page down
Scroll to top left of Cast window	Home
Scroll to show last occupied cast member	End
Type-select by cast member	Type the cast member number

Text

Command	Shortcut
Bold	Ctrl+Alt+B
Italic	Ctrl+Alt+I
Underline	Ctrl+Alt+U

Script

Command	Shortcut
New Movie Script	Ctrl+Shift+U
Comment	Ctrl+Shift+. (period)
Uncomment	Ctrl+Shift+, (comma)

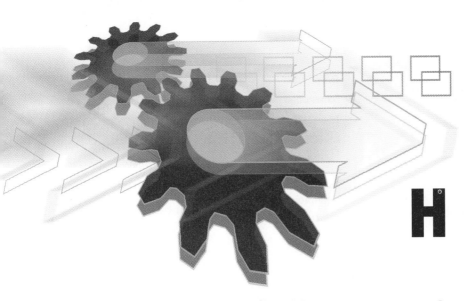

H

GUIDE TO XTRAS

This appendix contains an alphabetical list of Xtras for Director 5, 6, 7, 8 and 8.5. It starts off with an index list of Xtras by category and then goes into an alphabetical list that includes all the information about each Xtra.

Most of these Xtras will probably be upgraded to work with Director 8 by the time you read this. Some will not. Be sure to check with the company or on the Web to make sure the Xtra works with Director 8.

New Xtras are being created all the time. Check the Web sites listed in Appendix C, "Online Resources," for up-to-date information.

There are two great places on the Web to check for more Xtras. The first is the "Mile High Table O'Products" at http://www.updatestage.com/products.html. The second is Macromedia's own list of Xtras at http://www.macromedia.com/software/xtras/director/.

XTRA INDEX

3D

Dave's 3D Engine

Focus3D Xtra

QuickDraw 3D

RavWare OpenGL Xtra

ShapeShifter3D

Acrobat/PowerPoint

AcroViewer

MasterApp

RavWare PPViewer
Xtra

Authoring

Behavior Xtra

CastControl

RavWare MUIMaker

Speller, SpellerRT

Capturing and Exporting Graphics

DirectXport

f3Export Xtra

Grabber

RavImageExport Xtra

ScrnXtra

VSnap Xtra

CD-ROM/Projectors

AutoRun (PC) and
    AutoStart (Mac)

Border Xtra

BorderPatch

DropStart

Iconizer

Installed Fonts Xtra

LiveCD Xtra

RavWinShaper Xtra

RearWindow

Relaunch

WinGroup Xtra

XtrAgent

Databases

DAOTable

Datagrip

DDE Xtra

EasyBase

FileFlex

Index Xtra

Digital Video

DirectMedia

f3VideoCapture Xtra

ModMania

OnStage

QTIAW Xtra

Streaming Media Xtra

VCap Xtra

Video Mask

VideoSprite Xtra

Enhanced CD

CD Pro Xtra

ECD Xtra

Enhanced CD
Development Kit

External Devices

DirectComm

DirectControl

RavJoystick Xtra

RavWare GLU32 Xtra

zScript

Files

Attr Xtra

Attrib Xtra

BinaryIO Xtra

Buddy API

Buddy Zip

File IO

FileXtra

OSUtil

PickFolder Xtra

ProgressCopy

zOpen

Graphics and Effects

AdjustColors

AlphaMania

BitChecker

Blinker Xtra

BlurImage

CastEffects

CatCube

CatFlip

DM Star Field Effect

DM Waves Effect

Fireworks Import Xtra

Free Rotate

Gamma Control

PhotoCaster

TrackThemColors Xtra

Internet

BrowserController

CDLink

DirectConnection

DirectEmail

DirectFTP

FreePPP Control

HTML Xtra

LiveCD Xtra

Miscellaneous

Buddy Saver

CapsLock Xtra

ChartsInMotion Xtra

DateMaster

DateTime Xtra

TableMaker Xtra

TaskXtra

Printing

AcroViewer

mPrint

Print-O-Matic

Programming

Buddy API

ConvertData

DirectOS

Inspect

MasterApp

Ncrypt Xtra

OSUtil

System Tools Xtra

Versions XObject

zLaunch

Screen Resolution

DisplayRes

Resolution Xtra

Sound

Audio Xtra

Beatnik

bkMixer

DirectSound

DirectTTS

f3SoundFX Xtra

Promix Xtra

ShockTalk

SID6581

VolumeController Xtra

Yak Xtra

Transitions

CatBlur

CatFade

CatZoom

DirectTransition

DirectTransition3D

DM Transition Packs

DM Fade

User Interface

Dialogs Xtra

Popup Xtra

Precision Xtra

SetMouse Xtra

StyleUtil

ACROVIEWER

Description: View and print PostScript-quality PDF files using Adobe Acrobat viewers.

Developer: XtraMedia International

Web Address: http://www.xtramedia.com/xtras.shtml

Email: productInfo@xtramedia.com

Mailing Address: 1278 Glenneyre St., PMB #142, Laguna Beach, CA 92651-3103

ADJUSTCOLORS

Description: Performs color adjustments on graphics, including brightness, saturation, and RGB values of cast members.

Developer: Smoothware Design

Web Address: http://www.smoothware.com

Email: info@smoothware.com

Mailing Address: P.O. Box 0048, New York, NY 10023

Phone: 212-595-3190

ALPHAMANIA 2

Description: A sprite Xtra supporting dynamic Alpha-channel compositing of graphics.

Developer: Media Lab, Inc.

Web Address: http://www.medialab.com

Email: xtra-sales@medialab.com

Phone: 800-282-5361 or 303-774-0353

Fax: 303-485-9069

ATTR XTRA

Description: Makes it easy to set your files to read-only.

Developer: codeHorse

Web Address: http://www.codehorse.com/navproducts.html

Address: 47 Merriam Ave., Bronxville, NY 10708

Phone: 914-961-5636

Fax: 914-961-0450

ATTRIB XTRA

Description: Manipulates the file attributes of single files or complete file trees.

Developer: Media Connect

Web Address: http://www.mcmm.com

Address: Media Connect, Gratzmullerstr. 1, D-86150 Augsburg

Email: info@mcmm.com

Phone: 0049-821-34752-0

Fax: 0049-821-34752-49

AUDIO XTRA

Description: Records sound, plays back, and pauses.

Developer: Red Eye Software

Web Address: http://www.updatestage.com/xtras/xtrahome.html

Mailing Address: Red Eye Software, 3288 21st Street, #132, San Francisco, CA 94110

Email: sales@updatestage.com

AUTORUN (PC), AUTOSTART (MAC)

Description: Launches an application or an installer.

Developer: Dirigo Multimedia (Glenn M. Picher)

Web Address: http://www.maine.com/shops/gpicher/

Email: gpicher@maine.com

Mailing Address: 142 High Street, Suite 321, Portland, ME 04101

Phone: 207-767-8015

Fax: 207-775-4372

BEATNIK

Description: Enables you to play back and control MIDI files and Beatnik RMF files in Director.

Developer: Beatnik

Web Address: http://www.beatnik.com/software/xtra_director.html

Mailing Address: 2600 El Camino Real, San Mateo, Calif. 94403

Email Address: sales@beatnik.com

Phone: 650-295-2300

BEHAVIOR XTRA

Description: Automates the process of creating behaviors for Director.

Developer: Design Lynx

Web Address: http://www.designlynx.co.uk/xtras/

Email: xtras@designlynx.co.uk

Mailing Address: Newrella House, Curtis Road, Dorking, Surrey RH4 1DY

Phone: +44 (0) 1306 886337

Fax: +44 (0) 1306 877678

BINARYIO XTRA

Description: Reads, writes, and edits binary files. No chunk size limit.

Developer: Dirigo Multimedia (Glenn M. Picher)

Web Address: http://www.maine.com/shops/gpicher/

Email: gpicher@maine.com

Mailing Address: 142 High Street, Suite 321, Portland, ME 04101

Phone: 207-767-8015

Fax: 207-775-4372

BITCHECKER

Description: Finds cast members with incorrect palettes or bit depths.

Developer: Design Lynx

Web Address: http://www.designlynx.co.uk/xtras/

Email: xtras@designlynx.co.uk

Mailing Address: Newrella House, Curtis Road, Dorking, Surrey RH4 1DY

Phone: +44 (0) 1306 886337

Fax: +44 (0) 1306 877678

BKMIXER

Description: Controls CD audio, WAVE, and the system master volume on PC.

Developer: Burak KALAYCI

Web Address: http://www.updatestage.com/xtras/bkmixer.html

Email: support@updatestage.com

Mailing Address: 1341 Massachusetts Ave., Box 124, Arlington, MA 02476

Phone: 781-641-6043

Fax: 781-641-7068

BLINKER XTRA

Description: Makes sprites blink.

Developer: Penworks Corporation

Web Address: http://www.penworks.com

Email: sales@penworks.com

Mailing Address: P.O. Box 531, Holderness, NH 03245-0531

Phone: 1-800-PENWORX

Fax: 1-800-PW-FAX-NUM

BLURIMAGE

Description: Enables you to apply filters such as blur, motion-blur, emboss, invert, and find-edges.

Developer: Smoothware Design

Web Address: http://www.smoothware.com

Email: info@smoothware.com

Mailing Address: P.O. Box 0048, New York, NY 10023

Phone: 212-595-3190

BORDER XTRA AND BORDERPATCH

Description: Turns off the borders around the stage window or any MIAW.

Developer: Media Connect

Web Address: http://www.mcmm.com

Mailing Address: Media Connect, Gratzmullerstr. 1, D-86150 Augsburg

Email: info@mcmm.com

Phone: 0049-821-34752-0

Fax: 0049-821-34752-49

BROWSERCONTROLLER 2

Description: Controls Netscape or Internet Explorer.

Developer: Magister Ludi

Web Address: http://www.magisterludi.com/index.html?/xtras/

Email: info@magisterludi.com

Mailing Address: Via Natale Battaglia 8, 20127, Milan, ITALY

BUDDY API

Description: Includes a huge number of system calls to give you information about the user's system and change his or her computer's controls.

Developer: Magic Modules

Web Address: http://www.mods.com.au/default.htm

Email: gary@mods.com.au

Mailing Address: P.O. Box 550, Hamilton, Queensland, AUSTRALIA 4007

Phone: +61 0412 993612

Fax: +61 (7) 3256-4940

BUDDY SAVER

Description: An Xtra and installation maker for creating Windows screen savers.

Developer: Magic Modules

Web Address: `http://www.mods.com.au/default.htm`

Email: `gary@mods.com.au`

Mailing Address: P.O. Box 550, Hamilton, Queensland, AUSTRALIA 4007

Phone: +61 0412 993612

Fax: +61 (7) 3256-4940

BUDDY ZIP

Description: Zips and unzips files.

Developer: Magic Modules

Web Address: `http://www.mods.com.au/default.htm`

Email: `gary@mods.com.au`

Mailing Address: P.O. Box 550, Hamilton, Queensland, AUSTRALIA 4007

Phone: +61 0412 993612

Fax: +61 (7) 3256-4940

CAPSLOCK XTRA

Description: Returns the state of the Caps Lock key.

Developer: Scirius Development

Web Address: `http://www.scirius.com/HNorm/index.html`

Email: `xtras@scirius.com`

Mailing Address: Dresdner Straße 76a, D-04317 Leipzig, Germany

Phone: +49-341-6995741

Fax: +49-341-6995742

CASTCONTROL

Description: Controls the attachment and detachment of external cast libraries.

Developer: Paul Farry

Web Address: `http://www.powerup.com.au/~farryp/`

Email: `p.farry@kagi.com`

CASTEFFECTS

Description: Enables bitmap and cast manipulation from Lingo. Can transform, rotate, composite, and scale bitmaps and Casts.

Developer: Penworks Corporation

Web Address: http://www.penworks.com

Email: sales@penworks.com

Mailing Address: P.O. Box 531, Holderness, NH 03245-0531

Phone: 1-800-PENWORX

Fax: 1-800-PW-FAX-NUM

CATBLUR

Description: Adds blurred transitions on Windows machines.

Developer: CatEffects S.L.

Web Address: http://www.cateffects.com/xtras.html

Mailing Address: Doctor Esquerdo, 166 3° B, 28007 Madrid, Spain

Phone: +34 91.434.06.30

Fax: +34 91.434.06.30

Email: cesar@cateffects.com

CATCUBE

Description: Images can be mapped onto a cube.

Developer: CatEffects S.L.

Web Address: http://www.cateffects.com/xtras.html

Mailing Address: Doctor Esquerdo, 166 3° B, 28007 Madrid, Spain

Phone: +34 91.434.06.30

Fax: +34 91.434.06.30

Email: cesar@cateffects.com

CATFADE

Description: Smoothes out transitions.

Developer: CatEffects S.L.

Web Address: http://www.cateffects.com/xtras.html

Mailing Address: Doctor Esquerdo, 166 3° B, 28007 Madrid, Spain

Phone: +34 91.434.06.30

Fax: +34 91.434.06.30

Email: cesar@cateffects.com

CATFLIP

Description: Images can be mapped into a plane that spins either horizontally or vertically.

Developer: CatEffects S.L.

Web Address: http://www.cateffects.com/xtras.html

Mailing Address: Doctor Esquerdo, 166 3° B, 28007 Madrid, Spain

Phone: +34 91.434.06.30

Fax: +34 91.434.06.30

Email: cesar@cateffects.com

CATZOOM

Description: Adds a zoom transition on Windows machines.

Developer: CatEffects S.L.

Web Address: http://www.cateffects.com/xtras.html

Mailing Address: Doctor Esquerdo, 166 3° B, 28007 Madrid, Spain

Phone: +34 91.434.06.30

Fax: +34 91.434.06.30

Email: cesar@cateffects.com

CD PRO XTRA

Description: Enables some CD audio control.

Developer: Penworks Corporation

Web Address: http://www.penworks.com

Email: sales@penworks.com

Mailing Address: P.O. Box 531, Holderness, NH 03245-0531

Phone: 1-800-PENWORX

Fax: 1-800-PW-FAX-NUM

CDLINK

Description: Manages a Web connection over the PPP-TCP/IP protocol without requiring a browser.

Developer: Ideogram Design

Web Address: http://www.cdlink.com/

Email: developers@cdlink.com

Mailing Address: 15, traverse des Brucs, 06560 Valbonne Sophia Antipolis, FRANCE

Phone: 33-493-65-49-10

Fax: 33-493-65-47-92

CHARTSINMOTION XTRA

Description: Enables you to plot standard business charts in a window over a Director Stage.

Developer: XtraMedia International

Web Address: http://www.xtramedia.com/xtras.shtml

Email: productInfo@xtramedia.com

Mailing Address: 1278 Glenneyre St., PMB #142, Laguna Beach, CA 92651-3103

CONVERTDATA

Description: Adds bitwise manipulation of data values to Lingo.

Developer: Dirigo Multimedia (Glenn M. Picher)

Web Address: http://www.maine.com/shops/gpicher/

Email: gpicher@maine.com

Mailing Address: 142 High Street, Suite 321, Portland, ME 04101

Phone: 207-767-8015

Fax: 207-775-4372

DAOTABLE

Description: A complement to the Datagrip Xtra that enables you to see more information about Microsoft Access databases.

Developer: Paul Farry

Web Address: http://www.powerup.com.au/~farryp/

Email: p.farry@kagi.com

DATAGRIP

Description: Enables Director to communicate with Microsoft Access databases.

Developer: Sight and Sound Software

Web Address: http://www.datagrip.com/

DATEMASTER

Description: Enables you to retrieve dates in a consistent format.

Developer: Penworks Corporation

Web Address: http://www.penworks.com

Email: sales@penworks.com

Mailing Address: P.O. Box 531, Holderness, NH 03245-0531

Phone: 1-800-PENWORX

Fax: 1-800-PW-FAX-NUM

DATETIME XTRA

Description: Returns date- and time-related information.

Developer: Scirius Development

Web Address: `http://www.scirius.com/HNorm/index.html`

Email: `xtras@scirius.com`

Mailing Address: Dresdner Straβe 76a, D-04317 Leipzig, Germany

Phone: +49-341-6995741

Fax: +49-341-6995742

DAVE'S 3D ENGINE

Description: Positions sprites in 3D, performs translations/rotation/scaling on them; enables you to do sprite sorting, scaling, blending, and member changing of depth cues. Does not use Director 8.5's 3D engine, but instead uses pure Lingo.

Developer: Dave Cole

Web Address: `http://www.dubbus.com/devnull/`

Email: `dcole@sigma6.com`

DDE XTRA

Description: Enables Director to act as a Dynamic Data Exchange client.

Developer: Advanced Technology Center—University of Missouri-Columbia

Web Address: `http://www.atc.missouri.edu/software/`

Email: `ccjr@atc.missouri.edu`

DIALOGS XTRA

Description: Displays Open, Save, and PickFolder file dialog boxes.

Developer: Red Eye Software

Web Address: `http://www.updatestage.com/xtras/xtrahome.html`

Mailing Address: Red Eye Software, 3288 21st Street, #132, San Francisco, CA 94110

Email: `sales@updatestage.com`

DIRECTCOMM XTRA

Description: Provides direct access to communication resources such as serial ports, parallel ports, fax machines, and modems.

Developer: DirectXtras Llc.

Web Address: `http://www.directxtras.com/`

Email: `info@directxtras.com`

Mailing Address: P.O. Box 2645, Menlo Park, CA 94026

Phone: 1-800-445-3093, 415-505-8249

Fax: 801-858-5841

DIRECTCONNECTION XTRA

Description: Helps you control the process of allowing Mac and Windows users to connect to the Internet.

Developer: DirectXtras Llc.

Web Address: http://www.directxtras.com/

Email: info@directxtras.com

Mailing Address: P.O. Box 2645, Menlo Park, CA 94026

Phone: 1-800-445-3093, 415-505-8249

Fax: 801-858-5841

DIRECTCONTROL

Description: Enables Lingo control of analog and digital joysticks.

Developer: DirectXtras Llc.

Web Address: http://www.directxtras.com/

Email: info@directxtras.com

Mailing Address: P.O. Box 2645, Menlo Park, CA 94026

Phone: 1-800-445-3093, 415-505-8249

Fax: 801-8585841

DIRECTEMAIL XTRA

Description: Enables you to compose and send emails, with attachments.

Developer: DirectXtras Llc.

Web Address: http://www.directxtras.com/

Email: info@directxtras.com

Mailing Address: P.O. Box 2645, Menlo Park, CA 94026

Phone: 1-800-445-3093, 415-505-8249

Fax: 801-858-5841

DIRECTFTP XTRA

Description: Provides a Lingo interface for FTP.

Developer: DirectXtras Llc.

Web Address: http://www.directxtras.com/

Email: info@directxtras.com

Mailing Address: P.O. Box 2645, Menlo Park, CA 94026

Phone: 1-800-445-3093, 415-505-8249

Fax: 801-858-5841

DIRECTMEDIA XTRA

Description: Gives developers control over MPEG and AVI files.

Developer: Tabuleiro da Baiana

Web Address: http://xtras.tbaiana.com/

Email: tbaiana@tbaiana.com

Mailing Address: Rua Engenheiro Mario Pamponet, 280, Vila Beatriz, Sao Paulo - SP BRAZIL, 05448 - 010

Phone: +55 11 3871-5730

Fax: +55 11 3871-4025

DIRECTOS

Description: Provides access to a variety of functions on Mac and Windows.

Developer: DirectXtras Llc.

Web Address: http://www.directxtras.com/

Email: info@directxtras.com

Mailing Address: P.O. Box 2645, Menlo Park, CA 94026

Phone: 1-800-445-3093, 415-505-8249

Fax: 801-858-5841

DIRECTSOUND XTRA

Description: Enables the use of Microsoft's DirectSound API.

Developer: DirectXtras Llc.

Web Address: http://www.directxtras.com/

Email: info@directxtras.com

Mailing Address: P.O. Box 2645, Menlo Park, CA 94026

Phone: 1-800-445-3093, 415-505-8249

Fax: 801-858-5841

DIRECTTRANSITION XTRA

Description: Adds a whole set of transitions, including Avalanche, Bricks, Headline, Pivot, Shatter, Turn Table, and Zipper.

Developer: DirectXtras Llc.

Web Address: http://www.directxtras.com/

Email: info@directxtras.com

Mailing Address: P.O. Box 2645, Menlo Park, CA 94026

Phone: 1-800-445-3093, 415-505-8249

Fax: 801-858-5841

DIRECTTRANSITION3D XTRA

Description: Adds a whole set of 3D-like transitions, including accordion, bubble, flipboards, flush, fractal fade, fractal morph, fracture, page turn, and peel.

Developer: DirectXtras Llc.

Web Address: http://www.directxtras.com/

Email: info@directxtras.com

Mailing Address: P.O. Box 2645, Menlo Park, CA 94026

Phone: 1-800-445-3093, 415-505-8249

Fax: 801-858-5841

DIRECTTTS XTRA

Description: Allows you to turn text to speech.

Developer: DirectXtras Llc.

Web Address: http://www.directxtras.com/

Email: info@directxtras.com

Mailing Address: P.O. Box 2645, Menlo Park, CA 94026

Phone: 1-800-445-3093, 415-505-8249

Fax: 801-858-5841

DIRECTXPORT XTRA

Description: Enables you to export images into a wide variety of formats.

Developer: DirectXtras Llc.

Web Address: http://www.directxtras.com/

Email: info@directxtras.com

Mailing Address: P.O. Box 2645, Menlo Park, CA 94026

Phone: 1-800-445-3093, 415-505-8249

Fax: 801-858-5841

DISPLAYRES XTRA

Description: Controls Windows' display devices.

Developer: Dirigo Multimedia (Glenn M. Picher)

Web Address: http://www.maine.com/shops/gpicher/

Email: gpicher@maine.com

Mailing Address: 142 High Street, Suite 321, Portland, ME 04101

Phone: 207-767-8015

Fax: 207-775-4372

DM TRANSITION PACKS

Description: Provides a variety of transitions including rollup, fades, wormhole, laser, glass, and so on.

Developer: Dedalomedia Interactive

Web Address: http://www.dmtools.com/

Email: salesdm@dmtools.com

Mailing Address: B.go Padova 170, 35013 Cittadella PD, ITALY

Telephone: +39-049-941-44-11

Fax: +39-049-941-44-30

DM WAVES EFFECT

Description: Provides realistic ripples.

Developer: Dedalomedia Interactive

Web Address: http://www.dmtools.com/

Email: salesdm@dmtools.com

Mailing Address: B.go Padova 170, 35013 Cittadella PD, ITALY

Telephone: +39-049-941-44-11

Fax: +39-049-941-44-30

DM STAR FIELD EFFECT

Description: Provides animated star fields.

Developer: Dedalomedia Interactive

Web Address: http://www.dmtools.com/

Email: salesdm@dmtools.com

Mailing Address: B.go Padova 170, 35013 Cittadella PD, ITALY

Telephone: +39-049-941-44-11

Fax: +39-049-941-44-30

DM FADE

Description: Provides fade transitions.

Developer: Dedalomedia Interactive

Web Address: http://www.dmtools.com/

Email: salesdm@dmtools.com

Mailing Address: B.go Padova 170, 35013 Cittadella PD, ITALY

Telephone: +39-049-941-44-11

Fax: +39-049-941-44-30

DROPSTART

Description: Enables you to easily use the Mac QuickTime's AutoStart feature.

Developer: Dirigo Multimedia (Glenn M. Picher)

Web Address: http://www.maine.com/shops/gpicher/

Email: gpicher@maine.com

Mailing Address: 142 High Street, Suite 321, Portland, ME 04101

Phone: 207-767-8015

Fax: 207-775-4372

EASYBASE

Description: Enables you to create and use a database.

Developer: Klaus Kobald Software Design

Web Address: http://www.kobald.com/EasyBase/

Email: klaus@kobald.com

ECD XTRA

Description: Calculates disk space remaining after an audio session for enhanced CD.

Developer: European Enhanced CD Information Center

Web Address: http://members.tripod.com/~chief_raw_i/EECD/

ENHANCED CD DEVELOPMENT KIT

Description: Includes two XObjects that provide cross-platform CD audio and file system control from within Director.

Developer: Macromedia

Web Address: http://www.macromedia.com/software/xtras/director/

F3EXPORT XTRA

Description: Exports cast members in BMP and JPEG format.

Developer: Focus 3

Web Address: http://www.umminger.com/focus3/products_and_downloads.html

Email: hbdi@dnai.com

Phone: 510-548-7847

F3SOUNDFX XTRA

Description: Provides sound recording and effects.

Developer: Focus 3

Web Address: http://www.umminger.com/focus3/products_and_downloads.html

Email: hbdi@dnai.com

Phone: 510-548-7847

F3VIDEOCAPTURE XTRA

Description: Displays live video.

Developer: Focus 3

Web Address: http://www.umminger.com/focus3/products_and_downloads.html

Email: hbdi@dnai.com

Phone: 510-548-7847

FILEFLEX

Description: Provides a cross-platform database engine.

Developer: Component Software

Web Address: http://www.fileflex.com

Email: support@fileflex.com

Mailing Address: P.O. Box 201, Rocky Hill, NJ 08553

Phone: 609-497-4501

Fax: 609-497-4008

FILE IO

Description: Allows for the cross-platform reading and writing of files.

Developer: Macromedia

Web Address: http://www.macromedia.com/software/xtras/director/

FILEXTRA

Description: Provides a file enhancer.

Developer: Little Planet Publishing

Web Address: http://kblab.net/xtras/

Email: kent@littleplanet.com

FIREWORKS IMPORT XTRA

Description: Enables you to import Fireworks documents into Director and convert the JavaScript behaviors they use to Lingo.

Developer: Macromedia

Web Address: http://www.macromedia.com/software/xtras/director/

FOCUS3D XTRA

Description: Enables you to use QuickDraw3D images.

Developer: Focus 3

Web Address: http://www.umminger.com/focus3/products_and_downloads.html

Email: hbdi@dnai.com

Phone: 510-548-7847

FREE ROTATE

Description: Controls the rotation of a cast member in Lingo.

Developer: Smoothware Design

Web Address: http://www.smoothware.com

Email: info@smoothware.com

Mailing Address: P.O. Box 0048, New York, NY 10023

Phone: 212-595-3190

FREEPPP CONTROL

Description: Controls connections to the Internet.

Developer: Paul Farry

Web Address: http://www.powerup.com.au/~farryp/

Email: p.farry@kagi.com

GAMMA XTRA

Description: Solves the problem of images made on the Mac looking too dark when viewed in Windows.

Developer: Magister Ludi

Web Address: http://www.magisterludi.com/index.html?/xtras/

Email: info@magisterludi.com

Mailing Address: Via Natale Battaglia 8, 20127, Milan, ITALY

GRABBER

Description: Takes snapshots of the screen, stage, or area of the stage. Builds a new cast member by combining existing members either down or across.

Developer: Paul Farry

Web Address: http://www.powerup.com.au/~farryp/

Email: p.farry@kagi.com

HTML XTRA

Description: Enables the display of HTML on the stage.

Developer: Media Connect

Web Address: http://www.mcmm.com

Mailing Address: Media Connect, Gratzmullerstr. 1, D-86150 Augsburg

Email: info@mcmm.com

Phone: 0049-821-34752-0

Fax: 0049-821-34752-49

ICONIZER

Description: Enables you to customize the Projector icon from within Director.

Developer: Penworks Corporation

Web Address: http://www.penworks.com

Email: sales@penworks.com

Mailing Address: P.O. Box 531, Holderness, NH 03245-0531

Phone: 1-800-PENWORX

Fax: 1-800-PW-FAX-NUM

INDEX XTRA

Description: Provides text searches.

Developer: Media Connect

Web Address: http://www.mcmm.com

Mailing Address: Media Connect, Gratzmullerstr. 1, D-86150 Augsburg

Email: info@mcmm.com

Phone: 0049-821-34752-0

Fax: 0049-821-34752-49

INSPECT

Description: Complements the Message window and the debugger in Director.

Developer: codeHorse

Web Address: http://www.codehorse.com/navproducts.html

Mailing Address: 47 Merriam Ave., Bronxville, NY 10708

Phone: 914-961-5636

Fax: 914-961-0450

INSTALLED FONTS XTRA

Description: Returns a list of the user's installed fonts.

Developer: Red Eye Software

Web Address: http://www.updatestage.com/xtras/xtrahome.html

Mailing Address: Red Eye Software, 3288 21st Street, #132, San Francisco, CA 94110

Email: sales@updatestage.com

LIVECD XTRA

Description: Integrates Netscape-compatible plug-ins and HTML browsing into Director and Authorware.

Developer: Trevi Media

Web Address: http://www.trevimedia.com/products/livecd/livecd.html

Email: sales@trevimedia.com

Mailing Address: Trevi Media, Inc., 33 Bay Way, San Rafael, CA 94901

Phone: 1-415-459-0945

Fax: 1-415-459-0944

MASTERAPP

Description: Enables you to locate, launch, and control other applications from Director and Authorware.

Developer: Dirigo Multimedia (Glenn M. Picher)

Web Address: http://www.maine.com/shops/gpicher/

Email: gpicher@maine.com

Mailing Address: 142 High Street, Suite 321, Portland, ME 04101

Phone: 207-767-8015

Fax: 207-775-4372

MODMANIA

Description: Puts MPEG video into multimedia products.

Developer: Paul Farry

Web Address: http://www.powerup.com.au/~farryp/

Email: p.farry@kagi.com

MPRINT DESIGNER XTRA

Description: Enables you to generate elaborate reports from Authorware and Director.

Developer: MEDIA Shoppe

Web Address: http://www.mediashoppe.com/xtras/

Mailing Address: 203 W. 8th Ave., Suite 320, Amarillo, TX 79101

Email Address: support@mediashoppe.com

Phone: 806-371-0033

Fax: 806-371-0264

NCRYPT XTRA

Description: Encrypts and decrypts files and text on-the-fly.

Developer: MEDIA Shoppe

Web Address: http://www.mediashoppe.com/xtras/

Mailing Address: 203 W. 8th Ave., Suite 320, Amarillo, TX 79101

Email Address: support@mediashoppe.com

Phone: 806-371-0033

Fax: 806-371-0264

ONSTAGE

Description: Provides full-motion video and DVD.

Developer: Visible Light

Web Address: http://www.visiblelight.com/products/onstage/

Email: sales@visiblelight.com

Phone: 407-327-5700 or 1-800-596-4494

Fax: 407-327-5006

OSUTIL

Description: Moves, renames, or copies files from Lingo.

Developer: Paul Farry

Web Address: http://www.powerup.com.au/~farryp/

Email: p.farry@kagi.com

PHOTOCASTER 3

Description: Imports PhotoShop layers into Director as separate cast members.

Developer: Media Lab, Inc.

Web Address: http://www.medialab.com

Email: xtra-sales@medialab.com

Phone: 800-282-5361 or 303-774-0353

Fax: 303-485-9069

PICKFOLDER XTRA

Description: Enables folders to be chosen.

Developer: Dirigo Multimedia (Glenn M. Picher)

Web Address: http://www.maine.com/shops/gpicher/

Email: gpicher@maine.com

Mailing Address: 142 High Street, Suite 321, Portland, ME 04101

Phone: 207-767-8015

Fax: 207-775-4372

POPUP XTRA

Description: Creates custom pop-up menus on-the-fly.

Developer: Red Eye Software

Mailing Address: Red Eye Software, 3288 21st Street, #132, San Francisco, CA 94110

Web Address: http://www.updatestage.com/xtras/xtrahome.html

Email: sales@updatestage.com

PRECISION XTRA

Description: Enables you to receive mouse events at the pixel level.

Developer: Penworks Corporation

Web Address: http://www.penworks.com

Email: sales@penworks.com

Mailing Address: P.O. Box 531, Holderness, NH 03245-0531

Phone: 1-800-PENWORX

Fax: 1-800-PW-FAX-NUM

PRINT-O-MATIC

Description: Provides a Mac and Windows printing tool.

Developer: Electronic Ink

Web Address: http://www.printomatic.com

Email: ink@crestedbutte.net

Mailing Address: P.O. Box 3473, Crested Butte, CO 81223

Phone: 970-349-1747

PROGRESSCOPY

Description: Displays a progress bar while it is copying files.

Developer: Dirigo Multimedia (Glenn M. Picher)

Web Address: http://www.maine.com/shops/gpicher/

Email: gpicher@maine.com

Mailing Address: 142 High Street, Suite 321, Portland, ME 04101

Phone: 207-767-8015

Fax: 207-775-4372

PROMIX XTRA

Description: A comprehensive set of tools targeted directly at sound cards.

Developer: MEDIA Shoppe

Web Address: http://www.mediashoppe.com/xtras/

Mailing Address: 203 W. 8th Ave., Suite 320, Amarillo, TX 79101

Email Address: support@mediashoppe.com

Phone: 806-371-0033

Fax: 806-371-0264

QTIAW XTRA

Description: Allows you to display QuickTime movies in a native QuickTime window rather than on the Stage.

Developer: Media Connect

Web Address: http://www.mcmm.com

Address: Media Connect, Gratzmullerstr. 1, D-86150 Augsburg

Email: info@mcmm.com

Phone: 0049-821-34752-0

Fax: 0049-821-34752-49

QUICKDRAW 3D

Description: Provides 3D modeling for Director.

Developer: Macromedia

Web Address: http://www.macromedia.com/software/xtras/director/

RAVIMAGEEXPORT XTRA

Description: Enables Director developers to change the shape of the display window for a projector.

Developer: RavWare

Web Address: http://www.ravware.com/

Email: info@ravware.com

Mailing Address: P.O. Box 3084, Glen Ellyn, IL 60138-3084

RAVJOYSTICK XTRA

Description: Gives you the ability to use regular and force feedback joysticks, steering wheels, touch screens, and other gaming devices.

Developer: RavWare

Web Address: http://www.ravware.com/

Email: info@ravware.com

Mailing Address: P.O. Box 3084, Glen Ellyn, IL 60138-3084

RAVWARE GLU32 XTRA

Description: Calls 32-bit DLLs from Lingo. Provides for direct access to system calls.

Developer: RavWare

Web Address: http://www.ravware.com/

Email: info@ravware.com

Mailing Address: P.O. Box 3084, Glen Ellyn, IL 60138-3084

RAVWARE MUIMAKER

Description: Enables you to visually design a dialog box and then generates the Lingo code for it.

Developer: RavWare

Web Address: http://www.ravware.com/

Email: info@ravware.com

Mailing Address: P.O. Box 3084, Glen Ellyn, IL 60138-3084

RAVWARE OPENGL XTRA

Description: Gives you the capability to use the OpenGL API with Director.

Developer: RavWare

Web Address: http://www.ravware.com/

Email: info@ravware.com

Mailing Address: P.O. Box 3084, Glen Ellyn, IL 60138-3084

RAVWARE PPVIEWER XTRA

Description: Allows you to control Microsoft PowerPoint Viewer 97.

Developer: RavWare

Web Address: http://www.ravware.com/

Email: info@ravware.com

Mailing Address: P.O. Box 3084, Glen Ellyn, IL 60138-3084

RAVWINSHAPER XTRA

Description: Enables Director developers to change the shape of the display window for a projector.

Developer: RavWare

Web Address: http://www.ravware.com/

Email: info@ravware.com

Mailing Address: P.O. Box 3084, Glen Ellyn, IL 60138-3084

REARWINDOW

Description: Enables you to display a window behind the Director Stage.

Developer: XtraMedia International

Web Address: http://www.xtramedia.com/xtras.shtml

Email: productInfo@xtramedia.com

Mailing Address: 1278 Glenneyre St., PMB #142, Laguna Beach, CA 92651-3103

RELAUNCH

Description: Quits Director application, runs another application, and then restarts original application.

Developer: Dirigo Multimedia (Glenn M. Picher)

Web Address: http://www.maine.com/shops/gpicher/

Email: gpicher@maine.com

Mailing Address: 142 High Street, Suite 321, Portland, ME 04101

Phone: 207-767-8015

Fax: 207-775-4372

RESOLUTION XTRA

Description: Allows you to change the screen resolution and depth and then change it back without disturbing the position of the desktop icons.

Developer: Andrade Arts

Web Address: http://andradearts.com/

Email: mark@andradearts.com

Mailing Address: Mark Andrade, 12626 Milton Street, Los Angeles, CA 90066

SCRNXTRA

Description: Provides a screen-capture tool.

Developer: Little Planet Publishing

Web Address: http://kblab.net/xtras/

Email: kent@littleplanet.com

SETMOUSE XTRA

Description: Sets the mouse to any location on the screen.

Developer: Scirius Development

Web Address: http://www.scirius.com/HNorm/index.html

Email: xtras@scirius.com

Mailing Address: Dresdner Straße 76a, D-04317 Leipzig, GERMANY

Phone: +49-341-6995741

Fax: +49-341-6995742

SHAPESHIFTER 3D

Description: Adds a simple 3D creation tool in the authoring environment that can create Shockwave 3D files and members.

Developer: Tabuleiro da Baiana

Web Address: http://xtras.tbaiana.com/

Email: tbaiana@tbaiana.com

Mailing Address: Rua Engenheiro Mario Pamponet, 280, Vila Beatriz, Sao Paulo - SP BRAZIL, 05448 - 010

Phone: +55 11 3871-5730

Fax: +55 11 3871-4025

SHOCKTALK

Description: Incorporates spoken user interactions.

Developer: Digital Dreams

Web Address: http://www.surftalk.com/shocktalk/index.html

SID6581

Description: Enables you to include Commodore 64 SID music files as Director cast members.

Developer: Paul Farry

Web Address: http://www.powerup.com.au/~farryp/

Email: p.farry@kagi.com

SPELLER, SPELLERPRO, SPELLERRT

Description: Spell checks all text cast members. The "RT" version can do this while the projector is running.

Developer: Design Lynx

Web Address: http://www.designlynx.co.uk/xtras/

Email: xtras@designlynx.co.uk

Mailing Address: Newrella House, Curtis Road, Dorking, Surrey RH4 1DY

Phone: +44 (0) 1306 886337

Fax: +44 (0) 1306 877678

STREAMING MEDIA XTRA

Description: Plays Windows Media Files inside Shockwave movies.

Developer: Tabuleiro da Baiana

Web Address: http://xtras.tbaiana.com/

Email: tbaiana@tbaiana.com

Mailing Address: Rua Engenheiro Mario Pamponet, 280, Vila Beatriz, Sao Paulo - SP BRAZIL, 05448 - 010

Phone: +55 11 3871-5730

Fax: +55 11 3871-4025

STYLEUTIL

Description:Takes an editable field and creates the Rich Text Format (RTF) required to import the Styles field into Director.

Developer: Paul Farry

Web Address: http://www.powerup.com.au/~farryp/

Email: p.farry@kagi.com

SYSTEM TOOLS XTRA

Description: 32-bit scripting Xtra for accessing common Windows API functions for Windows 95/98/NT.

Developer: MEDIA Shoppe

Web Address: http://www.mediashoppe.com/xtras/

Mailing Address: 203 W. 8th Ave., Suite 320, Amarillo, TX 79101

Email Address: support@mediashoppe.com

Phone: 806-371-0033

Fax: 806-371-0264

TABLEMAKER XTRA

Description: Enables you to view spreadsheet data over the Director Stage.

Developer: XtraMedia International

Web Address: http://www.xtramedia.com/xtras.shtml

Email: productInfo@xtramedia.com

Mailing Address: 1278 Glenneyre St., PMB #142, Laguna Beach, CA 92651-3103

TASKXTRA

Description: Manages automated functions.

Developer: Little Planet Publishing

Web Address: http://kblab.net/xtras/

Email: kent@littleplanet.com

TRACKTHEMCOLORS XTRA

Description: Tracks multiple objects in a video according to their color value, brightness, or pattern.

Developer: Smoothware Design

Web Address: http://www.smoothware.com

Email: info@smoothware.com

Mailing Address: P.O. Box 0048, New York, NY 10023

Phone: 212-595-3190

VCAP XTRA

Description: Provides video capture from a Video for Windows capture card.

Developer: Penworks Corporation

Web Address: http://www.penworks.com

Email: sales@penworks.com

Mailing Address: P.O. Box 531, Holderness, NH 03245-0531

Phone: 1-800-PENWORX

Fax: 1-800-PW-FAX-NUM

VERSIONS XOBJECT

Description: Determines QuickTime, DOS, and Windows file version numbers.

Developer: Dirigo Multimedia (Glenn M. Picher)

Web Address: http://www.maine.com/shops/gpicher/

Email: gpicher@maine.com

Mailing Address: 142 High Street, Suite 321, Portland, ME 04101

Phone: 207-767-8015

Fax: 207-775-4372

VIDEO MASK

Description: Lets you apply video masks to live video.

Developer: Smoothware Design

Web Address: http://www.smoothware.com

Email: info@smoothware.com

Mailing Address: P.O. Box 0048, New York, NY 10023

Phone: 212-595-3190

VIDEOSPRITE XTRA

Description: Displays live video in a sprite.

Developer: Penworks Corporation

Web Address: http://www.penworks.com

Email: sales@penworks.com

Mailing Address: P.O. Box 531, Holderness, NH 03245-0531

Phone: 1-800-PENWORX

Fax: 1-800-PW-FAX-NUM

VOLUMECONTROLLER XTRA

Description: Provides smooth control of volume.

Developer: Magister Ludi

Web Address: http://www.magisterludi.com/index.html?/xtras/

Email: info@magisterludi.com

Mailing Address: Via Natale Battaglia 8, 20127, Milan, ITALY

VSNAP XTRA

Description: Provides video preview and single frame capture from a Video for Windows capture card.

Developer: Penworks Corporation

Web Address: http://www.penworks.com

Email: sales@penworks.com

Mailing Address: P.O. Box 531, Holderness, NH 03245-0531

Phone: 1-800-PENWORX

Fax: 1-800-PW-FAX-NUM

WINGROUP XTRA

Description: Enables you to create, edit, and delete entries in the Windows Start menu.

Developer: Media Connect

Web Address: http://www.mcmm.com

Mailing Address: Media Connect, Gratzmullerstr. 1, D-86150 Augsburg

Email: info@mcmm.com

Phone: 0049-821-34752-0

Fax: 0049-821-34752-49

XTRAGENT

Description: Enables the use of Microsoft's Agent technology in Director applications.

Developer: DirectXtras Llc.

Web Address: http://www.directxtras.com/

Email: info@directxtras.com

Mailing Address: P.O. Box 2645, Menlo Park, CA 94026

Phone: 1-800-445-3093, 415-505-8249

Fax: 801-858-5841

YAK XTRA

Description: Adds a "speak" command to Lingo, which speaks any text string using text-to-speech.

Developer: Electronic Ink

Web Address: http://www.printomatic.com

Email: ink@printomatic.com

Phone: 970-349-1747

Mailing Address: P.O. Box 3473, Crested Butte, CO 81224

ZLAUNCH

Description: Enables you to launch external applications from Director.

Developer: Zeus Productions

Web Address: http://www.zeusprod.com/

Email: sales@zeusprod.com

Phone: 1-800-797-2968

ZOPEN

Description: Opens and prints documents. Locates external applications such as browsers.

Developer: Zeus Productions

Web Address: http://www.zeusprod.com/

Email: sales@zeusprod.com

Phone: 1-800-797-2968

ZSCRIPT

Description: Controls AppleScript-able applications.

Developer: Zeus Productions

Web Address: http://www.zeusprod.com/

Email: sales@zeusprod.com

Phone: 1-800-797-2968

LINGO REFERENCE

Whenever you have a large, complex programming language such as
Lingo, it is useful to have an alphabetical reference. Every Director 8.5
owner already has one in the form of the Lingo Dictionary book that
comes with the program, or the Lingo Dictionary in the online help.This
appendix is meant to be a complement to the official documents. In
many cases I have simpler entries for quick reference, and in some cases
I have more detailed entries. I also tried to do a better job of categoriz-
ing and cross-referencing than the official manuals.

Here is a description of what each entry contains:

- **Topic**—Which part of Director the keyword relates to. This
  is truly a "topic," not a "type." For instance, *the
  systemDate* is shown relating to the topic "Date & Time"
  rather than as a "system property."

- **Type**—Command, function, property, and so on.

- **Description**—A short sentence or paragraph to give you an
  idea of what the keyword is and how to use it.

- **Syntax Sample**—A segment of Lingo code that shows the
  keyword in use. Sometimes it's a complete example, and
  other times it's a code snippet. The purpose is to quickly
  relay to the readers how the syntax works. Sometimes I
  use an ... to show a space where you can insert other code
  into the example. Other times, I use the *put* command to
  show the syntax in use in the Message window.

- **See Also**—References to other keywords.

* **See Chapter/Appendix**—If the keyword is specifically discussed in a chapter, that chapter is listed here. I also refer to chapters that deal with similar keywords or the same topic, even if that specific keyword does not appear in that chapter.

This list also contains some undocumented keywords. Keep in mind that these are unsupported by Macromedia, which means they could disappear in an updated version very easily, and might not work in some situations.

#

Symbols

Special Character

Used as the first character of any symbol. Symbols are commonly used as properties in lists. They are also used by Lingo to identify properties of sprites and members. Also used as an optional character in front of hexadecimal color values in the *rgb* function.

```
addProp myList, #mySymbol, 7
if member(7).type = #vectorShape
then...
sprite(7).color = rgb("#FFFFFF")
```

See Also: *symbol, rgb*

&

Strings

Special Character

Concatenates two strings.

```
myString = "abc"&"def"
myString = stringOne&stringTwo
```

See Also: *&&, after, before, into*

See Chapter/Appendix: 16

&&

Strings

Special Character

Concatenates two strings and places a space between them.

```
myString = "abc"&&"def"
myString = wordOne&&wordTwo
```

See Also: *&, after, before, into*

See Chapter/Appendix: 16

( )

Logic

Special Character

Used to set order of precedence in operations. Also used to surround parameters with objects or function calls.

```
(5+6)*6
sprite(7).member = member("my mem-
ber")
addTwoNumbers(a,b)
```

*

Math

Operator

Multiplies two numbers. When given a number and list, each item in the list will be multiplied by that number. When given two lists, each item in the first list will be multiplied by the corresponding item in the second list. When given two 3D vectors, this will return the dot product of the two vectors. If you multiply a 3D transform by a 3D vector, you will get a new vector that is the original vector with the changes specified in the transform. If you multiply a number by a vector, you will get a new vector with the appropriate change in magnitude.

```
n = 4*5
n = a*b
```

See Also: *+, -, /*

See Chapter/Appendix: 13

+   Math
Operator

Adds two numbers. When given a number and a list, the number will be added to each item in the list. When given two lists, each item in the list will added to its corresponding item in the second list. When given two vectors, this will add the components of the vectors.

```
n = 4+5
n = a+b
```

See Also: *, -, /

See Chapter/Appendix: 13

,   Misc
Special Character

Used to separate items in various Lingo syntax such as function calls, handler definitions, *global* and *property* statements, lists, and so on.

```
n = addTwoNumbers(a,b)
m = member(memberNumber,castLibNumber)
list = [1,2,3,4]
```

-   Math
Operator

Subtracts two numbers. When given a number and a list, the subtraction will be performed using the number and each item of the list, and a new list returned. If given two lists, then a new list will be returned with the subtraction performed on each corresponding item. If given two 3D vectors, then this will subtract the components of the vectors.

```
n = 4-5
n = a-b
```

See Also: +, *, /

See Chapter/Appendix: 13

.   Misc
Special Character

Used in syntax that refers to the properties of an object. Also used as a decimal point in numbers.

```
n = text.length
m = member(1).type
p = sprite(7).loc
n = 4.5
```

..   Strings
Special Character

Used to refer to a consecutive run of items in chunk expressions.

```
t = myText.word[3..7]
t = myText.char[1..80]
t = myText.item[4..6]
```

See Also: *char, word, line, item*

See Chapter/Appendix: 16

/   Math
Operator

Divides two numbers. If given two lists, then each item in the first list will be divided by the corresponding item in the second list and a new list returned. If given a number and list, then the division will be performed using the number and each item in the list and a new list will be returned. If given a 3D vector and a number, this will divide each of the components of the vector by the number and return a new vector. You cannot divide two vectors.

```
n = 4/5
n = a/b
```

See Also: +, -, *

See Chapter/Appendix: 13

:   Misc
Special Character

Used in property lists to separate the property name from its value. Used in *case* statements.

`list = [#a: 1, #b: 2]`

See Also: *[]*, *case*

<   Logic
Operator

Less than operator.

`If 4 < 5 then...`
`if a < b then...`

See Also: <=, >, =, <>

See Chapter/Appendix: 13

<=   Logic
Operator

Less than or equal to operator.

`If 4 <= 5 then...`
`if a <= b then...`

See Also: <, =, >, <>

See Chapter/Appendix: 13

<>
Logic
Operator

Not equal operator.

`If 4 <> 5 then...`
`if a <> b then...`

See Also: =, <, <=, >, >=

See Chapter/Appendix: 13

=   Logic
Operator

Equals operator.

`If 4 = 5 then...`
`if a = b then...`

See Also: <>, <, <=, >, >=

See Chapter/Appendix: 13

>   Logic
Operator

Greater than operator.

`If 4 > 5 then...`
`if a > b then...`

See Also: <, >=, =, <>

See Chapter/Appendix: 13

>=   Logic
Operator

Greater than or equal to operator.

`If 4 >= 5 then...`
`if a >= b then...`

See Also: >, <, =, <>

See Chapter/Appendix: 13

[ ]   List
Special Character

Used to surround a list declaration or to refer to an item in a list.

`[4,5,6], [#a: 1, #b: 2], text.char[1], myList[5]`

See Also: :

See Chapter/Appendix: 13

\   Misc

Special Character

Used to continue a command on the next line.

```
if member("myMember").text = "test"
then  go to \
frame 1
```

See Also: ¬

See Chapter/Appendix: 12

¬   Misc

Special Character

Used to continue a command on the next line. Obsolete. Use \ instead.

See Also: \

---

abbr, abbrev, abbreviated   Date & Time

Modifier

Modifies the date and time properties to return shorter versions.

```
put the date
— "3/7/00"
put the long date
— "Tuesday, March 7, 2000"
put the abbr date
— "Tue, Mar 7, 2000"
```

See Also: *date, time*

See Chapter/Appendix: 21

---

abor   Programming

Command

Exits the handler and also terminates the handler that called the current one, and so on back to the original event handler, exiting that as well.

```
on myHandler param
  if gMyGlobal  = #idle then abort
```

```
  . . .
end
```

See Also: *exit, exit repeat, halt*

---

abs   Math

Function

Returns the absolute value of a number. Has the effect of removing the negative sign from negative numbers.

```
put abs(-7)
—7
```

See Chapter/Appendix: 13

---

activateApplication   Movie, MIAW

Event Handler

Handler gets called when the projector or Director is brought from the background to the foreground. You need to set your preferences to "Animate in Background" while in Director. This is useful when you make a projector and need to check system properties after the user has switched applications and has come back to your projector.

```
on activateApplication
  alert "Welcome back!"
end
```

See Also: *deactivateApplication, activateWindow*

---

activateWindow   MIAW

Event Handler

Called when a window is made active by first appearing, or by a user action such as clicking on the window.

```
on activateWindow
  go to frame "Window Init"
end
```

See Also: *deactivateWindow, openWindow, closeWindow*

See Chapter/Appendix: 24

active3DRenderer

3D, Misc

Property

Returns the sytem 3D rendering engine currently being used to display 3D members. In Shockwave, users can right+Click the movie and change this on the fly. Possible values are #openGL, #directX7_0, #directX5_2, and #software. The #software value means that the user is not using 3D drivers at all. You can always get this value, but you can only attempt to set it if no 3D sprite is on the Stage at the moment.

```
on startMovie
  if the active3Drenderer = #software
then
    alert "You may want to install
DirectX or OpenGL before viewing this
movie."
  end if
end
```

See Also: *renderDeviceList, getRendererServices*
See Chapter/Appendix: 39

activeCastLib

Score Recording

Property

The number of the most recently accessed cast library. Useful for building authoring tools that need to perform an action based on the author's member selection.

```
put the activeCastLib
— 1
```

See Also: *castLib, selectedMembers*
See Chapter/Appendix: 26

activeWindow

MIAW

Property

The active window object. Returns *(the stage)* if it is the Stage.

```
forget(the activeWindow)
```

See Also: *open, activateWindow, activeWindow, close, forget, frontWindow, moveWindow*
See Chapter/Appendix: 24

actor

OOP

Function

Undocumented Lingo. It seems that the value of *actor(1)* returns the memory location of the next object to be added to *the actorList*. Unconfirmed.

```
put actor(1)
— <actor 1 a96fce4>
```

See Also: *actorList, new*
See Chapter/Appendix: 26

actorList

OOP

Property

A special list of child objects to which you can make additions. Each object in the list receives a "stepFrame" message each frame.

```
myChild = new(script "myParent")
add the actorList, myChild
```

See Also: *new, actor*
See Chapter/Appendix: 24

add

List

Command

Adds an item to a linear list. If the list has been sorted with the *sort* command, the item is added in the proper location. Otherwise, it is added at the end of the list.

```
list = [1,2,3]
put list
— [1, 2, 3]
add list, 4
put list
— [1, 2, 3, 4]
list.add(5)
put list
— [1, 2, 3, 4, 5]
```

See Also: *append, addProp, deleteAt, setAt, sort*

See Chapter/Appendix: 13

---

add   See *textureLayer*

---

addAtList   Command

Adds an item to a linear list at a specific location.

```
list = [1,2,3]
put list
— [1, 2, 3]
addAt list, 2, 99
put list
— [1, 99, 2, 3]
list.addAt(4,999)
put list
— [1, 99, 2, 999, 3]
```

See Also: *add, append, addProp, deleteAt*

See Chapter/Appendix: 23

---

addBackdrop   3D, Cameras
                                           Command

Adds a 2D bitmap graphic as a background to a 3D sprite when viewed through that camera. You can add more than one backdrop to a camera view. The first parameter should be a texture reference, the second parameter a location, and the third parameter a rotation.

```
myTexture =
member("my3Dmember").newTexture("My
Texture",#fromCaqstMemmber,member("my
texture bitmap"))
member("my3Dmember").camera[1].addBack
drop(myTexture,point(100,0),90)
```

See Also: *newTexture, removeBackdrop, backdrop, insertBackdrop, overlay*

---

addCamera   3D, Cameras
                                           Command

Takes a camera that exists inside a 3D member and adds it to the list of cameras associated with that sprite. If you give this command a second parameter, then the camera will be inserted into the list of cameras at that position.

```
sprite(1).addCamera(sprite(1).member.c
amera("myCamera"))
```

See Also: *newCamera, deleteCamera, cameraCount*

---

addChild   3D, Grouping
                                           Command

This command will attach a model or other object to another model or other object. From then on, when the "parent" object moves, the child will too.

You can add an optional second parameter to this command. If you use #preserveWorld, then the model remains in the same place as it is attached to its parent. If you use #preserveParent, then the world coordinates of the model are changed taking the new parent as the center of the world for that model.

```
sprite(1).member.model("parent
model").addChild(sprite(1).member.mode
l("child model"))
```

See Also: *parent, child*

See Chapter/Appendix: 39

addModifier

3D, Models

Command

This will add a modifier to a model. Modifiers can be used for collision detection, ink effects, mesh deform or animation.

```
sprite(1).member.model("my
model").addModifier(#meshDeform)
```

See Also: *bonesPlayer, collision, inker, keyFramePlayer, lod, meshDeform, sds, toon, removeModifier*

See Chapter/Appendix: 39

addOverlay

3D, Cameras

Command

This command takes a texture and creates a layer that floats above the 3D image when viewed through that camera. This can be used to create a 2D layers meant to be in front of the 3D view, like the bars between window panes in a cockpit.

```
sprite(1).camera.addOverlay(sprite(1).
member.texture("my texture"))
```

See Also: *removeOverlay, addBackdrop*

See Chapter/Appendix: 39

addProp

List

Command

Adds a property name and a value to a property list. If the list has been sorted, the property is added at the proper location.

```
list = [#a: 1, #b: 2, #c: 3]
put list
— [#a: 1, #b: 2, #c: 3]
addProp list, #d, 4
put list
— [#a: 1, #b: 2, #c: 3, #d: 4]
list.addProp(#e,5)
put list
— [#a: 1, #b: 2, #c: 3, #d: 4, #e: 5]
```

See Also: *add, deleteProp, getProp, getAProp, setProp, setAProp, sort*

See Chapter/Appendix: 13

addToWorld

3D, Models

Command

Models can be removed and added back to the 3D world. This is different than removing or adding a model to the 3D member. Models can be in the 3D member, but not be present in the member's world for display. You can use the *removeFromWorld* command to remove a model and speed up the member, and then use the *addToWorld* command to make it appear again.

```
sprite(1).member.model("my
model").addToWorld()
```

See Also: *removeFromWorld*

addVertex

Vector

Command

Inserts a vertex point into a vector shape member. After the vertex number and the vertex point, you can optionally add two lists that have the x and y position of the curve handles.

```
addVertex(member ("myVector"), 5,
point(50,50))
member("myVector").addVertex(5,point(5
0,50))
member("myVector").addVertex(5,point(5
0,50),[5,5],[10,10])
```

See Also: *deleteVertex, moveVertex, vertexList, newCurve*

See Chapter/Appendix: 20

after   Strings

Expression

Enables you to use the *put* command to append one string onto another.

```
myString = "Hello"
put "." after myString
put myString
— "Hello."
```

See Also: *put, before, into*

See Chapter/Appendix: 13

alert   Misc, Debug

Command

Brings up a dialog box that shows a string of text and an OK button. Movie stops while the box is present.

```
alert "Danger!"
```

See Chapter/Appendix:

20, 24

alertHook   Debug

Event Handler, Property

Enables you to set a script member as the one that handles error messages when they occur. Also the name of the event handler that must be in that script to receive the error messages.

When the *on alertHook* handler is called, it should return a value. A value of -1 halts the movie with no dialog box in Director and shows a stop/continue dialog box in projectors. A value of 0 presents an error message, halts the movie in Director, and shows a stop/continue dialog box in projectors. A value of 1 halts the movie and brings up the debug window if in Director but continues the movie in projectors. A value of 2 brings up the script window in Director but

quits projectors. In practice, I have never been able to get a value of 1 to actually bring up the debug window. Instead, it brings up the script window.

Warning: When you use *the alertHook*, it also captures *alert* commands, so you cannot use them normally. However, *alert* commands inside the *on alertHook* handler work as expected.

```
on startMovie
  the alertHook = script("Error
Handler")
end
```

```
on alertHook me, err, msg
  alert "Error:"&&msg
  return 1
end
```

See Chapter/Appendix: 33

alignment   Text, Field

Property

Text or field member property that determines text alignment. Possible values for a field are "left", "right", and "center", while the possible values for a text member are #left, #right, #center, and #full.

```
member("myText").alignment = #center
```

See Also: *text, lineHeight, font, fontSize, fontStyle, fi XEdLineSpace*

See Chapter/Appendix: 16

allowCustomCaching   Playback

Property

For future use.

allowGraphicMenu   Playback Property

If this is set to *FALSE*, Shockwave context menus will be text-only. If *TRUE*, the default, Shockwave may use graphics in the context menu.

```
on prepareMovie
  the allowGraphicMenu = FALSE
end
```

allowSaveLocal   Playback Property

If set to *FALSE*, the user should not be able to save the movie through context menus in Shockwave. Although this property exists, it is questionable whether it will ever be used to override the HTML tag properties that allow and disallow saving. Better to use those to be safe.

```
on prepareMovie
  the allowSaveLocal = FALSE
end
```

See Chapter/Appendix: 36

allowTransportControl   Playback Property

For future use.

allowVolumeControl   Playback Property

When set to *FALSE*, disables volume controls in Shockwave.

```
on prepareMovie
  the allowVolumeControl = FALSE
end
```

allowZooming   Playback Property

When set to *FALSE*, your movie cannot be stretched in Shockwave or in ShockMachine.

```
on prepareMovie
  the allowZooming = FALSE
end
```

alphaThreshold   Bitmap Property

A value from 0 to 255 that tells Director when to detect a click on a bitmap according to the value in the Alpha channel. A 0 makes all pi XEls detect hits, where a 255 makes only opaque pi XEls detect hits.

```
member("my32bitimage").alphaThreshold
= 128
```

See Also: *useAlpha*

ambient   3D, Shader Property

The *ambient* property of a shader determines how ambient lights reflect off of the surface.

```
sprite(1).member.shader("my
shader").ambient = rgb("FF0000")
```

See Also: *diffuse, specular, ambientColor*

See Chapter/Appendix: 39

ambientColor   3D, Light Property

This is the color and intensity of the ambient light in the 3D member. The ambient light appears to come from all directions and shine on all objects evenly.

```
sprite(1).member.ambientColor =
rgb("CCCCCC")
```

See Also: *directionalColor*

ancestor OOP

Property

Defines an ancestor to a parent script. All instances of that parent have the handlers of its ancestor made available for use.

```
the ancestor of me = new(script
"myAncestor")
```

See Also: *new, me*

See Chapter/Appendix: 23

and Logic

Operator

Returns *TRUE* if both expressions are *TRUE*; returns *FALSE* otherwise.

```
if (a = 1) and (b = 2) then...
```

See Also: *or, not*

See Chapter/Appendix: 13

angle 3D, Particle System

Property

This *emitter* property will determine how far away from the direction of emission that a particle might shoot out from. The default value of 180 degrees means that the particle could come from any direction. A value of 90 degrees would mean that the particle would come out of only one hemisphere, while a value of 0 would mean that all particles would be emitted from exactly the same direction.

```
sprite(1).member.modelResource("my
particle system").emitter.angle = 90
```

See Also: emitter, direction

See Chapter/Appendix: 39

angleBetween 3D, Math

Function

Returns the angle in degrees between two vectors.

```
v1 = vector(25,0,0)
v2 = vector(0,25,0)
put v1.angleBetween(v2)
— 90.0000
```

animationEnabled 3D, Animation

Property

If set to *FALSE*, then any animation in the 3D member will be disabled.

```
member("my 3D
member").animationEnabled = FALSE
```

antiAlias Text, Vector, Flash

Property

Determines whether a text, Flash, or vector member is drawn to the screen with anti-aliasing to smooth edges. Can be used as a sprite property for Vector Shape sprites.

```
member("myVector").antiAlias = TRUE
```

See Also: *Quality*

See Chapter/Appendix: 20

append List

Command

Adds a value to a linear list. Adds the value to the end, even if the list has been sorted.

```
list = [1,2,3]
put list
— [1, 2, 3]
append list, 4
put list
— [1, 2, 3, 4]
```

```
list.append(5)
put list
— [1, 2, 3, 4, 5]
```

See Also: *add*

See Chapter/Appendix: 13

---

applicationPath   System

Property

Returns the full path to the Director application or the projector. The returned path ends with a path delimiter, either a colon (:) on the Mac or a slash (\) in Windows.

```
put the applicationPath
— "Powerbook HD:Director 8:"
```

See Also: *moviePath, movie, fileName*

---

appMinimize   System

Command

This command minimizes the projector. On the Mac, it moves the application to the background.

```
on mouseUp
  appMinimize
end
```

See Also: *activateApplication*

---

atan   Math

Function

Returns the arctangent of a number in radians.

```
put atan(3.0/6.0)
— 0.4636
```

See Also: *sin, cos, tan*

---

attenuation   3D, Lights

Property

A property of 3D point and spot lights. This oddly-formatted property determines how fast the light fades as it gets further from the source. The vector format is used not as a vector, but the three values define the constant, linear or quadratic amount of fading. Use one value and set the others to 0. If using linear or quadratic, then set the value to something very small, like .00001.

```
sprite(1).member.light("my
light").attenuation = vector(1,0,0)
```

See Also: *color*

---

auto   3D, LOD

Property

When set to *TRUE*, the level of detail in a model will automatically change to reflect processor speed. This requires that *targetFrameRate* is set to *TRUE*. If not, the LOD will be determined by the distance of the model from the camera.

```
sprite(1).member.model("my
model").lod.auto = TRUE
```

See Also: bias, lod

---

autoBlend   3D, Animation, Bones

Property

When turned on, this allows 3D member animations to blend from one animation to another. Can be used with the *keyframePlayer* or *bonesPlayer*.

```
sprite(1).member.model("my
model").keyframePlayer.autoblend =
TRUE
```

See Also: blendFactor, blendTime, keyframePlayer

autoCameraPosition　　　3D, Text

Property

When turned on, the camera in a 3D text member will adjust itself to show all of the text.

```
sprite(1).member.autoCameraPosition =
TRUE
```

See Also: displayMode

autoMask　　　Cursor

Property

Determines whether the white pi XEls in an animated cursor are transparent.

```
member("cursor").autoMask = TRUE
```

See Also: *cursor*

autoTab　　　Text, Field

Property

Determines whether users can press the Tab key in an editable field or text member and automatically move the insertion point to the next field or text member.

```
member("text").autoTab = TRUE
```

See Also: *keyboardFocusSprite*

See Chapter/Appendix: 16

axisAngle　　　3D, Math

Function

Returns the axis, as a vector, and the amount of rotation of a 3D transform. This is just another way of representing a transform that could be useful in mathematical calculations. This gives you more control over a rotation, whereas the *rotate* command will always perform a rotation first on the x, then on the y and then on the z axis. This allows you to define an arbitrary axis to rotate around.

back　　　3D, Primitives

Property

Whether the back side of a 3D box primitive is present or not.

```
sprite(1).member.modelResource("my box
resource").back = FALSE
```

See Also: front, left, right, top, bottom, topCap, bottomCap, newModelResource

backcolor　　　Sprite, Text, Field

Property

Old syntax enabling you to specify the background color of a sprite, or the background color of a text or field member. The color number must be between 0 and 255 and correspond to the movie's palette. Use *bgColor* instead.

```
sprite(1).backcolor = 35
```

See Also: *bgColor, color*

See Chapter/Appendix: 18

backdrop　　　3D, Camera

Property

Refers to one of the backdrops applied to a camera. A backdrop appears as a 2D image behind the 3D world. It remains steady as the camera might swing around to show other parts of the world.

```
sprite(1).camera.backdrop[1].source =
myTexture
```

See Also: *loc, source, scale, rotation, regPoint, blend, count, overlay*

BACKSPACE　　　Strings

Constant

The equivalent of the character generated by the Delete key on the Mac and the Backspace key in Windows. It is also *numtoChar(8)*.

```
on keyDown
  if the key = BACKSPACE then
    beep()
    dontpassevent
  end if
end
```

See Chapter/Appendix: 16

beep   Misc, Sound
Command

Creates a number of system beeps. The sound depends on the user's system settings. If a number is included, that is the number of beeps created; otherwise, just one beep is performed.

```
on mouseUp
  beep(3)
end
```

See Chapter/Appendix: 17

beepOn   Misc, Sound
Property

If set to *TRUE*, a beep occurs when the user tries to click where there is no active sprite. Default is *FALSE*. An active sprite is one that has a script attached to it.

```
on startMovie
  the beepOn = TRUE
end
```

before   Strings
Expression

Enables you to use the *put* command to place a string at the beginning of another string.

```
myString = "Hello!"
put "Well, " before myString
```

```
put myString
— "Well, Hello!"
```

See Also: *put, after, into*

See Chapter/Appendix: 13, 16

beginRecording   Score Recording
Command

Signifies the start of a Score-recording session.

```
beginRecording
  sprite(7).loc = 100
  updateFrame
endRecording
```

See Also: *endRecording, updateFrame*

See Chapter/Appendix: 26

beginSprite   Behaviors
Event Handler

This handler is e XEcuted immediately before the sprite first appears.

```
on beginSprite me
  pMyProperty  = 1
  sprite(me.spriteNum).ink = 36
end
```

See Also: *endSprite, prepareFrame*

See Chapter/Appendix: 14

bevelDepth   3D, Text
Property

The amount of beveling on the chacters in a 3D text member. The *bevelType* of the member must be #miter or #round.

```
member("my 3D text").bevelDepth = 7
```

See Also: bevelType, extrude3D

bevelType   3D, Text
                                       Property

The type of beveling to use on a 3D text member. The options are #none, #miter or #round.

```
member("my 3D text").bevelType =
#miter
```

See Also: bevelDepth, extrude3D

bgColor   Sprite, Text, Field, Vector,
                                  Movie, Color
                                       Property

Enables you to specify the background color of a sprite, or the background color of a text, field, or vector shape member. You can set it to an *rgb* structure or a *paletteIndex*. You can also set the *bgColor* of the Stage.

```
sprite(1).bgColor = rgb(255,0,0)
  (the stage).bgColor = rgb("FF0000")
```

See Also: *rgb, paletteIndex, color*

See Chapter/Appendix: 18

bias   3D, LOD
                                       Property

This is the percentage of polygons that must stay in a model when the *lod.auto* property is set to *TRUE*.

```
sprite(1).member.model("my
model").lod.bias = 50
```

See Also: auto, lod

birth   OOP
                                       Command

Old syntax for creating an object from a parent script. Use *new* instead.

See Also: *new*

See Chapter/Appendix: 23

bitAnd   Math
                                       Function

Takes two numbers and performs a logical AND on the bits and returns the result.

```
a =  5  —  5=0101
b =  4  —  4=0100
put bitAnd(a,b)
—  4
```

See Also: *bitOr, bitXor, bitNot*

bitmapSizes   Font
                                       Property

Returns a list of bitmap sizes included with a font cast member.

```
put member("myFont").bitmapSizes
—  [9, 10, 12, 14, 18, 24]
```

See Also: *recordFont, characterSet, originalFont*

See Chapter/Appendix: 16

bitNot   Math
                                       Function

Takes two numbers and performs a logical NOT on the bits and returns the result. Numbers are 32-bit, so the operation reverses all 32 bits and often returns a negative number as a result.

```
a =  1
put bitNot(a)
—  -2
```

See Also: *bitOr, bitXor, bitAnd*

bitOr   Math
                                       Function

Takes two numbers and performs a logical OR on the bits and returns the result.

```
a =  5  —  5=0101
b =  6  —  6=0110
```

```
put bitOr(a,b)
— 7
```

See Also: *bitAnd, bitXor, bitNot*

---

bitRate   Shockwave Audio
                               Property

Returns the bitrate, in Kbps, of a streaming sound. Returns 0 when not streaming.

```
if member("mySWA").bitRate > 16
then...
```

See Also: *bitsPerSample*

---

bitsPerSample   Shockwave Audio
                               Property

Returns the original bit depth of the sound. Works only while streaming. Typical values are 8 and 16.

```
if member("mySWA").bitsPerSample
then...
```

See Also: *bitRate*

---

bitXor   Math
                               Function

Takes two numbers and performs a logical "exclusive or" on the bits and returns the result.

```
a =  5 — 5=0101
b =  6 — 6=0110
put bitXOr(a,b)
— 3
```

See Also: *bitOr, bitAnd, bitNot*

---

blend   Sprite
                               Property

A value of 0 to 100 determines how much the sprite's pi XEls should blend with the ones behind it. Works with many inks, particularly the Blend ink.

```
sprite(7).blend = 50
```

See Also: *ink, blendLevel*

See Chapter/Appendix: 18

---

blend   3D, Shader
                               Property

The blend percentage for a 3D shader. The *transparent* property of the shader must be turned on. This also works for overlays and backdrops.

```
sprite(1).member.shader("my
shader").blend = 50
```

See Also: *transparent*

---

blendLevel   Sprite
                               Property

A value of 0 to 255 determines how much the sprite's pi XEls should blend with the ones behind it. Same as *blend* but with a different scale.

```
sprite(7).blendLevel = 128
```

See Also: *ink, blend*

See Chapter/Appendix: 18

---

blue   Color
                               Property

Extracts the blue property from an *rgb* color object.

```
myColor = rgb("336699")
put myColor
— rgb( 51, 102, 153 )
put myColor.blue
— 153
```

See Also: *green, red, color, rgb*

See Chapter/Appendix: 18

blendConstant, blendConstantList
3D, Shader

Property

The *blendConstantList* contains eight values that determine how up to eight textures blend together to create the shader. Using *blendConstant* will affect only the first layer.

```
sprite(1).member.model("my
model").blendConstantList[2] = 50
```

See Also: *blendSource, blendFunction*

blendFactor
3D, Animation, Bones

Property

If you wish to blend bones player animation in a non-linear manner, set *autoblend* to *FALSE* and use the *blendFactor* property of the bones player to determine how much the current animation acts like the previous, rather than the current, animation. This can be used with either the *keyframesPlayer* or the *bonesPlayer* objects.

```
sprite(1).member.model("my
model").keyframePlayer.blendFactor =
50
```

See Also: autoblend, keyframePlayer

blendFunction, blendFunctionList
3D, Shader

Property

A shader can have up to eight different textures that blend with each other. The *belndFunctionList* defines what type of blending to use on each of these texture layers. Possible values are #multiply, #add, #replace, and #blend.

```
sprite(1).member.shader("my
shader").blendFunctionList[2] = #add
```

See Also: blendConstant, blendSource

blendRange
3D, Particle System

Property

The amount of opacity that a particle starts its life with (*blendRange.start*) and ends its life with (*blendRange.end*).

```
sprite(1).member.model("my parti-
cles").blendRange.start = 100
sprite(1).member.model("my parti-
cles").blendRange.end = 0
```

See Also: colorRange, emitter

blendSource, blendSourceList
3D, Shader

Property

A shader can have up to eight textures that blend together. The *blendSourceList* defines whether any of these texture use the alpha channel information to further define the blend. The possible values for each item in this list are #alpha or #constant. If #constant, then the *blendConstantList* is used to define a uniform blend over the entire texture.

```
sprite(1).member.shader("my
shader").blendSourceList[2] = #alpha
```

See Also: *blendFunction, blendConstant*

blendTime
3D, Animation, Bones

Property

The time between motions in the play list of bones player animation. This can be used with either the *keyframesPlayer* or the *bonesPlayer* objects.

```
sprite(1).member.model("my
model").keyframePlayer.blendTime = 500
```

See Also: autoBlend, blendFactor

bone   3D, Bones
Object

Refers to a bone embedded into a model when it
was made with a 3D program.

See Also: *bonesPlayer*

bonesPlayer   3D, Bones
Object

Provides access to various bits of information
about the bones embedded into a model when it
was created in a 3D program. You cannot create
a bonesPlayer modifier in Lingo. It must be
added by a third-party 3D program.

```
x = sprite(1).member.model("my
model").bonesPlayer.currentTime
```

See Also: autoBlend, blendTime, blendFactor,
bone, currentLoopState, currentTime,
lockTransition, playing, playlist, positionReset,
rootLock, rotationReset

border   Field
Property

The size of the black line around a field member.

```
member("myField").border = 1
```

See Also: *margin, boxType, boxDropShadow,
dropShadow*

See Chapter/Appendix: 16

bottom   Sprite, Misc
Property

The bottom vertical position of the sprite.
Corresponds to the bottom of the *rect* of a
sprite. Also a property of *rect* objects.

```
put sprite(1).rect
— rect(102, 143, 277, 233)
```

```
put sprite(1).bottom
— 233
put sprite(1).rect.bottom
— 233
```

See Also: *top, left, right, height, rect*

See Chapter/Appendix: 18

bottom   3D, Primitives
Property

Whether the bottom side of a 3D box primitive is
present or not.

```
sprite(1).member.modelResource("my box
resource").bottom = FALSE
```

See Also: back, front, left, right, top, topCap,
bottomCap, newModelResource

bottomCap   3D, Primitives
Property

Whether the bottom side of a 3D cylinder primitive is present or not.

```
sprite(1).member.modelResource("my
cylinder resource").bottomCap = FALSE
```

See Also: *back, front, left, right, top, bottom,
topCap, newModelResource*

bottomRadius   3D, Primitives
Property

The radius of the bottom circle in a cylinder
primitive.

```
sprite(1).member.modelResource("my
cylinder resource").bottomRadius = 10
```

See Also: *topRadius, radius*

bottomSpacing   Text

Property

A number indicating any extra spacing after a paragraph in a text member. Also works with negative values.

```
member("myText").line[2].bottomSpacing
= 12
```

See Also: *topSpacing, fi XEdLineSpace*

See Chapter/Appendix: 16

boundary   3D, Inker

Property

Whether or not a line is drawn at the edges of a model. Can also be used with the *toon* modifier.

```
sprite(1).member.model("my
model").inker.boundary = TRUE
```

See Also: *lineColor, lineOffset, silhouettes, creases, inker, toon*

boundingSphere   3D, Math

Function

Returns a list with the center of an object, a vector, and the radius of the object, a number value. This will give you an idea of how much space an object takes up and what other objects it may touch. You can also use it with groups.

```
s = sprite(1).member.model("my
model").boundingSphere
```

boxDropShadow   Field

Property

The offset of the black drop shadow around a field member. Values from 0 to 255.

```
member("myField").boxDropShadow = 1
```

See Also: *margin, boxType, border, dropShadow*

See Chapter/Appendix: 16

boxType   Text, Field

Property

The type of text box used for text members and fields. Possible values are #adjust, #fi XEd, #scroll, and #limit. #adjust adjusts the bottom of the member to make sure all text is visible. #scroll shows a system scrollbar to the right side of the text. #limit limits editable text input to the size of the member.

```
member("myText").boxType = #fi XEd
```

See Also: *editable, rect*

See Chapter/Appendix: 16

breakLoop   Sound

Command

Tells a sound in a sound channel to play out the rest of its looping sequence and then continue with the rest of the sound. It works only when the sound playing has *loopStartTime* and *loopEndTime* set and the loop is in the process of occurring.

```
sound(1).breakLoop()
```

See Also: *loopStartTime, loopEndTime, loopCount, loopRemaining*

See Chapter/Appendix: 17

brightness   3D, Shader

Property

The amount of white in a #newsprint or #engraver shader.

```
sprite(1).member.model("my
model").shader.brightness = 10
```

See Also: *newShader, engraver, newsprint*

broadcastProps

Flash, Vector

Property

Determines whether changes made to a Flash or vector shape member are immediately shown in the sprites present on the Stage, or whether they are used the next time a sprite appears using that member.

```
member("myVector").broadcastProps =
FALSE
```

See Chapter/Appendix: 20

browserName

Network

Command, Property, Function

As a command, enables you to set the default browser used by *gotoNetPage*. As a function, enables you to get the name of the default browser. In an alternate form, enables you to decide whether the browser launches automatically with the *gotoNetPage* command.

```
put browserName()
— "Powerbook HD:Netscape Communicator
Folder:Netscape Communicator"
browserName(#enabled, TRUE)
browserName myNewBrowserPath
```

See Also: *gotoNetPage*

See Chapter/Appendix: 22

bufferSize

Flash

Property

Determines how many bytes of a linked Flash movie can be loaded into memory at any one time. Works only when the *preload* property of the member is *FALSE*. Default is 32,768. Setting it higher results in slower loading, but might improve performance.

```
member("myFlash").bufferSize = 64000
```

See Also: *preload*

See Chapter/Appendix: 20

build

3D, Mesh

Command

This command completes the construction of a mesh model resource. To create a mesh model resource, you must first determine the vertex list, the color list, and the faces. Then, you must determine the normals of each face. Then you can use the *build* command to assemble the mesh.

See Also: *generateNormals, newMesh, face, colorList*

buttonsEnabled

Flash

Property

Determines whether the buttons in a Flash sprite are enabled.

```
sprite(7).buttonsEnabled = FALSE
```

See Also: *actionsEnabled*

See Chapter/Appendix: 20

buttonStyle

System

Property

If 0, users can click button members and roll over other members to highlight them. If *FALSE*, only the button first clicked is highlighted. Setting this to 1 means that *on mouseUp* handlers will not be called when the user clicked down on another space and then clicked up on the button.

```
the buttonStyle = 1
```

See Also: *checkBoxAccess, checkBoxType, buttonType*

buttonType

Button

Property

The type of button for a button member. Values can be #pushButton, #checkBox, or #radioButton.

```
member("myButton").buttonType =
#checkBox
```

See Also: *checkBoxAccess, checkBoxType, buttonStyle*

bytesStreamed

3D, Streaming

Function

Returns the number of bytes of a 3D member that have arrived

```
if sprite(1).member.bytesStreamed >
sprite(1).member.streamsize then...
```

See Also: streamSize, state

call

OOP

Command

Can call a handler in a parent script instance or a sprite behavior instance. Can use a single instance or a list of instances. In the second case, no error message is sent when the handler does not exist. You can also send parameters. You can even use a variable as a reference to the handler.

```
call(#myHandler, myScriptInstance,
param1)
call(#myHandler,
[myScript1,myScript2], param1,param2)
```

See Also: *callAncestor, sendSprite, sendAllSprites*

See Chapter/Appendix: 23

callAncestor

OOP

Command

Same as call, but sends the message or messages directly to an object's ancestor(s).

See Also: *call*

See Chapter/Appendix: 23

callFrame

Flash

Command

This command will tell the Flash movie in a sprite to run the ActionScript code placed on the specified frame. It is similar to the Flash 4 *call* command.

```
sprite(1).callFrame(7)
```

See Also: *tellTarget*

See Chapter/Appendix: 20

camera

3D, Camera

Object

Refers to a camera object in a member, or the single camera being used by a sprite.

```
sprite(1).camera =
sprite(1).member.camera("my camera")
```

See Also: cameraCount, cameraPosition, cameraRotation, addCamera, deleteCamera

cameraCount

3D, Camera

Function

Returns the number of cameras in the member used by the sprite.

See Also: camera, addCamera, deleteCamera

cameraPosition

3D, Camera

Property

A shortcut to get and set the location of the default camera.

```
sprite(1).member.cameraPosition = vec-
tor(0,0,0)
```

See Also: camera, cameraRotation

cameraRotation

3D, Camera

Property

A shortcut to get and set the orientation of the default camera.

```
sprite(1).member.cameraRotation = vec-
tor(90,0,0)
```

See Also: camera, cameraLocation

cancelIdleLoad

Memory
Command

Cancels loading of members with a specific tag number.

```
cancelIdleLoad(1)
```

See Also: *idleLoadTag*

See Chapter/Appendix: 34

case

Programming
Structure

Starts a *case* statement. Is followed by a test value and then *of*. Following lines list possible values, followed by a colon. Can use an *otherwise* statement to deal with all other possible values. The whole structure must end with an *end case*.

```
case a of
  1: beep
  2:
    beep
    go to frame 1
  3,4:
    halt
  otherwise:
    go to frame 7
end case
```

See Also: *if*

See Chapter/Appendix: 13

castLib

Casts
Object

Defines a cast object. Can accept a name or number.

```
put castLib(2)
— (castLib 2)
put castLib(2).name
— "Database"
```

See Also: *castLibNum*

castLibNum

Member, Sprite
Property

Returns the cast library number of the member or the member used by the sprite. You can set the sprite to use the member in the same position in a different cast library.

```
put member(1).castLibNum
— 1
sprite(7).castLibNum = 2
```

See Also: *memberNum, member*

castLibs

Casts
Function

When used as *the number of castLibs*, it returns the number of cast libraries.

```
put the number of castlibs
— 2
```

See Also: *castLibNum*

castMemberList

Cursor
Property

The list of members used by an animated cursor.

```
put member("myCursor").castMemberList
```

See Also: *cursor*

See Chapter/Appendix: 21

center

Digital Video
Property

A value of *TRUE* centers the video when the *crop* property is also *TRUE*.

```
member("myVideo").center = TRUE
```

See Also: *crop*

centerRegPoint   Vector, Flash, Bitmap
                                                    Property

When set to *TRUE*, the registration point is automatically centered when the sprite is resized.

```
member("myVector").centerRegPoint =
FALSE
```

See Also: *regPoint, originMode, originPoint*

See Chapter/Appendix: 20

centerStage   Movie
                                                    Property

When *TRUE*, the Stage is centered on the monitor when the movie is opened.

```
on prepareMovie
  the centerStage = TRUE
end
```

See Also: *fixStageSize*

changeArea   Transition
                                                    Property

With this property you can set a transition member to affect either the whole Stage or just the changed area.

```
member("myTransition").changeArea =
TRUE
```

See Also: *transitionType, chunkSize*

channelCount   Sound
                                                    Property

Returns the number of channels in a sound. Typical values are 1 and 2, with 2 usually meaning a stereo sound.

```
put member("mySound").channelCount
```

See Chapter/Appendix: 17

char   Strings
                                                  Expression

Used to specify a single character or range of characters in a string chunk.

```
myString = "Hello World."
put myString.char[7]
— "W"
put myString.char[4..8]
— "lo Wo"
```

See Also: *word, line, item, chars*

See Chapter/Appendix: 16

characterSet   Font
                                                    Property

This property returns a string that specifies the characters included with a font member. You can specify the characters when creating a font member.

```
put member("myFont").characterSet
— "1234567890.- "
```

See Also: *recordFont, bitmapSizes, originalFont*

See Chapter/Appendix: 16

charPosToLoc   Text, Field
                                                    Function

Returns the point location of a character in a text or field member. It is relative to the upper-left corner of the member.

```
put charPosToLoc(member("myText"),7)
— point(36, 9)
```

See Also: *locToCharPos, locVToLinePos, linePosToLocV, mouseChar*

See Chapter/Appendix: 16

chars

Strings
Function

Returns a range of characters in a string. Obsolete. Use *char* instead.

```
put chars("Hello World",4,8)
— "lo Wo"
```

See Also: *char*

See Chapter/Appendix: 16

charSpacing

Text
Property

Specifies additional or less spacing between characters in a text member. For instance, a value of 1 would be an additional point between characters.

```
put
member("myText").char[5..9].charSpacin
g
— 0
member("myText").char[5..9].charSpacin
g = 5
```

See Also: *fi XEdLineSpace*

See Chapter/Appendix: 16

charToNum

Strings
Function

Converts a character to its ASCII character value.

```
put charToNum("A")
— 65
```

See Also: *numToChar, integer, value*

See Chapter/Appendix: 16

checkBoxAccess

Button
Property

A system property. When set to 0, users can check and uncheck check bo XEs and radio buttons. When set to 1, users can only check them. When set to 2, users can't do either.

```
the checkBoxAccess = 0
```

See Also: *checkBoxType, hilite*

See Chapter/Appendix: 15

checkBoxType

Button
Property

A system property. Enables you to determine what a checked check box looks like. 0 puts an "X" inside it, 1 puts a small black box inside it, and 2 fills the box completely.

```
the checkBoxType = 1
```

See Also: *checkBoxAccess, hilite*

See Chapter/Appendix: 15

checkMark

Menu
Property

A menu item property. It enables you to check and uncheck a single menu item.

```
the checkMark of menuitem 1 of menu 1
= TRUE
```

See Also: *menuitem, installMenu*

See Chapter/Appendix: 21

child

3D, Grouping
Function

A way to refer to a model that is the child of another model.

```
sprite(1).member.model("my
model").child[1].rotate(90,0,0)
```

See Also: addChild, parent

chunkSize   Transition

Property

Determines the smoothness of a transition member. Values are 1 to 128, with 1 being the smoothest, but slowest.

```
member("myTransition").chunkSize = 4
```

See Also: *transitionType, changeArea, puppetTransition*

---

clearAtRender   3D, Camera

Property

If you set this property to *FALSE*, then models in the 3D world will leave trails as objects move or change.

```
sprite(1).camera.colorBuffer.clearAtRe
nder = FALSE
```

See Also: colorBuffer, clearValue

---

clearValue   3D, Camera

Property

If *clearAtRender* is set to *TRUE*, then this is the color used to clear the screen before each redraw. The default is black.

```
sprite(1).camera.colorBuffer.clearValu
e = rgb("FFFFFF")
```

See Also: colorBuffer, clearAtRender

---

clearCache   Network

Command

Clears Director's or a projector's network cache. This does not affect a browser's cache when used in Shockwave.

```
clearCache
```

See Also: *cacheDocVerify, cacheSize*

---

clearError   Flash

Command

Resets the error state of a streaming Flash movie.

```
clearError(member("myFlash"))
```

See Also: *state, getError*

---

clearFrame   Score Recording

Command

Clears all the sprites from the current frame during Score recording.

```
clearFrame
```

See Also: *beginRecording, updateFrame*

See Chapter/Appendix: 26

---

clearGlobals   System

Command

Sets the value of all globals to *VOID*.

```
clearGlobals
```

See Also: *global, showGlobals*

---

clickLoc   Mouse

Property

Returns a point with the location of the last mouse click. Works only from the object clicked, such as a sprite or frame, and inside an *on mouseUp* or *on mouseDown* handler.

```
on mouseUp me
  if (the clickLoc).locH <
sprite(me.spriteNum).locH then
    — means that the user clicked to
the left of the registration point
  end if
end
```

See Also: *mouseLoc, clickOn*

clickMode Flash

Property

When set to #boundingBox, clicks and rollovers are detected anywhere in a Flash sprite's rectangle. When set to #object, clicks and rollovers are detected when over a filled portion of the sprite. When set to #opaque, the behavior is like #object if the sprite's ink is Background Transparent and is like #boundingBox otherwise.

```
member("myFlash").clickMode = #object
```

See Chapter/Appendix: 20

clickOn Mouse

Property

Returns the number of the sprite that was last clicked. Returns a 0 if no sprite was clicked. Sprites must have some behavior applied to them, if even just a comment in an empty script, to effect a change to *the clickOn* when clicked.

```
if the clickOn = 7 then
  go to frame "other"
end if
```

See Also: *clickLoc, rollover*

clone 3D, Models

Command

Creates an identical copy of a model in the same place. It shares the model resource, shaders, and textures with the original model.

```
sprite(1).member.model("my
model").clone("my new model")
```

See Also: cloneDeep,
cloneModelFromCastMember

cloneDeep 3D, Models

Command

Creates a copy of a model, like the *clone* command, but also makes a copy of the model resources used and any children of the model.

```
sprite(1).member.model("my
model").cloneDeep("my new model")
```

See Also: clone, cloneModelFromCastMember

cloneModelFromCastmember 3D, Models

Command

Makes a copy of a model from another member inside the current member. Same as *cloneDeep*.

```
sprite(1).member.cloneModelFromCastmembe
r("my new model", "my old model", mem-
ber("old model member"))
```

See Also: clone, loadFile

cloneMotionFromCastmember 3D, Animation

Command

Makes a copy of a motion from another cast member.

```
sprite(1).member.cloneMotionFromCastmemb
er("my new motion", "my old motion",
member("old model member"))
```

close MIAW

Command

Hides a MIAW. The MIAW is still there; you need to use *forget* to really get rid of it.

```
on mouseUp
  close window ("myWindow")
end
```

See Also: *open, forget*

See Chapter/Appendix: 24

closed Vector

Property

TRUE makes the vector shape closed, and fills it with a solid color or a gradient.

```
member("myVector").closed = TRUE
```

See Chapter/Appendix: 20

closeWindow MIAW

Event Handler

Called when the movie is running as a MIAW and the window is closed.

```
on closeWindow
  forget(the activeWindow)
end
```

See Also: *openWindow, activateWindow*

See Chapter/Appendix: 24

closeXLib Xtras

Command

Disposes of an Xtra that has been loaded into memory.

```
closeXlib "FileIO"
```

See Also: *openXLib*

See Chapter/Appendix: 25

collision 3D, Collision Detection

Modifier

When you add the collision detection modifier to a model, handlers will be called in the event that another object with a collision modifier collides with this model. The #collideAny and #collideWith events must be run through *registerForEvent* before they are able to be recognized.

See Also: *registerForEvent, addModifier*

See Chapter/Appendix: 39

collisionData 3D, Collision Detection

Special

Although *collisionData* is listed as an entry in Director 8.5's documentation, there is no such thing. They use it to define the one paramater returned to a handler set to handle collision callbacks by *registerForEvent* or *registerScript*. In fact, you could call this paramater anything you want, like "myCollisionInformation" for instance.

Whatever you call the parameter, you can get four sub-properties of this unusual object. The *modelA* and *modelB* properties are references to the two models involved in the collision. The *pointOfContact* is the location of the collision. The *collisionNormal* is a vector in the direction of the collision.

Oddly enough, you can also use this object to eXEcute two commands: *resolveA* and *resolveB*. You can set these to *TRUE* or *FALSE* to override the collision resolution settings and stop or not stop either model or both from moving after the collision.

```
on myCollisionHandler me,
myCollisionData
  put myCollisionData.modelA,
myCollisionData.modelB
end
```

See Also: *registerForEvent, registerScript, setCollisionCallback*

See Chapter/Appendix: 39

collisionNormal See *collisionData*

color

Misc, Sprite, Text, Field, Vector, Color

Object

A *color* object can be either an *rgb* structure or a *paletteIndex* structure. You can use the color function to create these objects as well.

This keyword is also a property of sprites, 3D lights and fog, and of text, field, and vector shape members.

```
myColor = color(#rgb,255,255,255)
myColor = color(#paletteIndex,35)
sprite(7).color = rgb(255,0,0)
```

See Also: *colorType, rgb, paletteIndex, red, green, blue, bgColor, foreColor*

See Chapter/Appendix: 18

---

colorBufferDepth   See *getRendererServices*

colorDepth

System

Property

The current color depth of the user's monitor. Usually 8, 16, 24, or 32. You can set this property on a Mac and some Windows machines.

```
if the colorDepth < 16 then
  alert "You're still using 8-bit? Get
with it!"
end if
```

See Also: *switchColorDepth, depth*

See Chapter/Appendix: 34

---

colorList   3D, Mesh

Property

You can use this list to set the colors of the faces in a mesh model.

See Also: *face, mesh*

---

colorRange.start,
colorRange.end   3D, Particle Systems

Property

The starting and ending color of a particle.

```
sprite(1).member.modelResource("my
particle system").colorRange.start =
rgb("FF0000")
```

See Also: blendRange, sizeRange, tweenMode

See Chapter/Appendix: 39

---

colors   3D, Mesh

Property

This is a reference to a color used to color in a face of a mesh model.

See Also: face, colorList

---

colorSteps   3D, Model, Shader

Property

This property of a *toon* model or a *painter* shader lets you set the number of colors used to draw the model to either 2, 4, 8 or 16.

```
sprite(1).member.model("my
model").toon.colorSteps = 2
```

See Also: *highlightPercentage,*
shadowPercentage, toon, painter

See Chapter/Appendix: 39

---

colorType   Misc, Color

Property

A property of a color structure. Returns #rgb if it's an *rgb* structure and #paletteIndex if it's a *paletteIndex* structure. The best part is that you can set this property to convert between them.

```
mmyColor = rgb(255,0,0)
put myColor.colorType
— #rgb
myColor.colorType = #paletteIndex
put myColor
— paletteIndex( 35 )
```

See Also: *color, rgb, paletteIndex*

See Chapter/Appendix: 18

commandDown

Keyboard
Property

Returns *TRUE* if the user is holding down the ⌘ key on the Mac or the Ctrl key in Windows.

```
if the commandDown then...
```

See Also: *controlDown, optionDown, shiftDown, keyPressed*

See Chapter/Appendix: 16

comments

Member
Property

Returns the comments text for the member. This text is entered in the property inspector by the movie creator. It usually is removed when a Shockwave movie is created, but you can choose to include comments in Shockwave movies in the Publish Settings.

```
if member("myMember").comments con-
tains "alternative" then...
```

See Also: *creationDate, modifiedBy, modifiedDate, name*

compressed

3D, Shader
Property

When a bitmap member is used as a texture, and the bitmap member is compressed, then the *compressed* property of the texture is *TRUE* until the texture is first used, as which point it will be decompressed. If you try to set it to *FALSE*, then the bitmap will be decompressed immediately. If it is *FALSE* and then set to *TRUE* again, the decompressed bitmap will be released from memory until it is needed again.

```
sprite(1).member.texture("my tex-
ture").compressed = FALSE
```

See Also: *texture*

constrainH

Sprite
Function

Takes a sprite number and an integer as parameters. If the number is outside the horizontal boundaries of the sprite, it returns the value of the left or right side. Otherwise, it returns the integer unchanged.

```
sprite(me.spriteNum).locH =
constrainH(7,the mouseH)
```

See Also: *constrainV*

constraint

Sprite
Property

A value of greater than 0 constrains the location of a sprite to the bounding box of another sprite. A value of 0 means no constraint.

```
sprite(7).constraint = 6
```

constrainV

Sprite
Function

Takes a sprite number and an integer as parameters. If the number is outside the vertical boundaries of the sprite, it returns the value of the top or bottom side. Otherwise, it returns the integer unchanged.

```
sprite(me.spriteNum).locV =
constrainV(7,the mouseV)
```

See Also: *constrainV*

contains

Strings
Operator

Determines whether a string is found anywhere inside another.

```
if myString contains ".com" then...
```

See Also: *=, offset, starts*

See Chapter/Appendix: 16

controlDown

Keyboard

Property

Returns *TRUE* if the user is holding down the Control key on the Mac or the Ctrl key in Windows.

```
if the controlDown then...
```

See Also: *commandDown optionDown, shiftDown, keyPressed*

See Chapter/Appendix: 16

controller

Digital Video

Property

Enables you to test for and turn on or off the control strip for a QuickTime video. Does not work with Video for Windows.

```
member("myVideo").controller = TRUE
```

See Also: *directToStage*

See Chapter/Appendix: 19

copyPi XEls

Image

Command

Enables you to copy a rectangle from one image to a rectangle or quad-defined area in another. The first parameter is the source image, the second is the destination source or rect, the third is the source rect, and the last is a list of properties that modify the copy. The properties you can specify in that list are #color, #bgColor, #ink, #blendLevel, #dither, #useFastQuads, #maskImage, and #maskOffset. These properties modify the copy in the same way they modify a sprite's appearance on the Stage.

```
myImage.copyPi
XEls(myOtherImage,rect(50,50,150,150),
rect(0,0,100,100))
myImage.copyPi
XEls(myOtherImage,[point(50,50),point(
150,50),
```

```
point(170,150),point(70,150)])
myImage.copyPi
XEls(myOtherImage,rect(50,50,150,150),
rect(0,0,100,100),[#color:
rgb("FF0000"),#ink: 41])
```

See Also: *ink, color, fill, image*

See Chapter/Appendix: 18

copyrightInfo

Shockwave Audio

Property

Returns the copyright information embedded into a Shockwave Audio file. Sound must be pre-loaded or playing first.

```
member("myText").text =
member("mySWA").copyrightInfo
```

See Chapter/Appendix: 17

copyToClipBoard

Member

Command

Copies the media of a member to the computer's clipboard.

```
copyToClipBoard(member("myText"))
```

See Also: *pasteClipBoardInto*

cos

Math

Function

Returns the cosine of an angle. Angle must be in radians.

```
put cos(1.0)
— 0.5403
put cos(pi)
— -1.0000
put cos(2*pi)
— 1.0000
```

See Also: *sin, tan, atan, pi*

See Chapter/Appendix: 13

count

List, Strings, Misc, 3D

Property

Returns the number of items in a list. Returns the number of properties in a script object. Returns the number of globals with *(the globals)*, and the number of chunks with strings.

```
list = [1,2,3,4,5]
put list.count
— 5
myText = "This is a test."
put myText.word.count
— 4
```

See Also: *showGlobals, length*

See Chapter/Appendix: 13

cpuHogTicks

System

Property

Works on the Mac only. Determines how often Director allows the CPU to process other tasks. Default is 20. Set lower to enable the computer to run more smoothly in general, higher to have Director hog the CPU, thereby producing smoother animation.

```
on startMovie
  the cpuHogTicks = 40
end
```

See Chapter/Appendix: 34

creaseAngle

3D, Inker

Property

How sensitive *inker* and *toon* modifiers are to drawing lines at creases in the model. The range is -1 to 1.

```
sprite(1).member.model("my
model").inker.creaseAngle = .5
```

See Also: *creases, lineColor, lineOffset, useLineOffset*

creases

3D, Inker

Property

Whether lines are drawn at creases when a model is using the *inker* or *toon* modifier.

```
sprite(1).member.model("my
model").inker.creases = TRUE
```

See Also: *creaseAngle, lineColor, lineOffset, useLineOffset*

See Chapter/Appendix: 39

createMask

Image

Function

Makes a gradient image from an image. This can then be used with the #maskImage modifier of the *copyPi XEls* command.

```
member("myImage").image.copyPi
XEls(member("otherImage").image, \
rect(0, 0, 100, 100),
member("Happy").rect, \
[#maskImage:member("myGradient").image
.createMask()])
```

See Also: *copyPi XEls, createMatte*

See Chapter/Appendix: 18

createMatte

Image

Function

Makes a matte image from an image. This matte image can then be used with the #maskImage modifier of the *copyPi XEls* command. You need to use one parameter with *createMatte*—a value between 0 and 256 that determines how much of the Alpha channel to use as the matte.

```
member("myImage").image.copyPi
XEls(member("otherImage").image, \
rect(0, 0, 100, 100),
member("Happy").rect, \
```

```
[#maskImage:member("myMatte").image.cr
eateMatte(128)])
```

See Also: *copyPi XEls, createMask*

See Chapter/Appendix: 18

---

creationDate   Member

Property

Returns a date object that shows the creation date of the member.

```
put member(1).creationDate
— date( 2000, 1, 22 )
```

See Also: *comments, modifiedDate, modifiedBy*

See Chapter/Appendix: 26

---

crop   Bitmap

Command

Crops an image to the size of the rectangle specified. If used on a member, behaves like the Director 7 *crop* command and crops a bitmap member to a new rectangle.

```
myImage = member("picture").image
myImage.crop(rect(50,50,100,100))
member("picture").image = myImage
```

See Also: *image, copyPi XEls, fill, picture*

See Chapter/Appendix: 18

---

crop   Digital Video

Property

When *FALSE*, the digital video is scaled to fit the sprite rectangle. When *TRUE*, the video is presented at 100%, but is cropped by the sprite rectangle.

```
member("myVideo").crop = TRUE
```

See Also: *center*

See Chapter/Appendix: 19

---

cross, crossProduct   3D, Math

Function

Takes two vectors and returns a vector that is perpendicular to them.

```
myVector = vector(1,0,0).cross(vec-
tor(0,1,0))
put myVector
— vector( 0.0000, 0.0000, 1.0000 )
```

See Also: *crossProduct, perpendicularTo*

---

cuePassed   Sound

Event Handler

This handler is called when a cue point is passed in a sound. It sends the sound channel number, the number of the cue point, and the name of the cue point into the handler. If used by a frame behavior, you can insert the *me* parameter as the first parameter.

```
on cuePassed channelNum, cuePointNum,
cuePointName
  member("lyrics").text = cuePointName
end
```

See Also: *cuePointNames, cuePointTimes, isPastCuePoint*

See Chapter/Appendix: 17

---

cuePointNames   Sound, Digital Video

Property

Returns a list of cue point names in a sound member.

```
myCues =
member("mySound").cuePointNames
```

See Also: *cuePointTimes, cuePassed, isPastCuePoint*

See Chapter/Appendix: 17

cuePointTimes   Sound, Digital Video

Property

Returns a list with the time of each cue point, in milliseconds. Each item corresponds to the same item in the *cuePointNames* list.

```
myCueTimes =
member("mySound").cuePointTimes
```

See Also: *cuePointNames, cuePassed, isPastCuePoint*

See Chapter/Appendix: 17

currentLoopState   3D, Animation

Property

Whether the keyframePlayer or the bonesPlayer animation loops.

```
sprite(1).member.model("my
model").keyframePlayer.currentLoopStat
e = TRUE
```

See Also: *loop, play, queue, playList*

currentSpriteNum   Behaviors

Property

Returns the number of the sprite whose script is currently running. Works only in behaviors or cast scripts. It is obsolete and *me.spriteNum* should be used instead.

```
sprite(the currentSpriteNum).ink = 36
```

See Also: *spriteNum, me*

currentTime   Sound, Digital Video, 3D

Property

Returns the current time, in milliseconds, of a sound or digital video sprite. This also works for animation in a 3D member.

```
if sprite(1).currentTime =
sprite(1).member.duration then go next
```

See Also: *movieTime, duration*

See Chapter/Appendix: 17, 19

cursor   Cursor

Command

Enables you to use a number, 1-bit bitmap, pair of 1-bit bitmaps, or animated cursor member as a cursor.

```
cursor(4)
cursor([member("myCursor")])
cursor([member("myCursor"),
member("myMask")])
cursor(member("myAnimatedCursor"))
```

See Chapter/Appendix: 21

cursor   Sprite

Property

Enables you to set a cursor to be used when the cursor is over a sprite. To remove this property, set it to -1.

```
on beginSprite me
  sprite(me.spriteNum).cursor = 3
end
```

See Chapter/Appendix: 21

cursorSize   Cursor

Property

For animated cursor members, enables you to set the cursor size to 16 or 32.

```
member("myAnimatedCursor").cursorSize
= 32
```

See Also: *cursor*

See Chapter/Appendix: 21

curve Vector
Property

This property extracts a single continuous line from a *vertexList* of a vector shape member. It enables you to get and set this line. You can also use *the vertexList* property, which returns a list of all the continuous lines in a vector shape, separated by #newcurve items.

```
put member("myVector").curve[1]
— [[#vertex: point(3.0000, -
20.0000)], [#vertex: point(141.0000, -
20.0000)], [#vertex: point(141.0000,
110.0000)], [#vertex: point(3.0000,
110.0000)]]
```

See Also: *vertex, vertexList*

See Chapter/Appendix: 20

date System
Property

Reads the user's computer clock and returns the date in various formats. You can use "abbr", "long", and "short" as modifiers. The actual result depends on the date settings on the user's computer.

```
put the date
— "3/18/00"
put the short date
— "3/18/00"
put the long date
— "Saturday, March 18, 2000"
put the abbr date
— "Sat, Mar 18, 2000"
```

See Also: *abbr, long, short, time, systemDate*

See Chapter/Appendix: 21

date Date & Time
Object

An object type. Can accept an integer, a string, or three integers initially. Object converts to a series of three integers: *year, month,* and *day.*

```
d = date(20000312)
put d
— date( 2000, 3, 12 )
d = date(2000,3,17)
put d.year
— 2000
put d.day
— 17
```

See Also: *day, month, year, seconds, systemDate*

See Chapter/Appendix: 21

day Date & Time
Property

A property of a *date* object.

```
d = date(2000,3,17)
put d.day
— 17
```

See Also: *date, month, year, seconds, systemDate*

See Chapter/Appendix: 21

deactivateApplication Movie, MIAW
Event Handler

Handler gets called when the projector or Director is sent to the background. You need to set your preferences to "Animate in Background" while in Director. This is useful when you make a projector and need to check system properties when the user has switched applications.

```
on deactivateApplication
  alert "Goodbye!"
end
```

See Also: *activateApplication, activateWindow*

deactivateWindow

MIAW

Event Handler

Called when a window is the active window, but is then deactivated because the user clicks on another window or another window opens.

```
on deactivateWindow
sound(1).play(member("close window
sound"))
```

See Also: *activateWindow, openWindow, closeWindow*

See Chapter/Appendix: 24

debug

3D, Misc

Property

If *TRUE*, then a bounding sphere and a XEs of a model will be shown. This wil not work in software rendering mode.

```
sprite(1).member.model("my
model").debug = TRUE
```

See Also: *boundingSphere*

See Chapter/Appendix: 39

decayMode

3D, Camera

Property

Defines how fog density builds. Values can be either #linear, #exponential or #exponential2.

```
sprite(1).camera.fog.decayMode = #lin-
ear
```

See Also: *camera, fog*

See Chapter/Appendix: 39

defaultRect

Flash, Vector

Property

The default size for sprites created using that Flash or vector shape member, or for existing sprites that have not been stretched. Works only

when the *defaultRectMode* is set to #fi XEd. This property automatically changes *defaultRectMode* to #fi XEd when it is changed.

```
member("myFlash").defaultRect =
rect(0,0,100,100)
```

See Also: *defaultRectMode*

See Chapter/Appendix: 20

defaultRectMode

Flash, Vector

Property

Either #Flash or #fi XEd. The first means that the real size of the member will be used in non-stretched sprites. The second means that the *defaultRect* property will be used.

```
member("myFlash").defaultRectMode =
#Flash
```

See Also: *defaultRect*

See Chapter/Appendix: 20

delay

Navigation

Command

Place in an *on exitFrame* or *on enterFrame* handler to extend the playback time of a frame by a number of ticks.

```
on exitFrame
  if pMyProperty = 2 then
    delay 60
  end if
end
```

See Also: *ticks*

delete

Strings

Command

Deletes a chunk expression from a string.

```
delete myString.word[2].char[5]
```

See Also: *char, word, line, item*

See Chapter/Appendix: 16

deleteAll   List

                                              Command

Removes all items from a list.

```
deleteAll myList
```

See Also: *deleteAt*

See Chapter/Appendix: 13

deleteAt   List

                                              Command

Removes a single item from a linear or property list.

```
deleteAt(myList,7)
myList.deleteAt(7)
```

See Also: *addAt, getAt*

See Chapter/Appendix: 13

deleteCamera   3D, Camera

                                              Command

Removes a camera from the member.

```
sprite(1).member.deleteCamera("cam-
era")
```

See Also: *camera, newCamera*

See Chapter/Appendix: 39

deleteFrame   Score Recording

                                              Command

Removes the current frame and moves all frames after the current frame down one during Score recording.

```
beginRecording
  deleteFrame
endRecording
```

See Also: *beginRecording, updateFrame*

See Chapter/Appendix: 26

deleteGroup   3D, Groups

                                              Command

Deletes a group from the 3D member. The models in the group are removed from the world, but still exist in the member and may be added back to the world.

```
sprite(1).member.deleteGroup("my
group")
```

See Also: *newGroup*

See Chapter/Appendix: 39

deleteLight   3D, Lights

                                              Command

Removes the light from the 3D member,

```
sprite(1).member.deleteLight("my
light")
```

See Also: *newLight*

See Chapter/Appendix: 39

deleteModel   3D, Models

                                              Command

Removes a model from the 3D world and from the member.

```
sprite(1).member.deleteModel("my
model")
```

See Also: *deleteModelResource, newModel, removeFromWorld*

See Chapter/Appendix: 39

deleteModelResource

                                          3D, Models

                                              Command

Deletes a model resource from the member. Models that use the resource lose their geometry so they become invisible.

```
sprite(1).member.deleteModelResource("
my model resource")
```

See Also: *deleteModel, removeFromWorld*

See Chapter/Appendix: 39

---

deleteMotion   3D, Animation

Command

Removes a motion from the member.

```
sprite(1).member.removeMotion("my
motion")
```

See Also: *newMotion*

---

deleteOne   List

Command

Removes the first value in the list that matches the value given to this command.

```
deleteOne myList, valueToDelete
myList.deleteOne(valueToDelete)
```

See Also: *deleteAt, deleteProp*

See Chapter/Appendix: 13

---

deleteProp   List

Command

Removes the first property in a property list that matches the property given to this command.

```
deleteProp myList, propToDelete
myList.deleteProp(propToDelete)
```

See Also: *deleteAt*

See Chapter/Appendix: 13

---

deleteShader   3D, Shader

Command

Removes a shader from the member.

```
sprite(1).member.deleteShader("my
shader")
```

See Also: *newShader, shaderList, deleteTexture*

See Chapter/Appendix: 39

---

deleteTexture   3D, Shader

Command

Removes a texture from the member.

```
sprite(1).member.deleteTexture("my
texture")
```

See Also: *deleteShader, newTexture*

See Chapter/Appendix: 39

---

deleteVertex   Vector

Command

Removes a vertex point from a Vector shape member.

```
deleteVertex(member("myVector"), 2)
member("myVector").deleteVertex(2)
```

See Also: *addVertex, moveVertex, vertexList, curve*

See Chapter/Appendix: 20

---

density   3D, Shader

Property

The number of lines or dots used by an engraver or newsprint shader.

```
sprite(1).member.shader("my
shader").density = 20
```

See Also: *newShader*

See Chapter/Appendix: 39

depth   Bitmap
                                           Property

Returns the bit depth of a bitmap member.

```
if member("myBitmap").depth > 8
then...
```

See Also: *colorDepth*

See Chapter/Appendix: 18

depth   3D, Subdivision Surfaces
                                           Property

The maximum resolution (depth of recursion)
that a model can display when using subdivision
surfaces.

```
sprite(1).member.model("my
model").sds.depth = 2
```

See Also: *sds*, *tension*

See Chapter/Appendix: 39

deskTopRectList   System
                                           Property

Returns a list of rectangles that corresponds to
the monitor(s) connected to the computer.

```
put the desktopRectList
— [rect(0, 0, 1024, 768)]
```

See Also: *rect, sourceRect, drawRect*

See Chapter/Appendix: 21

diffuse   3D, Shader, Lights
                                           Property

The color of a shader surface as used by diffuse
lighting. Along with *ambient*, this setting determines the color of a model.

```
sprite(1).member.shader("my
shader").diffuse = rgb("FF0000")
```

See Also: *ambient, diffuseColor,
useDiffuseWithTexture, specular*

See Chapter/Appendix: 39

diffuseColor   3D, Lights
                                           Property

The color blended with the first texture of the
first shader in a member.

```
sprite(1).member.diffuseColor =
rgb("FF0000")
```

See Also: *diffuse, useDiffuseWithTexture*

See Chapter/Appendix: 39

3D,   th▸
                                                is
See Also: pl

See Chapter/Appendix:

diffuseLightMap   3D, Shader
                                           Property

The texture to use for diffuse light mapping in a
shader.

```
sprite(1).member.shader("my
shader").diffuseLightMap =
sprite(1).member.texture("my texture")
```

See Also: *textureModeList, glossMap,
reflectionMap, specularLightMap*

digitalVideoTimeScale   Digital Video
                                           Property

A system property that contains a units-per-sec-
ond timescale that Director uses to track video.
A value of 0 means that Director uses the scale
of the currently playing video.

```
on beginSprite me
  the digitalVideoTimeScale = 0
end
```

See Also: *movieTime, duration, movieRate*

See Chapter/Appendix: 19

digitalVideoType

Digital Video
Property

Returns #quickTime or #videoForWindows.

```
put member("myVideo").digitalVideoType
— #quickTime
```

See Chapter/Appendix: 19

direction

3D, Particle System
Property

The direction in which particles are emitted. The *angle* must be set to something less than 180 degrees or the *direction* really doesn't matter.

```
sprite(1).member.modelResource("my
particle system").emitter.direction =
vector(0,1,0)
```

See Also: *angle*

See Chapter/Appendix: 39

directionalColor

3D, Light
Property

The color of the default directional light in a 3D member.

```
sprite(1).member.directionalColor =
rgb("CCCCCC")
```

See Also: *ambientColor, directionalPreset*

directionalPreset

3D, Lights
Property

The direction of the default directional light in a member. Possible values are: #topLeft, #topRight, #topCenter, #bottomLeft,

#bottomRight, #bottomCenter, #middleLeft, #middleRight, #middleCenter, or #none.

```
sprite(1).member.directionalPreset =
#topRight
```

See Also: *directionalColor*

directToStage

Flash, Vector, Digital
Video, Animated GIF, 3DF
Property

Whether the member or sprite is drawn directly to the Stage, speeding up playback, but not using sprite inks. Sprites using this appear on top of other sprites, regardless of their ordering in the Score.

```
member("myVideo").directToStage = TRUE
sprite(7).directToStage = TRUE
```

See Chapter/Appendix: 19, 20

displayFace

3D, Text
Property

Which of the three parts of 3D text to show. A complete list would include #font, #back and #tunnel.

```
sprite(1).member.displayFace =
[#front, #tunnel, #back]
```

See Also: *extrude3D, displayMode*

See Chapter/Appendix: 4

displayMode

3D, Text
Property

For a text member, set this to #Mode3D to display the text as 3D, #ModeNormal is the default.

```
sprite(1).member.displayMode = #Mode3D
```

See Also: *displayFace, extrude3D*

See Chapter/Appendix: 4

distanceTo
3D, Math
Function

Returns the distance between two vector points.

```
v1 = vector(9,14,7)
v2 = vector(4,1,-6)
put v1.distanceTo(v2)
— 19.0526
```

See Also: *magnitude*

See Chapter/Appendix: 39

distribution
3D, Particle System
Property

How particles are emitted over time. The possible values are #linear or #gaussian.

```
sprite(1).member.modelResource("my
particle system").emitter.distribution
= #gaussian
```

See Also: *region*

See Chapter/Appendix: 39

dither
Bitmap
Property

If *TRUE*, a 16-bit or higher bitmap is dithered when shown on an 8-bit screen. This results in a better image, but slower performance.

```
member("myBitmap").dither = TRUE
```

See Also: *depth*

See Chapter/Appendix: 18

do
Programming
Command

This powerful command takes a string and eXEcutes it as a Lingo command. You can include any Lingo syntax, including calls to your own handlers.

```
myString = "gMyGlobal = 7 + 2"
do myString
```

```
put gMyGlobal
— 9
```

See Also: *value*

dontPassEvent
Programming
Command

Made obsolete by *stopEvent*. Prevents an event, such as a *mouseUp*, from passing to the next message level. For instance, a behavior can prevent the message from passing to the movie script. This is considered obsolete because messages are never passed on, unless the *pass* command is used.

See Also: *stopEvent, pass*

dot, dotProduct
3D, Math
Function

Returns a number that is the sum of the products of two vectors. If both vectors have the length of 1, then the result is the cosine of the angle between the vectors.

```
v1 = vector(1,1,0)
v2 = vector(0,1,1)
put v1.dot(v2)
— 1.0000
```

See Also: getNormalized, crossProduct

doubleClick
Mouse
Property

Returns a *TRUE* if the last two mouse clicks were very close together. An odd property, because a true double-click needs to occur on the same object, whereas this property can return *TRUE* if the two clicks occurred on different sprites.

```
if the doubleClick then...
```

See Also: *mouseDown, mouseUp*

downloadNetThing　　　　　Network

Command

Transfers a file from an Internet location to the local disk. Use *netDone* to see whether the operation is complete. Does not work in Shockwave for security reasons.

```
gNetID =
downloadNetThing("http://clevermedia.c
om/images/cmad3.gif", "temp.gif")
```

See Also: *netDone*

See Chapter/Appendix: 22

drag　　　　　3D, Particle System

Property

How much momentum is lost for each step in the particle system movement. This must be set to some value for *wind* to have any affect.

```
sprite(1).member.modelResource("my
particle system").drag = 50
```

See Also: *wind*, *gravity*

See Chapter/Appendix: 39

draw　　　　　Image

Command

Draws a line, rectangle, or oval in an image object. You need to specify a starting x and y location, an ending x and y location, and an optional set of parameters. These parameters include #lineSize, #color, and #shapeType. The #shapeType can be #line, #oval, #rect, or #roundRect. These are unfilled shapes. Use the *fill* command to draw filled shapes.

```
myImage = member("picture").image
myImage.fill(10,20,50,60,[#color:
rgb("FF0000"), #shapeType: #line,
#lineSize: 2])
```

See Also: *image, fill, copyPi XEls, setPi XEl*

See Chapter/Appendix: 18

drawRect　　　　　MIAW

Property

Returns the rectangle of a window. You can set this property too, which results in the scaling of bitmaps and some other sprites.

```
put window("myMIAW").drawRect
put (theStage).drawRect
```

See Also: *sourceRect*

See Chapter/Appendix: 24

dropShadow　　　　　Field

Property

The offset of the black shadow under text in a field member.

```
member("myField").dropShadow = 4
```

See Also: *margin, boxType, boxDropShadow, border*

See Chapter/Appendix: 16

duplicate　　　　　Member

Command

Creates a copy of a member. It places it in the next available member slot, or in a specific slot if specified.

```
duplicate member("myMember")
duplicate
member("myMember"),member("newMember",
"otherCast")
```

See Also: *new, erase*

duplicate　　　　　List, Image, 3D

Function

Returns a new list, identical to the one it is given. This is needed because lists are objects, so setting a variable equal to a list creates only another pointer to the same list, rather than a new list. It will also create a new, duplicate image from an image object. It also works with 3D vectors.

```
newList = duplicate(myist)
```

duplicateFrame
Score Recording
Command

During Score recording, this creates a new frame, identical to the current one, and places it after the current one. It also advances the playback head one frame.

```
on beginRecording
  duplicateFrame
end
```

See Also: *beginRecording, updateFrame*

See Chapter/Appendix: 26

duration
Transition, Digital Video, Shockwave Audio, 3D
Property

The length of the transition (milliseconds), video (ticks), SWA (ticks, only while streaming), or 3D motion.

```
if sprite(7).movieTime =
sprite(7).member.duration then...
```

See Also: *percentPlayed, movieTime, movieRate*

See Chapter/Appendix: 19

editable
Text, Field, Sprite
Property

When *TRUE*, the text or field member can be edited by the users. If not *TRUE* as a member property, the member can still be edited if the sprite property is *TRUE*.

```
Member("myText"). editable = TRUE
sprite(7).editable = TRUE
```

See Also: *autoTab*

See Chapter/Appendix: 16

editShortCutsEnabled
Text
Property

If set to *TRUE*, this enables users to use standard cut, copy, and paste shortcuts while typing in editable text members. Default is *TRUE*.

```
the editShortCutsEnabled = FALSE
```

See Also: *editable*

See Chapter/Appendix: 18

elapsedTime
Sound
Property

Returns the time, in milliseconds, that the sound has been playing. This time includes any looping.

```
if sound(1).elapsedTime > 60000
then...
```

See Also: *currentTime*

See Chapter/Appendix: 17

else
Programming
Structure

Enables alternative conditions to be set up inside an *if* statement.

```
if a = 4 then
  go to frame "this"
else if a = 7 then
  go to frame "that"
else
  go to frame "other"
end if
```

See Also: *if*

See Chapter/Appendix: 13

emissive
3D, Sahder
Property

This property will add light to the surface used by the shader. The light won't be coming from any source, but the surface will act as if the light is there anyway. This is a good way to brighten a model's surface independent of the lighting in a scene.

```
sprite(1).member.shader('my
shader").emissive = rgb("FF0000")
```

See Also: *shininess*

See Chapter/Appendix: 39

emitter 3D, Particle System

Object

The *emitter* keyword must be used to access various particle system properties.

```
sprite(1).member.modelResource("my
particle system").emitter.angle = 5
```

See Also: *angle, numParticles, mode, loop, minSpeed, maxSpeed, region, distribution, path, pathStrength*

See Chapter/Appendix: 39

EMPTY Strings

Constant

Any empty string with 0 length. Same as " ".

```
if myString = EMPTY then...
```

See Also: *SPACE, VOID, voidP, length*

See Chapter/Appendix: 16

emulateMultiButtonMouse Mouse

Property

If *TRUE*, a Control+click on the Mac acts like a right mouse button click on Windows.

```
the emulateMultiButton Mouse = TRUE
```

See Also: *rightMouseDown, rightMouseUp*

enabled Menu

Property

A menu item property that allows you to enable or disable a single menu item.

```
the enabled of menuitem 1 of menu 1 =
TRUE
```

See Also: *menuitem, installMenu*

See Chapter/Appendix: 21

enabled 3D

Property

The *enabled* property can be used to turn on or off fog, collision detection or subdivision surfaces.

```
sprite(1).member.model("my
model").collision.enabled = FALSE
```

See Also: *collision, fog, sds*

See Chapter/Appendix: 39

enableHotSpot QTVR

Command

Allows you to enable or disable a hotspot in a QTVR movie.

```
EnableHotSpot(sprite(7),myHotSpot,TRUE
)
```

end Programming

Misc

The line that marks the end of a handler. Also used as *end if, end case,* and *end repeat* to mark the end of those structures.

See Also: *if, case, repeat*

endAngle   3D, Primitives

Property

Together with *startAngle*, this indicates the amount of a sphere or cylinder primitive to draw.

```
sprite(1).member.modelResource("my
sphere resource").endAngle = 180
```

See Also: startAngle

See Chapter/Appendix: 39

endColor   Vector

Property

Destination color of a gradient. Has an effect only when the *fillMode* is set to #gradient.

```
Member("myVector").endColor =
rgb(255,0,0)
```

See Also: *fillMode, fillColor, fillCycles, fillDirection, fillOffset, fillScale,* closed

See Chapter/Appendix: 20

endFrame   Sprite

Property

Returns the last frame of a sprite span.

```
put sprite(7).endFrame
```

See Also: *startFrame*

endRecording   Score Recording

Command

Used to signify the end of a Score recording session.

See Also: *beginRecording, updateFrame*

See Chapter/Appendix: 26

endSprite   Behaviors

Event Handler

This event handler is called when the movie moves out of a frame, and on to one that does not contain the sprite.

```
on endSprite me
  gScore = 0
end
```

See Also: *beginSprite*

endTellTarget   Flash

Command

This command will end the targeting begun by *tellTarget*.

See Also: *tellTarget*

See Chapter/Appendix: 20

endTime   Sound

Property

The duration of a sound, in milliseconds.

```
if sound(1).endTime > 60000 then...
```

See Also: *startTime*

See Chapter/Appendix: 17

ENTER   Strings

Constant

Represents the character generated by the Enter key on the numeric keypad.

```
on keyUp me
  if the key = ENTER then beep
end
```

See Also: *RETURN*

See Chapter/Appendix: 16

enterFrame   Behaviors

Event Handler

This handler is called just after Director draws the current frame, but before any idle time occurs.

```
on enterFrame me
  if sprite(me.spriteNum).locH > 640
then...
end
```

See Also: *prepareFrame, exitFrame, idle*

See Chapter/Appendix: 13

environment   System

Property

Returns a list containing *platform, runMode, colorDepth,* and other information.

```
put the environment
— [#shockMachine: 0,
#shockMachineVersion: "", #platform:
"Macintosh,PowerPC", #runMode:
"Author", #colorDepth: 32,
#internetConnected: #online,
#uiLanguage: "English", #osLanguage:
"English", #productBuildVersion:
"178"]
```

See Also: *platform, runMode, colorDepth*

See Chapter/Appendix: 21

erase   Casts

Command

Enables you to remove a member from a Cast.

```
erase member("myUselessMember")
```

See Also: *duplicate, new, move*

error   3D, Subdivision Surfaces

Property

The amount of error allowed when rendering the model using subdivision surfaces.

```
sprite(1).member.model("my
model").sds.error = 0
```

See Also: *sds*

See Chapter/Appendix: 39

EvalScript   Shockwave

Event Handler

Receives events sent by the browser from JavaScript or VBScript "EvalScript()" functions. Accepts parameters as well. Can also use a *return* command to send a value back to the browser when it is done.

```
on EvalScript myParam
  if myParam = "Jump Button" then
    go next
  end if
end
```

See Also: *externalEvent*

See Chapter/Appendix: 22

eventPassMode   Flash

Property

Determines how events such as mouse clicks are passed through a Flash sprite or member to the sprite's behavior. Possible values are #passAlways, #passButton, #passNotButton, and #passNever. The #passButton and #passNotButton buttons refer to when a button in the Flash movie is clicked.

```
on beginSprite me
sprite(me.spriteNum).eventPassMode =
#passNever
```

See Chapter/Appendix: 20

exit Programming
Command

Exits the current handler without e XEcuting any more commands. The handler that called the current one, if any, continues.

```
on myHandler
  if gMyGlobal > 7 then exit
  gMyGlobal = gMyGlobal + 1
  myOtherHandler(gMyGlobal)
end
```

See Also: *abort*

exit repeat Programming
Command

Ends the current repeat loop immediately, skipping any code left in that instance of the loop and starting with the first line of code after the loop.

```
repeat while myVar < 7
  if myVar = 3 then exit repeat
  myVar = myOtherHandler(myVar)
end repeat
```

See Also: *repeat*

See Chapter/Appendix: 13

exitFrame Behaviors
Event Handler

This handler is called just before Director leaves the current frame.

```
on exitFrame me
  sprite(me.spriteNum).locH =
sprite(me.spriteNum).locH + 1
end
```

See Also: *enterFrame, beginSprite, endSprite, idle*

See Chapter/Appendix: 13, 14

exitLock Navigation
Property

If this system property is set to *TRUE*, users cannot use the keys such as ⌘+Q, Ctrl+Q, ⌘+., Ctrl+., or Esc to quit a projector.

```
the exitLock = TRUE
```

See Chapter/Appendix: 21

exp Math
Function

Returns the natural logarithm base, e, to the power given.

```
put exp(3)
— 20.0855
```

See Also: *log*

See Chapter/Appendix: 13

externalEvent Shockwave
Command

Sends a string to the browser, which it interprets with JavaScript or VBScript.

```
externalEvent("myJavaScriptFunction()"
)
```

See Also: *EvalScript*

See Chapter/Appendix: 22

externalParamCount Shockwave
Function

Returns the number of parameters in the <EMBED> or <OBJECT> tag for a Shockwave movie.

```
numParams = externalParamCount()
```

See Also: *externalParamName, externalParamValue*

See Chapter/Appendix: 22

externalParamName

Shockwave

Function

Returns the name of a specific parameter from the <EMBED> or <OBJECT> tag in the browser.

```
paramName = externalParamName(2)
```

See Also: *externalParamName, externalParamCount*

See Chapter/Appendix: 22

externalParamValue

Shockwave

Function

Returns the value of a specific parameter from the <EMBED> or <OBJECT> tag in the browser.

```
paramName = externalParamValue(2)
```

See Also: *externalParamCount, externalParamValue*

See Chapter/Appendix: 22

extractAlpha

Image

Function

Returns an 8-bit image that corresponds to the Alpha channel of the image specified.

```
myAlpha =
member("myImage").image.extractAlpha()
```

See Also: *setAlpha, useAlpha*

See Chapter/Appendix: 18

extrude3D

3D, Text

Command

Creates a 3D model resource from a text member and then places it in a 3D member.

```
my3Dtext = member("my text member").
extrude3D(member("my 3D member"))
member("my 3D member").newModel("my 3D
text model",my3Dtext)
```

See Also: *displayMode*

See Chapter/Appendix: 4, 39

face

3D, Mesh

Object

Use the *face* object to work with properties of an individual face in a mesh object. This can also be used as a list that identifies the vertices in a face in a mesh deform.

```
sprite(1).member.modelResource("my
model resource").face.shader =
myShader
```

See Also: *colors, normals, shader, texture, vertices, newMesh, meshDeform*

See Chapter/Appendix: 39

fadeIn

Sound

Command

Silences the sound, and then gradually brings it up to its previous setting over a period of time in milliseconds.

```
sound(1).play(member("mySound"))
sound(1).fadeIn(2000)
```

See Also: *fadeOut, fadeTo*

See Chapter/Appendix: 17

fadeOut

Sound

Command

Gradually lowers a sound to a volume of 0 over a period of time in milliseconds.

```
sound(1).play(member("mySound"))
sound(1).fadeOut(2000)
```

See Also: *fadeIn, fadeTo*

See Chapter/Appendix: 17

fadeTo Sound
Command

Gradually brings a sound from its current volume to a new one over a period of time in milliseconds. Volume is a number from 0 to 255.

```
sound(1).fadeTo(128,2000)
```

See Also: *fadeIn, fadeOut*

See Chapter/Appendix: 17

FALSE Logic
Constant

Logical false. Use in *if*, *repeat*, *case*, or other logic statements. Equivalent to 0.

```
if myVar = FALSE then...
```

See Also: *if, repeat, case, TRUE*

See Chapter/Appendix: 13

far 3D, Camera
Property

The distance from the camera where the fog reaches its maximum density.

```
sprite(1).camera.fog.far = 1000
```

See Also: *near, fog*

See Chapter/Appendix: 39

field Field
Object

Old syntax that can be used to refer to field members the same way as *member* in many cases. It really refers to the text of the member, so it cannot be used as a member reference.

```
if field("myField") = "done" then...
```

See Also: *member*

fieldOfView QTVR
Property

The current field of view of a QTVR sprite in degrees.

```
sprite(7).fieldOfView = 60
```


fieldOfView 3D, Camera
Property

The field of view determines how the 3D world is mapped on to the 2D screen. The *projection* property must be set to #perspective. The default setting is 30. This is similar to using different lenses on a real-life camera.

```
sprite(1).camera.fieldOfView = 60
```

See Also: *projection*

See Chapter/Appendix: 39

fileName Casts, Member, MIAW
Property

Refers to the external file path of either a cast library, member, or MIAW. In many cases, can also be an Internet location.

```
member("myExternalVideo").fileName =
"newvideo.mov"
castLib("myCast").fileName = "new-
cast.cst"
```

See Also: *url, importFileInto*

fileSaveMode 3D, Misc
Property

This is an undocumented property of 3D members. Its default value is #saveOriginal, which means that any Lingo changes to the 3D models in a member will not be saved in the member permanently. However, if you use #saveMarked, then any models that are cloned will also be saved in the member. If you use #saveScene setting, then changes to existing models will be saved, but not new models created. If you use #saveAll, then all changes to the models will be saved.

```
sprite(1).member.fileSaveMode =
#saveAll
```

fill
Image
Command

Creates a filled rectangle in an image. The first four parameters are the left, top, right, and bottom sides of the rectangle. The fifth parameter can either be a color, or a short list with #shapeType, #lineSize, #color, and #bgColor. The shape types can be #rect, #oval, #roundRect, or #line. The #bgColor property specifies the color of the line or border, whereas #color specifies the color of the fill.

```
myImage = member("picture").image
myImage.fill(10,10,50,50,rgb("FF0000")
)
myImage.fill(25,25,35,35,[#shapeType:
#oval, #color: rgb("FF0000"),
#bgColor: rgb("0000FF"), #lineSize:
2])
```

See Also: *image, draw, copyPi XEls, setPi XEl*
See Chapter/Appendix: 18

fillColor
Vector
Property

The primary fill color for a closed vector shape member. Also the starting color if a gradient is used.

```
member("myVector").fillColor =
rgb(0,0,255)
```

See Also: *endColor, fillMode, fillCycles, fillDirection, fillOffset, fillScale,* gradientType, closed

See Chapter/Appendix: 20

fillCycles
Vector
Property

The number of cycles in a gradient fill of a closed vector shape member.

```
member("myVector"). fillCycles = 2
```

See Also: *endColor, fillColor, fillMode, fillDirection, fillOffset, fillScale,* gradientType, closed

See Chapter/Appendix: 20

fillDirection
Vector
Property

The number of degrees of rotation of a gradient fill for a closed vector shape member.

```
member("myVector").fillDirection = 90
```

See Also: *endColor, fillColor, fillMode, fillCycles, fillOffset, fillScale, closed*

See Chapter/Appendix: 20

filled
Shape
Property

Whether the shape member is filled.

```
member("myOval").filled = TRUE
```

See Also: *pattern, color*
See Chapter/Appendix: 20

fillMode
Vector
Property

The type of fill used by a closed vector shape member. Possible values are #none, #solid, and #gradient.

```
member("myVector").fillMode = #gradi-
ent
```

See Also: *endColor, fillColor, fillDirection, fillCycles, fillOffset, fillScale,* gradientType, closed

See Chapter/Appendix: 20

fillOffset   Vector

Property

The position offset of a fill in a closed vector shape.

```
member("myVector").fillOffset =
point(100,50)
```

See Also: *endColor, fillColor, fillDirection, fillMode, fillCycles, fillScale,* gradientType, closed

See Chapter/Appendix: 20

fillScale   Vector

Property

The scale of a gradient fill for a closed vector shape.

```
member("myVector").fillScale = 2
```

See Also: *endColor, fillColor, fillDirection, fillMode, fillCycles, fillOffset,* gradientType, closed

See Chapter/Appendix: 20

findEmpty   Casts

Function

When given a cast member, returns the next empty member in that Cast.

```
nextMemberToUse =
findEmpty(member("myBitmap"))
```

See Also: *erase, duplicate, move*

findLabel   Flash

Function

Returns the frame number in a Flash movie that is associated with the label name. Warning: This function does not always work on a sprite the first instant that the sprite appears. You may have trouble trying to use it in an *on beginSprite* handler.

```
sprite(7).frame =
findLabel(sprite(7),"myLabel")
```

See Also: *frame*

See Chapter/Appendix: 20

findPos   List

Function

Returns the position of a property in a property list, and returns *VOID* if it isn't in the property list.

```
put findPos(myList, #myProp)
put myList.findPos(#myProp)
```

See Also: *findPosNear*

See Chapter/Appendix: 13

findPosNear   List

Function

Returns the position of a property in a property list, or the value in a linear list. If the item isn't in the list, it returns the closest alphanumeric match. The list must be sorted first with the *sort* command.

```
put findPosNear(myList, myVal)
put myList.findPosNear(myVal)
```

See Also: *findPos, sort*

See Chapter/Appendix: 13

finishIdleLoad   Memory

Command

Forces idle loading to complete for members with a specific idle load tag.

```
finishIdleLoad 7
```

See Also: *idleLoadTag*

See Chapter/Appendix: 21

firstIndent   Text

Property

A property of a chunk inside a text member. It provides for a left indent at the start of new lines. Measured in pi XEls.

```
member("myText").line[1..3].firstIndent
= 18
```

See Also: *leftIndent, rightIndent*

See Chapter/Appendix: 16

fi XEdLineSpace   Text

Property

The line height of a specific line or all the lines in a text member. A value of 0 enables the line height to be determined by the font and size.

```
member("myText").line[1..7].fi
XEdLineSpace = 14
```

See Also: *lineHeight*

See Chapter/Appendix: 18

fi XEdRate   Animated GIF, Flash

Property

If the *playbackMode* property of a member or sprite is set to #fi XEd, this controls the frame rate. Default is 15 frames per second.

```
member("myGIF").fi XEdRate = 5
```

See Also: *playbackMode*

See Chapter/Appendix: 20

fixStageSize   Movie

Property

If *TRUE*, the Stage remains the same size when a new movie is loaded, even if that movie uses a different Stage size.

```
the fixStageSize = TRUE
```

See Also: *centerStage, drawRect*

See Chapter/Appendix: 21

flashRect   Flash, Vector

Property

Returns the original size of a Flash or vector shape member.

```
put member("myFlash").flashRect
```

See Also: *defaultRect, defaultRectMode, state*

See Chapter/Appendix: 20

flashToStage   Flash

Property

Returns the point on the Stage that matches a point in a Flash sprite.

```
put
flashToStage(sprite(7),point(50,30))
```

See Also: *stageToFlash, hitTest*

See Chapter/Appendix: 20

flat   3D, Shader

Property

When *flat* is set to *TRUE*, then only one color is used per face.

```
sprite(1).member.shader("my
shader").flat = TRUE
```

See Chapter/Appendix: 39

flipH   Sprite

Property

If *TRUE*, the sprite appears flipped horizontally on the Stage.

```
sprite(7).flipH = TRUE
```

See Also: *flipV*

See Chapter/Appendix: 18

flipV   Sprite

Property

If *TRUE*, the sprite appears flipped vertically on the Stage.

```
sprite(7).flipV = TRUE
```

See Also: *flipH*

See Chapter/Appendix: 18

float
Math
Function

Converts an integer or string to a floating point number.

```
put float(5)
— 5.0000
put float(".5")
— 0.5000
```

See Also: *floatPrecision, integer, value*

See Chapter/Appendix: 13

floatP
Math
Function

Tests an expression and returns *TRUE* if it is a floating point number.

```
a = 5
put floatP(a)
— 0
a = 5.0
put floatP(a)
— 1
```

See Also: *integerP, voidP, float*

See Chapter/Appendix: 13

floatPrecision
Math
Property

This system property determines how many decimal places are to be returned in any floating point number math. Default is 4. Values can go up to 15. A 0 means that all floating point functions will round to an integer. A negative number is the same as a positive one, but all floating point math uses absolute (positive) values.

```
a = 5.5
put a
— 5.5000
the floatPrecision = 2
put a
```

```
— 5.50
the floatPrecision = 0
put a
— 6
the floatPrecision = 8
put a
— 5.50000000
```

See Also: *float*

See Chapter/Appendix: 13

flushInputEvents
System, Mouse
Command

E XEcuting this command flushes the system of any input events, such as mouse clicks or keyboard presses. This is useful if you have a pause in your program caused by a long transition, loading time, or a long repeat loop. You can then use this command to throw away events that users might have triggered while waiting. Works only in projectors and Shockwave, not in Director.

```
on getMemberList
  — long repeat loop here
  list = []
  repeat with i = 1 to 100000
    add list, member(i,2).name
  end repeat
  — clear any clicks from impatient
user
  flushInputEvents()
  return list
end
```

fog
3D, Camera
Object

Refers to the fog settings of a camera.

```
sprite(1).camera.fog.near = 100
```

See Also: *near, far, color, decayMode, enabled*

See Chapter/Appendix: 39

font   Text, Field, Button

Property

The name of the font used by a member, or a chunk in a member.

```
member("myText").font = "Times"
member("myText").char[6..12].font =
"Courier"
```

See Also: *fontSize, fontStyle*

See Chapter/Appendix: 16

fontList   Fonts

Function

This undocumented property of a font member will return a list of all of the names of fonts on the computer.

```
put member("my font
member").fontList()
```

See Also: *outlineFontList*

fontSize   Text, Field, Button

Property

The size of the font used by a member, or a chunk in a member.

```
member("myText").fontSize = 12
member("myText").char[6..12].fontSize
= 14
```

See Also: *font, fontStyle*

See Chapter/Appendix: 16

fontStyle   Text, Field, Button

Property

The style(s) used by a member, or a chunk in a member. Field and buttons use a string such as "bold, italic," whereas text members use a list, such as [#bold, #italic].

```
member("myField").fontStyle = "Bold"
member("myText").fontStyle = [#bold]
```

See Also: *font, fontSize*

See Chapter/Appendix: 16

forecolor   Text, Field, Sprite

Property

Can be used to set the color of text in a field or text member to a palette index number. Can also be used to set the forecolor of a sprite. Made mostly obsolete by *color*.

```
member("myField").forecolor = 35
sprite(7).forecolor = 215
```

See Also: *color, backcolor*

See Chapter/Appendix: 18

forget   MIAW, Timeout

Command

Removes a MIAW or a timeout object from memory. If a variable refers to it, the *forget* command won't work until that variable is set to 0.

```
forget window("myMIAW")
timeout("myTimeout").forget()
```

See Also: *close, timeout*

See Chapter/Appendix: 24

frame   Movie

Property

The number of the current frame that is playing.

```
if the frame = 7 then...
go to the frame + 2
```

See Also: *frameLabel, marker, label, go*

See Chapter/Appendix: 13

frame

Flash

Property

The number of the current frame in the Flash movie sprite.

```
sprite(7).frame = 6
```

See Also: *findLabel, frameCount*

See Chapter/Appendix: 20

frameCount

Flash

Property

Returns the number of frames in a Flash member.

```
sprite(7).frame =
sprite(7).member.frameCount
```

See Also: *frame, findLabel*

See Chapter/Appendix: 20

frameLabel

Movie, Score Recording

Property

Returns the label of the frame that is currently playing. If there is no label on the current frame, it returns a 0. Can be set during Score recording.

```
if the frameLabel = "Chapter 1"
then...
```

See Also: *frame, labelList*

See Chapter/Appendix: 13

framePalette

Movie, Score Recording

Property

Returns the palette member used in the current frame. Can be set during Score recording.

```
the framePalette = -1
```

See Also: *puppetPalette, beginRecording, endRecording*

See Chapter/Appendix: 26

frameRate

Flash, Digital Video

Property

You can use this to get, but not set, the frame rate of a Flash member. You can set the frame rate of a digital video member from 0 to 255. A value of -1 sets the video to play at a normal rate, and a value of -2 sets the video to play as fast as possible.

```
if member("myVideo").frameRate = -1
then...
```

See Also: *fi XEdRate, movieRate, movieTime, playbackMode*

See Chapter/Appendix: 19, 20

frameReady

Shockwave

Function

Returns *TRUE* if a frame or range of frames have been loaded in Shockwave streaming. If no parameters are passed in, it returns *TRUE* only if all the members used in the Score are ready.

```
on exitFrame me
  if frameReady(10,90) then
    go to the frame + 1
  else
    go to the frame
  end if
end
```

See Also: *mediaReady*

See Chapter/Appendix: 22

frameReady

Flash

Function

Returns *TRUE* if a Flash sprite's frame has been loaded and is ready to play.

```
if frameReady(sprite(7),25) then...
```

See Chapter/Appendix: 20

frameScript   Movie, Score Recording
Property

Returns the member used in the Frame Script channel of the current frame. Can be set during Score recording. Made somewhat obsolete by *setScriptList*.

```
the frameScript = member("myScript")
```

See Also: *scriptInstanceList, setScriptList, beginRecording, endRecording*

See Chapter/Appendix: 26

frameSound1   Movie, Score Recording
Property

Returns the sound member used in the first sound channel of the current frame. Can be set during Score recording.

```
the frameSound1 = member("mySound")
```

See Also: *puppetSound*

See Chapter/Appendix: 26

frameSound2   Movie, Score Recording
Property

Returns the sound member used in the second sound channel of the current frame. Can be set during Score recording.

```
the frameSound2 = member("mySound")
```

See Also: *puppetSound*

See Chapter/Appendix: 26

framesToHMS   Misc
Function

Takes a number of frames and tempo and returns a string with hours, minutes, and seconds, as in "00:01:30.X." It requires two other parameters: one set to *TRUE* only when you want to compensate for NTSC video frame timing, and one set to

TRUE when the final portion (the X in the example string) is in frames or seconds.

```
put framesToHMS(2000,15,FALSE,FALSE)
— " 00:02:13.05 "
```

See Also: *HMStoFrames*

frameTempo   Movie, Score Recording
Property

Returns the tempo used in the current frame. Can be set during Score recording.

```
the frameTempo = 30
```

See Also: *puppetTempo, beginRecording, endRecording*

See Chapter/Appendix: 26

frameTransition   Movie, Score Recording
Property

Returns the transition member used in the current frame. Can be set during Score recording.

```
the frameTransition =
member("myTransitionMember")
```

See Also: *puppetTransition, beginRecording, endRecording*

See Chapter/Appendix: 26

freeBlock   System
Function

Returns the largest free block of memory available to the movie in bytes.

```
put freeBlock()
— 12492960
```

See Also: *freeBytes, memorySize, ramNeeded, size*

See Chapter/Appendix: 21

freeBytes
System
Function

Returns the total number of bytes available to the movie.

```
put freeBytes()
— 54048052
```

See Also: *freeBlock, memorySize, ramNeeded, size*

See Chapter/Appendix: 21

front
3D, Primitives
Property

Whether the front side of a 3D box primitive is present or not.

```
sprite(1).member.modelResource("my box
resource").front = FALSE
```

See Also: back, left, right, top, bottom, topCap, bottomCap, newModelResource

frontWindow
MIAW
Property

Returns the frontmost window. If the frontmost window is the Stage, it returns *(the stage)*. If a Director palette is frontmost, it returns *VOID*.

```
if the frontWindow =
window("myWindow") then...
```

See Also: *activeWindow, moveToFront*

See Chapter/Appendix: 24

generateNormals
3D, Mesh
Command

This command will create all the normals needed for a mesh object. You could create these yourself using the *normalList* as well. You can use #smooth or #flat as a parameter.

```
sprite(1).member.modelResource("my model
resource").generateNormals(#smooth)
```

See Also: *normalList, normals, build*

See Chapter/Appendix: 39

generateOutlines
Fonts
Command

This undocumented command will take a font member and a text string and create a list of vertices from the text. You can then apply this list of vertices to a vector member to recreate the text as a vector member. However, this only seems to work with a few letters at a time as the letters created are very large and a vector member has size limits.

```
myVertexList = member("Arial
*").generateOutlines("ABC")
member("my vector").vertexList =
myVertexList
```

getaProp
List
Function

Returns the value of a property in a property list. If the property is not present, it returns *VOID*.

```
list = [#a: 4, #b: 6, #c: 9]
put getAProp(list,#b)
— 6
put getAProp(list,#d)
— <Void>
```

See Also: *getAt, getProp*

See Chapter/Appendix: 13

getAt
List
Function

Returns the value at a specific position in a linear or property list. If the position is beyond the end of the list, it generates an error message.

```
list = [4,6,9]
put getAt(list,2)
— 6
```

```
put list.getAt(2)
— 6
put list[2]
— 6
```

See Also: *getProp*

See Chapter/Appendix: 13

getBehaviorDescription

Behaviors

Event Handler

The string returned from this behavior is used in the Behavior Inspector.

```
on getBehaviorDescription me
   return "This is my behavior."
end
```

See Also: *getBehaviorToolTip*

See Chapter/Appendix: 14

getBehaviorTooltip

Behaviors

Event Handler

Used to generate a ToolTip when the behavior is made part of a library.

```
on getBehaviorTooltip me
   return "My Behavior"
end
```

See Also: *getBehaviorDescription*

See Chapter/Appendix: 14

getBoneID

3D, Bones

Function

Returns the number of a named bone in a model resource.

```
myBoneNumber =
sprite(1).member.modelResource("my
model resource").getBoneID("my bone")
```

See Also: bone

getError

Shockwave Audio, Flash

Function

Returns an error code of a Shockwave audio member. 0 is okay, 1 is a memory error, 2 is a network error, 3 is a playback error, and 99 is another error. For Flash members, it returns symbols: #memory, #fileNotFound, #network, #fileFormat, and #other.

```
if getError(member("mySWA")) = 0
then...
```

See Also: *getErrorString, clearError, state*

See Chapter/Appendix: 17, 20

getErrorString

Shockwave Audio

Function

Takes a Shockwave audio error code from *getError* and returns a string that describes the error.

```
alert getErrorString(mySWAerror)
```

See Also: *getError*

See Chapter/Appendix: 17

getFlashProperty

Flash

Function

Acts like a "getProperty" action command in Flash and returns the property value from the Flash movie. Possible properties are #posX, #posY, #scaleX, #scaleY, #visible, #rotate, #alpha, #name, #width, #height, #target, #url, #dropTarget, #totalFrames, #currentFrame, and #lastframeLoaded. The first parameter is the target name, which you can leave as an empty string if you want to get a property at the global level. The second parameter is the property name.

```
ballX =
sprite(7).getFlashProperty("bouncing
ball",#posX)
```

See Also: *setFlashProperty, getVariable*

See Chapter/Appendix: 20

getFrameLabel   Flash
Function

Returns the name of a label in a Flash sprite, given the frame number.

```
if sprite(7).getFrameLabel(22) =
"Section 2" then...
```

See Also: *findLabel, frame*

See Chapter/Appendix: 20

getHotSpotRect   QTVR
Function

Returns the rectangle of a QTVR hotspot on the Stage.

```
if the mouseLoc =
getHotSpot(sprite(7),2) then...
```

getLast   List
Function

Returns the last value in a linear or property list.

```
list = [4,6,9]
put getLast(list)
— 9
put list.getLast()
— 9
```

See Also: *getAt, getOne, count*

See Chapter/Appendix: 13

getLatestNetID   Network
Function

Returns the network ID number of the most recent network command. This can then be used in functions such as *netDone*. This is obsolete because network ID numbers are now returned by the functions themselves.

```
getNetText("http://clevermedia.com")
gNetID = getLatestNetID()
```

See Also: *getNetText, postNetText, netAbort, netDone, netError*

See Chapter/Appendix: 22

getNetErrorString   Network
Function

Takes a network error code from *netError* and returns a short string description.

```
alert getNetErrorString(myNetError)
```

See Also: *netError*

See Chapter/Appendix: 22

getNetText   Network
Function

Starts retrieving a text file from the Internet. It returns a network ID for the operation.

```
gNetID = getNetText("http://clevermedia.
com")
```

See Also: *netTextResult, netDone*

See Chapter/Appendix: 22

getNormalized   3D, Math
Function

Takes a vector and returns a vector of length 1 that points in the same direction.

```
v = vector(5,5,0)
put v.getNormalized()
— vector( 0.7071, 0.7071, 0.0000 )
```

See Also: *normalize*

getNthFileNameInFolder   Misc
Function

When given a valid file path and a number, it returns the filename. If the number is greater than the number of files in the folder, it returns an empty string.

```
on getAllFiles
  list = []
  i = 1
  repeat while TRUE
    filename =
getNthFileNameInFolder(the pathname,i)
    if filename = "" then exit repeat
    add list, filename
    i = i + 1
  end repeat
  return list
end
```

See Also: @

See Chapter/Appendix: 29

getOne List Function

For a linear list, returns the position of the first item that is equal to the given value. For a property list, it returns the property. A 0 is returned if the value is not found.

```
list = [4,6,9]
put getOne(list,6)
— 2
put list.getOne(6)
— 2
put list.getOne(8)
— 0
```

See Also: *getAt, getProp, getPos*

See Chapter/Appendix: 13

getPi XEl Image Function

Returns a color that corresponds to the color of the pi XEl at a coordinate in a bitmap image. The first parameter can be a point structure, or you can make the first parameter the horizontal location and the second parameter the vertical location. If a final parameter, #integer, is included, a number is returned instead of a color. This number contains both color and Alpha channel information and can be used in *setPi XEl* to set another pi XEl to the same color. A 0 is returned if the location is outside the image area.

```
myImage = member("picture").image
myColor = myImage.getPi
XEl(point(50,30))
```

See Also: *setPi XEl*

See Chapter/Appendix: 18

getPlaylist Sound Function

Returns the list of members queued to play in a sound channel, excluding any sound currently playing. The returned value is a list of property lists, each containing information about the sound member and how it is to be played.

```
myList = sound(1).getPlayList()
if myList[1].member =
member("mySound") then...
```

See Also: *setPlayList, queue, play*

See Chapter/Appendix: 17

getPos List Function

Like *getOne*, but returns a position for property lists, not a property.

```
list = [#a: 7, #b: 9, #c: 14]
put getPos(list,9)
— 2
put list.getPos(9)
— 2
```

See Also: *getOne, findPos, findPosNear*

See Chapter/Appendix: 13

getPref
Shockwave
Function

Gets a preference file's contents. Preference files are used in Shockwave to store "cookies" of information without creating a security risk. Returns a *VOID* if that preference file does not exist.

```
myPref = getPref("clevermediaGame1")
```

See Also: *setPref*

See Chapter/Appendix: 22

getProp
List
Function

Returns the value of a property in a property list. If the property is not present, it generates an error message.

```
list = [#a: 4, #b: 6, #c: 9]
put getProp(list,#b)
— 6
put list.getProp(#b)
— 6
put list.b
— 6
put list[#b]
— 6
```

See Also: *getAt, getaProp*

See Chapter/Appendix: 13

getPropAt
List
Function

Returns the property at a specific position in a property list.

```
list = [#a: 6, #b: 19, #c: 22]
put getPropAt(list,2)
— #b
put list.getPropAt(2)
— #b
```

See Also: *getProp, getAProp, getAt*

See Chapter/Appendix: 13

getPropertyDescriptionList
Behaviors
Event Handler

Called when the behavior is dropped on or added to a sprite. The list returned is used to generate the Parameters dialog box.

```
on getPropertyDescriptionList me
  list = [:]
  addProp list, #pMyProp, [#comment:
"My Prop", #format: #integer,
#default: 7]
  return list
end
```

See Also: *getBehaviorDescription*

See Chapter/Appendix: 14

getRendererServices
3D, Misc
Function

Returns an object that contains all sorts of information about the computer's video software and the capabilities of the Director 3D engine. See the sample below for a list of all properties in Director 8.5.

```
put getRendererServices().renderer
— #openGL
put
getRendererServices().rendererDeviceLi
st
— [#openGL, #software]
put
getRendererServices().textureRenderFor
mat
— #rgba5551
put
getRendererServices().depthBufferDepth
— 24
put
getRendererServices().colorBufferDepth
— 32
put getRendererServices().modifiers
```

— [#collision, #bonesPlayer,
#keyframePlayer, #toon, #lod,
#meshDeform, #sds, #inker]
put getRendererServices().primitives
— [#sphere, #box, #cylinder, #plane,
#particle]

See Also: *active3Drenderer, preferred3Drenderer*

See Chapter/Appendix: 39

getStreamStatus

Network

Function

When given a network ID or URL, this function
returns a list with information about the
progress of streaming. The list includes #URL,
#state, #bytesSoFar, #bytesTotal, and #error.

```
list = getStreamStatus(gNetID)
if list.bytesSoFar > list.bytesTotal/2
then
  member("status").text = "Half done!"
end if
```

See Also: *tellStreamStatus*

See Chapter/Appendix: 22

getVariable

Flash

Function

Returns the value of the variable from a Flash
sprite.

```
myVar = sprite(7).getVariable("myVar")
```

See Also: *getFlashProperty, setVariable*

See Chapter/Appendix: 20

getWorldTransform

3D, Models

Function

This returns the transform of a model or other
object relative to the world center. It differs from
just getting the *transform* because the *transform*
is dependent on the parent if the model happens
to be grouped as a child of another model. The
getWorldTransform is always relative to the
whole 3D scene.

INDEX

Symbols

E

G

Q

R

Y-Z